Ordnance Survey Motoring Atlas of Great Britain

Contents

2 Route Planning Maps

2 Limited Interchange Motorway Junctions

5 Distances between Principal Towns

6 **Ordnance Survey 3 miles : 1 inch Maps**
for key see back cover; for legend see back flap

98 **Ordnance Survey 5 miles : 1 inch Maps**
for key see back cover; for legend see back flap

106 National Parks, Forest Parks and Long-distance Paths

106 Sheet Maps

106 National Grid

107 Town Centre Maps

107 Routes into London

108 Central London

116 Road Signs

117 Index

Inside front cover
Schematic Mileage Map

Back flap
Legend. Motoring Information (on reverse)

Back cover
Key to Maps on pages 6-105

Ordnance Survey

Temple Press

First published 1983 by

Ordnance Survey and Temple Press
Romsey Road, Maybush, Southampton SO9 4DH
Temple Press, an imprint of Newnes Books, 84-88 The Centre, Feltham, Middlesex, TW13 4BH

Third Edition 1986
First Impression 1986

The representation in this atlas of a road is no evidence of the existence of a right of way.

Newnes Books is a division of The Hamlyn Publishing Group Limited

ISBN 0 600 35171 8

Printed in Great Britain

Route Planning Maps

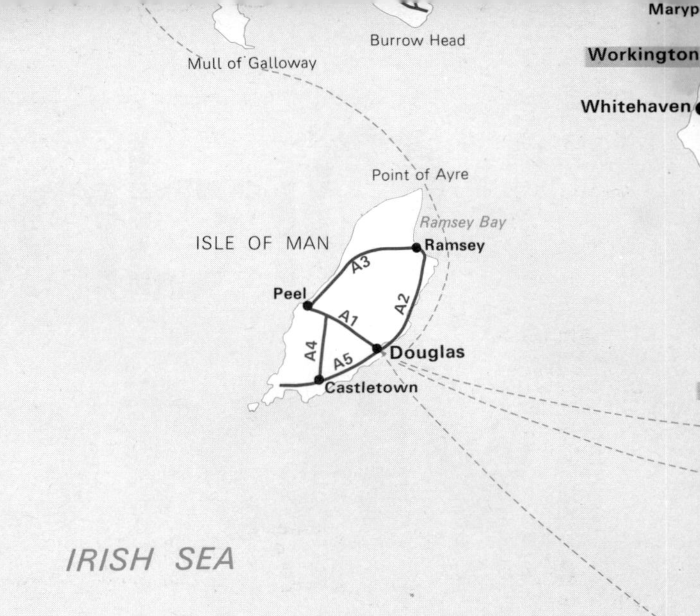

SELECTED MOTORWAY JUNCTIONS WITH LIMITED INTERCHANGE

M1-2
M1-4
M1-7
M1-17
M1-19
M1-46
M2-1
M3-8
M4-1
M4-29
M4-38-39
M4-41
M4-46
M5-10
M5-29
M6-5
M6-20
M6-24
M6-25
M6-30
M11-4
M11-5
M11-9
M11-13
M11-14
M20-M26
M25-A21
M27-10
M27-A33
M40-3
M40-7
M56-2
M53-11
M56-7-8
M56-9
M57-3
M58-1
M61-2-3
M62-14
M62-15
M62-23
M63-5
M63-9
M66-A56 A676
M63-10
M66-A56
M69-2
M180-1
A40(M)
A48(M)-29a
A58(M)-A660-A64(M)-A58
A57(M)-A34-A5103
A64(M)-A61-A64
A102(M)-A2203

Burrow Head
Mull of Galloway
Maryport
Workington
Whitehaven
Point of Ayre
Ramsey Bay
ISLE OF MAN
Ramsey
Peel
Douglas
Castletown
IRISH SEA
Amlwch
ANGLESEY
Holyhead
Menai Bridge
Llandudno
Conwy
Colwyn Bay
Abergele
Bangor
Caernarfon
Caernarfon Bay
Betws-y-Coed
Nefyn
Porthmadog
Ffestiniog
Pwllheli
Harlech
Bala
Barmouth
Dolgellau
Machynlleth
Tywyn
CAMBRIAN MOUNTAINS
CARDIGAN BAY
Aberystwyth
Aberaeron
Lampeter
Cardigan
Llanwrtyd Wells
Llandovery
Fishguard
ST GEORGE'S CHANNEL
St David's Head
St David's
St Brides Bay
Haverfordwest
Carmarthen
Llandeilo
Narberth
St Clears
Milford Haven
Pembroke Dock
Tenby
Carmarthen Bay
Llanelli
R Loughor
Neath
Swansea
Port Talbot
Swansea Bay
Porthcawl
Bridgend
Pontypridd
St Govan's Head
Cardiff-Wales Airport
BRISTOL CHANNEL
Ilfracombe
Lynton
Minehead
Barnstaple
Barnstaple or Bideford Bay
Bideford
South Molton
Hartland Point
Tiverton
Bude
Holsworthy
Crediton
Okehampton
Exeter
Launceston
Padstow
Wadebridge
Tavistock
Newton Abbot
Bodmin
Liskeard
Buckfastleigh
Torbay
Tor Bay
Newquay
St Austell
Plymouth
Totnes
Ivybridge
Whitsand Bay
Dartmouth
St Ives
Truro
Redruth
Bigbury Bay
Start Bay
Salcombe
Start Point
Penzance
Helston
Falmouth
Falmouth Bay
Mount's Bay
Land's End
Lizard Point

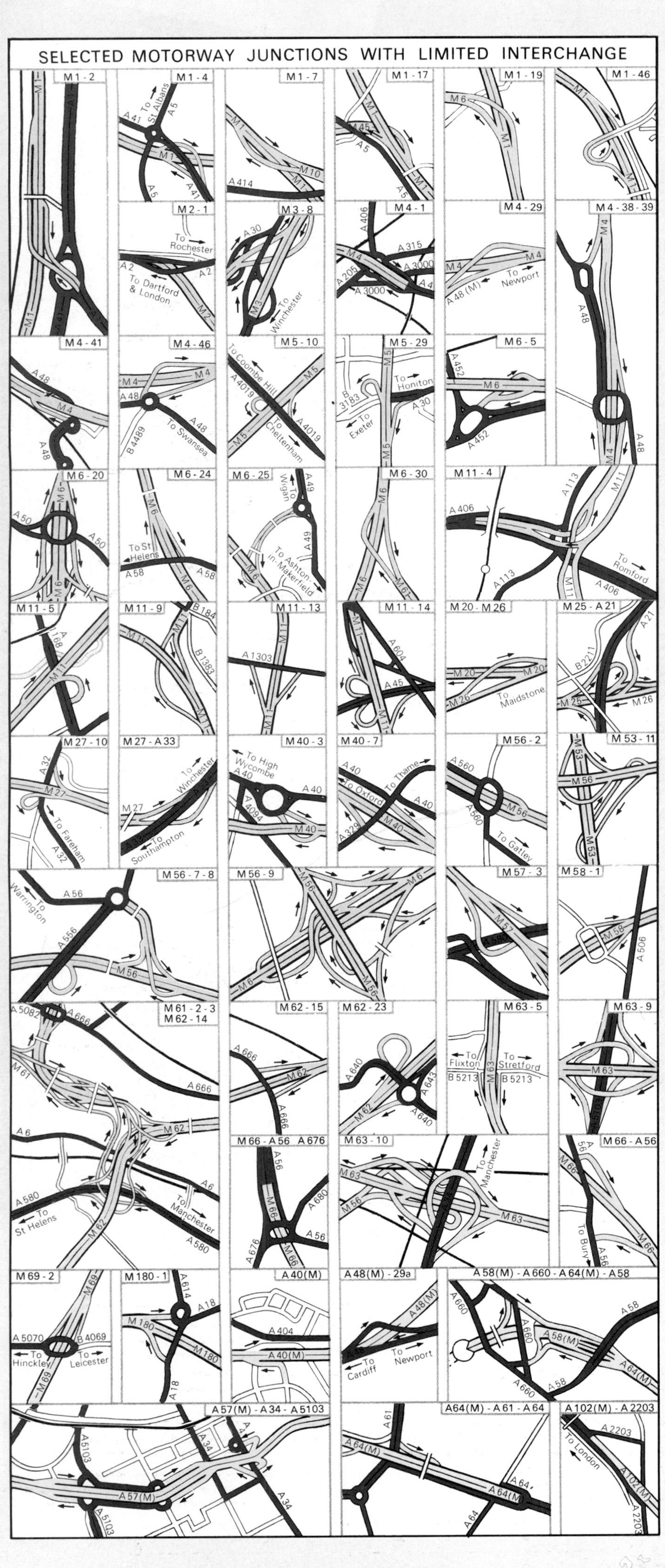

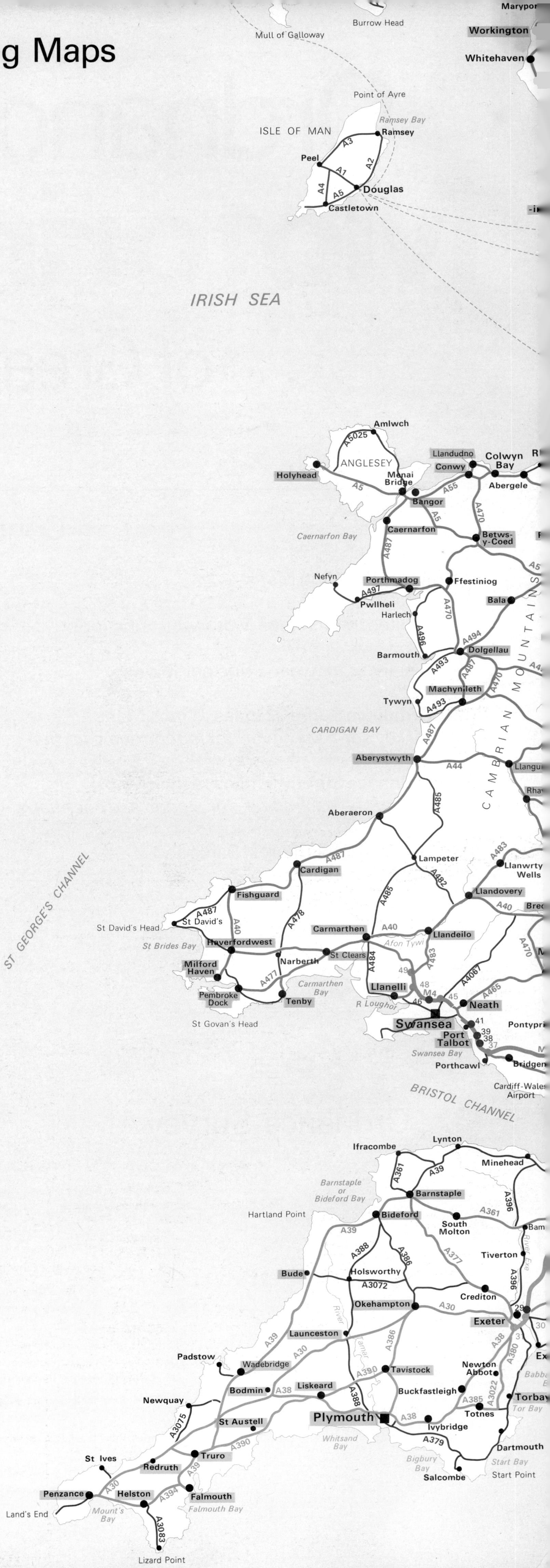

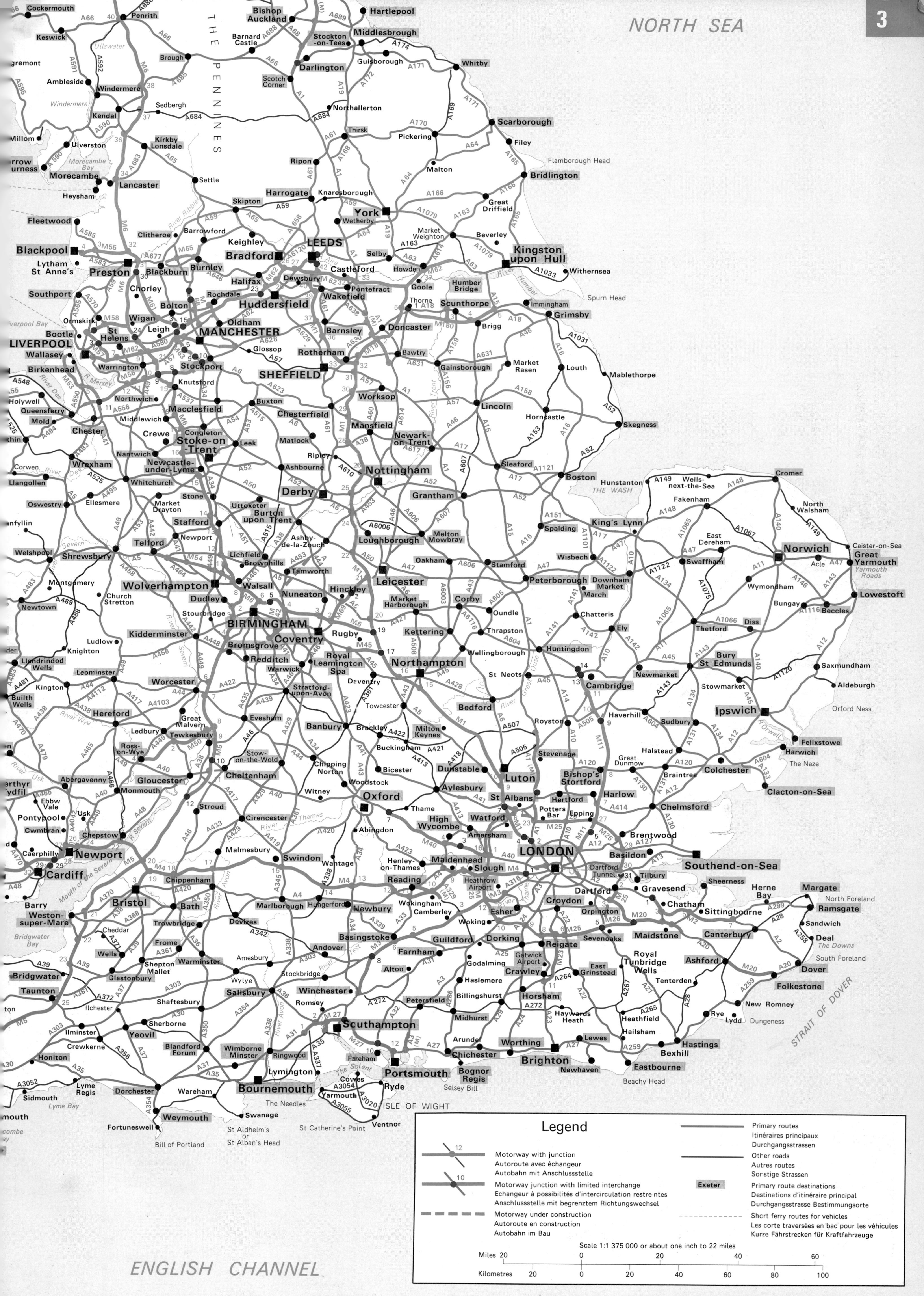
NORTH SEA
ENGLISH CHANNEL
THE PENNINES
Cockermouth
Penrith
Keswick
Ambleside
Windermere
Kendal
Sedbergh
Millom
Ulverston
Kirkby Lonsdale
Morecambe Bay
Morecambe
Lancaster
Heysham
Settle
Fleetwood
Blackpool
Lytham St Anne's
Preston
Blackburn
Clitheroe
Barrowford
Burnley
Chorley
Southport
Ormskirk
Wigan
Bolton
Bootle
St Helens
Leigh
LIVERPOOL
Wallasey
Birkenhead
Warrington
MANCHESTER
Oldham
Rochdale
Stockport
Glossop
Knutsford
Holywell
Queensferry
Mold
Chester
Northwich
Macclesfield
Middlewich
Crewe
Congleton
Stoke-on-Trent
Nantwich
Newcastle-under-Lyme
Leek
Wrexham
Corwen
Llangollen
Whitchurch
Oswestry
Ellesmere
Market Drayton
Stone
Stafford
Newport
Welshpool
Shrewsbury
Telford
Montgomery
Church Stretton
Newtown
Ludlow
Knighton
Llandrindod Wells
Builth Wells
Kington
Leominster
Hereford
Ledbury
Ross-on-Wye
Abergavenny
Monmouth
Pontypool
Cwmbran
Usk
Chepstow
Caerphilly
Newport
Cardiff
Barry
Weston-super-Mare
Bridgwater
Taunton
Bishop Auckland
Barnard Castle
Brough
Darlington
Scotch Corner
Stockton-on-Tees
Middlesbrough
Hartlepool
Guisborough
Whitby
Northallerton
Thirsk
Pickering
Scarborough
Filey
Malton
Ripon
Knaresborough
Harrogate
Skipton
York
Wetherby
Bridlington
Flamborough Head
Great Driffield
Market Weighton
Beverley
Kingston upon Hull
Withernsea
Keighley
Bradford
LEEDS
Selby
Howden
Castleford
Halifax
Dewsbury
Pontefract
Wakefield
Goole
Huddersfield
Thorne
Humber Bridge
Scunthorpe
Immingham
Grimsby
Spurn Head
Brigg
Barnsley
Doncaster
Rotherham
Bawtry
SHEFFIELD
Gainsborough
Market Rasen
Louth
Mablethorpe
Worksop
Lincoln
Horncastle
Skegness
Chesterfield
Mansfield
Buxton
Matlock
Newark-on-Trent
Ripley
Ashbourne
Nottingham
Derby
Sleaford
Boston
Grantham
Uttoxeter
Burton upon Trent
Ashby-de-la-Zouch
Loughborough
Melton Mowbray
Spalding
Hunstanton
THE WASH
Wells-next-the-Sea
Cromer
Fakenham
North Walsham
King's Lynn
East Dereham
Norwich
Caister-on-Sea
Great Yarmouth
Yarmouth Roads
Acle
Swaffham
Wisbech
Stamford
Oakham
Peterborough
Downham Market
Wymondham
Lowestoft
Bungay
Beccles
March
Chatteris
Thetford
Diss
Ely
Lichfield
Brownhills
Tamworth
Walsall
Wolverhampton
Dudley
Stourbridge
Kidderminster
BIRMINGHAM
Nuneaton
Hinckley
Leicester
Coventry
Rugby
Market Harborough
Corby
Oundle
Kettering
Thrapston
Wellingborough
Huntingdon
Bromsgrove
Redditch
Warwick
Royal Leamington Spa
Northampton
Daventry
Worcester
Stratford-upon-Avon
Great Malvern
Tewkesbury
Evesham
Towcester
Bedford
St Neots
Cambridge
Newmarket
Bury St Edmunds
Stowmarket
Saxmundham
Aldeburgh
Orford Ness
Ipswich
Felixstowe
Harwich
The Naze
Colchester
Clacton-on-Sea
Sudbury
Haverhill
Royston
Stevenage
Banbury
Brackley
Milton Keynes
Buckingham
Bicester
Chipping Norton
Stow-on-the-Wold
Cheltenham
Gloucester
Stroud
Cirencester
Woodstock
Witney
Oxford
Thame
Abingdon
Aylesbury
Dunstable
Luton
Bishop's Stortford
Great Dunmow
Braintree
Halstead
Harlow
Chelmsford
St Albans
Hertford
Potters Bar
Epping
Watford
High Wycombe
Amersham
Brentwood
Basildon
Southend-on-Sea
LONDON
Maidenhead
Henley-on-Thames
Slough
Heathrow Airport
Reading
Wantage
Swindon
Malmesbury
Chippenham
Bristol
Bath
Trowbridge
Devizes
Marlborough
Hungerford
Newbury
Wokingham
Camberley
Woking
Esher
Croydon
Dartford
Tilbury
Gravesend
Sheerness
Chatham
Sittingbourne
Herne Bay
Margate
North Foreland
Ramsgate
Sandwich
Deal
The Downs
South Foreland
Canterbury
Maidstone
Sevenoaks
Orpington
Reigate
Dorking
Guildford
Basingstoke
Farnham
Alton
Andover
Amesbury
Warminster
Frome
Shepton Mallet
Wells
Glastonbury
Cheddar
Bridgwater Bay
Wylye
Salisbury
Stockbridge
Winchester
Romsey
Southampton
Petersfield
Haslemere
Godalming
Gatwick Airport
Crawley
East Grinstead
Royal Tunbridge Wells
Ashford
Tenterden
Folkestone
Dover
New Romney
Rye
Lydd
Dungeness
STRAIT OF DOVER
Hastings
Bexhill
Eastbourne
Beachy Head
Hailsham
Heathfield
Lewes
Newhaven
Brighton
Worthing
Horsham
Haywards Heath
Billingshurst
Midhurst
Arundel
Chichester
Bognor Regis
Selsey Bill
Portsmouth
Fareham
Ryde
Cowes
Yarmouth
Ventnor
ISLE OF WIGHT
St Catherine's Point
The Needles
The Solent
Lymington
Ringwood
Bournemouth
Wimborne Minster
Blandford Forum
Swanage
St Aldhelm's or St Alban's Head
Wareham
Weymouth
Fortuneswell
Bill of Portland
Dorchester
Lyme Regis
Lyme Bay
Sidmouth
Honiton
Ilminster
Crewkerne
Yeovil
Sherborne
Shaftesbury
Ilchester
Legend
Motorway with junction
Autoroute avec échangeur
Autobahn mit Anschlussstelle
Motorway junction with limited interchange
Echangeur à possibilités d'intercirculation restreintes
Anschlussstelle mit begrenztem Richtungswechsel
Motorway under construction
Autoroute en construction
Autobahn im Bau
Primary routes
Itinéraires principaux
Durchgangsstrassen
Other roads
Autres routes
Sonstige Strassen
Exeter
Primary route destinations
Destinations d'itinéraire principal
Durchgangsstrasse Bestimmungsorte
Short ferry routes for vehicles
Les corte traversées en bac pour les véhicules
Kurze Fährstrecken für Kraftfahrzeuge
Scale 1:1 375 000 or about one inch to 22 miles
Miles 20 0 20 40 60
Kilometres 20 0 20 40 60 80 100

Cape Wrath
Butt of Lewis
Port of Ness
Durness
Tongue
A836
Melvich
Thurso
Dunnet Head
John o' Groats
Duncansby Head
Sinclair's Bay
Wick
A9
A882
A895
A897
A838
Scourie
Eddrachillis Bay
Altnaharra
A894
A836
Inchnadamph
Enard Bay
Stornoway
A857
ISLE OF LEWIS
A859
Tarbert
OUTER HEBRIDES
THE MINCH
Helmsdale
Lairg
A839
A835
A837
Golspie
Ullapool
Loch Broom
Bonar Bridge
Dornoch
Dornoch Firth
Tain
A832
Gairloch
Kinlochewe
A896
Achnasheen
A890
A835
Alness
Dingwall
Cromarty Firth
MORAY FIRTH
Sound of Harris
THE LITTLE MINCH
North Uist
A867
Lochmaddy
Sound of Monach
Uig
Loch Snizort
Dunvegan
A850
Portree
A863
Sligachan
ISLAND OF SKYE
Sound of Raasay
Inner Sound
Kyle of Lochalsh
South Uist
A865
Lochboisdale
Sound of Barra
Barra
Castle Bay
A851
Ardvasar
Sound of Sleat
Canna
Sound of Canna
Rhum
Sound of Rhum
Mallaig
Eigg
Sound of Arisaig
A830
Muck
INNER HEBRIDES
Coll
Arinagour
Tobermory
Tiree
Scarinish
ISLAND OF MULL
L Tuath
L Scridain
A849
A884
Sound of Mull
Firth of Lorn
Inverness
A833
A831
Drumnadrochit
Loch Ness
Invermoriston
A887
A87
Fort Augustus
Invergarry
Loch Lochy
A82
A86
Fort William
A861
Ballachulish
Loch Linnhe
A828
Oban
Dalmally
Tyndrum
A819
Inveraray
A83
A816
Lochgilphead
Colonsay
Scalasaig
JURA
A846
Sound of Jura
Port Askaig
ISLAY
A847
A846
Laggan Bay
Port Ellen
Kennacraig
Claonaig
Loch Fyne
A886
A815
Dunoon
Kyles of Bute
Rothesay
Island of Bute
Firth of Clyde
Kilbrannan Sound
Island of Arran
Brodick
Lamlash
A841
Campbeltown
Mull of Kintyre
NORTH CHANNEL
Nairn
A96
Forres
Elgin
Lossiemouth
Spey Bay
A940
A941
Charlestown of Aberlour
Keith
A95
Banff
A98
Kinnaird Head
Fraserburgh
Turriff
A947
A950
A952
Peterhead
Huntly
A97
A920
Oldmeldrum
A96
Ellon
A92
Kintore
Aberdeen
Grantown-on-Spey
Carrbridge
River Spey
A939
Aviemore
Kingussie
Newtonmore
A9
A889
Ballater
River Dee
Banchory
A980
A93
A957
Braemar
Stonehaven
MOUNTAINS
GRAMPIAN
Blair Atholl
Pitlochry
Loch Rannoch
River Tummel
Inverbervie
A94
Montrose
A934
A932
Forfar
Blairgowrie
A923
Aberfeldy
A826
A827
Killin
Loch Tay
A822
Dundee
Arbroath
Tay Bridge
Newport-on-Tay
Perth
Crieff
Lochearnhead
A85
Crianlarich
Firth of Tay
St Andrews Bay
St Andrews
Fife Ness
Crail
A917
Elie
A915
A914
A91
Auchtermuchty
Kinross
M90
Callander
A84
A821
River Forth
Dunblane
Stirling
Kincardine
A977
A985
Dunfermline
Kirkcaldy
A92
Forth Bridge
Firth of Forth
North Berwick
Dunbar
A198
A1
Loch Lomond
A82
A814
Loch Long
Greenock
Dumbarton
A811
A81
Erskine Bridge
GLASGOW
M8
M9
M80
M876
Falkirk
Airdrie
Edinburgh
Dalkeith
Paisley
Wemyss Bay
Largs
A760
River Clyde
Hamilton
M74
Wishaw
A71
A70
Penicuik
A701
A703
A68
A7
St Abb's Head
Eyemouth
Berwick-upon-Tweed
Lauder
A697
Strathaven
Lanark
A721
A702
Peebles
A72
Galashiels
River Tweed
Coldstream
Kelso
A698
Ardrossan
Irvine
A78
A736
A77
Kilmarnock
Biggar
A73
A74
Selkirk
A699
Jedburgh
Prestwick
Ayr
A70
Cumnock
A76
Sanquhar
Hawick
A6088
Maybole
Girvan
Moffat
River Annan
A713
A702
Langholm
Morpeth
Bedlington
Lockerbie
Loch Ryan
A714
New Galloway
A712
Dumfries
Newcastle upon Tyne
Newton Stewart
Castle Douglas
Dalbeattie
A710
Annan
Gretna Green
Longtown
A6071
A69
Hexham
River Tyne
Gateshead
Stranraer
A75
Gatehouse of Fleet
Wigtown
A747
A746
Kirkcudbright
A711
Solway Firth
Carlisle
Brampton
A689
Consett
Luce Bay
Whithorn
Burrow Head
Mull of Galloway
Alston
A596
M6
Maryport
A66
Cockermouth
Workington
Penrith
A686
Bishop Auckland
Keswick
Ullswater
Whitehaven
Barnard Castle
Brough
A685
Egremont
A591
A592
A595
THE PENNINES
Ambleside
Windermere
Scotch Corner
Point of Ayre
Ramsey Bay
ISLE OF MAN
Ramsey
A3
A2
Peel
A1
A4
A5
Douglas
Castletown
Sedbergh
A684
Kendal
A590
Millom
Ulverston
Kirkby Lonsdale
A683
A65
Barrow-in-Furness
Morecambe Bay
Morecambe
Lancaster
Heysham
Settle
Skipton
Fleetwood
A59
River Ribble
Barrowford
HEBRIDES or WESTERN ISLES
SEA OF THE HEBRIDES

ROAD DISTANCES IN KILOMETRES

(Upper right of the diagonal: kilometres; lower left: miles)

	London	Aberdeen	Aberystwyth	Ayr	Berwick-upon-Tweed	Birmingham	Blackpool	Bournemouth	Braemar	Brighton	Bristol	Cambridge	Cardiff	Carlisle	Doncaster	Dover	Dundee	Edinburgh	Exeter	Fishguard	Fort William	Glasgow	Gloucester	Great Yarmouth	Harwich	Holyhead	Inverness	John o' Groats	Kingston upon Hull	Kyle of Lochalsh	Land's End	Leeds	Leicester	Lincoln	Liverpool	Manchester	Newcastle upon Tyne	Norwich	Nottingham	Oban	Oxford	Plymouth	Portsmouth	Sheffield	Shrewsbury	Southampton	Stranraer	Swansea	York
London		810	340	634	544	169	364	161	776	84	185	87	269	484	256	114	658	608	277	418	800	639	175	206	122	407	863	1067	332	927	478	304	156	211	325	298	441	183	196	787	92	351	113	256	241	124	647	327	311
Aberdeen	503		716	285	293	676	496	908	95	895	793	737	789	356	554	927	108	201	916	790	266	233	753	797	813	707	169	373	586	304	1114	526	666	616	549	547	378	764	610	286	777	990	901	579	642	880	367	795	513
Aberystwyth	211	445		510	501	183	246	333	652	378	201	344	169	360	283	454	605	515	323	90	692	515	164	473	452	179	782	990	359	803	523	291	246	320	167	227	439	444	264	663	248	398	357	256	124	323	523	117	330
Ayr	394	177	317		216	465	290	702	230	718	595	575	615	150	378	748	188	117	734	600	214	53	531	647	707	491	320	528	404	341	917	341	481	441	343	341	240	615	441	201	568	792	692	394	433	671	82	589	344
Berwick-upon-Tweed	338	182	311	134		425	311	663	238	628	566	473	592	140	319	658	182	92	689	632	306	163	512	555	599	501	346	550	298	391	888	251	406	360	352	315	103	528	356	290	521	763	645	306	426	624	254	616	238
Birmingham	105	420	114	289	264		198	237	607	262	130	161	166	315	151	283	562	470	253	274	631	470	90	290	269	238	737	945	245	758	452	182	63	145	50	129	333	267	80	618	103	327	227	122	72	206	478	192	209
Blackpool	226	308	153	180	193	123		435	431	460	328	335	336	140	151	478	385	295	454	336	455	295	280	406	443	227	560	769	204	583	652	116	225	206	79	77	208	373	179	443	301	528	425	138	158	404	303	348	154
Bournemouth	100	564	207	436	412	147	270		843	148	132	248	188	552	378	280	757	707	132	377	867	707	159	367	283	463	961	1165	454	995	330	410	254	336	377	365	558	344	295	853	145	206	84	348	298	50	715	269	433
Braemar	482	59	405	143	148	377	268	524		859	737	686	756	291	499	890	84	146	859	742	201	177	674	768	811	632	121	325	494	256	1070	472	608	552	494	492	323	735	568	227	721	945	847	515	575	824	312	777	459
Brighton	52	556	235	446	390	163	286	92	534		220	171	293	568	340	132	782	692	267	468	884	723	214	290	206	501	946	1151	415	1011	465	388	240	295	412	381	525	262	280	871	159	341	77	340	335	98	731	357	394
Bristol	115	493	125	370	352	81	204	82	458	137		232	72	446	282	299	692	600	122	248	761	600	56	388	307	332	867	1075	375	888	322	312	193	275	259	259	463	356	233	748	119	196	156	259	166	122	608	137	340
Cambridge	54	458	214	357	294	100	208	154	426	106	144		288	425	187	201	629	539	354	435	740	58	198	132	108	399	793	998	262	867	538	233	109	137	270	243	370	100	134	727	134	423	200	193	233	211	587	349	241
Cardiff	167	490	105	382	368	103	209	117	470	182	45	179		465	317	383	710	620	195	180	781	620	90	420	396	348	884	1094	393	908	394	354	229	311	272	277	489	388	246	768	174	269	229	288	179	195	628	64	393
Carlisle	301	221	224	93	87	196	87	343	181	353	277	264	289		229	599	245	154	568	451	315	154	381	497	541	341	422	629	254	443	768	192	332	291	193	192	92	465	291	303	418	642	542	245	283	521	163	439	195
Doncaster	159	344	176	235	198	94	94	235	310	211	175	116	197	142		372	443	352	404	375	544	383	241	269	312	269	565	769	76	671	602	47	119	63	138	82	183	237	69	531	233	478	357	29	159	336	391	349	55
Dover	71	576	282	465	409	176	297	174	553	82	186	125	238	372	231		813	723	399	533	914	753	290	298	201	546	977	1181	446	1041	589	418	270	325	439	412	555	280	311	901	206	465	209	370	356	230	761	441	425
Dundee	434	67	376	117	113	349	239	495	52	486	430	391	441	152	275	505		90	814	695	204	134	628	711	755	586	212	417	438	299	1014	415	562	505	438	436	267	679	512	188	665	888	790	468	531	768	269	721	402
Edinburgh	378	125	320	73	57	292	183	439	91	430	373	335	385	96	219	449	56		724	605	232	71	538	621	665	496	254	459	348	348	924	325	455	415	348	346	177	589	422	198	575	798	700	378	441	678	200	631	312
Exeter	172	569	201	456	428	157	282	82	534	166	76	220	121	353	251	248	506	450		370	884	723	179	478	399	454	995	1197	497	1011	198	435	315	398	381	380	586	454	356	858	229	74	190	381	288	169	731	259	462
Fishguard	260	491	56	373	393	170	209	234	461	291	154	270	112	280	233	331	432	376	230		782	605	246	563	542	269	872	1080	451	893	568	381	336	410	257	317	529	531	354	753	330	444	404	346	214	346	613	116	420
Fort William	497	165	430	133	190	392	283	539	125	549	473	460	485	196	338	568	127	144	549	486		163	697	813	856	657	106	314	570	127	1081	507	647	607	509	507	407	781	607	79	734	958	858	560	599	837	296	755	510
Glasgow	397	145	320	33	101	292	183	439	110	449	373	360	385	96	238	468	83	44	449	376	101		536	652	695	496	267	475	409	288	922	346	486	446	348	346	238	620	446	148	573	797	697	399	438	676	135	594	349
Gloucester	109	468	102	330	318	56	174	99	419	133	35	123	56	237	150	180	390	334	111	153	433	333		330	286	290	811	1011	272	824	378	256	137	219	203	203	407	299	177	682	84	253	174	203	124	150	552	143	283
Great Yarmouth	128	495	294	402	345	180	252	228	477	180	241	82	261	309	167	185	442	386	297	350	505	405	205		132	504	834	1038	333	940	676	315	225	206	386	330	452	32	229	800	251	552	319	267	362	330	660	473	323
Harwich	76	505	281	439	372	167	275	176	504	128	191	67	246	336	194	125	469	413	248	337	532	432	178	82		507	877	1081	373	983	597	359	217	249	378	385	496	117	241	843	203	473	235	301	354	246	660	430	463
Holyhead	253	439	111	305	311	148	141	288	393	311	206	248	216	212	167	339	364	308	282	167	408	308	180	313	315		763	970	344	784	652	264	262	322	148	200	398	472	275	644	336	528	463	240	166	439	504	296	303
Inverness	536	105	486	199	215	348	318	597	75	588	539	493	549	262	351	607	132	158	618	542	66	166	504	518	545	474		208	602	135	1193	579	742	687	615	600	431	801	692	185	829	1069	953	632	705	932	402	861	566
John o' Groats	663	232	615	328	342	587	478	724	202	715	668	620	680	391	478	734	259	285	744	671	195	295	628	645	672	603	129		806	304	1397	784	898	892	822	805	636	1006	896	393	1033	1271	1157	837	912	1136	610	1069	771
Kingston upon Hull	206	364	223	251	185	152	127	282	307	258	233	163	244	158	47	277	272	216	309	280	354	254	198	169	232	214	374	501		697	678	89	195	71	209	153	195	240	145	557	309	571	433	105	235	412	417	425	60
Kyle of Lochalsh	576	189	499	212	243	471	362	618	159	628	552	539	564	275	417	647	186	216	628	555	79	179	512	584	611	487	84	189	433		1210	634	774	734	636	634	512	908	734	206	861	1085	985	687	726	964	423	882	637
Land's End	297	692	325	570	552	281	405	205	665	289	200	334	245	477	374	366	630	574	123	353	672	573	235	420	371	405	741	868	421	752		634	515	597	581	581	785	678	555	1070	441	143	388	581	488	367	930	459	661
Leeds	189	327	181	212	156	113	72	255	293	241	194	145	220	119	29	260	258	202	270	237	315	215	159	196	223	164	360	487	55	394	394		153	109	121	64	148	283	113	494	270	509	393	53	175	373	354	365	39
Leicester	97	414	153	299	252	39	140	158	378	149	120	68	142	206	74	168	349	283	196	209	402	302	85	140	135	163	461	558	121	481	320	95		82	161	148	301	192	40	632	117	389	241	100	135	220	494	254	174
Lincoln	131	383	199	274	224	90	128	209	343	183	171	85	193	181	39	202	314	258	247	255	377	277	136	128	155	200	427	554	44	456	371	68	51		90	135	256	169	56	592	200	472	323	74	188	303	454	336	121
Liverpool	202	341	104	213	219	93	49	234	307	256	161	168	169	120	86	273	272	216	237	160	316	216	126	240	235	92	382	511	130	395	361	75	100	118		56	249	354	158	496	253	455	377	116	93	356	356	246	159
Manchester	185	340	141	212	196	80	48	227	306	237	161	151	172	119	51	256	271	215	236	197	315	215	126	205	239	124	373	500	95	394	361	40	92	84	35		212	298	101	494	232	455	356	61	111	335	354	301	103
Newcastle upon Tyne	274	235	273	149	64	207	129	347	201	326	288	230	304	57	114	345	166	110	364	329	253	148	253	281	308	247	268	395	121	318	488	92	187	159	155	132		425	253	375	418	660	542	201	323	521	254	513	135
Norwich	114	475	276	382	328	166	232	214	457	163	221	62	241	289	147	174	422	366	282	330	485	385	186	20	73	293	498	625	149	564	427	176	119	105	220	185	264		196	768	233	552	299	235	330	311	628	441	291
Nottingham	122	379	164	274	221	50	111	183	353	174	145	83	153	181	43	193	318	262	221	220	377	277	110	142	150	171	430	557	90	456	345	70	25	35	98	63	157	122		594	158	430	282	60	132	261	467	272	124
Oban	489	178	412	125	180	384	275	530	141	541	465	452	477	188	330	560	117	123	533	468	49	92	424	497	524	400	134	244	346	128	665	307	393	368	308	307	233	477	369		721	945	845	546	586	824	283	742	497
Oxford	57	482	154	353	324	64	187	90	448	99	74	83	108	260	145	128	413	357	142	205	456	356	52	156	126	209	515	642	192	535	274	168	73	124	157	144	260	145	98	448		298	124	217	171	103	583	227	291
Plymouth	218	615	247	492	474	203	328	128	587	212	122	263	167	399	297	289	552	496	46	276	595	495	157	343	294	328	664	790	355	674	89	316	242	293	283	283	410	343	267	587	185		264	455	362	243	805	332	536
Portsmouth	70	560	222	430	401	141	264	52	526	48	97	124	142	337	222	130	491	435	118	251	533	433	108	198	146	288	592	719	269	612	24	244	150	201	234	221	337	186	175	525	77	164		341	298	34	705	293	415
Sheffield	159	360	159	245	190	76	86	216	320	211	161	120	179	152	18	230	291	235	237	215	348	248	126	166	187	149	393	520	65	427	361	33	62	46	72	38	125	146	37	339	135	283	212		132	320	423	322	84
Shrewsbury	150	399	77	269	265	45	98	185	357	208	103	145	111	176	99	221	330	274	179	133	372	272	77	225	220	103	438	567	146	451	303	109	84	117	58	69	201	205	82	364	106	225	185	82		274	446	190	214
Southampton	77	547	201	417	388	128	251	31	512	61	76	131	121	324	209	143	477	421	105	215	520	420	93	205	153	273	579	706	256	599	228	232	137	188	221	208	324	193	162	512	64	151	21	199	170		684	259	394
Stranraer	402	228	325	51	158	297	188	444	194	454	378	365	390	101	243	473	167	124	454	331	184	84	343	410	410	313	250	379	259	263	578	220	307	282	221	220	158	390	290	176	362	500	438	263	277	425		602	357
Swansea	203	494	73	366	383	119	216	167	483	222	85	217	40	273	217	274	448	392	161	72	469	369	89	294	267	184	535	664	264	548	285	227	158	209	153	187	319	274	169	461	141	206	182	200	118	161	374		404
York	193	319	205	214	148	130	96	269	285	245	211	150	244	121	34	264	250	194	287	261	317	217	176	201	288	188	352	479	37	396	411	24	108	75	99	64	84	181	77	309	181	333	258	52	133	245	222	251	

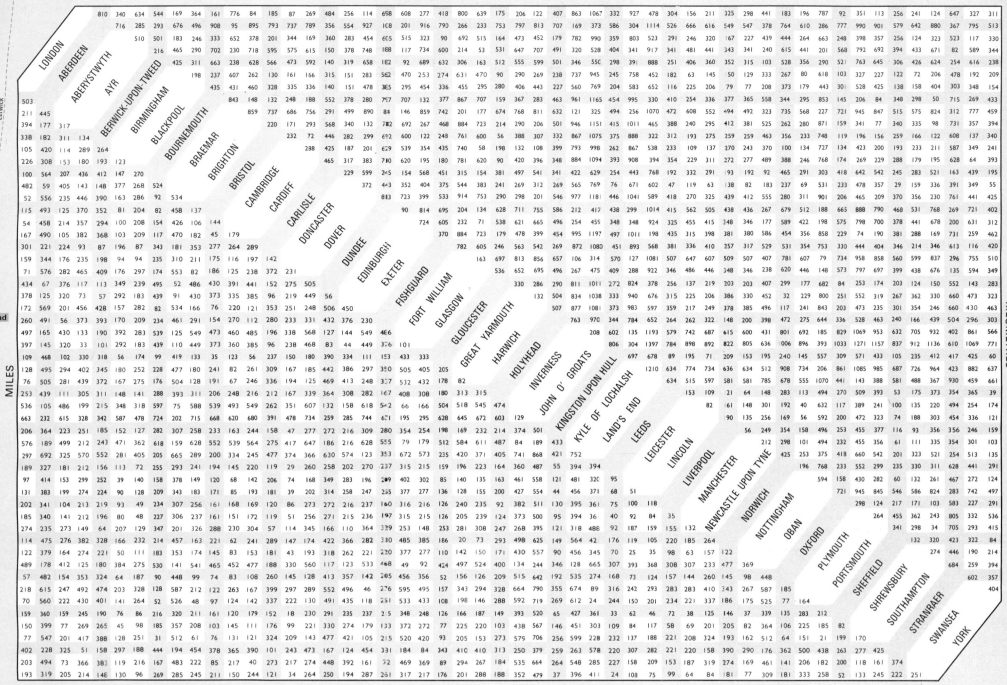

The distances given in this chart are those obtained by using motorways, primary routes and main roads

ROAD DISTANCES IN MILES

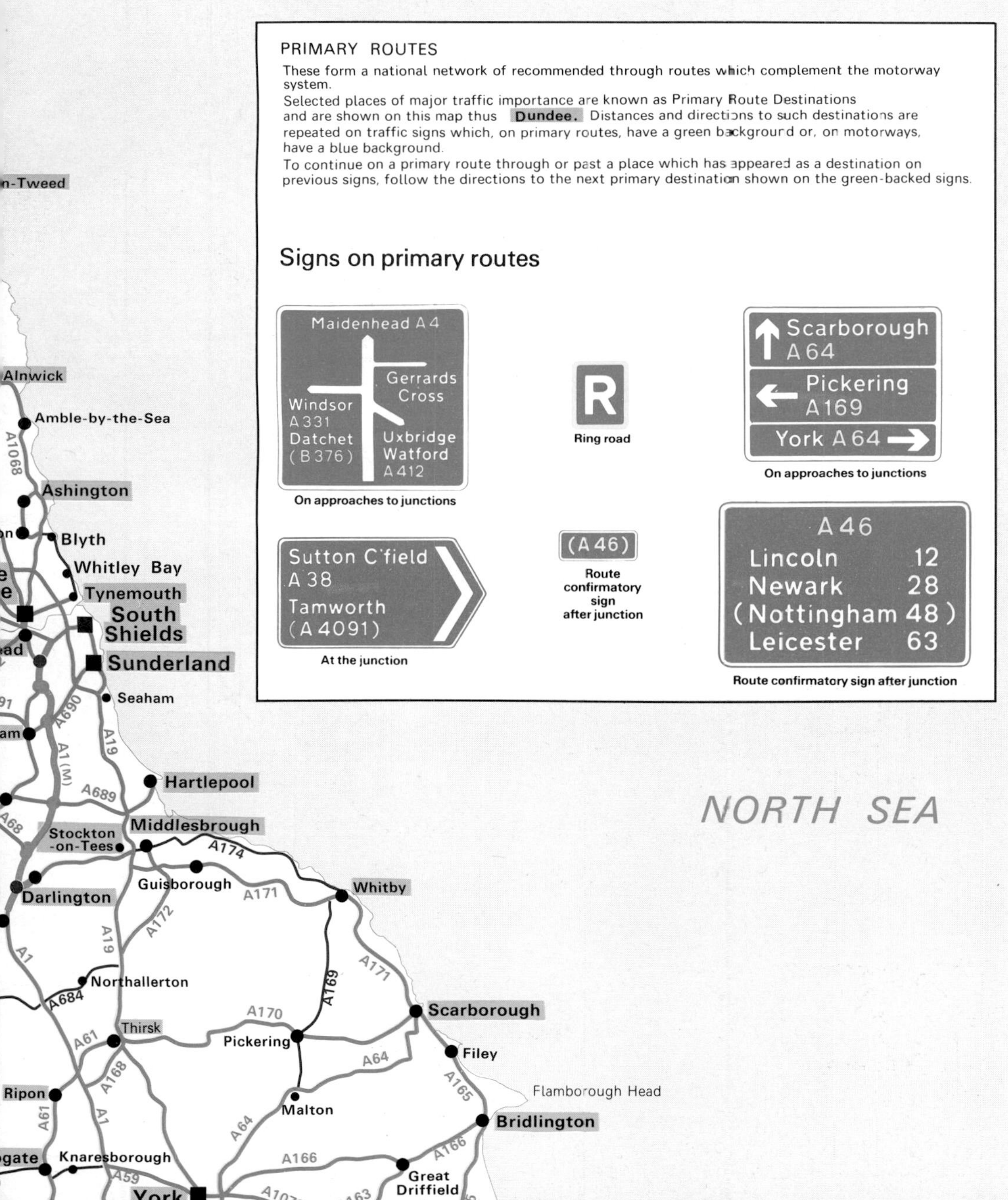
PRIMARY ROUTES
These form a national network of recommended through routes which complement the motorway system.
Selected places of major traffic importance are known as Primary Route Destinations and are shown on this map thus Dundee. Distances and directions to such destinations are repeated on traffic signs which, on primary routes, have a green background or, on motorways, have a blue background.
To continue on a primary route through or past a place which has appeared as a destination on previous signs, follow the directions to the next primary destination shown on the green-backed signs.
Signs on primary routes
Maidenhead A4
Gerrards Cross
Windsor A331 Datchet (B376)
Uxbridge Watford A412
On approaches to junctions
R
Ring road
Scarborough A64
Pickering A169
York A64
On approaches to junctions
Sutton C'field A38
Tamworth (A 4091)
At the junction
(A 46)
Route confirmatory sign after junction
A 46
Lincoln 12
Newark 28
(Nottingham 48)
Leicester 63
Route confirmatory sign after junction
NORTH SEA
Lerwick
Alnwick
Amble-by-the-Sea
Ashington
Blyth
Whitley Bay
Tynemouth
South Shields
Sunderland
Seaham
Hartlepool
Middlesbrough
Stockton-on-Tees
Darlington
Guisborough
Whitby
Northallerton
Thirsk
Pickering
Scarborough
Filey
Malton
Flamborough Head
Bridlington
Ripon
Knaresborough
York
Wetherby
Great Driffield
A1068
A19
A1(M)
A689
A174
A171
A172
A169
A170
A684
A61
A168
A1
A64
A165
A166
A59
A1079
A163

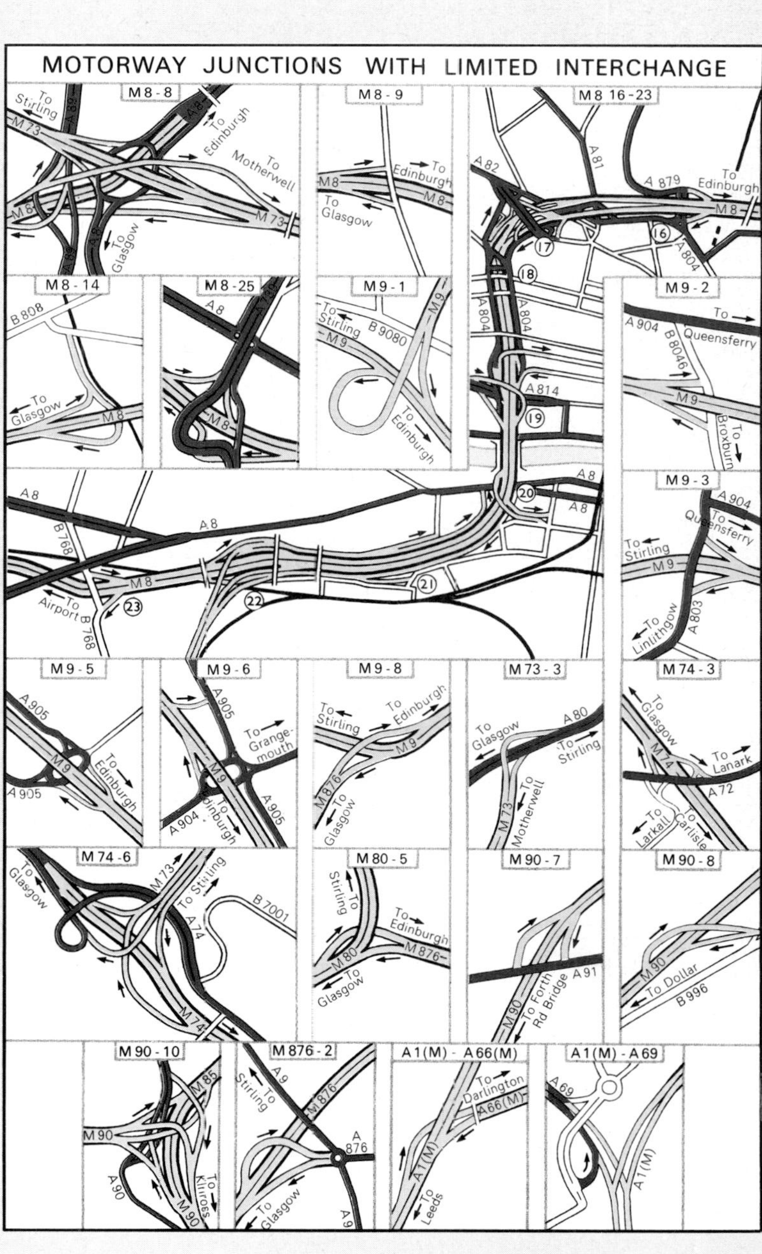
MOTORWAY JUNCTIONS WITH LIMITED INTERCHANGE
M8-8
M8-9
M8 16-23
M8-14
M8-25
M9-1
M9-2
M9-3
M9-5
M9-6
M9-8
M73-3
M74-3
M74-6
M80-5
M90-7
M90-8
M90-10
M876-2
A1(M)-A66(M)
A1(M)-A69
To Stirling
To Edinburgh
To Motherwell
To Glasgow
To Queensferry
To Grangemouth
To Lanark
To Dollar
To Kinross
To Darlington
To Leeds

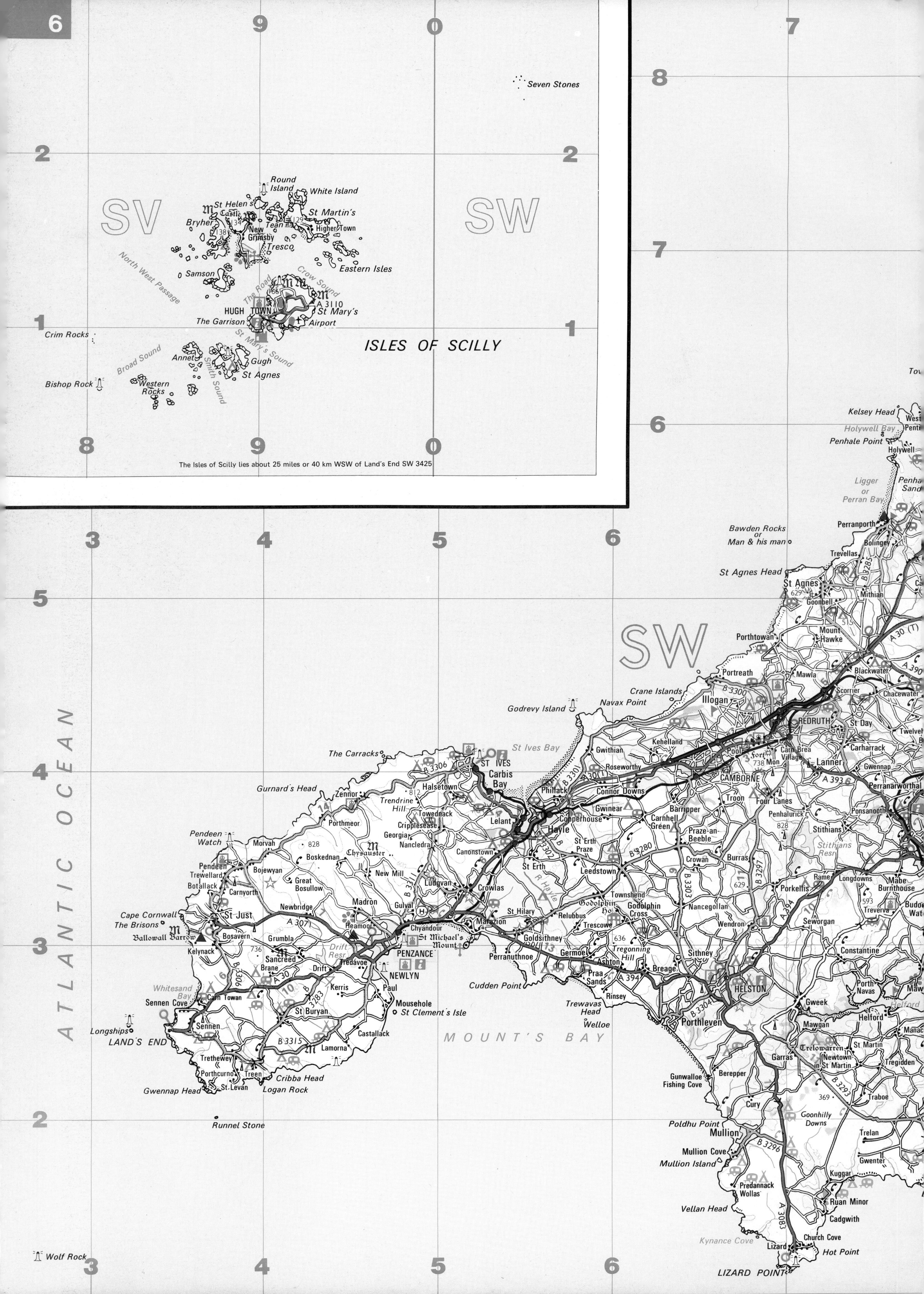
Seven Stones
Round Island
White Island
St Helen's
Castle
Bryher
St Martin's
Tean
Higher Town
New Grimsby
Tresco
Eastern Isles
Samson
North West Passage
Crow Sound
The Road
HUGH TOWN
St Mary's
A 3110
The Garrison
Airport
Crim Rocks
ISLES OF SCILLY
Broad Sound
St Mary's Sound
Annet
Smith Sound
Gugh
St Agnes
Bishop Rock
Western Rocks
SV
SW
The Isles of Scilly lies about 25 miles or 40 km WSW of Land's End SW 3425
Kelsey Head
Holywell Bay
Penhale Point
Holywell
Ligger or Perran Bay
Perranporth
Bolingey
Bawden Rocks or Man & his man
Trevellas
St Agnes Head
St Agnes
Goonbell
Mithian
Mount Hawke
Porthtowan
Portreath
Mawla
Blackwater
Scorrier
Chacewater
Crane Islands
Navax Point
Illogan
Godrevy Island
REDRUTH
St Day
St Ives Bay
Gwithian
Kehelland
Carn Brea Village
Lanner
Carharrack
The Carracks
ST IVES
Carbis Bay
Roseworthy
Pool
CAMBORNE
Gwennap
Gurnard's Head
Zennor
Trendrine Hill
Halsetown
Phillack
Connor Downs
Troon
Four Lanes
Perranarworthal
Towednack
Lelant
Gwinear
Barripper
Penhalurick
Ponsanooth
Pendeen Watch
Morvah
Porthmeor
Cripplesease
Georgia
Nancledra
Hayle
Copperhouse
Carnhell Green
Praze-an-Beeble
Stithians
Stithians Resr
Pendeen
Trewellard
Botallack
Bojewyan
Boskednan
Chysauster
Canonstown
St Erth Praze
St Erth
Leedstown
Crowan
Burras
Great Bosullow
New Mill
Ludgvan
Crowlas
Townshend
Porkellis
Longdowns
Mabe Burnthouse
Carnyorth
Cape Cornwall
The Brisons
St Just
Ballowall Barrow
Newbridge
Madron
Gulval
Godolphin
Godolphin Cross
Nancegollan
St Hilary
Relubbus
Treverva
Bosavern
Grumbla
Heamoor
Chyandour
St Michael's Mount
Marazion
Trescowe
Goldsithney
Wendron
Seworgan
Kelynack
Sancreed
Drift Resr
PENZANCE
Perranuthnoe
Germoe
Tregonning Hill
Sithney
Constantine
Brane
Drift
Tredavoe
NEWLYN
Ashton
Praa Sands
Breage
HELSTON
Whitesand Bay
Carn Towan
Kerris
Paul
Cudden Point
Rinsey
Porth Navas
Sennen Cove
St Buryan
Mousehole
St Clement's Isle
Trewavas Head
Welloe
Gweek
Helford
Longships
Sennen
LAND'S END
Castallack
MOUNT'S BAY
Porthleven
Mawgan
Trelowarren
St Martin
Lamorna
Newtown-in-St Martin
Tregidden
Trethewey
Porthcurno
Treen
Cribba Head
Gunwalloe Fishing Cove
Berepper
Garras
Gwennap Head
St Levan
Logan Rock
Traboe
Cury
Goonhilly Downs
Runnel Stone
Poldhu Point
Mullion
Trelan
Mullion Cove
Mullion Island
Gwenter
Kuggar
Predannack Wollas
Ruan Minor
Vellan Head
Cadgwith
Kynance Cove
Church Cove
Lizard
Hot Point
LIZARD POINT
Wolf Rock
ATLANTIC OCEAN
A 30
A 3047
A 393
A 394
A 3083
A 307
A 30
A 3074
B 3300
B 3301
B 3302
B 3280
B 3303
B 3297
B 3306
B 3311
B 3283
B 3315
B 3304
B 3296
B 3293
B 3285

8
9
0
1
2
Camelford
Delabole
Crowdy Reservoir
Laneast
Trewen
River Inny
Polyphant
Port Isaac Bay
Port Isaac
Rumps Point
Pentire Point
Port Quin Bay
Portquin
Portgaverne
Pendoggett
Tregeare Rounds
St Teath
Helstone
Michaelstow
Rough Tor
Altarnun
Lewannick
Brown Willy
Garrow Tor
Codca
Trebartha
North Hill
Gulland Rock
New Polzeath
Padstow Bay
Polzeath
Trebetherick
Trelights
St Endellion
Tredrizzick
St Minver
Trelill
St Breward
BODMIN MOOR
Bolventor
Gunver Head
Trevose Head
Quies
Crugmeer
Rock
Chapel Amble
St Kew
St Kew Highway
St Tudy
Row
De Lank River
Constantine Bay
Trevone
PADSTOW
Treyarnon
St Merryn
Shop
Little Petherick
Bodieve
Trevanson
WADEBRIDGE
Egloshayle
St Mabyn
Blisland
Temple
Dozmary Pool
River Fowey
Kilmar Tor
Bathpool
Henwood
Rilla Mill
Siblyback Lake Resr
The Hurlers
Minions
Upton Cross
Caradon Hill
Darite
Porthcothan Bay
St Breock
St Issey
Colliford Lake Resr
Maidenwell
Park Head
Penrose
Rumford
Tredinnick
Burlawn
Washaway
Helland
Bedruthan Steps
St Eval
St Ervan
St Breock Downs
R Camel
Common Moor
Trethevy Quoit
Tremar
Warleggan
St Neot
Cardinham
BODMIN
Trenance
Rutherbridge
Nanstallon
St Lawrence
Mount
St Cleer
Berryl's Point
St Mawgan
Rosenannon
Withiel
Ley
Dobwalls
Merrymeet
Watergate Bay
Talskiddy
Vale of Mawgan or Lanherne
St Wenn
Tregurrian
St Mawgan Airfield
Tregonetha
Lanivet
Lanhydrock House
Bodmin Parkway Sta
East Taphouse
Doublebois
LISKEARD
Newquay Bay
Fistral Bay
St Columb Minor
St Columb Major
Castle an Dinas
Victoria
Braddock
St Pinnock
Menheniot
NEWQUAY
Porth Resr
Colan
Trebudannon
Belowda
Lockengate
Redmoor
Castle
Boconnoc
St Keyne
Crantock
Mountjoy
Ruthvoes
Trevarren
Roche
Bilberry
Herodsfoot
Trewidland
Kestle Mill
St Columb Road
Indian Queens
Lanlivery
Luxulyan
LOSTWITHIEL
Trerice
Carines
Cubert
Fraddon
St Dennis
Hensbarrow Downs
Bugle
Stenalees
Duloe
Widegates
St Enoder
Whitemoor
Penpillick
St Winnow
Lerryn
Bocaddon
St Newlyn East
Retew
Trevisco
Nanpean
Penwithick
Sandplace
Muchlarnick
Mount
Rejerrah
Summercourt
Foxhole
Carthew
Trethurgy
Golant
Lanreath
Pelynt
Morval
Newlyn Downs
Mitchell
Brighton
High Street
St Blazey
Tywardreath
Penpoll
LOOE
St Martin
Downderry
Goonhavern
Carland Cross
St Stephen
ST AUSTELL
Par
Highway
Trenewan
Looe Bay
Zelah
New Mills
Trewoon
Charlestown
Polkerris
Ferry
FOWEY
Polruan
Lansallos
Polperro
St George's or Looe Island
Talland Bay
St Allen
Trispen
Laddock
Coombe
St Mewan
Polgooth
Porthpean
Menabilly
Pencarrow Head
Grampound Road
Sticker
St Austell Bay
Gribbin Head
St Erme
Grampound
Trenarren
Black Head
SX
Shortlanesend
Probus
Creed
Pentewan
Mevagissey Bay
St Ewe
Polmassick
Tresillian
Kenwyn
Merther
River Fal
Mevagissey
Threemilestone
TRURO
St Clement
Tregony
Portmellon
Trewarthenwick
Trevarrick
Chapel Point
Kea
Malpas
St Michael Penkevil
Ruan Lanihorne
St Michael Caerhays
Gorran Haven
Playing Place
Old Kea
Lamorran
Portholland
Boswinger
Penare
Carnon Downs
Ferry
Philleigh
Veryan
Portloe
Veryan Bay
Dodman Point
Penpoll
Trelissick
Feock
Devoran
Carclew
Carne
Gerrans Bay
Nare Head
Mylor Bridge
Carrick Roads
Trewithian
St Just in Roseland
PENRYN
Gerrans
Portscatho
Flushing
FALMOUTH
St Mawes
Greeb Point
Castle
Bohortha
Pendennis Point
Zone Point
Penjerrick
Falmouth Bay
Mawnan Smith
Rosemullion Head
St Anthony-in-Meneage
Nare Point
Porthallow
Porthoustock
Manacle Point
St Keverne
The Manacles
Coverack
Black Head
ENGLISH CHANNEL
A30 (T)
A39 (T)
A38 (T)
A390
A387
A3058
A3059
A3075
A3076
A3078
A389
B3314
B3266
B3267
B3274
B3276
B3254
B3359
B3269
B3268
B3273
B3287
B3289
B3284
B3253
B3082
5
4
3
2
6
7
8

Widemouth Bay
Marhamchurch
Bridgerule
Pyworthy
Hollacombe
Graddon Moor
SS
Halwill Junction
Coppathorne
Dizzard Point
Poundstock
Whitstone
Clawton
Halwill
Beaworthy
Tregole
Trewint
St Gennys
Week St Mary
North Tamerton
Quoditch
Cambeak
Crackington
Wainhouse Corner
Jacobstow
Tetcott
Lana
Ashwater
Broadbury
Luffincott
Eworthy
Germansweek
South Wheatley
Clubworthy
West Curry
Northcott
Chapmans Well
Virginstow
Boasley Cross
Fire Beacon Point
Marshgate
Canworthy Water
Bennacott
Boyton
East Panson
Bratton Clovelly
Boscastle
Lesnewth
Otterham
Warbstow
Brazacott
St Giles on the Heath
Tintagel Head
Castle
Trevalga
Tremaine
North Petherwin
Polapit Tamar
Broadwoodwidger
Tintagel
Bossiney
Hallworthy
Treneglos
Yeolmbridge
Werrington
Cross Green
Thrushelton
Treknow
Trewarmett
Trewassa
Davidstow
Tremail
Tresmeer
Egloskerry
Stowford
Lewdown
Start Point
Tregeare
Langore
Red Down
St Stephens
LAUNCESTON
Lifton
Portgate
Lewtrenchard
Treligga
St Clether
Tinhay
Lydford
Delabole
Camelford
Crowdy Reservoir
Laneast
Tregadillett
Coryton
Port Isaac Bay
Trewen
River Inny
Lawhitton
Marystow
Helstone
Polyphant
South Petherwin
Kelly
Chillaton
North Brentor
Black
Portgaverne
St Teath
Rough Tor
Altarnun
Lewannick
Bradstone
Pendoggett
Tregeare Rounds
Michaelstow
Brown Willy
Codda
Milton Abbot
Garrow Tor
Dunterton
Trelill
St Breward
BODMIN MOOR
Bolventor
Trebartha
North Hill
Coad's Green
Lezant
Treburley
St Kew
Lamerton
St Kew Highway
St Tudy
Row
De Lank River
Sydenham Damerel
Bray Shop
Kilmar Tor
Bathpool
Stoke Climsland
Luckett
Latchley
TAVISTOCK
Blisland
Temple
Henwood
Rilla Mill
Linkinhorne
Dozmary Pool
St Mabyn
River Fowey
WADEBRIDGE
Egloshayle
Colliford Lake Resr
Siblyback Lake Resr
Upton Cross
South Hill
Downgate
Chilsworthy
Whitchurch
Kit Hill
St Ann's Chapel
Gunnislake
The Hurlers
Minions
Kelly Bray
Helland
Maidenwell
Caradon Hill
Golberdon
Albaston
Higher Walreddon
Washaway
Haye
Pensilva
Darite
Common Moor
Trevigro
Harrowbarrow
Horrabridge
Cardinham
Warleggan
Trethevy Quoit
Callington
Cotehele Ho
Buckland Monachorum
Yelverton
BODMIN
Mount
St Neot
St Cleer
Tremar
Calstock
Crapstone
Nanstallon
St Ive
St Dominick
Buckland Abbey
St Lawrence
Merrymeet
Bere Alston
Ley
Milton Combe
Dobwalls
St Mellion
Lanivet
Bodmin Parkway Sta
East Taphouse
Doublebois
LISKEARD
Quethiock
Pillaton
Lopwell
Lanhydrock House
St Pinnock
Bere Ferrers
Braddock
Menheniot
Cargreen
Lockengate
Redmoor
Castle
Tamerton Foliot
Hatt
Landulph
Boconnoc
St Keyne
Botusfleming
Trewidland
Tideford
Landrake
Herodsfoot
LOSTWITHIEL
Trematon
Lanlivery
Crownhill
Bugle
Luxulyan
Duloe
Markwell
SALTASH
St Stephens
Budeaux
Stenalees
Hessenford
St Germans
PLYMOUTH
St Winnow
Lerryn
Sandplace
Widegates
Polbathic
Penwithick
Penpillick
Bocaddon
Lanreath
Muchlarnick
Morval
Sheviock
TORPOINT
Devonport
Carthew
Trethurgy
Golant
Pelynt
LOOE
St Martin
Seaton
Crafthole
Antony
St Blazey
Penpoll
Downderry
Portwrinkle
Ferry
ST AUSTELL
Tywardreath
Highway
Trenewan
St John
Par
Mount Edgecumbe
Drake's Island
Polkerris
Ferry
Looe Bay
WHITSAND BAY
Freathy
Millbrook
Hooe
Charlestown
FOWEY
Polruan
St George's or Looe Island
The Sound
Menabilly
Castle
Lansallos
Talland Bay
Kingsand
Polgooth
Porthpean
Polperro
Cawsand
Plymouth Breakwater
Pencarrow Head
St Austell Bay
Gribbin Head
Rame
Penlee Point
Heybrook Bay
Trenarren
Black Head
Rame Head
Great Mew Stone
Pentewan
Mevagissey Bay
PLYMOUTH to
Roscoff 6-7 hrs
Santander 24 hrs
Mevagissey
Portmellon
Chapel Point
Gorran Haven
Penare
Dodman Point
Eddystone Rocks
ENGLISH

9
Exbourne
Honeychurch
North Tawton
Sampford Courtenay
Jacobstowe
Inwardleigh
Folly Gate
OKEHAMPTON
Castle
Okehampton Camp
Okehampton Common
Meldon
Meldon Resr
Sourton
Yes Tor
High Willhays
Bridestowe and Sourton Common
Thorndon Cross
Sticklepath
South Tawton
South Zeal
Belstone
Taw Green
Cosdon Hill
Throwleigh
Wonson
Gidleigh
Whiddon Down
Spreyton
Hittisleigh
Hillerton
Itton
Nymet Tracey
Bow
Zeal Monachorum
Clannaborough Barton
Coleford
Colebrooke
Knowle
CREDITON
Yeoford
Sandford
Upton Hellions
Creedy Park
Shobrooke
Stockleigh Pomeroy
Efford
Thorverton
Nether Exe
Up Exe
Silverton
Bradninch
Hele
Brampford Speke
Upton Pyne
Stoke Canon
Rewe
Cowley
Newton St Cyres
Hookway
Uton
EXETER
Pinhoe
Poltimore
Broadclyst
Dog Village
Whimple
Rockbeare
Exeter Airport
Budlake
Westwood
Clyst Honiton
Sowton
Clyst St Mary
Aylesbeare
Farringdon
Whipton
Countess Wear
Alphington
Topsham
Clyst St George
Woodbury Salterton
Woodbury
Ebford
Exton
Lympstone
Black Hill
Exminster
Powderham
Castle
Kenton
Starcross
Cockwood
EXMOUTH
Littleham
Dawlish Warren
DAWLISH
Ide
Longdown
Whitestone
Pathfinder Village
Tedburn St Mary
Cheriton Bishop
Crockernwell
Drewsteignton
Easton
Chagford
Dunsford
Doccombe
Bridford
Christow
Kennick Resr
Tottiford Reservoir
Trenchford Reservoir
Shillingford St George
Duchideock
Doddiscombsleigh
Kennford
Kenn
Higher Ashton
Lower Ashton
Whiteway Ho.
Trusham
Hennock
Moretonhampstead
North Bovey
Lettaford
Manaton
Lustleigh
Frenchbeer
Fernworthy Reservoir
Hangingstone Hill
Amicombe Hill
Sittaford Tor
Cut Hill
DARTMOOR
FOREST
DARTMOOR
Grimspound
Hameldown Tor
Postbridge
Bellever
Rough Tor
Cocks Hill
Cudliptown
Great Mis Tor
Settlement
Merrivale
Two Bridges
HM Prison
Princetown
Sampford Spiney
West Dart River
Hexworthy
Dartmeet
Poundsgate
Babeny
Cator Court
Widecombe in the Moor
Haytor Vale
Rippon Tor
Ponsworthy
Buckland in the Moor
Ilsington
Bovey Tracey
Chudleigh Knighton
Chudleigh
Ashcombe
Ideford
Luton
Little Haldon
Heathfield
Coldeast
Teigngrace
Preston
Kingsteignton
Bishopsteignton
Holcombe
TEIGNMOUTH
Shaldon
Netherton
Combeinteignhead
Stokeinteignhead
Haccombe
BABBACOMBE BAY
Maidencombe
Coffinswell
Sigford
Bickington
NEWTON ABBOT
East Ogwell
West Ogwell
Abbotskerswell
Kingskerswell
North Whilborough
Barton
Babbacombe
TORQUAY
Hope's Nose
Shiphay
Cockington
Ipplepen
Compton
Marldon
Woodland
Denbury
Torbryan
Forder Green
Broadhempston
Staverton
Landscove
Woolston Green
ASHBURTON
Holne
Buckfast
Abbey
BUCKFASTLEIGH
Dean
Dean Prior
Dartington
Dartington Hall
Cott
Littlehempston
Berry Pomeroy
Blagdon
TORBAY
PAIGNTON
TOR BAY
Goodrington
Hydrofoil - Passenger Only
TORBAY to Seasonal
Alderney 2 hrs
Guernsey 2 hrs
Jersey 3 hrs
Venford Resr
Whiteworks
Walkhampton
Burrator Reservoir
Dousland
Sheepstor
Meavy
Cater's Beam
Ryder's Hill
Abbot's Way
Avon Dam Resr
SX
SY
Shaugh Prior
Shell Top
Ugborough Moor
Didworthy
Wotter
Lee Moor
Cornwood
Drakeland Corner
Lutton
Harford
Ugborough Beacon
Sparkwell
Ivybridge
Bittaford
Lee Mill
South Brent
Rattery
Tigley
TOTNES
Collaton St Mary
Stoke Gabriel
Harberton
Sharpham Ho
Belsford
Avonwick
Lincombe
Diptford
North Huish
Ugborough
Harbertonford
Crabadon
Ashprington
Tuckenhay
Cornworthy
Galmpton
Berry Head
BRIXHAM
Sharkham Point
Elburton
Westlake
Ermington
Brixton
Yealmpton
Modbury
Brownston
Curtisknowle
Moreleigh
Halwell
Washbourne
Allaleigh
Dittisham
Capton
Hillhead
Britannia RN College
Ferry
Kingswear
Scabbacombe Head
Woodford
Blackawton
DARTMOUTH
Castle
Mew Stone
Holbeton
Newton Ferrers
Noss Mayo
Wembury
Stoke Point
Kingston
St Ann's Chapel
Loddiswell
Aveton Gifford
Woodleigh
Hutcherleigh
East Allington
Bowden
Stoke Fleming
Strete
Ringmore
Bigbury
Churchstow
Goveton
Harleston
Slapton
Bigbury-on-Sea
Burgh Island
Bigbury Bay
Buckland
West Alvington
KINGSBRIDGE
Sherford
START BAY
Stokenham
Torcross
Bantham
Thurlestone
South Milton
West Charleton
Chillington
Woolston
Galmpton
Ford
Beeson
Beesands
Hope
Bolt Tail
Malborough
South Pool
SALCOMBE
East Portlemouth
Kellaton
Hallsands
South Allington
START POINT
East Prawle
Bolt Head
Prawle Point
CHANNEL
6
7
8
9
0

BRISTOL CHANNEL
North West Point
LUNDY
South West Point
Rat Island
ILFRACOMBE
Bull Point
Lee
Slade
Rockham Bay
Morte Point
Mortehoe
Woolacombe
Trimstone
Morte Bay
Baggy Point
Pickwell
North Buckland
Georgeham
Croyde Bay
Croyde
Knowle
Saunton
Braunton
Heanton Punchardon
Wrafton
Braunton Burrows
Chivenor
BARNSTAPLE
OR
BIDEFORD BAY
Bideford Bar
Fremington
River Taw
Yelland
Appledore
Instow
Bickleton
NORTHAM
Westward Ho!
Tapeley
Westleigh
Horwood
HARTLAND POINT
Titchberry
Windbury Point
Abbotsham
BIDEFORD
East-the-Water
Woodtown
Alverdiscott
Hartland Quay
Stoke
Hartland
Clovelly
Clovelly Dykes
Dyke
Buck's Mills
Fairy Cross
Landcross
Littleham
Millford
Philham
Elmscott
Buck's Cross
Parkham
Weare Giffard
South Hole
Woolfardisworthy
Parkham Ash
Buckland Brewer
Monkleigh
Melbury
Frithelstock
Knaps Longpeak
Welcombe
Meddon
Ashmansworthy
Little Torrington
Gooseham
Eastcott
East Putford
Morwenstow
Higher Sharpnose Point
Shop
Youlstone
Dinworthy
West Putford
Stibb Cross
Langtree
Bulkworthy
Woodford
Bradworthy
Abbots Bickington
Peters Marland
Lower Sharpnose Point
Upper Tamar Lake
Newton St Petrock
Winswell
Coombe
Kilkhampton
Sutcombe
Alfardisworthy
Lower Tamar Lake
Soldon Cross
River Waldon
Milton Damerel
Stibb
Shebbear
BUDE
Poughill
Holsworthy Beacon
Thornbury
Buckland Filleigh
Flexbury
Bude Haven
STRATTON
Grimscott
Bradford
Chilsworthy
BAY
Launcells
Pancrasweek
Cookbury
Sheepwash
HOLSWORTHY
Holemoor
Black Torrington
Highampton
Marhamchurch
Widemouth Bay
Bridgerule
Pyworthy
Hollacombe
Graddon Moor
Coppathorne
Halwill Junction
Dizzard Point
Poundstock
Halwill
Beaworthy
Northlew
Whitstone
Clawton
River Claw
River Tamar
River Deer
Tregole
Trewint
Week St Mary
St Gennys
North Tamerton
Quoditch
Broadbury
Cambeak
Crackington
Wainhouse Corner
Jacobstow
Tetcott
Lana
Ashwater
Eworthy
Germansweek
Luffincott
Chapmans Well
Boasley Cross
South Wheatley
Clubworthy
West Curry
Northcott
Virginstow
Fire Beacon Point
Marshgate
Bennacott
East Panson
Bratton Clovelly
Boscastle
Lesnewth
Otterham
Canworthy Water
Brazacott
Boyton
St Giles on the Heath
River Wolf
Castle
Tintagel Head
Trevalga
Warbstow
Tremaine
North Petherwin
Polapit Tamar
Broadwoodwidger
River Thrushel
Bossiney
Tintagel
Hallworthy
River Ottery
Werrington
Thrushelton
Trewassa
Treneglos
Yeolmbridge
Cross Green
Trewarmett
Treknow
Davidstow
Tremail
Tresmeer
Egloskerry
Stowford
Lewdown
Start Point
Tregeare
Langore
River Carey
Red Down
St Stephens
LAUNCESTON
Lifton
Portgate
Lewtrenchard
Treligga
St Clether
Castle
Tinhay
Lydford
Delabole
Camelford
Laneast
Tregadillett
Coryton
Crowdy Reservoir
River Inny
Trewen
Port Isaac Bay
Lawhitton
Marystow
Port Isaac
Helstone
Polyphant
South Petherwin
River Tamar
Kelly
Chillaton
North Brentor
Portgaverne
Rough Tor
St Teath
Tregeare Rounds
Altarnun
Lewannick
Bradstone
Pendoggett
Michaelstow
Brown Willy
Milton Abbot
Garrow Tor
Lezant
Dunterton
Trelill
Codda

6 7 8 9 0

Foreland Point
Heddon's Mouth
Woody Bay
LYNTON
Countisbury
Lynmouth
Combe Martin Bay
Trentishoe
Martinhoe
Culbone Hill
Toll
Porlock Bay
Porlock
Selworthy Beacon
North Hill
Allerford
Selworthy
MINEHEAD
Hele
Combe Martin
Berrynarbor
Kemacott
Barbrook
Brendon
Cheriton
Heale
Parracombe
Kentisbury
Furzehill
Shallowford
Brendon Common
Luccombe
Alcombe
Dunster
Blue Anchor
Blue Anchor Bay
Old Cleeve
Blackmoor Gate
Patchole
Pinkworthy Pond
EXMOOR
Wootton Courtenay
Dunkery Hill
Castle
Carhampton
Timberscombe
Withycombe
Washford
Bittadon
East Down
Wistlandpound Resr
Arlington
Challacombe
FOREST
River Exe
Croydon Hill
Rodhuish
Milltown
Muddiford
Loxhore
Shoulsbarrow Common
Simonsbath
Exford
Luckwell Bridge
Wheddon Cross
Roadwater
Luxborough
Knightacott
Bratton Fleming
Leworthy
Burcombe
EXMOOR
Lype Hill
BRENDON HILLS
Kingsbridge
Marwood
Prixford
Shirwell
Lydcott
Long Holcombe
Withypool
Withypool Common
Treborough
Ashford
Stoke Rivers
Goodleigh
Brayford
North Heasley
North Radworthy
Winsford Hill
Winsford
Exton
Bridgetown
Withiel Florey
BARNSTAPLE
Newport
Gunn
Charles
Heasley Mill
South Radworthy
Liscombe
Brompton Regis
Wimbleball Lake
Clatworthy Reservoir
Fremington
Bishop's Tawton
Landkey
West Buckland
East Buckland
Twitchen
Molland Common
Dane's Brook
Hawkridge
Tawstock
Swimbridge
North Molton
Molland
West Anstey
Dulverton
Haddon Hill
Upton
Huish Champflower
Newton Tracey
Filleigh
East Anstey
Battleton
Bury
Skilgate
Chipstable
Heydon Hill
Hiscott
Ensis
Herner
Cobbaton
Chapleton
Chittlehampton
R Mole
River Yeo
Yeo Mill
Brushford
Waterow
Morebath
SOUTH MOLTON
Ash Mill
Oldways End
Exebridge
Petton
Yarnscombe
Umberleigh
Clapworthy
George Nympton
Bishop's Nympton
Knowstone
Shillingford
Clayhanger
Atherington
Warkleigh
Satterleigh
Alswear
Mariansleigh
Roachill
Bampton
Sherwood Green
High Bickington
Chittlehamholt
Romansleigh
Rose Ash
Oakford
Huntsham
Ashbrittle
Portsmouth Arms Sta
Meshaw
Creacombe
Stoodleigh Beacon
Stoodleigh
Cove
St Giles in the Wood
King's Nympton
Northcote Manor
Rackenford
Kingscott
Roborough
Cadbury Barton
King's Nympton Sta
Burrington
Week
Little Dart River
Loxbeare
Chevithorne
Uplowman
Whitnage
Elstone
Lutworthy
Washfield
Bolham
Chettiscombe
Beaford
Riddlecombe
Chulmleigh
Witheridge
Templeton
Calverleigh
TIVERTON
Sampford Peverell
Worlington
Cheldon
Ashreigney
Nomansland
Withleigh
Halberton
Merton
Dolton
Huish
Chawleigh
Thelbridge Barton
Washford Pyne
Cruwys Morchard
Tiverton Junction Sta
Ashley
Eggesford Sta
Ash Thomas
Hollacombe
Dowland
Filleigh
Pennymoor
Way Village
Puddington
Black Dog
Eastington
Wembworthy
Woolfardisworthy
Poughill
Upham
Cadeleigh
Butterleigh
Stockstowe
Meeth
Iddesleigh
Winkleigh
Coldridge
Lapford
Nymet Rowland
Morchard Bishop
Kennerleigh
Bickleigh
Cullompton
Brushford
Oldborough
Stockleigh English
Cheriton Fitzpaine
Colebrooke
Monkokehampton
Broadwoodkelly
Morchard Road Sta
East Village
Cadbury
Hatherleigh
Bondleigh
East Leigh
Down St Mary
Mutterton
Bradninch
Westcott
Zeal Monachorum
Newbuildings
Stockleigh Pomeroy
Honeychurch
Copplestone
Sandford
Upton Hellions
Up Exe
Silverton
Hele
Langford
Plymtree
Clyst Hydon
Exbourne
North Tawton
Bow
Clannaborough Barton
Knowle
Creedy Park
Thorverton
Jacobstowe
Sampford Courtenay
Nymet Tracey
Coleford
CREDITON
Shobrooke
Efford
Nether Exe
Clyst St Lawrence
Budlake
Inwardleigh
Itton
Colebrooke
Rewe
Westwood
Hillerton
Yeoford
Uton
Hookway
Newton St Cyres
Brampford Speke
Stoke Canon
Whimple
Folly Gate
Spreyton
Upton Pyne
Poltimore
Broadclyst
Dog Village
Cowley
Taw Green
OKEHAMPTON
Hittisleigh
Tedburn St Mary
Whitestone
EXETER
Pinhoe
Rockbeare
South Tawton
South Zeal
Sticklepath
Whiddon Down
Pathfinder Village
Exeter Airport
Thorndon Cross
Castle
Okehampton Camp
Belstone
Cheriton Bishop
Whipton
Clyst Honiton
Sowton
Meldon
Cosdon Hill
Crockernwell
Longdown
Clyst St Mary
Aylesbeare
Okehampton Common
Meldon Resr
Yes Tor
High Willhays
Throwleigh
Ide
Countess Wear
Alphington
Farringdon
Sourton
Bridestowe
Bridestowe and Sourton Common
Wonson
Drewsteignton
River Teign
Easton
Gidleigh
Dunsford
Shillingford St George
Duchideock
Exminster
Topsham
Clyst St George
Woodbury Salterton
Woodbury
Chagford
Doccombe
Bridford
Doddiscombsleigh
Kennford
Ebford
Exton
Hangingstone Hill
Amicombe Hill
Frenchbeer
Fernworthy Reservoir
Moretonhampstead
Christow
Kennick Resr
Higher Ashton
Kenn
Powderham
Lympstone
Black Hill
Lettaford
North Bovey
Trenchford Reservoir
Tottiford Reservoir
Lower Ashton
Whiteway Ho
Kenton
Castle
Sittaford Tor
Cut Hill
Trusham
Starcross
DARTMOOR
Grimspound
Hameldown Tor
Manaton
Lustleigh
Hennock
Chudleigh
Ashcombe
Cockwood
EXMOUTH
Littleham
Cocks Hill
Rough Tor
FOREST
Postbridge
Bellever
Bovey Tracey
Dawlish Warren
Cudliptown
Peter Tavy
Haytor

SX

Withycombe
Washford
Williton
West Quantoxhead
Holford
Nether Stowey
Fiddington
Dunball
Woolavington
Cossington
Croydon Hill
Rodhuish
Sampford Brett
Bicknoller
Cannington
Chilton Trinity
Chilton Polden
Catcott
Wheddon Cross
Luckwell Bridge
Luxborough
Roadwater
QUANTOCK
Charlynch
BRIDGWATER
Bawdrip
Stawell
Lype Hill
BRENDON HILLS
Kingsbridge
Monksilver
Stogumber
Crowcombe
HILLS
Spaxton
Four Forks
Dufleigh Resr
Wembdon
Chedzoy
Sutton Mallet
Greinton
Treborough
Hawkridge Resr
Lower Aisholt
Enmore
Durleigh
Sedgemoor
Westonzoyland
Winsford
Elworthy
Lower Vexford
Flaxpool
Exton
Bridgetown
Withiel Florey
Willett
West Bagborough
Courtway
Goathurst
Huntworth
Middlezoy
Brompton Regis
Wimbleball Lake
Clatworthy Reservoir
Brompton Ralph
Lydeard St Lawrence
Tolland
Combe Florey
East Combe
Cothelstone
Broomfield
North Petherton
Northmoor Green or Moorland
Othery
Clatworthy
Tarr
Cushuish
North Newton
Dulverton
Haddon Hill
Upton
Huish Champflower
Langley Marsh
Ash Priors
Bishops Lydeard
Fulford
Kingston St Mary
Thurloxton
West Monkton
Burrow Bridge
Athelney
Lyng
Stathe
Battleton
Bury
Heydon Hill
Chipstable
Fitzhead
Halse
Cheddon Fitzpaine
Monkton Heathfield
Hedging
Durston
Stoke St Gregory
Langport
Brushford
Skilgate
Wiveliscombe
VALE OF TAUNTON DEANE
Staplegrove
River Tone
Meare Green
Waterrow
Milverton
Heathfield
Creech St Michael
Knapp
Curry Rivel
Drayton
Exebridge
Morebath
Oake
Norton Fitzwarren
Ruishton
North Curry
West Sedge Moor
Petton
Bathealton
Hillfarrance
Bradford-on-Tone
TAUNTON
Thornfalcon
Shillingford
Clayhanger
Langford Budville
Nynehead
Trull
Stoke St Mary
Fivehead
Bampton
Ashbrittle
Appley
Thorne St Margaret
Runnington
Staplehay
Orchard Portman
West Hatch
Wrantage
Curry Mallet
Isle Brewers
Hambridge
Oakford
Huntsham
Hockworthy
Hoiywell Lake
West Buckland
Hatch Beauchamp
Beer Crocombe
Isle Abbotts
Cove
WELLINGTON
Pitminster
Corfe
Westport
Stoodleigh
Holcombe Rogus
Sampford Arundel
Angersleigh
Blagdon Hill
Staple Fitzpaine
Puckington
Barrington
Wrangway
Ford Street
Luxhay Reservoir
Bickenhall
Ashill
Ilton
Shepton Beauchamp
Westleigh
Burlescombe
Monument
BLACK DOWN HILLS
Curland
Staple Hill
Loxbeare
Washfield
Chevithorne
Uplowman
Whitnage
Nicholashayne
Clayhidon
Windmill Hill
ILMINSTER
Seavington St Michael
Bolham
Chettiscombe
Appledore
Rosemary Lane
Churchstanton
Fyfett
Broadway
Calverleigh
TIVERTON
Sampford Peverell
Culmstock
Culm Valley
Stapley
Buckland St Mary
Horton
Donyatt
Kingstone
Dinnington
Withleigh
Halberton
Uffculme
Hemyock
Dowlish Wake
Smithincott
Hackpen Hill
Bolham Water
Churchinford
Bishopswood
Combe St Nicholas
Tiverton Junction Sta
Ash Thomas
Willand
Ashill
Abbey
Smeatharpe
Marsh
Chillington
Whitestaunton
Wadeford
Cudworth
Blackborough
Sheldon
Chaffcombe
Cadeleigh
Butterleigh
Kentisbeare
Dunkeswell
Newcott
Yarcombe
Wambrook
CHARD
Cricket St Thomas
Bickleigh
Cullompton
Black Down
Upottery
Rawridge
Luppitt
Forton
Wayford
Colebrook
Dulford
Kerswell
Beacon
Stockland
Tatworth
South Chard
Winsham
Cadbury
Mutterton
Westcott
Broadhembury
Chardstock
Forde Abbey
Drimpton
Bradninch
Plymtree
Norman's Green
Hembury
Monkton
Thorncombe
Hele
Langford
Clyst Hydon
Higher Tale
Payhembury
Combe Raleigh
Cotleigh
Membury
Tytherleigh
Burstock
Up Exe
Silverton
Awliscombe
HONITON
Churchill
Pilsdon Pen
Thorverton
Nether Exe
Clyst St Lawrence
Cheriton
Buckerell
Dalwood
Smallridge
Hawkchurch
Bettiscombe
Brampford Speke
Rewe
Budlake
Westwood
Talaton
Feniton
Offwell
Wilmington
AXMINSTER
Marshwood
Upton Pyne
Stoke Canon
Broadclyst
Whimple
Fenny Bridges
ROMAN ROAD
Gittisham
Shute
Kilmington
Cowley
Poltimore
Dog Village
Fairmile
Alfington
Wootton Fitzpaine
Whitchurch Canonicorum
EXETER
ISCA
Pinhoe
Rockbeare
OTTERY ST MARY
Farway
Northleigh
Whitford
Ryall
Exeter Airport
West Hill
Broad Down
Musbury
Charmouth
Whipton
Clyst Honiton
Sowton
Marsh Green
Wiggaton
Colyton
Southleigh
Uplyme
Combpyne
Morcombelake
Chideock
Aylesbeare
Tipton St John
Sidbury
Blackbury Castle
Colyford
LYME REGIS
Ide
Countess Wear
Clyst St Mary
Farringdon
Venn Ottery
Harcombe
SEATON
Axmouth
Rousdon
Seatown
Harpford
Bowd
Sidford
Newton Poppleford
Topsham
Clyst St George
Woodbury Salterton
Beer
Seaton Bay
Beer Head
Vicarage
Hawkerland
Salcombe Regis
Branscombe
Exminster
Ebford
Woodbury
Colaton Raleigh
SIDMOUTH
LYME
Kennford
Exton
Yettington
Kenn
R Kenn
Black Hill
Powderham
Lympstone
East Budleigh
Otterton
Kenton
Castle
R Exe
Starcross
Littleham
EXMOUTH
BUDLEIGH SALTERTON
Ashcombe
Cockwood
Dawlish Warren
Luton
DAWLISH
Little Halden
Bishopsteignton
Holcombe
TEIGNMOUTH
Shaldon
Combeinteignhead
Stokeinteignhead
BABBACOMBE BAY
Coffinswell
Maidencombe
0
1
2
3
4

GLASTONBURY
STREET
Evercreech
Bruton
Castle Cary
WINCANTON
MERE
Stourhead
Stourton
White Sheet Hill
Great Ridge
ROMAN ROAD
Keysley Down
Chicklade
Hindon
Fonthill Bishop
SOMERTON
GILLINGHAM
SHAFTESBURY
Cadbury Castle
Queen Camel
Sparkford
Ilchester
Yeovilton
YEOVIL
Montacute House
SHERBORNE
Milborne Port
Templecombe
Stalbridge
Marnhull
Sturminster Newton
BLACKMOOR VALE
South Petherton
Martock
Merriott
CREWKERNE
Misterton
Sutton Bingham Reservoir
Yetminster
Beaminster
Broadwindsor
Netherbury
Maiden Newton
Cerne Abbas
The Giant
Minterne Magna
Piddletrenthide
Milton Abbas
Winterborne Stickland
BLANDFORD FORUM
Blandford Camp
CRANBORNE CHASE
Shillingstone
Hod Hill
Okeford Fitzpaine
Bulbarrow Hill
Bingham's Melcombe
Bere Regis
Tolpuddle
Puddletown
Charminster
DORCHESTER
DVRNOVARIA
Maiden Castle
Winterborne Abbas
Bradpole
BRIDPORT
West Bay
Bothenhampton
Burton Bradstock
Eggardon Hill
Abbotsbury
Chesil Beach
Chickerell
WEYMOUTH
WEYMOUTH BAY
Wyke Regis
Portland Harbour
Castle
WEST BAY
FORTUNESWELL
Easton
ISLE OF PORTLAND
Weston
Southwell
BILL OF PORTLAND
ENGLISH CHANNEL
SY
Osmington
Ringstead Bay
Durdle Door
Lulworth Cove
West Lulworth
Lulworth Camp
Worbarrow Bay
Tyneham
PURBECK HILLS
Wool
Bovington Camp
Moreton
Wareham Forest
WAREHAM
Sandford
Broad Bench
WEYMOUTH to
Guernsey 4½-6½ hrs
Jersey 7¼-9¼ hrs
Seasonal
Cherbourg 4 hrs
5
6
7
8
9

Codford St Peter
Codford St Mary
Yarnbury Castle
Winterbourne Stoke
Amesbury
Newton Tony
Palestine
Stacey
Sherrington
Deptford
Berwick St James
Wilsford
Lake
Great Durnford
Allington
Boscombe
Fullerton
Chilbolton
Stockton
Bapton
Wylye
Steeple Langford
Stapleford
Upper Woodford
Idmiston
Over Wallop
Middle Wallop
Danebury
Nether Wallop
Leckford
Longstock
Great Ridge
ROMAN ROAD
Hanging Langford
Little Langford
Stoford
Middle Woodford
Lower Woodford
Gomeldon
Porton
Winterbourne Gunner
Winterbourne Dauntsey
Winterbourne Earls
Figsbury Ring
Crawley
Chicklade
Great Wishford
South Newton
Grovely Wood
Lopcombe Corner
Middle Winterslow
Stockbridge
Berwick St Leonard
Fonthill Bishop
Teffont Magna
Ford
Old Sarum
The Common
Whiteshoot Hill
Broughton
Hindon
Chilmark
Dinton
Baverstock
WILTON
West Winterslow
Pitton
Houghton
Up Somborne
Sparsholt
Fonthill Gifford
Ridge
Teffont Evias
Barford St Martin
Wilton Ho
Quidhampton
Laverstock
West Tytherley
King's Somborne
Ashley
Chicksgrove
Burcombe
Compton Chamberlayne
Netherhampton
SALISBURY
Farley
East Tytherley
Lockerley Hall
Horsebridge
Sutton Mandeville
Fovant
Chiselbury
Harnham
Britford
East Grimstead
Brook
Farley Mount
Monument
Pitt Down
Hatch
Swallowcliffe
Stratford Tony
Coombe Bissett
Alderbury
West Dean
Lockerley
Mottisfont Abbey
Michelmersh
Standon
Castle
Ansty
Donhead St Andrew
Broad Chalke
Odstock
Nunton
Bodenham
West Grimstead
Whaddon
Dean Hill
East Dean
Braishfield
White Sheet Hill
Bishopstone
Homington
Odstock Down
Charlton
Carter's Clay
Kent's Oak
Timsbury
Hursley
Ebbesbourne Wake
Alvediston
Whiteparish
Newtown
Ampfield
Berwick St John
Bowerchalke
Downton
Morgan's Vale
Newton
Awbridge
Abbotswood
Ludwell
Rockbourne Down
Wick Down
Wick
Melchet Court
Sherfield English
ROMSEY
North Baddesley
Winkelbury
Woodminton
Martin Drove End
Woodfalls
Redlynch
Landford Manor
East Wellow
Broadlands House
Chilworth
Castle Ditches
North Charford
Breamore House
Lover
Landford
Plaitford
West Wellow
EASTLEIGH
Martin
Tidpit
Whitsbury
Upper Street
Hale
Canada
Toothill
Tollard Royal
Rushmore Ho
Woodyates
Rockbourne
Breamore
Nomansland
Lee
Upton
Rownhams
Bassett
Deanland
Pentridge
Pentridge Hill
Woodgreen
Nursling
Ower
Sixpenny Handley
Damerham
Bramshaw
Newbridge
CRANBORNE CHASE
Farnham
Sandleheath
Godshill
Fritham
Calmore
Testwood
Portswood
Monkton Up Wimborne
Fordingbridge
Brook
Cadnam
Copythorne
TOTTON
Shirley
Stubhampton
Chettle
Cashmoor
Cranborne
Stuckton
Blissford
Rufus Stone
Bartley
Millbrook
Tarrant Gunville
Hyde
Netley Marsh
Toll
Eling
Gussage St Michael
Gussage All Saints
Wimborne St Giles
Edmondsham
Alderholt
Bickton
North Gorley
Broomy Lodge
Stoney Cross
Minstead
Woodlands
SOUTHAMPTON
Tarrant Hinton
Long Crichel
Circles
South Gorley
Newtown
Ashurst
Pooksgreen
Marchwood
Tarrant Launceston
Verwood
Ibsley
Linwood
NEW FOREST
Lyndhurst Road Sta
Blandford Camp
Tarrant Monkton
Manswood
Moor Crichel
Woodlands
Ringwood Forest
Moyles Court
Emery Down
Lyndhurst
Dibden
Hythe
Horton
Linford
Tarrant Rawston
Witchampton
Hinton Martell
Chalbury Common
Three Legged Cross
Blashford
Picket Post
Bank
Denny Lodge
Beaulieu Road Sta
Dibden Purlieu
Tarrant Rushton
Mannington
Ashley Heath
Ringwood
Burley Lodge
Beaulieu Heath
Gaunt's Common
Burley Street
New Park
Holbury
Tarrant Keyneston
Stanbridge
Holt
West Moors
St Ives
Avon Castle
Burley
Balmerlawn
Hill Top
Abbey
Tarrant Crawford
Broom Hill
Due to open Late 1986
Bisterne Close
Kingston
Brockenhurst
Beaulieu
Spetisbury
Badbury Rings
Clapgate
St Leonards
Shapwick
Tadden
Colehill
Trickett's Cross
Setley
East Boldre
Exbury
Sturminster Marshall
Pamphill
WIMBORNE MINSTER
Stapehill
Ferndown
Parley Common
Avon
Ripley
Thorney Hill
Beaulieu Heath
Bucklers Hard
Almer
Hampreston
Longham
Bournemouth (Hurn) Airport
Parley Cross
Wootton
Sway
Battramsley
Norleywood
East End
Lychett Matravers
Corfe Mullen
Bearwood
West Parley
Sopley
Bransgore
Bashley
Boldre
Portmore
Morden
Hurn
Neacroft
East Morden
Broadstone
Canford Heath
Ensbury
New Milton
Hordle
LYMINGTON
Beacon Hill
Moordown
Burton
Hinton
Highcliffe
Barton on Sea
Lytchett Minster
Upton
Waterloo
Winton
Everton
Lymore
Lower Pennington
Slepe
Newtown
Branksome
Pokesdown
CHRISTCHURCH
Downton
Keyhaven
Newtown Bay
Holton Heath
Hamworthy
Wick
Southbourne
Mudeford
Christchurch Bay
Hamstead
Parkstone
Branksome Park
Westbourne
Boscombe
BOURNEMOUTH
HENGISTBURY HEAD
Milford on Sea
Sconce Pt
Yarmouth
Cranmore
Shalfleet
Sandford
POOLE
Poole Harbour
Canford Cliffs
Hurst Castle
Norton
Colwell Bay
Norton Green
Ningwood
Newbridge
WAREHAM
Arne
Brownsea Island
POOLE BAY
Totland
Totland Bay
Freshwater
Wellow
Sandbanks
ISLE
Calbourne
Ridge
Ferry
Alum Bay
Freshwater Bay
Shalcombe
Stoborough
THE NEEDLES
Brook
Brighstone Forest
Stoborough Green
Wytch Heath
Newton Heath
Studland Bay
Compton Bay
Toll
Moortown
Norden
Mottistone
Brighstone
East Creech
ISLE OF PURBECK
Studland
The Foreland or Handfast Point
The Undercliff
PURBECK HILLS
Castle
Corfe Castle
Nine Barrow Down
Ballard Point
Chilton Chine
Church Knowle
Brighstone Bay
Kingston
Swanage Bay
Kimmeridge
Harman's Cross
SWANAGE
Peveril Point
Langton Matravers
Durlston Bay
Worth Matravers
DURLSTON HEAD
Tilly Whim Caves
Seacombe Cliff
ST ALDHELM'S OR ST ALBAN'S HEAD
ENGLISH
0
1
2
3
4

15
Candover
Lower Wield
Bentworth
Holybourne
ALTON
Binsted
Wheatley
Frensham
Fushmoor
Wonston
East Stratton
Sutton Scotney
Stoke Charity
Micheldever
Micheldever Wood
Brown Candover
Upper Wield
Thedden Grange
Beech
Wyck
East Worldham
Kingsley
Sleaford
Churt
Thursley
Bowlhead Green
Brook
Northington
Hattingley
Medstead
Chawton
West Worldham
Lindford
Hindhead
Gibbet Hill
South Wonston
The Grange
South Town
Lower Farringdon
Upper Farringdon
Oakhanger
Bordon Camp
Whitehill
Headley
Grayshott
Worthy Down
Kings Worthy
Itchen Abbas
Old Alresford
Bighton
Soldridge
Four Marks
Selborne
Standford
Grayswood
Gundleton
North Street
Kitwood
Newton Valence
Blackmoor
Shottermill
Bramshott
HASLEMERE
Headbourne Worthy
Itchen Stoke
Ropley
East Tisted
Longmoor Camp
Camelsdale
Fisherstreet
Easton
Ovington
New Alresford
Bishop's Sutton
Ropley Dean
Monkwood
Liphook
WINCHESTER
Tichborne
Due to open Early 1987
Emshott
Greatham
Liss Forest
Linchmere
Kingsley Green
Cheriton
Bramdean
West Tisted
Hawkley
Langley
Chilcomb
New Cheriton
Liss
East Liss
Rake
Fernhurst
Northchapel
Oliver's Battery
Twyford
Compton
Shawford
Longwood Warren
Morestead
Hinton Ampner
Kilmeston
Privett
High Cross
Steep
Hill Brow
Milland
Lurgashall
Lickfold
Longwood Ho
Brockwood Park
Froxfield Green
Sheet
Henley
Otterbourne
West Meon
Langrish
Stroud
Rogate
Chithurst
Iping
Woolbeding
Easebourne
Lodsworth
Owslebury
Preshaw Ho
Warnford
East Meon
Ramsdean
Weston
PETERSFIELD
Trotton
Stedham
MIDHURST
Upperton
Colden Common
Fisher's Pond
Upham
Exton
Corhampton
Old Winchester Hill
Butser Hill
Nursted
Nyewood
East Harting
Tillington
Selham
Chandler's Ford
Bishopstoke
Dean
Meonstoke
Buriton
West Lavington
South Ambersham
Lower Upham
Brockbridge
War Down
South Harting
Elsted
Fair Oak
Wintershill
Bishop's Waltham
Droxford
Chidden
Uppark
Treyford
Bepton
Heyshott
Southampton (Eastleigh) Airport
Horton Heath
Palace
Durley
Swanmore
Soberton
Clanfield
Chalton
North Marden
Cocking
Graffham
East Lavington
Waltham Chase
Long Common
Hambledon
SOUTH DOWNS
West End
Curdridge
Shirrell Heath
Soberton Heath
Catherington
Compton
West Marden
East Marden
Chilgrove
Upwaltham
Shedfield
Hoe Gate
HORNDEAN
Blendworth
Finchdean
Singleton
Charlton
Hedge End
Botley
Newtown
Anthill Common
Denmead
Rowland's Castle
Forestside
West Dean
East Dean
Wickham
Hundred Acres
Cowplain
Stoughton
Sholing
Curbridge
Burridge
North Boarhunt
FOREST OF BERE
Walderton
Stansted Ho
The Trundle
Bursledon
Swanwick
Waterlooville
Woodend
Goodwood House
Lower Swanwick
Purbrook
HAVANT
Funtington
West Stoke
Lavant
Earlham
Netley
Hamble
Sarisbury
Park Gate
Locks Heath
Funtley
Boarhunt
Southwick
Westbourne
Woodmancote
East Ashling
Halnaker
Fontwell
SOUTHAMPTON WATER
Titchfield
Wallington
Ports Down
Bedhampton
Hambrook
West Ashling
Westhampnett
Strettington
Boxgrove
Warsash
FAREHAM
Portchester
Wymering
Drayton
Cosham
Langstone
Emsworth
Hermitage
Southbourne
Broadbridge
Tangmere
Aldingbourne
Norton
Nyton
Westergate
Eastergate
Oil Refinery
Fawley
Calshot Castle
Castle
Horsea Island
Portsmouth Harbour
Hilsea
North Hayling
Fishbourne
Bosham
CHICHESTER
Stubbington
Bridgemary
Whale Island
North End
Langstone Harbour
Stoke
Thorney Island
Chidham
Apuldram
Donnington
Merston
Colworth
Woodgate
Yapton
Blackfield
Hill Head
West Thorney
Runcton
Shripney
Calshot
Calshot Spit
Hardway
Portsea
PORTSEA ISLAND
HAYLING ISLAND
West Itchenor
Hunston
Mundam
Bersted
Flansham
Langley
Lee-on-the-Solent
GOSPORT
Fratton
Shipton Green
Birdham
Street End
Nyetimber
Felpham
Lepe
Stansore Point
Alverstoke
South Hayling
Chichester Harbour
Somerley
Sidlesham
BOGNOR REGIS
SOLENT
Stokes Bay
Southsea
Eastney
Hayling Bay
West Wittering
Highleigh
Pagham
Aldwick
Needs Ore Point
Cowes Roads
Gilkicker Point
PORTSMOUTH
Earnley
COWES
East Cowes
Osborne Bay
East Wittering
Church Norton
Gurnard Bay
Gurnard
Osborne Ho
SPITHEAD
Bracklesham Bay
Thorness Bay
Whippingham
PORTSMOUTH to
Le Havre 5½ hrs
Guernsey 6½-7 hrs
St Malo 8½-10 hrs
Jersey 9-9½ hrs
Seasonal
Cherbourg 4-6½ hrs
Ryde Roads
¾ hr
RYDE
Northwood
Fishbourne
Abbey
Puckpool Point
Selsey
Porchfield
Parkhurst
Parkhurst Forest
Wootton Bridge
Binstead
Nettlestone Point
Seaview
Nettlestone
The Priory
SELSEY BILL
Wootton Common
Havenstreet
Carisbrooke
Staplers
St Helens
NEWPORT
Bembridge Point
Bembridge
FORELAND
Castle
Downend
ISLE OF WIGHT
Bowcombe
Arreton
Alverstone
Brading
Blackwater
Whitecliff Bay
Culver Cliff
Gatcombe
Merstone
Newchurch
Yaverland
Chillerton
Rookley
SANDOWN
Sandown Bay
Shorwell
Branstone
Apse Heath
Godshill
Yafford
Kingston
SHANKLIN
Shanklin Chine
Little Atherfield
Appuldurcombe House
Luccombe Village
Roud
SZ
Pyle
Chale Green
Wroxall
Luccombe Chine
Atherfield Point
Stenbury Down
Bierley
DUNNOSE
Whale Chine
Chale
Whitwell
Chale Bay
Niton
VENTNOR
Blackgang Chine
St Lawrence
Blackgang
The Undercliff
Rocken End
ST CATHERINE'S POINT
CHANNEL

WARLINGHAM
Biggin Hill
Cudham
Knockholt
Otford
Kemsing
Heaverham
Ightham
Wrotham
Ryarsh
Addington
New Hythe
Aylesford
Tatsfield
Chevening
Dunton Green
Riverhead
Seal
Borough Green
Platt
Wrotham Heath
Offham
West Malling
East Malling
Royal British Legion Village
Ditton
MAIDSTONE
Woldingham
CATERHAM
Chaldon
Westerham
Brasted
Sundridge
SEVENOAKS
Knole
Ivy Hatch
Ightham Mote
Claygate Cross
Plaxtol
Mereworth
Wateringbury
East Barming
Teston
West Farleigh
East Farleigh
Loose
Mote Ho
Bearsted
Shepway
Godstone
Limpsfield
Oxted
Brasted Chart
Whitley Row
Ide Hill
Underriver
Shipbourne
Dunk's Green
West Peckham
Mereworth Castle
Nettlestead
Nettlestead Green
Coxheath
Boughton Monchelsea
REDHILL
Bletchingley
Tandridge
Hurst Green
Crockham Hill
Toy's Hill
Sevenoaks Weald
Hadlow
Yalding
Hunton
Linton
Nutfield
South Nutfield
Godstone Sta
South Godstone
Marlpit Hill
Four Elms
Bough Beech Resr
Chiddingstone Causeway
Hildenborough
Higham Wood
East Peckham
Hale Street
Benover
Chart Sutton
Redhill Aerodrome
Salfords
Crowhurst
Edenbridge
Leigh
TONBRIDGE
R Medway
Golden Green
Laddingford
Collier Street
Chainhurst
Blindley Heath
Penshurst Sta
R Eden
Hever
Chiddingstone
Penshurst Place
Penshurst
Bidborough
Whetsted
Tudeley
Five Oak Green
Paddock Wood
Milebush
Marden
Outwood
Horne
Lingfield
Marsh Green
Horley
Smallfield
Newchapel
Dormansland
Markbeech
Cowden Sta
Fordcombe
SOUTHBOROUGH
Speldhurst
Pembury
Matfield
Brenchley
Staplehurst
Burstow
Felcourt
Cowden
Blackham
Ashurst
Langton Green
Horsmonden
Curtisden Green
Copthorne
Felbridge
EAST GRINSTEAD
ROYAL TUNBRIDGE WELLS
Bayham Abbey
Cranbrook Common
Crawley Down
Sunnyside
Ashurstwood
ROMAN ROAD
Groombridge
Bells Yew Green
Lamberhurst
Scotney Castle
Goudhurst
Kilndown
Cranbrook
Sissinghurst
CRAWLEY
Worth
Turners Hill
Saint Hill
Forest Row
Weir Wood Resr
Hartfield
Upper Hartfield
Withyham
Eridge Green
Eridge Sta
Frant
Hartley
Selsfield Common
Worth Abbey
Coleman's Hatch
Friar's Gate
Boarshead
Cousley Wood
Wadhurst
Bewl Bridge Resr
Bedgebury Forest
West Hoathly
Sharpthorne
Wych Cross
ASHDOWN
FOREST
CROWBOROUGH
Mark Cross
Three Leg Cross
Flimwell
Iden Green
Hawkhurst
Four Throws
Balcombe
Ardingly
Highbrook
Horsted Keynes
Chelwood Gate
Rotherfield
Tidebrook
Ticehurst
The Moor
Sandhurst
Ardingly Resr
Danehill
Nutley
Mayfield
Stonegate
Hurst Green
Whitemans Green
Paxhill Park
Lindfield
Fairwarp
High Hurstwood
Witherenden Hill
Etchingham
Bodiam Castle
CUCKFIELD
HAYWARDS HEATH
Scaynes Hill
Sheffield Park Sta
Fletching
Maresfield
Five Ashes
River Rother
Burwash
Bateman's
River Dudwell
Salehurst
Ewhurst Green
Ansty
Buxted
Hadlow Down
Burwash Common
Robertsbridge
Staplecross
Newick
Uckfield
Cross in Hand
Broadoak
Cade Street
Oxley's Green
Darwell Resr
Vinehall Street
Cripp's Corner
Due to open Late 1985
Blackboys
Possingworth Park
HEATHFIELD
Punnett's Town
Brightling
Mountfield
Wivelsfield Sta
Wivelsfield
Wivelsfield Green
Chailey
Ridgewood
Framfield
Little London
Waldron
Netherfield
BURGESS HILL
R Ouse
Little Horsted
Rushlake Green
Dallington
Whatlington
South Street
Isfield
Horam
Warbleton
Hurstpierpoint
Spithurst
Halland
Vines Cross
Penhurst
BATTLE
Plumpton Green
Barcombe Cross
East Hoathly
Foul Mile
Ponts Green
Abbey
Ditchling
ROMAN ROAD
Streat
East Chiltington
Shortgate
Ashburnham Place
Bodle Street Green
Keymer
Hassocks
Westmeston
Barcombe
Cowbeech
Catsfield
Beauport Park
Clayton
Pyecombe
Plumpton
Cooksbridge
Chiddingly
Whitesmith
Hellingly
Herstmonceux
Windmill Hill
Crowhurst
Ditchling Beacon
Mount Harry
Hamsey
Ringmer
Laughton
Golden Cross
Ninfield
Lunsford's Cross
Hollington
Offham
South Malling
Cliffe Hill
LEWES
Glyndebourne
Horsebridge
Magham Down
Boreham Street
Stanmer
Patcham
Coldean
Mount Caburn
Glynde
Ripe
Upper Dicker
Chalvington
Michelham Priory
HAILSHAM
Royal Greenwich Observatory
Wartling
Hooe
Sidley
Bulverhythe
St Leonards
Falmer
Kingston near Lewes
Moulsecoomb
Iford
Rodmell
Beddingham
West Firle
Selmeston
Arlington Resr
Arlington
PEVENSEY
LEVELS
Little Common
BEXHILL
Preston
Bevendean
Woodingdean
Firle Beacon
Alciston
Berwick
Polegate
Hankham
Pevensey Castle
Pevensey Bay
Pevensey Bay
BRIGHTON
HOVE
Southease
Tarring Neville
Wilmington
Folkington
Stone Cross
Westham
Ovingdean
Telscombe
Saltdean
Piddinghoe
South Heighton
Alfriston
The Long Man
Langney
Kemp Town
Rottingdean
Denton
Willingdon
Hampden Park
Langney Point
Peacehaven
Bishopstone
Litlington
Jevington
Willingdon Hill
East Blatchington
NEWHAVEN
SEAFORD
Westdean
EASTBOURNE
NEWHAVEN to Dieppe 4 hrs
Friston
East Dean
BEACHY HEAD
SOUTH DOWNS
THE WEALD
TQ
TV
Royal Sovereign
ENGLISH CHANNEL
3
4
5
6
7
0
9

19
27
7 hrs
Warden Point
Warden
Leysdown on Sea
SHEPPEY
Isle of Harty
Shell Ness
The Swale
WHITSTABLE
Seasalter
Swalecliffe
HERNE BAY
REGVLBIVM
Reculver
Beltinge
Hillborough
Chestfield
Broomfield
Herne
Hoath
St Nicholas at Wade
Sarre
Marshside
Chislet
Upstreet
West Stourmouth
East Stourmouth
River Stour
South Channel
MARGATE
Long Nose Spit
Foreness Point
Westgate on Sea
Birchington
White Ness
NORTH FORELAND
St Peter's
BROADSTAIRS
ISLE OF THANET
Acol
Manston Aerodrome
Monkton
Minster
RAMSGATE
Cliffs End
Pegwell Bay
RAMSGATE to
Dunkirk 2½ hrs
North Goodwin
Sandwich Flats
Sandwich Bay
SANDWICH
Toll
THE SMALL DOWNS
Goodwin Sands
THE DOWNS
DEAL
Castle
Sholden
Walmer Castle
Kingsdown
Uplees
Oare
Luddenham Court
FAVERSHAM
Goodnestone
Graveney
Ospringe
Dargate
Yorkletts
Hernhill
Boughton Street
Dunkirk
Honey Hill
Blean
Rough Common
Tyler Hill
Hales Place
Broad Oak
Sturry
Fordwich
Hersden
Westbere
Grove
Stodmarsh
Preston
Elmstone
Westmarsh
Hoaden
RVTVPIAE
Great Stonar
Ash
Marshborough
Staple
Wickhambreaux
Wingham
CANTERBURY
DVROVERNVM
Harbledown
Chartham Hatch
Chartham
Thanington
Littlebourne
Zoo
Ickham
Bekesbourne
Patrixbourne
Bridge
Nackington
Adisham
Goodnestone
Woodnesborough
Eastry
Ham
Worth
Northbourne
Betteshanger
Tilmanstone
Knowlton
Chillenden
Nonington
Aylesham
Easole Street
Elvington
Womenswold
Barfrestone
Eythorne
Great Mongeham
Ripple
Sutton
East Studdal
Ringwould
Waldershare House
Shepherdswell
Sibertswold
Coldred
West Langdon
East Langdon
Whitfield
St Margaret's at Cliffe
Guston
West Cliffe
St Margaret's Bay
SOUTH FORELAND
South Goodwin
Military School
Temple Ewell
Lydden
Ewell Minnis
Alkham
Buckland
St Radegund's Abbey
West Hougham
DOVER
DVBRIS
Capel le Ferne
Hawkinge
Densole
Swingfield Minnis
Acrise Place
Wootton
Denton
Elham
Lyminge
Lymbridge Green
Rhodes Minnis
Paddlesworth
Etchinghill
Postling
Beachborough
Newington
Stanford
Stowting
Lymington Forest
Stelling Minnis
Bossingham
Derringstone
Upper Hardres Court
Lower Hardres
Kingston
Barham
Bishopsbourne
Petham
Waltham
Crundale
Sole Street
Hassell Street
Elmsted
STONE STREET
Hastingleigh
Brook
Wye
Olantigh
Godmersham
Bilting
Shalmsford Street
Chilham
Shottenden
Old Wives Lees
Selling
Sheldwich
Throwley
Badlesmere
Leaveland
Molash
Challock
Great Stour
Boughton Aluph
Boughton Lees
Eastwell Park
Westwell
Kennington
Hothfield
ASHFORD
Chart
Hinxhill
Willesborough
Sevington
Kingsnorth
Mersham
Cheeseman's Green
Brabourne
Brabourne Lees
Smeeth
Sellindge
Aldington
Aldington Frith
Bonnington
East Stour R.
Shadoxhurst
Bromley Green
Orlestone
Hamstreet
Bilsington
Ruckinge
Warehorne
Royal Military Canal
Lympne
Lympne Castle
Saltwood
Castle
HYTHE
Sandgate
Tolls
FOLKESTONE
East Wear Bay
FOLKESTONE to
Boulogne 1¾ hrs
DOVER to
Calais 1½ hrs
Boulogne 1¼-1¾ hrs
Dunkirk 2¼ hrs
Ostend 3½ hrs
Zeebrugge 4 hrs
Calais 35 mins
Boulogne 40 mins
STRAIT OF DOVER
Varne
Burmarsh
Newchurch
Snave
ROMNEY MARSH
Dymchurch
St Mary in the Marsh
St Mary's Bay
Ivychurch
Snargate
Brenzett
Brookland
Old Romney
Littlestone-on-Sea
Romney Sands
NEW ROMNEY
Greatstone-on-Sea
East Road
WALLAND MARSH
LYDD
Lydd Airport
Lydd-on-Sea
Denge Marsh
Denge Beach
DUNGENESS
Power Station
West Road
A 2 (T)
A 20 (T)
A 28
A 251
A 252
A 253
A 256
A 257
A 258
A 259 (T)
A 261
A 290
A 291
A 299
B 2068
B 2067
B 2070
B 2075
M 20
0
1
2
3
4
1
2
3
4
5
6
7

RHONDDA
Ystrad
Tylorstown
Ynysboeth
ABERCYNON
Penybryn
Hengoed
PONTLLANFRAITH
ABERCARN
CWMBRAN
Henllys
Llanfrechfa
Llandegveth
Tredunnock
Llangybi
Nelson
YSTRAD MYNACH
Llwynypia
Wattstown
Ynysybwl
Trealaw
Clydach Vale
TONYPANDY
Ynyshir
PORTH
Penygraig
Trehafod
Price Town
Nant-y-moel
Blaengarw
Wyndham
PONTYCYMER
Ogmore Vale
Ogmore Forest
Gilfach Goch
Cymmer
PONTYPRIDD
Tonyrefail
Treforest
Rhydyfelin
Senghenydd
Abertridwr
Llanbradach
BEDWAS
MACHEN
Trethomas
Pontymister
Crosskeys
RISCA
Caerleon
Lower Machen
Rogerstone
Rhiwderin
Bassaleg
NEWPORT
Llanwern
Bishton
Underwood
Magor
Pye Corner
Nash
Whitson
Goldcliff
Glynogwr
Llangeinor
Betws
Blackmill
Mynydd y Gaer
Bryncethin
Heol-y-Cyw
Brynna
Llanharan
Pencoed
Cefn Hirgoed
Coity
BRIDGEND
Coychurch
Treoes
Llangan
Ewenny
St Bride's Major
Colwinston
Llysworney
Llandow
Wick
Broughton
Monknash
Marcross
St Donats
Nash Point
Church Village
Castellau
Coedely
Beddau
Llantrisant
Llantwit Fardre
Efail Isaf
Pontyclun
Cross Inn
Creigiau
Groes-faen
Capel Llanilltern
Llanharry
Brynsadler
Llanild
St Mary Hill
Graig Penllyn
Llansannor
Ystradowen
Maendy
Penllyn
Pendoylan
Welsh St Donats
COWBRIDGE
Llanblethian
Llandough
St Hilary
Llanmihangel
St Mary Church
Beaupre Castle
Flemingston
Llanmaes
Llantwit Major
Eglwys-Brewis
St Athan
Boverton
Gileston
East Aberthaw
Rhoose
Porthkerry
Breaksea Point
Cardiff-Wales Airport
Llancarfan
Penmark
Bonvilston
Llantrithyd
St Nicholas
St Lythans
Castle Ditches
BARRY
Barry Island
Merthyr Dyfan
Wenvoe
St Andrews Major
Dinas Powys
Michaelston-le-Pit
Leckwith
Llandough
Sully
Sully Island
Lavernock Point
PENARTH
Lower Penarth
CARDIFF
Canton
Llandaff
Radyr
Pentyrch
Gwaelod-y-Garth
Taff's Well
Tongwynlais
Nantgarw
CAERPHILLY
Thornhill
Lisvane
Rudry
Draethen
Ruperra Castle
Llanishen
Pentwyn
Whitchurch
Heath
Roath
Rumney
St Mellons
Castleton
Marshfield
Coedkernew
Michaelstone-y-Fedw
St Brides Wentlooge
Peterstone Wentlooge
Newton
St Fagans
St George's
Peterston-super-Ely
St Bride's super-Ely
Ely
Middle Grounds
MOUTH OF THE SEVERN
CLEVEDON
Flat Holm
Steep Holm
Sand Point
Langford Grounds
Kingston Seymour
Wick St Lawrence
Bourton
Kewstoke
Worle
WESTON-SUPER-MARE
Weston Bay
Brean Down
Uphill
Locking
Hutton
Banwell
Bleadon
Christon
Loxton
Brean
Lympsham
Eastertown
Biddisham
Badgworth
East Brent
Berrow Flats
Gore Sand
Berrow
Brent Knoll
Rooks Bridge
Edithmead
BURNHAM-ON-SEA
Mark
Highbridge
Stert Flats
Steart
Huntspill
Watchfield
Bason Bridge
East Huntspill
Burtle
Westham
SS
BRIDGWATER BAY
Selworthy Beacon
North Hill
Allerford
Selworthy
MINEHEAD
Alcombe
Luccombe
Dunster
Wootton Courtenay
Dunkery Hill
Timberscombe
Carhampton
Blue Anchor Bay
Blue Anchor
Old Cleeve
WATCHET
Withycombe
Washford
Williton
East Quantoxhead
West Quantoxhead
Kilton
Kilve
Lilstock
Hinkley Point Power Sta
Stolford
Shurton
Stockland Bristol
Burton
Stringston
Stogursey
Combwich
Holford
Nether Stowey
Fiddington
Cannington
Chilton Trinity
BRIDGWATER
Wembdon
Dunball
Pawlett
Puriton
Woolavington
Cossington
Bawdrip
Chilton Polden
Edington
Catcott
Stawell
Chedzoy
Sutton Mallet
Moorlinch
Sedgemoor
Westonzoyland
Middlezoy
Othery
Wheddon Cross
Luckwell Bridge
Croydon Hill
Rodhuish
Roadwater
Luxborough
Sampford Brett
Bicknoller
Monksilver
Stogumber
Crowcombe
QUANTOCK HILLS
Flaxpool
Hawkridge Res.
Lower Aisholt
Spaxton
Four Forks
Enmore
Durleigh
Goathurst
North Petherton
Huntworth
Kingsbridge
Treborough
BRENDON HILLS
Lype Hill
Winsford
Exton
Bridgetown
Withiel Florey
Brompton Regis
Wimbleball Lake
Clatworthy Reservoir
Elworthy
Lower Vexford
Willett
Lydeard St Lawrence
Brompton Ralph
Tolland
Combe Florey
East Combe
West Bagborough
Courtway
Cothelstone
Broomfield
Cushuish
Kingston St Mary
Thurloxton
West Monkton
North Newton
Northmoor Green or Moorland
Burrow Bridge
Lyng
Athelney
Stathe
Dulverton
Bury
Skilgate
Haddon Hill
Upton
Huish Champflower
Clatworthy
Langley Marsh
Wiveliscombe
Fitzhead
Halse
Ash Priors
Bishops Lydeard
Cheddon Fitzpaine
Monkton Heathfield
Hedging
Durston
River Tone
Stoke St Gregory
Curry Rivel
Langport
Battleton
Brushford
Morebath
Exebridge
Chipstable
Waterow
Milverton
VALE OF TAUNTON DEANE
Heathfield
Staplegrove
Oake
Hillfarrance
Norton Fitzwarren
Bradford-on-Tone
TAUNTON
Creech St Michael
Ruishton
Knapp
North Curry
West Sedge Moor
Thornfalcon
Shillingford
Petton
Clayhanger
Bathealton
Langford Budville
Nynehead
Wrantage
Fivehead
Drayton

CHEPSTOW
Oldbury Sands
Tidal Reservoir
Shepperdine
Rockhampton
Oldbury-on-Severn
Beachley
Caerwent
Caldicot
Portskewett
Severn Road Bridge
Aust
Severn Tunnel Junction Station
THORNBURY
Tortworth
Wotton-under Edge
Kingswood
Charfield
North Nibley
Kingscote
Beverston
TETBURY
COTSWO
Tetbury Upton
Long Newnton
Doughton
Leighterton
Tresham
Alderley
Hillesley
Wickwar
Cromhall
Tytherington
Itchington
Rangeworthy
Iron Acton
Hawkesbury
Hawkesbury Upton
Oldbury on the Hill
Didmarton
Sopworth
Easton Grey
Shipton Moyne
Brokenborough
MALMESBURY
Sherston
Foxley
Norton
Luckington
Little Badminton
Badminton
Horton
Horton Court
English Stones
Severn Beach
Pilning
Redwick
Northwick
Olveston
Tockington
Almondsbury
Awkley
Welsh Grounds
Denny Island
Easter Compton
Frampton Cotterell
Engine Common
CHIPPING SODBURY
YATE
Old Sodbury
Dodington
Acton Turville
Alderton
Hullavington
Corston
Rodbourne
Startley
Patchway
Filton
Winterbourne
Coalpit Heath
Westerleigh
Wapley
Codrington
Tormarton
Littleton Drew
Grittleton
Stanton St Quintin
Upper Seagry
Sutton Benger
Leigh Delamere
Kington St Michael
Langley Burrell
Avonmouth
Shirehampton
Henbury
Hambrook
Mangotsfield
Pucklechurch
Hinton
Dyrham
Dyrham Park
West Littleton
Nettleton
West Kington
Castle Combe
Yatton Keynell
North Wraxall
Ford
Biddestone
CHIPPENHAM
West Tytherton
Battery Point
PORTISHEAD
Portbury
Pill
Ham Green
Clapton-in-Gordano
Weston-in-Gordano
Redcliff Bay
Abbots Leigh
Redland
Clifton
Stapleton
Soundwell
Siston
Doynton
Marshfield
Thickwood
KINGSWOOD
Bridge Yate
Wick
Hanham
Oldland
Cold Ashton
Colerne
Corsham
BRISTOL
Leigh Woods
Long Ashton
Failand
Wraxall
Cadbury Camp
Tickenham
Clevedon Court
Nailsea
Brislington
Knowle
Bishopsworth
Flax Bourton
Backwell
Farleigh
West End
Upton Cheyney
Langridge
St Catherine
Rudloe
Box
Upper Swainswick
North Stoke
Northend
Batheaston
KEYNSHAM
Bitton
Queen Charlton
Whitchurch
Saltford
Kelston
Weston
Charlcombe
BATH
Bathford
Bathampton
Monkton Farleigh
Atworth
Whitley
Shaw
Beanacre
Gastard
Neston
Lacock Abbey
Bowden Hill
Barrow Gurney
Chelvey
West Town
Dundry
Dundry Hill
North Wick
Norton Malreward
Compton Dando
Burnett
Corston
Newton St Loe
Twerton
Claverton
Norrington Common
Wraxall
Broughton Gifford
MELKSHAM
North End
Claverham
Brockley
Cleeve
Lulsgate Bottom
Bristol Airport
Felton
Winford
Norton Hawkfield
Stanton Drew
Stone Circles
Stanton Wick
Pensford
Hunstrete
Stanton Prior
Chew Magna
Congresbury
Wrington
Redhill
Ridgehill
Chew Stoke
Butcombe
Lower Langford
Nempnett Thrubwell
Blagdon Lake
Chew Valley Lake
Chelwood
Marksbury
Englishcombe
Inglesbatch
Odd Down
Monkton Combe
Bradford Leigh
BRADFORD-ON-AVON
Winsley
Staverton
Holt
Semington
Seend
Seend Cleeve
Churchill
Dolebury
Burrington
Blagdon
Bishop Sutton
Clutton
Farmborough
Timsbury
Priston
Southstoke
Combe Hay
Limpley Stoke
Freshford
Twinhoe
Wellow
Westwood
Trowle Common
Hilperton
Great Hinton
Ashton Common
Keevil
Bulkington
Star
Shipham
MENDIP HILLS
Ubley
Compton Martin
North Widcombe
South Widcombe
Temple Cloud
High Littleton
Hinton Blewett
Carlingcott
Camerton
Peasedown St John
Charterhouse
Farleigh Hungerford
TROWBRIDGE
Steeple Ashton
Winscombe
Axbridge
Cheddar Gorge
Cheddar
Cheddar Resr
Mendip Forest
West Harptree
East Harptree
Hallatrow
Farrington Gurney
Paulton
Clandown
Shoscombe
Norton St Philip
Tellisford
Wingfield
Southwick
West Ashton
Litton
MIDSOMER NORTON
RADSTOCK
Faulkland
Woolverton
Rode
North Bradley
Heywood
Chewton Mendip
Ston Easton
Kilmersdon
Hemington
Laverton
Hardington
Hawkeridge
Edington
Draycott
Priddy
Chilcompton
Emborough
Downside Abbey
Stratton-on-the-Fosse
Lullington
Rudge
Beckington
Buckland Dinham
Bratton
Bratton Camp
Nyland Hill
Clewer
Rodney Stoke
Green Ore
Cocklake
Westbury-sub-Mendip
Wookey Hole
Binegar
Gurney Slade
Holcombe
Mells
Great Elm
Oldford
Berkley
Dilton Marsh
WESTBURY
Westbury Leigh
Wedmore
River Axe
Easton
West Horrington
East Horrington
Ashwick
Nettlebridge
Coleford
Vobster
Whatley
Chantry
Upton Scudamore
Summer Down
Theale
Henton
Wookey
WELLS
Oakhill
Stoke St Michael
Leigh upon Mendip
Downhead
Nunney
FROME
Chapmanslade
Corsley
Corsley Heath
Cley Hill
WARMINSTER
Battlesbury
Scratchbury
Heath House
Mudgley
Dulcote
Dinder
Croscombe
SHEPTON MALLET
Waterlip
Dean
Cranmore
Leighton
Trudoxhill
Tytherington
West Woodlands
Longleat House
Horningsham
Boreham
Norton Bavant
Heytesbury
Coxley
Polsham
Worminster
Doulting
Crockerton
Sutton Veny
Tytherington
Westhay
Meare
Abbot's Fish House
Godney
Southway
Whitelake
North Wootton
West Compton
Pilton
East Compton
Chesterblade
Prestleigh
Wanstrow
Witham Friary
Gare Hill
Longbridge Deverill
GLASTONBURY
Evercreech
Stoney Stratton
Westcombe
Upton Noble
Maiden Bradley
Brixton Deverill
Shapwick
Abbey
West Pennard
East Pennard
Pylle
Batcombe
Milton Clevedon
Kingston Deverill
Monkton Deverill
Ashcott
STREET
West Bradley
Parbrook
Wraxall
Ditcheat
Lamyatt
Brewham
Kilmington
Norton Ferris
Great Ridge
Pedwell
Walton
Butleigh Wootton
Baltonsbury
Ham Street
Alhampton
Bruton
White Sheet Hill
Fort
Stourhead
Stourton
Alfred's Tower
Hardway
Keysley Down
Chicklade
Sedge Moor
Butleigh
Hornblotton Green
Cole
Berwick St Leonard
Fonthill Bishop
Compton Dundon
Southwood
Ansford
Pitcombe
Redlynch
West Knoyle
Hindon
Henley
Dundon
Barton St David
Alford
Castle Cary
Shepton Montague
Charlton Musgrove
Penselwood
Zeals
MERE
High Ham
Littleton
Kingweston
Lydford
Lovington
Barrow Street
The Green
Fonthill Gifford
SOMERTON
Keinton Mandeville
Galhampton
Bratton Seymour
WINCANTON
Bourton
Silton
Milton on Stour
East Knoyle
Low Ham
Pitney
Charlton Mackrell
Charlton Adam
Babcary
North Barrow
South Barrow
Yarlington
North Cadbury
Stoke Trister
Cucklington
Sedgehill
Newtown
Hatch
Kingsdon
Lyte's Cary
Compton Pauncefoot
Sparkford
Holton
Lattiford
GILLINGHAM
Wyke
Semley
Huish Episcopi
Weston Bampfylde
Blackford
South Cadbury
Cadbury Castle
North Cheriton
Buckhorn Weston
Motcombe
Donhead St Mary
Donhead St Andrew
Muchelney
Long Sutton
Podimore
Queen Camel
West Camel
Sutton Montis
South Cheriton
Horsington
SHAFTESBURY
Long Load
River Yeo
Ilchester
Yeovilton
Marston Magna
Charlton Horethorne
Corton Denham
Abbas Combe
Kington Magna
West Stour
East Stour
Ludwell
Chilton
ROMAN ROAD

FARINGDON
CRICKLADE
Ashton Keynes
Kemble
Shorncote
Cerney Wick
Latton
Ampney
Castle Eaton
Hannington Wick
Upper Inglesham
River Thames or Isis
Badbury Hill
Coleshill
Great Coxwell
Little Coxwell
Shellingford
Hatford
Charney Bassett
Lyford
R Ock
Oaksey
Crudwell
Eastcourt
Leigh
Hannington
HIGHWORTH
Watchfield
Longcot
Fernham
Stanford in the Vale
West Hanney
East Hanney
Denchworth
Goosey
Baulking
Long Newton
Hankerton
Upper Minety
Minety
Purton Stoke
Broad Blunsdon
Sevenhampton
Stanton Fitzwarren
Shrivenham
Uffington
Grove
WANTAGE
Ardington
Brokenborough
Charlton
Garsdon
Hattons Lodge
Purton
Blunsdon St Andrew
Haydon Wick
Stratton St Margaret
South Marston
West Challow
East Challow
Childrey
Sparsholt
Kingston Lisle
Woolstone
Compton Beauchamp
Bourton
MALMESBURY
Lea
Cleverton
Green Hill
Lydiard Millicent
VALE OF WHITE HORSE
Uffington Castle
Whitehorse Hill
Wayland's Smithy
Letcombe Regis
Letcombe Bassett
Segsbury
Ridge Way
Little Somerford
Brinkworth
Callow Hill
Hook
SWINDON
Ashbury
Idstone
Hinton Parva
Bishopstone
Wanborough
Liddington
Lambourn Downs
Farnborough
Fawley
South Fawley
Woolley Ho
Startley
Great Somerford
Dauntsey
Grittenham
WOOTTON BASSETT
Upper Seagry
Lower Stanton Quintin
Tockenham Wick
Elcombe
Wroughton
Badbury
Upper Lambourne
Lambourn
Brightwalton
Sutton Benger
Lyneham
Tockenham
Church End
Chiseldon
Liddington Castle
Christian Malford
Bradenstoke
Broad Town
Uffcott
Upper Upham
Baydon
Eastbury
East Garston
Chaddleworth
Foxham
Preston
Bushton
Clyffe Pypard
Woodsend
Aldbourne
Woodlands St Mary
Leckhampstead
Goatacre
Spirthill
Broad Hinton
Barbury Castle
Marlborough Downs
Great Shefford
East Tytherton
Hilmarton
Clevancy
Winterbourne Bassett
Hackpen Hill
Ogbourne St George
Ogbourne St Andrew
West Tytherton
Highway
Berwick Bassett
Weston
Welford
CHIPPENHAM
Bremhill
Compton Basset
Winterbourne Monkton
Rockley
Ramsbury
Whittonditch
Chilton Foliat
Hungerford Newtown
Wickham
Boxford
Studley
Yatesbury
Ogbourne Maizey
CALNE
Cherhill
Avebury
Stone Circle
Mildenhall
Axford
River Kennet
Littlecote
Derry Hill
Notton
Lacock Abbey
Bowood House
Mile Elm
Calstone Wellington
White Horse
Oldbury Castle
Beckhampton
West Kennett
Fyfield
MARLBOROUGH
Manton
Hungerford
Halfway
Stockcross
Sandy Lane
Blackland
Silbury Hill
Long Barrow
East Kennett
West Overton
Lockeridge
White Horse
Savernake Forest
Froxfield
Avington
Bowden Hill
Stockley
Morgan's Hill
Chisbury
Kintbury
Chittoe
Heddington
Wansdyke
Clench Common
Cadley
Little Bedwyn
Bagshot
Enborne
Bromham
Roundway Hill
Bishops Cannings
Tan Hill
Milk Hill
Huish
Durley
Great Bedwyn
Hamstead Marshall
Inkpen
Upper Green
MELKSHAM
Roundway
Horton
Allington
Stanton St Bernard
West Stowell
Oare
Wootton Rivers
Kennet and Avon Canal
Shalbourne
Ham
North End
Ball Hill
Sells Green
Rowde
Coate
DEVIZES
Alton Priors
Stibb Green
Wilton
West Woodhay
Walbury Hill
Woolton Hill
Seend Cleeve
Seend
Castle
All Cannings
Wilcot
Burbage
Rivar
Buttermere
East Woodhay
East End
Poulshot
Woodborough
Pewsey
Easton Royal
West Grafton
East Grafton
Marten
Combe
VALE OF PEWSEY
Great Hinton
Etchilhampton
Stert
Milton Lilbourne
Easton Hill
Wexcombe
Oxenwood
Tidcombe
Faccombe
Linkenholt
Ashmansworth
Potterne
Wedhampton
Patney
Beechingstoke
North Newton
Manningford Bruce
White Horse
Keevil
Bulkington
Potterne Wick
Chirton
Marden
Wilsford
Manningford Bohune
Pewsey Down
Fosbury
Vernham Street
Steeple Ashton
Marston
Worton
Urchfont
Charlton
Haydown Hill
Chute Causeway
Vernham Dean
Crux Easton
Eastcott
Rushall
Upavon
Collingbourne Kingston
Upton
Great Cheverell
Littleton Panell
Easterton
Ridge Way
Market Lavington
Collingbourne Ducis
Upper Chute
Lower Chute
Coulston
Erlestoke
Little Cheverell
West Lavington
Everleigh
Ibthorpe
Hurstbourne Tarrant
Binley
Edington
East Chisenbury
Tangley
Doles Wood
Stoke
St Mary Bourne
Black Heath
Compton
Compton Down
Enford
Castle
Ludgershall
Haxton Down
Sidbury
Littleton Down
Hatherden
Wildhern
Enford Down
Fittleton
North Tidworth
Enham-Alamein
Little London
West Lavington Down
Imber
West Down
Orcheston Down
Netheravon
South Tidworth
Clanville
Appleshaw
Penton Mewsey
Picket Piece
Hurstbourne Priors
Tilshead
Figheldean
Kimpton
Weyhill
ANDOVER
SALISBURY PLAIN
Hotel
Knighton Down
Milston
Shipton Bellinger
Fyfield
Thruxton
Due to open Early 1986
Andover Down
Longparish
Scratchbury
Orcheston
Durrington
Amport
Monxton
Anna Valley
Norton Bavant
Chitterne
Shrewton
Larkhill
Beacon Hill
Bulford Camp
Quarley
Upper Clatford
Middleton
Heytesbury
Woodhenge
Bulford
Bury Hill
Harewood Forest
Drayton Camp
Stonehenge
Abbey
Cholderton
Abbotts Ann
Knook
Upton Lovell
Codford St Peter
Codford St Mary
Yarnbury Castle
Winterbourne Stoke
Amesbury
Newton Tony
Grateley
Goodworth Clatford
Wherwell
Newton Stacey
Boyton
Sherrington
Wilsford
Berwick St James
Lake
Great Durnford
Allington
Boscombe
Palestine
Fullerton
Chilbolton
Deptford
Steeple Langford
Upper Woodford
Idmiston
Over Wallop
Middle Wallop
Danebury
Longstock
Leckford
Stockton
Bapton
Wylye
Wylye Valley
Stapleford
R Bourne
Nether Wallop
Great Ridge
Hanging Langford
Little Langford
Stoford
Middle Woodford
Gomeldon
Porton
Crawley
Chicklade
Grovely Wood
Great Wishford
Lower Woodford
Winterbourne Gunner
Lopcombe Corner
Stockbridge
Berwick St Leonard
Fonthill Bishop
Teffont Magna
South Newton
Winterbourne Dauntsey
Winterbourne Earls
Figsbury Ring
Middle Winterslow
The Common
Whiteshoot Hill
Up Somborne
Sparsholt
Hindon
Chilmark
Dinton
Baverstock
WILTON
Ford
Old Sarum
West Winterslow
Pitton
Broughton
Houghton
Ridge
Teffont Evias
Barford St Martin
Wilton Ho
Laverstock
West Tytherley
Ashley
King's Somborne
Fonthill Gifford
Chicksgrove
Burcombe
Quidhampton
Horsebridge
Tisbury
Compton Chamberlayne
SALISBURY
Farley
East Tytherley
Lockerley Hall
Brook
Farley Mount
Monument
Pitt Down
Sutton Mandeville
Fovant
Chiselbury
Netherhampton
Harnham
Hatch
Swallowcliffe
Coombe Bissett
Britford
East Grimstead
Alderbury
West Dean
Mottisfont
Abbey
Michelmersh
Standon
Stratford Tony
West Grimstead
Dean Hill
East Dean
Lockerley
Braishfield
Castle
Ansty
Donhead St Andrew
Broad Chalke
Odstock
Bodenham
Whaddon
Carter's Clay
Hursley
White Sheet Hill
Homington
Odstock Down
Nunton
Bishopstone
Charlton
Whiteparish
Kent's Oak
Timsbury
Ebbesbourne
Alvediston
Bowerchalke
Ludwell
Berwick St John
Newton
Awbridge
Ampfield
Abbotswood
Morgan's

Culham
Long Wittenham
Dorchester
Berinsfield
Sutton Courtenay
Appleford
Little Wittenham
Warborough
Shillingford
Steventon
Milton
Didcot
Harwell
East Hendred
East Hagbourne
West Hagbourne
Upton
Brightwell-cum-Sotwell
North Moreton
South Moreton
Aston Upthorpe
Aston Tirrold
Cholsey
WALLINGFORD
Crowmarsh Gifford
Benson
Ewelme
Berrick Salome
Brightwell Baldwin
Britwell Salome
Cuxham
Pyrton
Shirburn
Watlington
Christmas Common
Northend
Greenfield
Cookley Green
Russell's Water
Park Corner
Nuffield
Nettlebed
North Stoke
Ipsden
Stoke Row
Highmoor Cross
Checkendon
Woodcote
Cray's Pond
Shepherd's Green
Sonning Common
Rotherfield Peppard
Rotherfield Greys
Kidmore End
Tokers Green
Binfield Heath
Dunsden Green
Emmer Green
Play Hatch
Chilton
Blewbury
Moulsford
South Stoke
Streatley
Goring
Lower Basildon
Whitchurch Hill
Whitchurch
Mapledurham
Purley
Pangbourne
Upper Basildon
Tidmarsh
Sulham
Tilehurst
Calcot
Theale
Bradfield
Englefield
Southend
Sheffield Bottom
READING
Whitley
Caversham
Sonning
Woodley
Earley
Whistley Green
Twyford
Ruscombe
Hurst
Winnersh
Sindlesham
Shinfield
Arborfield
Arborfield Cross
Arborfield Garrison
Barkham
WOKINGHAM
Binfield
BRACKNELL
Easthampstead
North Ascot
Ascot
Sunninghill
Windlesham
Crowthorne
Finchampstead
Wick Hill
Eversley
Yateley
Sandhurst
Bagshot
Lightwater
CAMBERLEY
Frimley
Blackwater
Hawley
Fox Lane
Deepcut
Bisley
Knaphill
Brookwood
Pirbright
FARNBOROUGH
Cove
West Heath
Minley Manor
Hartley Wintney
Phoenix Green
Hartfordbridge
Hazeley
Bramshill
Heckfield
Mattingley
Stratfield Saye
Stratfield Turgis
Riseley
Swallowfield
Spencers Wood
Three Mile Cross
Grazeley
Beech Hill
Mortimer
Stratfield Mortimer
Silchester
Pamber Heath
Tadley
Little London
Pamber End
Bramley
Sherfield on Loddon
Hartley Wespall
Turgis Green
Church End
Rotherwick
Chineham
Old Basing
BASINGSTOKE
Hatch
Mapledurwell
Up Nately
Greywell
Newnham
Hook
North Warnborough
Odiham
Winchfield
Dogmersfield
FLEET
Church Crookham
Crookham Village
ALDERSHOT
Ash
Tongham
FARNHAM
Upper Hale
Heath End
Ewshot
Crondall
Long Sutton
South Warnborough
Upton Grey
Weston Patrick
Tunworth
Winslade
Cliddesden
Farleigh Wallop
Ellisfield
Herriard
Southrope
Lasham
Golden Pot
Shalden
Bentworth
Holybourne
ALTON
Chawton
Beech
Medstead
Four Marks
Ropley
Bishop's Sutton
New Alresford
Old Alresford
Itchen Abbas
Itchen Stoke
Ovington
Easton
WINCHESTER
Kings Worthy
Headbourne Worthy
South Wonston
Micheldever
Micheldever Station
Popham
Dummer
North Waltham
Steventon
Overton
Laverstoke
Whitchurch
Oakley
East Oakley
Deane
Quidhampton
North Oakley
Hannington
Kingsclere
Wolverton
Ramsdell
Baughurst
Heath End
Ashford Hill
Headley
Burghclere
Old Burghclere
Sydmonton
Ecchinswell
Newtown
Crookham
Brimpton
Wasing
Aldermaston
Aldermaston Wharf
Woolhampton
Midgham
THATCHAM
Cold Ash
Bucklebury
Upper Bucklebury
Chapel Row
Beenham
Stanford Dingley
Hermitage
Frilsham
Yattendon
Ashampstead
Hampstead Norreys
Compton
Aldworth
East Ilsley
West Ilsley
Catmore
Beedon
Stanmore
Peasemore
World's End
Downend
Chieveley
Winterbourne
Donnington
Shaw
NEWBURY
Greenham
Ufton Nervet
Sulhamstead
Burghfield
Burghfield Common
Wokefield Park
HENLEY-ON-THAMES
Remenham
Lower Shiplake
Shiplake
Wargrave
Harpsden
Hambleden
Medmenham
MARLOW
Bix
Middle Assendon
Lower Assendon
Stonor
Turville
Turville Heath
Pishill
Skirmett
Fingest
Frieth
Ibstone
Stokenchurch
Cadmore End
Lane End
HIGH WYCOMBE
West Wycombe
Hughenden Valley
Hazlemere
Tylers Green
Loudwater
Flackwell Heath
BEACONSFIELD
Wooburn Green
Bourne End
Little Marlow
Cookham
Cookham Dean
Cookham Rise
MAIDENHEAD
Taplow
Burnham
Bray
Holyport
WINDSOR
Dorney
Knowl Hill
Hare Hatch
Littlewick Green
White Waltham
Waltham St Lawrence
Shurlock Row
Warfield
Winkfield
Cranbourne
Windsor Forest
GREAT PARK
Whitehill
Bordon Camp
Headley
Grayshott
Hindhead
Shottermill
HASLEMERE
Liphook
Bramshott
Liss
Liss Forest
Greatham
Selborne
Empshott
Hawkley
Newton Valence
East Tisted
West Tisted
Cheriton
Tichborne
Hinton Ampner
Kilmeston
Bramdean
West Meon
Privett
Froxfield Green
Steep
PETERSFIELD
Rake
Milland
Fernhurst
Chiddingfold
Witley
Milford
Elstead
Tilford
Frensham
Rowledge
Churt
Thursley
Twyford
Shawford
Otterbourne
Owslebury
Morestead
Chilcomb
Longwood Warren
CHILTERN HILLS
NORTH DOWNS
Due to open Early 1987

Winslow
Steeple Claydon
Leighton Buzzard
Dunstable
Houghton Regis
Aylesbury
Tring
Wendover
Berkhamsted
Thame
Haddenham
Long Crendon
Princes Risborough
Chinnor
Chesham
Amersham
Hemel Hempstead
Watford
Chorleywood
Rickmansworth
High Wycombe
Beaconsfield
Gerrards Cross
Marlow
Henley-on-Thames
Maidenhead
Slough
Windsor
Uxbridge
Wallingford
Watlington
Reading
Wokingham
Bracknell
Ascot
Staines
Egham
Camberley
Woking
Weybridge
Chertsey
Sandhurst
Yateley
Windsor Great Park
Chiltern Hundreds
The Three Hundreds of Aylesbury
Heathrow Airport London
SP
SU

LUTON
Luton International Airport
STEVENAGE
Knebworth
Welwyn
WELWYN GARDEN CITY
HARPENDEN
Wheathampstead
Redbourn
HATFIELD
ST ALBANS
VERVLAMIVM
London Colney
Radlett
BOREHAMWOOD
POTTERS BAR
Brookmans Park
Cuffley
HERTFORD
Hertford Heath
WARE
HODDESDON
Broxbourne
CHESHUNT
WALTHAM ABBEY
Waltham Cross
Enfield Chase
ENFIELD
BARNET
EAST BARNET
SOUTHGATE
Winchmore Hill
EDMONTON
CHINGFORD
LOUGHTON
EPPING
Theydon Bois
HARLOW
BISHOP'S STORTFORD
SAWBRIDGEWORTH
STANSTED MOUNTFITCHET
Stansted Airport
GREAT DUNMOW
Much Hadham
Puckeridge
Buntingford
CHIPPING ONGAR
North Weald Bassett
BRENTWOOD
ROMFORD
HORNCHURCH
UPMINSTER
DAGENHAM
BARKING
ILFORD
WANSTEAD
WOODFORD
WALTHAMSTOW
TOTTENHAM
WOOD GREEN
FINCHLEY
EDGWARE
Mill Hill
STANMORE
HARROW
PINNER
RUISLIP
Eastcote
KENTON
Kingsbury
HENDON
Golders Green
HAMPSTEAD
WEMBLEY
WILLESDEN
NORTHOLT
GREENFORD
SOUTHALL
EALING
ACTON
HAMMERSMITH
PADDINGTON
MARYLEBONE
CAMDEN TOWN
ISLINGTON
STOKE NEWINGTON
HACKNEY
LEYTON
STRATFORD
WEST HAM
EAST HAM
BETHNAL GREEN
BOW
STEPNEY
POPLAR
LONDON
LONDINIUM
WESTMINSTER
KENSINGTON
CHELSEA
FULHAM
BERMONDSEY
LAMBETH
CAMBERWELL
BATTERSEA
DEPTFORD
GREENWICH
WOOLWICH
ERITH
RAINHAM
Purfleet
GRAYS
CLAPHAM
BRIXTON
WANDSWORTH
PUTNEY
RICHMOND
BARNES
CHISWICK
BRENTFORD
HOUNSLOW
ISLEWORTH
TWICKENHAM
FELTHAM
TEDDINGTON
KINGSTON UPON THAMES
SURBITON
WIMBLEDON
MERTON
MORDEN
MITCHAM
STREATHAM
LEWISHAM
CATFORD
ELTHAM
BEXLEY
CRAYFORD
DARTFORD
Greenhithe
SWANSCOMBE
SIDCUP
CHISLEHURST
BROMLEY
BECKENHAM
CROYDON
CARSHALTON
SUTTON
EWELL
EPSOM
ESHER
WALTON-ON-THAMES
NEW MALDEN
Chessington
WALLINGTON
PURLEY
COULSDON
WARLINGHAM
ORPINGTON
Farnborough
Biggin Hill
New Addington
Swanley
Eynsford
Kemsing
SEVENOAKS
LEATHERHEAD
Ashtead
Tadworth
Kingswood
Woldingham
Due to open Mid 1986

BRAINTREE
GREAT DUNMOW
BISHOP'S STORTFORD
STANSTED MOUNTFITCHET
Stansted Airport
SAWBRIDGEWORTH
HARLOW
Coggeshall
Kelvedon
WITHAM
Tiptree
Hatfield Peverel
MALDON
Heybridge
CHELMSFORD
Danbury
Writtle
Great Baddow
Galleywood
Due to open Late 1986
EPPING
CHIPPING ONGAR
North Weald Bassett
Ingatestone
South Woodham Ferrers
Hullbridge
BILLERICAY
BRENTWOOD
WICKFORD
RAYLEIGH
Rochford
Hockley
BASILDON
Laindon
ROMFORD
HORNCHURCH
UPMINSTER
ILFORD
BARKING
DAGENHAM
LONDON
WOOLWICH
SOUTH BENFLEET
Hadleigh
Leigh-on-Sea
SOUTHEND-ON-SEA
Shoeburyness
CANVEY ISLAND
Corringham
Stanford-le-Hope
Thames Haven
Tilbury
GRAYS
Purfleet
ERITH
BEXLEY
DARTFORD
CRAYFORD
Greenhithe
SWANSCOMBE
NORTHFLEET
GRAVESEND
SHEERNESS
Isle of Grain
Allhallows-on-Sea
Hoo St Werburgh
ROCHESTER
Strood
GILLINGHAM
CHATHAM
SITTINGBOURNE
SIDCUP
CHISLEHURST
Swanley
ORPINGTON
Farnborough
Eynsford
West Kingsdown
Due to open Mid 1986
Snodland
Aylesford
MAIDSTONE
SEVENOAKS
Otford
Kemsing
Borough Green
West Malling
NORTH DOWNS
River Medway
River Thames
Yantlet Dredged Channel
SHEERNESS to Vlissingen (Flushing)

CARMARTHEN
LLANDEILO
AMMANFORD
LLANELLI
GORSEINON
SWANSEA
PORT TALBOT
KIDWELLY
BURRY PORT
Whitland
St Clears
Laugharne
Pendine
Llansteffan
Ferryside
Pembrey
Trimsaran
Tumble
Cross Hands
Pontardulais
Pontardawe
Glanaman
Brynamman
Llandybie
Ffairfach
Loughor
Gowerton
Morriston
Clydach
Dunvant
Killay
Sketty
The Mumbles
Mumbles Head
Bishopston
Southgate
Pennard
Parkmill
Penmaen
Nicholaston
Oxwich
Oxwich Bay
Penrice
Horton
Port-Eynon
Port-Eynon Point
Port-Eynon Bay
Knelston
Reynoldston
Llanddewi
Rhossili
Rhossili Bay
WORMS HEAD
(Penrhyn-gwyr)
Llangennith
Burry Holms
Llanmadoc
Cheriton
Landimore
Llanrhidian
Llanrhidian Sands
Whiteford Point
Crofty
Pen-clawdd
Llanmorlais
Three Crosses
Swansea Airport
Upper Killay
Cefn Bryn
Long Cairn
Pwlldu Head
G O W E R
CARMARTHEN BAY
SWANSEA BAY
BRISTOL CHANN
Pendine Sands
Laugharne Sands
Cefn Sidan Sands
Pembrey Forest
East Marsh
Ginst Point
Cefn-Padrig
Helwick
Scarweather
SN
SS
BLACK
Dyffryn Tywi
Afon Tywi
Afon Taf
Afon Cothi
Afon Gwili
Gwendraeth Fach
Gwendraeth Fawr
River Loughor
Afon Llwchwr
(River Loughor)
Drefach
Felindre
Drefelin
Pentre-cwrt
Saron
Bancyffordd
Capel Iwan
Moelfre
Cwmpengraig
Rhos
Pencader
New Inn
Gwyddgrug
Dolgran
Alltwalis
Cwmduad
Hermon
Trelech
Llanfyrnach
Dinas
Blaenwaun
Llanwinio
Cwmbach
Cwmfelin Mynach
Gellywen
Llanboidy
Meidrim
Talog
Abernant
Newchurch
Merthyr
Cynwyl Elfed
Pen-y-bont
Llanpumsaint
Pontarsais
Rhydargaeau
Bronwydd Arms
Capel Gwyn
Llanfihangel uwch-Gwili
Plâs
Horeb
Brechfa
Gwernogle
Abergorlech
Llansawel
Edwinsford
Talley
Pen-y-garn
Mynydd Figyn
Cwmdu
Halfway
Llansadwrn
Llanwrda
Llangadog
Felindre
Dyffryn Ceidrych
Bethlehem
Trichrug
Capel Gwynfe
Manordeilo
Llanfynydd
Capel Isaac
Salem
Pantglas Hall
Felingwmuchaf
Court Henry
Penybanc
Dynevor Castle
Llanegwad
Llangathen
Nantgaredig
Capel Dewi
Abergwili
Llangunnor
Llanarthney
Golden Grove
Trapp
Llandyfan
Carmel
Pentre-Gwenlais
Maesybont
Porthyrhyd
Llanddarog
Cwmisfael
Cwmffrwd
Croesyceiliog
Llangain
Llanllwch
Bancyfelin
Llangynog
Llanddowror
Red Roses
Llandawke
Llansadurnen
Llanmiloe
Llanybri
Llangendeirne
Crwbin
Pontantwn
Llandefaelog
Pontyberem
Meinciau
Pont Henri
Pontyates
Mynydd y Garreg
Llansaint
Carway
Five Roads
Mynydd Sylen
Sylen
Llannon
Cefneithin
Gorslas
Drefach
Mynydd Cerrig
Pen-y-groes
Saron
Capel Hendre
Tycroes
Pontamman
Betws
Pantyffynnon
Garnant
Gwaun-Cae-Gurwen
Cwmllynfell
Mynydd y Gwair
Mynydd Garn-fach
Graig Fawr
Cefn Drum
Fforest
Hendy
Felinfoel
Llangennech
Dafen
Pwll
Llwynhendy
Grovesend
Pontlliw
Penllergaer
Llangyfelach
Felindre
Craigcefnparc
Cadle
Fforest-fach
Waunarlwydd
Landore
Llansamlet
Birchgrove
Glais
Works
Mynydd Pen-bre
West Cross
Black Pill
Newton
Llandovery
Castle
Abbey
Fort
ROMAN ROAD
A 40(T)
A 48(T)
A 484
A 485
A 476
A 483
A 4069
A 474
A 4070
A 4067
A 4118
A 4216
A 4217
B 4300
B 4310
B 4297
B 4306
B 4308
B 4309
B 4317
B 4312
B 4298
B 4299
B 4333
B 4459
B 4301
B 4302
B 4337
B 4314
B 4271
B 4295
B 4436
B 4247
31

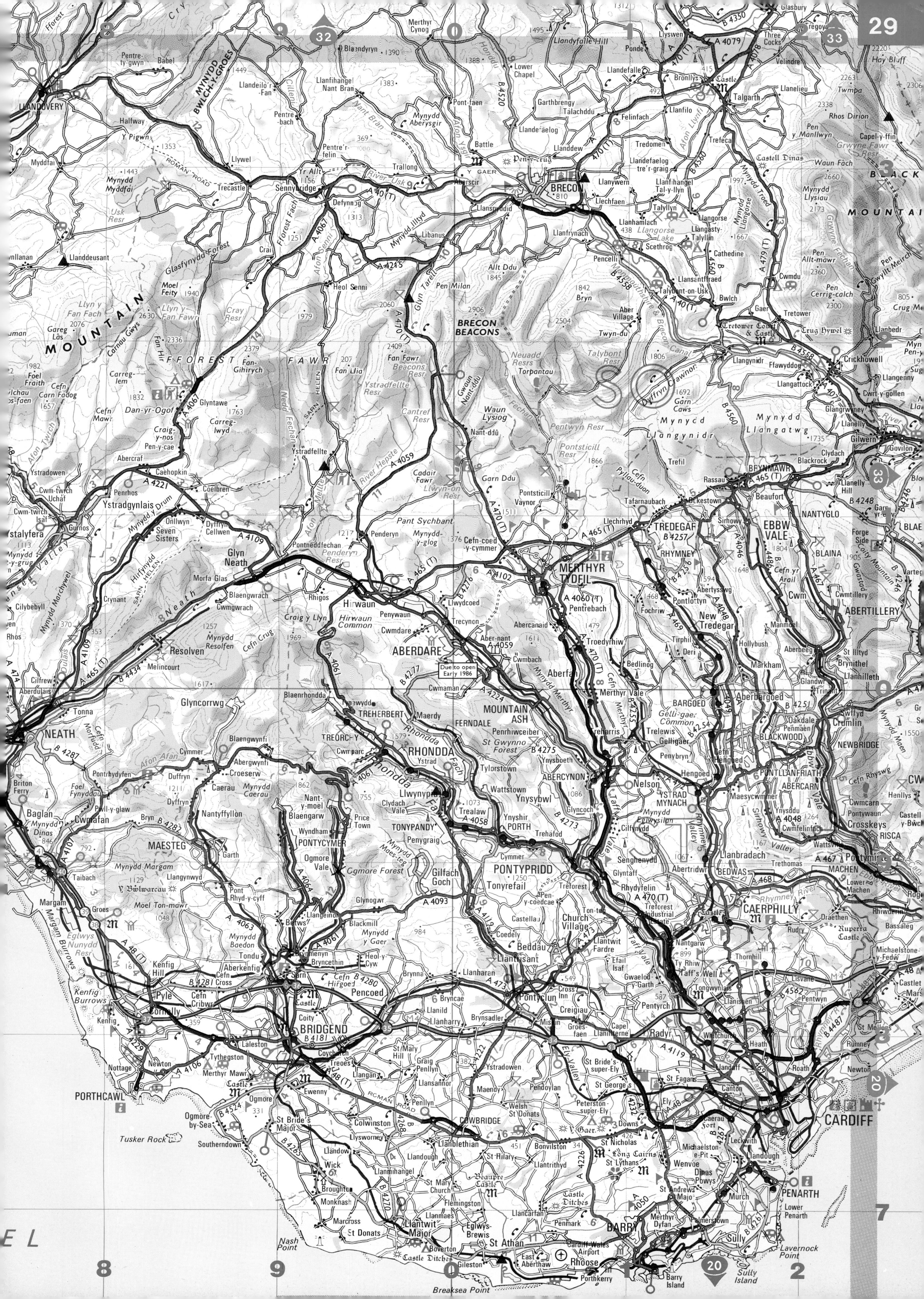

ST GEORGE'S CHANNEL
FISHGUARD to Rosslare................3½ hrs
PEMBROKE to Rosslare..................4¼ hrs
SM
SR
Cardigan Island
Cemaes Head
Gwbert
Pwllygranant
St Dogmaels
Abbey
Moylgrove
Monington
Trwyn-y-bwa
Glanrhyd
Bridell
STRUMBLE HEAD
DINAS HEAD
Carregwastad Point
Newport Bay
Tresinwen
Pen Caer
Pen Brush
Llanwnda
Fishguard Bay
Bryn-henllan
Parrog
Newport
Nevern
Felindre Farchog
GOODWICK
Harbour
FISHGUARD
Dinas Cross
Mynydd Carningli
Eglwyswrw
Penbwchdy
Manorowen
Mynydd Melyn
Afon Nyfer
Crosswell
Eglwyswen
Llanychaer
St Nicholas
Panteg
Scleddau
Brynberian
Pontfaen
Granston
Ynys Deullyn
Abercastle
MYNYDD PRESELI
Foel Eryr
Fort
Penclegyr
Trevine
Mathry
Jordanston
Trecwn
Cwmcerwyn
Porthgain
Square and Compass
Castlemorris
Mynachlog-ddu
Carreg-gwylan-fach
Abereiddy
Llanrhian
Croes-goch
Foel-drych
Berea
Puncheston
Rosebush
Penllechwen
Tretio
Treglemais
Letterston
Castlebythe
ST DAVID'S HEAD
Treleddyd-fawr
Carnhedryn
Treffynnon
Little Newcastle
Tufton
Henry's Moat
Maenclochog
Whitesand Bay or Porth-mawr
River Alun
River Solva
Welsh Hook
Wolf's Castle
Llangolman
Bishops and Clerks
Cath
Whitchurch
Middle Mill
Llandeloy
Hayscastle Cross
Ambleston
Wallis
Llys-y-frân Resr
Rhosson
St David's
Hayscastle
Rinaston
New Moat
Efailwen
Ramsey Island
Ramsey Sound
Solva
Treffgarne
Llys-y-frân
Llanycefn
Login
Penycwm
Dudwell Mt
Leweston
Walton East
Penffordd
Green Scar
Newgale
Wolfsdale
Western Cleddau
Spittal
Scolton
Clarbeston
Llandissilio
Roch
Camrose
Clarbeston Road
Bletherston
Rickets Head
Simpson Cross
Keeston
Gelli
Clunderwen
Llanfallteg
ST BRIDES BAY
Nolton Haven
Nolton
Pelcomb Cross
Crundale
Wiston
Bethesda
Castle
Llanddewi Velfrey
Druidston
Lambston
HAVERFORDWEST
Llawhaden
Robeston Wathen
Haroldston West
Portfield Gate
Conaston Bridge
Stack Rocks
Broad Haven
Merlin's Bridge
Uzmaston
NARBERTH
Crinow
Lampeter Velfrey
Little Haven
Walton West
Minwear
Talbenny
Boulston
Templeton
Skomer Island
Tower Point
Walwyn's Castle
Freystrop
Landshipping
Ludchurch
Wooltack Point
St Brides
Johnston
Hook
Martletwy
Tiers Cross
Llangwm
Yerbeston
Reynalton
Hasguard
Robeston Cross
Rosemarket
Hill Mountain
Thomas Chapel
Marloes
Oil Refinery
Steynton
Loveston
Kilgetty
BROAD SOUND
Herbrandston
MILFORD HAVEN
Houghton
Begelly
Gateholm Island
St Ishmael's
Lawrenny
Jeffreyston
Saundersfoot Station
Amroth
Dale
Waterston
Cresswell Quay
Cresselly
Dale Point
MILFORD HAVEN
Llanstadwell
NEYLAND
Burton
East Williamston
Saundersfoot
Skokholm Island
Toll
Redberth
Monkstone Point
Angle
Angle Bay
Refinery
Pembroke Dock
Power Sta
Cosheston
Carew Newton
Milton
Carew
New Hedges
St Ann's Head
Pwllcrochan
Carew Cheriton
Sheep Island
Rhoscrowther
PEMBROKE
Palace
Lamphey
St Florence
Gumfreston
TENBY
Hundleton
Freshwater West
Castlemartin
Hodgeston
Jameston
Penally
Giltar Point
St Twynnells
Freshwater East
Castle
Lydstep
Caldey Sound
Caldey Island
Warren
St Petrox
Trewent Point
Manorbier
Old Castle Head
Chapel Point
Linney Head
Stackpole
Crow Rock
Toes
The Wash
Bosherston
Stackpole Head
ST GOVAN'S HEAD

ABERAERON
NEW QUAY
Gilfachreda
Cross Inn
Cwmtydu
Ynys-Lochtyn
Llangranog
Llanarth
Oakford
Synod Inn
Llwyncelyn
Foss-y-ffin
Pennant
Monachty
Cilcennin
Cross Inn
Llangeitho
Penuwch
Bwlch-Llan
Trefilan
Cilliau-Aeron
Tal-sarn
Gartheli
Abermeurig
Capel Betws Lleucu
Llwyn-y-groes
Llanddewi Brefi
Dihewyd
Ystrad Aeron
Temple Bar
Mydroilyn
Caledrhydiau
Pont Creuddyn
Betws Bledrws
Llangybi
Llanfair Clydogau
Bryn Brawd
Craig Twrch
Aberporth
Parcllyn
Penbryn
Tresaith
Sarnau
Plwmp
Pentregat
Brynhoffnant
Talgarreg
Gorsgoch
Cribyn
Silian
LAMPETER
Cellan
Cwmann
Pentre-bach
Verwig
Blaenannerch
Tan-y-groes
Glynarthen
Tremain
Blaenporth
Penparc
Betws Ifan
Rhydlewis
Capel Cynon
Bwlch-y-fadfa
Castell Howell
Aber
Cwrtnewydd
Llanwnnen
CARDIGAN
Pantgwyn
Ponthirwaun
Beulah
Ffostrasol
Moel y Mor
Pont-Siân
Cwmsychbant
Llanwenog
Dre-fach
Pencarreg
Llanycrwys
Ffarmers
Cwrt-y-cadno
Ffaldybrenin
Llangoedmor
Llechryd
Llandygwydd
Troedyraur
Penrhiwpal
Maesllyn
Tre-groes
Rhydowen
Pren gwyn
Capel Dewi
Llanybydder
Mynydd Pencarreg
Castle
Afon Teifi
Cwm-cou
Cenarth
Llandyfriog
Aber-banc
Horeb
Penrh w-llan
Llandysul
Maesycrugiau
Llanllwni
Landre
Abercych
NEWCASTLE EMLYN
Newchapel
Cilwendeg
Penrherber
Henllan
Llangeler
Drefach
Pentre-cwrt
Llanfihangel-ar-arth
Pumsaint
Caio
Boncath
Felindre
Drefelin
Saron
Bancyffordd
Mynydd Llanllwni
Mynydd Llanbyther
Rhydcymerau
Blaenffos
Capel Iwan
Cwmpengraig
Pencader
New Inn
Lldiad-Nenog
Llansawel
Bwlchygroes
Freni-fawr
Clydey
Moelfre
Rhos
Gwyddgrug
Star
Cilrhedyn
Crymych
Tegryn
Dolgran
Gwernogle
Abergorlech
Edwinsford
Afon Cothi
Abbey
Talley
Hermon
Llanfyrnach
Cwmduad
Alltwalis
Brechfa
Pen-y-garn
Mynydd Figyn
Llansadwrn
Halfway
Cwmdu
Dinas
Trelech
Hermon
SN
Llanpumsaint
Pontarsais
Horeb
Llanfynydd
Capel Isaac
Blaenwaun
Llanwinio
Pen-y-bont
Cynwyl Elfed
Afon Duad
Rhydargaeau
Plâs
Pantglas Hall
Salem
Manordeilo
Felindre
Dyffryn Ceidrych
Bethlehem
Llanglydwen
Cefn-y-pant
Cwmbach
Cwmfelin Mynach
Talog
Newchurch
Felingwmuchaf
Penybanc
Fort Trichrug
Gellywen
Abernant
Bronwydd Arms
Llanfihangel uwch-Gwili
Capel Gwyn
Court Henry
Llanboidy
Afon Gronw
Afon Cynin
Nant Cynnen
Ffynnon-ddrain
Llanegwad
Dryslwyn
Langathen
Dynevor Castle
LLANDEILO
Dyffryn Tywi
Henllan Amgoes
Meidrim
Merthyr
Abergwili
Nantgaredig
Capel Dewi
Ffairfach
Cwmfelin Boeth
Llangynin
Sarnau
CARMARTHEN
Llangunnor
Llanarthney
Afon Twyi
Golden Grove
Trapp
Castle
Whitland
St Clears
Bancyfelin
Llanllwch
Cwmffrwd
Afon Cennen
Llandyfan
Afon Taf
Llangynog
Llangain
Croesyceiliog
Llanddarog
Porthyrhyd
Maesybont
Carmel
Pentre-Gwenlais
Llandybie
Llanddowror
Afon Cywyn
Cwmisfael
Gwendraeth Fach
Cefneithin
Gorslas
Pen-y-groes
Glanaman
Garnant
Banc Cwmhelen
Red Roses
Llandawke
Llanybri
Llangendeirne
Crwbin
Mynydd Cerrig
Drefach
Cross Hands
Saron
AMMANFORD
Pontamman
Betws
Mynydd y Betws
Llanstephan
Castle
Laugharne
Llansadurnen
Llandefaelog
Pontantwn
Pontyberem
Gwendraeth Fawr
Tumble
Capel Hendre
Tycroes
Pantyffynnon
Marros
Pendine
Llanmiloe
Ferryside
Meinciau
Pont Henri
Pontyates
Llannon
Ginst Point
East Marsh
Pendine Sands
Laugharne Sands
Llansaint
Mynydd y Garreg
Mynydd Sylen
Sylen
Mynydd y Gwair
Mynydd Garn-fach
Castle
KIDWELLY
Gwendraeth
Carway
Five Roads
Craig Fawr
Cefn Drum
Lliw Resrs
Cefn Sidan Sands
Pembrey Forest
Trimsaran
Fforest
Pontardulais
Pontardawe
Rhyd-y-fro
Mynydd Pen-bre
BURRY PORT
Hendy
Craigcefnparc
Felindre
Clydach
Felinfoel
Llangennech
Pembrey
Pwll
Dafen
Pontlliw
CARMARTHEN BAY
Cefn Padrig
Llwynhendy
Grovesend
Afon Lliw
LLANELLI
Penllergaer
Llangyfelach
Morriston
Afon Llwchwr (River Loughor)
Loughor
GORSEINON
Cadle
Llansamlet
SS
Whiteford Point
Llanrhidian Sands
Crofty
Gowerton
Fforest-fach
Landore
Pentre-dwr
Oil Refinery
Pen-clawdd
Waunarlwydd
Dunvant
SWANSEA
Llanmorlais
Llanmadoc
Cheriton
Landimore
Castle
Fort
Swansea Airport
Three Crosses
Sketty
Burry Holms
Llangennith
Llanrhidian
Upper Killay
Killay
Works
G O W E
Long Cairn
Ilston
Black Pill
River Loughor

Esgair Garthen
45
Bryn Garw
Pen-y-bwlch
Caban-coch Resr
Llanwrthwl
Llanyre
LLANDRINDOD WELLS
Penybont
Llandegley
Tregaron
Y Drum
Esgair Llyn-du
Esgair Ambor
Afon Claerwen
Drum Ddu
Newbridge-on-Wye
Howey
Disserth
Crossway
Gilwern Hill
Llandegley Rhos
Bryn Crwn
Drum yr Eira
Drygarn Fawr
Gorllwyn
Esgair Fraith
Llyn Berwyn
Esgair Cerrig
Gamallt
Llanddewi Brefi
Esgair Llethr
Camddwr
Bryn
Llanafan-fawr
Llansantffraed-in-Elwel
Irfon
Cefn Coch
Builth Road
Carneddau
Pen Rhiwclochdy
Bryn Brawd
Pen y Gurnos
Cefn Fannog
Abergwesyn
Afon Wye
Chwefru
Cilmery
Llanelwedd
Cregrina
Llanfaredd
Llyn Brianne Resr
Tywi Forest
Cwm Irfon
Beulah
Llanfechan
Garth
BUILTH WELLS
Tyn-y-graig
Rhulen
Llanbadarn-y-garreg
Aberedw
Craig Twrch
31
Afon Twrch
Mynydd Trawsnant
Llanwrtyd
Llangammarch Wells
Maesmynis
Llanddewi'r Cwm
Alltmawr
Llandeilo Hill
Ystradffin
LLANWRTYD WELLS
Drum-ddu
Llandeilo Graban
Ffarmers
Cwrt-y-cadno
Mynydd Mallaen
Afon Cothi
MYNYDD EPPYNT
Pentre Dolau Honddu
Gwenddwr
Erwood
Rhandirmwyn
Bryn Nicol
Cefn Llwydlo
Crychan Forest
Cledan
Bryn-du
Twyn Rhyd-car
Crickadarn
Llanstephan
Esgair Ferchon
Landre
Afon Tywi
Tirabad
Upper Chapel
Pumsaint
Caio
Cilycwm
Cynghordy
Gwryd
Boughrood
Fforest
Merthyr Cynog
Llandyfalle Hill
Llyswen
Porthyrhyd
Siloh
Blaendyryn
Honddu
Ponde
Pentre-ty-gwyn
Babel
MYNYDD BWLCH-Y-GROES
Llandeilo'r-Fan
Llanfihangel Nant Bran
Lower Chapel
Llandefalle
Bronllys
28
LLANDOVERY
29
Pont-faen
Garthbrengy
Talachddu
Llanfilo
Felinfach
Halfway
Y Pigwn
Cilieni
Pentre-bach
Nant Brân
Mynydd Aberysgir
Afon Ysgir
Llandefaelog
Tredomen
Llansadwrn
Llanwrda
ROMAN ROAD
Pentre'r-felin
Battle
Pen-y-crug
Llanddew
Llandefaelog tre'r-graig
Llanfihangel Tal-y-llyn
Halfway
Cilgwyn
Myddfai
Mynydd Myddfai
Llywel
Trecastle
Yr Allt
Sennybridge
Trallong
River Usk
Y GAER
Aberscir
BRECON
Llanywern
Llangadog
Defynnog
Llanspyddid
Llechfaen
Talyllyn
Felindre
Manordeilo
Pwll-y-Ceidrych
Usk Resr
Fforest Fach
Mynydd Illtyd
Libanus
Llanfrynach
Llanhamlach
Llangorse Lake
Llangasty-Talyllin
Bethlehem
Fort
Trichrug
Twynllanan
Llanddeusant
Glasfynydd Forest
Crai
Afon Senni
Scethrog
Pencelli
Dyffryn Tywi
LLANDEILO
Capel Gwynfe
Moel Feity
Llyn y Fan Fach
Llyn y Fan Fawr
Cray Resr
Heol Senni
Glyn Tarell
Pen Milan
Allt Ddu
Bryn
Ffairfach
Truman
Gareg Las
BLACK MOUNTAIN
Carnau Gwys
Fan Hir
FFOREST FAWR
Fan-Gihirych
Fan Fawr
Beacons Resr
Fan Llia
BRECON BEACONS
Aber Village
Twyn-du
Talybont-on-Usk
Trapp
Castle
Foel Fraith
Cefn Carn Fadog
Carreg-lem
Neuadd Resrs
Torpantau
Talybont Resr
Dyffryn Crawnon
Llandyfan
Bylchau Rhos-faen
Dan-yr-Ogof
Cefn Mawr
Glyntawe
Carreg-lwyd
SARN HELEN
Ystradfellte Resr
Cantref Resr
Nedd Fechan
Gwaun Nant-ddu
Waun Lysiog
Garn Caws
Mynydd Llangynidr
Craig-y-nos
Pen-y-cae
Nant-ddu
Pentwyn Resr
Pontsticill Resr
Brynamman
Glanaman
Garnant
Banc Cwmhelen
Cymllynfell
Ystradowen
Abercraf
Caehopkin
Ystradfellte
River Hepste
Cadair Fawr
Llwyn-on Resr
Garn Ddu
Trefil
Cefn Pyllau-duon
Betws
Gwaun-Cae-Gurwen
Mynydd y Betws
Cwm-twrch Uchaf
Cwm-twrch Isaf
Penrhos
Ystradgynlais
Coelbren
Pontsticill
Vaynor
Tafarnaubach
Dukestown
Pantyffynnon
Cefn Gwrhyd
Ystalyfera
Gurnos
Mynydd y Drum
Onllwyn
Seven Sisters
Dyffryn Cellwen
Pant Sychbant
Penderyn
Mynydd-y-glog
Cefn-coed-y-cymmer
Llechrhyd
TREDEGAR
RHYMNEY
Mynydd y Gwair
Mynydd Allt-y-grug
Cilmaengwyn
Swansea Valley
Glyn Neath
Pontneddfechan
Penderyn Resr
MERTHYR TYDFIL
Mynydd Garn-fach
Llangiwg
Hirfynydd
Morfa Glas
Rhigos
Hirwaun
Llwydcoed
Pentrebach
Pontlottyn
Lliw Resrs
Rhyd-y-fro
Crynant
Blaengwrach
Cwmgwrach
Craig y Llyn
Hirwaun Common
Penywaun
Trecynon
Fochriw
Pontardawe
Cilybebyll
Mynydd Marchywel
Vale of Neath
Mynydd Resolfen
Cefn Crug
Cwmdare
Abernant
Troedyrhiw
New Tredegar
Craigcefnparc
Alltwen
Rhos
Resolven
Melincourt
ABERDARE
Cwmbach
Tirphil
Deri
Felindre
Clydach
Faerdre
Glais
Bryn-Coch
Cilfrew
Aberdulais
Dulais
Aberaman
Cwmaman
Aberfan
Bedlinog
Merthyr Vale
Mynydd Merthyr
Blaenrhondda
Tynewydd
TREHERBERT
Maerdy
FERNDALE
MOUNTAIN ASH
BARGOED
Gelli-gaer Common
Glyncorrwg
Rhydding
Birchgrove
Tonna
Morriston
Llangyfelach
NEATH
Cefn Morfudd
Penrhiwceiber
Treharris
Trelewis
Gelligaer
Llansamlet
Skewen
TREORCHY
St Gwynno Forest
Pentre-dwr
Oil Refinery
Landore
Blaengwynfi
Cymmer
Abergwynfi
Cwmparc
RHONDDA
Ystrad
Rhondda Fach
Ynysboeth
Penybryn
Hengoed
SWANSEA
Briton Ferry
Pontrhydyfen
Duffryn
Croeserw
Caerau
Mynydd Caerau
Tylorstown
ABERCYNON
Nelson
YSTRAD MYNACH
Foel Fynyddau
Nant-y-moel
Llwynypia
Wattstown
Ynysybwl
Skettyy
Baglan
Mynydd Dinas
Pwll-y-glaw
Dyffryn
Nantyffyllon
Blaengarw
Price Town
Clydach Vale
Trealaw
Ynyshir
PORTH
Glyncoch
Mynydd Eglwysilan
Works
River Neath
PORT TALBOT
Cwmafan
Bryn
MAESTEG
Garth
Wyndham
PONTYCYMER
Ogmore
TONYPANDY
Penygraig
Trehafod
Cilfynydd
Senghenydd
Rhymney Valley
SN
SS

New Radnor
Kinnerton
Evenjobb
Burfa Camp
Nash
Rodd
Combe
Combe Moor
Shobdon
Lucton
Mortimer Cross
Eye
Luston
Kimbolton
Leysters
Kyre Park
Stoke Bliss
Old Radnor
Knill
Offa's Dyke
Titley
Staunton on Arrow
Kingsland
Eyton
Cobnash
Shirl Heath
Cholstrey
LEOMINSTER
Stockton
Bach Camp
Whyle
Grafton
Hatfield
Pudleston
Yardro
Walton
Burlingjobb
Llanfihangel-nant-Melan
Dolyhir
KINGTON
Hergest Ridge
Gladestry
Hergest
Huntington
Lyonshall
Marston
Pembridge
Eardisland
Lawton
Monkland
Steen's Bridge
Docklow
Stoke Prior
Humber Court
Grendon Green
Bredenbury
Bromyard Downs
Bromyard
Barewood
Moorcot
Luntley
Sollers Dilwyn
Haven
Stretford Court
Ivington
Ivington Green
Brierley
Wharton
Risbury
Marston Stannett
Kingswood
Holme Marsh
Broxwood
Dilwyn
Aulden
Upper Hill
Hope under Dinmore
Newton
Hegdon Hill
Pencombe
Stanford Bishop
Hengoed
Michaelchurch-on-Arrow
Newchurch
Upcott
Almeley
Weobley
Weobley Marsh
Sarnesfield
Westhope
Bowley
Bodenham
Maund Bryan
Ullingswick
Little Cowarne
Munderfield Row
Acton Beauchamp
Munderfield Stocks
Bryngwyn
Lower Welson
Brilley
Eardisley
Kinnersley
Ledgemoor
King's Pyon
Canon Pyon
Urdimarsh
The Vauld
Walker's Green
Stoke Lacy
Moreton Jeffries
Doly-cannau
Rhos-goch
Whitney-on-Wye
Ailey
Calver Hill
Norton Canon
Wormsley
Yarsop
Yazor
Wellington
Felton
Burley Gate
Much Cowarne
Clyro Hill
Painscastle
Toll
Winforton
Willersley
Letton
Letton Lake
River Wye
Moorhampton
Staunton on Wye
Mansell Gamage
Mansell Lacy
Tillington Common
Tillington
Moreton on Lugg
Marden
Sutton Walls
Sutton St Nicholas
Preston Wynne
Ocle Pychard
Castle Frome
Clifford
Priory Wood
Merbach
Bredwardine
Brobury
Monnington on Wye
Brinsop
Burghill
Westhide
Newtown
Clyro
Hardwicke
HAY-ON-WYE
The Bage
Bishopstone
Credenhill
Pipe and Lyde
Shelwick
Withington
Shucknall
Stretton Grandison
Canon Frome
Byford
Kenchester
Bridge Sollers
Stretton Sugwas
Swainshill
Holmer
Yarkhill
Ashperton
Llowes
Cusop
Dorstone
Moccas
Preston on Wye
Lulham
Upper Breinton
King's Acre
Lugwardine
Hagley
Weston Beggard
Bartestree
Tupsley
Dormington
Tarrington
Munsley
Cilwrch
Glasbury
Llanigon
Snodhill
Blakemere
Ploughfield
Canon Bridge
Tyberton
Lower Breinton
HEREFORD
Lower Bullingham
Hampton Bishop
Trumpet
Three Cocks
Tregoyd
Urishay Common
Peterchurch
Madley
Eaton Bishop
Shenmore
Clehonger
Dinedor
Mordiford
Aylton
Putley
Little Marcle
Velindre
Hay Bluff
Vowchurch
Kingstone
Allensmore
Grafton
Twyford Common
Holme Lacy
Woolhope
Llanelieu
Twmpa
Craswall
Michaelchurch Escley
Turnastone
Golden Valley
Thruxton
Callow
Fownhope
Rushall
Rhos Dirion
Upper Maes-coed
Middle Maes-coed
St Margarets
Kerry's Gate
Cockyard
Dewsall Court
Aconbury
Bolstone
Capler Camp
Sollers Hope
Much Marcle
Pen y Manllwyn
Capel-y-ffin
Grwyne Fawr Resr
Newton
Bacton
Didley
Kingsthorne
Little Birch
Little Dewchurch
Brockhampton
Ballingham
Castell Dinas
Waun Fach
BLACK MOUNTAINS
Llanveynoe
Lower Maes-coed
Abbey Dore
Wormbridge
Kilpeck
Much Dewchurch
Much Birch
Carey
Fawley Chapel
How Caple
Mynydd Llysiau
Priory
Llanthony
Longtown
Ewyas Harold
Howton
Wormelow Tump
Orcop Hill
Hoarwithy
Llandinabo
Kings Caple
Foy
Hole in the Wall
Kempley
Clodock
Mynydd Merddin
Hatterrall Hill
Bagwyllydiart
Llanwarne
Sellack
Brampton Abbotts
Upton Bishop
Crow Hill
Rowlestone
Pontrilas
Kentchurch Court
Orcop
Pencoyd
Llangua
Kentchurch
Michaelchurch
St Owen's Cross
Bridstow
Linton
Pen Allt-mawr
Pen Gwyllt Meirch
Walterstone
Grosmont Castle
White Rocks
St Weonards
Tretire
Peterstow
ROSS-ON-WYE
Bromsash
Aston Crews
Pen Cerrig-calch
Oldcastle
Cwmyoy
Hoaldalbert
River Monnow
Garway
Glewstone
Weston under Penyard
Crug Mawr
Pandy
Hom Green
Coughton
Pontshill
Gaer
Tretower
Stanton
Forest Coal Pit
Skenfrith
Broad Oak
Llangarron
Pencraig
Walford
Crug Hywel
Llanbedr
Llanvihangel Crucorney
Llangattock Lingoed
Crossway
Marstow
Goodrich
Kerne Bridge
Hope Mansell
Mitcheldean
Crickhowell
Mynydd Pen-y-fâl
Sugar Loaf
Bettws
Bont
Cross Ash
Llanrothal
Welsh Newton
Llangrove
Welsh Bicknor
Ruardean
Drybrook
Llangattock
Llangenny
Allt
Newcastle
Whitchurch
Symonds Yat
Brierley
Lydbrook
Ruardean Woodside
Cwrt-y-gollen
Mynydd Llanwenarth
Llantilio Pertholey
Llanvetherine
White Castle
Maypole
Llangattock-Vibon-Avel
Garnarew
English Bicknor
Mardy
ABERGAVENNY
Llantilio Crossenny
Rockfield
Dixton
Edge End
Cinderford
Flaxley
Gilwern
Govilon
Llanvapley
Llanvihangel-Ystern-Llewern
MONMOUTH
Christchurch
Berry Hill
Littledean
BRYNMAWR
Blackrock
Llanfoist
Blorenge
Llanddewi Rhydderch
Wernrheolydd
Penrhos
Staunton
Mile End
Broadwell
Ruspidge
Llanelly Hill
Beaufort
NANTYGLO
Llanellen
Llanarth
Dingestow
Wonastow
Coleford
FOREST OF DEAN
Upper Soudley
Garn-yr-erw
The Bryn
Tregare
Mitchel Troy
Penallt
Redbrook
Coalway
Newland
Milkwall
EBBW VALE
BLAENAVON
Forge Side
Coity Mountain
Llanvihangel Gobion
Raglan
Castle
Pen-y-clawdd
Cwmcarvan
Caer Llan
Clearwell
Parkend
Yorkley
BLAINA
Varteg
Llanover
Llanfair Kilgeddin
New Mills
Offa's Dyke
Ellwood
Whitecroft
Cefn yr Arail
Cwmavon
Mynydd Garnclochdy
Nant-y-derry
Bettws Newydd
Twyn-y-Sheriff
Kingcoed
Llangovan
Whitebrook
Trelleck
Trow Green
Bream
Blakeney
Cwm
Cwmtillery
ABERTILLERY
Penperlleni
Kemeys Commander
Gwehelog
Llandogo
St Briavels
Lydney
ABERSYCHAN
Little Mill
Llancayo
Monkswood
Llandenny
Llansoy
Llanishen
Parkhouse
Hewelsfield
Manmoel
Hollybush
Aberbeeg
Trevethin
Glascoed
Gwernesney
Trelleck Grange
Tintern Parva
Chapel Hill
Brockweir
Tintern Abbey
Aylburton
Alvington
Netherend
Woolaston
Markham
St Illtyd
Brynithel
Llanhi
Glandwr
Trinant
PONTYPOOL
USK
Llangwm
New Inn
Wolvesnewton
Devauden
Tidenham Chase
Lydney Sand
Aberbargoed
Griffithstown
Sebastapol
Llandegfedd Resr
Coed-y-paen
Gaer-fawr
Kilgwrrwg Common
Chepstow Park Wood
Boughspring
Stroat
Swffryd
Crumlin
Oakdale
Penmaen
BLACKWOOD
NEWBRIDGE
Mynydd Maen
Croesyceiliog
Llangybi
Llantrisant
Llanllowell
Newchurch
St Arvans
Woodcroft
Tutshill
Wibdon
Tidenham
Bevington
PONTLLANFRAITH
ABERCARN
Cefn Rhyswg
CWMBRAN
Llandegveth
Tredunnock
Pen-y-cae-mawr
Earlswood
Itton Common
Mynydd-bach
Newbridge-on-Usk
Tidal Reservoir
Shepperdine
Ynysddu
Cwmcarn
Pontywaun
Henllys
Llanfrechfa
Ponthir
Llantrisant
Wentwood
Llanvair-Discoed
Mounton
Shirenewton
CHEPSTOW
Sedbury
Oldbury Sands
Rockhampton
Oldbury-on-Severn
Crosskeys
RISCA
Castell-y-Bwch
Croes-y-mwyalch
CAERLEON
ISCA
Parc Seymour
Llanvaches
Pwllmeyric
Beachley
Littleton-on-Severn
Falfield
Whitfield
Wattsville
Malpas
Cat's Ash
Penhow
Caerwent
VENTA
Mathern
Morton
Milbury Heath
Trethomas
Bettws
Pontymister
Llanbeder
Highmoor
MACHEN
Sirhowy Valley

DROITWICH
Ombersley
Salwarpe
Hadzor
Feckenham
Astwood Bank
Studley
Stoke Bliss
Upper Sapey
Shelsley Walsh
Shelsley Beauchamp
Clifton upon Teme
Little Witley
Holt Heath
Holt
Bank Street
Wolferlow
High Lane
Harpley
Wichenford
Grimley
Hawford
Martin Hussingtree
Bradley Green
Sambourne
Coughton
Wall Hills
Collington
Thornbury
Tedstone Wafre
Tedstone Delamere
Martley
Sinton Green
Moseley
Shoulton
Hallow
Claines
Fernhill Heath
Oddingley
Hindlip
Himbleton
Stock Green
Holberrow Green
Stock Wood
Cookhill
Inkberrow
Alcester
Edvin Loach
Edwyn Ralph
Horsham
Berrow Green
Whitbourne
Tibberton
Huddington
Warndon
Crowle
Grafton Flyford
Kington
Abbots Morton
Arrow
Wixford
Exhall
Bredenbury
Bromyard Downs
Knightwick
Lulsley
Broad Green
Broadheath
Dines Green
WORCESTER
Broughton Hackett
Flyford Flavell
Rous Lench
Dunnington
Broom
Bromyard
Broadwas
Leigh
St Johns
Spetchley
Upton Snodsbury
North Piddle
Abberton
Iron Cross
Stanford Bishop
Linley Green
Alfrick
Suckley Hills
Rushwick
Whittington
White Ladies Aston
Church Lench
Salford Priors
Little Cowarne
Munderfield Row
Suckley
Acton Beauchamp
Bransford
Bowling Green
Powick
Norton
Naunton Beauchamp
Bishampton
Munderfield Stocks
Acton Green
Longley Green
Leigh Sinton
Littleworth
Peopleton
Stoulton
Throckmorton
Harvington
Cleeve Prior
Barcliff
Stoke Lacy
Moreton Jeffries
Much Cowarne
Bishop's Frome
Stifford's Bridge
Evesbatch
Storridge
Callow End
Kempsey
Pinvin
Wyre Piddle
Abbot's Salford
North Littleton
Cradley
Ridgeway Cross
Newland
Malvern Link
Madresfield
Kerswell Green
Pirton
Wadborough
Drakes Broughton
Lower Moor
Fladbury
Norton
Middle Littleton
Castle Frome
Fromes Hill
West Malvern
GREAT MALVERN
Clifton
Rhydd
Pershore
Wick
Offenham
South Littleton
Mathon
Guarlford
Severn Stoke
High Green
Croome Court
Besford
Cropthorne
Charlton
Newtown
Stretton Grandison
Wyche
Hanley Swan
Kinnersley
Defford
Birlingham
Little Comberton
EVESHAM
Aldington
Honeybourne
Bretforton
Canon Frome
Bosbury
Colwall Stone
Hanley Castle
Great Comberton
Bricklehampton
Hampton
Badsey
Yarkhill
Ashperton
Coddington
Colwall Green
Malvern Wells
Little Malvern
Earl's Croome
Eckington
Elmley Castle
Netherton
Wickhamford
Munsley
Wellington Heath
MALVERN HILLS
Upton upon Severn
Strensham
Bredon's Norton
Bredon Hill
Kersoe
Hinton on the Green
Willersey
Trumpet
LEDBURY
Welland
Naunton
Ashton under Hill
Sedgeberrow
Childswickham
Aylton
Eastnor
Ripple
Twyning Green
Overbury
Conderton
Aston Somerville
Putley
Little Marcle
Hollybush
Birts Street
Castlemorton
Longdon
Twyning
Bredon
Kemerton
Wormington
Broadway
Woolhope
Rushall
Preston
Sledge Green
Shuthonger
Beckford
Dumbleton
Buckland
Laverton
Stanton
Sollers Hope
Much Marcle
Donnington
Pendock
Bushley
Northway
Great Washbourne
Alderton
Snowshill
Ryton
Redmarley D'Abitot
Eldersfield
Forthampton
TEWKESBURY
Ashchurch
Teddington
Alstone
Toddington
Stanway
Dymock
Walton Cardiff
Fiddington
Oxenton
Dixton
Gretton
Didbrook
Hailes Abbey
Beckbury
Cutsdean
Kempley
Chaceley
Odda's Chapel
Deerhurst
Great
Ford
Hole in the Wall
Poolhill
Staunton
Tirley
Stoke Orchard
Gotherington
Langley Hill
Winchcombe
Farmcote
Brampton Abbotts
Apperley
Bishop's Cleeve
Temple Guiting
Crow Hill
Upton Bishop
Hasfield
Hardwicke
Cleeve Hill
Sudeley Castle
Gorsley
Upleadon
Ashleworth
The Leigh
Coombe Hill
Elmstone Hardwicke
Kineton
Rudhall
ROSS-ON-WYE
Linton
Kilcot
Newent
Tithe Barn
Norton
Swindon
Southam
Long Barrow
Charlton Abbots
Barton
Bromsash
Aston Ingham
Kent's Green
Hartpury
Boddington
Uckington
Prestbury
Guiting Power
Weston under Penyard
Aston Crews
Clifford's Mesne
Highleadon
Sandhurst
Staverton
Gloucester & Cheltenham (Staverton) Airport
Down Hatherley
Golden Valley
CHELTENHAM
Hawling
Coughton
Lea
May Hill
Taynton
Tibberton
Twigworth
Innsworth
Longford
Brockhampton
Sevenhampton
Pontshill
Glasshouse Hill
Maisemore
CHARLTON KINGS
Whittington
Syreford
Long Barrow
Salperton
Kerne Bridge
Hope Mansell
Mitcheldean
Huntley
Bulley
Highnam
Up Hatherley
Dowdeswell
Andoversford
Hazelton
Longhope
Birdwood
Churcham
Churchdown
Badgeworth
Leckhampton
Shipton
Turkdean
Ruardean
Ruardean Woodside
Drybrook
Blaisdon
Oakle Street
Minsterworth
GLOUCESTER
GLEVUM
Barnwood
Hucclecote
Shurdington
Ullenwood
Brierley
Lydbrook
Northwood Green
Hempsted
Matson
Brockworth
Upton St Leonards
Bentham
Coberley
Withington
Compton Abdale
Hampnett
Flaxley
Westbury-on-Severn
Elmore Back
Elmore
Farleys End
Tuffley
Whaddon
Prinknash Park
Great Witcombe
Roman Villa
Birdlip
Norbury
Cowley
Yanworth
Cinderford
Elton
Littledean
Quedgeley
Cranham
Colesbourne
Boxbush
Longney
Hardwicke
Brookthorpe
Brimpsfield
Elkstone
Chedworth
Fossebridge
Newnham
Ruspidge
Rodley
Haresfield
Sheepscombe
Syde
Coln St Dennis
FOREST OF DEAN
Upper Soudley
Arlingham
Upper Framilode
Harescombe
Whiteway
Winstone
Painswick
Coln Rogers
Coalway
Fretherne
Saul
Moreton Valence
Whitminster
The Camp
Miserden
Woodmancote
Rendcomb
Calmsden
Winson
Ablington
Parkend
Awre
Frampton on Severn
Pitchcombe
Duntisbourne Abbots
Duntisbourne Leer
North Cerney
Yorkley
The Noose
Randwick
Whiteshill
Slad
Sudgrove
Whitecroft
Blakeney
Stonehouse
STROUD
Bisley
Edgeworth
Duntisbourne Rouse
Bagendon
Arlington
Bream
New Grounds
Eastington
Eastcombe
Bournes Green
Daglingworth
Barnsley
Purton
Leonard Stanley
King's Stanley
Baunton
Lydney
Sharpness
Halmore
Cambridge
Slimbridge
Frocester
Woodchester
Thrupp
Chalford
Oakridge
Sapperton
Frampton Mansell
Stratton
CIRENCESTER
CORINIVM
Ampney Crucis
Ampney St Mary
Aylburton
Wanswell
Breadstone
Lower Cam
Coaley
Amberley
Hyde
Minchinhampton
Coates
Preston
Ampney St Peter
Alvington
Lydney Sand
Berkeley
Castle
Ham
The Quarry
Hetty Pegler's Tump
Cam
Nympsfield
Box
NAILSWORTH
Cherington
Tarlton
Source of the River Thames
Harnhill
Siddington
Driffield
Uley
Stinchcombe
Newport
Dursley
Horsley
Avening
Rodmarton
Ewen
South Cerney
Down Ampney
Bevington
Kingscote
Culkerton
Kemble
Shorncote
Cerney Wick
Latton
Shepperdine
Hill
Stone
North Nibley
Tetbury Upton
Ashley
Poole Keynes
Somerford Keynes
Oaksey
Ashton Keynes
CRICKLADE
Rockhampton
Tortworth
Wotton-under-Edge
Beverston
Crudwell
Eastcourt
Oldbury-on-Severn
Falfield
Whitfield
TETBURY
Long Newnton
Leigh
Charfield
Doughton
Hankerton
Upper Minety
Purton Stoke
Morton
Milbury Heath
Alderley
Leighterton
Shipton
COTSWOLD HILLS
VALE OF EVESHAM
VALE OF GLOUCESTER
VALE OF BERKELEY
RIVER SEVERN
Gloucester & Sharpness Canal
ROMAN ROAD
ERMIN WAY
FOSS WAY
AKEMAN STREET
RYKNILD STREET
GLOUCESTERSHIRE
M 5
M 50
A 44
A 38
A 40 (T)
A 417
A 419
A 429
A 435
A 46
A 48 (T)
21
33
37

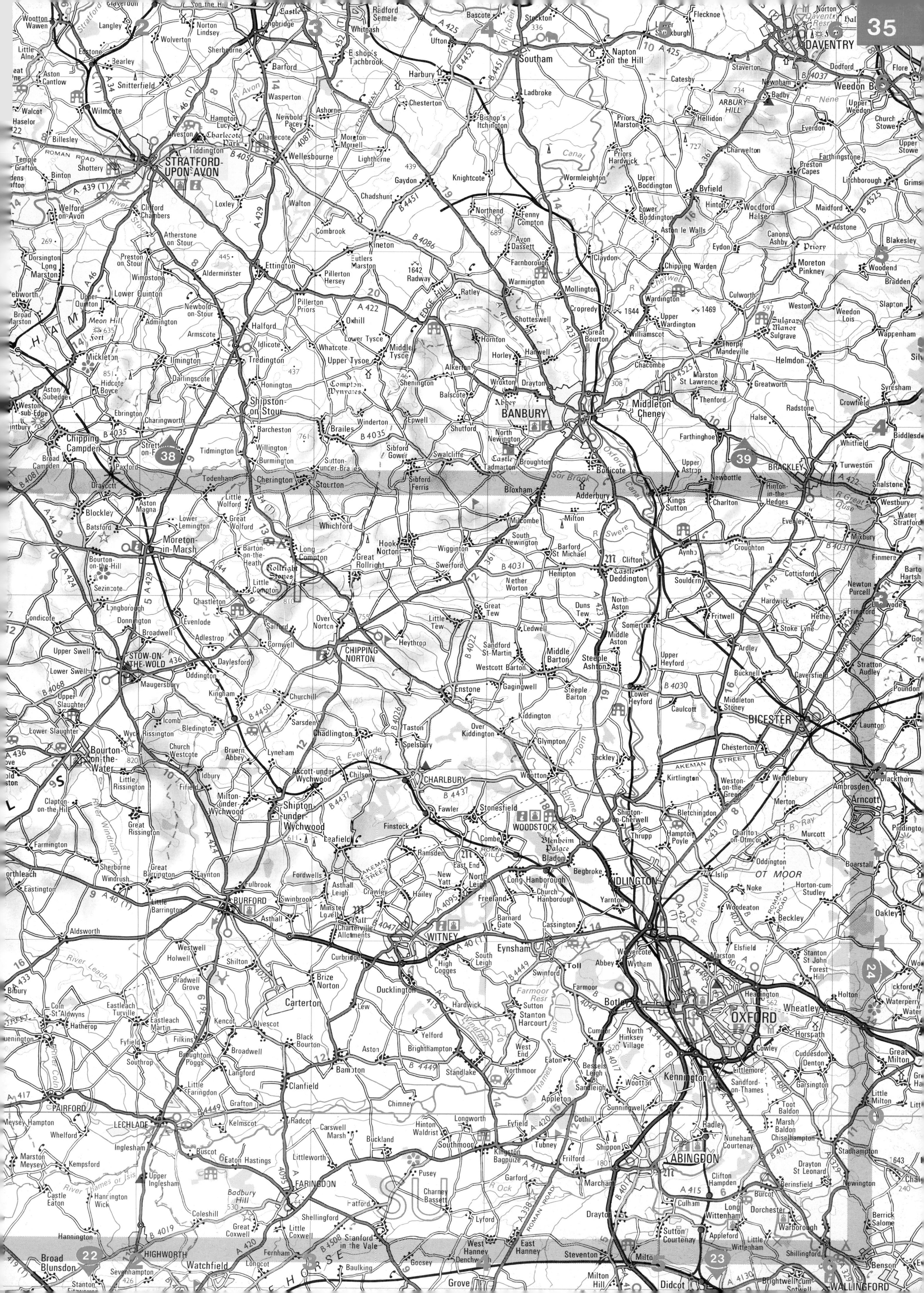

DAVENTRY
Southam
Napton on the Hill
Flecknoe
Radford Semele
Whitnash
Bishop's Tachbrook
Ufton
Harbury
Ladbroke
Staverton
Catesby
Badby
Newnham
Dodford
Weedon Bec
Flore
Barford
Wasperton
Chesterton
Bishop's Itchington
Priors Marston
Hellidon
Everdon
Stratford
Langley
Wolverton
Norton Lindsey
Sherbourne
Longbridge
Claverdon
Wootton Wawen
Little Alne
Edstone
Bearley
Aston Cantlow
Snitterfield
Wilmcote
Walcot
Haselor
Billesley
Hampton Lucy
Charlecote
Charlecote Park
Alveston
Tiddington
Newbold Pacey
Ashorne
Moreton Morrell
Wellesbourne
Lighthorne
STRATFORD-UPON-AVON
Temple Grafton
Binton
Shottery
ROMAN ROAD
Welford-on-Avon
Clifford Chambers
Loxley
Walton
Gaydon
Knightcote
Chadshunt
Priors Hardwick
Wormleighton
Upper Boddington
Lower Boddington
Byfield
Charwelton
Preston Capes
Farthingstone
Upper Stowe
Church Stowe
Litchborough
Woodford Halse
Hinton
Maidford
Adstone
Canons Ashby
Blakesley
Aston le Walls
Eydon
Priory
Moreton Pinkney
Woodend
Bradden
Northend
Fenny Compton
Avon Dassett
Farnborough
Claydon
Chipping Warden
Culworth
Weston
Slapton
Weedon Lois
Wappenham
Sulgrave Manor
Sulgrave
Atherstone on Stour
Preston on Stour
Combrook
Kineton
Dorsington
Long Marston
Wimpstone
Alderminster
Ettington
Eatington
Pillerton Hersey
Pillerton Priors
Butlers Marston
Radway
Ratley
EDGE HILL
Warmington
Mollington
Cropredy
Wardington
Upper Wardington
Williamscot
Shotteswell
Great Bourton
Hanwell
Horley
Hornton
Alkerton
Lower Quinton
Upper Quinton
Newbold-on-Stour
Admington
Armscote
Halford
Idlicote
Tredington
Oxhill
Lower Tysoe
Middle Tysoe
Upper Tysoe
Whatcote
Meon Hill
Mickleton
Ilmington
Darlingscote
Hidcote Boyce
Honington
Compton Wynyates
Shenington
Balscote
Wroxton
Drayton
Abbey
BANBURY
Middleton Cheney
Chacombe
Thorpe Mandeville
Marston St Lawrence
Thenford
Greatworth
Helmdon
Syresham
Crowfield
Radstone
Halse
Farthinghoe
Whitfield
Biddlesden
Aston Subedge
Weston-sub-Edge
Ebrington
Charingworth
Shipston-on-Stour
Barcheston
Brailes
Winderton
Epwell
Shutford
North Newington
Broughton
Castle
Tadmarton
Bodicote
Upper Astrop
Newbottle
BRACKLEY
Turweston
Shalstone
Chipping Campden
Broad Campden
Paxford
Tidmarton
Willington
Burmington
Sutton-under-Brailes
Sibford Gower
Swalcliffe
Sibford Ferris
Todenham
Cherington
Stourton
Bloxham
Adderbury
Sor Brook
Kings Sutton
Charlton
Hinton-in-the-Hedges
Westbury
Water Stratford
Draycott
Blockley
Aston Magna
Little Wolford
Great Wolford
Lower Lemington
Batsford
Moreton-in-Marsh
Whichford
Hook Norton
Milcombe
Milton
South Newington
Barford St Michael
Aynho
Croughton
Evenley
Mixbury
Finmere
Bourton-on-the-Hill
Sezincote
Barton-on-the-Heath
Long Compton
Great Rollright
Rollright Stones
Little Compton
Wigginton
Swerford
Nether Worton
Hempton
Clifton
Castle
Deddington
Souldern
Cottisford
Newton Purcell
Longborough
Donnington
Chastleton
Evenlode
Over Norton
Great Tew
Little Tew
Duns Tew
North Aston
Somerton
Fritwell
Hardwick
Hethe
Fringford
Condicote
Broadwell
Adlestrop
Salford
Cornwell
CHIPPING NORTON
Heythrop
Ledwell
Middle Aston
Ardley
Stoke Lyne
Upper Swell
Lower Swell
STOW-ON-THE-WOLD
Maugersbury
Daylesford
Oddington
Sandford St Martin
Westcott Barton
Middle Barton
Steeple Aston
Upper Heyford
Bucknell
Caversfield
Stratton Audley
Upper Slaughter
Lower Slaughter
Kingham
Churchill
Enstone
Gagingwell
Steeple Barton
Lower Heyford
Caulcott
Middleton Stoney
BICESTER
Launton
Poundon
Wyck Rissington
Icomb
Bledington
Sarsden
Chadlington
Taston
Spelsbury
Over Kiddington
Kiddington
Glympton
Tackley
Chesterton
Bourton-on-the-Water
Church Westcote
Bruern Abbey
Lyneham
Ascott-under-Wychwood
Chilson
CHARLBURY
Wootton
Kirtlington
Weston-on-the-Green
Wendlebury
AKEMAN STREET
Ambrosden
Arncott
Blackthorn
Little Rissington
Idbury
Fifield
Milton-under-Wychwood
Shipton-under-Wychwood
Fawler
Stonesfield
WOODSTOCK
Shipton-on-Cherwell
Bletchingdon
Merton
Clapton-on-the-Hill
Great Rissington
Finstock
Leafield
Ramsden
Combe
Blenheim Palace
Bladon
Thrupp
Hampton Poyle
Charlton on Otmoor
Murcott
Piddington
Farmington
Sherborne
Windrush
Great Barrington
Taynton
Fulbrook
Fordwells
Asthall Leigh
Crawley
New Yatt
North Leigh
Hailey
Long Hanborough
Church Hanborough
Freeland
Begbroke
KIDLINGTON
Yarnton
Islip
Oddington
OT MOOR
Noke
Boarstall
Horton-cum-Studley
Northleach
Eastington
Little Barrington
BURFORD
Swinbrook
Minster Lovell
Hall
Charterville Allotments
Asthall
WITNEY
Barnard Gate
Cassington
Woodeaton
Beckley
Oakley
Aldsworth
Westwell
Holwell
Shilton
Curbridge
High Cogges
South Leigh
Eynsham
Wolvercote
Wytham
Marston
Elsfield
Stanton St John
Forest Hill
Bibury
River Leach
Bradwell Grove
Brize Norton
Carterton
Ducklington
Swinford
Toll
Farmoor
Abbey
Botley
Headington
OXFORD
Wheatley
Holton
Waterperry
Coln St Aldwyns
Hatherop
Eastleach Turville
Eastleach Martin
Kencot
Alvescot
Lew
Hardwick
Farmoor Resr
Sutton
Stanton Harcourt
Cumnor
North Hinksey Village
Horspath
Great Milton
Fyfield
Filkins
Broadwell
Black Bourton
Yelford
Brighthampton
Aston
West End
Southrop
Broughton Poggs
Langford
Bampton
Standlake
Northmoor
Eaton
Bessels Leigh
Wootton
Cowley
Littlemore
Cuddesdon
Denton
Kennington
Sandford-on-Thames
Garsington
Little Faringdon
Clanfield
Chimney
Appleton
Sandleigh
Sunningwell
Toot Baldon
Little Milton
Marsh Baldon
Chiselhampton
PAIRFORD
Meysey Hampton
LECHLADE
Kelmscot
Grafton
Radcot
Carswell Marsh
Buckland
Hinton Waldrist
Longworth
Southmoor
Fyfield
Tubney
Cothill
Shippon
Radley
Nuneham Courtenay
Whelford
Inglesham
Buscot
Eaton Hastings
Littleworth
Kingston Bagpuize
Frilford
ABINGDON
Stadhampton
Marston Meysey
Kempsford
Upper Inglesham
FARINGDON
Pusey
Garford
Marcham
Drayton St Leonard
Castle Eaton
Hannington Wick
Badbury Hill
Charney Bassett
Clifton Hampden
Berinsfield
Newington
Coleshill
Hatford
Lyford
Drayton
Culham
Long Wittenham
Dorchester
Warborough
Berrick Salome
Hannington
Great Coxwell
Little Coxwell
Shellingford
Stanford in the Vale
Sutton Courtenay
Appleford
Little Wittenham
Shillingford
Broad Blunsdon
HIGHWORTH
Sevenhampton
Watchfield
Longcot
Fernham
Baulking
Goosey
West Hanney
Denchworth
East Hanney
Steventon
Milton
Milton Hill
Grove
Didcot
Brightwell-cum-Sotwell
WALLINGFORD
Benson
Stanton
SP
SU

NEWTOWN
BISHOP'S CASTLE
Clun Forest
Stretton
Craven Arms
Clun
KNIGHTON
LUDLOW
Leintwardine
Bringewood
PRESTEIGNE
Radnor Forest
New Radnor
LLANDRINDOD WELLS
KINGTON
LEOMINSTER
Pembridge
Weobley
Eardisley
HAY-ON-WYE
River Wye
HEREFORD
Golden Valley
Talgarth
BLACK MOUNTAINS
Hay Bluff
Llanthony
Priory
Pontrilas
Kentchurch Court
Grosmont
Ross-on-Wye
Llangorse Lake
Crickhowell
Skenfrith
Offa's Dyke
River Teme
R Lugg
River Monnow
SO

Monkhopton
Upton Cressett
Oldbury
BRIDGNORTH
Quatford
Eardington
Chetton
Middleton Priors
Ditton Priors
Neenton
Cleobury North
Brown Clee Hill
Burwarton
Aston Botterell
Loughton
Wheathill
Farlow
Oreton
Cleeton St Mary
Catherton
Neen Savage
Hopton Wafers
Doddington
Hints
Knowle
Coreley
Cleobury Mortimer
Milson
Neen Sollars
Nash
Boraston
Newnham
Rochford
Callows Grave
Hanley Child
Hanley William
Kyre Park
Stoke Bliss
Garmsley Camp
Bank Street
Wolferlow
Wall Hills
Thornbury
Edvin Loach
Edwyn Ralph
Bredenbury
Bromyard
Bromyard Downs
Little Cowarne
Munderfield Stocks
Stoke Lacy
Much Cowarne
Stretton Grandison
Yarkhill
Tarrington
Canon Frome
Castle Frome
Bishop's Frome
Evesbatch
Acton Beauchamp
Munderfield Row
Stanford Bishop
Suckley
Alfrick
Leigh
Bransford
Knightwick
Lulsley
Broadwas
Martley
Tedstone Wafre
Tedstone Delamere
Whitbourne
Horsham
Collington
Harpley
High Lane
Upper Sapey
Sapey Common
Shelsley Walsh
Shelsley Beauchamp
Clifton upon Teme
Woodbury Hill
Stanford Bridge
Stanford on Teme
Orleton
Eardiston
Stockton on Teme
Pensax
Lindridge
Frith Common
Mamble
Rock
Clows Top
Bayton
Pound Bank
Far Forest
Callow Hill
Bliss Gate
BEWDLEY
Wyre Forest
Buttonoak
Kinlet
Stottesdon
Chorley
Highley
Woodhill
Billingsley
Sidbury
Middleton Scriven
Glazeley
Chelmarsh
Sutton
Chelmarsh Resr
Hampton
Alveley
Quatt
Tuckhill
Six Ashes
Birdsgreen
Romsley
Kingsford
Shatterford
Upper Arley
Trimpley Resr
Trimpley
Habberley
Blakebrook
Wribbenhall
Ribbesford
STOURPORT-ON-SEVERN
Areley Kings
Dunley
The Village Abberley
Abberley Hill
Great Witley
Little Witley
Shrawley
Holt Heath
Holt
Wichenford
Sinton Green
Grimley
Moseley
Shoulton
Hallow
Claines
Berrow Green
Broad Green
Broadheath
Dines Green
WORCESTER
St Johns
Rushwick
Bowling Green
Powick
Leigh Sinton
Longley Green
Storridge
Acton Green
Stifford's Bridge
Cradley
Ridgeway Cross
Mathon
West Malvern
GREAT MALVERN
Malvern Link
Newland
Madresfield
Callow End
Guarlford
Wyche
Colwall Stone
Colwall Green
Coddington
Bosbury
Ashperton
Munsley
Trumpet
Aylton
Putley
Woolhope
LEDBURY
Little Marcle
Eastnor
Wellington Heath
Malvern Wells
Little Malvern
Welland
Hollybush
Birts Street
Castlemorton
Longdon
Preston
Rushall
Sollers Hope
Much Marcle
Donnington
Dymock
Kempley
Ryton
Redmarley D'Abitot
Eldersfield
Pendock
Poolhill
Staunton
How Caple
Hole in the Wall
Foy
Brampton Abbotts
Crow Hill
Upton Bishop
Gorsley
Linton
Rudhall
ROSS-ON-WYE
Bromsash
Kilcot
Newent
Upleadon
Aston Ingham
Aston Crews
Weston under Penyard
Clifford's Mesne
Kent's Green
Highleadon
Hartpury
Tibberton
Taynton
Lea
Coughton
Pontshill
Hope
Mitcheldean
Glasshouse Hill
Huntley
Bulley
Highnam
Maisemore
Sandhurst
Norton
Tithe Barn
Ashleworth
Hasfield
Tirley
Forthampton
Chaceley
Odda's Chapel
Deerhurst
Apperley
The Leigh
Coombe Hill
Boddington
Staverton
Down Hatherley
Twigworth
Innsworth
Longford
Gloucester-Cheltenham (Staverton) Airport
Up Hatherley
Golden Valley
Uckington
Swindon
Elmstone Hardwicke
Hardwicke
Stoke Orchard
Bishop's Cleeve
CHELTENHAM
CHARLTON KINGS
Prestbury
Southam
Cleeve Hill
Long Barrow
Charlton Abbots
Sudeley Castle
Winchcombe
Gotherington
Langley Hill
Fort
Guiting Power
Hawling
Brockhampton
Sevenhampton
Whittington
Syreford
Salperton
Naunton
Barton
Kineton
Temple Guiting
Farmcote
Cutsdean
Didbrook
Hailes Abbey
Beckbury
Stanway
Toddington
Dixton
Gretton
Alstone
Oxenton
Teddington
Alderton
Great Washbourne
Dumbleton
Wormington
Buckland
Laverton
Stanton
Snowshill
Broadway
Childswickham
Aston Somerville
Sedgeberrow
Hinton on the Green
Wickhamford
Badsey
Bretforton
Aldington
Honeybourne
EVESHAM
Hampton
South Littleton
Middle Littleton
North Littleton
Offenham
Harvington
Norton
Abbot's Salford
Cleeve Prior
Marlcliff
Bidford-on-Avon
Salford Priors
Iron Cross
Church Lench
Rous Lench
Dunnington
Broom
Wixford
Exhall
Arrow
Abbots Morton
Inkberrow
Kington
Alcester
Cookhill
Stock Wood
Holberrow Green
King's Coughton
Coughton
New End
Sambourne
Astwood Bank
Studley
Crabbs Cross
Headless Cross
Hunt End
Mappleborough Green
Winyates
REDDITCH
Holt End
Beoley
Alvechurch
Rowney Green
Portway
Wythall
Hopwood
Hollywood
Cofton Hackett
Barnt Green
Lickey
Lickey End
Catshill
Blackwell
BROMSGROVE
Tutnall
Aston Fields
Stoke Prior
Webheath
Woodgate
Bentley
Hanbury
Ham Green
Feckenham
Bradley Green
Stock Green
Himbleton
Huddington
Grafton Flyford
Flyford Flavell
North Piddle
Abberton
Bishampton
Throckmorton
Naunton Beauchamp
Peopleton
Pinvin
Wyre Piddle
Lower Moor
Fladbury
Cropthorne
Charlton
Little Comberton
Great Comberton
Elmley Castle
Netherton
Bricklehampton
Kersoe
Ashton under Hill
Conderton
Overbury
Kemerton
Beckford
Bredon's Norton
Bredon
Eckington
Strensham
Birlingham
Defford
Pershore
Besford
Drakes Broughton
Wadborough
Pirton
Stoulton
Littleworth
Norton
Whittington
Kempsey
Kerswell Green
Clifton
Rhydd
Severn Stoke
Hanley Swan
Hanley Castle
Kinnersley
Earl's Croome
Croome Court
High Green
Upton upon Severn
Naunton
Ripple
Twyning Green
Twyning
Shuthonger
Bushley
TEWKESBURY
Walton Cardiff
Ashchurch
Northway
Fiddington
Spetchley
Upton Snodsbury
White Ladies Aston
Broughton Hackett
Crowle
Tibberton
Warndon
Hindlip
Oddingley
Sale Green
Fernhill Heath
Hawford
Martin Hussingtree
Hadzor
Salwarpe
Ombersley
DROITWICH
Oldfield
Doverdale
Sytchampton
Dunhampton
Noutard's Green
Lincomb
Astley
Astley Cross
Crossway Green
Hartlebury
Elmley Lovett
Cutnall Green
Elmbridge
Upton Warren
Wychbold
Hampton Lovett
Rushock
Shenstone
Chaddesley Corbett
Dodford
Bournheath
Fairfield
Belbroughton
Drayton
Broome
Blakedown
Mustow Green
Stone
KIDDERMINSTER
Wilden
Franche
Wolverley
Cookley
Churchill
Caunsall
Blakeshall
Kinver
Whittington
STOURBRIDGE
Potter's Cross
Stourton
Amblecote
Wordsley
Enville
Kingswinford
Swindon
Bobbington
Halfpenny
Halfpenny Green
Heathton
Claverley
Roughton
Wombourne
Himley
The Village
TIPTON
DUDLEY
OLDBURY
WEST BROMWICH
SMETHWICK
BRIERLEY HILL
Quarry Bank
Rowley Regis
BLACKHEATH
Lye
HALESOWEN
Pedmore
Hagley
Clent
Clent Hills
Holy Cross
Romsley
Frankley
Illey
Woodgate
Harborne
Chad Valley
Selly Oak
Edgbaston
Moseley
Springfield
Bournville
King's Heath
King's Norton
Northfield
Longbridge
Rubery
Handsworth
Aston
Perry Barr
Hamstead
Great Barr
Beoley
Tanworth-in-Arden
Due to open Late 1986

Hamstead
Short Heath
Walmley
Lea Marston
Nether Whitacre
Church End
Galley Common
Hartshill
Weddington
NUNEATON
Attleborough
WEST BROMWICH
Erdington
Minworth
Over Whitacre
Ansley
Stockingford
Gravelly Hill
Tyburn
Water Orton
Shustoke
Arley
Burton Hastings
DUDLEY
OLDBURY
Handsworth
Aston
Castle Bromwich
Astley
Bramcote
Wolvey
SMETHWICK
Coleshill
BEDWORTH
BRIERLEY HILL
Rowley Regis
Quarry Bank
Tile Cross
Maxstoke
Fillongley
BIRMINGHAM
Corley Ash
Goodyers End
Bulkington
BLACKHEATH
Chad Valley
Yardley
Marston Green
Barnacle
Withybrook
Shilton
Lye
Sheldon
Corley
Neal's Green
Longford
HALESOWEN
Harborne
Edgbaston
Acock's Green
Birmingham Airport
National Exhibition Centre
Corley Moor
Keresley
Pedmore
Selly Oak
Moseley
Hawkes End
Foleshill
Ansty
Woodgate
Springfield
Olton
Elmdon
Bickenhill
Meriden
Allesley
Walsgrave on Sowe
Illey
Bournville
King's Heath
Hall Green
Four Oaks
Eastern Green
Hagley
Romsley
Frankley
Elmdon Heath
Hampton in Arden
Coombe Abbey
Clent
King's Norton
COVENTRY
Brinklow
Northfield
Eastcote
Berkswell
Binley
Binley Woods
Longbridge
Shirley
SOLIHULL
Barston
Copt Heath
Tile Hill
Rubery
Hollywood
Whitlock's End
Knowle
Balsall Common
Earlsdon
Brandon
Belbroughton
Lickey
Cofton Hackett
Hopwood
Bentley Heath
Stivichall
Willenhall
Ryton-on-Dunsmore
Wolston
Fairfield
Wythall
Cheswick Green
Dorridge
Fen End
Burton Green
Barnt Green
Earlswood
Baginton
Coventry Airport
Bournheath
Catshill
Lickey End
Portway
Hockley Heath
Chadwick End
Meer End
Stoneleigh
Stretton-on-Dunsmore
Dodford
Alvechurch
Due to open Late 1986
Honiley
KENILWORTH
Bubbenhall
Blackwell
Wood End
Kingswood
Wroxall
Beausale
Princethorpe
Bourton on Dunsmore
BROMSGROVE
Tutnall
Lapworth
Ashow
Weston under Wetherley
Wappenbury
Frankton
Beoley
Tanworth-in-Arden
Rowington
Cubbington
Marton
Aston Fields
REDDITCH
Holt End
Leek Wootton
Eathorpe
Birdingbury
Lowsonford
Haseley
Stoke Prior
Winyates
Ullenhall
Shrewley
Hatton
Upton Warren
Webheath
Mappleborough Green
Henley-in-Arden
Preston Bagot
Old Milverton
ROYAL LEAMINGTON SPA
Hunningham
Woodgate
Bentley
Headless Cross
Oldberrow
WARWICK
Union Canal
Offchurch
Long Itchington
Hunt End
Crabbs Cross
Budbrooke
Hanbury
Studley
Morton Bagot
Claverdon
Hampton on the Hill
Radford Semele
Bascote
Stockton
Ham Green
Wootton Wawen
Langley
Norton Lindsey
Longbridge
Whitnash
Ufton
Hadzor
Bradley Green
Feckenham
Astwood Bank
Sambourne
Little Alne
Wolverton
Sherbourne
Bishop's Tachbrook
Southam
Great Alne
Edstone
Bearley
Barford
Coughton
Aston Cantlow
Snitterfield
Harbury
Ladbroke
Oddingley
Holberrow Green
New End
King's Coughton
Wasperton
Sale Green
Himbleton
Stock Green
Stock Wood
Cookhill
Wilmcote
Chesterton
Huddington
Inkberrow
Alcester
Walcot
Haselor
Newbold Pacey
Ashorne
Bishop's Itchington
Grafton Flyford
Abbots Morton
Arrow
Billesley
Hampton Lucy
Alveston
Charlecote Park
Charlecote
Moreton Morrell
Kington
Exhall
Tiddington
Wellesbourne
Lighthorne
Broughton Hackett
Flyford Flavell
Wixford
Temple Grafton
Roman Road
Shottery
STRATFORD-UPON-AVON
Knightcote
Upton Snodsbury
North Piddle
Rous Lench
Dunnington
Ardens Grafton
Binton
Gaydon
White Ladies Aston
Abberton
Iron Cross
Broom
Welford-on-Avon
Clifford Chambers
Loxley
Walton
Chadshunt
Northend
Fenny Compton
Naunton Beauchamp
Church Lench
Salford Priors
Bidford-on-Avon
Atherstone on Stour
Combrook
Kineton
Avon Dassett
Peopleton
Bishampton
Abbot's Salford
Barton
Marlcliff
Cleeve Prior
Dorsington
Preston on Stour
Alderminster
Ettington
Butlers Marston
Farnborough
Pinvin
Throckmorton
Harvington
Long Marston
Wimpstone
Pillerton Hersey
Radway
Wyre Piddle
Norton
North Littleton
Pebworth
Lower Quinton
Upper Quinton
Newbold on Stour
Ratley
Warmington
Drakes Broughton
Lower Moor
Middle Littleton
Pillerton Priors
Pershore
Fladbury
Offenham
South Littleton
Broad Marston
Meon Hill
Admington
Halford
Oxhill
Shotteswell
Wick
Charlton
Aldington
Honeybourne
Armscote
Lower Tysoe
Besford
Cropthorne
EVESHAM
Mickleton
Ilmington
Idlicote
Whatcote
Middle Tysoe
Hornton
Hanwell
Birlingham
Little Comberton
Bretforton
Hidcote Boyce
Tredington
Upper Tysoe
Horley
Great Comberton
Bricklehampton
Hampton
Badsey
Darlingscote
Honington
Compton Wynyates
Shenington
Alkerton
Wroxton
Drayton
Elmley Castle
Netherton
Wickhamford
Aston Subedge
Shipston-on-Stour
Balscote
Eckington
Vale of Evesham
Weston sub-Edge
Ebrington
Epwell
BANBURY
Bredon's Hill
Bredon's Norton
Kersoe
Hinton on the Green
Willersey
Saintbury
Charingworth
Barcheston
Winderton
Brailes
Shutford
North Newington
Ashton under Hill
Sedgeberrow
Childswickham
Chipping Campden
Stretton-on-Fosse
Tidmington
Willington
Sibford Gower
Swalcliffe
Overbury
Broad Campden
Burmington
Sutton-under-Brailes
Castle Tadmarton
Broughton
Conderton
Aston Somerville
Broadway
Paxford
Todenham
Cherington
Stourton
Sibford Ferris
Bredon
Kemerton
Buckland
Draycott
Bloxham
Beckford
Wormington
Dumbleton
Laverton
Blockley
Stow Magna
Little Wolford
Great Washbourne
Stanton
Batsford
Lower Lemington
Great Wolford
Whichford
Milcombe
Northway
Teddington
Alderton
Snowshill
Moreton-in-Marsh
Long Compton
Hook Norton
Wiggington
South Newington
Ashchurch
Alstone
Toddington
Stanway
Bourton-on-the-Hill
Barton-on-the-Heath
Great Rollright
Swerford
Fiddington
Oxenton
Dixton
Gretton
Didbrook
Cutsdean
Sezincote
Little Compton
Nether Worton
Langley Hill
Greet
Hailes Abbey
Beckbury
Ford
Longborough
Chastleton
Great Tew
Stoke Orchard
Gotherington
Farmcote
Condicote
Donnington
Evenlode
Over Norton
Little Tew
Ledwell
Bishop's Cleeve
Winchcombe
Temple Guiting
Broadwell
Adlestrop
Salford
Heythrop
Hardwicke
Cleeve Hill
Sudeley Castle
Kineton
Upper Swell
STOW-ON-THE-WOLD
Cornwell
CHIPPING NORTON
Sandford St Martin
Elmstone Hardwicke
Swindon
Southam
Long Barrow
Barton
Lower Swell
Daylesford
Westcott Barton
Charlton Abbots
Guiting Power
Maugersbury
Oddington
Enstone
Gagingwell
Prestbury
Naunton
Upper Slaughter
Kingham
Churchill
Kiddington
CHELTENHAM
Brockhampton
Hawling
Lower Slaughter
Icomb
Bledington
Sarsden
Chadlington
Taston
Over Kiddington
Sevenhampton
Wyck Rissington
Spelsbury
CHARLTON KINGS
Whittington
Syreford
Long Barrow
Salperton
Notgrove
Bourton-on-the-Water
Church Westcote
Bruern Abbey
Lyneham
Ascott-under-
Glympton

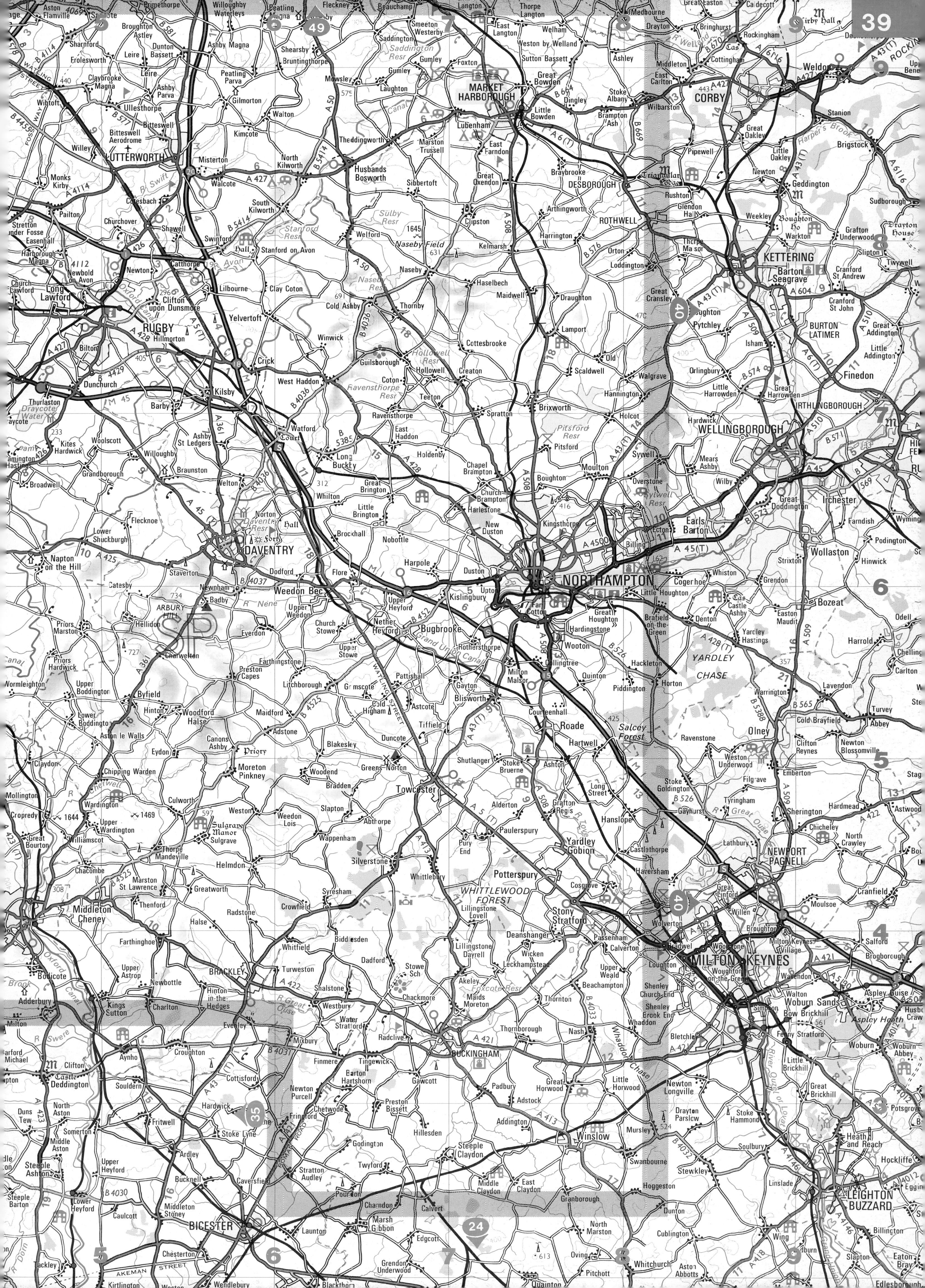

Aston Flamville
Primethorpe
Willoughby Waterleys
Peatling Magna
Fleckney
Beauchamp
Langton
Thorpe Langton
Medbourne
Great Easton
Caldecott
Kirby Hall
Broughton Astley
Smeeton Westerby
East Langton
Drayton
Bringhurst
Rockingham
Sharnford
Dunton Bassett
Ashby Magna
Shearsby
Saddington
Welham
Leire
Bruntingthorpe
Saddington Resr
Weston by Welland
Ashley
Middleton
Cottingham
Weldon
Frolesworth
Gumley
Foxton
Sutton Bassett
East Carlton
Claybrooke Magna
Peatling Parva
Ashby Parva
Mowsley
Laughton
MARKET HARBOROUGH
Great Bowden
Stoke Albany
Wilbarston
CORBY
Ullesthorpe
Gilmorton
Little Bowden
Dingley
Withcote
Walton
Brampton Ash
Stanion
Bitteswell
Bitteswell Aerodrome
Kimcote
Theddingworth
Lubenham
Marston Trussell
East Farndon
Great Oakley
Brigstock
Willey
LUTTERWORTH
Misterton
North Kilworth
Husbands Bosworth
Pipewell
Little Oakley
Monks Kirby
Walcote
Sibbertoft
Great Oxendon
Braybrooke
DESBOROUGH
Triangular Lodge
Newton
Geddington
Cotesbach
South Kilworth
Rushton
Sudborough
Pailton
Churchover
Shawell
Swinford
Stanford Resr
Sulby Resr
Clipston
Arthingworth
Glendon Hall
Weekley
Boughton Ho
Warkton
Grafton Underwood
Drayton House
Stretton under Fosse
Easenhall
Stanford on Avon
Welford
Naseby Field
Harrington
ROTHWELL
Thorpe Malsor
KETTERING
Slipton
Harborough Magna
Newbold on Avon
Newton
Catthorpe
Kelmarsh
Orton
Twywell
Church Lawford
Long Lawford
Clifton upon Dunsmore
Lilbourne
Clay Coton
Naseby
Haselbech
Maidwell
Loddington
Barton Seagrave
Cranford St Andrew
Naseby Resr
Cold Ashby
Thornby
Draughton
Great Cransley
Broughton
Cranford St John
RUGBY
Hillmorton
Yelvertoft
Lamport
Pytchley
Isham
BURTON LATIMER
Great Addington
Bilton
Winwick
Cottesbrooke
Little Addington
Crick
Guilsborough
Hollowell Resr
Hollowell
Old
Scaldwell
Walgrave
Orlingbury
Finedon
Dunchurch
West Haddon
Coton
Creaton
Hannington
Little Harrowden
Great Harrowden
Thurlaston
Draycote Water
Kilsby
Barby
Ravensthorpe Resr
Teeton
Brixworth
IRTHLINGBOROUGH
Ravensthorpe
Spratton
Holcot
Pitsford Resr
Hardwick
WELLINGBOROUGH
Kites Hardwick
Woolscott
Ashby St Ledgers
Watford
Watford Court
East Haddon
Pitsford
Sywell
Mears Ashby
Willoughby
Braunston
Long Buckby
Holdenby
Chapel Brampton
Moulton
Grandborough
Welton
Whilton
Great Brington
Boughton
Overstone
Sywell Resr
Wilby
Great Doddington
Irchester
Broadwell
Little Brington
Church Brampton
Harlestone
Norton
Daventry Resr
Hall
Fort
Flecknoe
Lower Shuckburgh
Brockhall
Nobottle
New Duston
Kingsthorpe
Earls Barton
Farndish
Wymington
Ecton
Billing
Wollaston
Podington
DAVENTRY
Napton on the Hill
Staverton
Dodford
Harpole
Duston
NORTHAMPTON
Whiston
Strixton
Hinwick
Catesby
Newnham
Weedon Bec
Flore
Upper Heyford
Kislingbury
Cogenhoe
Grendon
Badby
Arbury Hill
Upper Weedon
Nether Heyford
Bugbrooke
Far Cotton
Great Houghton
Little Houghton
Castle Ashby
Bozeat
Hellidon
Priors Marston
Everdon
Church Stowe
Hardingstone
Brafield on-the-Green
Denton
Easton Maudit
Odell
Charwelton
Upper Stowe
Rothersthorpe
Wootton
Yardley Hastings
Harrold
Priors Hardwick
Preston Capes
Farthingstone
Collingtree
Hackleton
YARDLEY CHASE
Chellington
Carlton
Wormleighton
Upper Boddington
Byfield
Litchborough
Pattishall
Gayton
Milton Malsor
Quinton
Piddington
Horton
Warrington
Lavendon
Lower Boddington
Hinton
Woodford Halse
Maidford
Grimscote
Cold Higham
Astcote
Blisworth
Courteenhall
Salcey Forest
Cold Brayfield
Turvey
Aston le Walls
Adstone
Tiffield
Roade
Olney
Abbey
Canons Ashby
Eydon
Priory
Blakesley
Duncote
Hartwell
Ravenstone
Clifton Reynes
Newton Blossomville
Claydon
Chipping Warden
Moreton Pinkney
Woodend
Greens Norton
Shutlanger
Stoke Bruerne
Ashton
Weston Underwood
Emberton
Mollington
Bradden
Towcester
Long Street
Stoke Goldington
Filgrave
Wardington
Culworth
Weston
Slapton
Alderton
Grafton Regis
Tyringham
Hardmead
Astwood
Cropredy
Upper Wardington
Sulgrave Manor
Sulgrave
Weedon Lois
Abthorpe
Paulerspury
Hanslope
Gayhurst
Sherington
Chicheley
Great Bourton
Williamscot
Thorpe Mandeville
Wappenham
Pury End
Yardley Gobion
Castlethorpe
Lathbury
North Crawley
NEWPORT PAGNELL
Chacombe
Helmdon
Silverstone
Potterspury
Haversham
Marston St Lawrence
Greatworth
Syresham
Whittlebury
WHITTLEWOOD FOREST
Cosgrove
Great Linford
Cranfield
Middleton Cheney
Thenford
Crowfield
Lillingstone Lovell
Stony Stratford
Wolverton
Willen
Moulsoe
Halse
Radstone
Deanshanger
Passenham
Broughton
Salford
Farthinghoe
Whitfield
Biddlesden
Wicken
Calverton
Bradwell
Woolstone
Milton Keynes Village
Lillingstone Dayrell
Leckhampstead
MILTON KEYNES
Brogborough
Bodicote
Upper Astrop
Newbottle
BRACKLEY
Turweston
Dadford
Stowe Sch
Akeley
Upper Weald
Loughton
Woughton on the Green
Wavendon
Adderbury
Kings Sutton
Charlton
Hinton-in-the-Hedges
Shalstone
Chackmore
Foxcote Resr
Maids Moreton
Beachampton
Thornton
Shenley Church End
Walton
Woburn Sands
Aspley Guise
Milton
Evenley
Westbury
Water Stratford
Shenley Brook End
Simpson
Bow Brickhill
Aspley Heath
Mixbury
Radclive
Thornborough
Nash
Whaddon
Bletchley
Fenny Stratford
Woburn
Barford St Michael
Clifton
Aynho
Croughton
Finmere
Tingewick
BUCKINGHAM
Whaddon Chase
Woburn Abbey
Castle
Deddington
Souldern
Cottisford
Barton Hartshorn
Gawcott
Padbury
Great Horwood
Little Horwood
Little Brickhill
Newton Purcell
Adstock
Newton Longville
Great Brickhill
Duns Tew
North Aston
Hardwick
Fritwell
Chetwode
Preston Bissett
Drayton Parslow
Stoke Hammond
Potsgrove
Somerton
Stoke Lyne
Fringford
Godington
Hillesden
Addington
Winslow
Mursley
Soulbury
Heath and Reach
Middle Aston
Steeple Claydon
Swanbourne
Hockliffe
Steeple Aston
Upper Heyford
Ardley
Twyford
Stewkley
Linslade
Stratton Audley
Middle Claydon
East Claydon
LEIGHTON BUZZARD
Bucknell
Caversfield
Hoggeston
Steeple Barton
Lower Heyford
Poundon
Granborough
Eggington
Caulcott
Middleton Stoney
Charndon
Calvert
Dunton
BICESTER
Marsh Gibbon
North Marston
Launton
Edgcott
Cublington
Wing
Billington
Chesterton
Grendon Underwood
Oving
Slapton
Eaton Bray
Tackley
Akeman Street
Pitchott
Whitchurch
Aston Abbotts
Kirtlington
Wendlebury
Blackthorn
Quainton
Edlesborough
Watling Street
Grand Union Canal
Oxford Canal
R Nene
R Avon
R Swift
R Great Ouse
R Welland
R Cherwell
R Swere
River Ouzel or Lovat
Harper's Brook
Rockingham
SP

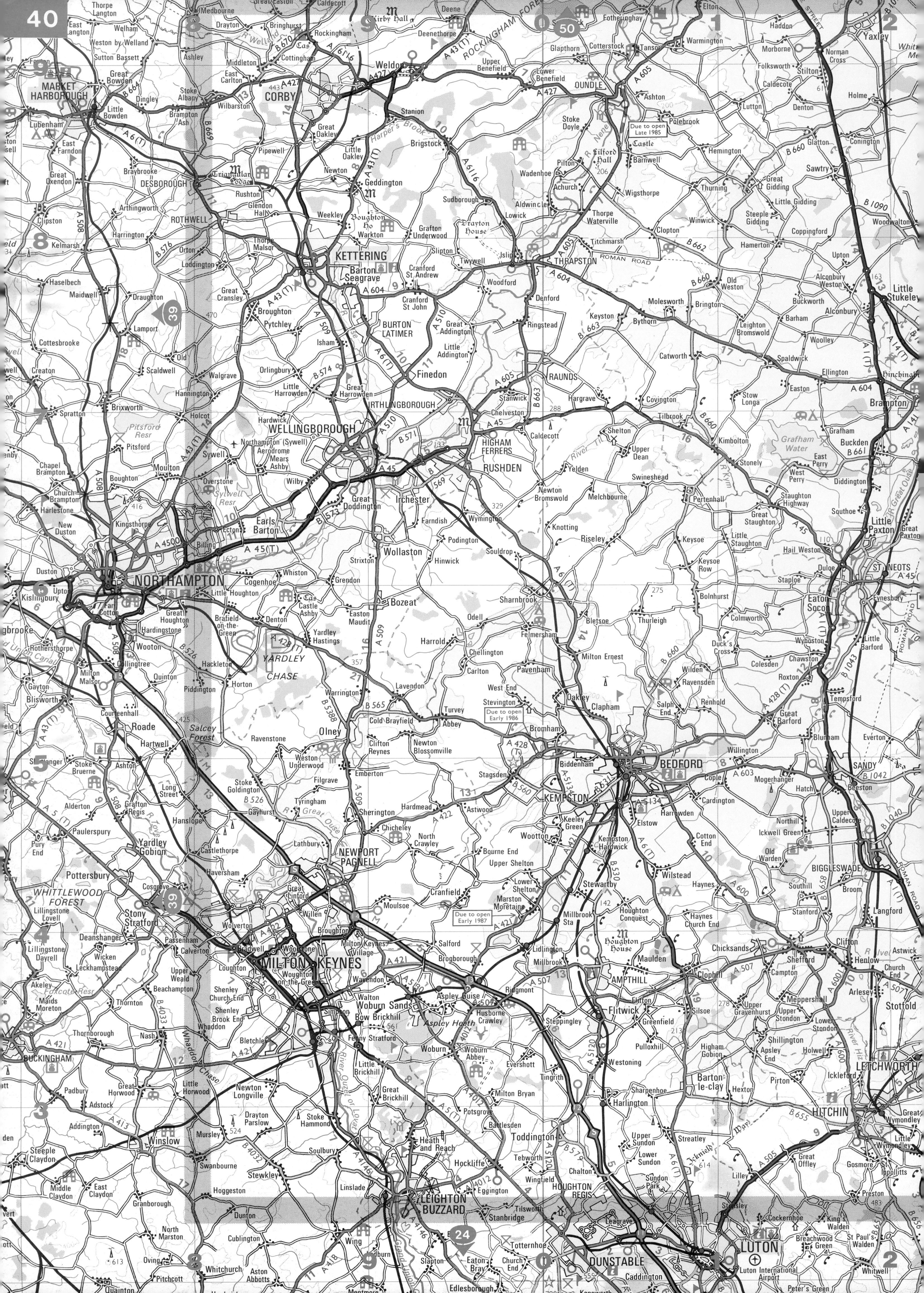

Ranson Moor
MIDDLE LEVEL
White Fen
Pondersbridge
Wimblington
B 1093
Benwick
Doddington
Ramsey Mereside
Manea
Apes Hall
Methwold Fens
Queen's Ground
Brandon Creek
Feltwell
Southery Fens
The Herne
Middle Moor
Wimblington Fen
Mare Fen
Brandon Bank
Feltwell Anchor
Ramsey St Mary's
Ramsey Forty Foot
Ramsey Hollow
RAMSEY
Forty Foot or Vermuden's Drain
Sixteen Foot Drain
Horseway
Purls Bridge
Welches Dam
CHATTERIS
Langwood Fen
New Bedford River or Hundred Foot Drain
Hundred Foot Washes
Fodder Fen
Littleport
Pymore
Burnt Fen
Hockwold Fens
Little Ouse River
Lakenheath Sta
BEDFORD LEVEL
SOUTH LEVEL
Shippea Hill Sta
Wangford Fen
Tick Fen
Bury
Upwood
Great Raveley
Somersham High North Fen
Horseley Fen
Little Downham
Chettisham
Prickwillow
Lakenheath
Warboys
Pidley Fen
Wardy Hill
Coveney
West Fen
Due to open Early 1986
Queen Adelaide
Mepal
Witcham
Little Raveley
Wistow
Fenton
Chatteris Fen
Sutton
A 142 Witchford
ELY
Middle Fen
Great Fen
Kenny Hill
The Delph
Mildenhall Fen
Wennington
Abbots Ripton
Broughton
Pidley
Somersham
Wentworth
Stuntney
Eriswell
Holywell Row
Beck Row
Kings Ripton
Oldhurst
Woodhurst
Colne
Earith
Hill Row Doles
Haddenham
Little Thetford
Broad Hill
Isleham Fen
Thistley Green
West Row
Mildenhall
Great Stukeley
HUNTINGDON
Hartford
Bluntisham
North Hill
Aldreth
Wilburton
Stretham
Barway
Soham
Isleham
Worlington
Priory
Barton Mills
Houghton
Hemingford Abbots
Needingworth
ST IVES
Holywell
Hemingford Grey
GODMANCHESTER
Over
Willingham
Smithey Fen
Chittering
North Fen
Soham Mere
Wicken
Fordham
Freckenham
Due to open Early 1987
Tuddenham
Upware
New River
Fordham Abbey
Chippenham
Herringswell
Fenstanton
Fen Drayton
Swavesey
Rampton
Abbey
Adventurers Fen
Little Fen
River Bank
Landwade
Kennett
Offord Cluny
Offord D'Arcy
Hilton
Conington
Longstanton
Cottenham
Burwell
Snailwell
Icknield Way
Kentford
Papworth St Agnes
Boxworth
Lolworth
Oakington
Westwick
Landbeach
Waterbeach
Reach
Exning
Moulton
Graveley
Elsworth
Bar Hill
Knapwell
Histon
Impington
Swaffham Prior
Newmarket Heath
NEWMARKET
Gazeley
Toseland
Yelling
Papworth Everard
Dry Drayton
Girton
Milton
Horningsea
Lode
Swaffham Bulbeck
Devil's Ditch
Ashley
Denham Castle
Dalham
Croxton
Eltisley
Madingley
Chesterton
Fen Ditton
Stow cum Quy
Bottisham
Cheveley
Highfields
Caxton
Hardwick
Coton
Little Wilbraham
Teversham
Stetchworth
Saxton Street
Ousden
Abbotsley
Cambridge Airport
Church End
Great Wilbraham
Dullingham
Woodditton
Ditton Green
Upend
Lidgate
Kirtling
Great Gransden
Little Gransden
Bourn
Caldecote
Comberton
Grantchester
Cherry Hinton
Fulbourn
Six Mile Bottom
Westley Waterless
Burrough Green
Kirtling Green
Waresley
Longstowe
Toft
Kingston
Barton
CAMBRIDGE
Trumpington
Brinkley
Cowlinge
Gog Magog Hills
Wandlebury
Great Eversden
Little Eversden
Hastingfield
Great Shelford
Weston Colville
Carlton
Great Bradley
Gamlingay
Hatley St George
Harlton
Hauxton
Stapleford
Steam Dyke
West Wratting
Weston Green
Little Bradley
Wimpole Hall
Arrington
Harston
Little Shelford
Babraham
ROMAN ROAD
Balsham
Little Thurlow
Potton
East Hatley
Croydon
New Wimpole
Orwell
Barrington
Newton
Sawston
Little Abington
Great Thurlow
Barnardiston
Cockayne Hatley
Shepreth
Foxton
Hildersham
Great Abington
West Wickham
Great Wratting
Tadlow
Wendy
Thriplow
Whittlesford
Pampisford
Horseheath
Withersfield
Wrestlingworth
Whaddon
Meldreth
Duxford
Linton
Kedington
Eyeworth
Fowlmere
Hinxton
Bartlow
HAVERHILL
Guilden Morden
Kneesworth
Melbourn
Hadstock
Shudy Camps
Castle Camps
Sturmer
Wixoe
Abington Pigotts
Bassingbourn
Ickleton
Stump Cross
Great Chesterford
Little Chesterford
Steeple Morden
Litlington
Edworth
Hinxworth
ROYSTON
Ashdon
Church End
Helions Bumpstead
Birdbrook
Little Walden
Steeple Bumpstead
Heydon
Ashwell
Great Chishill
Elmdon
Strethall
Littlebury
Caldecote
Barley
Chrishall
Sewards End
Stambourne Green
Stambourne
Therfield
Little Chishill
Littlebury Green
Audley End
SAFFRON WALDEN
Radwinter
Hempstead
Newnham
Bygrave
Kelshall
Reed
Dudenhoe End
Bridge Green
Wendens Ambo
Wimbish
Toppesfield
Barkway
Great Sampford
Cornish Hall End
Sandon
Langley
Arkesden
Newport
Wimbish Green
Gainsford End
BALDOCK
Wallington
Buckland
Nuthampstead
Wicken Bonhunt
Howlett End
Debden
Howe Street
Little Sampford
Mill End
Chipping
Anstey
Clavering
Rickling
Widdington
Debden Green
Finchingfield
Clothall
Meesden
Wyddial
Brent Pelham
Rushden
Weston
Thaxted
Little Bardfield
Wethersfield
Throcking
Berden
Quendon
Great Bardfield
Cottered
Great Hormead
Hare Street
Hall's Green
Cromer
Buntingford
Stocking Pelham
Shalford
Graveley
Aspenden
Furneux Pelham
Ugley
Henham
Ardeley
Westmill
East End
Ugley Green
Duton Hill
Lindsell
Bardfield Saling
Shalford Green
Walkern
Manuden
Broxted
Elsenham
Wood End
Braughing
Patmore Heath
Farnham Green
STANSTED MOUNTFITCHET
Great Easton
Bran End
Great Saling
STEVENAGE
Nasty
Albury
Farnham
Molehill Green
Butcher's Pasture
Stebbing
Panfield
Aston End
Benington
Puckeridge
Little Hadham
Little Easton
Aston
Standon
Birchanger
Stansted Airport
GREAT DUNMOW
Churchend
Rayne
Bragbury End
Dane End
Hadham Ford
Bury Green
STANE STREET
Takeley
Little Dunmow
Knebworth
Watton at
Colliers End
BISHOP'S STORTFORD
Felsted
R Chelmer

Methwold Fens
Queen's Ground
Mundford
52
Shropham
Brandon Creek
B 1386
Feltwell
183
Wretham
Great Hockham
Puddledock
Brandon Bank
Feltwell Anchor
Castle
Grime's Graves
Peddars Way
Eccles Road
Wilby
Harling Road Sta
Larling
Hockwold Fens
Hockwold cum Wilton
Weeting
Santon Downham
Quidenham
Burnt Fen
Little Ouse River
Lakenheath Sta
Brandon
Croxton
Bridgham
East Harling
Kenninghall
Banham
FORD LEVEL
Brandon Park
Wangford Fen
Shippea Hill Sta
Priory
THETFORD
Brettenham
North Lopham
Fersfield
Thetford Warren
A 1066
Lakenheath
Wangford Warren
B 1382
Prickwillow
Queen Adelaide
Rushford
South Lopham
Bressingham
Garboldisham
Gasthorpe
The Delph
Lakenheath Warren
ELY
Middle Fen
Kenny Hill
Elveden
Euston
Hopton
Blo' Norton
Great Fen
Mildenhall Fen
Eriswell
Barnham
Coney Weston
Thelnetham
Redgrave
Stuntney
Holywell Row
Market Weston
Wortham
Broad Hill
Beck Row
Little Fakenham
Barningham
Hinderclay
Thistley Green
Rickinghall
Botesdale
Isleham Fen
West Row
Mildenhall
Hepworth
Soham Mere
Soham
Isleham
Worlington
Honington
Sapiston
Bardwell
Wattisfield
Barton Mills
Due to open Late 1986
Icklingham
Troston
Ixworth Thorpe
Stanton
Walsham Le Willows
Gislingham
Freckenham
Tuddenham
Ingham
Ampton
Great Livermere
Wicken
Fordham
Lackford
West Stow
Culford
Ixworth
Four Ashes
Fordham Abbey
Chippenham
Herringswell
Cavenham
Flempton
Langham
Finningham
Little Fen
Hengrave
Timworth Green
Stowlangtoft
Badwell Ash
Westhorpe
Landwade
Kennett
Icknield Way
Great Ashfield
Wyverstone
Burwell
Snailwell
Fornham All Saints
Fornham St Martin
Great Barton
Pakenham
Hunston
Wyverstone Street
Bacton
Reach
Kentford
Risby
A 45 (T)
Stanton Street
Earl's Green
Exning
Higham
Thurston
Norton
Moulton
BURY ST EDMUNDS
Westley
Tostock
Elmswell
Haughley Green
Swaffham Prior
Newmarket Heath
NEWMARKET
Gazeley
Barrow
Little Saxham
Ward Green
Gipping
Denham Castle
Great Saxham
Horringer
Ickworth House
Blackthorpe
Kingshall Street
Beyton
Woolpit
Wetherden
Old Newton
Swaffham Bulbeck
Ashley
Dalham
Denham
Rushbrooke
Rougham Green
Hessett
Drinkstone
Haughley
Cheveley
Dunstall Green
Chevington
Sicklesmere
Bradfield St George
Drinkstone Green
Harleston
Stowupland
Saxon Street
Ousden
Little Welnetham
Great Welnetham
Rattlesden
STOWMARKET
Stetchworth
Woodditton
Hargrave
Hawstead
Whepstead
Bradfield St Clare
Gedding
Poystreet Green
Buxhall
Great Finborough
Combs Ford
Combs
Great Wilbraham
Dullingham
Ditton Green
Upend
Lidgate
Bradfield Combust
Felsham
Kirtling
Depden Green
Chedburgh
Six Mile Bottom
Westley Waterless
Burrough Green
Kirtling Green
Thorns
Rede
Great Green
High Street Green
Wickhambrook
Brockley Green
Lawshall
Cockfield
Thorpe Green
Battisford
Brinkley
Cowlinge
Clopton Green
Wickham Street
Steam Dyke
Weston Colville
Carlton
Great Bradley
Denston
Hawkedon
Hartest
Shimpling Street
Brettenham
Battisford Tye
Ringshall
Weston Green
Stradishall
Stansfield
Thorpe Morieux
Charles Tye
Barking
Little Bradley
Boxted
Shimpling
Alpheton
Preston St Mary
Hitcham
Cross Green
Wattisham
West Wratting
Little Thurlow
Great Thurlow
Great Bricett
Ringshall Stocks
Balsham
Kettlebaston
Stanstead
Bridge Street
Lavenham
Bildeston
Nedging Tye
Offton
Hildersham
West Wickham
Barnardiston
Hundon
Poslingford
Glemsford
Kentwell Hall
Brent Eleigh
Monks Eleigh
Chelsworth
Naughton
Great Wratting
Withersfield
Horseheath
Chilton Street
Cavendish
Semer
Whatfield
Linton
Bartlow
Kedington
Long Melford
Milden
Elmsett
HAVERHILL
Clare
Acton
Little Waldingfield
Lindsey
Shudy Camps
Foxearth
Great Waldingfield
Kersey
Castle Camps
Sturmer
Wixoe
Stoke by Clare
Belchamp St Paul
Borley
Ashdon
Helions Bumpstead
Ashen
Ovington
SUDBURY
Edwardstone
HADLEIGH
Birdbrook
Belchamp Otten
Groton
Church End
Steeple Bumpstead
Ridgewell
Belchamp Walter
Bulmer
Great Cornard
Newton
Boxford
Little Walden
Stambourne Green
Little Yeldham
Middleton
Layham
Sewards End
Hempstead
Stambourne
Great Yeldham
Gestingthorpe
Bulmer Tye
Assington
Polstead
Great Wenham
Raydon
Radwinter
Toppesfield
Great Henny
Twinstead
Holton St Mary
SAFFRON WALDEN
Wimbish
Great Sampford
Cornish Hall End
Gainsford End
Castle Hedingham
Wickham St Paul
Lamarsh
Stoke-by-Nayland
Higham
Wimbish Green
Great Maplestead
Alphamstone
Nayland
Thorington Street
Stratford St Mary
East Bergholt
Howlett End
Debden
Little Sampford
Howe Street
Sible Hedingham
Little Maplestead
Pebmarsh
Bures
Dedham
Debden Green
Finchingfield
Mount Bures
Little Horkesley
Langham Hall
Thaxted
Little Bardfield
Wethersfield
Blackmore End
HALSTEAD
Langham
Wormingford
Great Bardfield
Colne Engaine
Great Horkesley
Ardleigh
Gosfield
Wakes Colne
Chappel
Fordham
Shalford
Beazley End
Earls Colne
Colne Valley
West Bergholt
Mile End
Duton Hill
Broxted
Lindsell
Bardfield Saling
Shalford Green
High Garrett
Greenstead Green
Fordstreet
Ardleigh Resr
Crockleford Heath
Great Easton
Bran End
Great Saling
Bocking Churchstreet
Great Tey
Aldham
Eight Ash Green
COLCHESTER
Elmstead Market
Molehill Green
Butcher's Pasture
Stebbing
Panfield
Stisted
Stanway
Beacon End
Bocking
BRAINTREE
Little Easton
GREAT DUNMOW
Churchend
Rayne
Bradwell
Marks Tey
Shrub End
Old Heath
WIVENHOE
Little Dunmow
Coggeshall
Copford Green
Takeley
Bannister Green
Black Notley
Feering
Easthorpe
Blackheath
Rowhedge
Felsted
Cressing
Birch
Layer de
Fingringhoe
Silver End
Kelvedon
Alresford
26

NORTH SEA
LOWESTOFT
Pakefield
Kirkley
Oulton Broad
Carlton Colville
Gisleham
Kessingland
Burgh St Peter
Aldeby
R. WAVENEY
Gillingham
Geldeston
Kirby Row
Broome
BECCLES
Barnby
Worlingham
North Cove
Mutford
Hulver Street
Rushmere
Ellough
Henstead
Benacre
Sotterley
Shadingfield
Wrentham
Covehithe
South Cove
Stoven
Clay Common
Brampton
Brampton Sta
Uggeshall
Wangford
Reydon
SOUTHWOLD
Walberswick
Blythburgh
Blyford
Holton
Mells
Wenhaston
Thorington
Bramfield
Dunwich
Darsham
Westleton
Yoxford
Sibton
Peasenhall
Middleton
Theberton
Eastbridge
Leiston Abbey
LEISTON
Sizewell
Aldringham
Thorpeness
Knodishall
Coldfair Green
Friston
Sternfield
SAXMUNDHAM
Kelsale
Carlton
Rendham
Sweffling
Snape
Farnham
Stratford St Andrew
Great Glemham
Little Glemham
Marlesford
Blaxhall
Tunstall
Tunstall Forest
Iken
ALDEBURGH
Aldeburgh Bay
High Street
Sudbourne
River Alde
Chillesford
Butley
Orford
Castle
Orford Ness
Boyton
R. Ore
Hollesley
Hollesley Bay
Shottisham
Sutton
Alderton
Bawdsey
Shipwash
Rough Tower
Sunk
Rendlesham Forest
Rendlesham
Campsey Ash
WICKHAM MARKET
Pettistree
Ufford
Eyke
Bromeswell
Melton
Sutton Hoo Tumuli
WOODBRIDGE
Martlesham
Martlesham Heath
Waldringfield
Newbourn
Hemley
R. Deben
Kirton
Falkenham
Trimley St Martin
Trimley St Mary
Walton
Old Felixstowe
FELIXSTOWE
Levington
Nacton
Bucklesham
Kesgrave
Brightwell
Rushmere St Andrew
IPSWICH
Chantry
Belstead
Wherstead
Freston
Woolverstone
R. Orwell
Chelmondiston
Shotley
Erwarton
Shotley Gate
Holbrook
Tattingstone
Alton Water Resr
Stutton
Harkstead
Holbrook Bay
RIVER STOUR
Brantham
Cattawade
Seafield Bay
Manningtree
Mistley
Wrabness
Parkeston
HARWICH
Harwich Harbour
Ramsey
Bradfield
Little Oakley
Great Oakley
Wix
Horsleycross Street
Horsley Cross
Stones Green
Beaumont
Little Bentley
Great Bentley
Tendring
Frating Green
Weeley
Weeley Heath
Thorpe le-Soken
Kirby Cross
Kirby
Horsey Island
Hamford Water
The Naze
WALTON-ON-THE-NAZE
FRINTON-ON-SEA
Aingers Green
Thorrington
Capel St Mary
Chattisham
Hintlesham
Bramford
Sproughton
Flowton
Somersham
Little Blakenham
Great Blakenham
Baylham
Claydon
Akenham
Henley
Barham
Coddenham
Needham Market
Creeting St Mary
Crowfield
Helmingham
Hall
Gosbeck
Ashbocking
Hemingstone
Swilland
Witnesham
Grundisburgh
Tuddenham
Westerfield
Castle Hill
Playford
Great Bealings
Little Bealings
Burgh
Clopton
Debach
Bredfield
Hasketon
Otley
Dallinghoo
Charsfield
Letheringham
Easton
Hoo
Monewden
Hacheston
Parham
Kettleburgh
Cretingham
Brandeston
Framsden
Pettaugh
Stonham Aspal
Earl Stonham
Little Stonham
Mickfield
Middlewood Green
Winston
Debenham
Ashfield
Earl Soham
Wetherup Street
Mendlesham Green
Mendlesham
Aspall
Kenton
Monk Soham
Bedfield
Saxtead
Saxtead Green
FRAMLINGHAM
Castle
Brabling Green
Cransford
Bruisyard
Dennington
Badingham
Worlingworth
Tannington
Brundish
Brundish Street
Fingal Street
Athelington
Horham
Wilby
Stradbroke
Laxfield
Ubbeston Green
Heveningham
Huntingfield
Cratfield
Silverley's Green
Ashfield Green
Pixey Green
Walpole
Cookley
HALESWORTH
Chediston
Linstead Parva
Wissett
Spexhall
Rumburgh
Westhall
Cox Common
Redisham
Ilketshall St Lawrence
Ilketshall St Andrew
Ilketshall St Margaret
Ringsfield
Barsham
Shipmeadow
Mettingham
BUNGAY
Flixton
Earsham
Ditchingham
Hedenham
Topcroft
Topcroft Street
Hempnall Green
Fritton
Stratton St Michael
Long Stratton
Morningthorpe
Shelton
Shelton Green
Hardwick
North Green
Alburgh
Denton
Homersfield
Wortwell
Redenhall
Starston
St Margaret South Elmham
St Michael South Elmham
All Saints South Elmham
St Cross South Elmham
St James South Elmham
Mendham
Withersdale Street
Weybread
Metfield
Fressingfield
Little Whittingham Green
HARLESTON
Needham
Rushall
Pulham Market
Pulham St Mary
Bush Green
Tivetshall St Margaret
Tivetshall St Mary
Great Moulton
Aslacton
Wacton
Forncett St Peter
Forncett End
Bunwell
Carleton Rode
New Buckenham
Gissing
Vinfarthing
Shelfanger
Burston
Shimpling
Dickleburgh
Thorpe Abbotts
Brockdish
Syleham
Hoxne
Wingfield
Denham
Billingford
Scole
DISS
Roydon
Palgrave
Thrandeston
Stuston
Oakley
Brome
Brome Street
EYE
Yaxley
Mellis
Thornham Parva
Thornham Magna
Wickham Street
Stoke Ash
Wickham Skeith
Thwaite
Brockford Street
Braiseworth
Occold
Thorndon
Rishangles
Bedingfield
Southolt
Redlingfield
Denham Street
Wetheringsett
Forward Green
Abbey
ROMAN ROAD
STONE STREET
R. Blyth
R. Dove
R. Waveney
River Deben
R. Alde
TM

FELIXSTOWE to
Zeebrugge 5-8 hrs

HARWICH to
Hook of Holland 6½-8½ hrs
Esbjerg 20 hrs
Kristiansand 22-24 hrs
Hamburg 21 hrs
Gothenburg 24 hrs

Penrhyn Mawr
Tŷ-hen
Porthor
Bryncroes
Botwnnog
Rhedyn
Nanhoron
Llanbedrog
Mynytho
Trwyn Llanbedrog
54
Rhydlios
Rhoshirwaun
999
Llawr Dref
Llangian
St Tudwal's Road
Capel Carmel
Castell Odo
Braich Anelog
B 4413
Rhiw
Abersoch
Llanengan
Porth Neigwl or Hell's Mouth
628
Llwchmynydd
Aberdaron
Sarn Bach
Braich y Pwll
Bwlchtocyn
St Tudwal's Islands
Uwchmynydd
Ynys Gwylan-fawr
Bardsey Sound
Trwyn yr Wylfa
Pen y Cil
Cilan Uchaf
Trwyn Cilan
548
Bardsey Island (Ynys Enlli)
A 499
2
3
4
5
6
2
1
0
9
8
7
6
SH
SN
Llanfair
Llandanwg
Pen-sarn
Llanbedr
Morfa Dyffryn
Coed Ystumgwern
Burial Chamber
Llanenddwyn
Dyffryn Ardudwy
Tal-y-bont
A 496
BARMOUTH
The Bar
Barmouth Bay
Fairbourne
Llwyngwril
Llangelynnin
Rhoslefain
116
Llanfendigaid
Aber Dysynni
A 493
TYWYN
Caethle
Aberdyfi
Aberdovey Bar
CARDIGAN BAY
Ynyslas
Borth
Upper Borth
B 4572
Llangorwen
485
A 487
ABERYSTWYTH
Llanbadarn
The Bar
Pen Dinas
Penparcau
Rhydyfelin
Llanfarian
147
Blaenplwyf
Rhôd-mâd
447
B 4576
Llanddeiniol
Carreg Ti-pw
Llanrhystud
Llansantffraid
Rhydrosser
Llanon
Nebo
Aberarth
Bethania
1129
Cross Inn
ABERAERON
B 4577
Pennant
617
Monachty
B 4337
Penuwch
80
A 482
Foss-y-ffin
NEW QUAY
30
31
Llwyncelyn
Cilcennin
Gilfachreda
405
Oakford
Bwlch-Llan
Llangeitho

CAMBRIAN MOUNTAINS
CADAIR IDRIS
PLYNLIMON (Pumlumon Fawr)
DOLGELLAU
MACHYNLLETH
LLANIDLOES
NEWTOWN
LLANFYLLIN
LLANDRINDOD WELLS
Rhayader
Devil's Bridge
Llanuwchllyn
Llanymawddwy
Dinas Mawddwy
Mallwyd
Corris
Aberdyfi
Llanbrynmair
Carno
Caersws
Llangurig
Staylittle
Dylife
Pontrhydfendigaid
Strata Florida
Tregaron
Llanfair Caereinion
Llangadfan
Lake Vyrnwy
Dyfnant Forest
Llyn Clywedog
Nant-y-moch Resr
Craig Goch Resr
Claerwen Resr
Caban-coch Resr
Elan Village
St Harmon
Llanbister
Crossgates
Blaenhafren Source of River Severn
Source of River Wye (Afon Gwy)
SJ
SO

Groes
Llangynhafal
Cilcain
Gwernaffield
MOLD
Mynydd Isa
Airport
Lache
Rowton
Bylchau
Peniel
Llanrhaeadr
Pentre
Llanynys
Gellifor
Moel Fammau
Cadole
BUCKLEY
Broughton
Bretton
Saighton
Nantglyn
Pant-pastynog
Ffridd Fawr
Tafarn-y-Gelyn
Maeshafn
Gwernymynydd
Penyffordd
Kinnerton
Eccleston
Eaton Hall
Bruera
Gorsedd Brân
Rhewl
Moel y Gaer
Foel Fenlli
Llanferres
Nercwys
Padeswood
Dodleston
Llyn Brân
Llanbedr-Dyffryn-Clwyd
Pontybodkin
Leeswood
Hope
Alford
Milton Green
Llyn Brenig
Llanfwrog
RUTHIN
Treuddyn
Caergwrle
Burton Green
Rossett
Pulford
Handley
Cyffylliog
Bontuchel
Eryrys
Cefn-y-bedd
Churton
Coddington
Mynydd Hiraethog
Efenechtyd
Llanfair Dyffryn Clwyd
Graianrhyd
Llanarmon-yn-Ial
Llanfynydd
Ffrith
Llay
Farndon
Alwen Resr
Nilig
Cefn Du
Clocaenog
Graig-fechan
Rhydtalog
Gresford
Holt
Barton
Clocaenog Forest
Pentre-celyn
Bwlchgwyn
Brymbo
Moss
Borras Head
Crewe
Stretton
Pentre-llyn-cymmer
Clawdd-newydd
Nantclwyd Hall
Moel Garegog
Llandegla
Pen-y-stryt
Minera
Brynteg
Gwersyllt
Llan-y-pwll
Isycoed
Due to open Late 1986
Derwen
Llanelidan
Esclusham Mountain
Coedpoeth
Bersham
WREXHAM
Rhosnesni
Wrexham Industrial Estate
Llanfihangel Glyn Myfyr
Melin-y-Wig
CYRN-Y-BRAIN
World's End
Eglwyseg Mountain
Rhostyllen
Marchwiel
Bowling Bank
Horton Green
Shocklach
Bettws Gwerfil Goch
Bryneglwys
Moel Morfydd
Llantysilio Mountain
Maesyrychen Mountain
Pentredwr
Ruabon Mountain
Rhosllanerchrugog
Cross Lanes
Bangor is-y-coed
Chorlton Lane
Worthenbury
Ty-nant
Maerdy
Gwyddelwern
Rhewl
Threapwood
Llangwm
Carrog
Llantysilio Hall
Valle Crucis Abbey
Castell
Penycae
Crabtree Green
Tallarn Green
Afon Alwen
Druid
Plas Isaf
Corwen
R. Dee (Afon Dyfrdwy)
Berwyn
Garth
Acrefair
Ruabon
River Dee
Glan-yr-afon
Glyndyfrdwy
Llangollen Canal
Cefn-mawr
Newbridge
Erbistock
Foel Goch
Wenallt
Cynwyd
LLANGOLLEN
Overton
Horseman's Green
Froncysyllte
Pentre
Halton
Lightwood Green
Hanmer
Sarnau
Moel Fferna
Penley
Knolton
Pontfadog
Chirk Castle
Chirk
Ifton Heath
Llandderfel
Glyn Ceiriog
Plâs Nantyr
Llwynmawr
River Ceiriog
Bronygarth
Dudleston Heath
Llandrillo
Crogen
Cefn Coch
Pale
Pandy
Weston Rhyn
Preesgweene
St Martin's
Bryn Du
Ellesmere
The Mere
Welshampton
Rhos-y-gwaliau
Pentre
Tregeiriog
Craignant
Selattyn
Gobowen
New Marton
Perthy
Lyneal
Llanarmon Dyffryn Ceiriog
Llechrydau
Foel Wen
Dinam
Mynydd Tarw
Foel Rhiwlas
Hengoed
Hindford
Welsh Frankton
Tetchill
Lee
Colemere
Rhiwlas
Lower Frankton
B E R W Y N
Pont Cwm Pydew
Tyn-y-ffridd
Llawnt
Old Oswestry
Whittington
Llangadwaladr
Rhydycroesau
Babbinswood
Kenwick
Wolverley
English Frankton
Pistyll Rhaeadr
Y Clogydd
Mynydd Mawr
Moelfre
OSWESTRY
Middleton
Hordley
Lower Hordley
Cockshutt
Loppington
Tai-bach
Llansilin
Morda
Rednal
Bagley
Craig Rhiwarth
Pennant-Melangell
Pencraig
Llangynog
Cefn Coch
Llanrhaeadr-ym-Mochnant
Trefonen
Ball
Haughton
West Felton
Petton
Afon Tanat
Llangedwyn
Maesbury Marsh
Wykey
River Perry
Weston Lullingfields
Alltforgan
Penybontfawr
Hirnant
Penygarnedd
Rhos-y-brithdir
Pen-y-bont
Nantmawr
Morton
Llynclys
Woolston
Eardiston
Stanwardine in the Fields
The Berth
Cedig
Ty-uchaf
Llanyblodwel
Crickheath
Knockin
Baschurch
Llyn Efyrnwy
Abernaint
Llanfechain
Pant
Maesbrook
Kinnerley
Ruyton-XI-Towns
Walford
Prescott
Bodfach Hall
Llansantffraid-ym-Mechain
Llanymynech
Hotel
Abertridwr
LLANFYLLIN
Afon Cain
Domgay
Great Ness
Little Ness
Nesscliffe
Yeaton
Hen Gerrig
Llanwddyn
Tycrwyn
Bwlch-y-cibau
Four Crosses
Llandrinio
Crosslanes
Pentre
Felton Butler
Ensdon
Fitz
Pen y Ffrid Gownwy
Ddôl Cownwy
Llanfihangel-yng-Ngwynfa
Waen-fâch
Deuddwr
Melverley
Dyfnant Forest
Pont Llogel
Dolwar Hall
Sarnau
Arddleen
Shrawardine
Forton
Moel y Llyn
Mynydd y Gadfa
Afon Efyrnwy (River Vyrnwy)
Trefnanney
Crew Green
Alberbury
Montford
Bicton
Meifod
Pentre'r beirdd
Geuffordd
Criggion Fort
Ford
A 458 (T)
Afon Twrch
Dolanog
Pontrobert
Middletown
Rowton Castle
SHREWSBURY
Foel
Pool Quay
Wollaston
Cardeston
Llangadfan
Guilsfield
Garreg Bank
Stretton Heath
Halfway House
Nox
Cruckton
Afon Banwy
Llanerfyl
Yockleton
Pen Coed
Buttington
Vennington
Cruckmeole
Hanwood
Four Crosses
Glascoed
Westbury
Stoney Stretton
Edge
Lea
Dolwen
Melin-y-grug
Melin-y-ddôl
Cyfronydd
WELSHPOOL (Trallwng)
Powis Castle
Offa's Dyke
Hope
Long Mountain
Rowley
Caus Castle
Westley
Farley
Annscroft
Nant yr Eira
Afon Banwy
Llanfair Caereinion
Castle Caereinion
Leighton
Aston Rogers
Asterley
Pleaeley
Longden
Bryn y Castell
Mynydd Waun Fawr
Short Cross
Minsterley
Pontesbury
Trelystan
Brockton
Binweston
Worthen
Oaks
Stapleton
Ffridd
Llwynderw
Fron
Ploxgreen
Habberley
Manafon
Llanllugan
Pant-y-ffridd
River Rhiw
Kingswood
Leigh
Church Pulverbatch
Marton
Snailbeach
Pulverbatch
Rhyd
Llanwyddelan
Berriew
River Severn
Forden
Betton
Hope
Afon Rhiw
Adfa
New Mills
Vaynor Park
Rorrington
Meadowtown
Esgair Cwmowen
Mynydd Clogau
Wotherton
Black Marsh
Gravels
Pennerley
Picklescott
Woolstaston
Tregynon
Brooks
Garthmyl
Chirbury
Middleton
Shelve
Plas Llysyn
Carno
Llyn Mawr
Llyn y Tarw
Offa's Dyke
Priest Weston
The Bog
Stiperstones
Ratlinghope
Bettws Cedewain
Ffridd Faldwyn
MONTGOMERY
The Marsh
Corndon Hill
Bridges
Bwlch-y-ffridd
ROMAN ROAD
Castle
Abermule
Llandyssil
Clatter
Llanwnog
Church Stoke
Hyssington
Linley Hill
All Stretton
Cefn-y-coed
Norbury
Church Stretton
Caersws
ROMAN ROAD
Llanllwchaiarn
Llanmerewig
More
Wentnor
Little Stretton
Trefeglwys
NEWTOWN
Sarn
Snead
Lydham
Asterton
Minton
L O N G M Y N D
The Port Way
Canal
A 483 (T)
A 5 (T)
A 5104
A 525
A 539
A 494 (T)
A 495
A 4083
A 528
A 458 (T)
A 470 (T)
A 489
A 490
A 488
B 4391
B 4393
B 4396
B 4500
B 4580
B 4390
B 4386
B 4385
B 4388
B 4389
B 4392
B 4397
B 5105
B 5437
B 4401
B 4402
B 4579
B 5069
B 5068
B 4382
B 4395
B 4568
B 4569
B 4499
B 4387
B 4370
1698
1703
1644
1543
1275
1083
1330
1079
1466
1531
1297
1241
1240
1676
1818
1354
1848
1839
1614
1677
2004
1285
1893
1942
2066
1838
1294
1848
1330
2265
1490
2712
2226
1167
1356
1715
1753
1256
2185
1991
1118
1768
1772
1276
490
1168
1009
992
1169
1084
1324
1419
911
1193
230
339
1049
514
1444
1590
1647
1320
1760
1683
1349
1305
847
869
1158
406
0
1
2
3
4
5
6
45
55
56
36

5 6 7 8 9

Duddon Clotton Budworth Hebden Green Bottom Flash Brereton Green Brereton Heath Hulme Walfield CONGLETON Macclesfield Rushton Spencer Heaton River Dane

Eaton Rushton Wettenhall Church Minshull Eccleston Green Bradwall Green Elworth Arclid Green Astbury Key Green Timbersbrook Hightown

Hargrave Huxley Tarporley Tilstone Fearnall Tiverton Warmingham SANDBACH Brookhouse Green Fourlanes End Brownlow Heath Newtown Rudyard Resr Meerbrook

Newton Castle Alpraham Calveley Bradfield Green Wheelock Hassall Green Gillow Heath Biddulph Moor Tittesworth Resr

Tattenhall Beeston Bunbury Radio Telescope Wardle Aston juxta Mondrum Worleston Winterley Hassall Rode Heath Scholar Green Mow Cop BIDDULPH Horton Rudyard

Chowley Burwardsley Spurstow Barbridge CREWE Haslington ALSAGER Church Lawton KIDSGROVE Knypersley LEEK

Peckforton Haughton Moss Rease Heath Crewe Hall Hardings Wood Harriseahead Blackwood Hill

Harthill Bulkeley Fuller's Moor Burland Acton Wistaston Radway Green Talke Newchapel Brindley Ford Brown Edge Longsdon Horse Bridge

Bickerton Faddiley NANTWICH Willaston Shavington Weston Barthomley Goldenhill Endon Caldon Canal

Cholmondeley Castle Ravensmoor Butt Green Hough Balterley Red Street Tunstall Norton-in-the-Moors Stanley Cheddleton

Chorley Stapeley Chorlton Audley Baddeley Green Bagnall Basford Green

Hampton Heath Walgherton Wybunbury Betley Chesterton Burslem Milton Abbey Hulton Wetley Rocks Consall

Bickley Moss Newtown Halmer End Alsagers Bank Hanley

No Man's Heath Wrenbury Llangollen Canal Hatherton Wrinehill Leycett Cellarhead

MALPAS Norbury Aston Blakenhall Madeley Heath Silverdale Bucknall Werrington

Marbury Newhall Marley Green Hankelow Checkley Madeley Keele NEWCASTLE UNDER-LYME STOKE-ON-TRENT Fenton

Higher Wych Wirswall Audlem Buerton Onneley Longton Dilhorne

Grindley Brook WHITCHURCH Burleydam Woore Clayton Caverswall

Wilkesley Coxbank Pipe Gate Aston Baldwin's Gate Whitmore Hanford Hanchurch Lightwood Meir Blythe Bridge Forsbrook Draycott in the Moors

Broughall Adderley Knighton Trentham Rough Close Meir Heath Cresswell

Ash Magna Alkington Shavington Park Norton in Hales Blackbrook Maer Tittensor Barlaston Fulford

Fenn's Moss Tilstock Ightfield Calverhall Mucklestone Chapel Chorlton Beech

Welsh End Hollinwood Prees Higher Heath Betton Loggerheads Ashley Ashley Heath Cranberry Swynnerton Moddershall Middleton Green

Longslow Almington Hookgate Podmore Standon Fort Oulton Cotwalton

Whixall Prees Moreton Say Bletchley Hales Chatcull Cotes STONE Hilderstone Garshall Green

Darliston Fauls Longford MARKET DRAYTON Fairoak Wetwood Millmeece B 5027

Paddolgreen Edstaston Ternhill Sutton Chipnall Slindon Yarnfield Milwich Coton

Newtown Prees Green Stoke Heath Woodseaves Rosehill Croxton Sugnall Aston-By-Stone Fradswell

Wollerton Cheswardine Sturbridge Norton Bridge Burston Sandon

Wem Aston Marchamley Weston Hodnet Wistanswick Lockleywood Soudley Bishop's Offley Eccleshall Chebsey Whitgreave Yarlet Gayton

Lee Brockhurst Bury Walls Stoke on Tern Mill Green Shropshire Union Canal Adbaston Wootton River Sow Great Bridgeford Weston

Preston Brockhurst Booley High Hatton Ollerton Tinstock Ellerton Knighton High Offley Shebdon Ellenhall Salt Hopton

Alderton Clive Stanton upon Hine Heath Peplow Child's Ercall Lawnhead Seighford STAFFORD Ingestre

Yorton Grinshill Moreton Corbet Ellerdine Heath Eaton upon Tern Howle Sambrook Weston Jones Woodseaves Norbury Ranton Coton Clanford Tixall

Shawbury Edgebolton Great Bolas Edgmond Marsh Puleston Sutton Long Compton Derrington Doxey Weeping Cross

Merrington Muckleton Rowton Tibberton Forton Gnosall Haughton Walton-on-the-Hill Milford

Preston Gubbals Hadnall Great Wytheford Cherrington Edgmond Aqualate Mere Aqualate Hall Gnosall Heath Coppenhall Brocton

Albrighton Astley Poynton Green Walton Waters Upton Aceney Longford NEWPORT Allimore Green Dunston Acton Trussell Bednall

High Ercall Crudgington Church Aston Chetwynd Aston Moreton Church Eaton Bradley Cannock Chase

Battlefield Haughton Roden Longdon on Tern Kynnersley Levedale

Uffington Rodington Sleapford Preston upon the Weald Moors Lilleshall Woodcote Great Chatwell Orslow High Onn Brindley Heath

Marsh Green Due to open Early 1986 Abbey Heath Hill Weston Heath Brineton Marston Mitton Penkridge

Withington Admaston Eyton upon the Weald Moors Donnington Wheaton Aston Whiston Huntington

Upton Magna Walcot Wrockwardine Hadley Sheriffhales Blymhill Lapley

Wellington Oakengates Crackleybank Weston-under-Lizard Watling Street Belvide Resr Stretton

Atcham Attingham Norton Uppington Arleston Hollinswood Bishop's Wood Horsebrook Kiddemore Green Gailey Hatherton Four Crosses

Bayston Hill Wroxeter Viroconium Lawley Oldpark TELFORD Boscobel House Brewood Standeford Cheslyn Hay

Berrington Rushton The Wrekin Horsehay Dawley Shifnal Tong Chillington Hall Coven Landywood

Cross Houses Donnington Eaton Constantine Upper Longwood Little Wenlock Stirchley The Wyke Shareshill

Condover Cantlop Leighton Coalbrookdale Cosford Station Codsall Wood Codsall

Cound Cressage Abbey Sutton Hill Kemberton Featherstone Essington

Pitchford Golding Acton Pigott Sheinton Iron-Bridge Coalport Brockton Grindle Ryton Albrighton Bilbrook Oaken Lane Green Oxley Bushbury

Dorrington Castle Acton Burnell Benthall Boningale Ashmore Park

Frodesley Homer Wyke Broseley Sutton Maddock Beckbury Wergs

Longnor Ruckley Kenley Harley Priory Barrow Willey Norton Burnhill Green Patshull Hall Tettenhall WEDNESFIELD

Leebotwood Stretton Westwood MUCH WENLOCK River Severn Stockton Badger Ackleton WOLVERHAMPTON Perton WILLENHALL

Enchmarsh Church Preen Hughley Plaish Presthope Nordley Pattingham Trescott BILSTON

Caer Caradoc Easthope Bourton Acton Round Astley Abbots The Walls Shipley Blakenhall DARLASTON

Cardington Gretton Longville in the Dale Haughton Worfield Hilton Lower Penn COSELEY WEDNESBURY

Hope Bowdler Brockton Aston Eyre Morville Tasley Roughton Seisdon Trysull SEDGLEY

East Wall Weston Monkhopton BRIDGNORTH Claverley Wombourne

Rushbury Shipton Upton Cressett Oldbury Heathton Halfpenny Green Airport Himley TIPTON

Ticklerton

A 51 A 534 A 530 A 49(T) A 41(T) A 525 A 495 A 442 A 53 A 529 A 5(T) A 458 A 454 A 449 A 34(T) A 50 A 500(T) A 52 A 5035 A 5005 A 519 A 518 A 5013 A 520 A 523(T) A 464 A 4169 A 4380 B 5074 B 5077 B 5071 B 5415 B 5026 B 5062 B 5063 B 5065 B 5476 B 5395 B 5367 B 5066 B 5405 B 5012 B 4394 B 4378 B 4368 B 4373 B 4176 B 4379 M 6 M 54 Roman Road Watling Street

57 48 37

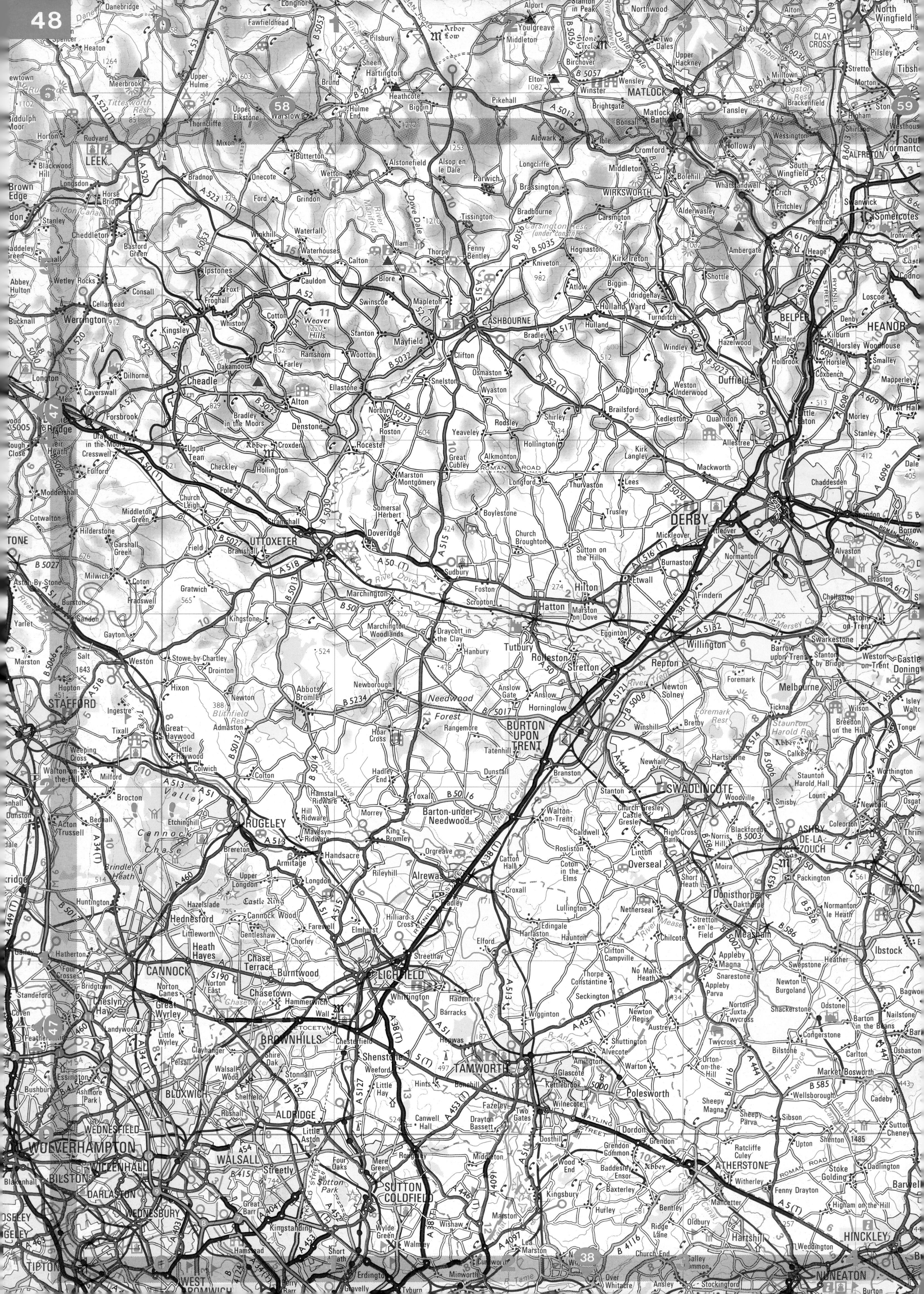
Danebridge
Longnor
Alport
Stanton in Peak
Northwood
Alton
North Wingfield
Fawfieldhead
Arbor Low
Youlgreave
Middleton
Stone Circle
Two Dales
Ashover
Clay Cross
Heaton
Pilsbury
Upper Hackney
Pilsley
Meerbrook
Upper Hulme
Sheen
Hartington
Birchover
Elton
Winster
Wensley
Matlock
Milltown
Stretton
Tittesworth Resr
Brund
Heathcote
Pikehall
Ogston Resr
Brackenfield
Biddulph Moor
Upper Elkstone
Warslow
Hulme End
Biggin
Brightgate
Bonsall
Matlock Bath
Tansley
Thorncliffe
Aldwark
Lea
Wessington
Horton
Rudyard
Leek
Mixon
Ible
Holloway
Alfreton
Butterton
Cromford
South Wingfield
Blackwood Hill
Alstonefield
Alsop en le Dale
Longcliffe
Middleton
Brown Edge
Longsdon
Bradnop
Onecote
Wetton
Parwich
Brassington
Wirksworth
Bolehill
Whatstandwell
Crich
Swanwick
Horse Bridge
Ford
Grindon
River Manifold
Dove Dale
Tissington
Bradbourne
Carsington
Alderwasley
Fritchley
Somercotes
Caldon Canal
Stanley
Cheddleton
Carsington Resr (under constn)
Pentrich
Ironville
Winkhill
Waterfall
Ilam
Thorpe
Fenny Bentley
Hognaston
Ambergate
Hage
Basford Green
Waterhouses
Calton
Kniveton
Kirk Ireton
Abbey Hulton
Wetley Rocks
Ipstones
Cauldon
Blore
Shottle
Consall
Atlow
Biggin
Idridgehay
Loscoe
Cellarhead
Foxt
Froghall
Swinscoe
Mapleton
Ashbourne
Hulland Ward
Belper
Denby
Heanor
Bucknall
Werrington
Cotton
Weaver Hills
Whiston
Stanton
Hulland
Turnditch
Kilburn
Horsley Woodhouse
Kingsley
Mayfield
Bradley
Windley
Hazelwood
Milford
Smalley
Oakamoor
Farley
Ramshorn
Wootton
Clifton
Holbrook
Horsley
Coxbench
Longton
Dilhorne
Cheadle
Snelston
Osmaston
Duffield
Caverswall
Alton
Ellastone
Wyaston
Mugginton
Weston Underwood
Meir
Forsbrook
Bradley in the Moors
Denstone
Norbury
Roston
Rodsley
Shirley
Brailsford
Kedleston
Quarndon
Little Eaton
Morley
West Hallam
Stanley
Blythe Bridge
Draycott in the Moors
Croxden
Rocester
Yeaveley
Hollington
Allestree
Cresswell
Upper Tean
Kirk Langley
Fulford
Checkley
Marston Montgomery
Great Cubley
Alkmonton
Roman Road
Mackworth
Chaddesden
Dale
Moddershall
Fole
Longford
Thurvaston
Lees
Church Leigh
Middleton Green
Somersal Herbert
Boylestone
Trusley
Derby
Cotwalton
Stramshall
Hilderstone
Uttoxeter
Doveridge
Church Broughton
Mickleover
Littleover
Stone
Garshall Green
Bramshall
Field
Sutton on the Hill
Burnaston
Normanton
Alvaston
Elvaston
Aston-By-Stone
Milwich
Coton
Gratwick
Sudbury
Etwall
Fradswell
Marchington
Foston
Hilton
Findern
Chellaston
Burston
Sandon
Scropton
Hatton
Marston on Dove
Kingstone
Trent and Mersey Canal
Aston-on-Trent
Yarlet
Gayton
Marchington Woodlands
Draycott in the Clay
Egginton
Willington
Swarkestone
Weston
Salt
Marston
Hanbury
Tutbury
Rolleston
Stretton
Repton
Barrow upon Trent
Stanton by Bridge
Weston-on-Trent
Castle Donington
Stowe-by-Chartley
Drointon
Hopton
Hixon
Newborough
Abbots Bromley
Needwood
Anslow Gate
Anslow
Newton Solney
Foremark
Melbourne
Stafford
Newton
Ingestre
Blithfield Resr
Forest
Horninglow
Foremark Resr
Ticknall
Wilson
Tixall
Admaston
Hoar Cross
Rangemore
Burton upon Trent
Winshill
Bretby
Staunton Harold Resr
Breedon on the Hill
Great Haywood
Little Haywood
Weeping Cross
Colwich
Tatenhall
Hartshorne
Calke
Walton-on-the-Hill
Milford
Colton
Hadley End
Dunstall
Branston
Newhall
Staunton Harold Hall
Worthington
Brocton
Hamstall Ridware
Yoxall
Stanton
Swadlincote
Woodville
Smisby
Lount
Acton Trussell
Bednall
Cannock Chase
Etchinghill
Rugeley
Hill Ridware
Morrey
Barton-under-Needwood
Walton-on-Trent
Church Gresley
Castle Gresley
Blackfordby
Norris Hill
Coleorton
Ashby-de-la-Zouch
Mavesyn Ridware
King's Bromley
Orgreave
Caldwell
High Cross Bank
Moira
Brereton
Armitage
Handsacre
Rosliston
Linton
Overseal
Brindley Heath
Upper Longdon
Longdon
Rileyhill
Alrewas
Catton Hall
Coton in the Elms
Short Heath
Packington
Huntington
Castle Ring
Fradley
Croxall
Netherseal
Donisthorpe
Oakthorpe
Hazelslade
Hednesford
Cannock Wood
Lullington
Nomanton le Heath
Gentleshaw
Farewell
Hilliard's Cross
Elmhurst
Edingale
Stretton en le Field
Measham
Littleworth
Chorley
Elford
Harlaston
Haunton
Chilcote
Hatherton
Heath Hayes
Chase Terrace
Streethay
Clifton Campville
Appleby Magna
Ibstock
Cannock
Burntwood
Lichfield
Thorpe Constantine
No Man's Heath
Swepstone
Heather
Norton Canes
Four Crosses
Bridgtown
Standeford
Cheslyn Hay
Chasetown
Hammerwich
Whittington
Hademore
Seckington
Snarestone
Appleby Parva
Newton Burgoland
Great Wyrley
Chasewater
Wall
Barracks
Newton Regis
Norton-Juxta-Twycross
Shackerstone
Odstone
Coven
Landywood
Letocetum
Austrey
Barton in the Beans
Nailstone
Little Wyrley
Brownhills
Chesterfield
Hopwas
Wigginton
Shuttington
Congerstone
Featherstone
Shenstone
Tamworth
Alvecote
Twycross
Pelsall
Clayhanger
Shire Oak
Weeford
Amington
Orton-on-the-Hill
Bilstone
Carlton
Essington
Walsall Wood
Stonnall
Hints
Glascote
Warton
Kettlebrook
Market Bosworth
Bushbury
Ashmore Park
Bloxwich
Little Hay
Bonehill
Polesworth
Wellsborough
Shelfield
Wilnecote
Sheepy Magna
Wednesfield
Rushall
Aldridge
Canwell Hall
Fazeley
Drayton Bassett
Two Gates
Watling Street
Sheepy Parva
Sibson
Cadeby
Wolverhampton
Little Aston
Dosthill
Dordon
Grendon
Upton
Shenton
Sutton Cheney
Walsall
Four Oaks
Middleton
Grendon Common
Ratcliffe Culey
Willenhall
Streetly
Mere Green
Roughley
Wood End
Baddesley Ensor
Atherstone
Roman Road
Stoke Golding
Dadlington
Bilston
Sutton Park
Sutton Coldfield
Kingsbury
Baxterley
Witherley
Fenny Drayton
Barwell
Darlaston
Great Barr
Bentley
Mancetter
Higham on the Hill
Wednesbury
Marston
Hurley
Ridge Lane
Oldbury
Wishaw
Wylde Green
Kingstanding
Lea Marston
Hartshill
Hinckley
Tipton
Hamstead
Short Heath
Walmley
Church End
Galley Common
Weddington
West Bromwich
Erdington
Minworth
Curdworth
Nether Whitacre
Over Whitacre
Ansley
Stockingford
Nuneaton
Gravelly
Tyburn
River Dove
River Trent
River Blithe
River Mease
R. Sence
R. Anker
R. Tame
R. Derwent
Ashby Canal
Coventry Canal
Trent and Mersey Canal

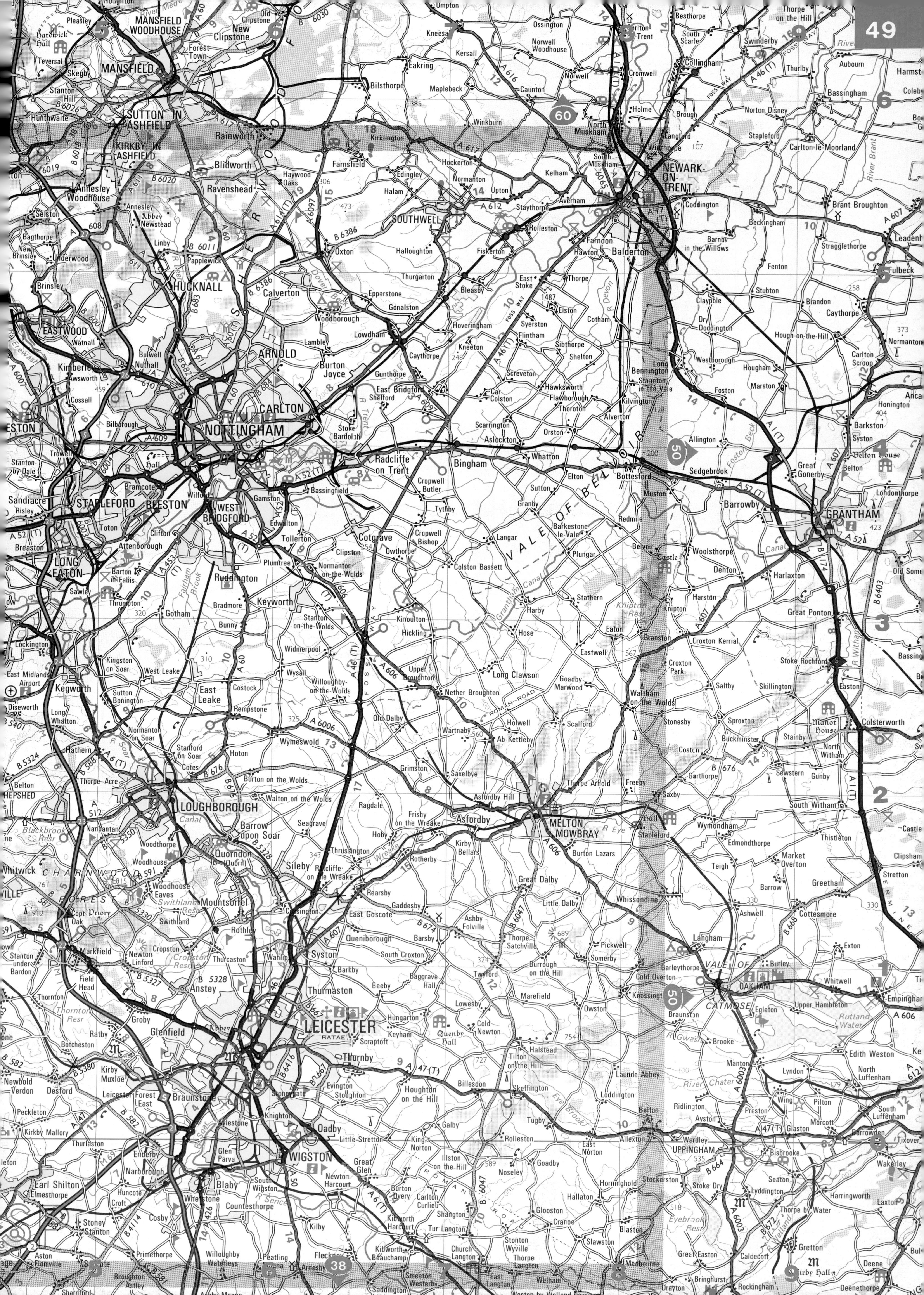
NOTTINGHAM
LEICESTER
LOUGHBOROUGH
MELTON MOWBRAY
GRANTHAM
NEWARK-ON-TRENT
MANSFIELD
VALE OF BELVOIR

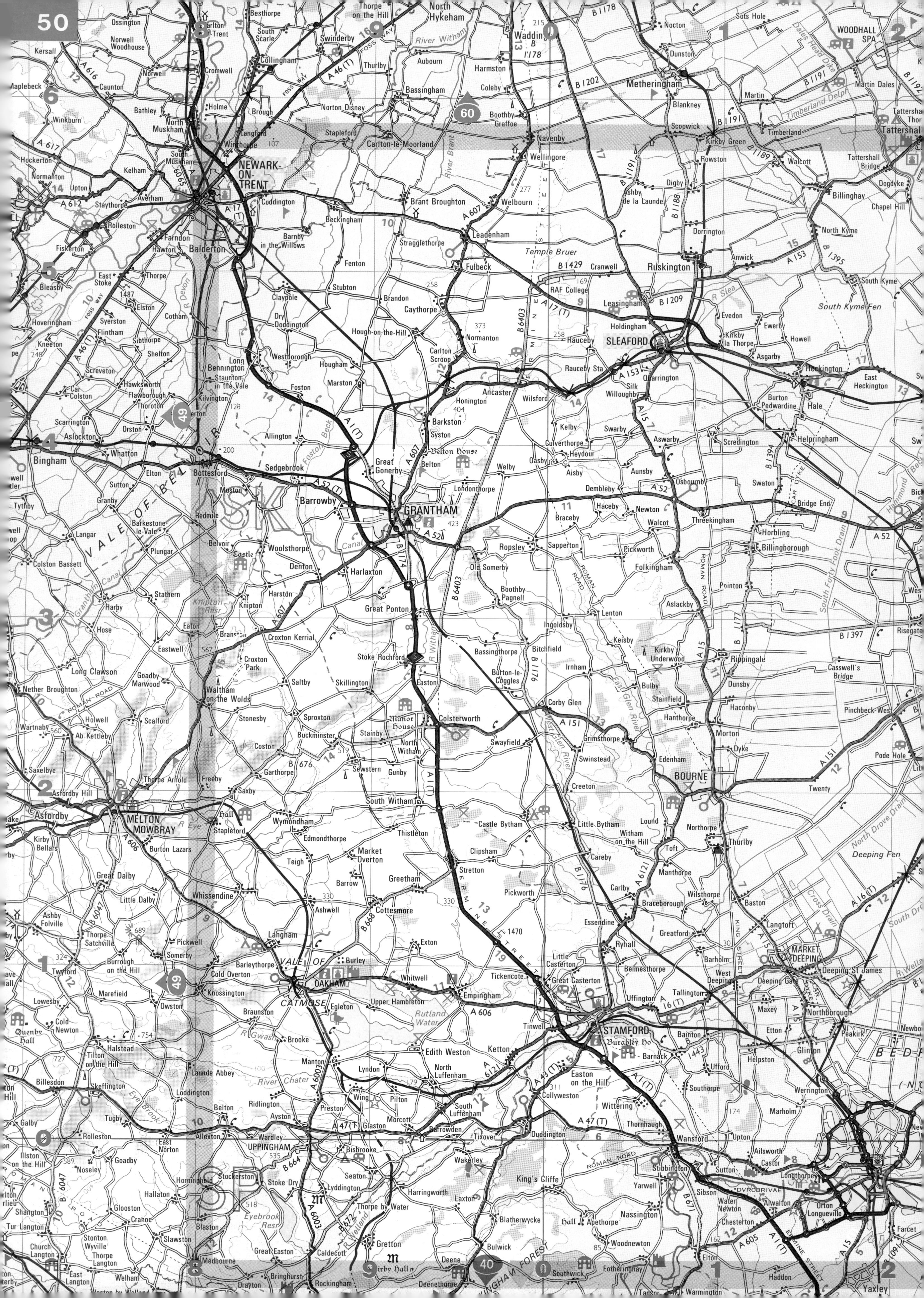
Ossington
Besthorpe
Thorpe on the Hill
North Hykeham
Waddington
Nocton
Sots Hole
WOODHALL SPA
Carlton-on-Trent
South Scarle
Swinderby
FOSS WAY
River Witham
Norwell Woodhouse
Kersall
Collingham
Thurlby
Aubourn
Harmston
Dunston
Cromwell
Norwell
Maplebeck
Caunton
Bassingham
Coleby
Metheringham
Martin Dales
Martin
Holme
Bathley
Norton Disney
Brough
Boothby Graffoe
Blankney
Timberland Delph
Tattershall Thorpe
Winkburn
North Muskham
Stapleford
Carlton-le-Moorland
River Brant
Navenby
Scopwick
Kirkby Green
Timberland
Tattershall
Langford
Winthorpe
Wellingore
Rowston
Walcott
Tattershall Bridge
Hockerton
South Muskham
NEWARK-ON-TRENT
Kelham
Normanton
Upton
Averham
Staythorpe
Coddington
Brant Broughton
Welbourn
Ashby de la Launde
Digby
Dogdyke
Billinghay
Chapel Hill
Rolleston
Beckingham
Leadenham
Dorrington
North Kyme
Fiskerton
Farndon
Hawton
Balderton
Barnby in the Willows
Stragglethorpe
Temple Bruer
Anwick
Fenton
Fulbeck
Cranwell
Ruskington
Bleasby
East Stoke
Thorpe
Elston
Stubton
Claypole
Brandon
Caythorpe
RAF College
Leasingham
South Kyme
South Kyme Fen
Evedon
Syerston
Cotham
Hoveringham
Flintham
Sibthorpe
Dry Doddington
Hough-on-the-Hill
Normanton
Holdingham
Rauceby
SLEAFORD
Ewerby
Kirkby la Thorpe
Howell
Kneeton
Shelton
Westborough
Hougham
Carlton Scroop
Asgarby
Heckington
East Heckington
Screveton
Car Colston
Hawksworth
Flawborough
Long Bennington
Staunton in the Vale
Marston
Rauceby Sta
Quarrington
Silk Willoughby
Thoroton
Kilvington
Foston
Ancaster
Wilsford
Honington
Burton Pedwardine
Hale
Scarrington
Aslockton
Orston
Bottesford
Allington
Barkston
Syston
Kelby
Swarby
Culverthorpe
Heydour
Aswarby
Scredington
Helpringham
Bingham
Whatton
Elton
Sedgebrook
Great Gonerby
Belton
Belton House
Welby
Oasby
Aisby
Aunsby
Osbournby
Dembleby
Swaton
Sutton
Muston
Barrowby
Londonthorpe
GRANTHAM
Haceby
Newton
Bridge End
Tythby
Granby
Redmile
Barkestone-le-Vale
Braceby
Walcot
Threekingham
Horbling
Billingborough
VALE OF BELVOIR
Langar
Plungar
Belvoir
Castle
Woolsthorpe
Denton
Harlaxton
Ropsley
Sapperton
Pickworth
Folkingham
Colston Bassett
Old Somerby
Grantham Canal
Harby
Stathern
Knipton
Knipton Resr
Harston
Great Ponton
Boothby Pagnell
Pointon
Aslackby
Hose
Eaton
Branston
Croxton Kerrial
Ingoldsby
Lenton
Keisby
Kirkby Underwood
Rippingale
Risegate
Eastwell
Croxton Park
Stoke Rochford
Bassingthorpe
Bitchfield
Irnham
Long Clawson
Goadby Marwood
Waltham on the Wolds
Saltby
Skillington
Easton
Burton-le-Coggles
Bulby
Casswell's Bridge
Dunsby
Nether Broughton
Stainfield
Haconby
Pinchbeck West
Holwell
Scalford
Stonesby
Sproxton
Manor House
Colsterworth
Corby Glen
Hanthorpe
Morton
Wartnaby
Ab Kettleby
Coston
Buckminster
Stainby
North Witham
Swayfield
Grimsthorpe
Swinstead
Edenham
Dyke
Pode Hole
Saxelbye
Thorpe Arnold
Freeby
Garthorpe
Sewstern
Gunby
BOURNE
Twenty
Asfordby Hill
Saxby
Creeton
Asfordby
MELTON MOWBRAY
Hall
Stapleford
Wymondham
South Witham
Castle Bytham
Little Bytham
Lound
Northorpe
Thurlby
Kirby Bellars
Burton Lazars
Edmondthorpe
Thistleton
Witham on the Hill
Toft
Deeping Fen
Teigh
Market Overton
Clipsham
Careby
Great Dalby
Barrow
Stretton
Manthorpe
Whissendine
Greetham
Pickworth
Carlby
Wilsthorpe
Baston
Little Dalby
Ashwell
Cottesmore
Braceborough
Langtoft
Ashby Folville
Thorpe Satchville
Pickwell
Langham
Exton
Essendine
Greatford
MARKET DEEPING
Deeping St James
Somerby
Burley
Ryhall
Barholm
Twyford
Burrough on the Hill
Barleythorpe
VALE OF CATMOSE
OAKHAM
Whitwell
Tickencote
Little Casterton
Great Casterton
Belmesthorpe
West Deeping
Tallington
Deeping Gate
Cold Overton
Knossington
Egleton
Upper Hambleton
Empingham
Uffington
Maxey
Northborough
Marefield
Lowesby
Owston
Braunston
Rutland Water
Tinwell
STAMFORD
Bainton
Etton
Peakirk
Cold Newton
Quenby Hall
Halstead
Brooke
Edith Weston
Ketton
Burghley Ho
Barnack
Glinton
Tilton on the Hill
Manton
Lyndon
North Luffenham
Easton on the Hill
Ufford
Helpston
Billesdon
Skeffington
Launde Abbey
River Chater
Collyweston
Southorpe
Werrington
Loddington
Wing
Pilton
South Luffenham
Wittering
Marholm
Tugby
Belton
Ridlington
Preston
Ayston
Glaston
Morcott
Barrowden
Thornhaugh
Galby
Rolleston
Allexton
Wardley
East Norton
UPPINGHAM
Bisbrooke
Tixover
Duddington
Wansford
Upton
Ailsworth
Castor
Illston on the Hill
Goadby
Noseley
Wakerley
Roman Road
King's Cliffe
Stibbington
Sutton
Longthorpe
Stockerston
Horninghold
Seaton
Stoke Dry
Lyddington
Harringworth
Yarwell
Sibson
Hallaton
Laxton
Water Newton
Alwalton
Orton Longueville
Shangton
Glooston
Cranoe
Eyebrook Resr
Thorpe by Water
Blatherwycke
Apethorpe
Nassington
Chesterton
Tur Langton
Blaston
Church Langton
Stonton Wyville
Thorpe Langton
Slawston
Great Easton
Caldecott
Gretton
Bulwick
Woodnewton
Elton
Farcet
Medbourne
Bringhurst
Deene
Kirby Hall
Southwick
Fotheringhay
East Langton
Welham
Drayton
Rockingham
Deenethorpe
Haddon
Yaxley
Warmington
Tansor
DVROBRIVAE
ERMINE STREET
KING STREET
ROMAN ROAD
Car Dyke
South Forty Foot Drain
North Drove Drain
Cross Drain
East Glen River
West Glen River
Foston Beck
R Witham
R Slea
R Eye
R Gwash
R Welland
Eye Brook
Dales Head Dyke
A1(T)
A17(T)
A46(T)
A607
A52(T)
A52
A153
A15
A151
A606
A6003
A47(T)
A43(T)
A16(T)
A6121
A612
A617
A616
A6097
A605
B1178
B1202
B1191
B1189
B1188
B1429
B1209
B6403
B1394
B1177
B1397
B1174
B1176
B676
B668
B6047
B664
B672
B671
B1443
B1091
B1395
49
60
40
SK
TF
SP
0
1
2
3
4
5
6
8
9

SKEGNESS
Wainfleet All Saints
Wainfleet Bank
Wainfleet Sand
Gibraltar
Croft Marsh
Seacroft
Havenhouse Sta
Thorpe St Peter
Thorpe Fendykes
Steeping River
Great Steeping
Irby in the Marsh
Bratoft
Toynton St Peter
Toynton Fen Side
Toynton All Saints
Keal Cotes
East Kirkby
Revesby
Miningsby
Moorby
Wood Enderby
Haltham
Bain
Mareham le Fen
Tumby
Coningsby
Tumby Woodside
New Bolingbroke
Stickford
Stickney
Midville
New Leake
Eastville
East Fen
Friskney
Lade Bank
Carrington
New York
West Fen
Northlands
Wildmore Fen
Leake Commonside
Old Leake
Wrangle
Friskney Flats
Sibsey
Frithville
Gipsey Bridge
River Witham
Langrick
Fishtoft Drove
Frith Bank
Hilldyke
Hobhole Drain
Leverton
Leake Hurn's End
Benington
Brothertoft
Boston Deeps
Long Sand
Lynn Deeps
BOSTON
Haltoft End
Butterwick
Freiston
Butterwick Low
Hubbert's Bridge
Frampton West End
Kirton Holme
Fishtoft
Scrane End
The Haven
Wyberton
Frampton
Kirton End
Kirton
Sandholme
Skeldyke
Sea Bank
THE WASH
Roger Sand
Toft Sand
Black Buoy Sand
Gat Sand
Mare Tail
Old South
TF
Wigtoft
Sutterton
Fosdyke
Bicker Haven
Quadring
Gosberton
Surfleet Seas End
Surfleet
Pinchbeck
River Welland
Holbeach St Marks
Holbeach St Matthew
Whaplode River
Dawsmere
Holbeach Marsh
Gedney Marsh
Gedney Drove End
Moulton Seas End
Saracen's Head
Holbeach Bank
Holbeach Hurn
Gedney Dyke
Lutton
Westor
Whaplode
HOLBEACH
Fleet Hargate
Fleet
Gedney
Chapelgate
Long Sutton
Gedney Broadgate
Sutton Bridge
Guy's Head
Moulton
Weston Hills
Whaplode Fen
Delph Bank
Sutton Crosses
Old Lynn Channel
Seal Sand
Peter Black Sand
Bulldog Sand
Breast Sand
Ongar Hill
Terrington Marsh
Terrington St Clement
Clenchwarton
West Lynn
HUNSTANTON
Holme next the Sea
Thornham
Ringstead
Heacham
Sedgeford
Snettisham
Southgate
Ingoldisthorpe
Shernborne
Dersingham
Anmer
Sandringham
Wolferton
West Newton
Flitcham
Babingley River
Castle Rising
North Wootton
Hillington
Congham
Roydon
South Wootton
Gaywood
Grimston
Pott Row
KING'S LYNN
Ashwicken
Gayton
Cowbit
Moulton Chapel
New River
Holbeach St Johns
Sutton St James
South Holland Main Drain
Tydd St Mary
Tydd Gote
Four Gotes
River Nene
Walpole St Andrew
Walpole St Peter
Tilney All Saints
Tilney High End
Terrington St John
St John's Highway
Tilney St Lawrence
Saddle Bow
West Winch
Middleton
East Winch
East Walton
North Runcton
Blackborough End
West Bilney
Pentney
Setchey
Narborough
River Nar
Tydd St Giles
Tydd St Giles Fen
Newton
Whaplode Drove
Holbeach Drove
Sutton St Edmund
Fitton End
West Walton
Walpole Highway
Walton Highway
Marshland
Wiggenhall St Germans
Wiggenhall St Mary the Virgin
Wiggenhall St Mary Magdalen
St John's Fen End
Wormegay
Tottenhill
Watlington
Great Postland
Gedney Hill
Gorefield
Leverington
Dowsdale
Crowland
North Fen
Church End
WISBECH
Walsoken
Marshland St James
Runcton
South Runcton
Shouldham
Marham
Parson Drove
Wisbech St Mary
Emneth
Emneth Hungate
Marshland Fen
Stowbridge
Wallington Hall
Shouldham Thorpe
Roman Road
Morris Fen
Wryde Croft
Murrow
Tholomas Drove
Elm
Holly End
Middle Level Main Drain
Stow Bardolph
Fincham
Barton Bendish
Thorney
Bedford Level
Waldersey
Friday Bridge
Outwell
Stow Bardolph Fen
Barroway Drove
Wimbotsham
Stradsett
Crimplesham
Eye
Guyhirn
Ring's End
Laddus Fens
Upwell
DOWNHAM MARKET
Bexwell
Boughton
Denver
Due to open Mid 1936
Wereham
Oxborough
PETERBOROUGH
North Side
Morton's Leam
River Nene
Twenty Foot River
West Fen
Westry
Euximoor Fen
Three Holes
Popham's Eau
Nordelph
West Dereham
Stoke Ferry
Whittington
Eldernell
WHITTLESEY
Fen Causeway
Old Croft River
South District
Upwell Fen
Fordham
Hilgay
Wretton
River Wissey
Eastrea
Coates
MARCH
Binnimoor Fen
Christchurch
Ten Mile Bank
Turves
Lakesend
Old Bedford River
River Delph
Southery
Methwold Hythe
Methwold
King's Delph
Flag Fen
TL
Town End
Upwell Fen
Hilgay Fen
Welney
Bedford Level
Ranson Moor
Methwold Fens
Queen's Ground
Middle Level
White Fen
Pondersbridge
Wimblington
Sixteen Foot Drain
Brandon Creek
Sea Bank
Devil's Dyke
Brancaster
Titchwell
Fring
Bircham
Peddars Way
A 158
A 52
A 16 (T)
A 155
A 153
B 1183
B 1195
B 1192
B 1184
A 1121
B 1181
A 17 (T)
A 151
B 1357
B 1359
B 1390
B 1165
B 1168
A 1073
B 1166
B 1040
A 47 (T)
B 1443
A 605
B 1093
B 1095
A 141
B 1099
B 1098
B 1101
A 1101
B 1187
A 1122
A 10
A 134
A 1078
A 148
A 149
B 1439
B 1153
B 1440
B 1145
B 1094
B 1100
B 1160
B 1106
B 1112
B 1386
52
61
41
1
2
3
4
5
6
7

NORTH SEA
THE WASH
BRANCASTER ROADS
Brancaster Bay
Holkham Bay
Blakeney Point
LYNN DEEPS
Seal Sand
Peter Black Sand
Bulldog Sand
SKEGNESS
Gibraltar
HUNSTANTON
Holme next the Sea
Thornham
Titchwell
Brancaster
Burnham Deepdale
Burnham Norton
Burnham Market
Burnham Overy Staithe
Burnham Overy Town
Burnham Thorpe
Holkham Hall
WELLS-NEXT-THE-SEA
Salt Marshes
Stiffkey
Morston
Blakeney
Cley next the Sea
Newgate
Cockthorpe
Wiveton
Langham
Glandford
Warham
Wighton
Binham Priory
Westgate
Saxlingham
Field Dalling
Letheringsett
Ringstead
Docking
North Creake
Abbey
Stanhoe
Waterden
Little Walsingham
Great Walsingham
Lower Green
Bale
Sharrington
Hindringham
Brinton
Thornage
Heacham
Sedgeford
Fring
South Creake
North Barsham
Houghton St Giles
East Barsham
Great Snoring
Thursford
Gunthorpe
Stody
Briningham
Snettisham
Southgate
Bircham Newton
Barmer
Bircham Tofts
Syderstone
West Barsham
Little Snoring
Barney
Swanton Novers
Melton Constable
Ingoldisthorpe
Shernborne
Great Bircham
Bagthorpe
Kettlestone
Dersingham
Sculthorpe
Dunton
Fulmodeston
Anmer
Tattersett
Shereford
FAKENHAM
Hempton
Little Ryburgh
Great Ryburgh
Stibbard
Wood Norton
Hindolveston
Sandringham
Wolferton
West Newton
Hall
East Rudham
West Rudham
Tatterford
Toftrees
Flitcham
New Houghton
Harpley
Helhoughton
Colkirk
Castle Rising
Babingley River
Hillington
West Raynham
East Raynham
Oxwick
Guist
Foulsham
Ongar Hill
North Wootton
Castle
Little Massingham
South Raynham
Gateley
Twyford
Themelthorpe
Congham
Great Massingham
Whissonsett
Bintree
Clenchwarton
South Wootton
Gaywood
Roydon
Grimston
Weasenham St Peter
Weasenham All Saints
Horningtoft
Brisley
North Elmham
Cathedral
Foxley
Bawdeswell
Pott Row
Massingham Heath
Wellingham
Tittleshall
Stanfield
Billingford
West Lynn
KING'S LYNN
Ashwicken
Gayton
Gayton Thorpe
Rougham
Mileham
East Bilney
Beetley
Worthing
Tilney All Saints
Great Ouse
Saddle Bow
West Winch
East Winch
Middleton
West Lexham
East Lexham
Litcham
Bittering
Longham
Gressenhall
Mill Street
Swanton Morley
Lyng
Elsing
River Wensum
North Runcton
Blackborough End
West Bilney
East Walton
West Acre
Castle Acre
Priory
Newton
South Acre
Great Dunham
Beeston
Hoe
Woodgate
Wiggenhall St Germans
Wiggenhall St Mary the Virgin
Tilney St Lawrence
Setchey
Pentney
Narborough
Great Palgrave
Little Dunham
Great Fransham
Wendling
EAST DEREHAM
North Tuddenham
Wiggenhall St Mary Magdalen
River Nar
Wormegay
Sporle
Little Fransham
Scarning
Toftwood
Mattishall Burgh
Tottenhill
Watlington
Marham
Devil's Dyke
SWAFFHAM
Necton
Daffy Green
Clint Green
Yaxham
Mattishall
Runcton Holme
South Runcton
Shouldham
Shouldham Thorpe
Beachamwell Warren
Westfield
Whinburgh
Welborne
Wallington Hall
Stowbridge
Stow Bardolph
ROMAN ROAD
Bradenham
Shipdham
Runhall
Fincham
Holme Hale
North Pickenham
Garvestone
Wimbotsham
Barton Bendish
Beachamwell
Letton Hall
Thuxton
Reymerston
Crimplesham
Stradsett
Cockley Cley
South Pickenham
Ashill
Cranworth
Southburgh
Hardingham
Bexwell
DOWNHAM MARKET
Barroway Drove
Boughton
Saham Toney
Woodrising
Wicklewood
Hackford
Denver
Oxborough
Gooderstone
Ovington
Carbrooke
Hingham
Due to open Mid 1986
Wereham
Hilborough
Great Cressingham
Deopham
Nordelph
West Dereham
Stoke Ferry
Little Cressingham
WATTON
Scoulton
Fordham
Wretton
Whittington
Foulden
Merton
Griston
Little Ellingham
Deopham Green
Hilgay
River Wissey
Bodney
Caston
Rockland St Peter
Ten Mile Bank
Northwold
Great Ellingham
Hilgay Fen
Southery
Methwold Hythe
Methwold
Cranwich
Thompson
Stow Bedon
Rockland All Saints
Besthorpe
Ickburgh
Methwold Fens
Southery Fens
Queen's Ground
Mundford
Breckles
Shropham
ATTLEBOROUGH
Brandon
Great Hockham
Puddledock
PEDDARS WAY
A 149
A 148
A 1067
A 1078
A 10 (T)
A 47 (T)
A 1065
A 134
A 122
A 1075
B 1153
B 1155
B 1355
B 1454
B 1105
B 1388
B 1156
B 1354
B 1110
B 1146
B 1145
B 1439
B 1440
B 1135
B 1108
B 1077
B 1106
B 1112
B 1160
B 1386
B 1147
51
42
6
7
8
9
0
5
4
3
2
1

1
2
3
4
5
6
5
4
3
2
1
0
Haisborough
SHERINGHAM
West Runton
CROMER
Foulness
Overstrand
Kelling
Weybourne
Upper Sheringham
Beeston Regis
East Runton
Sidestrand
Trimingham
Bodham
West Beckham
East Beckham
Aylmerton
Felbrigg
Crossdale Street
Northrepps
HOLT
Gresham
Baconsthorpe
Roughton
Gimingham
Mundesley
Sustead
Southrepps
Bessingham
Hanworth
Thorpe Market
Paston
Edgefield
Plumstead
Matlaske
Thurgarton
Alby Hill
Gunton Sta
Gunton Hall
Trunch
Bacton
Aldborough
Antingham
Knapton
Keswick
Walcott
Little Barningham
Wickmere
Suffield
Bradfield
Swafield
Edingthorpe
Calthorpe
Erpingham
Saxthorpe
Itteringham
Colby
NORTH WALSHAM
Witton Bridge
Ridlington
Happisburgh
Corpusty
Spa Common
Crostwight
Whimpwell Green
Banningham
Ingworth
Happisburgh Common
Blickling
Felmingham
Hempstead
Oulton
Heydon
Dulton Street
AYLSHAM
Tuttington
Westwick
Honing
East Ruston
Lessingham
Sea Palling
Wood Dalling
Burgh next Aylsham
Skeyton
Waxham
Ingham
Salle
Southgate
Cawston
Swanton Abbot
Worstead
Dilham
Smallburgh
Stalham
Reepham
Marsham
Brampton
Stalham Green
Hickling
Sloley
Sutton
Hickling Green
Horsey
Scottow
Lamas
Little Hautbois
Eastgate
The Heath
Buxton
Tunstead
Barton Turf
Hickling Heath
Hundred Stream
Brandiston
Sco Ruston
Neatishead
Catfield
Hevingham
Stratton Strawless
Coltishall
Irstead
Somerton
Winterton-on-Sea
Swannington
Horstead
Potter Heigham
Martham
Hemsby Hole
Waterloo
Hainford
Belaugh
Ludham
Bastwick
Alderford
Hoveton
Horning
Hemsby
Newport
Felthorpe
Frettenham
Wroxham
R. Thurne
Repps
Rollesby
Morton
Attlebridge
Horsford
Newton St Faith
Upper Street
Thurne
Ormesby St Margaret
Scratby
Weston Longville
Crostwick
Woodbastwick
California
Taverham
Horsham St Faith
Spixworth
Rackheath
Salhouse
Ranworth
Clippesby
Ormesby St Michael
Ringland
Burgh St Margaret (Fleggburgh)
Drayton
Norwich Airport
South Walsham
Caister-on-Sea
Hellesdon
Catton
New Rackheath
Panxworth
Billockby
Thrigby
Filby
Mautby
Costessey
Honingham
Sprowston
Little Plumstead
Hemblington
Upton
Castle
West Caister
Easton
New Costessey
Thorpe End
North Burlingham
Stokesby
West End
Great Plumstead
Acle
Runham
Marlingford
Colton
River Yare
Thorpe St Andrew
Blofield
Lingwood
Damgate
River Bure
Bowthorpe
Brundall
Beighton
Tunstall
A 47 (T)
Barford
Bawburgh
Earlham
NORWICH
Postwick
Strumpshaw
South Burlingham
Halvergate Marshes
Breydon Water
Colney
Trowse Newton
Halvergate
Berney Arms Sta
Burgh Castle
GREAT YARMOUTH
YARMOUTH ROADS
Wramplingham
Little Melton
Eaton
Lakenham
Surlingham
Buckenham
Hassingham
Freethorpe
GREAT YARMOUTH to Scheveningen 8 hrs
High Green
Cringleford
Kirby Bedon
Bramerton
Southwood
Wickhampton
Kimberley Ho
Hethersett
Keswick
Arminghall
Framingham Pigot
Cantley
ROMAN FORT
Bradwell
Crownthorpe
Caistor St Edmund
Rockland St Mary
Claxton
River Yare
Limpenhoe
Belton
Gorleston-on-Sea
Ketteringham
Swardeston
Framingham Earl
Hellington
Hobland Hall
WYMONDHAM
East Carleton
Dunston
Yelverton
Ashby St Mary
Langley Street
Reedham
Swainsthorpe
Stoke Holy Cross
Poringland
Bergh Apton
Thurton
Hardley Street
Ferry
Norton Marshes
Fritton
Mulbarton
Howe
Chedgrave
R. Chet
Priory
Hopton on Sea
Bracon Ash
Shotesham
Brooke
Loddon
Norton Subcourse
Lower Thurlton
Wreningham
Newton Flotman
Mundham
Thurlton
Thorpe
Herringfleet
Lound
Blundeston
Corton
Spooner Row
Ashwellthorpe
Flordon
Saxlingham Nethergate
Kirstead Green
Seething
Hales
Raveningham
Haddiscoe
Somerleyton
Hapton
Tasburgh
ROMAN ROAD
Tacolneston
Forncett St Mary
Hempnall
Thwaite St Mary
Kirby Cane
Toft Monks
Maypole Green
Oulton
Forncett End
Thurston
Stratton St Michael
Woodton
Wheatacre
Bunwell
Stockton
Burgh St Peter
Carleton Rode
Forncett St Peter
Long Stratton
Fritton
Hempnall Green
Topcroft Street
Hedenham
Ellingham
Kirby Row
Geldeston
Gillingham
Aldeby
River Waveney
Oulton Broad
LOWESTOFT
Morningthorpe
Wacton
Shelton
Ditchingham
Broome
43

54
HOLYHEAD to
Dun Laoghaire 3½ hrs
Dublin 3½ hrs
The Skerries
West Mouse
Middle Mouse
Carmel Head
Wylfa Power Station
Cemlyn Bay
Cemaes Bay
Cemaes
Llanbadrig
Porthllechog
Bull Bay
AMLWCH
Amlwch Port
Point Lynas
Pengorffwysfa
Penysarn
Parys Mountain
Ynys Dulas
Dulas
Dulas Bay
City Dulas
Gadfa
Rhosybol
Capel Parc
Brynrefail
Din Lligwy
Moelfre
Burial Chamber
Llanallgo
Marian-glas
Maenaddwyn
Llandyfrydog
Ceidio
Llyn Alaw
Rhosgoch
Bodewryd
Llanfechell
Mynydd Mechell
Carreglefn
Llanfflewyn
Llanbabo
Tregele
Llanfairynghornwy
Llanrhyddlad
Church Bay
Rhydwyn
Llanfaethlu
Llanddeusant
Elim
Llanfwrog
Llantrisant
Llanerchymedd
HOLYHEAD BAY
North Stack
South Stack
Salt Island
Holyhead Mountain
Standing Stones
HOLYHEAD
Penrhos
Penrhyn Mawr
Trearddur
Llanfachraeth
Pen-llyn
Carmel
Llyn Llywenan
Llechcynfarwy
Llanynghenedl
Trefor
Bodedern
Capel Coch
Brynteg
Benllech
Red Wharf Bay
Llanbedrgoch
Tregaian
Llanddyfnan
Dyffryn
Caergeiliog
ANGLESEY
Llangwyllog
Llynfaes
Llanfihangel yn Nhowyn
Four Mile Bridge
Bodior
Rhoscolyn
Bryngwran
Llanfairyneubwll
Valley Airfield
Tywyn Trewan
Cymyran Bay
Rhosneigr
Capel Gwyn
Gwalchmai
Bodffordd
Heneglwys
Rhosmeirch
Cefni Resr
LLANGEFNI
Talwrn
Pentraeth
Pen-y-garnedd
Llansadwrn
Llanddona
Llanfaes
BEAUMARIS
Rhoscefnhir
Ceint
Penmynydd
Llandegfan
MENAI BRIDGE
BANGOR
Llandegai
Penrhyn Castle
Llanfaelog
Ty Croes Station
Cerrigceinwen
Llangristiolus
Pentre Berw
Llanfairpwllgwyngyll
Gaerwen
Bodorgan Station
Trefdraeth
Afon Cefni
Malltraeth Marsh
Llyn Coron
Llangadwaladr
Aberffraw
Hermon
Bodorgan
Malltraeth
Malltraeth Sands
Malltraeth Bay
Llangaffo
Llanddaniel Fab
Chambered Cairn
Brynsiencyn
Vaynol Hall
Glasinfryn
Y Felinheli
Pentir
Tregarth
Dwyran
Newborough
Newborough Warren
Llanddwyn Island
Menai Strait
Llanddeiniolen
Rhiwlas
Dinas Dinorwig
Bethel
Penisa'r Waun
Deiniolen
CAERNARFON
Pont-rug
ROMAN FORT
Llanrug
Cwm-y-glo
Clwt-y-bont
Dinorwig
Abermenai Point
The Bar
Caeathro
Llanberis
Llanfaglan
Bontnewydd
Waunfawr
Moel Eilio
Betws Garmon
Salem
Rhostryfan
Rhosgadfan
Llanwnda
Penffridd
Groeslon
Moel Tryfan
Mynydd Mawr
Llyn Cwellyn
Carmel
Llandwrog
SNOWDON
Nantlle
Talysarn
Penygroes
Llyn Nantlle Uchaf
Rhyd-Ddu
Ffridd Uchaf
CAERNARFON BAY
Pontllyfni
Trwyn Maen Dylan
Llanllyfni
Nebo
Nasareth
Clynnog-fawr
Tai'n Lôn
Garnedd-goch
Llyn Cwm Dulyn
Bwlch Mawr
Upper Clynnog
Pant-glas
Afon Dwyfach
Beddgelert
Pass of Aberglaslyn
Moel Hebog
Trevor
Gurn Ddu
Trwyn y Gorlech
Yr Eifl
Tre'r Ceiri
Llanaelhaearn
Cennin
Bryncir
Garn Dolbenmaen
Dolbenmaen
Llanfihangel-y-pennant
Moel-ddu
Llyn Cwmystradllyn
Golan
Llithfaen
Pen-sarn
Carreg Ddu
Porth Dinllaen
Pistyll
Llwyndyrys
Llangybi
Rhoslan
Prenteg
Garreg
Penmorfa
Tremadog
Morfa-Nefyn
Nefyn
Fron
Llanarmon
Afon Dwyfor
Pentrefelin
Llanystumdwy
PORTHMADOG
Morfa Bychan
Minffordd
Portmeirion
Borth-y-Gest
Porth Ysgolaig
Edern
Garn Boduan
Boduan
Rhos-fawr
Y Ffôr
Chwilog
Rhos-y-llan
Tudweiliog
Llandudwen
Llannor
Efailnewydd
Abererch
CRICCIETH
Castle
Pen-ychain
Traeth Bach
Llanfihangel-y-traethau
Morfa Harlech
Porth Colmon
Penrhyn Colmon
Dinas
Carn Fadrun
Garn
Rhyd-y-clafdy
PWLLHELI
Carreg yr Imbill
Tremadog Bay
Llangwnnadl
Llaniestyn
Sarn Meyllteyrn
Penrhos
Y Gamlas
LLEYN PENINSULA
Penrhyn Mawr
Ty-hen
Bryncroes
Botwnnog
Rhedyn
Nanhoron
Llanbedrog
Trwyn Llanbedrog
Mynytho
Harlech
Porthor
Rhydlios
Rhoshirwaun
Llanfair
Braich Anelog
Capel Carmel
Castell Odo
Rhiw
Llawr Dref
Llangian
St Tudwal's Road
Abersoch
Llandanwg
Pen-sarn
Porth Neigwl or Hell's Mouth
Llanengan
Sarn Bach
Llwchmynydd
Aberdaron
Llanbedr
Braich y Pwll
Uwchmynydd
Ynys Gwylan-fawr
Bwlchtocyn
St Tudwal's Islands
Morfa Dyffryn
Bardsey Sound
Pen y Cil
Cilan Uchaf
Trwyn yr Wylfa
Trwyn Cilan
Coed Ystumgwern
Llanenddwyn
Dyffryn Ardudwy
44

Great Ormes Head
(Pen-y-Gogarth)
Puffin Island
Penmon
Toll
LLANDUDNO
Little Ormes Head
Penrhyn Bay
Rhôs-on-Sea
CONWY BAY
Conwy Sands
Dutchman Bank
Penmaen Swatch
Due to open Early 1985
COLWYN BAY
Llandudno Junction
Mochdre
Old Colwyn
Llysfaen
Llanddulas
Abergele Roads
Kinmel Bay
Towyn
Pensarn
ABERGELE
RHYL
PRESTATYN
West Hoyle Bank
Welsh Channel
Point of Ayr
Talacre
Mostyn
Gronant
Gwespyr
Gwaenysgor
Meliden
Llanasa
Gop Hill
Trelawnyd
Dyserth
Moel Hiraddug
Whitford
Rhuddlan
Castle
Pengwern
Bodelwyddan
Cwm
Rhuallt
Llyn Helyg
Pen-y-cefn
St Asaph (Lanelwy)
Lowther College
Tremeirchion
Caerwys
Afon-wen
Ysceifiog
Llannerch Hall
Graig
Trefnant
Bodfari
Henllan
DENBIGH
Afon Clywedog
Penycloddiau
Llangwyfan
Llandyrnog
Llangynhafal
Llanrhaeadr
Pentre
Peniel
Gellifor
Llanynys
Part-pastynog
Ffridd Fawr
Rhewl
Llanbedr-Dyffryn-Clwyd
RUTHIN
Llanfwrog
Bontuchel
Cyffylliog
Efenechtyd
Llanfair Dyffryn Clwyd
Clocaenog
Clocaenog Forest
Nilig
Cefn Du
Clawdd-newydd
Nantclwyd Hall
Derwen
Llanelidan
Melin-y-Wig
Gwyddelwern
Bettws Gwerfil Goch
Maerdy
Ty-nant
Carrog
Corwen
Druid
Plas Isaf
Cynwyd
Glan-yr-afon
Sarnau
Cefn-ddwysarn
Llandderfel
Crogen
Llandrillo
Pale
Cefn Coch
BERWYN
Dinam
Pont Cwm Pydew
Pistyll Rhaeadr
Y Clogydd
Pencraig
Pennant Melangell
Craig Rhiwarth
Llangynog
Afon Tanat
Penybontfawr
Penygarnedd
Hirnant
Alltforgan
Cefn Coch
Llanrhaeadr-ym-Mochnant
Moel Ffenod
Foel Wen
Mynydd Tarw
Tyn-y-ffridd
Mynydd Mawr
Llanarmon Dyffryn Ceiriog
PENMAENMAWR
Dwygyfylchi
CONWY
Llansanffraid Glan Conwy
Deganwy
Llanrhos
Llandrillo-yn-Rhos
Penrhyn-side
Tywyn
Bryn-y-maen
Llanelian-yn-Rhôs
Rhyd-y-foel
Gwrych Castle
St George
Dolwen
Betws-yn-Rhos
Moelfre Isaf
Mynydd Bodrochwyn
Glascoed
Roman Road
River Elwy
Bont-newydd
Llannefydd
Cefn Berain
Moelfre Uchaf
Llanfair Talhaiarn
Afon Aled
Llangernyw
Llansannan
Tan-y-fron
Groes
Bylchau
Nantglyn
Gorsedd Brân
Llyn Brân
Bryn Trillyn
Llyn Brenig
Mynydd Hiraethog
Alwen Resr
Pentre-llyn-cymmer
Cefn-brîth
Llanfihangel Glyn Myfyr
Cerrigydrudion
Glasfryn
Pentrefoelas
Rhydlydan
Hafod-Dinbych
Llyn Alwen
Moel Llyn
Llyn Aled
Aled Isaf Resr
Moel Seisiog
Gwytherin
Pandy Tudur
Afon Cledwen
Rhos-y-mawn
Mwdwl Eithin
Gell
Trofarth
Dawn
Pentrefelin
Tal-y-cafn
Graig
Eglwysbach
Llanddoged
Pentre-tafarn-y-fedw
LLANRWST
Melin-y-coed
Oaklands
Nebo
Capel Garmon
Fairy Glen
Glan-Conwy
Conwy Falls
Penmachno
Ysbyty Ifan
Afon Machno
Afon Conwy
Llyn Conwy
Garn Prys
Ty Mawr-Cwm
Afon Ceirw
Gellioedd
Llangwm
Gylchedd
Carnedd y Filiast
Migneint
Arenig Fach
Carnedd Iago
Llyn Celyn
Frongoch
Afon Tryweryn
Rhiwlas
BALA
Llanfor
Llanycil
Rhos-y-gwaliau
Llyn Tegid or Bala Lake
Llangower
Llanuwchllyn
Cwm Cynllwyd
Foel Figenau
Foel y Geifr
Ty-nant
Dyrysgol
Cwm Croes
Foel Rhudd
Bwlch y Groes
Aran Benllyn
Aran Fawddwy
Rhydymain
Foel Goch
Wenallt
Craig y Hyrddod
Llyn Arenig-Fawr
Arenig Fawr
Moel Llyfnant
Afon Llafar
Moel y Feidiog
Mynydd Bryn-llech
Mynydd Bach
Bronaber
Trawsfynydd
Cwm Prysor
Llyn Trawsfynydd
Moel Ysgyfarnogod
Cwm Bychan
Roman Steps
Rhinog Fawr
Cwm Nantcol
Llyn Hywel
Y Llethr
Afon Eden
Sarn Helen
Cefndeuddwr
Rhobell Fawr
Afon Gamlan
Llyn Bodlyn
Diffwys
Ganllwyd
Y Garn
Llanfachreth
Afon Wnion
Maentwrog
Gellilydan
Craig Gyfynys
Graig Wen
FFESTINIOG
Rhaeadr Cynfal
BLAENAU FFESTINIOG
Rhiwbryfdir
Tanygrisiau
Tanygrisiau Resr
Moelwyn Mawr
Cnicht
Glanaber Terrace
Pen y Bedw
Moel Penamnen
Dolwyddelan
Pentre-bont
Pont-y-pant
Carnedd Moel-siabod
Mynydd Cribau
Llyn Elsi Resr
BETWS-Y-COED
Swallow Falls
Pont Cyfyng
Capel Curig
Afon Llugwy
GLYDER FAWR
GLYDER FACH
Pen-y-benglog
Llyn Ogwen
Nant Ffrancon
CARNEDD DAFYDD
CARNEDD LLEWELYN
Ffynnon Llugwy Resr
Pen Llithrig-y-wrâch
Llyn Cowlyd Resr
Llyn Crafnant Resr
Trefriw
Afon Ddu
Llyn Eigiau Resr
Afon Porth-llwyd
Dolgarrog
Dulyn Resr
Afon Dulyn
FOEL-FRAS
Drosgl
Moel Wnion
Aber Falls
Llanllechid
Rachub
BETHESDA
Llanbedr-y-cennin
Tal-y-Bont
Vale of Conwy
Afon Conwy
Drum
Tal y Fan
Roewen
Ty'n-y-groes
Roman Road
Henryd
Aber
LLANFAIRFECHAN
Lavan Sands (Traeth Lafan)
Llyn Llydaw
Llyn Gwynant
Plas Gwynant
Y Cribau
Yr Arddu
Rhyd
Penrhyndeudraeth
Llanfrothen
SJ
SNOWDONIA

LIVERPOOL to
Dublin.......................7-8¾ hrs
Belfast...........................9 hrs
LIVERPOOL BAY
Marshside Sands
Angry Brow
SOUTHPORT
Crossens
Banks
Tarleton
Marshside
Churchtown
Mere Brow
Holmeswood
Birkdale
Bescar Lane Station
Rufford
Tarlscough
Scarisbrick
New Lane
Burscough Bridge
Burscough
Ainsdale
Shirdley Hill
Pinfold
Halsall
Freshfield
Formby Hills
Mad Wharf
FORMBY
ORMSKIRK
Haskayne
Great Altcar
Westhead
Aughton
Aughton Park
Scarth Hill
River Alt
Hightown
Ince Blundell
Lydiate
Bickerstaffe
MAGHULL
Lunt
CROSBY
Hall Road Sta
Thornton
Sefton
Netherton
Melling
RAINFORD
Blundellsands
CROSBY
Great Crosby
Ford
Aintree
KIRKBY
Kirkby Industrial Estate
Great Burbo Bank
CHANNEL
Waterloo
Seaforth
LITHERLAND
BOOTLE
Knowsley
New Brighton
Wharf
Knowsley Hall
West Derby
WALLASEY
Toll
HUYTON-WITH-ROBY
East Hoyle Bank
Mockbeggar
Moreton
Seacombe
LIVERPOOL
Tunnels
HOYLAKE
Upton
Toll
Childwall
West Hoyle Bank
Greasby
BIRKENHEAD
Rock Ferry
Welsh Channel
Point of Ayr
West Kirby
Frankby
Grange
Woolton
Prenton
New Ferry
Allerton
Hunt's Cross
Halewood
Caldy
Storeton
Port Sunlight
Garston
Talacre
Thurstaston
Irby
BEBINGTON
Speke
Mostyn Bank
Pensby
Barnston
Liverpool Airport
PRESTATYN
RHYL
Gronant
Gwespyr
Ffynnongroyw
HESWALL
Bromborough
Hale
Gwaenysgor
Meliden
Llanasa
Dawpool Bank
Thornton Hough
Eastham Sands
Dungeon Banks
Kinmel Bay
Gop Hill
Trelogan
Mostyn
RIVER DEE (AFON DYFRDWY)
Gayton
Raby
Eastham
Towyn
Trelawnyd
Glan-y-don
Holywell Bank
Gayton Sands
Parkgate
Dyserth
Offa's Dyke
Whitford
Downing
Willaston
ELLESMERE PORT
Ince Banks
ABERGELE
Rhuddlan
Moel Hiraddug
Llyn Helyg
Greenfield
Childer Thornton
Pengwern
Cwm
Carmel
NESTON
Oil Refinery
Ince
St George
Bodelwyddan
Gorsedd
HOLYWELL
Ness
Thornton-le-Moors
Lowther College
St Asaph (Llanelwy)
Rhuallt
Pen-y-cefn
Brynford
Milwr
Bagillt Bank
Bagillt
Ledsham
Whitby
Little Stanney
Moelfre Isaf
Glascoed
Tremeirchion
Babell
Castle
FLINT
Burton
Capenhurst
Stoak
Mynydd Hiraethog
Llannerch Hall
Caerwys
Afon-wen
Halkyn Mountain
Pentre Halkyn
Puddington
White Sands
Wervin
Picton
Bridge Trafford
Llannefydd
Graig
Ysceifiog
Lixwm
Halkyn
Shotwick
Works
Backford
Mollington
Cefn Berain
Bont-newydd
Trefnant
Bodfari
Vale of Clwyd
Nannerch
Rhes-y-cae
Flint Mountain
CONNAH'S QUAY
Northop Hall
Shotton
Saughall
Mickle Trafford
Guilden Sutton
Henllan
Afon Clwyd
Rhosesmor
Hendre
Northop
Queensferry
Castle
Sealand
Upton
Blacon
Hoole
DENBIGH
Penycloddiau
Rhydymwyn
Soughton (Sychdyn)
Ewloe
Mancot
Sandycroft
Hawarden
CHESTER
Littleton
Christleton
Llangwyfan
Moel Llys-y-coed
Mynydd Isa
Drury
Handbridge
Lache
Rowton
Castle
Groes
Llandyrnog
Cilcain
Broughton
Bretton
Tan-y-fron
Llangynhafal
Gwernaffield
MOLD
BUCKLEY
Saighton
Bylchau
Peniel
Llanrhaeadr
Pentre
Moel Famau
Tafarn-y-Gelyn
Cadole
Gwernymynydd
Llong
Penyffordd
Eccleston
Kinnerton
Llanynys
Gellifor
Maeshafn
Padeswood
Eaton Hall
Bruera
Nantglyn
Gorsedd Brân
Pant-pastynog
Ffridd Fawr
Moel y Gaer
Foel Fenlli
Llanferres
Nercwys
Dodleston
Bryn Trillyn
Llyn Brân
Rhewl
Llanbedr-Dyffryn-Clwyd
Leeswood
Aldford
Milton Green
RUTHIN
Pontybodkin
Hope
Pulford
Burton Green
Rossett
Handley
Mynydd Hiraethog
Llyn Brenig
Cyffylliog
Llanfwrog
Bontuchel
Treuddyn
Caergwrle
Efenechtyd
Llanfair Dyffryn Clwyd
Eryrys
Graianrhyd
Llanarmon-yn-Iâl
Llanfynydd
Ffrith
Cefn-y-bedd
Llay
Churton
Coddington
Alwen Resr
Nilig
Cefn Du
Clocaenog
Graig-fechan
Pentre-celyn
Rhydtalog
Bwlchgwyn
Brymbo
Moss
Gwersyllt
Gresford
Farndon
Holt
Barton
Clocaenog Forest
Clawdd-newydd
Moel Garegog
Brynteg
Borras Head
Crewe
Pentre-llyn-cymmer
Nantclwyd Hall
Llandegla
Minera
Stretton
Llan-y-pwll
Derwen
Llanelidan
Esclusham Mountain
Coedpoeth
Rhosnesni
Isycoed
WREXHAM
Wrexham Industrial
Llanfihangel

LEYLAND
Tockholes
Haslingden
RAWTENSTALL
BACUP
Walsden
Much Hoole
Clayton-le-Woods
Whittle-le-Woods
Whitehill
Hoddlesden
DARWEN
Helmshore
Waterfoot
Shawforth
Bretherton
Wheelton
Brinscall
Edenfield
Croston
Euxton
White Coppice
Anglezarke Moor
Turton Moor
Entwistle Sta.
Crowthorn School
Stubbins
Cowm Resr
WHITWORTH
Summit
CHORLEY
Belmont Resr
Edgworth
RAMSBOTTOM
Eccleston
Charnock Richard
Limbrick
Chapeltown
Turton Bottoms
Mawdesley
Heskin Green
Belmont
Winter Hill
Egerton
Summerseat
LITTLEBOROUGH
Rivington
Greenmount
Norden
Coppull
ADLINGTON
Toppings
Walmersley
ROCHDALE
Wrightington Bar
Grimeford Village
Bradshaw
Limefield
Firgrove
MILNROW
HORWICH
Tottington
Parbold
Appley Bridge
STANDISH
BOLTON
BURY
Newhey
Newburgh
Shevington Moor
Blackrod
Harwood
HEYWOOD
Red Rock
Haigh
Ainsworth
Shevington
Aspull
Fishpool
SHAW
Dalton
Roby Mill
Lostock Junction
Hollins
ROYTON
Gathurst
Marylebone
Wingates
RADCLIFFE
Birch
MIDDLETON
Delph
SKELMERSDALE
WIGAN
WESTHOUGHTON
FARNWORTH
LITTLE LEVER
WHITEFIELD
OLDHAM
ORRELL
Up Holland
KEARSLEY
PRESTWICH
CHADDERTON
Lees
Greenfield
INCE-IN-MAKERFIELD
HINDLEY
ATHERTON
Higher End
Hindley Green
Little Hulton
Walkden
Blackley
FAILSWORTH
Bryn Gates
TYLDESLEY
Pendlebury
Cheetham Hill
Broughton
Harpurhey
BILLINGE
ABRAM
LEIGH
Boothstown
Worsley
SWINTON
MOSSLEY
Crank
Garswood
ASHTON-UNDER-LYNE
Moss Bank
ASHTON-IN-MAKERFIELD
Astley Green
ECCLES
MANCHESTER
STALYBRIDGE
GOLBORNE
Lowton
Lowton Common
Lately Common
SALFORD
DROYLSDEN
DUKINFIELD
ST HELENS
HAYDOCK
Barton Moss
Glazebury
Trafford Park
Gorton
Audenshaw
Mottram in Longdendale
Eccleston
Earlestown
Kenyon
Culcheth
Chat Moss
URMSTON
STRETFORD
Rusholme
DENTON
HYDE
NEWTON-LE-WILLOWS
IRLAM
Flixton
Levenshulme
Thatto Heath
Croft
Ashton upon Mersey
Chorlton-cum-Hardy
Haughton Green
Broadbottom
PRESCOT
Sutton Leach
Risley
Carrington
Withington
Burnage
Reddish
Bredbury
Gee Cross
Clock Face
Fearnhead
Cadishead
Hollinfare
Carrington Moss
Heaton Moor
BOMILEY
Chisworth
Rainhill
Bold Heath
Orford
Partington
SALE
Didsbury
Compstall
WARRINGTON
Woolston
Toll
Warburton
Broadheath
STOCKPORT
MARPLE
Cronton
Great Sankey
Martinscroft
Heatley
Dunham Town
Timperley
GATLEY
CHEADLE
Heaviley
Mellor
Farnworth
Penketh
Thelwall
ALTRINCHAM
HALE
WYTHENSHAWE
HAZEL GROVE
Hough Green
Bowdon
CHEADLE HULME
High Lane
NEW MILLS
Ditton
Grappenhall
LYMM
Broomedge
Bollington
Halebarns
Heald Green
BRAMHALL
Stockton Heath
Higher Walton
Appleton Thorn
High Legh
Ashley
Manchester Airport
Middlewood Station
Poynton
Disley
Newtown
WIDNES
Moore
Daresbury
Swerton Heath
Bucklow Hill
Rostherne
Styal
Handforth
Woodford
Higher Poynton
RUNCORN
Norton
Halton
Hatton
Stretton
Tatton Hall
New Mills
Morley Green
Dean Row
Wood Lanes
Adlington
Lyme Park
Preston Brook
Arley
Mere
WILMSLOW
Weston
Whitley
Antrobus
Bate Heath
Knolls Green
Pott Shrigley
FRODSHAM
Sutton Weaver
Dutton
Aston
Great Budworth
Mobberley
KNUTSFORD
ALDERLEY EDGE
Mottram St Andrew
Prestbury
BOLLINGTON
Comberbach
Pickmere
Ollerton
Kerridge
Little Leigh
Anderton
Nether Alderley
Tytherington
Rainow
Helsby
Newton
Kingsley
Acton Bridge
Barnton
Wincham
Marston
Plumley
Marthall
Lostock Gralam
Chelford
Lamaload Resr
Alvanley
Crowton
Weaverham
NORTHWICH
Lower Peover
Parkgate
Monk's Heath
Henbury
Broken Cross
MACCLESFIELD
Dunham-on-the-Hill
Norley
Broken Cross
Swan Green
Peover Heath
Hartford
Hatchmere
Langley
Manley
Cuddington
Lach Dennis
Blackden Heath
Mouldsworth
Sandiway
Davenham
Radio Telescope
Siddington
Warren
Sutton Lane Ends
Delamere Station
Moulton
Withington Green
Oakgrove
Ashton
Eddisbury Hill
Whitegate
Byley
Goostrey
Gawsworth
Foxwist Green
Twemlow Green
Gleadsmoss
Wildboarclough
Great Barrow
Delamere
Bostock Green
Cranage
Kelsall
Tarvin
Oscroft
Willington Corner
Salterswall
Sproston Green
Holmes Chapel
Swettenham
Marton
Allgreave
Wharton
Rodeheath
Wincle
North Rode
Quarrybank
Cotebrook
Little Budworth
WINSFORD
MIDDLEWICH
Eaton
Bosley
Danebridge
Duddon
Hebden Green
Brereton Heath
Hulme Walfield
Burton
Clotton
Rushton
Brereton Green
CONGLETON
Rushton Spencer
Waverton
Hargrave
Tarporley
Occlestone Green
Key Green
Timbersbrook
Heaton
Huxley
Wettenhall
Bradwall Green
Elworth
Arclid Green
Brookhouse Green
Astbury
Hightown
Tiverton
Tilstone Fearnall
Church Minshull
Warmingham
SANDBACH
Newtown
Rudyard Resr
Meerbrook
Newton
Castle
Alpraham
Calveley
Bradfield Green
Fourlanes End
Brownlow Heath
Tittesworth Resr
Tattenhall
Beeston
Wheelock
Hassall Green
Gillow Heath
Biddulph Moor
Burwardsley
Bunbury
Radio Telescope
Winterley
Hassall
Scholar Green
Rode Heath
BIDDULPH
Mow Cop
Horton
Rudyard
Chowley
Spurstow
Wardle
Aston juxta Mondrum
Worleston
Church Lawton
Knypersley
Peckforton
Barbridge
CREWE
Haslington
ALSAGER
LEEK
Harthill
Haughton Moss
KIDSGROVE
Harriseahead
Blackwood Hill
Rease Heath
Crewe Hall
Hardings Wood
Newchapel
Brindley Ford
Longsdon
Bulkeley
Radway Green
Brown Edge
Caldon Canal
Horse Bridge
Fuller's Moor
Burland
Wistaston
Talke
Golden Hill
Stanley
Bickerton
Acton
Willaston
Weston
Endon
Duckington
Faddiley
Barthomley
Tunstall
Cheddleton
Cholmondeley Castle
NANTWICH
Shavington
Red Street
Baddeley Green
Stockton Brook
Ravensmoor
Butt Green
Hough
Balterley
Audley
Bagnall
Basford Green
Chorley
Chorlton
Hampton
Wybunbury

RAWTENSTALL
BACUP
TODMORDEN
BRIGHOUSE
LIVERSEDGE
HECKMONDWIKE
SOWERBY BRIDGE
66
ELLAND
MIRFIELD
RAMSBOTTOM
WHITWORTH
SD
LITTLEBOROUGH
RIPPONDEN
HUDDERSFIELD
ROCHDALE
MILNROW
SLAITHWAITE
Linthwaite
Golcar
Almondbury
BURY
HEYWOOD
Marsden
MELTHAM
Honley
KIRKBURTON
BOLTON
MIDDLETON
SHAW
ROYTON
HOLMFIRTH
Shepley
FARNWORTH
KEARSLEY
RADCLIFFE
WHITEFIELD
PRESTWICH
CHADDERTON
OLDHAM
57
Saddleworth Moor
Black Hill
FAILSWORTH
MOSSLEY
SWINTON
MANCHESTER
ASHTON-UNDER-LYNE
STALYBRIDGE
ECCLES
SALFORD
DROYLSDEN
DUKINFIELD
Tintwistle
Hollingworth
MIDHOPE MOORS
HOWDEN MOORS
Bleaklow Hill
URMSTON
STRETFORD
DENTON
HYDE
Hadfield
GLOSSOP
IRLAM
Chat Moss
Carrington Moss
SALE
STOCKPORT
ROMILEY
MARPLE
Featherbed Top
Kinder Scout
HIGH PEAK
ALTRINCHAM
HALE
GATLEY
WYTHENSHAWE
CHEADLE
CHEADLE HULME
HAZEL GROVE
BRAMHALL
High Lane
NEW MILLS
Hayfield
Low Leighton
Manchester Airport
Handforth
Poynton
Disley
Edale
Mam Tor
Castleton
WILMSLOW
Lyme Park
WHALEY BRIDGE
Chapel-en-le-Frith
KNUTSFORD
Mobberley
ALDERLEY EDGE
Prestbury
BOLLINGTON
Dove Holes
Tideswell
Chelford
MACCLESFIELD
BUXTON
Goyt's Moss
Shining Tor
Goostrey
Holmes Chapel
Ashford in the Water
BAKEWELL
MIDDLEWICH
Monyash
CONGLETON
Longnor
SANDBACH
Elworth
Biddulph Moor
Hartington
BIDDULPH
CREWE
ALSAGER
KIDSGROVE
LEEK
Brown Edge
Alstonefield
48
Haslington
Shavington
Audley
Endon
Cheddleton
Dove Dale

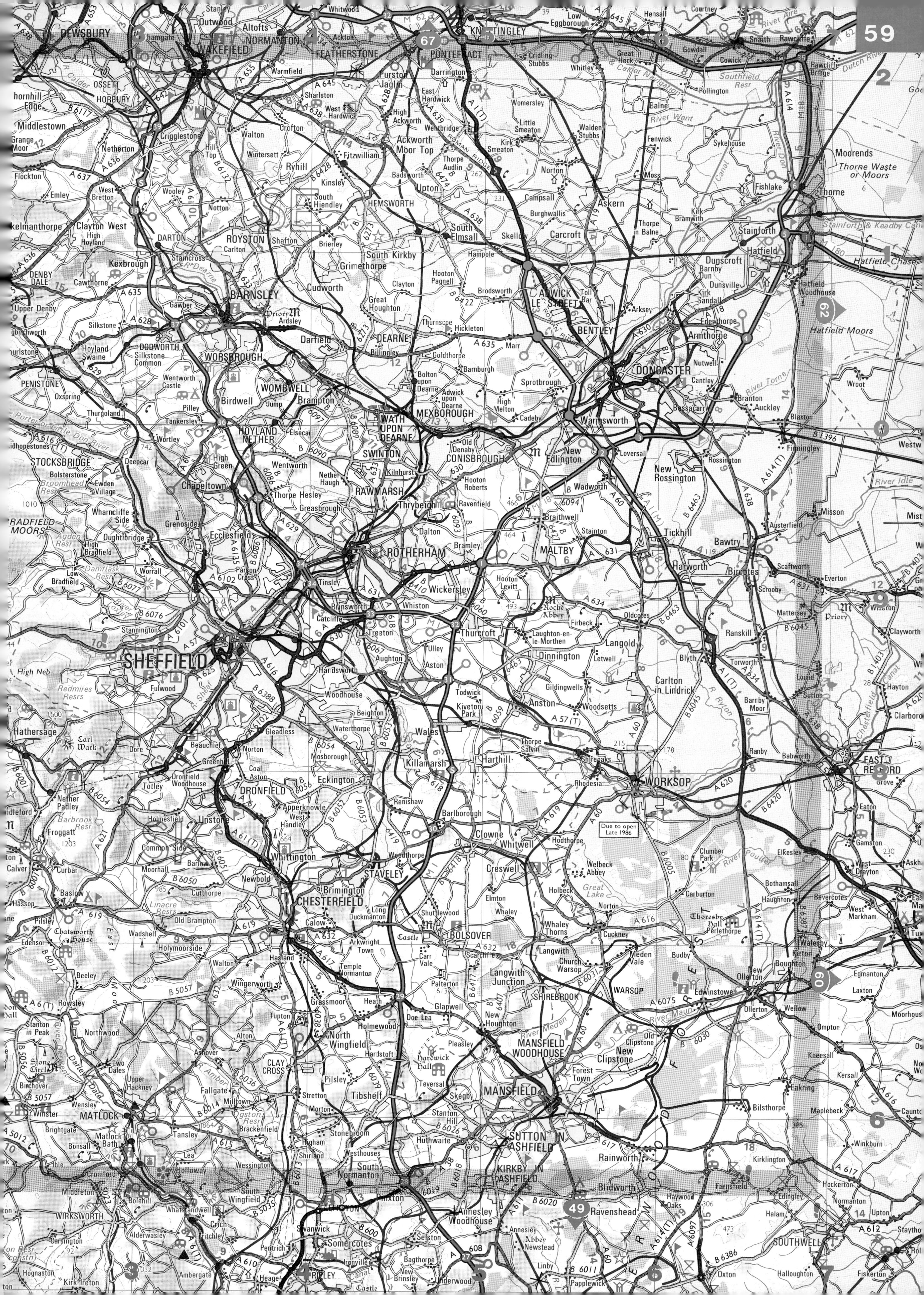
DEWSBURY
WAKEFIELD
NORMANTON
Altofts
Outwood
Stanley
FEATHERSTONE
PONTEFRACT
KNOTTINGLEY
Whitwood
Ackton
Low Eggborough
Hensall
Courtney
Snaith
Rawcliffe
Gowdall
Cowick
Great Heck
Whitley
Cridling Stubbs
Darrington
Purston Jaglin
Warmfield
Sharlston
West Hardwick
East Hardwick
Womersley
Pollington
Balne
Southfield Resr
River Went
River Aire
Dutch River
Rawcliffe Bridge
OSSETT
HORBURY
Thornhill Edge
Middlestown
Grange Moor
Netherton
Crigglestone
Walton
Crofton
High Ackworth
Wentbridge
Little Smeaton
Walden Stubbs
Fenwick
Sykehouse
Moorends
Thorne Waste or Moors
Thorne
Hill Top
Wintersett
Fitzwilliam
Ackworth Moor Top
Thorpe Audlin
Kirk Smeaton
ROMAN RIDGE
Flockton
Emley
West Bretton
Wooley
Notton
Ryhill
Kinsley
Badsworth
Upton
Norton
Moss
Fishlake
South Hiendley
HEMSWORTH
Campsall
Askern
Kirk Bramwith
Clayton West
High Hoyland
DARTON
ROYSTON
Carlton
Shafton
Brierley
South Kirkby
South Elmsall
Burghwallis
Skellow
Carcroft
Thorpe in Balne
Stainforth
Hatfield
Stainforth & Keadby Canal
Hatfield Chase
Kexbrough
Staincross
Grimethorpe
Hampole
DENBY DALE
Cawthorne
BARNSLEY
Gawber
Cudworth
Hooton Pagnell
Clayton
Brodsworth
ADWICK LE STREET
Toll Bar
Dunscroft
Barnby Dun
Dunsville
Kirk Sandall
Hatfield Woodhouse
Upper Denby
Silkstone
Priory
Ardsley
Great Houghton
Thurnscoe
Hickleton
BENTLEY
Arksey
Edenthorpe
Armthorpe
Hatfield Moors
Hoyland Swaine
DODWORTH
Silkstone Common
WORSBROUGH
Darfield
DEARNE
Billingley
Goldthorpe
Marr
DONCASTER
Nutwell
Cantley
Wroot
PENISTONE
Oxspring
Wentworth Castle
WOMBWELL
Birdwell
Jump
Brampton
Bolton upon Dearne
Barnburgh
Adwick upon Dearne
High Melton
Sprotbrough
Warmsworth
Cadeby
Branton
Auckley
Bessacarr
River Torne
Blaxton
Thurgoland
Pilley
Tankersley
HOYLAND NETHER
Elsecar
WATH UPON DEARNE
MEXBOROUGH
Old Denby
CONISBROUGH
New Edlington
Loversall
Rossington
New Rossington
Finningley
Westwood
Wortley
STOCKSBRIDGE
Bolsterstone
Deepcar
High Green
Wentworth
SWINTON
Kilnhurst
Nether Haugh
Hooton Roberts
Wadworth
River Idle
Broomhead Resr
Ewden Village
Chapeltown
Thorpe Hesley
RAWMARSH
Thrybergh
Ravenfield
Braithwell
Stainton
Tickhill
Austerfield
Misson
BRADFIELD MOORS
Wharncliffe Side
Grenoside
Ecclesfield
Greasbrough
Dalton
Bramley
MALTBY
Bawtry
Agden Resr
High Bradfield
Oughtibridge
ROTHERHAM
Harworth
Bircotes
Scaftworth
Everton
Low Bradfield
Damflask Resr
Worrall
Parson Cross
Tinsley
Wickersley
Hooton Levitt
Roche Abbey
Firbeck
Oldcotes
Scrooby
Mattersey
Wiseton
Brinsworth
Catcliffe
Whiston
Stannington
Treeton
Thurcroft
Laughton-en-le-Morthen
Langold
Ranskill
Clayworth
SHEFFIELD
High Neb
Redmires Resrs
Fulwood
Ulley
Aston
Aughton
Dinnington
Letwell
Blyth
Torworth
Lound
Hardsworth
Woodhouse
Todwick
Kiveton Park
Gildingwells
Carlton in Lindrick
Barnby Moor
Hayton
Beighton
Anston
Woodsetts
Hathersage
Carl Wark
Dore
Beauchief
Gleadless
Waterthorpe
Wales
Thorpe Salvin
Harthill
Shireoaks
Ranby
Babworth
EAST RETFORD
Greenhill
Norton
Mosbrough
Killamarsh
Rhodesia
WORKSOP
Totley
Dronfield Woodhouse
Coal Aston
DRONFIELD
Eckington
Grove
Nether Padley
Barbrook Resr
Apperknowle
West Handley
Renishaw
Barlborough
Eaton
Froggatt
Holmesfield
Unstone
Clowne
Whitwell
Hodthorpe
Due to open Late 1986
Gamston
Common Side
Whittington
Woodthorpe
Welbeck Abbey
Clumber Park
River Poulter
Elkesley
West Drayton
Calver
Curbar
Moorhall
Barlow
STAVELEY
Creswell
Bothamsall
Baslow
Cutthorpe
Newbold
Brimington
Holbeck
Great Lake
Carburton
Haughton
Bevercotes
Hassop
Linacre Resrs
CHESTERFIELD
Long Duckmanton
Shuttlewood
Elmton
Whaley
Norton
Thoresby Hall
Perlethorpe
West Markham
Pilsley
Old Brampton
Calow
Castle
BOLSOVER
Whaley Thorns
Cuckney
Chatsworth House
Wadshelf
Arkwright Town
Scarcliffe
Langwith
Meden Vale
Budby
Walesby
Edensor
Holymoorside
Hasland
Carr Vale
Church Warsop
Kirton
Beeley
Walton
Temple Normanton
Palterton
Langwith Junction
WARSOP
Boughton
Egmanton
Rowsley
Wingerworth
Grassmoor
Heath
Glapwell
SHIREBROOK
Edwinstowe
New Ollerton
Laxton
Stanton in Peak
Northwood
Tupton
Doe Lea
New Houghton
Ollerton
Wellow
Moorhouse
Alton
Holmewood
River Maun
River Meden
Ompton
Stone Circle
Two Dales
Ashover
North Wingfield
Pleasley
MANSFIELD WOODHOUSE
Old Clipstone
New Clipstone
Birchover
Upper Hackney
CLAY CROSS
Hardstoft
Hardwick Hall
Forest Town
Kneesall
Kersall
Fallgate
Pilsley
Teversal
Winster
Wensley
MATLOCK
Milltown
Stretton
Tibshelf
Skegby
MANSFIELD
Eakring
Bilsthorpe
Maplebeck
Caunton
Ogston Resr
Brightgate
Bonsall
Matlock Bath
Tansley
Brackenfield
Morton
Stonebroom
Stanton Hill
Huthwaite
SUTTON IN ASHFIELD
Rainworth
Winkburn
Kirklington
Ible
Cromford
Lea
Holloway
Wessington
Higham
Shirland
Westhouses
South Normanton
KIRKBY IN ASHFIELD
Blidworth
Farnsfield
Hockerton
Edingley
Normanton
Upton
Middleton
WIRKSWORTH
Bolehill
Whatstandwell
South Wingfield
Pinxton
Annesley Woodhouse
Ravenshead
Haywood Oaks
Halam
SOUTHWELL
Staythorpe
Carsington
Alderwasley
Crich
Fritchley
Swanwick
Somercotes
Selston
Annesley
Abbey Newstead
Hognaston
Kirk Ireton
Ambergate
Pentrich
RIPLEY
Heage
Ironville
Bagthorpe
New Brinsley
Underwood
Linby
Papplewick
Oxton
Halloughton
Fiskerton
SHERWOOD FOREST
Castle
A 1(M)
M 1
M 18
M 62
M 180

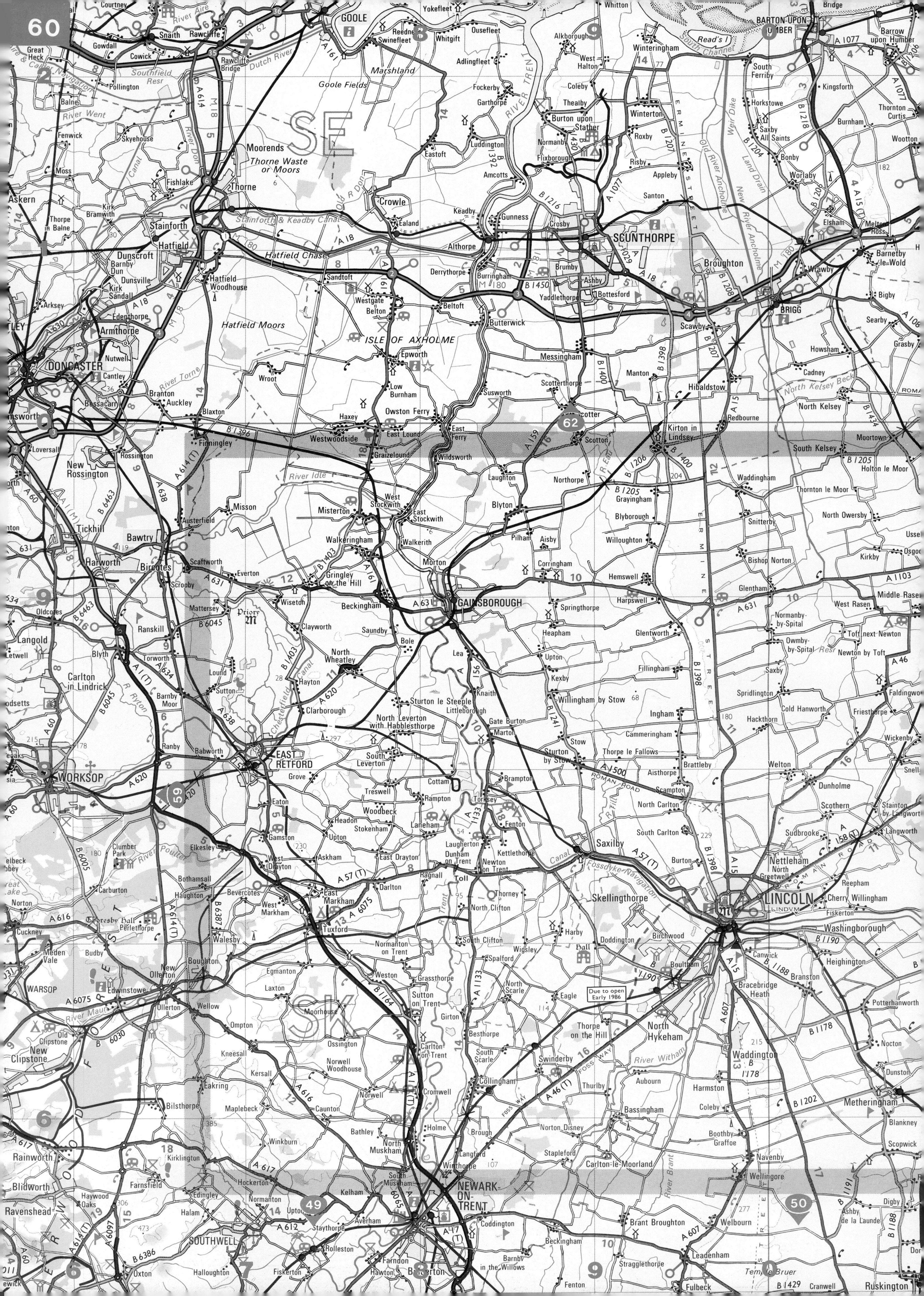
Courtney
River Aire
Snaith
Rawcliffe
GOOLE
Yokefleet
Whitton
Bridge
BARTON-UPON-HUMBER
Barrow upon Humber
Great Heck
Gowdall
Cowick
Rawcliffe Bridge
Dutch River
Reedness
Swinefleet
Whitgift
Ousefleet
Alkborough
West Halton
Winteringham
Read's I.
South Channel
South Ferriby
Kingsforth
Pollington
Southfield Resr
Marshland
Goole Fields
Adlingfleet
Fockerby
Garthorpe
Coleby
Thealby
Burton upon Stather
Winterton
Horkstowe
Thornton Curtis
Balne
River Went
Saxby All Saints
Burnham
Wootton
Fenwick
Skyehouse
Moorends
Thorne Waste or Moors
SE
Eastoft
Luddington
Normanby
Roxby
Flixborough
Risby
Appleby
Bonby
Worlaby
Moss
Fishlake
Thorne
Amcotts
Old River Ancholme
New River Ancholme
Weir Dike
Land Drain
Askern
Kirk Bramwith
Crowle
Santon
Thorpe in Balne
Stainforth
Stainforth & Keadby Canal
Ealand
Keadby
Gunness
Crosby
SCUNTHORPE
Elsham
Melton Ross
Hatfield
Dunscroft
Barnby Dun
Dunsville
Kirk Sandall
Hatfield Chase
Althorpe
Broughton
Barnetby le Wold
Hatfield Woodhouse
Sandtoft
Derrythorpe
Burringham
Brumby
Ashby
Bottesford
Yaddlethorpe
Wrawby
Bigby
Arksey
Edenthorpe
Westgate
Belton
Beltoft
BRIGG
Armthorpe
Hatfield Moors
Butterwick
Scawby
Searby
ISLE OF AXHOLME
Grasby
DONCASTER
Nutwell
Cantley
Epworth
Messingham
Howsham
Cadney
Wroot
Manton
North Kelsey Beck
River Torne
Branton
Bessacarr
Low Burnham
Susworth
Scotterthorpe
Hibaldstow
Auckley
Blaxton
Haxey
Owston Ferry
Scotter
North Kelsey
Redbourne
Loversall
Finningley
Westwoodside
East Lound
East Ferry
Scotton
Kirton in Lindsey
Moortown
Rossington
Graizelound
Wildsworth
South Kelsey
New Rossington
River Idle
Laughton
Northorpe
Holton le Moor
Waddingham
Thornton le Moor
Misson
West Stockwith
Blyton
Grayingham
Misterton
East Stockwith
Blyborough
North Owersby
Tickhill
Austerfield
Walkeringham
Walkerith
Pilham
Aisby
Willoughton
Snitterby
Bawtry
Harworth
Bircotes
Scaftworth
Everton
Gringley on the Hill
Morton
Corringham
Hemswell
Bishop Norton
Kirkby
Scrooby
Glentham
Middle Rasen
Oldcotes
Mattersey
Priory
Wiseton
Beckingham
GAINSBOROUGH
Springthorpe
Harpswell
West Rasen
Normanby-by-Spital
Ranskill
Clayworth
Saundby
Heapham
Glentworth
Toft next Newton
Langold
Blyth
Torworth
Bole
North Wheatley
Lea
Upton
Owmby-by-Spital
Newton by Toft
Fillingham
Carlton in Lindrick
Lound
Hayton
Chesterfield Canal
Kexby
Saxby
Sutton
Barnby Moor
Clarborough
Sturton le Steeple
Littleborough
Knaith
Willingham by Stow
Ingham
Spridlington
Cold Hanworth
Faldingworth
Friesthorpe
River Ryton
North Leverton with Habblesthorpe
Gate Burton
Marton
Cammeringham
Hackthorn
Ranby
Babworth
EAST RETFORD
South Leverton
Stow
Sturton by Stow
Thorpe le Fallows
Brattleby
Wickenby
WORKSOP
Grove
Cottam
Brampton
ROMAN ROAD
Aisthorpe
Scampton
Welton
Dunholme
Treswell
Rampton
Torksey
North Carlton
Scothern
Stainton by Langworth
Eaton
Woodbeck
Headon
Stokenham
Laneham
Fenton
South Carlton
Sudbrooke
Langworth
Clumber Park
River Poulter
Gamston
Upton
Elkesley
Askham
Laughterton
Kettlethorpe
Saxilby
Nettleham
North Greetwell
West Drayton
East Drayton
Dunham on Trent
Newton on Trent
Canal
Fossdyke Navigation
Burton
Reepham
Welbeck Abbey
Bothamsall
Ragnall
Toll
Haughton
Bevercotes
Darlton
East Markham
Thorney
Skellingthorpe
Carburton
West Markham
North Clifton
LINCOLN
LINDVM
Cherry Willingham
Fiskerton
Great Lake
Norton
Thoresby Hall
Perlethorpe
Tuxford
Washingborough
Cuckney
Walesby
South Clifton
Harby
Doddington
Birchwood
Meden Vale
Budby
Normanton on Trent
Wigsley
Hall
Canwick
Heighington
Egmanton
Spalford
Boultham
Branston
WARSOP
Edwinstowe
New Ollerton
Boughton
Laxton
Weston
Grassthorpe
North Scarle
Eagle
Bracebridge Heath
Due to open Early 1986
River Maun
Ollerton
Wellow
Sutton on Trent
SK
Moorhouse
Girton
Potterhanworth
Old Clipstone
New Clipstone
Ompton
Besthorpe
Thorpe on the Hill
North Hykeham
Ossington
Kneesall
Norwell Woodhouse
Carlton-on-Trent
South Scarle
Swinderby
River Witham
Waddington
Nocton
Kersall
FOSS WAY
Aubourn
Dunston
Eakring
Norwell
Cromwell
Collingham
Thurlby
Harmston
Metheringham
Bilsthorpe
Maplebeck
Caunton
Bassingham
Coleby
Blankney
Rainworth
Kirklington
Winkburn
Bathley
Holme
North Muskham
Brough
Norton Disney
Boothby Graffoe
Scopwick
Langford
Stapleford
Carlton-le-Moorland
Navenby
River Brant
Blidworth
Farnsfield
Hockerton
Winthorpe
South Muskham
NEWARK-ON-TRENT
Wellingore
Edingley
Haywood Oaks
Normanton
Kelham
Digby
Ravenshead
Halam
Upton
Averham
Coddington
Brant Broughton
Welbourn
Ashby de la Launde
SOUTHWELL
Staythorpe
Rolleston
Beckingham
Leadenham
Farndon
Barnby in the Willows
Hawton
Balderton
Halloughton
Oxton
Fiskerton
Stragglethorpe
Fenton
Fulbeck
Temple Bruer
Cranwell
Ruskington
ERMINE STREET
SHERWOOD FOREST
M62
M18
M180
M181
A1(M)
A1(T)
A15
A15(T)
A18
A46(T)
A57(T)
A60
A161
A607
A614(T)
A620
A631
A638
A1077
A1103
A1133
A1500
A6075
A616
A617
A6097
A612
A17(T)
B1396
B1398
B1400
B1205
B1206
B1207
B1208
B1216
B1241
B1178
B1188
B1190
B1202
B1164
B1403
B6045
B6463
B6387
B6386
B1429
B1191
B1188
B1434
B1204
B1218
B1206
B1450
B1392
A6065
59
49
50
62
2
3
4
5
6
7
8
9
0

KINGSTON UPON HULL tc
Rotterdam (Europoort)..........14 hrs
Zeebrugge..........15 hrs
NORTH SEA
RIVER HUMBER
MOUTH OF THE HUMBER
SPURN HEAD
Sunk Island Sands
TA
TF
THE WOLDS
ROMAN ROAD
GRIMSBY
CLEETHORPES
Immingham
Humberston
Killingholme
Habrough
Stallingborough
Healing
Great Coates
Laceby
Scartho
New Waltham
Waltham
Holton le Clay
Tetney
Tetney Lock
North Cotes
Marshchapel
Donna Nook
Grainthorpe
North Somercotes
Saltfleet
Caistor
Nettleton
Rothwell
Binbrook
MARKET RASEN
Tealby
Ludford
LOUTH
Keddington
Legbourne
Mablethorpe
MABLETHORPE
Trusthorpe
Sutton on Sea
Sandilands
Theddlethorpe St Helen
Gas Terminal
ALFORD
Bilsby
Huttoft
Anderby Creek
Chapel St Leonards
Hogsthorpe
Ingoldmells
Ingoldmells Point
Skegness (Ingoldmells) Aerodrome
Seathorne
SKEGNESS
Croft Marsh
Wainfleet All Saints
Gibraltar
Wainfleet Sand
Friskney
Friskney Flats
Wrangle
Old Leake
Sibsey
Stickney
Eastville
East Fen
West Fen
Wildmore Fen
Coningsby
Tattershall
WOODHALL SPA
HORNCASTLE
SPILSBY
Wragby
Bardney
Billinghay
North Kyme
Anwick
Tetford
Belchford
Ruckland
Burgh le Marsh
Orby Marsh
Timberland Delph
River Witham
River Bain
Steeping River
Covenham Resr
Fulstow
Ludborough
North Thoresby
Wold Newton
Humber
Bull
Spurn
Kilnsea
Easington
Skeffling
Patrington
Welwick
Holmpton
Sunk Island
Goxhill
East Halton
Ulceby
Kirmington
Keelby
Brocklesby
Great Limber
Riby
Aylesby
Irby Upon Humber
Barnoldby le Beck
Swallow
Cabourne
Cuxwold
Beelsby
Hatcliffe
Grainsby
Ashby cum Fenby
Brigsley
Bradley
Thoresway
Thorganby
Swinhope
Normanby le Wold
Claxby
Stainton le Vale
Walesby
Kirmond le Mire
Linwood
Legsby
North Willingham
Sixhills
Kelstern
Welton le Wold
South Elkington
North Elkington
Fotherby
Utterby
North Ormsby
Covenham St Mary
Covenham St Bartholomew
Yarburgh
Alvingham
Cockerington
Conisholme
South Somercotes
Skidbrooke
Saltfleetby St Clement
Saltfleetby All Saints
Saltfleetby St Peter
Theddlethorpe All Saints
Grimoldby
Manby
Stewton
Little Carlton
Great Carlton
Gayton le Marsh
Strubby
Maltby le Marsh
Beesby
Withern
South Reston
Authorpe
Muckton
Little Cawthorpe
Raithby
Tathwell
Haugham
Burwell
Belleau
Aby
Saleby
Markby
Thorpe
Anderby
Mumby
Farlesthorpe
Cumberworth
Willoughby
Sloothby
Addlethorpe
Winthorpe
Welton le Marsh
Candlesby
Scremby
Orby
Bratoft
Irby in the Marsh
Thorpe St Peter
Croft
Seacroft
Havenhouse Sta
Wainfleet Bank
Thorpe Fendykes
Steeping
Great Steeping
Halton Holegate
Ashby by Partney
Hundleby
Raithby
Mavis Enderby
Old Bolingbroke
Keal
Toynton All Saints
Toynton Fen Side
Toynton St Peter
East Kirkby
Keal Cotes
Revesby
Miningsby
Hareby
Asgarby
Hameringham
Lusby
Mareham on the Hill
High Toynton
Hagworthingham
Greetham
Ashby
Somersby
Salmonby
Fulletby
West Ashby
Hemingby
Baumber
Minting
Gautby
Wispington
Edlington
Thimbleby
Langton
Thornton
Horsington
Bucknall
Southrey
Stixwould
Sots Hole
Martin Dales
Martin
Timberland
Walcott
Tattershall Bridge
Tattershall Thorpe
Dogdyke
Chapel Hill
Scrub Hill
New York
Tumby
Tumby Woodside
New Bolingbroke
Carrington
Midville
New Leake
Northlands
Leake Commonside
Frithville
Gipsey Bridge
Stickford
Mareham le Fen
Haltham
Kirkby on Bain
Roughton
Wood Enderby
Moorby
Dalderby
Hatton
Great Sturton
Sotby
Panton
Langton by Wragby
Apley
Stainfield
Goulceby
Market Stainton
Donington on Bain
Benniworth
Hainton
South Willingham
Burgh on Bain
East Barkwith
East Torrington
West Torrington
Wickenby Airport
Holton cum Beckering
Fulnetby
Rand
Scamblesby
Salmonby
Swaby
South Thoresby
South Ormsby
Driby
Brinkhill
Well
Ulceby
Claxby
Harrington
Aswardby
Langton
Sausthorpe
Skendleby
Old Leake

Due to open Early 1986
YORK
EBVRACVM
Towthorpe
Sand Hutton
Buttercrambe
Underdale
Fridaythorpe
Wetwang
Garton-on-the-Wolds
GREAT DRIFFIELD
Huntington
Skirpenbeck
Bugthorpe
Stockton on the Forest
Upper Helmsley
ROMAN ROAD
Youlthorpe
Huggate
Tibthorpe
Kirkburn
Wansford
Skelton
Rawcliffe
New Earswick
Warthill
Stamford Bridge
Bishop Wilton
Gate Helmsley
Full Sutton
Great Givendale
Skerne
Holtby
Low Catton
High Catton
Fangfoss
Brigham
Murton
Dunnington
Bolton
Meltonby
North Dalton
Bainton
Hutton Cranswick
Rotsea
Yapham
Millington
Kexby
Wilberfoss
Warter
Middleton-on-the-Wolds
Watton
Heslington
Fulford
Newton upon Derwent
Barmby Moor
Pocklington
Lund
Kilnwick
Beswick
Watton Beck
Elvington
Allerthorpe
Nunburnholme
Lockington
Bishopthorpe
Crockey Hill
Sutton upon Derwent
Burnby
Holme on the Wolds
River Hull
Aike
Acaster Malbis
Naburn
Pocklington Canal
Thornton
Hayton
Londesborough
South Dalton
Scorborough
Deighton
Wheldrake
Melbourne
Bielby
Everingham
Shiptonthorpe
Goodmanham
Etton
Leconfield
Arram
Escrick
East Cottingwith
Seaton Ross
Cherry Burton
River Ouse
Thorganby
Market Weighton
BEVERLEY
Tickton
Stillingfleet
Laytham
River Foulness
Molescroft
Bishop Burton
Sancton
Kelfield
Ellerton
Skipwith
Holme-on-Spalding-Moor
Woodmansey
Aughton
Cawood
Riccall
North Duffield
Harlthorpe
Foggathorpe
North Cliffe
North Newbald
Walkington
Wistow
Bubwith
South Cliffe
High Hunsley
Bentley
Gunby
Willitoft
River Derwent
COTTINGHAM
Barlby
Osgodby
Breighton
Spaldington
Bursea
Hotham
Little Weighton
Skidby
Selby
Toll
Lund
South Duffield
North Cave
Wressle
Riplingham
Cliffe
Hemingbrough
Brind
Portington
West End
South Cave
Willerby
Thorpe Willoughby
Brayton
Sandholme
Gilberdyke
Newport
Walling Fen
Selby Canal
Newsholme
Howden
Eastrington
Staddlethorpe
Ellerker
Brantingham
Kirk Ella
Barlow
Burn
Long Drax
Barmby on the Marsh
Elloughton
Swanland
Asselby
Balkholme
Anlaby
Chapel Haddlesey
Camblesforth
Drax
Kilpin
Welton
Temple Hirst
Broomfleet
Brough
Laxton
North Ferriby
HESSLE
Hirst Courtney
Newland
Carlton
Airmyn
Hook
Saltmarshe
Blacktoft
Faxfleet
Hensall
Humber Bridge
Whitton
GOOLE
River Aire
Yokefleet
BARTON-UPON-HUMBER
Reedness
Ousefleet
Barrow upon Humber
Snaith
Rawcliffe
Swinefleet
Whitgift
Alkborough
Read's I.
Gowdall
Great Heck
Cowick
Rawcliffe Bridge
Dutch River
South Channel
Winteringham
West Halton
Adlingfleet
Southfield Resr
Aire & Calder Navigation
Pollington
Marshland
South Ferriby
Goole Fields
Coleby
Kingsforth
Fockerby
Balne
Garthorpe
Thealby
Winterton
Horkstowe
Thornton Curtis
River Went
Burton upon Stather
River Trent
Saxby All Saints
Burnham
Fenwick
Skyehouse
Roxby
Wootton
Moorends
Eastoft
Luddington
Normanby
Thorne Waste or Moors
Flixborough
Risby
Appleby
Bonby
Moss
Fishlake
Amcotts
Worlaby
Askern
Thorne
Crowle
Santon
Old River Ancholme
Weir Dike
Land Drain
New River Ancholme
Ermine Street
Kirk Bramwith
Keadby
Elsham
Melton Ross
Gunness
Crosby
Stainforth & Keadby Canal
Thorpe in Balne
Stainforth
Ealand
SCUNTHORPE
Hatfield
Althorpe
Barnetby le Wold
Dunscroft
Hatfield Chase
Broughton
Wrawby
Barnby Dun
Derrythorpe
Dunsville
Hatfield Woodhouse
Sandtoft
Burringham
Brumby
Ashby
Bottesford
Yaddlethorpe
Kirk Sandall
Westgate
Belton
Beltoft
Arksey
Edenthorpe
Butterwick
Scawby
BRIGG
Bigby
Searby
Armthorpe
Hatfield Moors
ISLE OF AXHOLME
Grasby
Howsham
DONCASTER
Nutwell
Epworth
Messingham
Cantley
Wroot
Manton
Cadney
Scotterthorpe
Hibaldstow
North Kelsey Beck
River Torne
Low Burnham
Susworth
Branton
Auckley
North Kelsey
Bessacarr
Blaxton
Owston Ferry
Scotter
Redbourne
Haxey
East Ferry
Kirton in Lindsey
Moortown
Loversall
Finningley
Westwoodside
East Lound
Scotton
Rossington
South Kelsey
New Rossington
Graizelound
Wildsworth
Holton le Moor
River Idle
Laughton
Northorpe
Waddingham
Thornton le Moor
Grayingham
West Stockwith
Misson
Misterton
East Stockwith
Blyton
Blyborough
North Owersby
Snitterby
Austerfield
Tickhill
Bawtry
Walkeringham
Walkerith
Pilham
Aisby
Willoughton
Usselby
Kirkby
Osgodby
Harworth
Bircotes
Scaftworth
Everton
Gringley on the Hill
Morton
Corringham
Bishop Norton
Hemswell
Scrooby
Glentham
Wiseton
GAINSBOROUGH
Harpswell
Middle Rasen
West Rasen
Oldcotes
Mattersey
Priory
Beckingham
Springthorpe
Normanby-by-Spital
Tealby
Ranskill
Clayworth
Saundby
Heapham
Glentworth
Tofts next Newton
Langold
Bole
Owmby-by-Spital
Newton by Toft
Letwell
Blyth
Torworth
North Wheatley
Lea
Upton
Fillingham
Carlton
Lound
Hayton
Kexby
Saxby
Canal
M 62
M 18
M 180
M 181
A 1(M)
A 1(T)
A 19
A 19(T)
A 59
A 64(T)
A 63
A 63(T)
A 166
A 163
A 164
A 614
A 1079(T)
A 1034
A 1035
A 1174
A 1105
A 1077
A 15
A 15(T)
A 18
A 161
A 159
A 1029
A 631
A 638
A 614(T)
A 630
A 60
A 634
A 156
A 46
A 1103
A 1084
A 180
A 1237
A 1036
B 1248
B 1249
B 1246
B 1228
B 1222
B 1230
B 1233
B 1231
B 1206
B 1218
B 1204
B 1207
B 1208
B 1398
B 1400
B 1450
B 1216
B 1205
B 1434
B 1396
B 1403
B 6463
B 6045
67
68
59
60
5
4
3
2
1
0
9
6
7
8

Great Kelk
Lissett
Ulrome
Skipsea
Castle
Beeford
North Frodingham
Dunnington
Atwick
HORNSEA
Brandesburton
Seaton
Hornsea Mere
Rolston
Sigglesthorne
Leven
Catwick
Goxhill
Mappleton
Rise
Great Hatfield
Long Riston
Withernwick
Meaux
New Ellerby
South Skirlaugh
Old Ellerby
West Newton
Aldbrough
Burton Constable
Holderness Drain
Swine
Coniston
Flinton
Garton
Ganstead
Sproatley
Humbleton
Sutton on Hull
Bilton
Lelley
Owstwick
Elstronwick
Tunstall
Preston
Burton Pidsea
Roos
Marfleet
Waxholme
KINGSTON UPON HULL
HEDON
Burstwick
Rimswell
WITHERNSEA
Halsham
Thorngumbald
Paull
Keyingham
Ottringham
Winestead
Hollym
East Halton Skitter
Paull Holme Sands
Foulholme Sands
Cherry Cobb Sands
Salthaugh Grange
Patrington
Holmpton
Out Newton
Welwick
Skeffling
Easington
Sunk Island
The Old Hall
Sunk Island Sands
Kilnsea
RIVER HUMBER
Goxhill
East Halton
Killingholme
Oil Refinery
Ulceby
Habrough
Immingham
Croxton
Kirmington
Brocklesby
Stallingborough
GRIMSBY
SPURN HEAD
Bull
Spurn
Humber
MOUTH OF THE HUMBER
Healing
Keelby
Great Limber
Great Coates
CLEETHORPES
Aylesby
R. Freshney
Riby
Laceby
Bradley
Scartho
Humberston
Irby Upon Humber
Barnoldby le Beck
New Waltham
Holton le Clay
Swallow
Waltham
Caboume
Beelsby
Brigsley
Tetney Lock
Caistor
Ashby cum Fenby
Cuxwold
Hatcliffe
Tetney
North Cotes
Nettleton
Rothwell
Grainsby
Marshchapel
East Ravendale
Donna Nook
North Thoresby
Fulstow
Grainthorpe
Thorganby
Thoresway
Wold Newton
Covenham Resr
North Somercotes
Swinhope
Canal
Ludborough
Covenham St Bartholomew
Normanby le Wold
Claxby
Stainton le Vale
Binbrook
Covenham St Mary
South Somercotes
Saltfleet
Utterby
Kirmond le Mire
Yarburgh
North Ormsby
Skidbrooke
Walesby
Fotherby
Alvingham
Saltfleetby St Clement
North Elkington
Tealby
Kelstern
Cockerington
Saltfleetby All Saints
MARKET RASEN
Ludford
South Elkington
Keddington
Saltfleetby St Peter
Theddlethorpe St Helen
North Willingham
Welton le Wold
LOUTH
Grimoldby
Theddlethorpe All Saints
Gas Terminal
Sixhills
Stewton
Manby
Linwood
Legsby
Burgh on Bain
Little Carlton
Great
NORTH SEA
KINGSTON UPON HULL to
Rotterdam (Europoort) 14 hrs
Zeebrugge 15 hrs

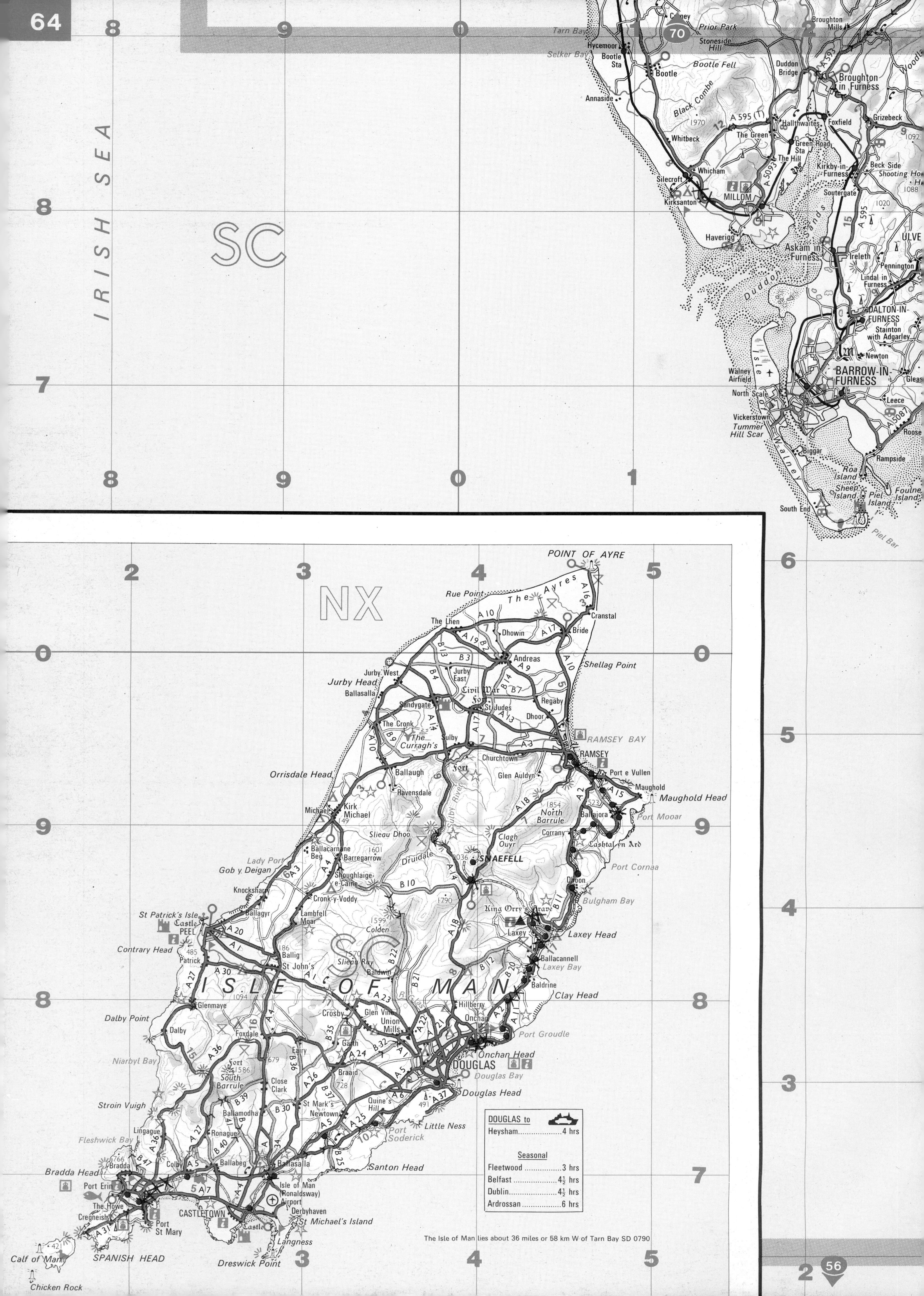
IRISH SEA
SC
NX
70
56
Bootle
Bootle Fell
Black Combe
Broughton in Furness
Whicham
Silecroft
MILLOM
Haverigg
Askam in Furness
Duddon Sands
Isle of Walney
Walney Airfield
BARROW-IN-FURNESS
DALTON-IN-FURNESS
Roa Island
Piel Island
Sheep Island
South End
Rampside
Piel Bar
POINT OF AYRE
The Ayres
Rue Point
Bride
Cranstal
Andreas
Shellag Point
Jurby Head
Jurby West
Jurby East
Sandygate
Civil War Fort
St Judes
The Cronk
The Curragh's
Sulby
RAMSEY BAY
RAMSEY
Port e Vullen
Maughold
Maughold Head
Port Mooar
Orrisdale Head
Ballaugh
Ravensdale
Churchtown
Glen Auldyn
Kirk Michael
North Barrule
Ballajora
Slieau Dhoo
Clagh Ouyr
Cashtal yn Ard
SNAEFELL
Lady Port
Gob y Deigan
Ballacarnane Beg
Barregarrow
Druidale
Port Cornaa
Dhoon
Shoughlaige-e-Caine
Cronk-y-Voddy
Knockshary
Bulgham Bay
King Orry's Grave
Laxey
Laxey Head
St Patrick's Isle
Castle
PEEL
Ballagyr
Lambfell Moar
Colden
Contrary Head
Patrick
Ballig
St John's
Slieau Ruy
Baldwin
Ballacannell
Laxey Bay
Baldrine
Clay Head
ISLE OF MAN
Glenmaye
Dalby Point
Dalby
Foxdale
Crosby
Glen Vine
Union Mills
Hillberry
Onchan
Port Groudle
Niarbyl Bay
South Barrule
Eairy
Garth
Onchan Head
DOUGLAS
Douglas Bay
Douglas Head
Close Clark
Braaid
Stroin Vuigh
Ballamodha
St Mark's
Newtown
Quine's Hill
Little Ness
Port Soderick
Lingague
Fleshwick Bay
Ronague
Bradda Head
Bradda
Colby
Ballabeg
Ballasalla
Santon Head
Port Erin
The Howe
Cregneish
Port St Mary
CASTLETOWN
Isle of Man (Ronaldsway) Airport
Derbyhaven
St Michael's Island
Castle
Langness
Calf of Man
SPANISH HEAD
Dreswick Point
Chicken Rock
DOUGLAS to
Heysham....4 hrs
Seasonal
Fleetwood....3 hrs
Belfast....4½ hrs
Dublin....4½ hrs
Ardrossan....6 hrs
The Isle of Man lies about 36 miles or 58 km W of Tarn Bay SD 0790

MORECAMBE
BAY
Cartmel Wharf
Mort Bank
Lancaster Sound
Yeoman Wharf
Humphrey Head Point
Cartmel Sands
Warton Sands
SD
HEYSHAM to
Douglas 4 hrs
FLEETWOOD to
Douglas 3 hrs
(seasonal)
HEYSHAM LAKE
Shoulder of Lune
Sunderland Point
River Lune
Bernard Wharf
North Wharf
Rossall Point
FLEETWOOD
Knott End-on-Sea
Preesall
Stalmine
Hambleton
CLEVELEYS
THORNTON
POULTON-LE-FYLDE
Bispham
Carleton
North Shore
BLACKPOOL
Normoss
Staining
Great Marton
South Shore
Blackpool Airport
St Annes
Ansdell
Salter's Bank
LYTHAM ST ANNE'S
Lytham
Warton
Warton Aerodrome
Banks Sands
Great Bank
Marshside Sands
Crossens
Banks
Marshside
Churchtown
Mere Brow
Sollom
Tarleton
Hesketh Bank
Hundred End
Becconsall
Longton
Walmer Bridge
Much Hoole
Bretherton
Croston
Hutton
New Longton
Higher Penwortham
PRESTON
FULWOOD
Sharoe Green
Ribbleton
Walton-le-Dale
BAMBER BRIDGE
Farington
Midge Hall
LEYLAND
Clayton-le-Woods
Whittle-le-Woods
Euxton
Gregson Lane
Higher Walton
Brindle
Wheelton
BLACKBURN
Pleasington
Hoghton
Feniscowles
Tockholes
Withnell
Brinscall
DARWEN
Lower Darwen
Ryal Fold
Hoddlesden
Turton Moor
Entwistle Sta
Crowthorn School
Helmshore
HASLINGDEN
Haslingden Grane
ACCRINGTON
OSWALDTWISTLE
CHURCH
CLAYTON-LE-MOORS
RISHTON
GREAT HARWOOD
Baxenden
Belthorn
Rising Bridge
Samlesbury
Samlesbury Aerodrome
Samlesbury Bottoms
Mellor
Mellor Brook
Osbaldeston
Balderston
Salesbury
Wilpshire
Copster Green
Ribchester
Grimsargh
Haighton Green
Goosnargh
LONGRIDGE
Knowle Green
Alston Resr
Hurst Green
Stonyhurst College
New Row
Billington
Whalley
Wiswell
Sabden
Barrow
Pendleton
Great Mitton
CLITHEROE
Chatburn
Worston
Low Moor
Waddington
West Bradford
Grindleton
Sawley
Browsholme Hall
Bashall Eaves
Walker Fold
Hesketh Lane
Chipping
Longridge Fell
Whitechapel
Inglewhite
Beacon Fell
Claughton
Bilsborrow
St Michael's on Wyre
Great Eccleston
Elswick
Inskip
Cuddy Hill
Barton
Broughton
Catforth
Woodplumpton
Roseacre
Wharles
Esprick
Singleton
Weeton
Wesham
KIRKHAM
Treales
Westby
Plumpton
Wrea Green
Salwick Sta
Lea Town
Cottam
Newton
Clifton
Moss Side
Higher Ballam
FRECKLETON
Hardhorn
Out Rawcliffe
Ratten Row
Nateby
Garstang
Churchtown
Catterall
Eagland Hill
Pilling
Pilling Lane
Stake Pool
Winmarleigh
Cockerham
Braides
Forton
Scorton
Thurnham Hall
Glasson
Overton
Middleton
Heaton
HEYSHAM
Nuclear Power Sta
MORECAMBE
Torrisholme
Hest Bank
Bolton-le-Sands
Slyne
LANCASTER
Scotforth
Galgate
Dolphinholme
Abbeystead
Street
Quernmore
Clougha
Brow Top
Littledale
Haylot Fell
Blanch Fell
Ward's Stone
Mallowdale Fell
Tarnbrook Fell
Tarnbrook
Wolfhole Crag
Lee
Marshaw
Hawthornthwaite Fell
Blaze Moss
Whins Brow
Sykes
Hareden
Dunsop Bridge
Newton
Slaidburn
FOREST OF BOWLAND
Sykes Fell
Bleasdale Moors
Oakenclough
Calder Vale
Fair Snape Fell
Wolf Fell
Whitewell
Easington Fell
Crossdale Fell
White Hill
Stocks Resr
Gisburn Forest
Tosside
Catlow Fell
Bottom Head
Thrushgill
Salter
Goodber Common
Tatham Fells
Burn Moor
Burn Moor Fell
Lowgill
Whit Moor
Caton Moor
Caton
Brookhouse
Crossgill
Claughton
Halton
Aughton
Nether Kellet
Over Kellet
Capernwray
CARNFORTH
Borwick
Warton
Yealand Conyers
Yealand Redmayne
Priest Hutton
Silverdale
Arnside
Burton-in-Kendal
Holme
Beetham
Storth
Milnthorpe
Heversham
Leasgill
Levens
Sedgwick
Gatebeck
Stainton
Endmoor
Crooklands
Hincaster
Natland
Oxenholme
Old Hutton
Killington
Middleton
Rigmaden Park
Barbon
Old Town
Lupton
Scout Hill
Farleton
Kearstwick
Hutton Roof
Casterton
KIRKBY LONSDALE
Biggins
Whittington
Newton
Nether Burrow
Cowan Bridge
Ireby
Masongill
Westhouse
Tunstall
Cantsfield
Burton in Lonsdale
Ingleton
Arkholme
Melling
Wennington
Tatham
Hornby
Gressingham
Wray
Low Bentham
High Bentham
Newby
Clapham
Austwick
Lawkland
Keasden
Eldroth
River Wenning
Ingleborough
Simon Fell
Newby Moss
Chapel-le-Dale
Scales Moor
Leck Fell
Bullpot Fm
WHERNSIDE
Crag Hill
Calf Top
Dent
Gawthrop
Cowgill
Stone House
Rise Hill
Garsdale
East Baugh Fell
Millthrop
Ingmire Hall
Deepdale
Blea Moor
Ribble Head
Selside
Grange-over-Sands
Kents Bank
Allithwaite
Flookburgh
Cark
Holker
Cartmel
Lindale
Meathop
Field Broughton
Ayside
High Newton
Witherslack
Witherslack Hall
Mill Side
Cartmel Fell
Bowland Bridge
Crosthwaite
Brigsteer
Sizergh Castle
Lakeside
Finsthwaite
Stavely-in-Cartmel
Newby Bridge
Backbarrow
Haverthwaite
Greenodd
Penny Bridge
Spark Bridge
Colton
Oxen Park
Rusland
Lowick
Broughton Beck
Arrad Foot
Canal Foot
Bardsea
Baycliff
Aldingham
Ravenstown
Water Yeat

East Baugh Fell
Mossdale Moor
Applersett
Hardraw
High Shaw
Sedbusk
Hawes
Askrigg
Newbiggin
Woodhall
Castle
Redmire
Preston-under-Scar
Leyburn
Constable Burton
Garsdale
Rise Hill
Widdale Fell
Gayle
Burtersett
Bainbridge
WENSLEYDALE
Swinithwaite
Bolton Hall
Wensley
Harmby
Spennithorne
Finghall
Cowgill
Dent
Dentdale
Stone House
Wold Fell
Dodd Fell
Wether Fell
ROMAN ROAD
Countersett
Semer Water
Marsett
Carpley Green
Thornton Rust
Aysgarth
West Witton
Middleham
Thornton Steward
Thornton Resr
West Burton
Thoralby
Penhill
Agglethorpe
Coverham
East Witton
River Cover
River Ure
Jervaulx Abbey
Stalling Busk
Newbiggin
Melmerby
Carlton
Caldbergh
Harland Hill
Carlton Moor
Deepdale
Gayle Moor
Cragdale Moor
Bishopdale Beck
Walden
West Scrafton
Ellingstring
Low Ellington
High Ellington
WHERNSIDE
Blea Moor
Cam Fell
Oughtershaw
Beckermonds
Middle Tongue
LANGSTROTHDALE CHASE
Kidstones
Walden Head
Horsehouse
Coverdale
Colsterdale Moor
Colsterdale
Healey
Fearby
Masham
Ribble Head
Cray
Buckden Pike
Cover Head Bents
Braidley
Hindlethwaite Moor
Woodale
Great Haw
Masham Moor
Swinton
Ilton
Scales Moor
Sike Moor
Cam Beck
Hubberholme
Buckden
Little Whernside
Scar House Resr
Brown Ridge
Leighton Resr
Roundhill Resr
Chapel-le-Dale
High Birkwith
Foxup
Halton Gill
Plover Hill
Angram Resr
THE PENNINES
Selside
Simon Fell
Ingleborough
Horton Moor
New Houses
Pen-y-ghent
Litton
Starbotton
Great Whernside
River Skirfare
River Wharfe
Middlesmoor
Lofthouse
Hambleton Hill
Ingleton
Newby Moss
Horton in Ribblesdale
Darnbrook Fell
Littondale
Arncliffe
Kettlewell
Riggs Moor
How Stean Beck
Stean
Greygarth
Dallowgill Moor
Lumley Moor Resr
Newby
Moughton
Fountains Fell
Hawkswick
Conistone Moor
Stean Moor
Nidderdale
Ramsgill
Clapham
Austwick
Wharfe
Helwith Bridge
Grassington Moor
Goathwaite Resr
Heathfield Moor
Wath
Pateley Moor
River Wenning
Feizor
Lawkland
Stainforth
Malham Tarn
Kilnsey
Conistone
Hebden Moor
Keasden
Eldroth
Stackhouse
Langcliffe
Bordley
Grassington
Grimwith Resr
Pateley Bridge
Bewerley
Wilsill
Glasshouses
Burn Moor Fell
Giggleswick
Settle
Kirkby Fell
Malham
Threshfield
Hebden
River Dibb
Greenhow Hill
Burn Moor
Wham
Linton
River Wharfe
Hanlith
Thorpe
Burnsall
Dacre Banks
Catlow Fell
Black Hill
Mearbeck
Kirkby Malham
Winterburn Resr
Cracoe
Appletreewick
Pock Stones Moor
River Washburn
Dacre
Rathmell
Long Preston
Airton
Calton
Hetton
Rylstone
Barden Resrs
Earl Seat
Barden Fell
Brown Bank Head
Thornthwaite
Long Gill
Otterburn
Winterburn
West End
Thruscross Resr
Gisburn Forest
Wigglesworth
Ribblesdale
Hellifield
Bell Busk
Flasby
Embsay Moor
Forest
Stocks Resr
Tosside
Tosside Beck
Eshton
Coniston Cold
Halton East
Bolton Abbey
Bolton Priory
Blubberhouses
Fewston Resr
Fewston
SD
Halton West
Ribble
Gargrave
Embsay Resr
Embsay
Round Hill
Swinsty Resr
Slaidburn
Nappa
Bank Newton
Thorlby
Draughton
Beamsley
Timble
River Hodder
Paythorne
Newsholme
West Marton
East Marton
Broughton
Chelker Resr
Langbar
March Ghyll Resr
Jack Hill
Horton
SKIPTON
Easington Fell
Holden
Bolton-by-Bowland
Gisburn
Bracewell
Elslack
Carleton
Addingham
Middleton
ILKLEY
Denton
Askwith
Weston
Farnley
OTLEY
Thornton-in-Craven
Low Bradley
RUMBALDS MOOR
WHARFEDALE
Sawley
Abbey
BARNOLDSWICK
EARBY
Cononley
Kildwick
SILSDEN
Ilkley Moor
Burley in Wharfedale
Grindleton
West Bradford
Rimington
Salterforth
Kelbrook
Lothersdale
AIREDALE
Glusburn
Steeton
Menston
Waddington
Downham
Weets Hill
Whitemoor Resr
Sutton-in-Craven
Riddlesden
East Morton
GUISELEY
Chatburn
Worston
Foulridge
Cowling
Utley
Low Moor
CLITHEROE
Pendle Hill
Blacko
Laneshaw Resr
Laycock
KEIGHLEY
River Aire
Hawksworth
YEADON
Rawdon
Roughlee
Barley
COLNE
Laneshaw Bridge
Eldwick
BAILDON
Great Mitton
Pendleton
Churn Clough Resr
Newchurch in Pendle
BARROWFORD
TRAWDEN
KEIGHLEY MOOR
Oakworth
BINGLEY
Leeds & Liverpool Canal
Barrow
Sabden
THE FOREST OF PENDLE
Wheatley Lane
THE FOREST OF TRAWDEN
Harden
Cullingworth
Wilsden
SHIPLEY
Calverley
Wiswell
Whalley
NELSON
Fence
Sabden Brook
Haworth
Billington
Higham
BRIERFIELD
Boulsworth Hill
Oxenhope
Farsley
Read
Gawthorpe Hall
Harle Syke
Swinden Resr
Haworth Moor
Denholme
Langho
Simonstone
PADIHAM
Walshaw Dean Resrs
Wadsworth Moor
Thornton
GREAT HARWOOD
Altham
BURNLEY
Worsthorne
Thornton Moor Resr
Clayton
Wilpshire
Calder
Hurstwood Resr
Widdop Resr
Hebden Water
Warley Moor Resr
BRADFORD
CLAYTON-LE-MOORS
Hapton
Huncoat
Towneley Hall
Gorple Resrs
Brownhill
RISHTON
Merecleugh
Heptonstall Moor
QUEENSBURY
Buttershaw
Birkenshaw
CHURCH
Hameldon Hill
Clowbridge Resr
Walk Mill
Holme Chapel
Pecket Well
Slack
Shelf
Oakenshaw
ACCRINGTON
Due to open Early 1986
Dunnockshaw
Deerplay Moor
Heptonstall
Wainstalls
Illingworth
Ovenden
Northowram
Wyke
OSWALDTWISTLE
Baxenden
Love Clough
Heald Moor
Mytholm
HEBDEN BRIDGE
Midgley
Luddenden
Hipperholme
CLECKHEATON
Gomersal
Rising Bridge
FOREST OF ROSSENDALE
Weir
Cornholme
Lydgate
Eastwood
Mytholmroyd
HALIFAX
Belthorn
Crawshawbooth
Clough Foot
Lower Darwen
HASLINGDEN
Haslingden Grane
Acre
RAWTENSTALL
BACUP
Britannia
TODMORDEN
Mankinholes
Cragg Vale
Southowram
LIVERSEDGE
HECKMONDWIKE
BRIGHOUSE
Sowerby
SOWERBY BRIDGE
Greetland
Hoddlesden
Ogden Resr
Helmshore
Stacksteads
Waterfoot
Gorpley Resr
Walsden
Withens Clough Resr
Warland Resr
Lumb
Mill Bank
Robertown
Rastrick
ELLAND
Ravensthorpe
Barkisland
Stainland
Holywell Green
MIRFIELD
Upper Hopton
Shawforth
Warland
Soyland Moor
RIPPONDEN
Edenfield
Cowm Resr
Water
Watergrove Resr
WHITWORTH
Entwistle
Crowthorn School
Stubbins
Summit
Calderbrook
Rochdale Canal

Helmsley Moor
HAMBLETON HILLS
Bedale
Aiskew
Leeming
Northallerton
Thirsk
Sowerby
Kilburn
Byland Abbey
Coxwold
Newburgh Priory
Rievaulx Abbey
Helmsley
Kirkbymoorside
Hovingham
Howardian Hills
Easingwold
Ripon
Fountains Abbey
Newby Hall
Boroughbridge
Aldborough
Knaresborough
Harrogate
Marston Moor 1644
Wetherby
Tadcaster
York
Haxby
Strensall
Stamford Bridge
Dunnington
Fulford
Bishopthorpe
Selby
Sherburn in Elmet
Castleford
Pontefract
Knottingley
Wakefield
Leeds
Pudsey
Morley
Dewsbury
Batley
Horsforth
Rothwell
Normanton
Featherstone
Snaith
Rawcliffe
Drax
Howden
Due to open Early 1986
Due to open Mid 1987
SE

WHITBY
Saltwick Bay
Stainsacre
Sneaton
Hawsker
Ugglebarnby
Ness Point or North Cheek
Sneatonthorpe
Fylingthorpe
Robin Hood's Bay
Old Peak or South Cheek
Ravenscar
Fylingdales Moor
Burn Howe Rigg
Staintondale
Harwood Dale
Cloughton Newlands
Cloughton Wyke
Cloughton
Cromer Point
Burniston
Silpho
Langdale End
Toll
SCALBY
Scalby Ness Rocks
Hackness
Everley
Castle
SCARBOROUGH
Black Rocks
Osgodby
Cayton Bay
Eastfield
Sawdon
Hutton Buscel
Ayton
Irton
Ebberston
Seamer
Cayton
The Wyke
Snainton
Wykeham
Brompton
Lebberston
Gristhorpe
FILEY
Filey Bay
R Hertford
Flixton
Folkton
Yedingham
THE CARRS
Willerby
Staxton
Muston
Ganton
Sherburn
Holiday Camp
Hunmanby
East Heslerton
West Heslerton
Reighton Sands
Fordon
Reighton
Speeton
Crab Rocks
Wintringham
Wold Newton
Foxholes
Burton Fleming
Bempton
Danes Dyke
Holiday Camp
FLAMBOROUGH HEAD
Place Newton
Butterwick
Willy Howe
Grindale
Flamborough
Helperthorpe
Weaverthorpe
Thwing
Gypsey Race
Duggleby
West Lutton
Boynton
Sewerby
Kirby Grindalythe
Duggleby Howe
Langtoft
Rudston
BRIDLINGTON
ROMAN ROAD
Carnaby
Hilderthorpe
Sledmere
Kilham
Haisthorpe
BRIDLINGTON BAY
THE WOLDS
Burdale
Hall
Burton Agnes
Harpham
Fraisthorpe
Ruston Parva
Fimber
Lowthorpe
Gransmoor
Barmston
Fridaythorpe
Wetwang
Garton-on-the-Wolds
Nafferton
Lissett
GREAT DRIFFIELD
Kelk Beck
Great Kelk
Ulrome
Wansford
Foston on the Wolds
Old Howe
Huggate
Tibthorpe
Kirkburn
Skerne
Castle
Skipsea
Canal
Beeford
Brigham
North Frodingham
North Dalton
Bainton
Hutton Cranswick
Rotsea
Dunnington
Hempholme
Bewholme
Atwick
Middleton-on-the-Wolds
Watton
Watton Beck
Kilnwick
Burshill
HORNSEA
Lund
Beswick
Lockington
Brandesburton
Seaton
Holme on the Wolds
Aike
River Hull
Hornsea Mere
South Dalton
Scorborough
Sigglesthorpe
Rolston
Canal
Leven
Catwick
Etton
Arram
Goxhill
Mappleton
Goodmanham
Leconfield
Routh
Great Hatfield
Cherry Burton
Long Riston
Rise
Tickton
Market
Withernwick
BEVERLEY
NORTH SEA
OV
TA
A 171
A 165
A 170
A 1039
A 64(T)
A 166
A 163
A 164
A 1035
A 1079(T)
B 1416
B 1261
B 1258
B 1249
B 1229
B 1255
B 1259
B 1253
B 1254
B 1248
B 1251
B 1252
B 1242
B 1244
B 1243
B 1246
62
63

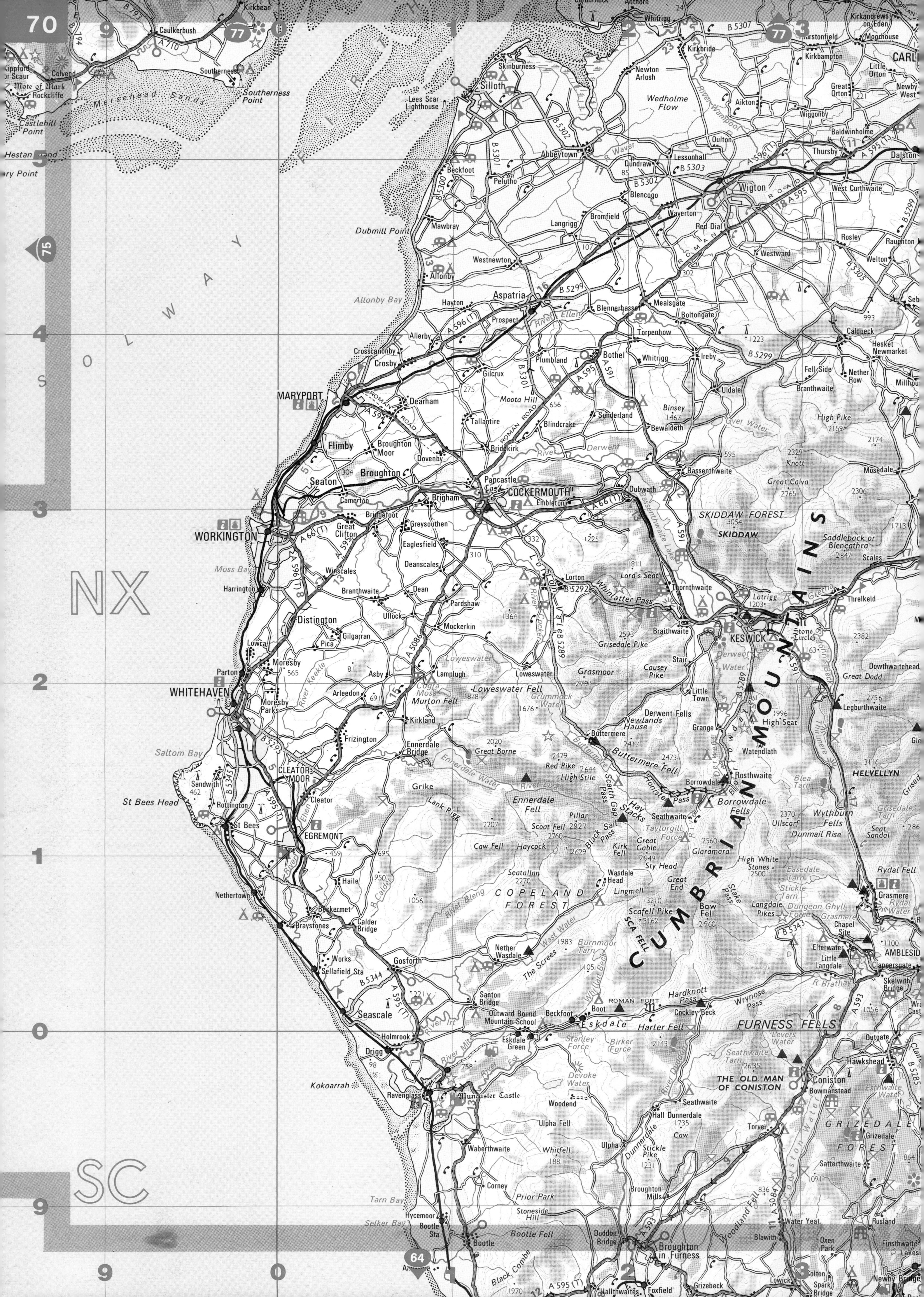

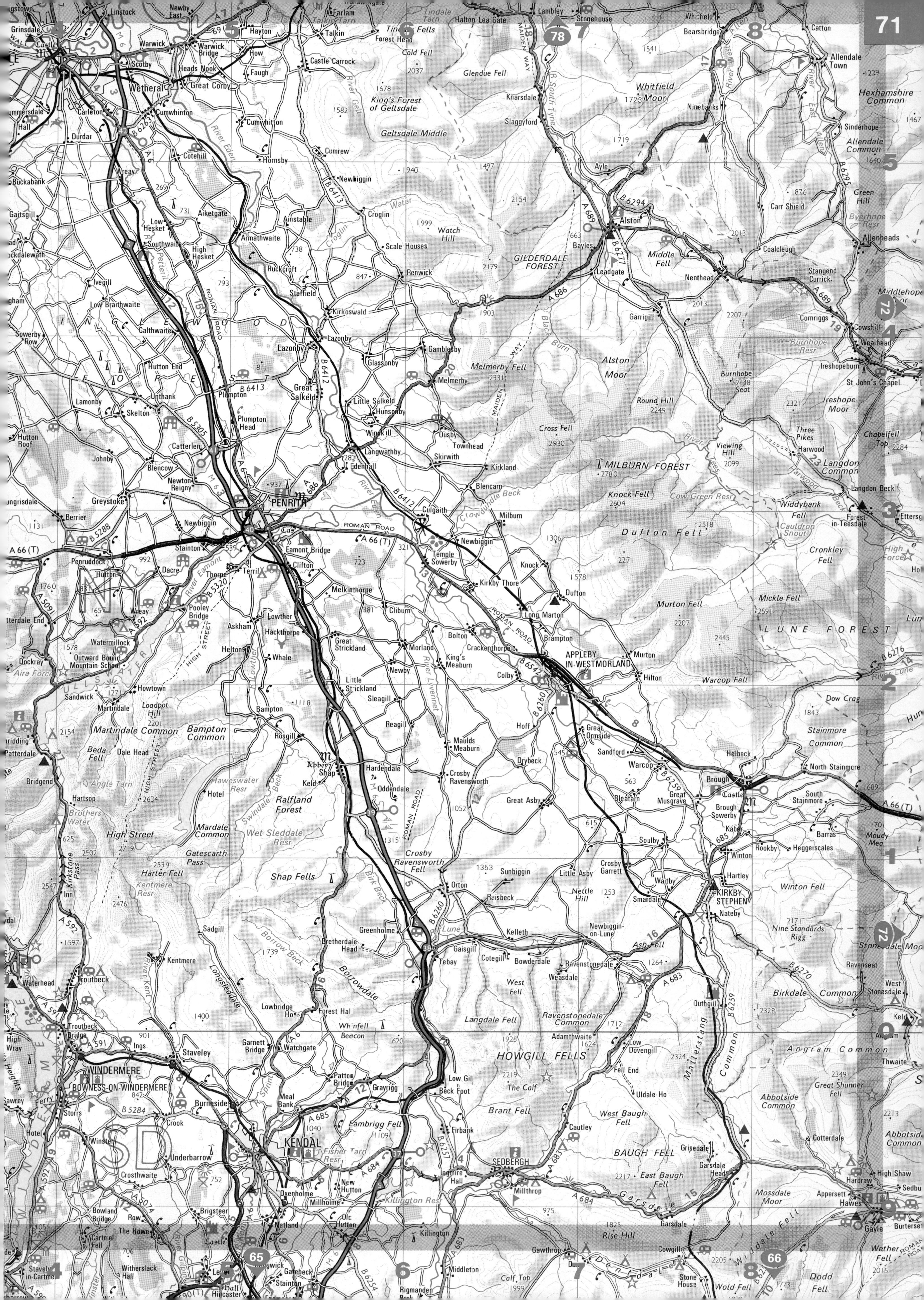
Linstock
Newby East
Grinsdale
Hayton
Farlam
Tindale
Talkin Tarn
Talkin
Tindale Fells
Forest Head
Halton Lea Gate
Lambley
Stonehouse
Whitfield
Bearsbridge
Catton
Allendale Town
Warwick
Warwick Bridge
Scotby
How
Heads Nook
Castle Carrock
Cold Fell
Glendue Fell
Whitfield Moor
Wetheral
Great Corby
Faugh
King's Forest of Geltsdale
Knarsdale
Ninebanks
Hexhamshire Common
Carleton
Cumwhinton
Cumwhitton
Slaggyford
Sinderhope
Durdar
Geltsdale Middle
Allendale Common
Cotehill
Cumrew
Hornsby
Ayle
Wreay
Newbiggin
Buckabank
Croglin
Alston
Green Hill
Carr Shield
Byerhope Resr
Gaitsgill
Low Hesket
Aiketgate
Ainstable
Watch Hill
Allenheads
Southwaite
Armathwaite
Scale Houses
Bayles
Middle Fell
Coalcleugh
High Hesket
Ruckcroft
GILDERDALE FOREST
Leadgate
Renwick
Nenthead
Stangend Currick
Ivegill
Staffield
Middlehope
Low Braithwaite
Kirkoswald
Garrigill
Cornriggs
Cowshill
INGLEWOOD FOREST
Calthwaite
Lazonby
Gamblesby
Alston Moor
Wearhead
Sowerby Row
Burnhope Resr
Glassonby
Melmerby Fell
Melmerby
Ireshopeburn
Hutton End
Burnhope Seat
St John's Chapel
Plumpton
Great Salkeld
Round Hill
Ireshope Moor
Unthank
Little Salkeld
Lamonby
Skelton
Hunsonby
Plumpton Head
Cross Fell
Three Pikes
Hutton Roof
Ousby
Viewing Hill
Chapelfell Top
Winskill
Townhead
Harwood
Catterlen
Langwathby
Skirwith
MILBURN FOREST
Langdon Common
Johnby
Blencow
Edenhall
Kirkland
Newton Reigny
Blencarn
Langdon Beck
Knock Fell
Cow Green Resr
Widdybank Fell
Greystoke
PENRITH
Culgaith
Forest in-Teesdale
Berrier
Newbiggin
Milburn
Cauldron Snout
Dufton Fell
Stainton
Eamont Bridge
Temple Sowerby
Cronkley Fell
High Force
Penruddock
Hutton
Dacre
Clifton
Knock
Thorpe
Terril
Kirkby Thore
Dufton
Melkinthorpe
Murton Fell
Mickle Fell
Pooley Bridge
Lowther
Cliburn
Long Marton
Wreay
Askham
Hackthorpe
Bolton
Crackenthorpe
Brampton
LUNE FOREST
Watermillock
Helton
Great Strickland
Morland
Outward Bound Mountain School
Whale
King's Meaburn
APPLEBY-IN-WESTMORLAND
Murton
Dockray
Aira Force
ULLSWATER
Newby
Colby
Hilton
Warcop Fell
Howtown
Little Strickland
Sandwick
Martindale
Loadpot Hill
Sleagill
Dow Crag
Bampton
Martindale Common
Bampton Common
Reagill
Hoff
Great Ormside
Stainmore Common
Patterdale
Beda Fell
Dale Head
Rosgill
Maulds Meaburn
Sandford
Warcop
Helbeck
North Stainmore
Bridgend
Angle Tarn
Haweswater Resr
Shap
Hardendale
Drybeck
Crosby Ravensworth
Brough
Castle
Hartsop
Hotel
Ralfland Forest
Keld
Oddendale
Great Asby
Bleatarn
Great Musgrave
Brough Sowerby
South Stainmore
Brothers Water
Swindale Beck
Mardale Common
Wet Sleddale Resr
Kaber
Barras
High Street
Soulby
Winton
Rookby
Heggerscales
Moudy Mea
Gatescarth Pass
Crosby Ravensworth Fell
Sunbiggin
Little Asby
Crosby Garrett
Harter Fell
Shap Fells
Hartley
Kentmere Resr
Orton
Raisbeck
Nettle Hill
Waitby
KIRKBY STEPHEN
Winton Fell
Kirkstone Pass
Inn
Smardale
Nateby
Sadgill
Borrow Beck
Greenholme
Bretherdale Head
Kelleth
Newbiggin-on-Lune
Nine Standards Rigg
Stonesdale Moor
Tebay
Gaisgill
Cotegill
Bowderdale
Ash Fell
Ravenseat
Waterhead
Troutbeck
Kentmere
Borrowdale
Ravenstonedale
Weasdale
West Fell
Outhgill
West Stonesdale
Longsleddale
Birkdale Common
Lowbridge Ho
Forest Hal
Whinfell Beacon
Langdale Fell
Ravenstonedale Common
Keld
Troutbeck Bridge
Ings
Staveley
Garnett Bridge
Watchgate
Adamthwaite
Low Dovengill
Mallerstang Common
High Wray
WINDERMERE
HOWGILL FELLS
Angram Common
Thwaite
BOWNESS-ON-WINDERMERE
Patton Bridge
Grayrigg
Low Gill
Beck Foot
Fell End
The Calf
Great Shunner Fell
Storrs
Burneside
Meal Bank
Uldale Ho
Abbotside Common
Crook
Lambrigg Fell
Brant Fell
West Baugh Fell
Hotel
Winster
KENDAL
Fisher Tarn Resr
Firbank
Caution
Cotterdale
Underbarrow
BAUGH FELL
Grisedale
Crosthwaite
SEDBERGH
Garsdale Head
High Shaw
Oxenholme
Ingmire Hall
East Baugh Fell
Hardraw
New Hutton
Millthrop
Mossdale Moor
Appersett
Bowland Bridge
Row
Brigsteer
Millholme
Killington Resr
Garsdale
Hawes
The Howe
Natland
Old Hutton
Rise Hill
Gayle
Burtersett
Cartmel Fell
Killington
Widdale Fell
Witherslack Hall
Levens
Gatebeck
Gawthrop
Cowgill
Dentdale
Wether Fell
Staveley-in-Cartmel
Stainton
Middleton
Calf Top
Stone House
Dodd Fell
Hincaster
Rigmaden
Wold Fell
SD
NY
65
66
72
78

SUNDERLAND
NORTH SEA
SEAHAM
HOUGHTON LE-SPRING
HETTON-LE-HOLE
PETERLEE
NZ
HARTLEPOOL
Tees Bay
BILLINGHAM
REDCAR
MARSKE-BY-THE-SEA
SALTBURN-BY-THE-SEA
STOCKTON-ON TEES
MIDDLESBROUGH
GUISBOROUGH
LOFTUS
Whitby
NORTH YORK MOORS
CLEVELAND HILLS
SE
NORTHALLERTON
Kirkbymoorside

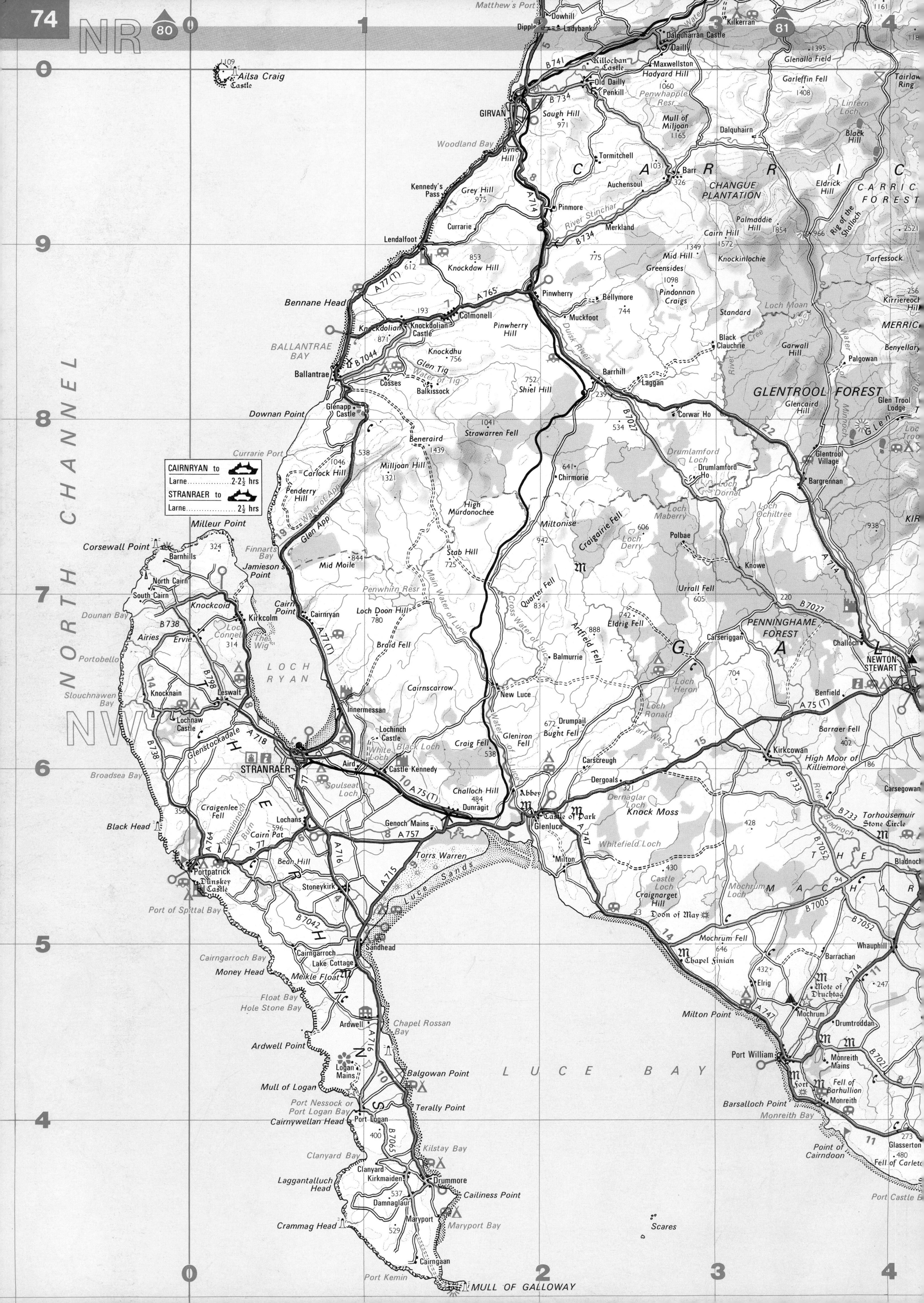
NR
80
81
NW
CAIRNRYAN to
Larne.............2-2½ hrs
STRANRAER to
Larne.............2½ hrs
NORTH CHANNEL
Ailsa Craig
Castle
Matthew's Port
Dowhill
Dipple
Ladybank
Kilkerran
Dalquharran Castle
Dailly
Maxwellston
Killochan Castle
Hadyard Hill
Old Dailly
Penkill
Penwhapple Resr
GIRVAN
Saugh Hill
Mull of Miljoan
Dalquhairn
Glenalla Field
Garleffin Fell
Tairlaw Ring
Linfern Loch
Black Hill
Woodland Bay
Byne Hill
Tormitchell
Barr
CHANGUE PLANTATION
Kennedy's Pass
Grey Hill
Auchensoul
Eldrick Hill
CARRICK FOREST
Pinmore
River Stinchar
Palmaddie Hill
Rig of the Shalloch
Currarie
Merkland
Cairn Hill
Lendalfoot
Knockdaw Hill
Mid Hill
Knockinlochie
Tarfessock
Greensides
Pindonnan Craigs
Pinwherry
Bellymore
Kirriereoch Hill
Bennane Head
Colmonell
Muckfoot
Standard
Loch Moan
MERRICK
Knockdolian
Knockdolian Castle
Pinwherry Hill
Dusk River
Black Clauchrie
River Cree
Garwall Hill
Benyellary
BALLANTRAE BAY
Knockdhu
Glen Tig
Water of Tig
Palgowan
Ballantrae
Cosses
Balkissock
Shiel Hill
Barrhill
Laggan
GLENTROOL FOREST
Glencaird Hill
Glen Trool Lodge
Downan Point
Glenapp Castle
Corwar Ho
Strawarren Fell
Beneraird
Currarie Port
Carlock Hill
Milljoan Hill
Chirmorie
Drumlamford Loch
Drumlamford Ho
Loch Dornal
Glentrool Village
Bargrennan
Penderry Hill
Water of App
High Murdonochee
Loch Maberry
Loch Ochiltree
Milleur Point
Glen App
Miltonise
Craigairie Fell
Loch Derry
Polbae
Corsewall Point
Barnhills
Finnarts Bay
Jamieson's Point
Mid Moile
Stab Hill
Knowe
North Cairn
South Cairn
Knockcoid
Kirkcolm
Penwhirn Resr
Main Water of Luce
Cross Water of Luce
Quarter Fell
Urrall Fell
Dounan Bay
Cairn Point
Cairnryan
Loch Doon Hill
Eldrig Fell
PENNINGHAME FOREST
Airies
Ervie
Loch Connell
The Wig
Artfield Fell
Carseriggan
Challoch
NEWTON STEWART
Portobello
Braid Fell
Balmurrie
LOCH RYAN
Slouchnawen Bay
Knocknain
Leswalt
Cairnscarrow
Loch Heron
Benfield
Lochnaw Castle
Innermessan
New Luce
Loch Ronald
Barraer Fell
Glenstockadale
Lochinch Castle
Black Loch
White Loch
Craig Fell
Drumpail
Bught Fell
Gleniron Fell
Tarf Water
Kirkcowan
High Moor of Killiemore
STRANRAER
Aird
Castle Kennedy
Carscreugh
Dergoals
Broadsea Bay
Soulseat Loch
Challoch Hill
Dunragit
Abbey
Glenluce
Castle of Park
Dernaglar Loch
Knock Moss
Carsegowan
Torhousemuir Stone Circle
Craigenlee Fell
Black Head
Cairn Pat
Lochans
Genoch Mains
Whitefield Loch
Bladnoch
Torrs Warren
Bean Hill
Milton
Luce Sands
Portpatrick
Dunskey Castle
Stoneykirk
Castle Loch
Craignarget Hill
Mochrum Loch
Port of Spittal Bay
Doon of May
Cairngarroch Bay
Cairngarroch
Sandhead
Mochrum Fell
Whauphill
Money Head
Lake Cottage
Chapel Finian
Barrachan
Meikle Float
Elrig
Mote of Druchtag
Float Bay
Hole Stone Bay
Milton Point
Mochrum
Drumtroddan
Chapel Rossan Bay
Ardwell
Ardwell Point
LUCE BAY
Port William
Monreith Mains
Logan Mains
Balgowan Point
Fell of Barhullion
Mull of Logan
Fort
Monreith
Port Nessock or Port Logan Bay
Terally Point
Barsalloch Point
Monreith Bay
Cairnywellan Head
Port Logan
Kilstay Bay
Point of Cairndoon
Glasserton
Fell of Carleton
Clanyard Bay
Clanyard
Kirkmaiden
Drummore
Laggantalluch Head
Cailiness Point
Damnaglaur
Port Castle Bay
Crammag Head
Maryport
Maryport Bay
Scares
Cairngaan
Port Kemin
MULL OF GALLOWAY

NS
NX
Windy Standard
Craignane
Blacklorg Hill
Corse Hill
Durisdeer
Big Hill of Glenmount
Loch Muck
Campbell's Hill
CARSPHAIRN
Brockloch Rig
Windy Standard
Polskeoch
Countam
Cairnkinna Hill
Enoch
Benbrack
Waterhead Hill
Alhang
Ox Hill
Blackcraig Hill
Chanlockfoot
FOREST
Drumlanrig Castle
Holestane
Morton Castle
Bellybought Hill
Loch Finlas
Lamford Hill
Cairnsmore of Carsphairn
Colt Hill
Countam
Tibber's Castle
Carronbridge
Loch Bradan Resr
Loch Doon
Dodd Hill
Big Corlae
Benbrack
Auchenbrack
Gatelawbridge
Craiglee
Castle
Black Craig
Beninner
Benbuie
Shinnel Water
Scar Water
Burnhead
Thornhill
Penpont
Dalwhat Water
Bennan
Manquhill Hill
Wether Hill
Water of Ken
Carsphairn
Fort
Tynron
Keir Mill
Great Hill
Loch Riecawr
Cairn Avel
Marscalloch Hill
Closeburn
Loch Macaterick
Meaul
Gala Lane
Keir Hills
Moniaive
Kirkland
Motte of Dinning
Macaterick
Gairy Craig
Knowehead
Kendoon Loch
Culmark Hill
Castlemaddy
Thorny Hill
THE GLENKENS
Glenhoul
Wether Hill
DALMACALLAN FOREST
Mullwharchar
Corserine
Loch Harrow
Forrest Lodge
Carsfad Loch
Bogrie Hill
Loch Enoch
Round Loch of the Dungeon
RHINNS OF KELLS
Millfire
Loch Dungeon
Earlstoun
Lochinvar
Loch Urr
Dunscore
Dalswinton
L. Neldricken
Earlstoun Loch
Blackcraig Hill
Cairn Water
Steilston Hill
L. Valley
Cooran Lane
Drumbuie
Bogue
Barr Hill
Glenlee
St John's Town of Dalry
Loch Dee
Brockloch Hill
Bennan
Balmaclellan
Cairngarroch
NEW GALLOWAY
Kenmure Castle
Terregles
Darnaw
Clatteringshaws Loch
Cairnsmore or Black Craig of Dee
Benbrack
Craig
Corsock
Shawhead
Brockloch Hill
Ironmacannie
Cargenbridge
Knocknevis
River Dee or Black Water of Dee
Lochfoot
CAIRN EDWARD
Loch Ken
Drumrash
Crocketford or Ninemile Bar
Lochrutton Loch
Round Fell
Shaw Hill
Auchenreoch Loch
Milton Loch
Auchinleck
Fell of Fleet
FOREST
Mossdale
Parton
Urr Water
Craignelder
Stroan Loch
Mabie
Lochaber Loch
Kirkpatrick Durham
Springholm
Milton
Loch Grannoch
Airie Hill
Beeswing
Palnure Burn
Craiglowrie
Loch Skerrow
Woodhall Loch
Tower
Loch Arthur
CAIRNSMORE OF FLEET
Old Bridge of Urr
Lotus Hill
Sweetheart Abbey
Crossmichael
Clarebrand
Haugh of Urr
Kirkgunzeon
L O W A Y
Lochenbreck Loch
Laurieston
Townhead of Greenlaw
Clints of Dromore
LAURIESTON FOREST
Mote of Urr
Long Fell
Palnure
Big Water of Fleet
White Top of Culreoch
Glentoo Loch
Bargatton Loch
Threave Castle
CASTLE DOUGLAS
Meikle Hard Hill
Cree
Carlingwark Loch
DALBEATTIE
Maidenpap
Boreland Hill
Loch Whinyeon
Pibble Hill
Stey Fell
Bengray
GLENGAP FOREST
Loch Mannoch
Bridge of Dee
Rhonehouse or Kelton Hill
Creetown
Miefield
Gelston
DALBEATTIE FOREST
Caulkerbush
Glen
Ringford
Palnackie
Wigtown Sands
Cairnharrow
GATEHOUSE OF FLEET
WIGTOWN
Anwoth
Screel Hill
Tower
Kippford or Scaur
Colvend
Carsluith
Cairn Holy
Cardoness Castle
Twynholm
Bengairn
Mote of Mark
Rockcliffe
Castle
Tongland
Rough Island
Mersehead Sands
Baldoon Sands
Girthon
Due to open Early 1986
Barcloy Hill
Castlehill Point
Ravenshall Point
Sandgreen
Fleet Bay
KIRKCUDBRIGHT
Auchencairn
Auchencairn Bay
Hestan Island
Islands of Fleet
Innerwell Port
Knockbrex
St Mary's Isle
Kirkcarswell
Balcary Point
Borgue
Rascarrel
Rascarrel Bay
Garlieston
WIGTOWN BAY
Dundrennan
Abbey
Orroland
Eggerness Point
Townhead
Borness
Ross
Kirkcudbright Bay
Netherlaw
Port Mary
Borness Point
Balmae
Wall Hill
Abbey Head
Little Ross
Port Allen
Priory
Portyerrock Bay
Cairn Head
Isle of Whithorn
St Ninian's Chapel
BURROW HEAD
S O L W
A702
A713
A762
A712
A702
A713
A75(T)
A711
A755
A710
A746
A750
A747
B729
B7000
B794
B795
B793
B796
B736
B727
B7004
B7052
B7063
B793
76
70
5
6
7
8
9
0
9
8
7
6
5
4

Mauchline
Catrine
Sorn
Netherwood
Black Hill
Glenbuck
Hill 1527
Douglas
Roberton Law 1238
Startup Hill
Broad Hill
Smallburn
Muirkirk
Kames
Limmerhaugh
A 70
B 743
Glespin
Carmacoup
Pagie Hill
Backstane Hill
Roberton
Culter
Shawwood
Airds Moss
Urit Hill
Auchensaugh Hill
Middle Muir
Duncangill Head
B 705
Cairn Table
1945
Crawfordjohn
Abington
Fort
Tewsgill Hill
82
Cronberry
Lugar
B 7036
1631 Wardlaw Hill
Common Hill
Drake Law 1586
Camps Water
Auchinleck
Ochiltree
HOLMHEAD
Logan
CUMNOCK
Glenmuir
Glenmuirshaw
Cairn Kinny
Duneaton Water
Kirkton
Crawford
Henge
1805
Glenmuir Water
Dalblair
White Hill
1568 Mount Stuart
Spango Hill 1392
Netherthird
1527 Auchtitench Hill
Fingland
LOWTHER
1621 Rake Law
1814 Wellgrain Dod
B 7040
Elvanfoot
Clyde Law 1790
Elvan Water
Skares
Carsgailoch Hill
1199
NS
Kirkland Hill 1675
Wedder Dod 1460
ROMAN CAMP
ROMAN FORTLET
Pathhead
New Cumnock
Mansfield
1559
Kirkland
Leadhills
Dun Law
Stood Hill 1926
Wanlockhead
Watermeetings
Dalgig
Connel Park
Afton Bridgend
B 741
Bankglen
A 76 (T)
Kirkconnel
B 740
1591 Conrig Hill
Green Lowther
2403
1653
River Nith
Waterhead
Burnside
The Knipe
1886 Hare Hill
Crawick
1556
B 797
Lowther Hill
Wintercleuch Fell
81
Dalleagles
SANQUHAR
Ulzieside
Auchengruith
Thirstane Hill 1912
1999
1859
Benty Cowan Hill
Quintin Knowe
Kello Water
Mid Hill
1737
Mennock
Euchan Water
1473 Cairn Hill
2108 Comb Law
LOWTHER HILLS
1866 Enoch Hill
Prickenny Hill
Milray Hill
Craigdarroch
Blackcraig Hill
2298
Well Hill 1987
Benbrack
Windy Standard
1646 Craignane
White Knowes
Afton Resr
2232
Blacklorg Hill
Shiel Hill 1567
Enterkinfoot
ROMAN FORTLET
Ballencleuch Law
2268
1818
Durisdeer
Campbells Hill
CARSPHAIRN
Corse Hill
Cairnkinna Hill 1817
Wedder Law
2191
Craighoar Hill 1898
Kinnelhead
1485
Brockloch Rig
Windy Standard 2290
Polskeoch
Countam
Enoch
Gana Hill 2191
Benbrack
Waterhead Hill
1768
Alhang
Ox Hill 1657
1639 Blackcraig Hill
Chanlockfoot
744
Holestane
Drumlanrig Castle
Morton Castle
Bellybought Hill
1453
1432
2286 Queensberry
Wee Queensberry
FOREST
Colt Hill 1963
Countam 1640
Tibber's Castle
Carronbridge
Lamford Hill
Cairnsmore of Carsphairn 2614
Corlae
Benbrack 1906
979
Locherben
Minnygap Height 1308
Dodd Hill
Beninner
Benbuie 1788
Shinnel Water
Auchenbrack
Gatelawbridge
Bennan
Burnhead
Thornhill
997
1150
Holehouse Hill
Black Craig
1256
Manquhill Hill
Dalwhat Water
Scar Water
1222
Penpont
2042
1747
Wether Hill
Fort
Keir Mill
Whitefau Hill
Carsphairn
Marscalloch Hill
Water of Ken
617
Tynron
1157 Great Hill
Brownmoor Hill
FOREST OF AE
Cairn Avel
B 729
15
Knowehead
Kirkland
Moniaive
A 702
Keir Hills 1172
Closeburn
Motte of Dinning
Gairy Craig
Kendoon Loch
Castlemaddy
A 713
886
Culmark Hill
1369
Glenmaid Moor
Ae
Parkgate
Thorny Hill
Glenhoul
1127
Wether Hill 1263
DALMACALLAN FOREST
Loch Harrow
Forrest Lodge
Carsfad Loch
Bogrie Hill 1417
712
R. Nith
Millfire
Loch Dungeon
B 7000
Lochinvar
13
1368
Loch Urr
Dunscore
Dalswinton
Earlstoun
Earlstoun Loch
17
B 729
Duncow
Amisfield
2448
Drumbuie
A 702
Blackcraig Hill 1332
Cairn Water
787
Garroch
Bogue
Barr Hill
1224
A 76 (T)
Kirkton
Tinwald
Locharbriggs
12
St John's Town of Dalry
Holywood
Glenlee
NX
Brockloch Hill
1285
A 762
A 712
Balmaclellan
Lincluden College
75
Bennan 1249
A 712
NEW GALLOWAY
Terregles
A 709
A 75 (T)
A 701 (T)
Darnaw
Clatteringshaws Loch
Cairnsmore or Black Craig of Dee
Kenmure Castle
631
Craig
1306
Corsock
Shawhead
DUMFRIES
Ironmacannie
15
9
A 75 (T)
Cargenbridge
Brockloch Hill
Knocknevis
River Dee or Black Water of Dee
A 762
1067
Loch Ken
A 713
Urr Water
695
A 712
Crocketford or Ninemile Bar
605
Lochfoot
Lochrutton Loch
Kingholm Quay
Racks
Round Fell
CAIRN EDWARD
Shaw Hill
1255
Auchenreoch Loch
Milton Loch
Cargen
312
Fell of Fleet 1544
FOREST
Mossdale
Stroan Loch
Drumrash
Parton
B 794
Milton
818
Mabie
Lochaber Loch
Loch Grannoch
14
Kirkpatrick Durham
Springholm
Beeswing
Loch Arthur
Glencaple
Craiglowrie
Airie Hill 955
Loch Skerrow
Woodhall Loch
Old Bridge of Urr
Tower
Lotus Hill
Kirkconnell
Bankend
2331
W
A
Y
Crossmichael
520
Kirkgunzeon
14
Sweetheart Abbey
New Abbey
343
Clarebrand
Haugh of Urr
220
Lochenbreck Loch
Laurieston
Townhead of Greenlaw
B 795
Mote of Urr
Long Fell 1256
Loch Kindar
Overton
Clints of Dromore
638
LAURIESTON FOREST
B 795
Glentoo Loch
A 713
B 794
A 711
Meikle Hard Hill
Criffel 1868
1126
White Top of Culreoch
Bargatton Loch
Threave Castle
CASTLE DOUGLAS
A 745
1032 Maidenpap
Boreland Hill
Loch Whinyeon
Carlingwark Loch
598
DALBEATTIE
767
Pibble Hill
Stey Fell
GLENGAP FOREST
Loch Mannoch
Bengray 1202
719
Bridge of Dee
Rhonehouse or Kelton Hill
Carsethorn
A 762
A 75 (T)
Gelston
B 736
B 793
Kirkbean
B 796
Glen
75
DALBEATTIE FOREST
Caulkerbush
A 710
Cairnharrow
Anwoth
GATEHOUSE OF FLEET

MOFFAT
LOCKERBIE
LOCHMABEN
ANNAN
Gretna
Longtown
LANGHOLM
HAWICK
SELKIRK
Brampton
CARLISLE
ETTRICK FOREST
CRAIK FOREST
ESKDALEMUIR FOREST
CASTLE O'ER FOREST
NEWCASTLETON FOREST
KERSHOPE FOREST
ESKDALE
LIDDESDALE
TEVIOTDALE
ANNANDALE
NT
NY
Eastriggs
Canonbie
Newcastleton
Ecclefechan
Eskdalemuir
Tweedsmuir
St Mary's Loch
Talla Resr
Megget Resr
Hart Fell
White Coomb
Ettrick Pen
Priestside Bank
Solway Moss
Bowness-on-Solway
Port Carlisle
HADRIAN'S WALL
83
84
70
71
78

SELKIRK
Philiphaugh
Rutherford
Maxton
Bowmont Forest
Town Yetholm
Kirk Yetholm
Kirknewton
Yeavering Bell
Akeld
Longnewton
Midlem
Peniel Heugh
Linton Hill
Linton
Crookhouse
Kale Water
Coldsmouth Hill
Hethpool
Newton Tors
Fredden Hill
DERE STREET
Nisbet
Eckford
Morebattle
Crookedshaws Hill
White Law
Steer Rig
Clerklands
Riddell
Lilliesleaf
Belses
Ancrum
Crailing
Bonjedward
Castle
Cessford
The Curr
Preston Hill
Cold Law
College Burn
Ashkirk
Greenhouse
Chesters
Woll
Lanton
Crailinghall
Whitton
Hownam Law
Fort
The Schil
Langleeford
Minto Hills
Minto
Hassendean
Newton
JEDBURGH
Abbey
Howgate
Mowhaugh
Sourhope
THE CHEVIOT
Auchope Cairn
Hedgehope Hill
Horsleyhill
Knowetownhead
Dunion Hill
Hundalee
Hownam
Craik Moor
Comb Fell
Drinkstone Hill
Appletreehall
Denholm
Bedrule
Ferniehirst Castle
Oxnam
Chatto
Cock Law
Smasha Hill
Burnfoot
Oxnam Water
Swinside Hall
R Breamish
Shill Moor
Wilton Dean
Rubers Law
Mossburnford
Bairnkine
Whitestone Hill
Mozie Law
Windy Gyle
Bloodybush Edge
HAWICK
Motte
Kirkton
Hallrule
Mervinslaw
Falla
ROMAN CAMPS
Beefstand Hill
Loft Hill
Cushat Law
Branxholm Park
Bonchester Bridge
Abbotrule
Woden Law
Wether Cairn
White Hill
Branxholme
Hobkirk
A 6088
Chesters
Jed Water
Philip Law
Blindburn
Bell Hill
Newmill
Broadhaugh
Deerlee Knowe
Leithope Forest
Grindstone Law
Biddlestone
Shillmoor
R Coquet
Dodburn
Allan Water
Carter Bar
Arks Edge
Leap Hill
Hungry Law
Ravens Knowe
Linshiels
Alwinton
The Pike
Green Law
WAUCHOPE FOREST
Windy Crag
Crigdon Hill
Harbottle
Sharperton
Wyndburgh Hill
Fanna Hill
Carlin Tooth
Knox Knowe
Catcleugh Resr
Ridlees Cairn
Holystone
Maiden Paps
Leap Hill
Lamblair Hill
Needs Law
Hartshorn Pike
Girdle Fell
REDESDALE FOREST
Ellis Crag
Dour Hill
Corby Pike
Watty Bell's Cairn
North Yardhope
Cauldcleuch Head
Greatmoor Hill
Sandy Edge
Kielderhead Moor
Sills
Peel Fell
Oh Me Edge
Toll
Saughtree Fell
Redesdale Camp
BREMENIVM
ROMAN ROAD
Rushy Knowe
Rochester
Blackman's Law
Hindhope Law
Deadwater
Saughtree
Wether Lair
Horsley
Blakeman's Law
Otterburn Camp
Billsmoor Park
Din Fell
Castle
Hermitage
Arnton Fell
Larriston
Foulmire Heights
Kielder Burn
Emblehope Moor
Rooken Edge
Elishaw
Newlands
Kielder
Kielder Castle
Monkside
Wainhope
Blakehope Fell
Otterburn
Elsdon
Roan Fell
Steele Road
Larriston Fells
Earl's Seat
Blackburn Common
Padon Hill
North Birny Fell
Black Knowe
KIELDER
Bakethin Resr
Highfield
Highgreen Manor
Troughend Common
Old Town
Raylees
Old Castleton
Wilson's Pike
FOREST
Hawkhope
Gatehouse
LIDDESDALE
Newcastleton
Caplestone Fell
Kielder Water
Falstone
Greenhaugh
West Woodburn
HABITANCVM
NEWCASTLETON FOREST
Black Knowe
Glendhu Hill
Rough Pike
Ridsdale
Kershope Burn
The Rigg
Reeker Pike
Bower
Hesleyside
Bellingham
Chirdon Burn
Redesmouth
Kershopefoot
Sighty Crag
Black Knowe
Bewcastle Fells
KERSHOPE FOREST
Black Lyne
Hopehouse
Carrycoats Hall
Nook
Clintburn
Thockrington
Arthur Seat
The Flatt
Paddaburn Moor
WARK
Blacka Burn
Colt Crag Resr
Catlowdy
Crossings
Blackpool Gate
White Preston
Churnsike Lodge
Birtley
Wark
Warks Burn
Stonehaugh
Whygate
Chipchase Castle
Great Swinburne
Park End
Gunnerton
Haggbeck
Roughsike
Bewcastle
ROMAN FORT
White Lyne
Butterburn
Nunwick
Barrasford
Spadeadam Forest
Black Fell
Simonburn
Chollerton
Haughton Common
River Lyne
Stapleton
Middle Shield Park
ROMAN ROAD
Humshaugh
Spadeadam Fm
River Irthing
Broomlee Lough
Greenlee Lough
BROCOLITIA
Wiley Sike
GILVRNVM
Low Brunton
Boltonfellend
Kirkcambeck
Thirlwall Common
Whiteside
VERCOVICIVM
HADRIAN'S WALL
VALLUM
Wall
West Hall
Gilsland Spa
Crag Lough
Newbrough
Fourstones
Kirklinton
Hethersgill
King Water
CAMBOGLANNA
Thirlwall Castle
Gilsland
Greenhead
STANEGATE
Acomb
Smithfield
Banks
Lanercost Priory
Haltwhistle
Melkridge
Henshaw
Bardon Mill
Haydon Bridge
CORSTOPITVM
Walton
Naworth Castle
Low Row
Plenmeller
Willimontswick
R South Tyne
Low Gate
HEXHAM
Scaleby
Newtown
Brampton
Denton Fell
R Allen
Irthington
Carlisle Airport
Featherstone Castle
Rowfoot
Plenmeller Common
Milton
Crosby-On-Eden
Newby East
Hallbankgate
Farlam
Tindale
Midgeholme
Tindale Tarn
Lambley
Stonehouse
Whitfield
Dye Ho
Dalton
Talkin Tarn
Hayton
Talkin
Tindale Fells
Forest Head
Halton Lea Gate
Cold Fell
Bearsbridge
Catton
Allendale
Whitley Chapel
Warwick Bridge
Warwick
MAIDEN WAY
East Allen
NT
NY
THE CHEVIOT HILLS
REDESDALE
A 699
A 68 (T)
A 698
A 7 (T)
B 6400
B 6359
B 6405
B 6358
B 6357
B 6401
B 6436
B 6351
B 6399
B 6318
B 6320
B 6319
B 6531
B 6305
B 6304
B 6264
A 69 (T)
A 689
A 686
A 6079
A 6071
A 68
A 696
B 6342
84
77
71
5
6
7
8
9
2
1
0
9
8
7
6

NORTH SEA
Wooler
Chillingham
Lilburn Tower
Middle Moor
Beadnell
Beadnell Bay
Snook Point
Embleton
Embleton Bay
Dunstanburgh Castle
Craster
Howick
Boulmer
ALNWICK
Hulne Priory
Hulne Park
Alnmouth
Alnmouth Bay
Shilbottle
Warkworth
Coquet Island
AMBLE-BY-THE-SEA
Hauxley Haven
Hadston Carrs
Rothbury
Thrunton Wood
Biggles' Pillar
Felton
Druridge Bay
Widdrington
Cresswell
Lynemouth
ASHINGTON
Beacon Point
NEWBIGGIN-BY-THE-SEA
MORPETH
BEDLINGTON
BLYTH
Seaton Sluice
St Mary's or Bait Island
Cramlington
Seaton Delaval
WHITLEY BAY
Ponteland
Darras Hall
Newcastle Airport
LONGBENTON
TYNEMOUTH
GOSFORTH
NEWCASTLE UPON TYNE
WALLSEND
SOUTH SHIELDS
JARROW
HEBBURN
NEWBURN
BLAYDON
Corbridge
PRUDHOE
WHICKHAM
GATESHEAD
FELLING
Whitburn
BOLDON
ROWLANDS GILL
SUNDERLAND
HARWOOD FOREST
Bolam Lake
Due to open Mid 1986
NEWCASTLE UPON TYNE to
Seasonal
Bergen .... 23½ hrs
Esbjerg .... 18-20½ hrs
Stavanger .... 17-18½ hrs
Gothenburg .... 25-27½ hrs

KENNAGRAIG to
Port Askaig 2¾ hrs
Port Ellen 2¼ hrs
(seasonal)
Skervuile Lighthouse
99
Point of Knap
Ormsary Ho
Stonefield Castle Hotel
Barmore Island
Druimdrishaig
Point Cill Maluaig
Dubh Chreag
Loch Chaorunn Resr
Meall Reamhar
Cruach an Tailleir
Loch nan Torran
Miller's Bay
Loch a' Chaoruinn
Cretshengan
Cruach Lagain
Cruach an Locha
Achaglachgach Forest
Kilberry Head
Kilberry
Carse Ho
Dunmore
Port Mór
Ardpatrick
Ardpatrick Ho
Loch Stornoway
Ardpatrick Point
Gartnagrenach
Kilchamaig
Whitehouse
Kennacraig
West Loch Tarbert
Rhu
Tarbert
West Tarbert
East Loch Tarbert
Mealdarroch Point
Portavadie
Millhouse
Kames
Kyles of Bute
Asgog Loch
Asgog Bay
Eilean Aoidhe
Kilbride Bay
Ardlamont Ho
Ardlamont Bay
Ardlamont Point
Cnoc na Carraige
Fionn Phort
Camas na Ceardaich
Guallann Mhór
Cnoc a' Bhaile-shios
Rubha Leathan
Cnoc na Meine
Torran Tùrach
Windy Hill
Island of Bute
St Colmac
Kildavanan
Ettrick Bay
Straad
St Ninian's Point
Quien Hill
Inchmarnock
Ardscalpsie Point
Scalpsie Bay
Stravanan Bay
Glenrisdell
Skipness
Skipness Point
Skipness Bay
Claonaig
Claonaig Bay
Portachoillan
Dunskeig Bay
Duns
Clachan
Ronachan Ho
Cruach nam Fiadh
Cnoc Creagach
Fuar Larach
Loch Ciaran
Cnoc Donn
Ballochroy
Loch Garasdale
Sound of Bute
Dunagoil
Eascairt Point
(Summer only) Loch Ranza
An Dubh-sgeir
Port Mór
Gamhna Gigha
Eilean Garbh
Rubh' a' Chàirn Bhàin
West Tarbert Bay
East Tarbert Bay
Tarbert
Creag Bhan
Druimyeon Bay
Gigha Island
Ardminish
Ardminish Bay
Sound of Gigha
20 mins
Craro Island
Leim
Gròb Bàgh
Gigalum Island
Cara Island
Mull of Cara
Rhunahaorine
Cruach Mhic-Gougain
Narachan Burn
Crossaig Glen
Crossaig
Cour Bay
Cour
Beinn Bhreac
Largie Castle
Tayinloan
Killean
Cnoc nan Craobh
Carradale Water
Sunadale
Grogport
Beacharr
A' Chlèit
Clachaig Water
Cruach nan Gabhar
Brackley
Eilean Grianain
Muasdale
Diollaid Mhòr
Cnoc nan Gabhar
Carradale
Beinn Bhreac
Glenacardoch Point
Belloch
Barr Water
Barr Glen
Arnicle
Dippen
Torris Dale
Port Righ
Port a' Bhorrain
Glenbarr
Blary Hill
Beinn an Tuirc
Torrisdale Castle
Carradale Point
Carradale Bay
Cleongart
Rubha nan Sgarbh
Saddell Glen
Meall Buidhe
Abbey
Saddell
Saddell Bay
A' Chruach
Bellochantuy Bay
Bellochantuy
Killocraw
Cnoc Buidhe
Lussa Loch
Sgreadàn Hill
Ugadale
Ugadale Point
Port Corbert
Tangy Loch
NR
Skeroblingarry
Cairn
Glen Lussa
Glenlussa Water
Black Bay
Kilchenzie
Ranachan Hill
Ardnacross Bay
Peninver
Darlochan
Machrihanish Airfield
Machrihanish Bay
Machrihanish Water
Machrihanish
Campbeltown Loch
Island Davaar
Campbeltown
Drumlemble
Kildalloig
Tirfergus Hill
Knocknaha
Beinn Ghuilean
Earadale Point
The Slate
Achinhoan Head
Cnoc Moy
Rubha Dùin Bhàin
Cnoc Odhar
Kerran Hill
Feochaig
Rubha a' Mharaiche
Remuil Hill
Glen Breackerie
Breackerie Water
Conie Glen
Conieglen Water
Johnston's Point
Tod Hill
A' Church
Strone Water
Strone Glen
Carrine
Cnoc Mór
Cairn
Polliwilline Bay
Macharioch
Beinn na Lice
Glemanuilt Hill
Carskiey
Southend
Keil Point
Brunerican Bay
Cove Point
Port Mean
Mull of Kintyre
Rubha Chlachan
Sheep Island
Black Point
Sanda Island
Kilbrannan Sound
Rubha Creagan Dubha
Cock of Arran
Lochranza
Catacol
Catacol Bay
Meadhonach
Doire Bhuidhe
Torr Nead an Eoin
Millstone Point
Rubha Airigh Bheirg
Meall nan Damh
Mid Thundergay
N Glen Sannox
Mid Sannox
Sannox Bay
Glen Sannox
Pirnmill
Caisteal Abhail
Cir Mhòr
Corrie
Loch Tanna
Beinn Bharrain
Whitefarland Point
Goat Fell
Beinn Tarsuinn
Imachar
Island of Arran
Balliekine
Sail Chalmadale
Glen Iorsa
Glen Rosa
Merkland Point
Dougarie Point
Dougarie
Beinn Lochain
Garbh Thorr
An Tunna
Glencloy
Brodick
Brodick Bay
Strathwhillan
Machrie Bay
Auchagallon
Machrie Water
A' Chruach
Tormore
Stone Circles
Burial Chamber
Ballymichael
Beinn Bhreac
Clauchlan Point
Margnaheglish
Lamlash
Lamlash Bay
Holy Island
Torbeg
Shiskine
Cnoc a Chapuill
Drumadoon Point
Drumadoon Bay
Blackwaterfoot
Kingscross
Kingscross Point
Tighvein
Knockenkelly
Kilpatrick
Sliddery Water
Cairn
Whiting Bay
Brown Head
The Torr
Cnoc Reamhar
Largymore
Bennecarrigan
Kilmory Water
Largybeg
Largybeg Point
Port na Feannaiche
Sliddery
Dippin
Dippin Head
Lagg
Kilmory
Sliddery water Foot
Torrylin
Bennan
Kildonan
Torrylinwater Foot
Sound of Pladda
Bennan Head
Pladda
74
Ailsa Craig
Castle

Dunan
86
Power Sta
Inverkip
Garvock
Bishopton
Rossland
Bishopton Sta
87
BEARSDEN
Drumchapel
Castle Toward
Toward
Port Bannatyne
Toward Point
Wemyss Bay
Leap Moor
Kilmacolm
Inchinnan
CLYDEBANK
Upper Skelmorlie
Skelmorlie
Creuch Hill
North Burnt Hill
Duchal Moor
Caider Dam
Quarrier's Homes
Bridge of Weir
Barochan Ho
Georgetown
RENFREW
Glasgow Airport
Partick
Govan
Rothesay Bay
Bogany Point
Castle
Blackhouse Moor
Queenside Muir
Carruth Ho
Ranfurly
Houston
Brookfield
Linwood
PAISLEY
ROTHESAY
Ascog
Knock Castle
Hill of Stake
Heathfield
Kilbarchan
Elderslie
JOHNSTONE
Pollokshields
Routenburn
Girtley Hill
Waterhead Moor
Mistylaw Muir
Kaim Dam
Millikenpark
Glenburn
Kerrycroy
Scoulag Point
Upper Scoulag
Howwood
Waterside
Nitshill
Pollokshaws
Cathcart
Tomont End
LARGS
Largs Bay
Irish Law
Ladyland Moor
Burnt Hill
Lochwinnoch
Church
Mountstuart
Fort
Harelaw Resr
Nether Kirkton
BARRHEAD
Thornliebank
Clarkston
Bruchag Point
GREAT CUMBRAE ISLAND
Portrye
Barr Castle
Barcraigs Resr
Neilston
Patterton Sta
Busby
Kingarth
Muirhead Resr
Kelburn
Whitehill
Balgray Resr
Newton Mearns
Kilchattan Bay
Kilchattan
MILLPORT
Fairlie
Castle
Camphill Resr
Kilbirnie
Kilbirnie Loch
Uplawmoor
Neilston Pad
Netherplace
Waterfoot
Church
Torr
Mor
Ore Terminal
Fairlie Roads
The Tan
Kaim Hill
Knockendon Resr
Glengarnock
Beith
Gateside
Lugton
Halket
Harelaw Dam
Earn Water
Jackton
Garroch Head
Little Cumbrae Island
Castle
Hunterston Ho
Campbelton
Power Station
Baidland Hill
Rye Water
Drakemyre
The Den
Barrmill
Burnhouse
Long Loch
Gabroc Hill
Fullwood
Lochcraig Resr
Eaglesham
Gull Point
Crosbie
Caaf Resr
Highfield
Dalry
Dunlop
Corsehouse Resr
Ballageich Hill
Dunwan Dam
Portencross
Farland Head
West Kilbride
Ardneil Bay
Seamill
Munnock Resr
Dusk Water
Auchentiber
Lugton Water
Lochgoin Resr
Melowther Hill
C U N N I N G H A M E
STEWARTON
Craigendunton Resr
Corse Hill
Busbie Muir Resr
Dalgarven
Burnfoot Resr
Rough Hill
82
F I R T H O F C L Y D E
KILWINNING
Montgreenan
Fenwick
Waterside
Whitelee Forest
Horse Isle
Annick Water
Rowallan Castle
Whitelee Hill
ARDROSSAN
STEVENSTON
Cunninghamhead
Kilmaurs
Craufurdland Castle
SALTCOATS
Moscow
1 hr
ARDROSSAN to
Douglas ....6 hrs
(seasonal)
IRVINE
Springside
Knockentiber
KILMARNOCK
NEWMILNS
DARVEL
Irvine Bay
Crosshouse
Dreghorn
R Irvine
Hurlford
GALSTON
GREENHOLM
Loudoun Hill
NS
Drybridge
Gatehead
Riccarton
Earlston
Shortlees
Dundonald
Sornhill
Barassie
Bogend
Craigie
Middleyard
Little Hartmidd
Loans
Symington
Carnell
TROON
Lady Isle
Meikle Craigs
Millburn
Blackside
Auchmillan
Rosemount
Cessnock Water
Mossgiel
Monkton
Prestwick Airport
Tarbolton
Mauchline
Sorn
Catrine
PRESTWICK
New Prestwick
Failford
Shawwood
St Quivox
Mossblown
River Ayr
Airds Moss
Annbank
Stair
Whitletts
Lugar Water
AYR
Wallacetown
Trabboch
Trabbochburn
Auchinleck
Lugar
Sundrum
Ochiltree
HOLMHEAD
Logan
CUMNOCK
Belston
Doonfoot
Heads of Ayr
Burns Cott
Coylton
Hillhead
Drongan
Netherthird
Alloway
Burnock Water
Martnaham Loch
Fisherton
Doonholm
Skares
Castle
Dunure
Brown Carrick Hill
Newark Castle
Sinclairston
Sauchrie
Culroy
Dalrymple
Hollybush
Littlemill
Carsgailoch Hill
Drumshang
Minishant
Rankinston
Knoweside
Cairntable
Water of Coyle
Stannery Knowe
New Cumnock
Connel Park
Culzean Bay
Polnessan
Kilmein Hill
KYLE FOREST
Waterhead
River Nith
Culzean Castle
MAYBOLE
Patna
Burnside
Dalleagles
Maidenhead Bay
Crossraguel Abbey
Kirkmichael
Waterside
Benty Cowan Hill
76
Maidens
Kirkoswald
Loch Spallander Resr
River Doon
Benbeoch
Turnberry Bay
Turnberry
Girvan Water
Crosshill
Dalmellington
Enoch Hill
Milray Hill
Brest Rocks
Straiton
Bogton Loch
Bellsbank
Benbrack
Prickenny Hill
Matthew's Port
Dersalloch Hill
Windy Standard
Craignane
Dowhill
Dipple
Ladybank
Kilkerran
CARSPHAIRN
Dalquharran Castle
Dailly
Ness Glen
Campbells Hill
Brockloch Rig
Big Hill of Glenmount
Killochan Castle
Maxwellston
Glenalla Fell
Loch Muck
Benbrack
Waterhead Hill
Hadyard Hill
Garleffin Fell
74
Old Dailly
Tairlaw Ring
75
FOREST
Penkill
Penwhapple Resr
Loch Finlas
Lamford
Cairnsmore of

Inchmurrin
Gartocharn
Croftamie
Boquhan
Ballikinrain Castle
Killearn
Fintry
Loch Walton
Cringate Law
Cairnoch Hill
Carron Valley Resr
Carron Valley Forest
Dunipace
Rhu
HELENSBURGH
Arden
Balloch
Balloch Castle
Craighat
Dumgoyne
Earl's Seat
CAMPSIE FELLS
Strathblane Hills
Birkenburn Resr
Kilsyth Hills
Tomtain
High Banton
Head of Dennyloanhead
Rosneath Point
Craigendoran
Colgrain
Darleith Ho
Alexandria
Jamestown
Auchencarroch
Auchineden Hill
Duntreath Castle
Netherton
Clachan of Campsie
Bonhill
Dumbarton Muir
Burncrooks Resr
Blanefield
Strathblane
Balgrochan
Banton
KILSYTH
Banknock
Ardmore
Renton
Geilston
Kilmannan Resr
Lennoxtown
Milton of Campsie
Queenzieburn
GREENOCK
Cardross
Pillar Bank
KILPATRICK HILLS
Cochno Loch
Mugdock Resr
Mugdock
Bellsmyre
Dullatur
Croy
ANTONINE WALL
PORT GLASGOW
Newark Castle
Finlaystone
DUMBARTON
Milton
Loch Humphrey
Greenside Resr
Jaw Resr
MILNGAVIE
Blairskaith
Birdston
R. Kelvin
Twechar
Eastfield
CUMBERNAULD
Bowling
Old Kilpatrick
Erskine Br Toll
Duntocher
Faifley
Torrance
Bardowie
Balmore
Forth and Clyde Canal
KIRKINTILLOCH
Waterside
Condorrat
Gryfe Resrs
Bardrainney
Langbank
Auchendores Resr
Leperstone Resr
BEARSDEN
Lenzie
Cadder
Mollinsburn
Luggiebank
Bishopton
Rossland
Bishopton Sta
ERSKINE
Inchinnan
Drumchapel
Bishopbriggs
Auchinloch
Lumloch
Bridgend
Annathill
Riggend
Wattston
Strathgryfe
Kilmacolm
Barochan Ho
CLYDEBANK
Yoker
Temple
Muirhead
Stepps
Marnock
Glenboig
Stand
Georgetown
RENFREW
Ferry
Springburn
Garnkirk
Gartcosh
Glenmavis
Airdriehill
Duchal Moor
Quarrier's Homes
Bridge of Weir
Houston
Glasgow Airport
Partick
Tunnel
Govan
GLASGOW
Lochwood
COATBRIDGE
Calder Dam
Carruth Ho
Queenside Muir
Ranfurly
Brookfield
Linwood
PAISLEY
Ferry
Coatdyke
Craigneuk
Hill of Stake
Heathfield
Kilbarchan
Locher Water
Elderslie
JOHNSTONE
Pollokshields
Shettleston
Baillieston
Old Monkland
Calderbank
Chapelhall
River Calder
Kaim Dam
Millikenpark
Glenburn
White Cart Water
RUTHERGLEN
Carmyle
Birkenshaw
Viewpark
Mossend
Holytown
Mistylaw Muir
Howwood
Waterside
Nitshill
Pollokshaws
Cathcart
Newton
Uddingston
Bothwell
Bellshill
New Stevenson
Cleland
Lochwinnoch
Ladyland Moor
Burnt Hill
Church
Fort
Harelaw Resr
Nether Kirkton
BARRHEAD
Thornliebank
Cambuslang
Flemington
Carmunnock
Stonefield
Barcraigs Resr
Barr Castle
Clarkston
Patterton Sta
Busby
Nerston
MOTHERWELL
Whitehill
Neilston
Balgray Resr
Newton Mearns
Rogerton
Castle
High Blantyre
Craigneuk
Kilbirnie
Uplawmoor
Neilston Pad
Netherplace
Waterfoot
Thorntonhall
EAST KILBRIDE
HAMILTON
Kilbirnie Loch
Beith
Harelaw Dam
Low Waters
Rye Water
Glengarnock
Gateside
Lugton
Halket
Earn Water
Jackton
Eaglesham
Meikle Earnock
Overtown
The Den
Barrmill
Long Loch
Lochcraig Resr
Quarter
Larkhall
Drakemyre
Highfield
Burnhouse
Gabroc Hill
Ballageich Hill
Auldhouse
Limekilnburn
Millheugh
Strutherhill
Dalry
Dusk Water
Dunlop
Fullwood
Corsehouse Resr
Dunwan Dam
Melowther Hill
Lochgoin Resr
Chapelton
Ashgill
Swinhill
Auchentiber
Lugton Water
STEWARTON
CUNNINGHAME
NS
Corse Hill
Udstonhead
Stonehouse
Glassford
Dalgarven
Burnfoot Resr
Craigendunton Resr
Rough Hill
Strathaven
Draffan
KILWINNING
Montgreenan
Fenwick
Waterside
Whitelee Forest
Whitelee Hill
Sandford
Blackwood
Rowallan Castle
Cunninghamhead
Annick Water
Calder Water
Avon Water
Caldermill
STEVENSTON
Kilmaurs
Craufurdland Castle
Moscow
Stobieside
Kype Muir
Lesmahagow
IRVINE
Springside
Knockentiber
Crosshouse
KILMARNOCK
NEWMILNS
DARVEL
Loudoun Hill
Drumclog
Hawkwood Hill
Logan Water
Stockbriggs
Irvine Bay
Dreghorn
R Irvine
Hurlford
GALSTON
GREENHOLM
Glengavel Water
Auchingilloch
Tod Law
Nethan
Drybridge
Gatehead
Riccarton
Shortlees
Earlston
Dundonald
Sornhill
Mill Rig
Glengavel Resr
Nutberry Hill
Barassie
Loans
Bogend
Craigie
Middleyard
Carnell
Little Hartmidden
Twopenny Knowe
Bibblon Hill
Symington
Blackside
Middlefield Law
Hagshaw Hill
TROON
Meikle Craigs
Rosemount
Millburn
Auchmillan
Cessnock Water
Netherwood
Black Hill
Glenbuck
Hareshaw Hill
Monkton
Prestwick Airport
Tarbolton
Mossgiel
Mauchline
Catrine
Sorn
River Ayr
Limmerhaugh
Smallburn
Muirkirk
Carmacoup
Urit Hill
PRESTWICK
Failford
Kames
New Prestwick
St Quivox
Mossblown
Stair
Shawwood
Airds Moss
Cairn Table
AYR
Whitletts
Annbank
Lugar Water
Lugar
Cronberry
Wardlaw Hill
Wallacetown
Trabboch
Sundrum
Trabbochburn
Ochiltree
Auchinleck
Glenmuir
Cairn Kinny
Belston
HOLMHEAD
Logan
Glenmuirshaw
Glenmuir Water
Doonfoot
Firth of Ayr
Burns Cott
Alloway
Coylton
Hillhead
Drongan
CUMNOCK
Dalblair
Mount Stuart
Fisherton
Doonholm
Martnaham Loch
Burnock Water
Skares
Netherthird
Auchtitench Hill
Fingland
Brown Carrick Hill
Newark Castle
Sinclairston
Kirkland Hill
Sauchrie
Culroy
Dalrymple
Dalmellington
Littlemill
Rankinston
Carsgailoch Hill
Lathhead
New Cumnock
Mansfield
Kirkland

87
81
76

Kincardine
Valleyfield
DUNFERMLINE
KINGHORN
Pettycur
BURNTISLAND
Culross
Torryburn
Crossford
Aberdour
Blair Cas
Longannet Point
Charlestown
Limekilns
Rosyth
INVERKEITHING
Dalgety Bay
Inchcolm
Inchkeith
Oxcars
Stenhousemuir
Larbert
Skinflats
Carron
GRANGEMOUTH
BO'NESS
Grangepans
Carriden
FALKIRK
Camelon
Bonnybridge
High Bonnybridge
Greenhill
Glen Village
Redding
Reddingmuirhead
Brightons
Shieldhill
Maddiston
California
Linlithgow Bridge
LINLITHGOW
Philpstoun
Old Philpstoun
Blackness
Hopetoun Ho
The Binns
QUEENSFERRY
North Queensferry
Forth Road Bridge
Forth Br
Inch Garvie
Cramond Island
Inchmickery
Dalmeny
Newton
Dundas Castle
Kirkliston
Cramond
Cramond Bridge
Granton
Black Rocks
Leith
EDINBUR
Portobello
Duddingston
Craigmillar
Liberton
Gilmerton
Jawcraig
Slamannan
Avonbridge
Westfield
Torphichen
Bridgend
Winchburgh
Ecclesmachan
Uphall
Broxburn
Edinburgh Airport
Ingliston
Gogar
Newbridge
Ratho Station
Ratho
Corstorphine
Craiglockhart
Colinton
Juniper Green
Currie
Balerno
Fairmilehead
Kaimes
Straiton
LOANHEAD
BONNYRIGG
LASSWADE
Bilston
Roslin
Rosewell
Auchendinny
PENICUIK
Milton Bridge
Silverburn
Limerigg
Binniehill
Longriggend
ARMADALE
BATHGATE
Boghall
Deans
Uphall Station
LIVINGSTON
Bonnington
Hermiston
Wilkieston
East Calder
Kirknewton
Oakbank
Dedridge
Livingston Village
Bellsquarry
Polbeth
Blackburn
Seafield
Whiteside
Blackridge
Westrigg
Forrestfield
Harthill
Eastfield
WHITBURN
East Whitburn
Longridge
Stoneyburn
Addiewell
West Calder
Breich
Kirk of Shotts
Salsburgh
Shotts
Fauldhouse
Greenburn
Stane
Hartwood
Dykehead
Allanton
Bonkle
Newmains
WISHAW
Waterloo
Bogside
Law
Castlehill
Carluke
Yieldshields
Roadmeetings
Kilcadzow
Braidwood
Rosebank
Crossford
Hazelbank
Cartland
Nemphlar
Kirkfieldbank
LANARK
New Lanark
Auchenheath
Kirkmuirhill
Hawksland
Brocketsbrae
Ravenstruther
Carstairs
Carstairs Junction
Pettinain
Carnwath
Newbigging
Walston
Libberton
Shieldhill
Quothquan
Thankerton
BIGGAR
Symington
Coulter
Elsrickle
Candy Mill
Skirling
Dolphinton
Blyth Bridge
Castlecraig
Drochil Castle
Romannobridge
Mountain Cross
Halmyre Mains
West Linton
Carlops
Newhall
Leadburn
Cowdenburn
Waterheads
Howgate
Eddleston
PEEBLES
Neidpath Castle
Kings Muir
Cardrona
Glentress Forest
Hallyne
Stobo
Kirkton Manor
Broughton
Drumelzier
Tinnis Castle
Bellspool
Posso
Stanhope
Tweedsmuir
Crook Inn
Hearthstane
Wiston
Lamington
Roberton
Abington
Crawford
Elvanfoot
Leadhills
Douglas
Douglas Water
Rigside
Uddington
Happendon
Coalburn
Braehead
Crawfordjohn
Kirkton
Glespin
Middle Muir
Tinto
Tinto Hills
Culter Fell
Broad Law
Dollar Law
Cappercleuch
Rodono Hotel
Tibbie Sheils Inn
St Mary's Loch
Megget Resr
Talla Resr
Talla Linnfoots
Meggethead
Glenbreck
Fruid Resr
Tweed's Well Source of R. Tweed
Mountbenger
Dryhope
Tushielaw Inn
Ettrick
Ramseycleuch
Crosslee
PENTLAND HILLS
FIRTH OF FORTH
NT
Due to open Early 1986

Fidra
Bass Rock
NORTH BERWICK
Craigleith
Eyebroughy
Tantallon Castle
St Baldred's Boat
Dirleton
North Berwick Law
Auldhame
Gullane Bay
Gullane
Scoughall
Kingston
Inchkeith
Whitekirk
St Baldred's Cradle
Aberlady Bay
Tyne Mouth
Aberlady
Drem
Tyninghame
Gosford Bay
Gosford Ho
DUNBAR
Black Rocks
Spittal
Ballencrieff
Athelstaneford
Preston
West Barns
Broxburn
Barns Ness
Leith
EAST LINTON
EDINBURGH
COCKENZIE AND PORT SETON
Longniddry
Garleton Hills
Traprain
Skateraw
Power Station
PRESTONPANS
Seton Ho
Huntington
Hailes Castle
Spott
Thorntonloch
Portobello
Elvingston
HADDINGTON
Traprain Law
Luggate Burn
Pitcox
Brunt Hill
Dry Burn
MUSSELBURGH
TRANENT
Due to open Late 1986
Stenton
Innerwick
Duddingston
Gladsmuir
Papple
Inveresk
Wallyford
Macmerry
New Winton
Whitelaw Hill
Cocklaw Hill
Cockburnspath
Craigmillar
Due to open Early 1986
Elphinstone
Samuelston
Garvald
Oldhamstocks
Danderhall
Whitecraig
Millerhill
New Town
Bolton
Ormiston
Braid Hills
Gilmerton
Pencaitland
Dunbar Common
Bransly Hill
Carfrae
Kaimes
Cousland
Gifford
Danskine
Ecclaw
DALKEITH
West Saltoun
East Saltoun
Yester Ho
Yester Castle
Straiton
Peaston Bank
Heart Law
LOANHEAD
BONNYRIGG AND LASSWADE
Eskbank
Mayfield
Oxenfoord Castle
Peaston
Gilchriston
Spartleton Edge
Longyester
Bilston
Polton
Newtongrange
Pathhead
Whiteadder Resr
Roslin
Rosewell
Newlandrig
Hopes Resr
Abbey St Bathans
Auchendinny
Arniston Engine
Crichton
Humbie
Fala Dam
Blegbie
Lammer Law
Meikle Says Law
Cranshaws
Cranshaws Hill
Gorebridge
Crichton Castle
Fala
LAMMERMUIR HILLS
Ellemford
PENICUIK
Carrington
North Middleton
Tynehead
Soutra Mains
Crib Law
Temple
Fala Moor
Cairn
Edgelaw Resr
Middleton
Hunt Law
Dye Water
Longformacus
Gilston
Blythe Edge
Watch Water Resr
Rosebery Resr
Falahill
Gladhouse Resr
Twinlaw Cairns
Dirrington Great Law
MOORFOOT HILLS
Heriot
Oxton
Hotel
Forts
Torfichen Hill
Dirrington Little Law
Leader Water
Gavinton
Scoured Rig
Collie Law
Portmore Loch
Polwarth
Hule Moss
Fountainhall
Edgarhope Wood
Hare Faulds
Blythe
Westruther
Dun Law
Thirlestane Castle
LAUDER
Halliburton
Fogo
Blackhope Scar
Torquhan
Lauder Common
Thirlestane
Houndslow
Ladyside Height
Eden Water
Greenlaw
Killochyett
Stow
Lugate Water
Milkieston Rings
Whitehope Law
Nether Blainslie
Legerwood
Dunslair Heights
Windlestraw Law
Gordon
Lambden
Glentress Forest
Black Law
Great Law
Broch
Hume
PEEBLES
Bowland
Fans
Kings Muir
Priesthope Hill
William Law
Langshaw
Sweethope Hill
Blackhaugh
Knowes Hill
Buckholm
Mellerstain Ho
Stichill
Lee Pen
Walkerburn
Earlston
Nenthorn
Ednam
Cardrona
Cardrona Forest
INNERLEITHEN
Clovenfords
Meigle Hill
GALASHIELS
Smailholm
Hendersyde Park
Traquair House
Elibank and Traquair Forest
Lowood
Gattonside
Redpath
Tower
Sprouston
Wallace's Hill
Traquair
Ashiestiel Hill
Caddonfoot
Abbotsford
Abbey
Newstead
Bemersyde
Floors Castle
KELSO
Kirkhouse
Yair Hill Forest
Boleside
MELROSE
Eildon Hills
Clintmains
Maxwellheugh
Glen Ho
Minch Moor
Newtown St Boswells
Dryburgh Abbey
Makerstoun
Trows
Broomy Law
Cauldshiels Hill
Lindean
St. Boswells
Roxburgh
Blakelaw
Blake Muir
Broadmeadows
Linglie Hill
Bowden
Rutherford
Heiton
Deuchar Law
Newark Castle
SELKIRK
Maxton
Bowmont Forest
Yarrow
Yarrow Water
Fastheugh Hill
Bowhill
Philiphaugh
Midlem
Longnewton
Crookhouse
Douglas Burn
Peniel Heugh
Yarrow Feus
Sundhope
Eckford
Mountbenger
Etttrickbridge
Riddell
Lilliesleaf
Belses
Ancrum
Nisbet
Morebattle
Dryhope
Hotel
ETTRICK FOREST
Clerklands
Crailing
Cessford
Kirkhope
Greenhouse
Bonjedward
Black Knowe Head
Ashkirk
Woll
Chesters
Lanton
Crailinghall
Whitton
Gilmanscleuch
Akermoor Loch
Minto Hills
Newton
JEDBURGH
Hassendean
Minto
Shaws Under Loch
Horsleyhill
Knowetownhead
Dunion Hill
Hundalee
Hownam
Drinkstone Hill
Denholm
Oxnam
Crosslee
Tushielaw Inn
Dun Knowe
Appletreehall
Bedrule
Ferniehirst Castle
Swinside Hall
Chatto
Ramsey Knowe
Hellmoor Loch
Smasha Hill
Burnfoot
Rubers Law
Mossburnford
Redfordgreen
Borthwickshiel
Wilton Dean
Bairnkine
Ettrick
Alemoor Loch
Ramseycleuch
Roberton
HAWICK
Hallrule
Falla
DERE STREET
NT

8
9
0
1
2
8
7
6
5
4
3
2
NORTH SEA
NU
Reed Point
Siccar Point
Wheat Stack
Fast Castle
Telegraph Hill
ST ABB'S HEAD
Meikle Black Law
Lumsdaine
Cross Law
Coldingham Moor
Forts
Northfield
St Abbs
Coldingham Bay
Grantshouse
Coldingham
Priory
B 6438
Buss Craig
EYEMOUTH
Houndwood
Eye Water
Ale Water
Cairncross
A 1107
A 1(T)
Reston
Ayton
Castle
Burnmouth
Horseley Hill
Fort
Auchencrow
B 6438
Marygold
B 6437
Lamberton Beach
Lintlaw
Preston
B 6355
Chirnsidebridge
Lamberton
Chirnside
Foulden
Clappers
Halidon Hill
Edrom
Whiteadder Water
A 6105
Allanton
Hutton
BERWICK-UPON-TWEED
B 6460
Paxton
B 6461
Blackadder Water
Blackadder
Tweedmouth
Spittal
R Tweed
Loanend
East Ord
Redshin Cove
Whitsome
Fishwick
Horncliffe
Longridge Towers
Scremerston
New Horndean
Murton
Swinton
Ladykirk
Cas
Norham
A 698
Thornton
Aller Dean
Cheswick Black Rocks
MERSE
Swintonmill
Shoresdean
Shoreswood
West Allerdean
Cheswick
DEVIL'S CAUSEWAY
A 1(T)
Goswick
Simprim
Grindon
B 6354
Ancroft
Felkington
Emmanuel Head
Leitholm
Leet Water
A 6112
B 6437
Haydon Dean
Haggerston
Castle
HOLY ISLAND
Berrington
Beal
Holy Island
Lindisfarne
Holy Island Sands
Castle
Castle Point
Priory
Duddo
Castle Heaton
Bowsden
Guile Point
Lennel
COLDSTREAM
Barmoor Castle
B 6353
Kyloe
Kyloe Hills
Fenwick
Cornhill-on-Tweed
Pallinsburn Ho
Etal
Lowick
Fort
Birgham
Castle
Crookham
Buckton
Carham
Wark
Learmouth
B 6353
Fort
FARNE ISLANDS
Branxton
Ford
B 6525
Elwick
Ross
Staple Sound
Hadden
Pressen
Kimmerston
Holburn
Detchant
Budle Bay
Inner Sound
Middleton
Flodden
Waren Mill
Castle
Bamburgh
Downham
B 6352
Milfield
Fenton
Nesbit
Belford
Easington
Budle
Mindrum
Pawston
Housedon Hill
A 697
River Till
Fort
Hazelrigg
Spindlestone
Burton
Lempitlaw
Kilham
B 6351
Doddington
Fort
Mousen
Bradford
Seahouses
Hoselaw Loch
Lanton
Coupland
Horton
Bellshill
Lucker
Elford
North Sunderland
Shotton
R Glen
Weetwood Hall
B 6349
Warenton
Newham Hall
Beadnell
Kirknewton
Fort
Yeavering Bell
Akeld
B 6348
Fowberry Tower
Greendykes
B 6348
Adderstone
Swinhoe
Town Yetholm
Kirk Yetholm
Coldsmouth Hill
Hethpool
Humbleton
Wooler
Warenford
Newham
West Fleetham
Chatton
Beadnell Bay
Newstead
Chathill
Newton Tors
Fredden Hill
Haugh Head
Chillingham
Castle
High Newton by-the-Sea
Snook Point
White Law
Fort
Earle
DEVIL'S CAUSEWAY
Ellingham
Preston
Steer Rig
Middleton Hall
Lilburn Tower
Newtown
Hepburn
Fort
Brunton
St Mary's or Newton Haven
Crookedshaws Hill
Bowmont Water
College Burn
Preston Hill
Cold Law
Middleton
Middle Moor
Embleton Bay
The Curr
Harthope Burn
East Lilburn
Cateran Hill
Brownieside
Christon Bank
Hownam Law
Fort
The Schil
Langlee Crags
Ilderton
Roseden
Old Bewick
Fort
North Charlton
Embleton
Dunstanburgh Castle
Mowhaugh
THE CHEVIOT
Langleeford
West Ditchburn
Howgate
Sourhope
Auchope Cairn
Hedgehope Hill
Roddam
Wooperton
Harehope
South Charlton
Rock
Dunstan
New Bewick
Eglingham
B 6346
Craster
Craik Moor
Comb Fell
Dunmoor Hill
A 697
B 6347
B 1339
Rennington
79
Cock Law
R Breamish
Brandon
Beanley
Howick
Ingram
Powburn
Littlehoughton
Howick Haven
Mozie Law
Windy Gyle
Shill Moor
Greensidehill
Branton
Hulne Priory
Hulne Park
Bloodybush Edge
Glanton Pike
Titlington
Shawdon Hall
Longhoughton
Beefstand
Glanton
Denwick
Boulmer
A 1(T)
B 1340
B 1341

Benderloch
Ledaig
Ardmucknish Bay
Rubha Garbh-àird
Ledaig Point
Eilean Mòr
Dunstaffnage Castle
Dunbeg
Ganavan
Maiden Island
Dunollie
OBAN
Connel
Falls of Lora
Achnacloich
Black Crofts
Achnaba
Ardchattan Priory
Bonawe
Airds Bay
LOCH ETIVE
Beinn Mheadhonach
Glen Kinglass
Meall Garbh
Beinn nan Lus
Glen Liver
Glen Noe
BEN CRUACHAN
Beinn Eunaich
Glen Strae
Beinn Donachain
Beinn Mhic-Mhonaidh
Glen Orchy
Bridge of Orchy
Beinn Inverveigh
Beinn Dorain
Beinn Bhreac-liath
Beinn Odhar
Beinn Udlaidh
Glen Lochy
Clifton
Tyndrum
River Lochy
Beinn na Sròine
R Cononish
Strath of Orchy
Stronmilchan
Kilchurn Cas
Lochawe
Dalmally
Falls of Cruachan
Cruachan Resr
Beinn a' Bhùiridh
Pass of Brander
Taynuilt
Glen Nant
Tailor's Leap
Lusragan Burn
Black Lochs
Fearnoch Forest
Deadh Choimhead
Glen Lonan
Loch Nell
Beinn Ghlas
Cleigh
Kilmore
Glen Feochan
Loch Feochan
Sior Loch
A' Chruach
Abhainn Cam Linne
Loch Tromlee
Loch Nant
Innis Chonain
Ardanaiseig
Inishail
Kilchrenan
Annat
Hotel
Coillaig
Cladich
Teatle Water
Allt Fearna
Lochan Shira
Allt an Stacain
Beinn Bhalgairean
Meall nan Tighearn
Ben Lui
Beinn Dubhchraig
Fiarach
Falls of Falloch
Ben Glas
Troisgeach
Inverarnan
Ardlui
Pulpit Rock
Maol Breac
Beinn Bhuidhe
Lochan Sron Mòr
Beinn Ghlas
Rob Roy's House
Glen Shira
Clachan Hill
Glenfyne Lodge
Glen Fyne
Stuc Scardan
Cruach Mhòr
Tullich
Glen Aray
Allt Beochlich
Eredine Forest
Blarghour
Barr Mòr
Dubh Loch
Dun Corr-bhile
Clachan
Cairndow
Ardkinglas Ho
Binnein an Fhidhleir
BEN VORLICH
Loch Sloy
Inveruglas
Inversnaid Hotel
Rob Roy's Cave
BEINN IME
Rest and be thankful
Glen Kinglas
Beinn an Lochain
Stob an Eas
Ben Arthur
The Cobbler
Succoth
Arrochar
Tarbet
Cruach Tairbeirt
Glen Croe
Ben Donich
The Brack
Ardgartan
Ardgoil
Ardmay
Stuckgowan
LOCH LONG
Dunderave Point
Ardno
St Catherines
Hell's Glen
Cruach nan Capull
INVERARAY
Castle
An Suidhe
Am Buachaille
Dalchenna
Douglas Water
Creag a' Phuill
Beinn Bhreac
Portinnisherrich
Eredine
LOCH AWE
Inverinan
INVERINAN FOREST
Tom an t-Saighdeir
Loch Avich
Dalavich
Cruach Maolachy
Kilmelford
Glenmore
Braes of Lorn
Loch Tralaig
Meall Odhar
Carn Dearg
Loch Scammadale
Bragleenmore
Carn Duchara
Inverliever Forest
Inverliever Lodge
Cruach an Eachlaich
Barbreck House
Torran
Stone
Castle
Fincharn
Church
Ford
Ederline
Cruach Mhic Fhionnlaidh
Sidh Mor
Loch Gaineamhach
Beinn Dearg
Auchindrain
Loch Leacann
Dun Leacainn
Creagan an Eich
Creggans
Strachur
Strachur Bay
Mullach Coire a' Chuir
Drimsynie
Lochgoilhead
Beinn Lochain
Corrow
Cnoc Coinnich
Ardgoil Estate
The Saddle
Loch Goil
Clach Bheinn
Carrick
Furnace
Beinn Ghlas
Crarae
Glen Sluain
Newton
Invernoaden
Glenbranter
Glenbranter Forest
Beinn Bheula
Loch Eck
Strathlachlan
Castle Lachlan
Lachlan Bay
Garbhallt
Cruach nan Capull
Minard
Minard Forest
Tullochgorm
Minard Castle
KILMICHAEL FOREST
Dun Dubh
Gleann Airigh
Kilmichael Glassary
Bridgend
Loch Glashan
Scotston Hill
Asknish
Asknish Forest
Lochgair
LOCH FYNE
Lephinmore
Cruach an Lochain
Caol Ghleann
Strath nan Lùb
Creag Mholach
Beinn Bheag
Bernice
Beinn Mhòr
Cruach a' Bhuic
Creachan Mòr
Glen Finart
Portincaple
Garelochhead
Cnoc na h-Airighe
Glen Douglas
Doune Hill
Beinn a' Mhanaich
Beinn Eich
Edentaggart
Glen Luss
Beinn Chaorach
Beinn Ruisg
Aldochlay
Glen Fruin
Shandon
Faslane Bay
GARE LOCH
Dunans
Meall Dubh
Conchra
Glendaruel Forest
An Socach
Cruach Chuilceachan
Largiemore
Tom na h-Iolaire
Otter Ferry
Port Ann
Carrick
LOCHGILPHEAD
Kilmory Castle
Castleton
Ardrishaig
Loch Gilp
Caolard Rubha
Liath Eilean
Brenfield Bay
Inverneil Ho
Bàgh an t-Sailleir
Bàgh Tigh-an-Droighinn
Ballimore
Cruach nan Tarbh
Barr Ganuisg
Cruach nan Caorach
Kilfinan
Kilfinan Bay
Glendaruel
Clachan of Glendaruel
Cruach nan Cuilean
Balliemore
Glen Tarsan
Sgorach Mòr
Beinn Ruadh
Stronchullin Hill
Glen Massan
Strath Eachaig
Benmore
Cnoc a' Mhadaidh
Gairletter Point
Ardentinny
Coulport
Little Rahane
Ardpeaton
Clynder
Rosneath
Rhu
HELENSBURGH
Craigendoran
Kilmun
Blairmore
Strone
Strone Pt
Barons Pt
Cove Bay
COVE
KILCREGGAN
Rosneath Point
Holy Loch
Glen Lean
Clachaig
Dalinlongart Hill
Sandbank
Ardnadam
Hunter's Quay
Kirn
DUNOON
Auchenbreck
Dun Mòr
Cruach nan Capull
Glenstriven
Inverchaolain Glen
LOCH STRIVEN
Glen Kin
Beinn Bhreac
Craig Lodge
Loch Riddon
Buttock Pt
Colintraive
Altgaltraig
South Hall
KYLES OF BUTE
Port Leathan
Auchalick Bay
Melldalloch
Achafosson Burn
Erines
Sloc nam Feàrna
Ardmarnock Bay
Creag Mhòr
Ardmarnock Ho
Barr Liath
Port Driseach
Ferry
Tighnabruaich
Kames
Millhouse
Asgog Loch
Portavadie
Stonefield Castle Hotel
Barmore Island
East Loch Tarbert
Tarbert
Mealdarroch Point
Port a' Mhadaidh
West Tarbert
Eilean Aoidhe
Cnoc na Carraige
Asgog Bay
Kilbride Bay
Ardlamont Ho
Torran Tùrach
Windy Hill
Strone Point
Ardmaleish Point
Ardyne Point
Knockdow
Castle Toward
Toward
Toward Point
Innellan
Dunan
Corlarach Forest
Beinn Ruadh
Bullwood
Cloch Point
Kempock Point
GOUROCK
GREENOCK
Larkfield
Braeside
Loch Thom
Lunderston Bay
Ardgowan
Inverkip
Power Sta
Castle
Wemyss Bay
Leap Moor
Skelmorlie
Upper Skelmorlie
Creuch Hill
Gryfe Resrs
Garvock
Bardrainney
PORT GLASGOW
Newark Cast
Cardross
Pillar Bar
Ardmore
Colgrain
Darleit Ho
Duchal Moor
North Burnt Hill
Calder Dam
Carruth Ho
Port Bannatyne
Kames Bay
St Colmac
Kildavanan
Ettrick
Rothesay Bay
Bogany
Toward Point
ISLAND
FIRTH OF CLYDE
ARGYLL
NM
NR
90
99
80
81

Beinn Heasgarnich
Meall Tournie
Meall Ghaordie
Meall nan Tarmachan
91
Tullich Hill
Gleann a Chilleine
Meall nam Fuaran
Glen Lochay
Kenknock
Forest of Mamlorn
Creag Mhòr
B R E A D A L B A N E
Falls of Lochay
Boreland
Milton Morenish
Morenish
Ardeonaig
Corrymuckloch
Creag Mhòr
Hotel
Finlarig
Killin
Achmore
Meall a'Churain
Beinn Cheathaich
Ben Challum
Beinn nan Imirean
Creag Gharbh
Creag Uchdag
Fingen Burn
R. Almond
Auchnafree
Meall Reamhar
Auchnafree Hill
Ben Chonzie
Loch Lednock Resr
Meall Tarsuinn
Lochan Breaclaich
Allt Riobain
Auchlyne West Burn
R. Dochart
A 827
Auchlyne
Ardchyle
Hotel
Ledcharrie
Glen Dochart
Lochdochart House
Loch Iubhair
A 85
Beinn Leabhain
Glen Ogle
Glen Lednock
Spout Rolla
Invergeldie Burn
Invergeldie
Loch Turret Resr
Carn Chòis
Glen Turret
Strath Fillan
Benmore
Loch Dochart
Crianlarich
Meall a'Mhadaidh
Beich Burn
Sròn Mhòr
Glen Tarken
Loch Bottachan
R. Lednock
Falls of Keltie
Monzie
BEN MORE
Stob Binnein
Monachyle Glen
Meall an t-Seallaidh
Lochearnhead
Dalveich
LOCH EARN
Hotel
St Fillans
Dunira
Deil's Caldron
Comrie
Lawers
Ochtertyre
Hosh
CRIEFF
Castle
Edinample
Ardtrostan
Ardvorlich
Dundurn
Tullybannocher
Dalginross
Ross
R. Earn
Quoig
Lochlane
NN
Braes of Balquhidder
Balquhidder
Auchtoo
Craigruie
Monachylemore
Loch Voil
Kingshouse
Meall Reamhar
Ben Halton
BEN VORLICH
Beinn Tulaichean
Beinn a' Chroin
L. Doine
Inverlochlarig
Calair Burn
Ballimore
STRATHYRE FOREST
Glen Ampie
Strathyre
Hotel
FOREST OF GLENARTNEY
Glen Artney
Water of Ruchill
Culloch
Torlum
Torlum Wood
Drummond Castle
Balloch
88
Muthill
Fathan Glinne
Stob a' Choin
Beinn Each
Meall Odhar
Dalchruin
Tighnablair
Ochtermuthill
Machany Water
Beinn Bhreac
Benvane
Loch Lubnaig
Ardchullarie More
Findhu Glen
Creag Beinn nan Eun
Ben Clach
Coire Odhar
ROMAN FORTLET
Cruinn Bheinn
Meall Cala
Glen Finglas
Allt Gleann nam Meann
Uamh Bheag
Glenlichorn
River Knaik
Muir of Orchill
Garrick
Strath Gartney
Glen Finglas Resr
Gleann Casaig
Anie
Cromlet
Slymaback
Braco Castle
Braco
ROMAN FORT
Stronachlachar
LOCH KATRINE
Loch Arklet
Meall Gainmheich
Ellen's Isle
Ben An
BEN LEDI
Pass of Leny
Leny Ho
CALLANDER
Keltie Water
Bullie Burn
Goblin's Cave
The Trossachs
Hotel
Brig o' Turk
Coilantogle
Bochastle
Mickle Burn
Greenloaning
BEN VENUE
Hotel
A 821
Lendrick
Loch Venachar
A 81
R. Teith
Loch Mahaick
Braes of Doune
Allan Water
Loch Chon
Beinn Dubh
Loch Achray
Loch Drunkie
Annet Burn
Ardoch Burn
Kinbuck
ACHRAY FOREST
Beinn Dearg
Torrie Forest
Drumvaich
Burn of Cambus
Kilbryde Castle
Ashfield
Sheriff Muir
B 829
Kinlochard
Hotel
BEN LOMOND
Loch Ard
Menteith Hills
Loch Rusky
B 822
Lanrick Castle
B 8032
Deanston
DOUNE
A 820
DUNBLANE
Kippenross
Blairdenon Hill
Milton
Aberfoyle
Hotel
Port of Menteith
Priory
Castle
Ruskie
A 873
B 826
Thornhill
Goodie Water
Lake of Menteith
Blair Drummond
Sunnylaw
Dumyat Fort
Duchray Water
LOCH ARD FOREST
Rowardennan Lodge
Beinn Uird
Gartmore Ho
Gartmore
Dykehead
Cardross
B 8034
Flanders Moss
B 8031
Broch
Blairdrummond Moss
BRIDGE OF ALLAN
Blairlogie
ALVA
Menstrie
Drum of Clashmore
Rowardennan Forest
Beinn Bhreac
Kelty Water
Dalmary
Flanders Moss
River Forth
B 8075
Drip Moss
Causewayhead
Tullibody
Inchlonaig
Gualann
B 835
Buchlyvie
Arnprior
B 8037
Kippen
Cauldhame
A 811
Leckie
Gargunnock
Cambuskenneth
Abbey
STIRLING
Cambus
Moor Park
Conic Hill
Muir Park Resr
Carleatheran
Gargunnock Hills
Touch Hills
Cambusbarron
Gillies Hill
St Ninians
Fallin
Inchfad
Balmaha
Milton
Inchcailloch
Garadhban Forest
Buchanan Smithy
B 837
A 875
Chartershall
Bannockburn
Rossdhu House
Drymen
Balfron
Stronend
Earlsburn Resrs
North Third Resr
Cringate Law
Earl's Hill
Cowie
Ross Priory
Inchmurrin
Boquhan
B 818
Ballikinrain Castle
Endrick Water
Fintry
Loch Walton
Gartness
Croftamie
Gartocharn
Killearn
Cairnoch Hill
Loch Coulter Resr
Plean
B 9124
ROMAN ROAD
A 872
Arden
Castle
Balloch Castle
Balloch
NS
Craighat
Dumgoyne
Strath Blane
Earl's Seat
C A M P S I E   F E L L S
River Carron
Carron Valley Resr
R. Carron
B 818
Carron Bridge
Dunipace
Carron Valley Forest
DENNY
Larbert
Stenhousemuir
Auchencarroch
Jamestown
Alexandria
Bonhill
Auchineden Hill
Duntreath Castle
Strathblane Hills
A 809
Netherton
Blanefield
B 821
Birkenburn Resr
Tomtain
Kilsyth Hills
High Banton
Head of Muir
Dennyloanhead
Bonnybridge
Camelon
Dumbarton Muir
Burncrooks Resr
Clachan of Campsie
Balgrochan
Strathblane
Banton
KILSYTH
Banknock
Longcroft
High Bonnybridge
Greenhill
A 82 (T)
Renton
Kilmannan Resr
Lennoxtown
Queenzieburn
A 891
Milton of Campsie
Castlecary
ANTONINE WALL
Shieldhill
KILPATRICK HILLS
Bellsmyre
Cochno Loch
Mugdock
Mugdock Resr
Dullatur
Croy
Jawcraig
DUMBARTON
Milton
Loch Humphrey
Greenside Resr
Jaw Resr
Blairskaith
MILNGAVIE
Birdston
Kelvin
Twechar
Eastfield
CUMBERNAULD
Finlaystone
Bowling
B 8050
A 807
Torrance
Forth and Clyde Canal
KIRKINTILLOCH
B 8048
Waterside
Fannyside Lochs
Slamannan
River Avon
Langbank
Old Kilpatrick
Duntocher
Faifley
Bardowie
Balmore
Condorrat
Luggiebank
Erskine Br. Toll
BEARSDEN
Lenzie
Mollinsburn
Binniehill
Bishopton
Rossland
Drumchapel
Cadder
Bridgend
B 803
Erskine
Inchinnan
Bishopbriggs
Auchinloch
Annathill
Riggend
Greengairs
Limerigg
Kilmacolm
CLYDEBANK
Temple
Lumloch
Muirhead
Marnock
Wattston
Longriggend
Black Loch
Barochan Ho
Yoker
A 80 (T)
Stepps
Glenboig
Stand
Caldercruix
Hillend Resr
Georgetown
A 761
RENFREW
Glasgow Airport
Springburn
Garnkirk
Gartcosh
Glenmavis
Airdriehill
Blackridge
Bridge of Weir
Houston
Partick
Tunnel
82
Coatbridge
AIRDRIE
83
Forrestfield
Linwood
Govan
GLASGOW
Lilly Loch
Forrestburn Resr

Ardtalnaig
Glen Quaich
Milton
Amulree
Obney Hills
Gellyburn
Murthly
Meikleour
Kinclaven
Tullich Hill
Ardeonaig
Gleann a Chilleine
Loch Freuchie
Meall nam Fuaran
Creag Liath
Gibbieston
Obney
Waterloo
Muir of Thorn
Ardoch
Cargill
Bankfoot
Airntully
Gauls
West Tofts
Wolfhill
Stanley
Corrymuckloch
Meall nan Caorach
Glenshee
Finglen Burn
Auchnafree
R Almond
Creag Uchdag
Meall Reamhar
Logiealmond Lodge
Dunsinnan
Guildtown
Kinrossie
Ben Chonzie
Auchnafree Hill
Loch Lednoch Resr
Logiealmond
Harrietfield
Chapelhill
Newmiln
St Martins
Colenden
Meall Tarsuinn
Moneydie
Luncarty
Spout Rolla
Loch-Turret Resr
Invergeldie
Glen Lednock
Buchanty
Glenalmond
College
Pitcairngreen
Almondbank
Scone Palace
Old Scone
New Scone
Loch Boltachan
Càrn Chois
Glen Turret
Loch Meallbrodden
Busby
Falls of Keltie
Monzie
Keillour
Methven
Huntingtower
Glen Tarken
Hotel
St Fillans
Ardtrostan
Dunira
Deil's Caldron
Lawers
Ochtertyre
Castle
Hosh
Gilmerton
Cross
Fowlis Wester
Keillour Forest
Braegrum
Tibbermore
Perth
Kinnoull Hill
Kinfauns
Dundurn
Comrie
Tullybannocher
Dalginross
Ross
Quoig
Crieff
Lochlane
Madderty
Pow Water
Findo Gask
Milltown of Aberdalgie
Tarsappie
Elcho
Rhynd
Ben Halton
Balloch
Torlum
Torlum Wood
St David's
Clathy
Aberdalgie
Craigend
Moncreiffe Hill
Forest of Glenartney
Glen Artney
Culloch
Drummond Castle
Muthill
Chapel
Roman Road
Kirkton
Forteviot
Forgandenny
Bridge of Earn
Kintillo
Aberargie
Dalchruin
Tighnablair
Ochtermuthill
Machany Water
Kinkell Bridge
Strathallan Cas
R Earn
Aberuthven
Ardargie Ho Hotel
Fort
Dron
Glenfoot
Dunning
Balmanno Hill
Findhu Glen
Ben Clach
Creag Beinn nan Eun
Coire Odhar
Roman Fortlet
Muir of Orchill
Auchterarder
Craig Rossie
Rossie Ochill
Glenlichorn
River Knaik
Garrick
Muirtown
Kincardine Castle
Path of Condie
Glenfarg Resr
Arngask
Newton of Balcanquhal
Uamh Bheag
Cromlet
Braco Castle
Braco
Roman Fort
Slymaback
Hotel
Gleneagles Sta
Common of Dunning
Glenfarg
Bullie Burn
Blackford
Gleneagles
Corb Law
Middle Rigg
Duncrievie
Gateside
Muckle Burn
Greenloaning
Braes of Ogilvie
Glen Eagles
Steele's Knowe
Sim's Hill
Innerdouny Hill
Dochrie Hill
Hospital
Middleton
Burnside
Loch Mahaick
Braes of Doune
Allan Water
Wether Hill
Glendevon Resrs
Craigow
Upper Tillyrie
Kinbuck
Core Hill
Glen Devon
Glendevon
Burnfoot
Dalqueich
Milnathort
Castle
Balgedie
Drumyaich
Burn of Cambus
Kilbryde Castle
Ashfield
Sheriff Muir
South Queich
Lendrick Hill
Lanrick Castle
Doune
Deanston
Blairdenon Hill
Commonedge Hill
Yetts o' Muckhart
Carnbo
Kinross
Loch Leven
Castle
Dunblane
Ben Cleuch
King's Seat Hill
Muckhart
Drum
Tullibole Castle
St Serf's Island
Priory
Kippenross Ho
Blair Drummond
Castle Campbell
Rumbling Bridge
Crook of Devon
Coldrain
Gairney Bank
Ballingry
Sunnylaw
Dumyat Fort
Blairdrummond Moss
Bridge of Allan
Blairlogie
Alva
Tillicoultry
Dollar
Powmill
Cleish
Benarty Hill
Lochore
Menstrie
Causewayhead
Devonside
Blairingone
Cleish Hills
Loch Ore
Drip Moss
Leckie
Gargunnock
Fishcross
Coalsnaughton
Cult Hill
Hill End
Loch Glow
Glencraig
Cambuskenneth
Abbey
Stirling
Cambus
Tullibody
New Sauchie
Forest Mill
Kelty
Keilarsbrae
Balgonar
Knock Hill
Carleatheran
Touch Hills
Cambusbarron
Gillies Hill
St Ninians
Fallin
Alloa
Tower
Clackmannan
South Alloa
Kennet
Saline
Craigluscar Hill
Lassodie
Loch Fitty
Cowdenbeath
Gargunnock Hills
Chartershall
Bannockburn
Throsk
Cowstrandburn
Bowershall
Kingseat
Hill of Beath
Earlsburn Resrs
North Third Resr
Cowie
Dunmore
Blairhall
Carnock
Gowkhall
Townhill
Crossgates
Cringate Law
Earl's Hill
Tulliallan Cas
Devilla Forest
Moor Loch
Oakley
Milesmark
Wellwood
Dunfermline
Fordell
Donibristle
Plean
Airth
Kincardine
Valleyfield
Cairneyhill
Crossford
Pow Burn
Blair Cas
Abbey
Culross
Low Torry
Torryburn
Cairnoch Hill
Loch Coulter Resr
Roman Road
Power Station
Longannet Point
Torry Bay
Charlestown
Limekilns
Rosyth
Castle
Fordell Castle
Aberdour
Carron Valley Resr
R Carron
Stenhousemuir
Skinflats
Hillend
Dalgety
Dunipace
Carron Bridge
Larbert
Carron
Grangemouth
Bo'ness
Grangepans
Carriden
Inverkeithing
St Davids
Carron Valley Forest
Denny
Camelon
Falkirk
Muirhouses
St Margaret's Hope
Inverkeithing Bay
North Queensferry
Birkenburn Resr
Tomtain
High Banton
Head of Muir
Dennyloanhead
Bonnybridge
Kinneil Ho
Blackness
Hopetoun Ho
Forth Road Bridge
Inch Garvie
Forth Br
Kilsyth Hills
Kilsyth
Banton
Longcroft
High Bonnybridge
Glen Village
Redding
Champany
The Binns
Queensferry
Barnbougle Castle
Dalmeny
Queenzieburn
Banknock
Castlecary
Greenhill
Reddingmuirhead
Brightons
Linlithgow Bridge
Linlithgow
Old Philpstoun
Philpstoun
Newton
Dundas Castle
Antonine Wall
Dullatur
Croy
Shieldhill
Maddiston
Whitecross
Union Canal
Fort
Twechar
California
Bridgend
Winchburgh
Cumbernauld
Eastfield
Jawcraig
Loan
Forts
Kirkliston
Cramond Bridge
Kirkintilloch
Fannyside Lochs
Standburn
Lochcote Resr
Tower
Ecclesmachan
Edinburgh Airport
Ingliston
Gogar
Waterside
Condorrat
Slamannan
River Avon
Avonbridge
Westfield
Torphichen
Preceptory
B 8046
Newbridge
Ratho Station
Mollinsburn
Luggiebank
Binniehill
Cairnpapple
Uphall
Broxburn
Burnside
Ratho
Bridgend
Annathill
Riggend
Greengairs
Limerigg
Dechmont
Uphall Station
Union Canal
Wattston
Longriggend
Bathgate
Boghall
Deans
Bonnington
Long Hermiston
Juniper Green
Muirhead
Marnock
Glenboig
Stand
Caldercruix
Black Loch
Hillend Resr
Armadale
Whiteside
Livingston
Livingston Village
Wilkieston
Garnkirk
Gartcosh
Glenmavis
Airdriehill
Blackridge
Westrigg
East Calder
Lochwood
Plains
Forrestfield
Lilly Loch
Oakbank
Kirknewton
Balerno
Coatbridge
Airdrie
Hall
NN
NS
87
92
83

DUNDEE
CARNOUSTIE
MONIFIETH
BUDDON NESS
Barry Links
Broughty Ferry
TAYPORT
NEWPORT ON TAY
Tay Road Bridge
Tay Bridge
FIRTH OF TAY
TENTSMUIR FOREST
Invergowrie
Longforgan
CARSE OF GOWRIE
Dog Bank
Carthagena Bank
Leuchars
Earlshall
Guardbridge
Eden Mouth
ST ANDREWS BAY
ST ANDREWS
Kinkell Ness
Buddo Ness
Babbet Ness
Boarhills
Kingsbarns
Cambo Ness
Carr Brigs
Tullybothy Craigs
FIFE NESS
North Carr
CRAIL
West Ness
KILRENNY
ANSTRUTHER
PITTENWEEM
ST MONANCE
ELIE
EARLSFERRY
Chapel Ness
Saucher Point
Isle of May
NORTH SEA
NO
NEWBURGH
Lindores Loch
AUCHTERMUCHTY
PITMEDDEN FOREST
CUPAR
Dairsie or Osnaburgh
Pitscottie
Ceres
Springfield
LADYBANK
Howe of Fife
Kingskettle
FALKLAND
Lomond Hills
Freuchie
Largoward
Lathones
Peat Inn
Colinsburgh
Kilconquhar
Largo Law
LARGO BAY
Ruddons Point
Lower Largo
Lundin Links
Kennoway
LEVEN
METHIL
BUCKHAVEN
East Wemyss
West Wemyss
Macduff's Castle
MARKINCH
GLENROTHES
LESLIE
Thornton
Auchterderran
LOCHGELLY
Dysart
KIRKCALDY
Linktown
Seafield Tower
KINGHORN
Pettycur
BURNTISLAND
NT
FIRTH OF FORTH
Inchkeith
Oxcars
Inchmickery
Cramond Island
Granton
Leith
Black Rocks
EDINBURGH
Portobello
Duddingston
Morningside
Liberton
Gilmerton
Dalkeith
Musselburgh
PRESTONPANS
COCKENZIE AND PORT SETON
TRANENT
Due to open Late 1986
Due to open Early 1986
Longniddry
Gosford Bay
Aberlady Bay
Aberlady
Gullane Bay
Gullane
Dirleton
Eyebroughy
Fidra
NORTH BERWICK
Craigleith
Bass Rock
Tantallon Castle
St Baldred's Boat
Scoughall
Whitekirk
St Baldred's Cradle
Tyne Mouth
Tyninghame
DUNBAR
East Linton
Traprain Law
HADDINGTON
Athelstaneford
Drem
Garleton Hills
Gifford
Yester Ho
Pencaitland
Dunbar Common
Stenton
Broxburn
Spott
Lammermuir Hills

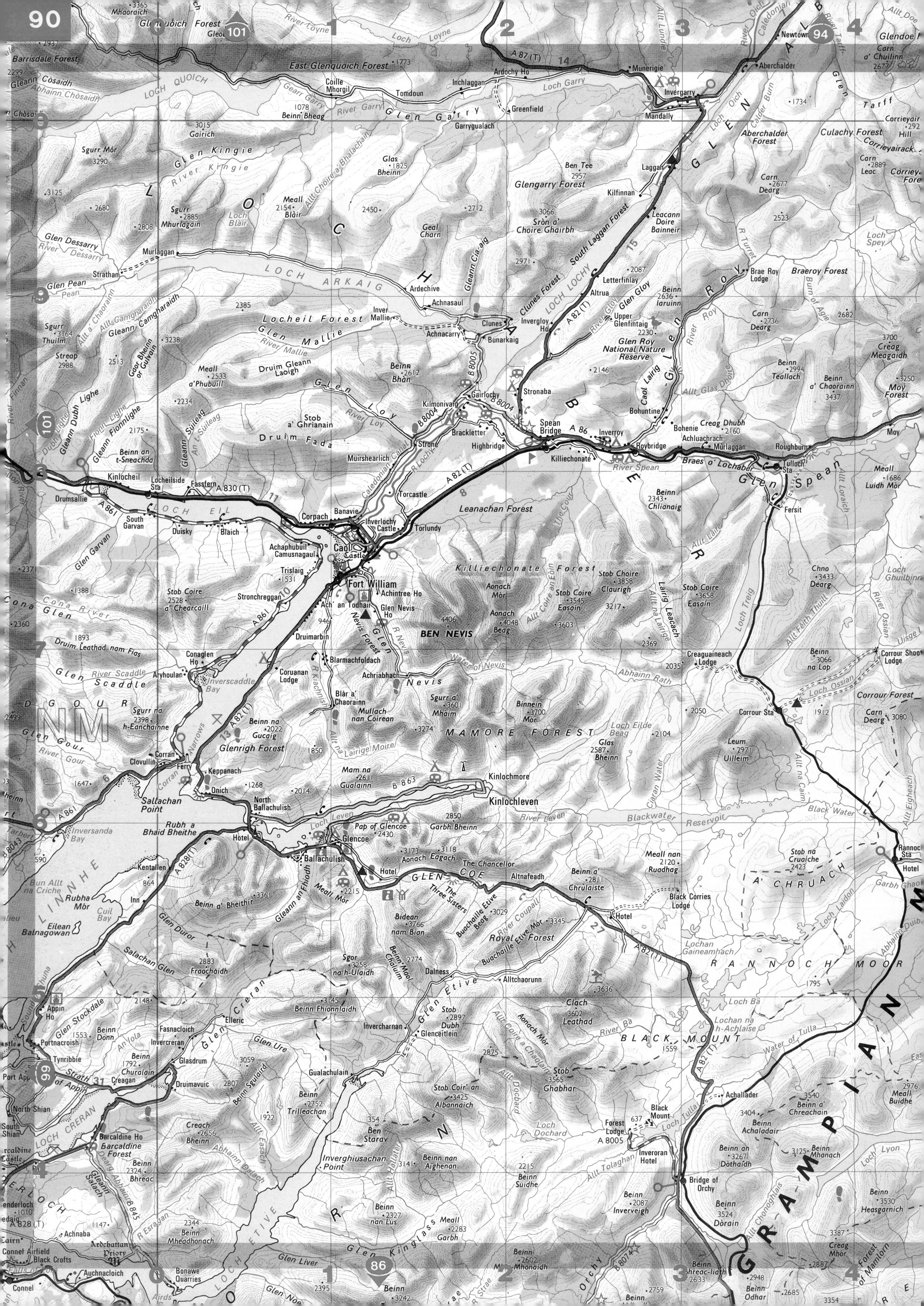

90
Glenquoich Forest
101
1
2
3
4
94
Barrisdale Forest
East Glenquoich Forest
Coille Mhorgil
Tomdoun
Inchlaggan
Ardochy Ho
Loch Garry
Munerigie
Invergarry
Mandally
Aberchalder
Newtown
Glendoe
LOCH QUOICH
Gleann Còsaidh
River Garry
Glen Garry
Greenfield
Garrygualach
Beinn Bheag
Gairich
Glen Kingie
River Kingie
Sgurr Mòr
Glas Bheinn
Ben Tee
Glengarry Forest
Laggan
Kilfinnan
Aberchalder Forest
Culachy Forest
Corrieyairack
Carn Dearg
Meall Blàir
Sgurr Mhurlagain
Loch Blair
Geal Charn
Sròn a' Choire Ghairbh
South Laggan Forest
Leacann Doire Bainneir
Loch Spey
Glen Dessarry
River Dessarry
Murlaggan
Strathan
LOCH ARKAIG
Gleann Cia-aig
Letterfinlay
LOCH LOCHY
Clunes Forest
Glen Pean
Ardechive
Achnasaul
Brae Roy Lodge
Braeroy Forest
Beinn Iaruinn
Glen Gloy
Altrua
Glen Roy
Locheil Forest
Inver Mallie
Clunes
Invergloy Ho
Upper Glenfintaig
Sgurr Thuilm
Gleann Camgharaidh
Glen Mallie
River Mallie
Achnacarry
Bunarkaig
Glen Roy National Nature Reserve
Creag Meagaidh
Streap
Gaor Bheinn or Gulvain
Meall a' Phubuill
Druim Gleann Laoigh
Beinn Bhan
Stronaba
Caol Lairig
Beinn Teallach
Beinn a' Chaorainn
Moy Forest
Gleann Dubh Lighe
Gleann Fionnlighe
Glen Loy
Gairlochy
Kilmonivaig
Stob a' Ghrianain
River Loy
Druim Fada
Strone
Brackletter
Spean Bridge
Inverroy
Bohuntine
Bohenie
Creag Dhubh
Achluachrach
Murlaggan
Roughburn
Moy
Beinn an t-Sneachda
Gleann Suileag
Muirshearlich
Caledonian Canal
Highbridge
Killiechonate
Roybridge
Braes o' Lochaber
Tulloch Sta
River Spean
Glen Spean
Kinlocheil
Locheilside Sta
Fassfern
A 830 (T)
LOCH EIL
Drumsallie
Torcastle
Leanachan Forest
Meall Luidh Mòr
Beinn Chlianaig
Fersit
South Garvan
Duisky
Blaich
Corpach
Banavie
Inverlochy Castle
Torlundy
Glen Garvan
Achaphubuil
Camusnagaul
Caol
Castle
Trislaig
Killiechonate Forest
Fort William
Stob Coire a' Chearcaill
Stronchreggan
Achintree Ho
Glen Nevis Ho
Ach' an Todhair
Aonach Mòr
Stob Choire Claurigh
Stob Coire Easain
Chno Dearg
Cona Glen
Aonach Beag
BEN NEVIS
Nevis Forest
Lairig Leacach
Loch Treig
Druimarbin
Druim Leathad nam Fias
Conaglen Ho
Blarmachfoldach
Water of Nevis
Glen Nevis
Achriabhach
Creaguaineach Lodge
Abhainn Rath
Beinn na Lap
Corrour Shooting Lodge
Glen Scaddle
River Scaddle
Aryhoulan
Inverscaddle Bay
Coruanan Lodge
Blàr a' Chaorainn
Sgurr a' Mhaim
Binnein Mòr
Loch Ossian
Corrour Forest
Corrour Sta
Sgurr na h-Eanchainne
Beinn na Gucaig
Mullach nan Coirean
MAMORE FOREST
Loch Eilde Beag
Carn Dearg
Glen Gour
River Gour
Glenrigh Forest
Lairige Moire
Glas Bheinn
Leum Uilleim
Clovullin
Corran
Ferry
Corran Narrows
Keppanach
Onich
Mam na Gualainn
Kinlochmore
Kinlochleven
Sallachan Point
North Ballachulish
Ciaran Water
Allt na Caim
Black Water
Rubh' a Bhaid Bheithe
Inversanda Bay
Hotel
Loch Leven
Pap of Glencoe
Garbh Bheinn
River Leven
Blackwater Reservoir
Glencoe
Ballachulish
Aonach Eagach
The Chancellor
Altnafeadh
Beinn a' Chrùlaiste
Meall nan Ruadhag
Stob na Cruaiche
Rannoch Sta
A' CHRUACH
Kentallen
Gleann an Fhiodh
Meall Mòr
GLEN COE
The Three Sisters
Black Corries Lodge
Inn
Rubha Mòr
Cuil Bay
Beinn a' Bheithir
Buachaille Etive Beag
Buachaille Etive Mòr
Royal Forest
Eilean Balnagowan
LINNHE
Glen Duror
Bidean nam Bian
River Coupall
Lochan Gaineamhach
Salachan Glen
Fraochaidh
Sgor na h-Ulaidh
Beinn Maol Chaluim
Dalness
Alltchaorunn
RANNOCH MOOR
Appin Ho
Glen Stockdale
Glen Creran
Beinn Fhionnlaidh
Glen Etive
Stob Dubh
Clach Leathad
Loch Ba
Lochan na h-Achlaise
Beinn Donn
Portnacroish
Fasnacloich
Invercreran
Elleric
Invercharnan
Glenceitlein
Aonach Mòr
River Ba
BLACK MOUNT
Water of Tulla
Tynribbie
Beinn Churalain
Creagan
Glasdrum
Glen Ure
Strath of Appin
Gualachulain
Stob Ghabhar
99
Druimavuic
Beinn Sgulaird
Beinn Trilleachan
Stob Coir' an Albannaich
Achallader
Beinn a' Chreachain
Beinn Achaladair
Meall Buidhe
North Shian
South Shian
Creach Bheinn
Ben Starav
Loch Dochard
Black Mount
Forest Lodge
A 8005
Loch Tulla
Barcaldine Ho
Barcaldine Forest
LOCH CREAN
Barcaldine Castle
Beinn Bhreac
Gleann Salach
Inverghiusachan Point
Beinn nan Aighenan
Beinn Suidhe
Inveroran Hotel
Allt Tolaghan
Beinn an Dòthaidh
Beinn Mhanach
Bridge of Orchy
GRAMPIAN
Benderloch
Beinn Inverveigh
Beinn Dòrain
Beinn Heasgarnich
A 828 (T)
Achnaba
Beinn Mheadhonach
Beinn nan Lus
Meall Garbh
Connel Airfield
Black Crofts
Ardchattan Priory
Glen Liver
Glen Kinglass
86
Beinn Mhonaidh
Beinn Mhòr
Forest of Mamlorn
Auchnacloich
Bonawe Quarries
LOCH ETIVE
Connel
Glen Noe
Beinn Eunaich
Beinn Odhar
Orchy
Beinn Chreag-liath

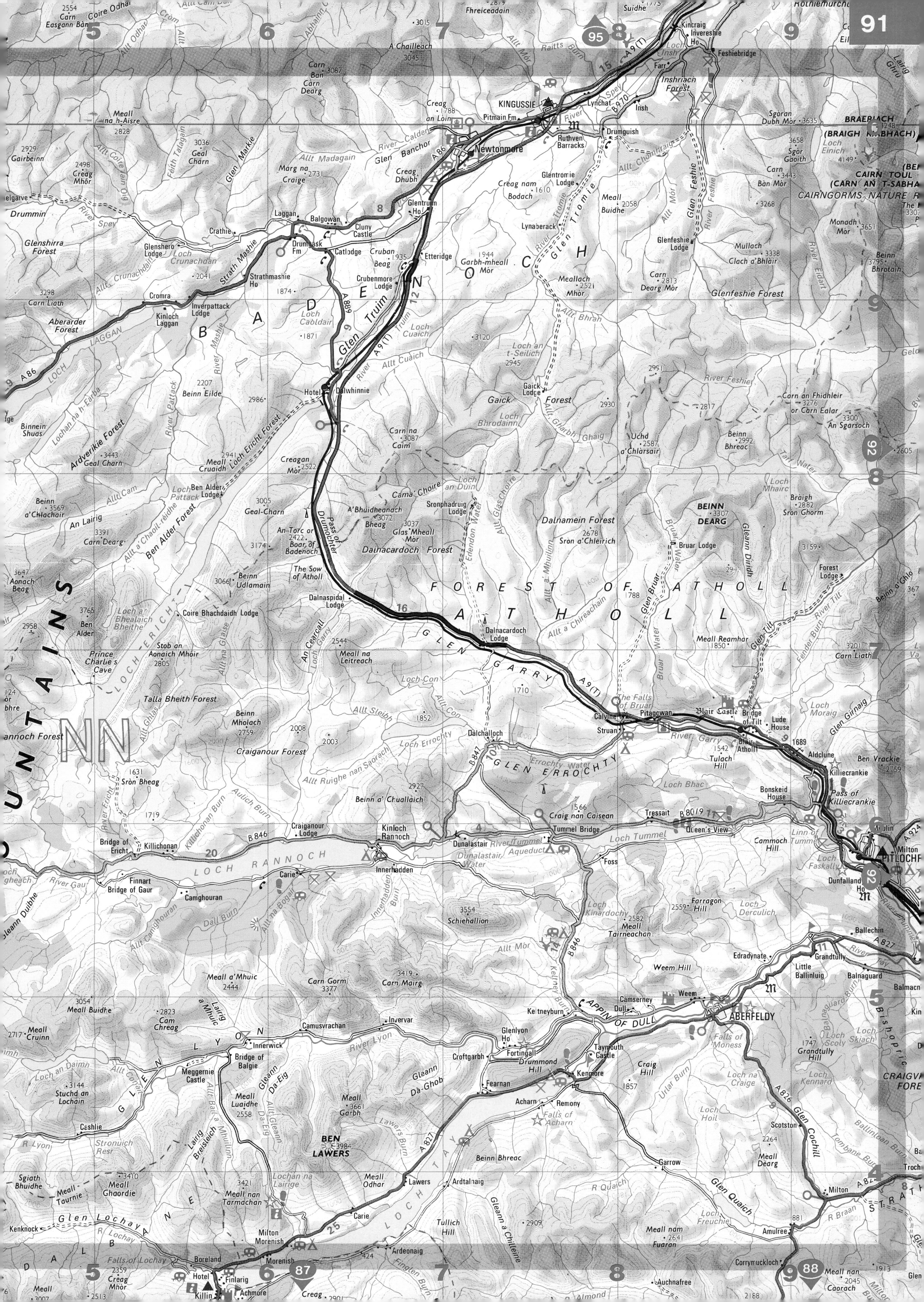
KINGUSSIE
Newtonmore
Kincraig
Insh
Feshiebridge
Inshriach Forest
Lynchat
Pitmain Fm
Ruthven Barracks
Drumguish
Glen Banchor
River Calder
Allt Madagain
Creag an Loin
Creag Dhubh
Glentruim Ho
Laggan
Balgowan
Cluny Castle
Crathie
Drummin
River Spey
Glenshirra Forest
Glenshero Lodge
Loch Crunachdan
Drumgask Fm
Catlodge
Strath Mashie
Strathmashie Ho
Cromra
Kinloch Laggan
Inverpattack Lodge
Carn Liath
Aberarder Forest
LOCH LAGGAN
A86
A9(T)
A889
Cruban Beag
Etteridge
Crubenmore Lodge
Glen Truim
Loch Caoldair
Loch Cuaich
Allt Cuaich
Dalwhinnie
Hotel
BADENOCH
Glentromie Lodge
Glen Tromie
River Tromie
Creag nam Bodach
Meall Buidhe
Lynaberack
Garbh-mheall Mòr
Meallach Mhòr
Allt Bhran
Loch an t-Seilich
Gaick Lodge
Gaick Forest
Loch Bhrodainn
Glen Feshie
River Feshie
Glenfeshie Lodge
Glenfeshie Forest
Carn Dearg Mòr
Mullach Clach a' Bhlàir
Sgòran Dubh Mòr
BRAERIACH (BRAIGH RIABHACH)
Loch Einich
Sgòr Gaoith
Carn Bàn Mòr
CAIRN TOUL (CARN AN T-SABHAIL)
CAIRNGORMS NATURE RESERVE
Monadh Mòr
Beinn Bhrotain
Carn an Fhidhleir or Carn Ealar
An Sgarsoch
Beinn Bhreac
Uchd a' Chlàrsair
Tarf Water
Loch Mhairc
Bràigh Sròn Ghorm
BEINN DEARG
Gleann Diridh
Bruar Lodge
Forest Lodge
Beinn a' Ghlo
Carn Liath
Meall Reamhar
Glen Tilt
Fender Burn
Beinn Eilde
River Pattack
Binnein Shuas
Lochan na h-Earba
Ardverikie Forest
Geal Charn
Loch Ericht Forest
Meall Cruaidh
Loch Pattack
Ben Alder Lodge
Ben Alder Forest
Beinn a' Chlachair
An Lairig
Carn Dearg
Geal-Charn
Creagan Mòr
Carn na Caim
Cama' Choire
Loch an Dùin
Sronphadruig Lodge
A' Bhuidheanach Bheag
Glas Mheall Mòr
Pass of Drumochter
An Torc or Boar of Badenoch
Dalnacardoch Forest
Edendon Water
Dalnamein Forest
Sron a' Chleirich
The Sow of Atholl
Beinn Udlamain
Aonach Beag
GRAMPIAN MOUNTAINS
FOREST OF ATHOLL
ATHOLL
Dalnaspidal Lodge
Loch Garry
GLEN GARRY
Dalnacardoch Lodge
Allt a' Chireachain
Glen Bruar
Bruar Water
Coire Bhachdaidh Lodge
Ben Alder
Loch a' Bhealaich Bheithe
LOCH ERICHT
Stob an Aonaich Mhòir
Prince Charlie's Cave
An Cearcall
Meall na Leitreach
Loch Con
Talla Bheith Forest
Beinn Mholach
Craiganour Forest
Allt Sleibh
Loch Errochty
Dalchalloch
GLEN ERROCHTY
Errochty Water
The Falls of Bruar
Calvine
Struan
Pitagowan
Blair Castle
Bridge of Tilt
Blair Atholl
Lude House
Tulach Hill
Aldclune
Killiecrankie
Pass of Killiecrankie
Ben Vrackie
Bonskeid House
Loch Bhac
Glen Girnaig
Loch Moraig
NN
Rannoch Forest
Sròn Bheag
Beinn a' Chuallaich
Allt Ruighe nan Saorach
Craig nan Caisean
Tummel Bridge
Tressait
Queen's View
Loch Tummel
Linn of Tummel
Cammoch Hill
Loch Faskally
PITLOCHRY
Dunfallandy Ho
Milton
Bridge of Ericht
Killichonan
Craiganour Lodge
Kinloch Rannoch
Dunalastair
Dunalastair Water
River Tummel
Aqueduct
Foss
LOCH RANNOCH
B846
B847
B8019
Finnart
Bridge of Gaur
River Gaur
Camghouran
Carie
Innerhadden
Schiehallion
Allt na Bogair
Dall Burn
Loch Kinardochy
Meall Tairneachan
Farragon Hill
Loch Derculich
Ballechin
A827
Grandtully
Little Ballinluig
Balnaguard
Edradynate
Weem Hill
Allt Mòr
Keltney Burn
Meall a' Mhuic
Carn Gorm
Carn Mairg
Meall Buidhe
Cam Chreag
Lairig a' Mhuic
Camusvrachan
Invervar
Innerwick
GLEN LYON
River Lyon
Bridge of Balgie
Meggernie Castle
Meall Cruinn
Loch an Daimh
Stuchd an Lochain
Cashlie
Stronuich Resr
Glenlyon Ho
Fortingall
Croftgarbh
Keltneyburn
APPIN OF DULL
Camserney
Dull
Weem
ABERFELDY
Falls of Moness
Grandtully Hill
Loch Scoly
Loch Skiach
Bishopric
CRAIGVINEAN FOREST
Taymouth Castle
Drummond Hill
Kenmore
Craig Hill
Loch Kennard
Loch na Craige
Urlar Burn
Fearnan
Acharn
Remony
Falls of Acharn
Loch Hoil
A826
Glen Cochill
Scotston
Meall Dearg
Ballinloan Burn
Meall Luaidhe
Gleann Da-Eig
Meall Garbh
Gleann Dà-Ghob
BEN LAWERS
Lairig Breisleich
LOCH TAY
Beinn Bhreac
Garrow
Glen Quaich
R Quaich
Loch Freuchie
Milton
R Braan
Amulree
Sgiath Bhuidhe
Meall Ghaordie
Meall nan Tarmachan
Lochan na Lairige
Meall Odhar
Lawers
Ardtalnaig
Gleann a' Chilleine
Tullich Hill
Meall nam Fuaran
Kenknock
Glen Lochay
R Lochay
BREADALBANE
Falls of Lochay
Boreland
Milton Morenish
Morenish
Carie
Ardeonaig
Finglen Burn
Creag Mhòr
Hotel
Finlarig
Killin
Achmore
Corrymuckloch
Auchnafree
Meall nan Caorach
Fhreiceadain
A' Chailleach
Carn Ban
Carn Dearg
Meall na h-Aisre
Gairbeinn
Creag Mhòr
Geal Charn
Glen Markie
Marg na Craige
Coire Odhar
Easgann Bàn
95
92
87
88
5
6
7
8
9
4

CAIRNGORM
CAIRNGORM MOUNTAINS
GRAMPIAN MOUNTAINS
BRAEMAR
FOREST OF MAR
Bynack More
Glen Avon
The Bruach
Forest of Glenavon
Stob an t-Sluichd
Loch Avon
Loch Builg
Brown Cow Hill
Carn Leac Saighdeir
Cairn Mona Gowan
Morven
Migvie
Logie Coldstone
Beinn a'Chaorainn
Shelter Stone
Loch Etchachan
BEN AVON
BEINN A'BHUIRD
BRAERIACH
BEN MACDUI (BEINN MACDUIBH)
CAIRN TOUL
Derry Cairngorm
Beinn Bhreac
Carn a'Mhaim
The Devil's Point
Carn Eas
Culardoch
Creag an Dail Bheag
River Gairn
Gairnshiel Lodge
Glen Fenzie
Peter's Hill
Culblean Hill
Glendavan House
Geallaig Hill
Glen Gairn
Culsh
Coilacriech
Milton of Tulloch
Muir of Dinnet
Bush Crathie
Crathie
Balmoral Castle
Abergeldie Castle
Bridge of Gairn
River Dee
Ballater
Glascorrie
Pannanich Hill
House of Glenmuick
Black Craig
Carn na Drochaide
Meall Gorm
Feardar Burn
Inver
Invercauld Ho
Easter Balmoral
Birkhall
Creag nan Gall
Girnock Burn
The Coyles of Muick
Aucholzie
Cairn Leuchan
Clachan Yell
Pollagach Burn
Water of Tanar
Glen Lui
Luibeg Water
Sgòr Mór
Creag Bhalg
Allanaquoich
Braemar
Castle
Ballochbuie Forest
Falls of Garbh Allt
Claybokie
Linn of Dee
Muir
Inverey
Tomintoul
Cairn Geldie
Geldie Burn
Ey Burn
The Colonel's Bed
Auchallater
Glen Gelder
Balmoral Forest
LOCHNAGAR
Conachcraig
River Muick
Glen Muick
Mount Keen
Carn Liath
Glen Ey
Clunie Water
Callater Burn
Glen Callater
Loch Callater
Creag nan Gabhar
Spittal of Glenmuick
Fasheilach
Glen Mark
Water of Mark
Hill of Saugh
Ladder Burn
Bynack
Carn Bhac
Baddoch
Sgòr Mór
White Mounth
Dubh Loch
Cairn Bannoch
Broad Cairn
Glas-allt-Shiel
Loch Muick
Allt Darrarie
Black Hill of Mark
Glen Lee
Invermark Lodge
Monawee
AN SOCACH
Carn an Tuirc
Tolmount
Loch Esk
Easter Balloch
Loch Lee
Inchgrundle
Beinn Iutharn Mhor
Loch nan Eun
Loch Vrotachan
Water of Unich
Lair of Aldararie
Carn an Righ
Glas Tulaichean
Gleann Mór
Carn a'Gheoidh
The Cairnwell
Devil's Elbow
GLAS MAOL
Caenlochan Forest
Glen Doll
Glendoll Forest
Glendoll Lodge
Braedownie
Muckle Cairn
Cruys
Glen Effock
Loch Brandy
Ben Tirran
Water of Saughs
Beinn a'Ghlo
Loch Loch
Glen Loch
Creag Leacach
Finalty Hill
River Isla
Mayar
Driesh
GLEN CLOVA
Clova
River South Esk
White Hill
Ben Gulabin
Dalmunzie Hotel
Meall a' Choire Bhuidhe
Carn an Daimh
Monamenach
Cairn Baddoch
Cairn Inks
Cairn of Barns
Wheen
Finbracks
Hill of Glansie
Loch Valigan
Ben Vuirich
Allt Glen Loch
Spittal of Glenshee
Hotel
Ben Earb
Auchavan
Loch Beanie
GLEN PROSEN
Rottal
Badandun Hill
Glen Finlet
Glen Damff
Glen Logie
Runtaleave
Glenprosen Village
Eskielawn
Hill of Couternach
Auld Darkney
Gleann Fearnach
Meall Uaine
Mealna Letter or Duchray Hill
Creag an t-Sithein
Dalnaglar Castle
Glen Shee
Forter
Glenmoy
Redheugh
NN
Tarvie
Straloch
Ben Vrackie
Glen Brerachan
Enochdhu
Cray
Folda
Lamh Dearg
Mount Blair
Brewlands Bridge
Glenhead Fm
Blackwater Reservoir
Easter Lednathie
Horniehaugh
Glenquiech
Newmill of Inshewan
Balvarran
Creag Dhubh
Ashintully Castle
Kirkmichael
Blacklunans
Kirkton of Glenisla
Cat Law
Dykehead
Cortachy
Castle
Memus
Milton of Edradour
PITLOCHRY
Hotel
B950
STRATHARDLE
Cairn Gibbs
Bellaty
Creigh Hill
Balintore
Pearsie
Burnside
Loch Broom
Meall Reamhar
Black Water
Dykend
Mile Hill
Balloch
Inverquharity
Shielhill
Dalcapon
Knock of Balmyle
FOREST OF ALYTH
Drumderg
Loch of Lintrathen
B951
Kinnordy
Northmuir
Tulliemet Ho
Ballintuim
Creag nam Mial
Blackcraig Castle
Balduff Hill
Bridge of Craigisla
Bridgend of Lintrathen
Kirkton of Kingoldrum
KIRRIEMUIR
Ballechin
River Tay
Tulliemet
Ballinluig
Logierait
Blackcraig Hill
Netherton
Tullymurdoch
Westmuir
Mosside
Balnaguard
Forest of Clunie
Blackcraig Forest
Bridge of Cally
Hotel
Bamff
Airlie Castle
Kirkton of Airlie
Mains of Ballindarg
Padanaram
Drumgley
Balmacneil
Kindallachan
Loch Ordie
Loch Benachally
Cochrage Muir
Hill of Alyth
Craigton
Leys of Cossans
Kincraigie
Guay
Dowally
Riemore Lodge
Benachally
Tullyfergus
Ruthven
Gateside
Bishopric
Loch Skiach
Dalguise
Deuchary Hill
Riechip
Middleton
Craighall
ALYTH
New Alyth
Ruthven House
Dean Water
Glamis Castle
Glamis
Douglastown
Lornty Burn
Rotmell Loch
Cardney Ho
Butterstone
Lornty
A926
A9412
STRATHMORE
Balhary
Leitfie
Thornton
Kirkton
CRAIGVINEAN FOREST
Forneth
Logie
BLAIRGOWRIE
RATTRAY
Kinloch
Charleston
Foffarty
Loch of Lowes
Concraigie
Clunie
Craigie
Balkeerie
Eassie
Inverarity
Dunkeld
Little Dunkeld
Dunkeld Ho
Cath
Snaigow Ho
Muirton of Ardblair
Rosemount
Kinloch
Meigle
Belmont Castle
Kirkinch
Wester Denoon
Milton
Gateside
Inver
Newtyle Hill
Kirkton of Lethendy
Lunan Burn
Arthurstone
Ark Hill
Nether Handwick
Gallowfauld
Ballinloan Burn
Ballinlick
Birnam
Spittalfield
A984
Ardler
Newbigging
Newtyle
Kinpurney Hill
Gallow Hill
SIDLAW HILLS
Trochry
Birnam Hill
Caputh
Delvine
Keillor
COUPAR ANGUS
STRATHBRAAN
Obney Hills
Stare Dam
Gellyburn
Murthly
Meikleour
R Tay
Kinclaven
R Isla
Markethill
Kettins
Hallyburton Ho
Long Loch
Kirkton of Auchterhouse
Coldstream
Balgray
Souterrain
Muir of Thorn
Ardoch
Campmuir
Leys
Kirkton of Tealing
Newbigging
East Mains
Creag Liath
Gibbieston
Obney
Waterloo
Cargill
Woodside
Burrelton
Pitcur
Lundie
Auchterhouse
Leoch
Glen Shee
Bankfoot
Airntully
Whitefield
Dronley
Kirkton of Strathmartine
Burnside of Duntrune
Glenshee
Gauls
Ordie Burn
West Tofts
Wolfhill
Saucher
King's
Littleton
Redmyre
Fowlis Easter
Muirhead
Birkhill
Camperdown
Downfield
Stanley
95
96
91
88
89

MORAY FIRTH
CROMARTY FIRTH
INVERGORDON
CROMARTY
Sutors of Cromarty
Blue Head
Mc Farquhar's Cave
North Sutor
Dunskeath Ness
Nigg
Sands of Nigg
Nigg Bay
Balnapaling
Castlecraig
Hill of Nigg
King's Cave
Pitcalnie
Chapelhill
Ankerville
Tarbat Ho
Kilmuir
Barbaraville
Balintraid
Saltburn
Port an Righ
Cromarty Bay
Udale Bay
Balblair
Jemimaville
Newton
Muirton
Upper Eathie
Balmungie
Whiteness Head
Rosemarkie
Rosemarkie Bay
FORTROSE
Cathedral
Chanonry Point
Fort George
Ardersier
Tradespark
NAIRN
Aulcearn
Gollanfield
Inverness Airport
Muir of the Clans
Milton of Gollanfield
Fisherton
Tornagrain
Alturlie Point
Castle Stuart
Newton
Croy
Dalcross
Cantraywood
Culloden Forest
Culloden Muir
Balloch
Newlands
Clava Cairns
Easter Muckovie
Kilravock Castle
Cawdor
Easter Galcantray
Cantraydoune
Assich Forest
Kirkton of Barevan
Mains of Clunas
Clunas Resr
Clephanton
Rosefield
Geddes Ho
Regoul
Piperhill
Culcharry
Mid Urchany
Laiken Forest
Littlemil
Redburn
Newlands of Fleenas Wood
Ardclach
Ferness
Glenferness Ho
Dulsie
Saddle Hill
Carn a' Chrasgie
Carn Sgùmain
Beinn Bhuidhe Mhòr
House of Daviot
Daviot
Carn nan Tri-tighearnan
Streens
River Findhorn
Beinn Bhreac
Moy Burn
Meall Mòr
Moy Hall
Loch Moy
Meall a' Bhreacraibh
Ruthven
Carn na h-Easgainn
Carn an t-Sean-liathanaich
Balvraid
Inverbrough
Tomatin
Carn a' Choire Mhòir
Carn Glas-choire
Beinn Bhreac
Findhorn Bridge
Carn nam Bain-tighearna
Kyllachy Ho
Glen Kyllachy
Corrievorrie
Slochd
Strathdearn
Dalmigavie Lodge
Glen Mazeran
Carn Phris Mhòir
Carn Dubh 'Ic an Deoir
Dalmigavie
River Dulnain
Carrbridge
Duthil
Dulnain Bridge
Skye of Curr
Drumuillie
Cullachie
Boat of Garten
East Croftmore
Loch Garten
Abernethy Forest
Kinveachy
Beinn Ghuilbin
Avielochan
Eil
Carn Sleamhuinn
Cnoc Fraing
Granish
Aundorach
Tore Hill
Tulloch
Auchgourish
Forest Lodge
Carn Coire na h-Easgainn
Geal-charn Mòr
Aviemore
Craigellachie
Coylumbridge
Inverdruie
The Queen's Forest
Glenmore Lodge
Glen More
Loch Morlich
River Luineag
Loch Alvie
Alvie
The Polchar
Rothiemurchus
Carn an Fhreiceadain
An Suidhe
Kincraig
Inverehie Ho
Loch Insh
Feshiebridge
Insh
Inshriach Forest
Lynchat
KINGUSSIE
Pitmain Fm
Raitts Burn
Allt Mòr
Carn Eilrig
Castle Hill
Lairig Ghru
CAIRN GORM
CAIRNGORM
Sgoran Dubh Mòr
BRAERIACH
Shelter Stone
Loch Avon
Beinn a' Chaorainn
Bynack More
Stac na h-Iolaire
Meall a' Bhuachaille
Carn Bheadhair
Geal Charn
Braes of Abernethy
Dorback Lodge
Baddoch
Lettoch
Nethy Bridge
Sliemore
Dell Lodge
River Nethy
Carn na Farraidh
Tom an t-Suidhe Mhòir
Carn Meadhonach
Bridge of Brown
Sgòr Gaoithe
Creagan a' Chaise
HILLS OF CROMDALE
Haughs of Cromdale
Cromdale
Speybridge
GRANTOWN-ON-SPEY
Glenbeg
Craggan
Beinn Mhòr
Achnahannet
Cottartown
Camerory
Creag Liath
Dellefure
Mains of Dalvey
Lettoch
Upper Derraid
Auchnagallin
Glenmore Loch
Carn Ruigh Chorrach
Lochindorb Lodge
Lochindorb
Carn na Lòine
Advie
Bridge of Avon
Scootmore Forest
Burn of Tulchan
Allt a' Gheallaidh
Larig Hill
Hill of Aitnoch
Aitnoch
Knock of Braemoray
Dorback Burn
River Divie
Carn Kitty
NJ
Beachans
Relugas
Loch Dallas
Hill of Tomechole
Mill Buie
Drumine Forest
Darnaway Forest
Milton
Conicavel
Whitemire
Boghole Fm
Altyre Woods
Altyre Ho
Newtyle Forest
Branchill
Dallas
Dallas Forest
Hill of the Wangie
Meikle Hill
Kellas
Pluscarden
Black Burn
Heldon Hill
Monaughty Forest
Pluscarden Priory
Barnhill
Rafford
Blervie Castle
Califer
FORRES
Sueno's Stone
Dyke
Brodie Castle
Kintessack
Cloddymoss
Culbin Forest
Kincorth Ho
Moy Ho
Findhorn
Findhorn Bay
Kinloss
Grange Hall
Springfield
Coltfield
Crook of Alves
Hempriggs
BURGHEAD
BURGHEAD BAY
Roseisle Forest
Roseisle
Cummingstown
Newtown
Hopeman
Duffus
Church
Gordonstoun
Duffus Castle
Quarrywood
Covesea Skerries
Newton
Miltonduff
Pittendreich
Paddockhaugh
Thornhill
Glenlatterach
Glenlatterach Resr
Leanoch Burn
Pikey Hill
Cairn Uish
Carn na Cailliche
Elchies Forest
Archiestown
Upper Knockando
Cardow
Knockando
Knockando Ho
Carron
Marypark
Bellehiglash
Cairnacay
Drumin
Glenlivet
Shenval
Strath Avon
River Avon
Carn Liath
Carn Daimh
Tomnavoulin
Knockandhu
Clashnoir
Braes
Chapelton
Fodderletter
Burn of Lochy
Tomintoul
Milton
Conglass Water
Blairnamarrow
Water of Ailnack
Water of Caiplich
Craig Veann
Cnap Chaochan Aitinn
Carn na Feannaige
Burn of Loin
Big Garvoun
GLEN AVON
The Bruach
Forest of Glenavon
Stob an t-Sluichd
BEN AVON
Loch Builg
Carn Ealasaid
Delnabo Lodge
Brown Hill
STRATHSPEY

103
Halliman Skerries
Covesea Skerries
BRANDERBURGH
LOSSIEMOUTH
Hopeman
Duffus
Gordonstoun
Boar's head Rock
Lossie Forest
SPEY BAY
PORTKNOCKIE
FINDOCHTY
Cullen Bay
Logie Head
Redhythe Point
Sandend Bay
Bauds of Cullen
CULLEN
Sandend
PORTSOY
Boyne Bay
Knock Head
Whitehills
BUCKIE
Rathven
Loch Spynie
Spynie Palace
Leuchars Ho
Quarrywood
Loch-hill
Kingston
Spey Bay
Portgordon
Garmouth
Nether Dallachy
Upper Dallachy
Slackhead
Bin of Cullen
Linmill
Fordyce
Durn Hill
Milton
Kirktown of Deskford
Easter Whyntie
Boyndie
Auds
ELGIN
Urquhart
Bogmoor
Lochs Crofts
Llanbryde
Auchenhalrig
Cairnfield House
Drybridge
Hill of Maud Crofts
Shiel Muir
Berryhillock
Wester Culbeuchly Crofts
Miltonduff
Pittendreich
Moss of Barmuckity
Mosstodloch
Broadley
Clochan
Craibstone
Toux
Oldtown of Ord
Paddockhaugh
Fochabers
Whiteash Hill Wood
Speymouth Forest
Aultmore
Millstone Hill
Lurg Hill
Cornhill
Thornshill
Longmorn
Blackhills
Dipple
Ordiequish
Whitewreath
Teindland Forest
Teindland
Inchberry
Wood of Ordiequish
Deerhill
Edingight Ho
Knock Hill
Gordonstown
Middle Witchyburn
Fattahead
Kellas
Glenlatterach
Glenlatterach Resr
Leanoch Burn
Glen of Rothes
Forgie
Broadrashes
Grange Crossroads
Crannach
Sillyearn
Bracobrae
Finnygaud
Lootcherbrae
Cranna
ABERCHIRDER
Pikey Hill
Cairn Uish
Newlands
Aultmore
Newmill
Hill of Mulderie
Davoch of Grange
Drumnagorrach
Knock
Glen Barry
Farmtown
ROTHES
River Spey
Mulben
KEITH
ISLA
Tauchers
Marnoch
Clunie
Carn na Cailliche
Cairn Cattoch
Burn of Rothes
Elchies Forest
Ben Aigan
Rosarie Forest
STRATH
The Bin Forest
River Isla
Milltown
Arndilly Ho
Hill of Towie
Little Pitlurg
The Balloch
Glen of Coachford
Ruthven
Yonder Bognie
Hillbrae
River Deveron
Inverkeithny
Auchininna
Whiteacen
Dandalieth
Maggieknockater
Towiemore
Fourman Hill
Bogniebrae
Archiestown
Ringorm
Craigellachie
Kininvie Ho
Drummuir Castle
Cairnie
Corse of Kinnoir
Upper Knockando
Cardow
Knockando
Knockando Ho
Midtown of Buchromb
CHARLESTOWN OF ABERLOUR
SPEY
The Bin
The Bin Forest
Daugh of Cairnborrow
Drumblair Ho
Lessendrum
Aucharnie
Balgaveny
Carron
Daugh of Kinermony
Balvenie Castle
Milltown of Auchindoun
Daugh of Invermarkie
Cairnborrow
Torry
HUNTLY
Castle
Corse
Drumblade
Marypark
Daugh of Carron
Milltown of Edinvillie
DUFFTOWN
Haugh of Glass
River Deveron
Geln of Artloch Croft
Clashmach Hill
Strath Bogie
STRATHBOGIE
Slioch
Brideswell
Denend
Ythanwells
Scootmore Forest
Bellehiglash
Beatshach
Meikle Conval
Auchindoun Castle
The Scalp
Bailieswards
Bridgend
Crofts of Shanquhar
Thomastown
Newtongarry Croft
Dullan Water
BEN RINNES
Glen Rinnes
Succoth
Tillathrowie
Coynachie
Kirkstile
Crofts of Backburn
Glens of Foudland
Hill of Tillymorgan
Bridge of Avon
Favillar
Glen Fiddich
Tomnaven
Clashindarroch Forest
Culdrain
Clashindarroch Forest
Hill of Foudland
Kirkton of Culsalmond
Colpy
Cairnacay
Achnastank
Glenfiddich Lodge
River Fiddich
Gartly
Largie
Wrangham
Bridgend
Inverharroch
Clashindarroch
Kirkney Water
Cults
Knockandy Hill
Picardy Stone
Glenfiddich Forest
Black Water
Drumin
Glenlivet
Shenval
Corryhabbie Hill
Tap o' Noth
Milton of Noth
Milton of Lesmore
Leith Hall
Kennethmont
B 9002
Ardlair
The Shevock
Aulton
Insch
Newton Ho
Ardoyne
Strath Avon
River Avon
Carn Liath
Cairn Muldonich
Mount of Haddoch
Round Hill
Cabrach
Aldunie
Rhynie
Cottown
Wheedlemont
Clatt
Duncanston
Leslie
Kirkton
Oyne
Carn Daimh
Tomnavoulin
Carn an t-Suidhe
Blackwater Forest
Craig Castle
Church
Knockespock Ho
Auchleven
Gadie Burn
Licklyhead Castle
Bennachie
River Livet
Cairnbrallan
Hill of Three Stones
The Buck
Coldwells Croft
Whitehaugh Forest
Suie Hill
Knockandhu
Clashnoir
Braes of Glenlivet
Chapeltown
Clova
Lumsden
CORREEN HILLS
Muckletown
Bodderletter
Lord Arthur's Cairn
Tullynessle
Keig
Castle Forbes
Tomintoul
Milton
LADDER HILLS
Carn Mor
Badenyon
Glenbuchat Lodge
Creag an Eunan
Mossat
Bridge of Alford
Montgarrie
HOWE OF ALFORD
Alford
Rorandle
Cairn William
Pitfichie Forest
Conglass Water
Moss Hill
Ladylea Hill
Belnacraig
Rinmore
Kildrummy
Castle
Milltown
Auchintoul
Asloun
Blairnamarrow
Carn Liath
The Socach
Water of Nochty
Kirkton of Glenbuchat
Water of Buchat
Bridge of Buchat
Castle
Glenkindie
Towie
Sinnahard
Milltown of Towie
Whitehouse
Pitmunie
Lecht Road
Breagach Hill
Glen Ernan
Bellabeg
Strathdon
Muir of Fowlis
Little Lynturk
Kirkton
Tillyfourie
Balck Hill
River Avon
Carn Ealasaid
Craig Veann
Ernan Water
Geal Charn
Inverernan Ho
Candacraig Ho
Heugh-head
Boultenstone
Frosty Hill
Milton of Cushnie
Leochel Cushnie
Ley
Orrdhead
Correnie Forest
Correnie Moor
Tornashean Forest
Craig of Bunzeach
Hillockhead
Craigievar Castle
Kintocher
Benaquhallie
Bankhead
Cock Bridge
Colnabaichin
Delnadamph Lodge
Castle
Corgarff
River Don
Tornahaish
Pressendye
Easter Davoch
Corse Ho
Comers
AVON
Carn Leac Saighdeir
Cairn Mona Gowan
Deskry Water
Migvie
Coynach
Douneside
Craskins
Craiglich
Tornaveen
Findrack Ho
Drumlasie
Brown Cow Hill
Loch Builg
Logie Coldstone
Morven
Tarland
Souterrain
Lumphanan
Motte
HILL
MOUNTAINS
CROMAR
Stone Circle
Coul
Milton of Auchinhove
Auchlossan
Torphins
Milton of Campfield
River Gairn
Gairnshiel Lodge
Fenzie
92
Peter's Hill
Culblean Hill
Glendavan House
Ordie
Loch Davan
Scar Hill
Mortlich
Mid Beltie

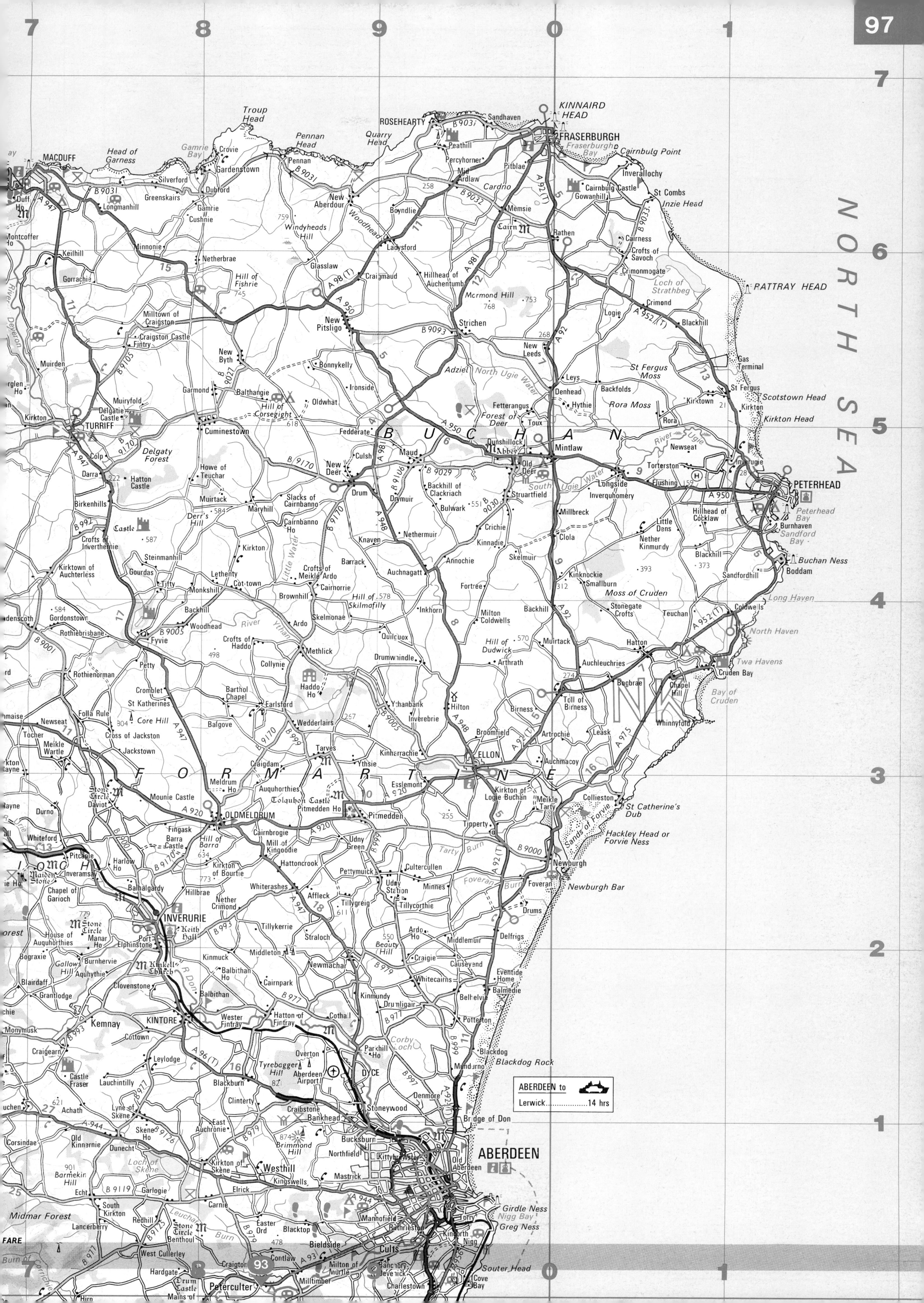

7
8
9
0
1
NORTH SEA
KINNAIRD HEAD
FRASERBURGH
Fraserburgh Bay
Cairnbulg Point
Inverallochy
Cairnbulg Castle
St Combs
Inzie Head
Sandhaven
ROSEHEARTY
Troup Head
Pennan Head
Quarry Head
Head of Garness
MACDUFF
Gamrie Bay
Crovie
Gardenstown
Pennan
Peathill
Percyhorner
Mid Ardlaw
Pitblae
Memsie
Cardno
Cairn
Rathen
Silverford
Dubford
Greenskairs
Gamrie
Cushnie
Longmanhill
New Aberdour
Boyndlie
Windyheads Hill
Woodhead
Ladysford
Minnonie
Netherbrae
Keilhill
Gorrachie
Hill of Fishrie
Glasslaw
Craigmaud
Hillhead of Auchentumb
Mormond Hill
Strichen
New Pitsligo
Milltown of Craigston
Craigston Castle
Fintry
New Byth
Muirden
Bonnykelly
Ironside
Adziel
North Ugie Water
New Leeds
Leys
Denhead
Hythie
Backfolds
Rora Moss
Rora
St Fergus Moss
Crimond
Loch of Strathbeg
Crimonmogate
Cairness
Crofts of Savoch
Logie
Blackhill
RATTRAY HEAD
Gas Terminal
St Fergus
Scotstown Head
Kirkton
Kirkton Head
Garmond
Balthangie
Hill of Corsegight
Oldwhat
Muiryfold
Delgatie Castle
TURRIFF
Cuminestown
Fetterangus
Forest of Deer
Toux
Fedderate
BUCHAN
Dunshillock
Abbey
Mintlaw
Old Deer
Newseat
River Ugie
Inverugie
Torterston
Flushing
PETERHEAD
Peterhead Bay
Sandford Bay
Burnhaven
Boddam
Buchan Ness
Delgaty Forest
Colp
Darra
Hatton Castle
Howe of Teuchar
New Deer
Culsh
Maud
Drum
Dumuir
Backhill of Clackriach
Bulwark
South Ugie Water
Longside
Inverquhomery
Stuartfield
Hillhead of Cocklaw
Little Dens
Nether Kinmundy
Blackhill
Sandfordhill
Birkenhills
Muirtack
Slacks of Cairnbanno
Maryhill
Cairnbanno Ho
Derr's Hill
Castle
Crofts of Invertherie
Knaven
Nethermuir
Crichie
Kinnadie
Millbreck
Clola
Annochie
Skelmuir
Kinknockie
Smallburn
Moss of Cruden
Long Haven
Steinmanhill
Kirkton
Gourdas
Tifty
Lethenty
Cot-town
Little Water
Crofts of Meikle Ardo
Cairnorrie
Barrack
Auchnagatt
Fortree
Kirktown of Auchterless
Monkshill
Brownhill
Hill of Skilmafilly
Inkhorn
Milton Coldwells
Backhill
Stonegate Crofts
Teuchan
Coldwells
North Haven
Gordonstown
Rothiebrisbane
Backhill
Woodhead
Fyvie
River Ythan
Ardo
Skelmonae
Quilquox
Crofts of Haddo
Methlick
Hill of Dudwick
Arthrath
Muirtack
Hatton
Auchleuchries
Twa Havens
Cruden Bay
Bay of Cruden
Petty
Rothienorman
Collynie
Drumwhindle
Cromblet
St Katherines
Barthol Chapel
Earlsford
Haddo Ho
Ythanbank
Inverebrie
Hilton
Toll of Birness
Birness
Bogbrae
Chapel Hill
Whinnyfold
Folla Rule
Core Hill
Newseat
Tocher
Meikle Wartle
Cross of Jackston
Jackstown
Balgove
Wedderlairs
Broomfield
Artrochie
Leask
Tarves
Ythsie
Kinharrachie
ELLON
Auchmacoy
Craigdam
FORMARTINE
Meldrum Ho
Auquhorthies
Esslemont
Kirkton of Logie Buchan
Meikle Tarty
Collieston
St Catherine's Dub
Stone Circle
Daviot
Mounie Castle
Tolquhon Castle
Pitmedden Ho
Pitmedden
Durno
OLDMELDRUM
Tipperty
Sands of Forvie
Hackley Head or Forvie Ness
Whiteford
Fingask
Barra Castle
Hill of Barra
Cairnbrogie
Mill of Kingoodie
Udny Green
Tarty Burn
Newburgh
Newburgh Bar
Pitcaple
Maiden Stone
Inveramsay
Harlow Ho
Kirkton of Bourtie
Hattoncrook
Pettymuick
Udny Station
Cultercullen
Minnes
Foveran Burn
Foveran
Chapel of Garioch
Balhalgardy
Hillbrae
Nether Crimond
Whiterashes
Affleck
Tillygreig
Tillycorthie
Drums
INVERURIE
Keith Hall
Stone Circle
Manar Ho
House of Auquhorthies
Port Elphinstone
Tillykerrie
Straloch
Ardo Ho
Middlemuir
Delfrigs
Bograxie
Burnhervie
Gallows Hill
Aquhythie
Kinkell Church
Kinmuck
Middleton
Beauty Hill
Newmachar
Craigie
Causeyend
Eventide Home
Balmedie
Blairdaff
Balbithan Ho
Clovenstone
Cairnpark
Whitecairns
Belhelvie
R. Don
Grantlodge
Balbithan
Kinmundy
Drumligair
Kemnay
KINTORE
Wester Fintray
Hatton of Fintray
Cothal
Potterton
Monymusk
Cottown
Craigearn
Leylodge
Overton
Parkhill Ho
Corby Loch
Blackdog
Blackdog Rock
Tyrebagger Hill
Aberdeen Airport
DYCE
Mundurno
Castle Fraser
Lauchintilly
Blackburn
Denmore
Achath
Lyne of Skene
Clinterty
Craibstone
Stoneywood
ABERDEEN to
Lerwick 14 hrs
Bankhead
Bridge of Don
Corsindae
Old Kinnernie
Skene Ho
East Auchronie
Dunecht
Brimmond Hill
Bucksburn
Loch of Skene
Kirkton of Skene
Westhill
Northfield
Kittybrewster
ABERDEEN
Old Aberdeen
Barmekin Hill
Echt
Garlogie
Mastrick
Elrick
Kingswells
Midmar Forest
South Kirkton
Carnie
Girdle Ness
Nigg Bay
Greg Ness
Lancerberry
Redhill
Stone Circle
Benthoul
Easter Ord
Blacktop
Mannofield
Torry
Ruthrieston
Kincorth
Nigg
FARE
Bieldside
West Cullerley
Contlaw
Cults
Hardgate
Craigton
Milton of Murtle
Bancory Devenick
Souter Head
Drum Castle
Peterculter
Milltimber
Charlestown
Cove Bay
93

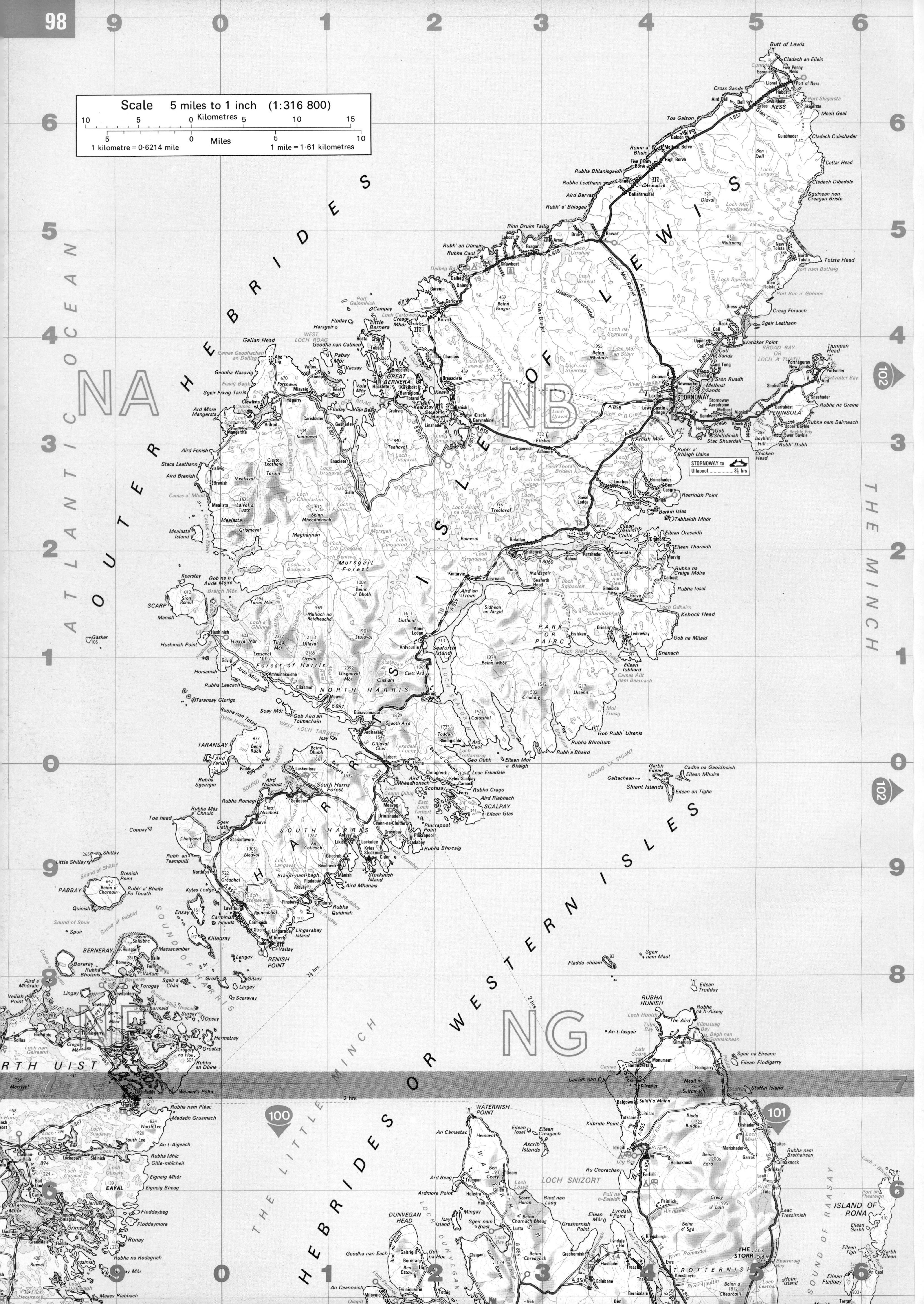
Scale 5 miles to 1 inch (1:316 800)
Kilometres
10 5 0 5 10 15
Miles
5 0 5 10
1 kilometre = 0·6214 mile
1 mile = 1·61 kilometres
NA
NB
NF
NG
ATLANTIC OCEAN
OUTER HEBRIDES
ISLE OF LEWIS
HARRIS
HEBRIDES OR WESTERN ISLES
THE MINCH
THE LITTLE MINCH
NORTH HARRIS
SOUTH HARRIS
Forest of Harris
Morsgail Forest
South Harris Forest
PARK OR PAIRC
STORNOWAY
STORNOWAY to Ullapool 3½ hrs
Butt of Lewis
Port of Ness
Tiumpan Head
EYE PENINSULA
BROAD BAY OR LOCH A TUATH
GREAT BERNERA
WEST LOCH ROAG
EAST LOCH ROAG
SCARP
TARANSAY
SOUND OF TARANSAY
WEST LOCH TARBERT
EAST LOCH TARBERT
LOCH SEAFORTH
SOUND OF SHIANT
Shiant Islands
SCALPAY
PABBAY
BERNERAY
SOUND OF HARRIS
RENISH POINT
NORTH UIST
EAVAL
RUBHA HUNISH
WATERNISH POINT
DUNVEGAN HEAD
LOCH DUNVEGAN
LOCH SNIZORT
TROTTERNISH
THE STORR
ISLAND OF RONA
SOUND OF RAASAY
100
101
102
9 0 1 2 3 4 5 6

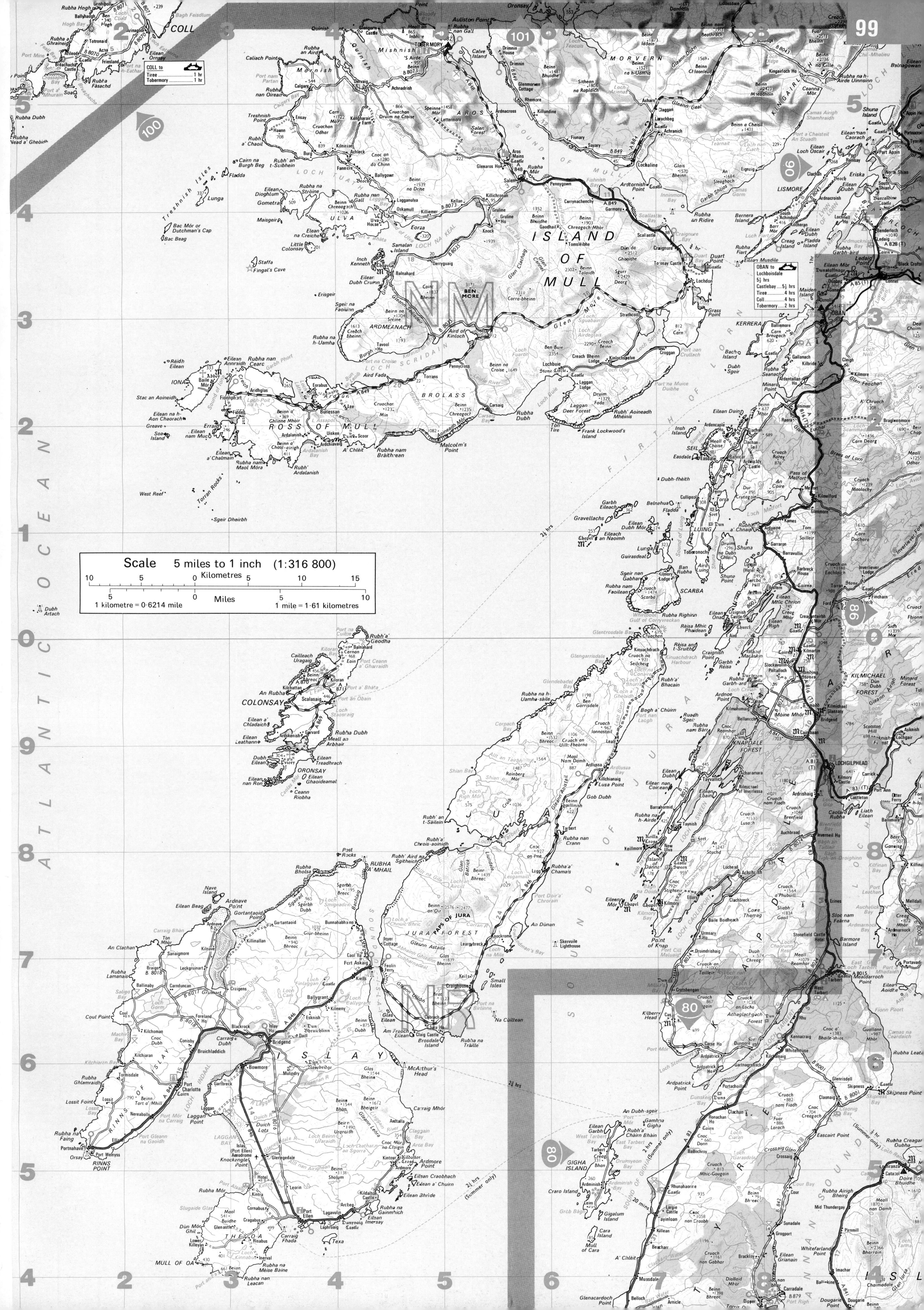
Scale 5 miles to 1 inch (1:316 800)
Kilometres
10 5 0 5 10 15
Miles
5 0 5 10
1 kilometre = 0·6214 mile
1 mile = 1·61 kilometres
COLL to
Tiree 1 hr
Tobermory 1 hr
OBAN to
Lochboisdale 5¾ hrs
Castlebay 5¼ hrs
Tiree 4 hrs
Coll 4 hrs
Tobermory 2 hrs
ATLANTIC OCEAN
ISLAND OF MULL
ROSS OF MULL
IONA
ULVA
Treshnish Isles
Staffa
Fingal's Cave
BEN MORE
TOBERMORY
MORVERN
SOUND OF MULL
LOCH TUATH
LOCH NA KEAL
LOCH SCRIDAIN
ARDMEANACH
BROLASS
KERRERA
OBAN
LISMORE
FIRTH OF LORN
SEIL
LUING
SCARBA
Gulf of Corryvreckan
COLONSAY
ORONSAY
JURA
PAPS OF JURA
JURA FOREST
SOUND OF JURA
SOUND OF ISLAY
ISLAY
RINNS OF ISLAY
LOCH INDAAL
LAGGAN BAY
THE OA
MULL OF OA
Port Ellen
Bowmore
Port Charlotte
Port Askaig
RINNS POINT
GIGHA ISLAND
SOUND OF GIGHA
KNAPDALE FOREST
LOCHGILPHEAD
KILMICHAEL FOREST
LOCH SWEEN
LOCH CAOLISPORT
Tarbert
West Tarbert
Point of Knap
Skervuile Lighthouse
Dubh Artach
Torran Rocks
Frank Lockwood's Island
KINTYRE
KILBRANNAN SOUND
Skipness Point
Carradale
Craighouse
Small Isles
McArthur's Head
Texa
NM
NR
100
101
98
80
90

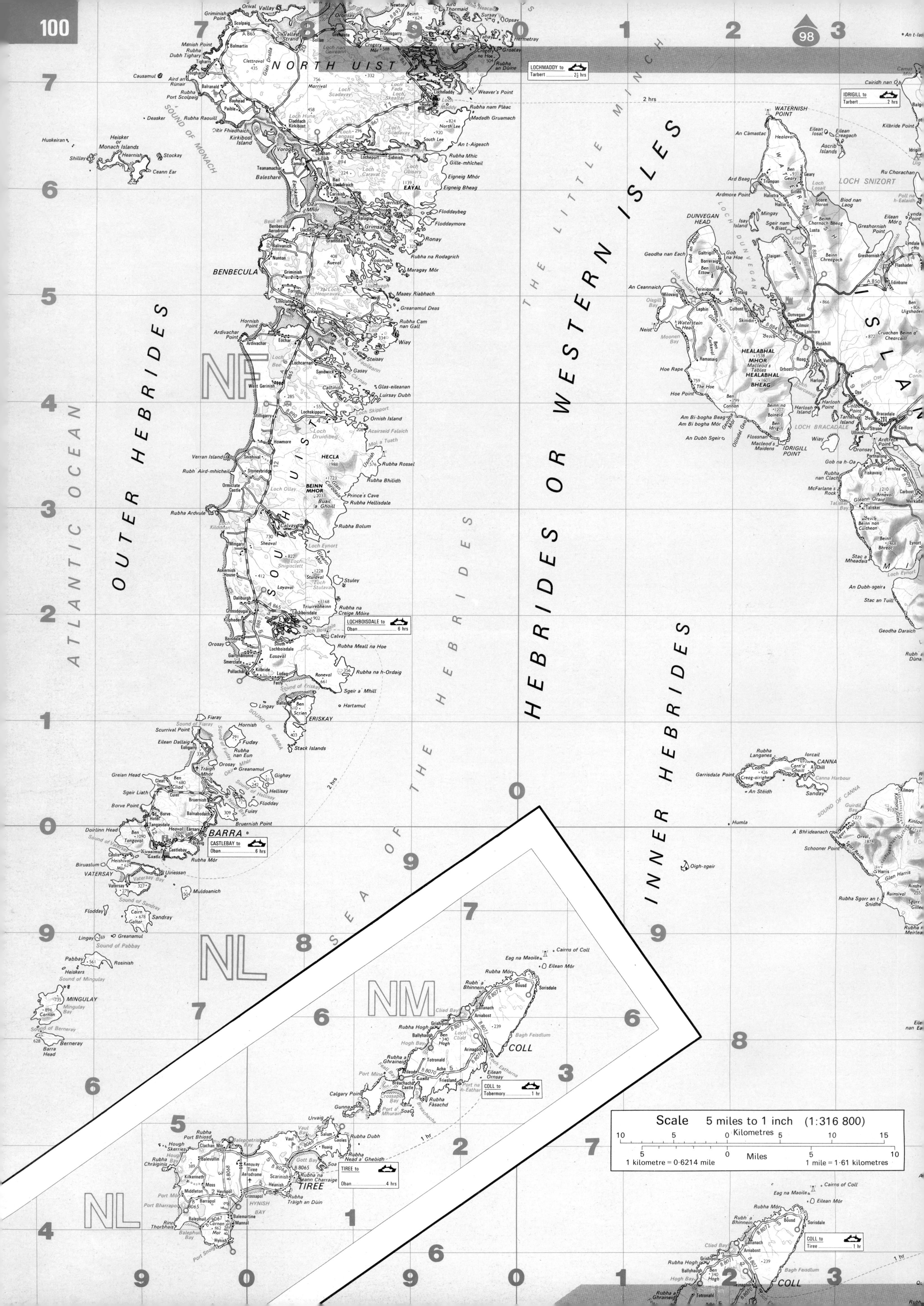

100
98
NORTH UIST
LOCHMADDY to Tarbert 2½ hrs
IDRIGILL to Tarbert 2 hrs
THE LITTLE MINCH
SOUND OF MONACH
Monach Islands
BENBECULA
OUTER HEBRIDES
ATLANTIC OCEAN
HEBRIDES OR WESTERN ISLES
SOUTH UIST
LOCHBOISDALE to Oban 6 hrs
HECLA
BEINN MHOR
EAVAL
ERISKAY
SOUND OF BARRA
BARRA
CASTLEBAY to Oban 6 hrs
VATERSAY
Sandray
Pabbay
MINGULAY
Berneray
Barra Head
SEA OF THE HEBRIDES
INNER HEBRIDES
WATERNISH POINT
LOCH SNIZORT
DUNVEGAN HEAD
LOCH DUNVEGAN
HEALABHAL MHOR
HEALABHAL BHEAG
IDRIGILL POINT
LOCH BRACADALE
CANNA
SOUND OF CANNA
Oigh-sgeir
Humla
NF
NL
NM
COLL
COLL to Tobermory 1 hr
TIREE
TIREE to Oban 4 hrs
HYNISH BAY
Scale 5 miles to 1 inch (1:316 800)
Kilometres
Miles
1 kilometre = 0·6214 mile
1 mile = 1·61 kilometres
COLL to Tiree 1 hr

NG
NH
NM
NN
ISLAND OF RONA
ISLAND OF RAASAY
SOUND OF RAASAY
INNER SOUND
SCALPAY
CROWLIN ISLANDS
SKYE
CUILLIN HILLS
BLA BHEINN
SOAY
RHUM
EIGG
MUCK
TROTTERNISH
THE STORR
GLAMAIG
Portree
Broadford
Kyle of Lochalsh
Mallaig
Fort William
BEN NEVIS
MAMORE FOREST
ARDNAMURCHAN
MOIDART
SUNART
ARDGOUR
KNOYDART
NORTH MORAR
SOUTH MORAR
ARISAIG
SOUND OF SLEAT
LOCH TORRIDON
LOCH CARRON
LOCH ALSH
LOCH DUICH
LOCH HOURN
LOCH NEVIS
LOCH MORAR
LOCH SHIEL
LOCH SUNART
LOCH QUOICH
LOCH ARKAIG
LOCH EIL
LOCH MAREE
LIATHACH
BEINN EIGHE
SLIOCH
FIVE SISTERS
BEINN FHADA OR BEN ATTOW
BEINN SGRITHEALL
ROIS-BHEINN
Applecross Forest
Torridon Forest
Coulin Forest
Attadale Forest
West Monar Forest
East Monar Forest
Glenshiel Forest
Cluanie Forest
Bunloinn Forest
Glengarry Forest
Loch Eil
Lochcarron
Strathcarron
Achnasheen
Kinlochewe
Gairloch
Glenfinnan
Lochailort
Spean Bridge
Kinlochleven
Glencoe
Tobermory
TOBERMORY to Oban 2 hrs

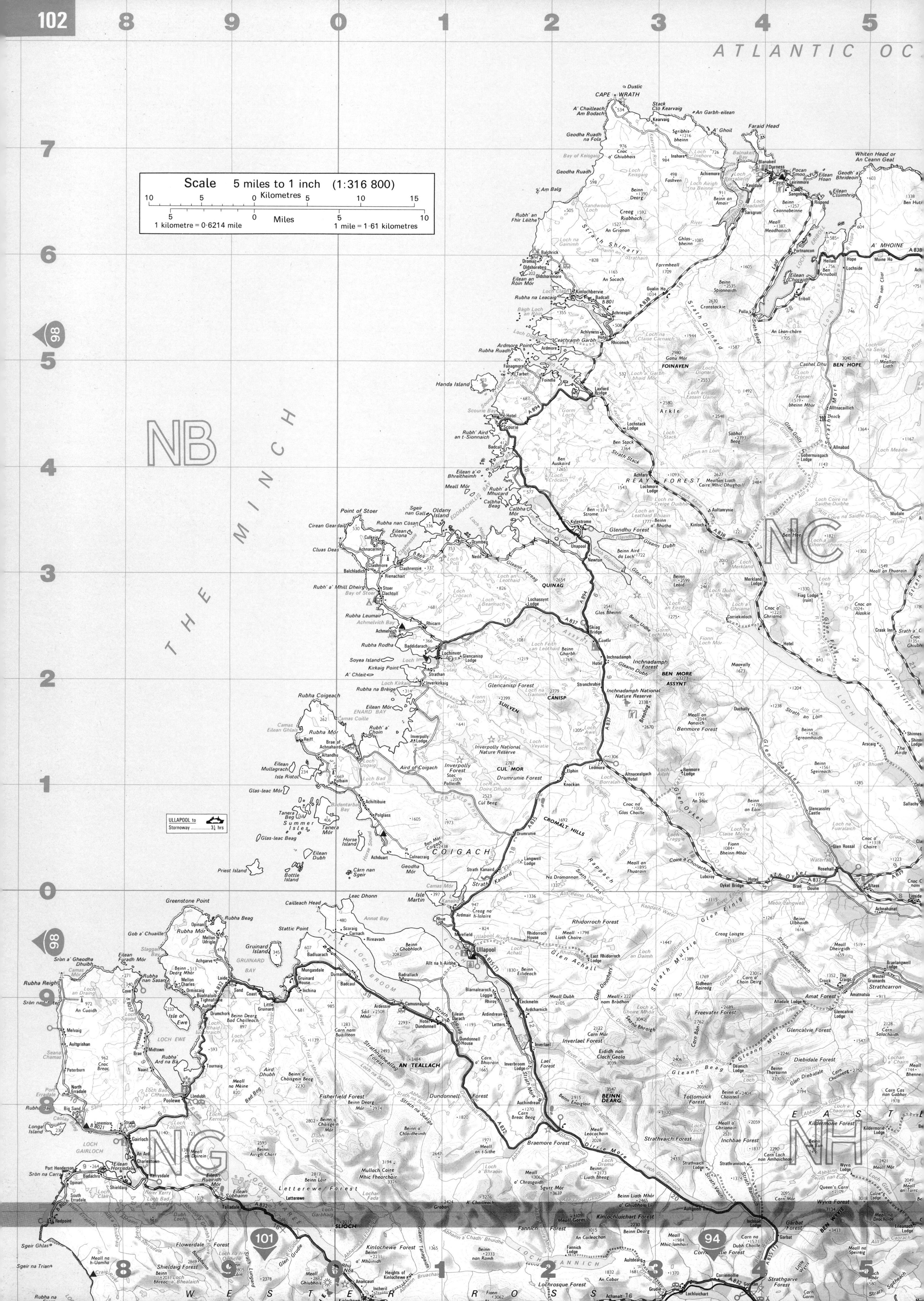
8
9
0
1
2
3
4
5
ATLANTIC OC
Scale 5 miles to 1 inch (1:316 800)
Kilometres
10 5 0 5 10 15
Miles
5 0 5 10
1 kilometre = 0·6214 mile
1 mile = 1·61 kilometres
98
NB
THE MINCH
NC
NG
NH
ULLAPOOL to Stornoway 3½ hrs
CAPE WRATH
Duslic
A' Chailleach Am Bodach
Stack Clò Kearvaig
An Garbh-eilean
Kearvaig
Faraid Head
Geodha Ruadh na Fola
Bay of Keisgaig
Geodha Ruadh
Balnakeil Bay
Balnakeil
Durness
Whiten Head or An Ceann Geal
Am Balg
Sandwood Loch
Strath Shinary
Rubh' an Fhir Leithe
Grudie River
Keoldale
Sangobeg
Rispond
Loch Eriboll
A' MHOINE
Balchrick
Oldshoremore
Eilean an Ròin Mòr
Rubha na Leacaig
Kinlochbervie
Badcall
Achriesgill
Polla
Strath Dionard
Strath Beag
Eriboll
Achlyness
Rhiconich
Ceathramh Garbh
Ardmore Point
Rubha Ruadh
FOINAVEN
Ganu Mòr
Cashel Dhu
BEN HOPE
Strathmore
Handa Island
Tarbet
Foindle
Fanagmore
Laxford Bridge
Arkle
Scourie Bay
Scourie
Rubh' Aird an t-Sionnaich
Badcall
Lochstack Lodge
Ben Stack
Strath Stack
Sàbhal
Glen Golly
Gobernuisgach Lodge
Eilean a' Bhreitheimh
Meall Mòr
Rubh' a' Mhucard
Calbha Mòr
Calbha Beag
Ben Auskaird
REAY FOREST
Achfary
Lochmore Lodge
Meallan Liath Coire Mhic Dhughaill
Loch More
Aultanrynie
Kinloch
Point of Stoer
Sgeir nan Gall
Oldany Island
Cirean Geardail
Rubha nan Còsan
Eilean Chrona
Culkein
Achnacarnin
Clashnessie
Cluas Deas
Clashmore
Balchladich
Drumbeg
Nedd
Kylestrome
Unapool
Glendhu Forest
Glen Coul
Ben Hee
Gleann Leireag
QUINAG
Newton
Rubh' a' Mhill Dheirg
Bay of Stoer
Stoer
Clachtoll
Rubha Leumair
Achmelvich Bay
Achmelvich
Rhicarn
Lochassynt Lodge
Loch Assynt
Glas Bheinn
Skiag Bridge
Rubha Rodha
Baddidarach
Lochinver
Glencanisp Lodge
Soyea Island
Kirkaig Point
A' Chleit
Strathan
Inverkirkaig
Ben More Assynt
Inchnadamph
Inchnadamph Forest
Gleann Dubh
Stronchrubie
Inchnadamph National Nature Reserve
Loch Shin
Glencanisp Forest
SUILVEN
CANISP
Rubha Coigeach
Rubha na Brèige
Eilean Mòr
ENARD BAY
Camas Coille
Camas Eilean Ghlais
Rubha Mòr
Reiff
Brae of Achnahaird
Altandhu
Inverpolly Lodge
Inverpolly National Nature Reserve
Inverpolly Forest
Benmore Forest
Duchally
Eilean Mullagrach
Isle Ristol
Polbain
Aird of Coigach
CUL MOR
Drumrunie Forest
Elphin
Knockan
Ledmore
Altnacealgach Hotel
Glen Oykel
Glen Cassley
Glas-leac Mòr
Achiltibuie
Polglass
Badentarbat Bay
Cùl Beag
Tanera Beg
Summer Isles
Tanera Mòr
Glas-leac Beag
Horse Island
Horse Sound
Ben Mor Coigach
COIGACH
Drumrunie
CROMALT HILLS
Rappach
Glen Rossal
Priest Island
Eilean Dubh
Bottle Island
Càrn nan Sgeir
Achduart
Culnacraig
Geodha Mòr
Strath Kanaird
Langwell Lodge
Oykel Bridge
Strath Oykel
Rosehall
Lubcroy
Isle Martin
Camas Mòr
Kanaird
Leac Dhonn
Glen Einig
Greenstone Point
Cailleach Head
Annat Bay
Rhue
Ardmair
Rhidorroch Forest
Rubha Beag
Opinan
Rubha Mòr
Mellon Udrigle
Stattic Point
Scoraig
Carnach
Rireavach
Morefield
Ullapool
Rhidorroch House
Glen Achall
East Rhidorroch Lodge
Strath Mulzie
Strath Cuileannach
Gob a' Chuaille
Slaggan Bay
Gruinard Island
GRUINARD BAY
LITTLE LOCH BROOM
LOCH BROOM
Badluarach
Dùn
Ben Ghobhlach
Allt na h-Airbhe
Beinn Eilideach
Strathcarron
Sròn a' Gheodha Dhuibh
Eilean Furadh Mòr
Achgarve
Mellon Charles
Laide
Gruinard House
Mungasdale
Inchina
Badcaul
Badrallach
Blarnalearoch
Loggie
Rhiroy
Leckmelm
Ardcharnich
Glen Douchary
Freevater Forest
Amat Forest
Rubha Reidh
Sròn na Gaoithe
Cove
Rubha nan Sasan
Aultbea
Drumchork
Isle of Ewe
Sand
Coast
Little Gruinard
Camusnagaul
Strath Beag
Dundonnell Hotel
Ardindrean
Letters
Inverlael
Inverlael Forest
Glencalvie Forest
Glencalvie Lodge
An Cuaidh
Melvaig
Aultgrishan
LOCH EWE
Midtown
Naast
Poolewe
Londubh
Inverewe
Tournaig
Sàil Mhòr
Ardessie
Carn nam Buailtean
Strath na Sealga
AN TEALLACH
Dundonnell House
Lael Forest
Inverbroom Lodge
Strath More
Diebidale Forest
Gleann Beag
Peterburn
North Erradale
Big Sand
Longa Island
Port Erradale
Rubha Ban
Loch Maree
LOCH GAIRLOCH
Gairloch
Strath
Charlestown
Flowerdale
Shieldaig
Kerrysdale
Port Henderson
Badachro
South Erradale
Redpoint
Fisherfield Forest
Beinn Dearg Mòr
Dundonnell Forest
BEINN DEARG
Auchindrean
Braemore Forest
Dirrie More
Strathvaich Forest
Inchbae Forest
Tollomuick Forest
EAST
Kildermorie Forest
Kildermorie Lodge
Letterewe Forest
Letterewe
Mullach Coire Mhic Fhearchair
Fannich
Sgurr Mòr
Kinlochluichart Forest
Strathvaich Lodge
Strath Vaich
Strath Rannoch
Wyvis Forest
Garbat Forest
BEN WYVIS
SLIOCH
Talladale
Kinlochewe Forest
Kinlochewe
Heights of Kinlochewe
Flowerdale Forest
Shieldaig Forest
Strath Lungard
Glen Grudie
Meall a' Ghiubhais
Fannich Lodge
Lochluichart
Corriemoillie Forest
Strathgarve Forest
Sgeir Ghlas
Sgeir na Trian
Rubha na Fearn
WESTER ROSS
101
94
Lochrosque Forest
Achnasheen
Lochluichart
Garve

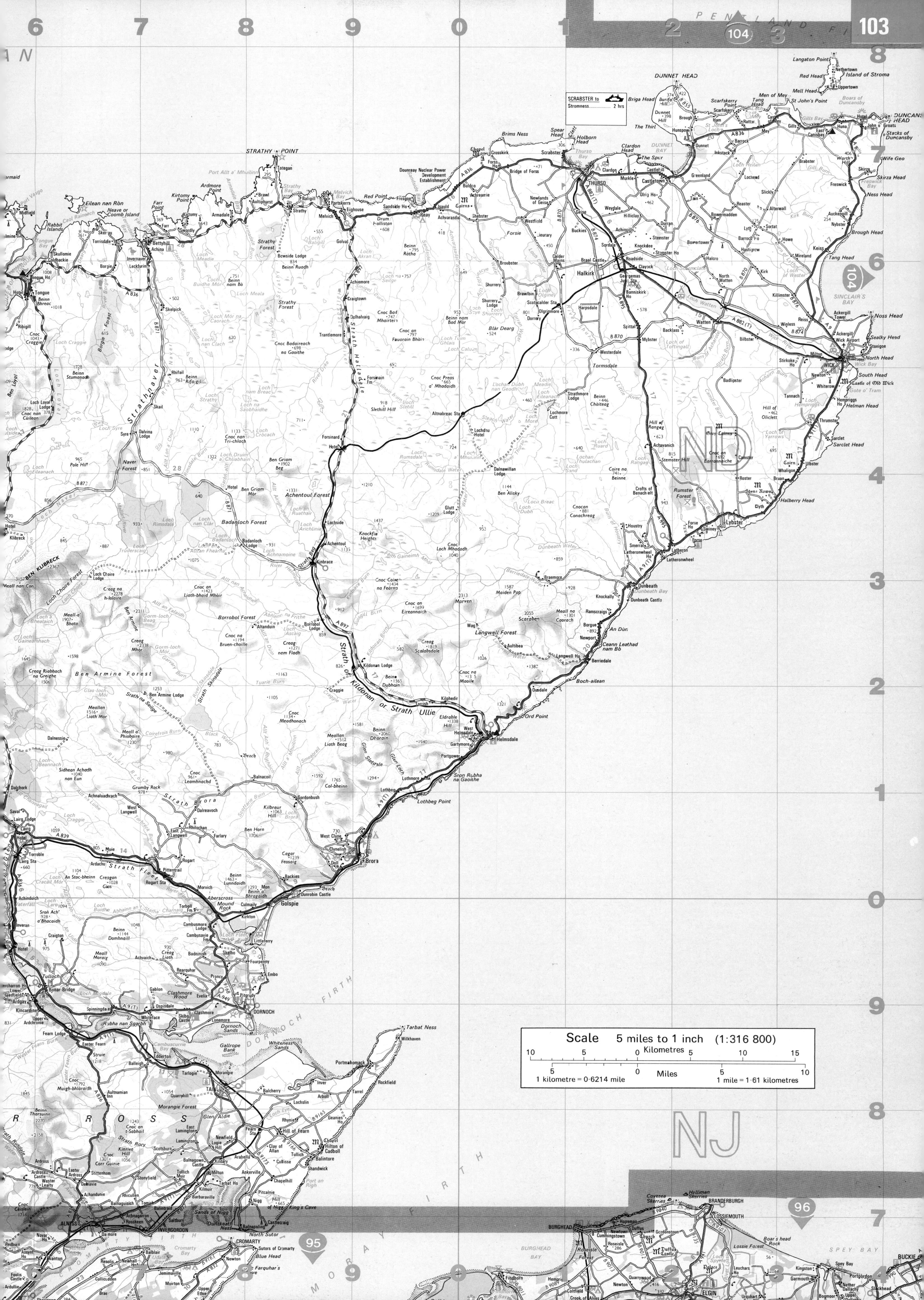

PENTLAND FIRTH
104
SCRABSTER to Stromness 2 hrs
DUNNET HEAD
DUNCANSBY HEAD
John o' Groats
Island of Stroma
STRATHY POINT
Thurso
Dounreay Nuclear Power Development Establishment
Halkirk
Castletown
Watten
Wick
SINCLAIR'S BAY
ND
Lybster
Latheronwheel
Dunbeath
Berriedale
Helmsdale
Brora
Golspie
Dornoch
DORNOCH FIRTH
Tain
Tarbat Ness
Portmahomack
Invergordon
Alness
Cromarty
MORAY FIRTH
Burghead
Lossiemouth
Elgin
Buckie
SPEY BAY
NJ
95
96
Strathnaver
Strath Halladale
Strath of Kildonan or Strath Ullie
Strath Fleet
Ben Klibreck
Ben Armine Forest
Tongue
Bettyhill
Lairg
Bonar Bridge
ROSS
Scale 5 miles to 1 inch (1:316 800)
Kilometres
Miles
1 kilometre = 0·6214 mile
1 mile = 1·61 kilometres

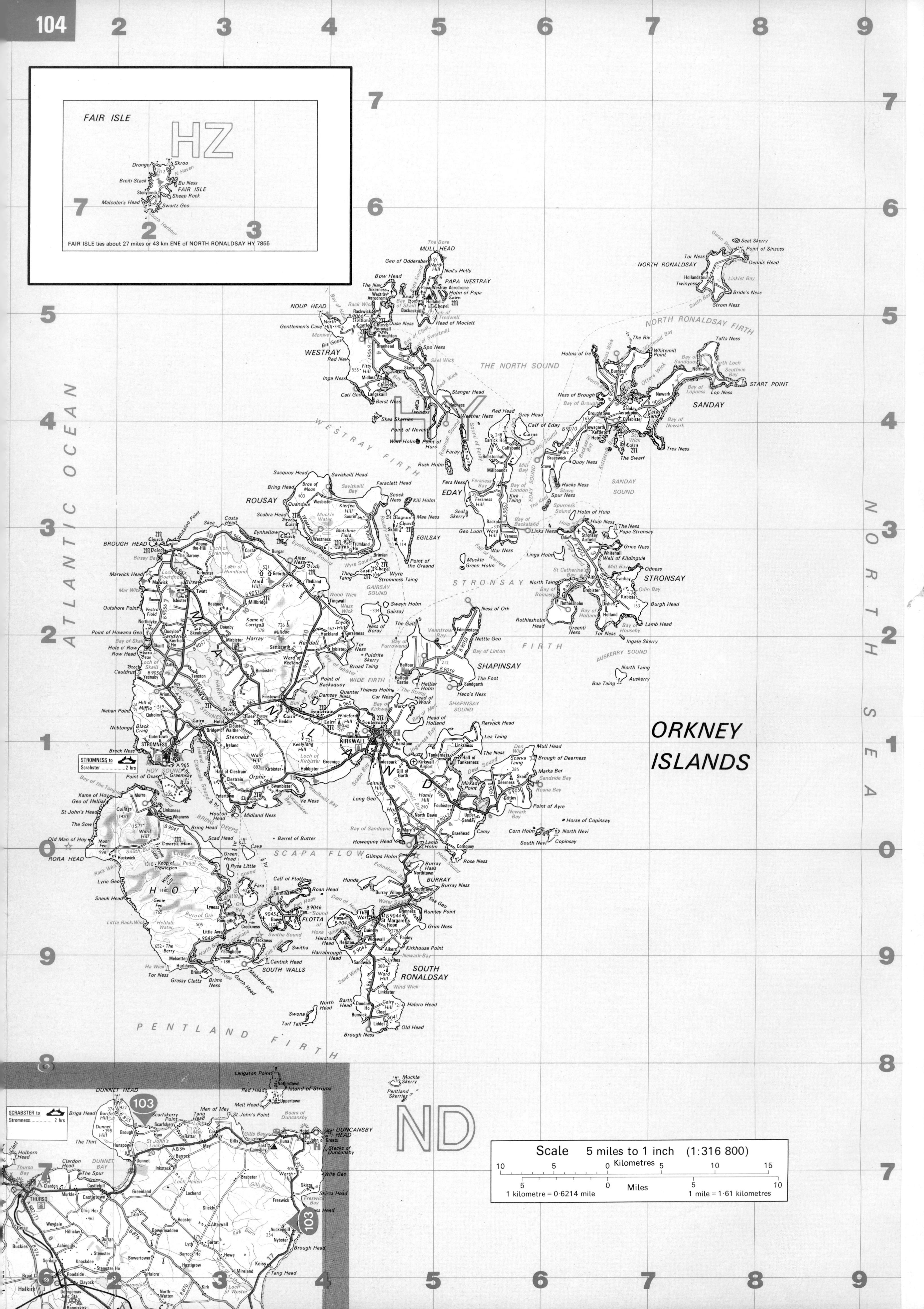

FAIR ISLE
HZ
Dronger
Skroo
N Haven
Breiti Stack
Bu Ness
FAIR ISLE
Stonybreck
Sheep Rock
Malcolm's Head
Swartz Geo
South Harbour
FAIR ISLE lies about 27 miles or 43 km ENE of NORTH RONALDSAY HY 7855
ATLANTIC OCEAN
NORTH SEA
ORKNEY ISLANDS
HY
ND
MULL HEAD
The Bore
Geo of Odderaber
North Hill
Neil's Helly
PAPA WESTRAY
Bow Head
The Nev
Aikerness
Papa Sound
Papa Westray Aerodrome
Holm of Papa
Holland
Cairn
Chapel
Backaskaill
NOUP HEAD
Rackwick
North Hill
Gentlemen's Cave
Pierowall
Ouse Ness
Head of Moclett
Bay of Tredwell
Bay of Cleat
Bay of Swartmill
Monivey
Bis Geos
Broughton
Spo Ness
WESTRAY
Red Nev
Fitty Hill
Skelwick
Skel Wick
Inga Ness
Midbea
Rack Wick
Cati Geo
Langskaill
Berst Ness
Stanger Head
Skea Skerries
Twiness
Rapness
Point of Nevers
Weather Ness
Sound of Faray
Wart Holm
Point of Huro
Faray
Rusk Holm
WESTRAY FIRTH
THE NORTH SOUND
Seal Skerry
Point of Sinsoss
Tor Ness
NORTH RONALDSAY
Dennis Head
Hollandstoun
Linklet Bay
Twinyess
Bride's Ness
South Bay
Strom Ness
NORTH RONALDSAY FIRTH
The Riv
Whitemill Bay
Tafts Ness
Whitemill Point
Holms of Ire
Otters Wick
North Loch
Scuthvie Bay
START POINT
Northwall
Ness of Brough
Newark
Bay of Lopness
Lop Ness
Bay of Brough
SANDAY
Sanday Aerodrome
Overbister
Red Head
Grey Head
Calf of Eday
Cata Sand
Bay of Newark
Carrick Ho
Cairns
Kettletoft
Calfsound
Wick
The Wart
Tres Ness
Braeswick
The Swarf
Bencottonhall
Stove
Quoy Ness
Millbounds
Mill Bay
Hacks Ness
Stove
Spur Ness
SANDAY SOUND
Fers Ness
Fersness Bay
EDAY
Bay of London
Kirk Taing
EDAY SOUND
Fersness Hill
Seal Skerry
Spurness Sound
Holm of Huip
Huip Ness
Backaland
Bay of Backaland
Links Ness
Huip Sound
The Ness
Papa Stronsay
Geo Luon
Ward Hill
Veness
Muckle Green Holm
War Ness
Fall of Warness
Stronsay Airfield
Whitehall
Grice Ness
Well of Kildinguie
Linga Holm
Mill Bay
Odness
St Catherine's Bay
STRONSAY
North Taing
Grobister
Everbay
Bay of Bomasty
Dishes
Kirbister
Odin Bay
Rothiesholm
Burgh Head
Holland
Bay of Holland
Rothiesholm Head
Lamb Head
Greenli Ness
Tor Ness
Bay of Houseby
Ingale Skerry
AUSKERRY SOUND
North Taing
Auskerry
Baa Taing
STRONSAY FIRTH
Sacquoy Head
Saviskaill Head
Bring Head
Broe of Moon
Saviskaill Bay
Faraclett Head
ROUSAY
Quandale
Wasbister
Kierfea Hill
Scock Ness
Kili Holm
Scabra Head
Muckle Water
Sourin
Mae Ness
Costa Head
Skea
Whitaloo Point
Brough Head
Westness
Blotchnie Fiold
Trumland
EGILSAY
Point of the Graand
BROUGH HEAD
Eynhallow
Eynhallow Sound
Birsay Bay
Loch of Swannay
Costa
Aiker Ness
Broch
Wyre
Marwick Head
Marwick
Loch of Boardhouse
Birsay
Kirbuster
Loch of Hundland
Mid Hill
Evie
Redland
Wyre Sound
The Taing
Stromness Taing
GAIRSAY SOUND
Mar Wick
Twatt
Beaquoy
Millbrigg
Wood Wick
Tingwall
Sweyn Holm
Gairsay
Outshore Point
Vestra Fiold
Isbister
Wass Wick
Kame of Corrigall
Enyaw Hill
Hackland
Gorseness
Ness of Boray
The Galt
Point of Howana Geo
Quoyloo
Sandwick
Skeabrae
Dounby
Milldoe
Veantrow Bay
Edmondstone
Nettle Geo
Hole o' Row
Bay of Skaill
Skaill
Kierfiold Ho
Harray
Merbister
Settiscarth
Rendall
Isbister
Tor Ness
Pulldrite Skerry
Bay of Furrowend
Bay of Linton
Row Head
Loch of Skaill
LOCH OF HARRAY
Ward of Redland
Broad Taing
Bay of Isbister
Balfour
Balfour Castle
SHAPINSAY
Cauldrus
Bimbister
Point of Backaquoy
WIDE FIRTH
Helliar Holm
Sandgarth
The Foot
Tenston
Quanter Ness
Damsay
Thieves Holm
Haco's Ness
Yesnaby
Car Ness
Finstown
Bay of Firth
Work
The String
Head of Work
SHAPINSAY SOUND
Hill of Miffia
Arion
LOCH OF STENNESS
Bay of Kirkwall
Bay of Meil
Neban Point
Quholm
Stone Circles
Maes Howe
Cairn Heddle
Wideford Hill
Head of Holland
Nebonga
Black Craig
Cairn
Hotel
Clouston
Bridge of Waithe
Stenness
Keelylong Hill
KIRKWALL
Berstane
Rerwick Head
Lea Taing
Outertown
Breck Ness
STROMNESS
Ireland
Loch of Kirbister
Greenigo
Inganess Bay
Linksness
Tankerness
The Ness
Den Wick
Mull Head
Brough of Deerness
STROMNESS to Scrabster 2 hrs
HOY SOUND
Graemsay
Ward Hill
Kirkwall Airport
Hall of Tankerness
Deer Sound
Scarva Taing
Marka Ber
Sandside Bay
Point of Oxan
Hall of Clestrain
Kirbister
Hobbister
Scapa Bay
Gill of Garth
Clestrain
Orphir
Gaitnip Hill
Mirkady Point
Deerness
Skaill
Bay of the Tongue
Kame of Hoy
Geo of Hellia
Morra
Petertown
Swanbister
Long Geo
Toab
Gritley
Roana Bay
St John's Head
Cuilags
Linksness
Houton Head
Houton
Midland Ness
Ve Ness
Waulkmill Bay
Hamly Hill
Foubister
Point of Ayre
Newark Bay
The Sow
Whaness
BRING DEEPS
Bring Head
Holm
North Dawn
Upper Sanday
Horse of Copinsay
Old Man of Hoy
Ward Hill
Dwarfie Stane
Scad Head
Cava
Barrel of Butter
Bay of Sandoyne
St Mary's
Braehead
Camy
Corn Holm
North Nevi
Moor Fea
Howequoy Head
Lamb Holm
Corrquoy
South Nevi
Copinsay
RORA HEAD
Rackwick
Green Head
SCAPA FLOW
Glimps Holm
Rose Ness
Rack Wick
Knap of Trowieglen
Rysa Little
Echnaloch Bay
Burray Haas
Northtown
Holm Sound
Lyrie Geo
Withi Gill
Fara
Calf of Flotta
Hunda
BURRAY
Burray Ness
HOY
Oil Terminal
Roan Head
Burray Village
Southtown
Sneuk Head
Genie Fea
Lyness
Water Sound
Sea Geo
Rumley Point
FLOTTA
Grimness
Little Rack Wick
Heldale Water
Burn of Ore
Rinnigill
Crockness
The Wart
St Margaret's Hope
Grim Ness
Little Ayre
Switha Sound
Hoxa
Quindry
Papley
The Berry
Longhope
Hackness
Herston Head
Widewall
Kirkhouse Point
Switha
Harrabrough Head
Aikers
Newark Bay
Melsetter
Cantick Head
Sandwick
Lythes
Ha Wick
Hurliness
Brims
SOUTH WALLS
SOUTH RONALDSAY
Tor Ness
Brims Ness
Garth Head
Grassy Cletts
Mishiatter Geo
Sand Wick
Ward Hill
Wind Wick
Linklater
North Head
Barth Head
Dundas Ho
Gairy Hill
Halcro Head
Swona
Burwick
Clett
Tarf Tail
Liddel
Old Head
Brough Ness
PENTLAND FIRTH
Langaton Point
Nethertown
Island of Stroma
Red Head
Uppertown
Mell Head
Muckle Skerry
Pentland Skerries
DUNNET HEAD
103
SCRABSTER to Stromness 2 hrs
Briga Head
Burifa Hill
Dunnet Hill
Scarfskerry
Scarfskerry Point
Men of Mey
Tang Head
St John's Point
Boars of Duncansby
Brough
Rattar
Castle of Mey
Gills Bay
Hotel
John o' Groats
DUNCANSBY HEAD
Stacks of Duncansby
The Thirl
Hunspow
St John's Loch
Mey
Gills
East Canisbay
Huna
Holborn Head
Thurso Bay
Clardon Head
DUNNET BAY
Dunnet
Barrock
Inkstack
Wife Geo
The Spur
Loch Heilen
Brabster
Warth Hill
Skirza
Skirza Head
Clardon
Castletown
Greenland
Lochend
Gill Burn
Freswick Bay
THURSO
Murkle
Olrig Ho
Slickly
Freswick
Weydale
Hillclay
Reaster
Alterwall
Auckengill
Nybster
Geise
Achingills
Durran
Bowermadden
Lyth
Sortat
Buckies
Stemster
Barrock Ho
Howe
Brough Head
Sordale
Knockdee
Stemster Ho
Bowertower
Hastigrow
Kirk Burn
Keiss
Braal Castle
Roadside
Clayock
Halcro
Mireland
Tang Head
Halkirk
Georgemas Junc Sta
Bannaskirk
North Watten
Kirk
Loch of Wester
Scale 5 miles to 1 inch (1:316 800)
Kilometres
10 5 0 5 10 15
Miles
5 0 5 10
1 kilometre = 0·6214 mile
1 mile = 1·61 kilometres

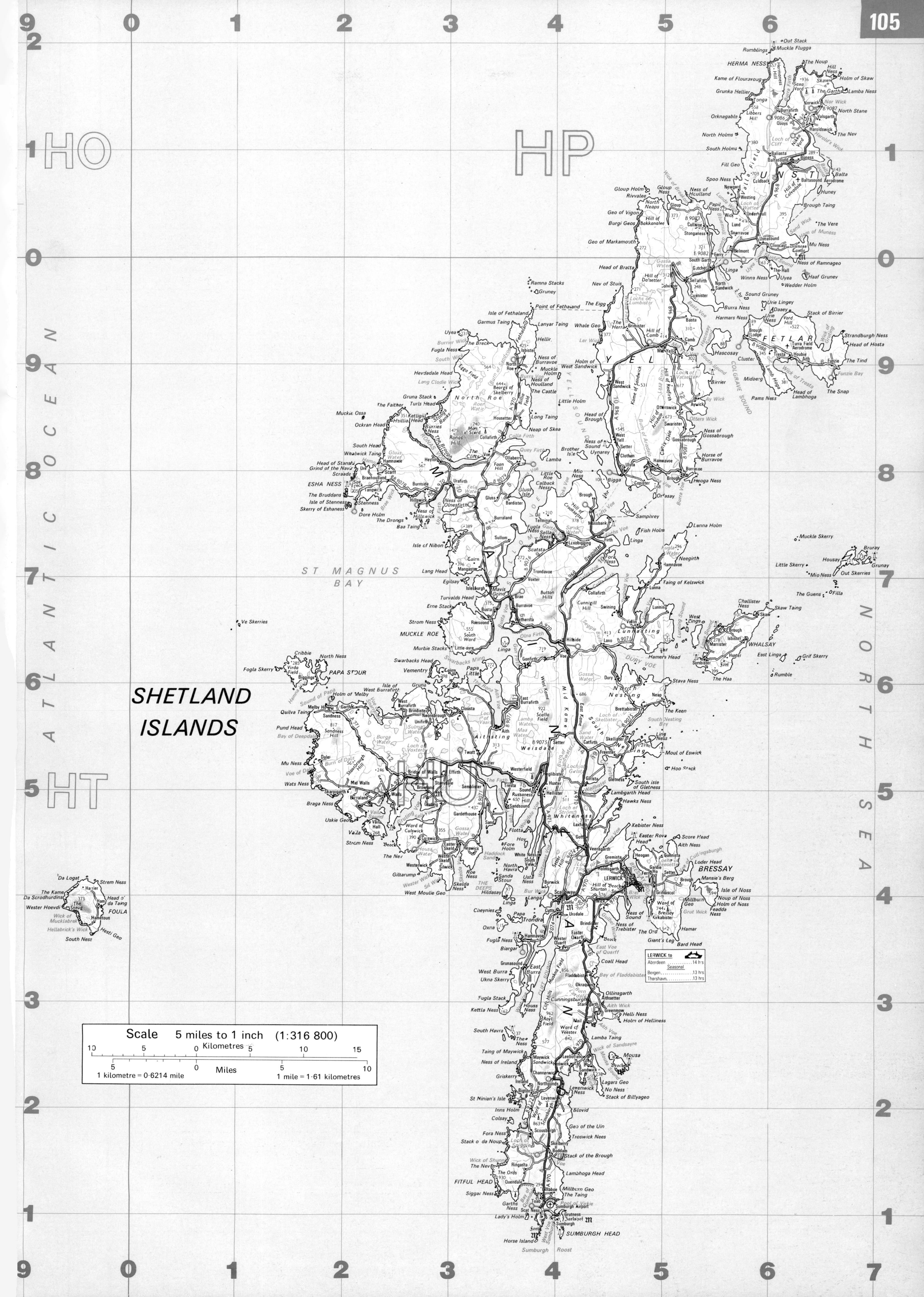
HO
HP
HT
HU
SHETLAND
ISLANDS
ATLANTIC OCEAN
NORTH SEA
ST MAGNUS
BAY
UNST
FETLAR
YELL
WHALSAY
BRESSAY
FOULA
PAPA STOUR
MUCKLE ROE
LERWICK
SUMBURGH HEAD
FITFUL HEAD
HERMA NESS
ESHA NESS
North Roe
Muckle Flugga
Out Stack
Ronas Hill
Yell Sound
Colgrave Sound
Sullom
Brae
Voe
Walls
Scalloway
Sumburgh Airport
Ve Skerries
LERWICK to
Aberdeen 14 hrs
Seasonal
Bergen 13 hrs
Thorshavn 13 hrs
Scale 5 miles to 1 inch (1:316 800)
Kilometres
10 5 0 5 10 15
5 0 Miles 5 10
1 kilometre = 0·6214 mile
1 mile = 1·61 kilometres

National Parks, Forest Parks and Long-distance Paths

KEY TO LONG DISTANCE PATHS

1 Pennine Way
2 Cleveland Way
3 Pembrokeshire Coast Path
4 Offa's Dyke Path
5 South Downs Way
6 North Downs Way
7 Ridgeway
8 South-West Peninsula Coast Path
  a Somerset & N Devon Coast Path
  b Cornwall Coast Path
  c South Devon Coast Path
  d Dorset Coast Path
9 Wolds Way
10 Millennium Way
11 West Highland Way
12 Speyside Way
13 Peddars Way and Norfolk Coast Path
14 Southern Upland Way

National Parks
Forest Parks and New Forest
Designated areas of outstanding natural beauty and National scenic areas (Scotland)
Long distance paths

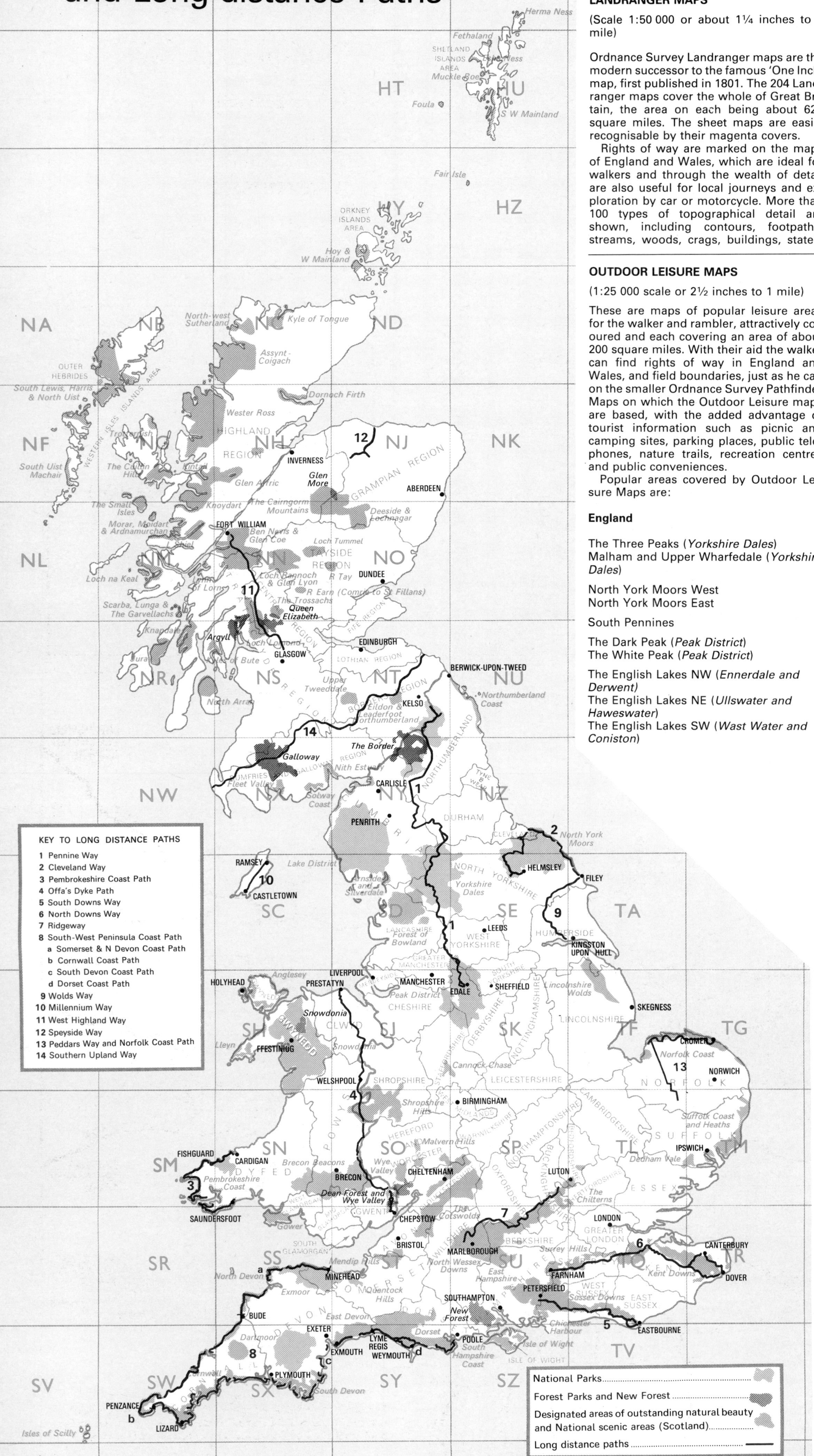

Ordnance Survey Sheet Maps

LANDRANGER MAPS

(Scale 1:50 000 or about 1¼ inches to 1 mile)

Ordnance Survey Landranger maps are the modern successor to the famous 'One Inch' map, first published in 1801. The 204 Landranger maps cover the whole of Great Britain, the area on each being about 620 square miles. The sheet maps are easily recognisable by their magenta covers.

Rights of way are marked on the maps of England and Wales, which are ideal for walkers and through the wealth of detail are also useful for local journeys and exploration by car or motorcycle. More than 100 types of topographical detail are shown, including contours, footpaths, streams, woods, crags, buildings, stately homes, ancient monuments, bus and coach stations, and selected camping and caravan sites, parking places and viewpoints.

Ordnance Survey keeps the Landranger series as up to date as possible – major changes are shown on reprints and as soon as there is significant overall change on a sheet a new edition is produced.

When Landrangers were first introduced in the 1970s the maps were simply photographic enlargements of the One Inch maps presented in a new format. Now nearly two thirds of the 204 maps have been redrawn after revision and issued as Second Series Landranger maps; the rest will be converted to Second Series style by 1990.

OUTDOOR LEISURE MAPS

(1:25 000 scale or 2½ inches to 1 mile)

These are maps of popular leisure areas for the walker and rambler, attractively coloured and each covering an area of about 200 square miles. With their aid the walker can find rights of way in England and Wales, and field boundaries, just as he can on the smaller Ordnance Survey Pathfinder Maps on which the Outdoor Leisure maps are based, with the added advantage of tourist information such as picnic and camping sites, parking places, public telephones, nature trails, recreation centres and public conveniences.

Popular areas covered by Outdoor Leisure Maps are:

England

The Three Peaks (*Yorkshire Dales*)
Malham and Upper Wharfedale (*Yorkshire Dales*)

North York Moors West
North York Moors East

South Pennines

The Dark Peak (*Peak District*)
The White Peak (*Peak District*)

The English Lakes NW (*Ennerdale and Derwent*)
The English Lakes NE (*Ullswater and Haweswater*)
The English Lakes SW (*West Water and Coniston*)
The English Lakes SE (*Windermere and Kendal*)

Wye Valley and Forest of Dean

South Devon

Purbeck

New Forest

Brighton and Sussex Vale

Isles of Scilly

Scotland

Aviemore and the Cairngorms

The Cuillin and Torridon Hills

Wales

Snowdonia National Park (*Snowdon*)

Snowdonia National Park (*Conwy Valley*)

Snowdonia National Park (*Harlech*)

Snowdonia National Park (*Bala*)

Snowdonia National Park (*Cader Idris/Dovey Forest*)

Brecon Beacons National Park (*Central*)

Brecon Beacons National Park (*Western*)

Brecon Beacons National Park (*Eastern*)

The National Grid

The National Grid provides a unique referencing system which can be applied to all maps of Great Britain, at all scales. Great Britain is divided into 100 kilometre grid squares, each of which is identified by a set of 2 letters shown on the adjoining map. The numbered values of the 100 kilometre grid lines indicate distances from the south west corner of the grid; these numbers are not used for map referencing, the 100 kilometre squares being indicated by the letters.

In the map section of this atlas each page is annotated with the set(s) of two letters identifying the 100 kilometre square(s) containing the page. These 100 kilometre squares are further sub-divided into smaller squares by grid lines spaced 10 kilometres apart, each of which is numbered from 0 to 9 in an easterly or northerly direction from the south west corner of each of the larger squares. Hence 100 smaller squares make up each lettered square as shown above.

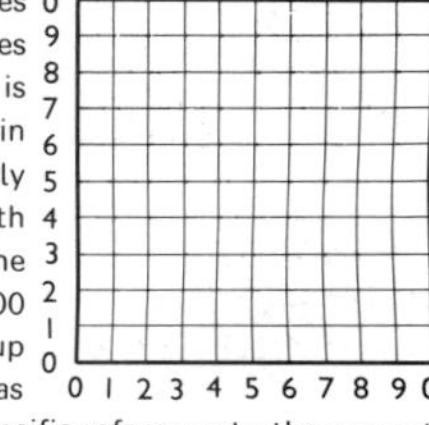

A more specific reference to the nearest kilometre may be achieved by visually estimating the number of tenths east and north from the south west corner of each 10 kilometre square.

The index lists the National Grid map references of all named features in the map section of the Atlas and an example of using the National Grid reference system is given on page 117.

Town Centre Maps

PAGE 110
- Aberdeen
- Birmingham
- Bournemouth
- Brighton
- Bristol
- Cambridge

PAGE 111
- Cardiff
- Coventry
- Dover
- Dundee
- Edinburgh
- Exeter

PAGE 112
- Central Glasgow
- Gloucester
- Great Yarmouth
- Inverness
- Leeds
- Leicester

PAGE 113
- Liverpool
- Manchester
- Middlesbrough
- Newcastle upon Tyne
- Norwich
- Nottingham

PAGE 114
- Oxford
- Plymouth
- Poole
- Portsmouth
- Salisbury
- Sheffield

PAGE 115
- Southampton
- Stoke-on-Trent
- Stratford-upon-Avon
- Swansea
- Wolverhampton
- York

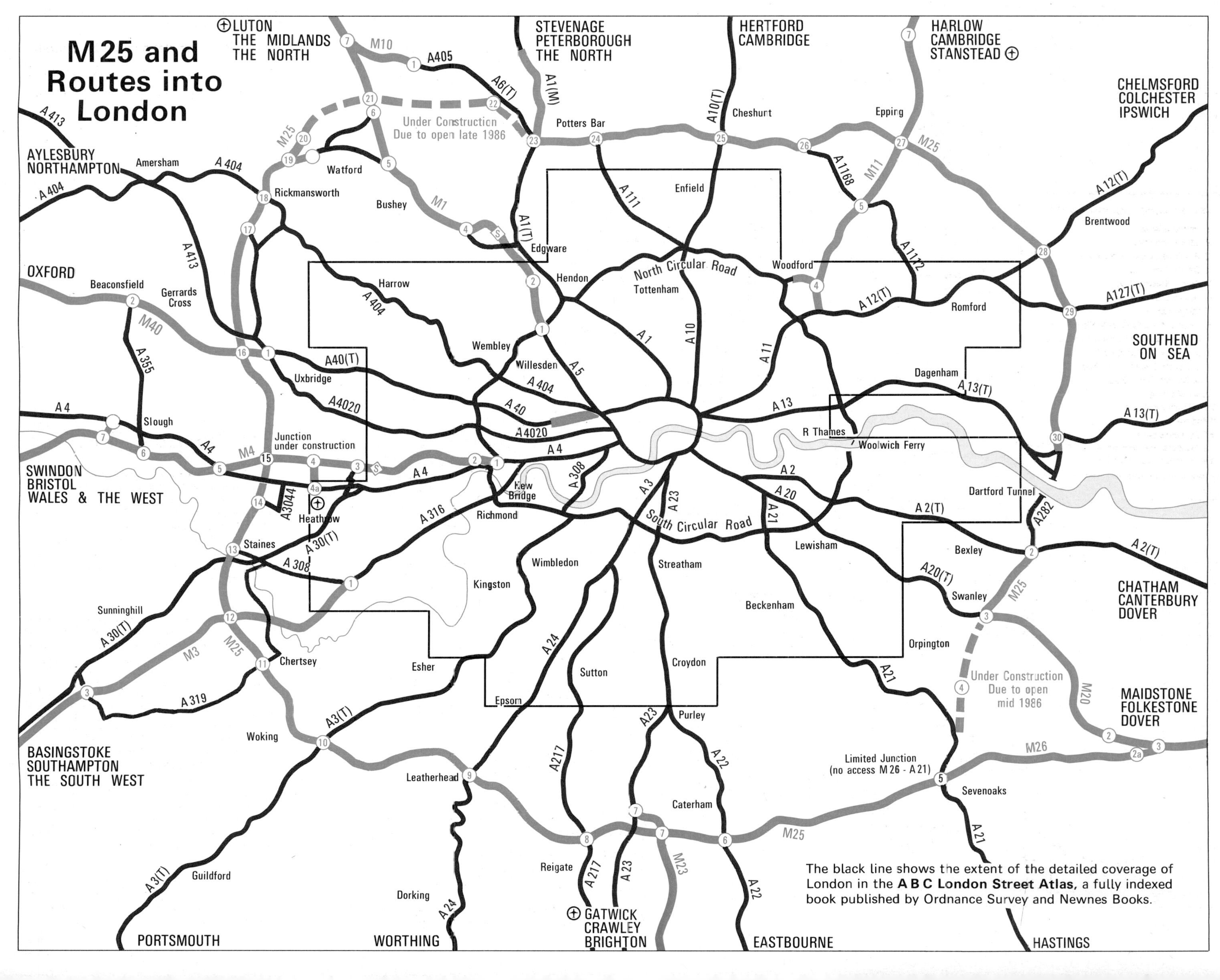

Lord's Cricket Gd
London Mosque
Boat Houses
Jetty
Boating Lake
The Holme
Tennis Court
INNER CIRCLE
Open Air Theatre
QUEEN MARY'S GARDENS
New Lodge
Tennis Courts
BEDFORD COLLEGE (Univ of London)
OUTER CIRCLE
CHESTER ROAD
National Temperance Hospital
Post Stone
PARK SQUARE GDNS
CRESCENT GDNS
PARK CRESCENT
Regent's Park
Great Portland Street
Warren Street
Euston Square
R Nat Ortho Hospl
London Foot Hospl
Lisson Green
Marylebone Station
Baker Street
Madame Tussaud's & Planetarium
Royal Academy of Music
London Clinic and Nursing Home
Florence Nightingale Hospital
Paddington Green Children's Hospl
Western Ophthalmic Hospl
Samaritan Hospl for Women
Lisson Grove
Edgware Road (Bakerloo)
Edgware Road (Met & Circle)
HARROW ROAD
Paddington Basin
St Mary's Hospital
Paddington
Hospital for Tropical Diseases
Nat Heart Hospital
Nat Hosp Speech Sciences
London Telecom tower
Middlesex Hospital
Fitzroy Nuffield Hospital
Wallace Collection
Wigmore Hall
Marylebone
Oxford Circus
OXFORD STREET
London Palladium
Bond Street
Marble Arch
Tyburn Tree (site of)
Speakers' Corner
BAYSWATER ROAD
Lancaster Gate
Westbourne Gate
Victoria Gate
Marlborough Gate
The Fountains
North Ride
Buck Hill Walk
The Long Water
Nursery
New Lodge
Pol Sta
Resr
Ring Tea House
Ranger's Lodge
Ranger's Cottage
HYDE PARK
Serpentine Lodge
Broad Walk
Lovers' Walk
Temple Lodge
Serpentine Bridge
Boat Houses
The Serpentine
Restaurant
Bandstand
War Meml
Statue
The Dell
Rotten Row
Hyde Park Corner
Mayfair
GROSVENOR SQUARE
Royal Academy of Arts
PICCADILLY
Green Park
Lancaster House
Queen Victoria Memorial
CONSTITUTION HILL
(Closed to traffic on Sundays)
BUCKINGHAM PALACE GARDENS
BUCKINGHAM PALACE
Queens Gallery
The Royal Mews
Albert Memorial
Alexandra Gate
Prince's Gate
Prince of Wales' Gate
Albert Gate
SOUTH CARRIAGE DRIVE
Bowling Greens
Knightsbridge
Imperial College
Science Museum
Geo Mus
British Museum (Natural History)
Victoria & Albert Museum
The Oratory
Brompton
BROMPTON ROAD
BELGRAVE SQUARE
SLOANE STREET
Westminster Cathedral
Victoria
Victoria Station

LONDON
LONDINIVM
RIVE
FINSBURY
Clerkenwell
Bloomsbury
Holborn
St Giles
Soho
Strand
St James
Lambeth
King's Reach
Euston Station
University College
University of London
British Museum
Coram's Fields
Mount Pleasant Post Office
City University
Central Markets (Smithfield)
St Bartholomew's Hospital
General Post Office
Central Criminal Court
St Paul's Cathedral
Lincoln's Inn Fields
Royal Courts of Justice
Inner Temple
Middle Temple
Somerset House
King's College
Covent Garden
National Gallery
Nelson's Column
Charing Cross
Cleopatra's Needle
Waterloo Bridge
Blackfriars Bridge
National Film Theatre
National Theatre
Queen Elizabeth Hall
Royal Festival Hall
Hayward Gallery
South Bank
Hungerford Bridge (Foot)
Waterloo Station
Horse Guards
Banqueting House
Treasury Buildings
Foreign, Commonwealth & Home Offices
Cenotaph
The County Hall
Westminster Bridge
New Palace Yard
Old Palace Yard
HOUSES OF PARLIAMENT
Westminster Abbey
New Scotland Yard
St Thomas' Hospital
Lambeth Palace
Archbishop's Park
Imperial War Museum
ST JAMES'S PARK
St James's Park Lake
Duck Island
The Victoria Tower Gardens
ROUTE RESTRICTIONS
(Some may not apply at all times and to all vehicles)
Main Roads and Bus Routes
One way traffic route
No access in direction of arrow
OXFORD STREET Open to buses and taxis only between 7am-7pm, Monday to Saturday
TOURIST INFORMATION
Royal Academy of Arts
Selected places of interest
Horse Guards
Information Centre
Railway Station
Underground Station
Bus/Coach Station
Parking
Hospital with casualty facilities
LONDON CENTRAL
Scale 1:10 000
(10 centimetres to 1 kilometre or about 6 inches to 1 mile)

ABERDEEN

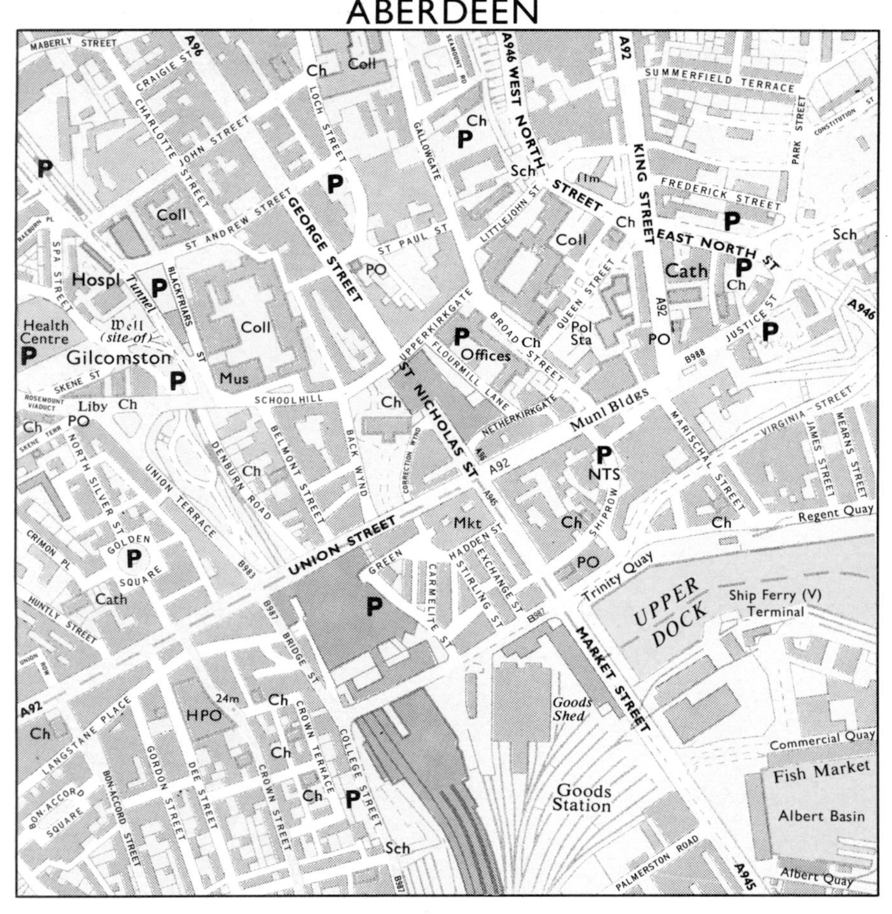

BIRMINGHAM (CENTRAL)

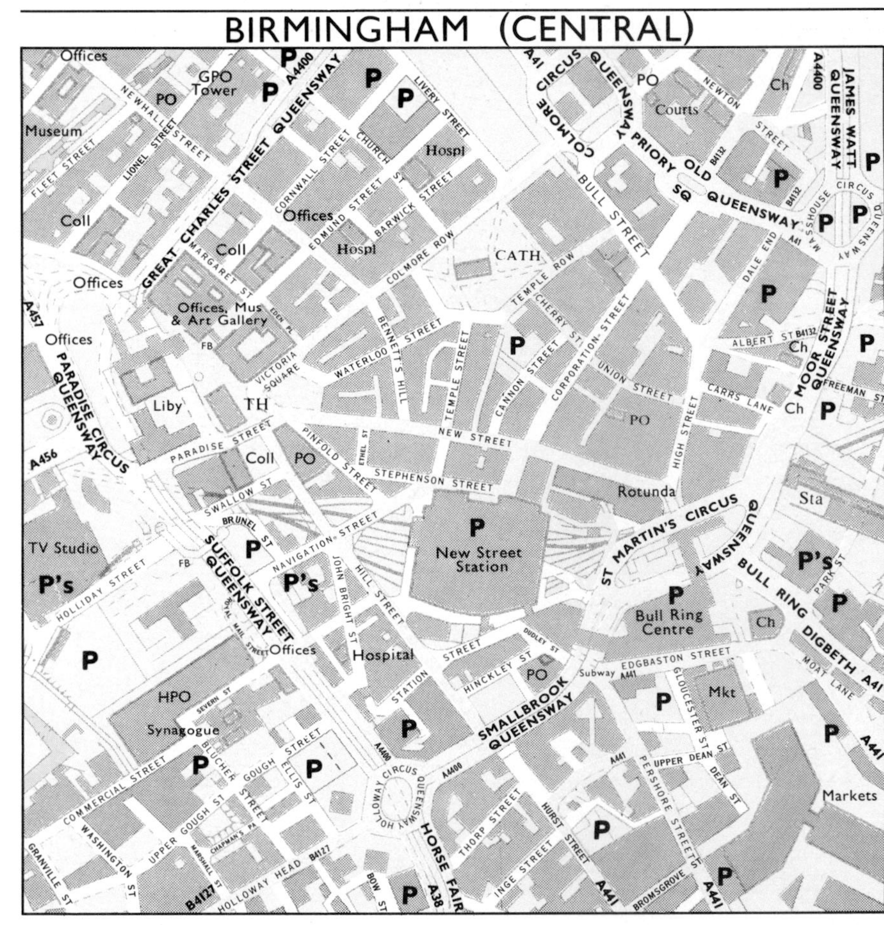

BOURNEMOUTH

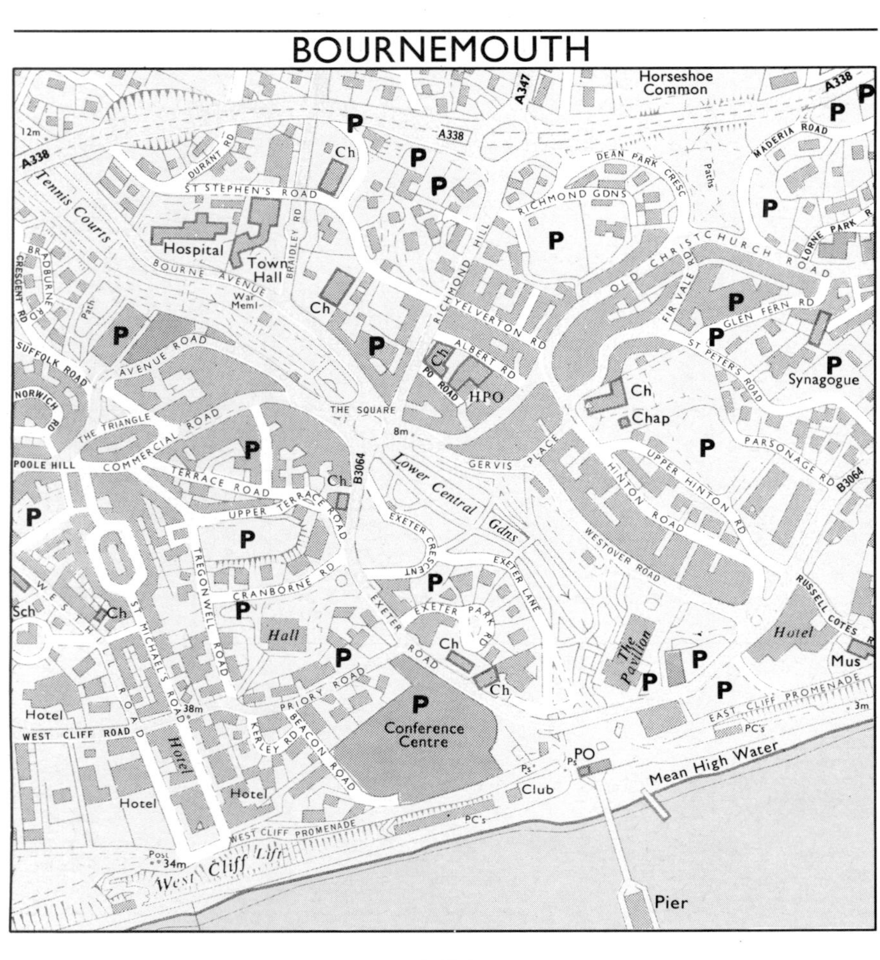

BRIGHTON

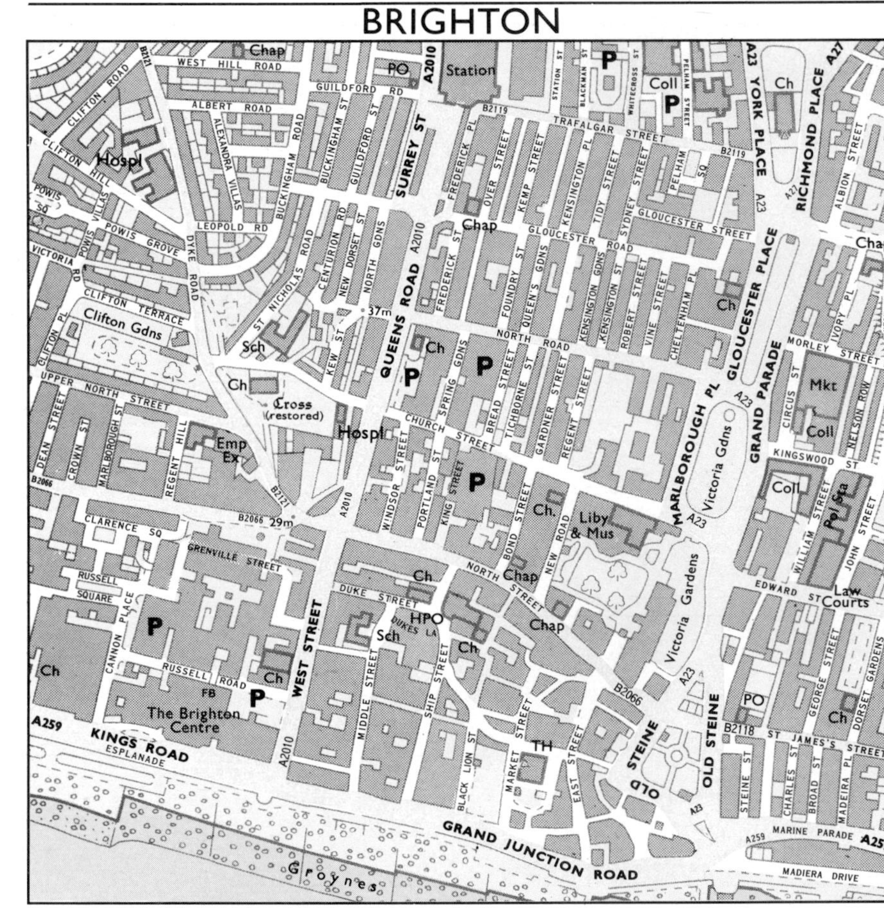

BRISTOL

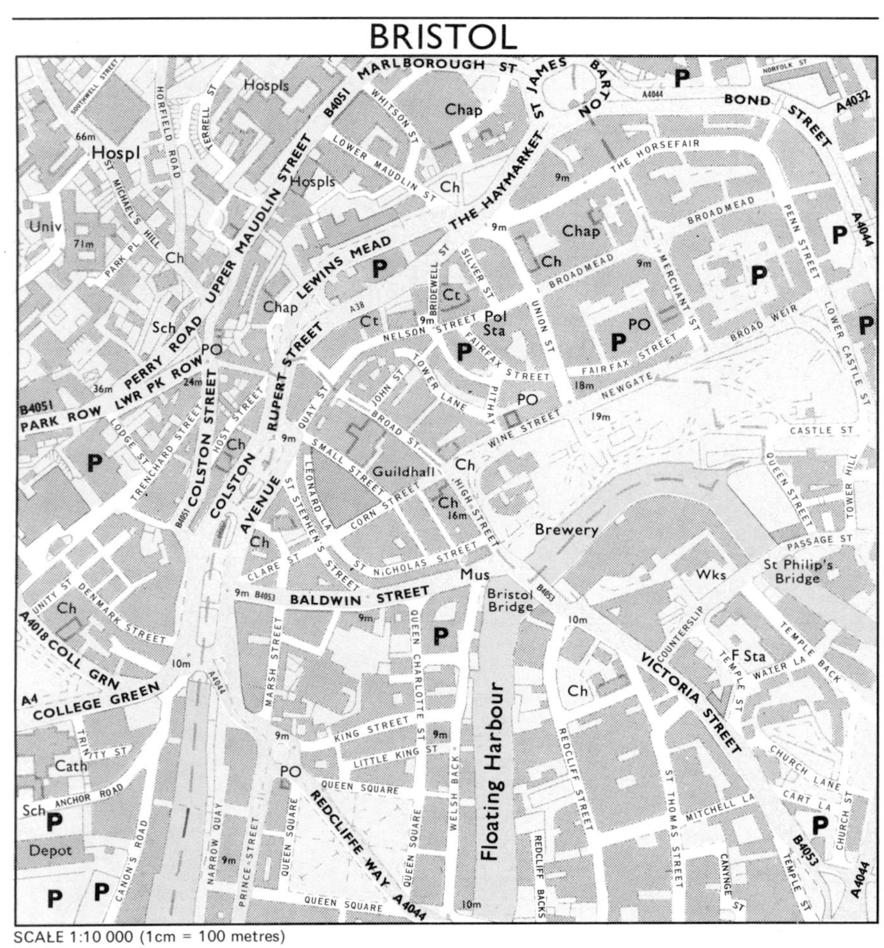

CAMBRIDGE

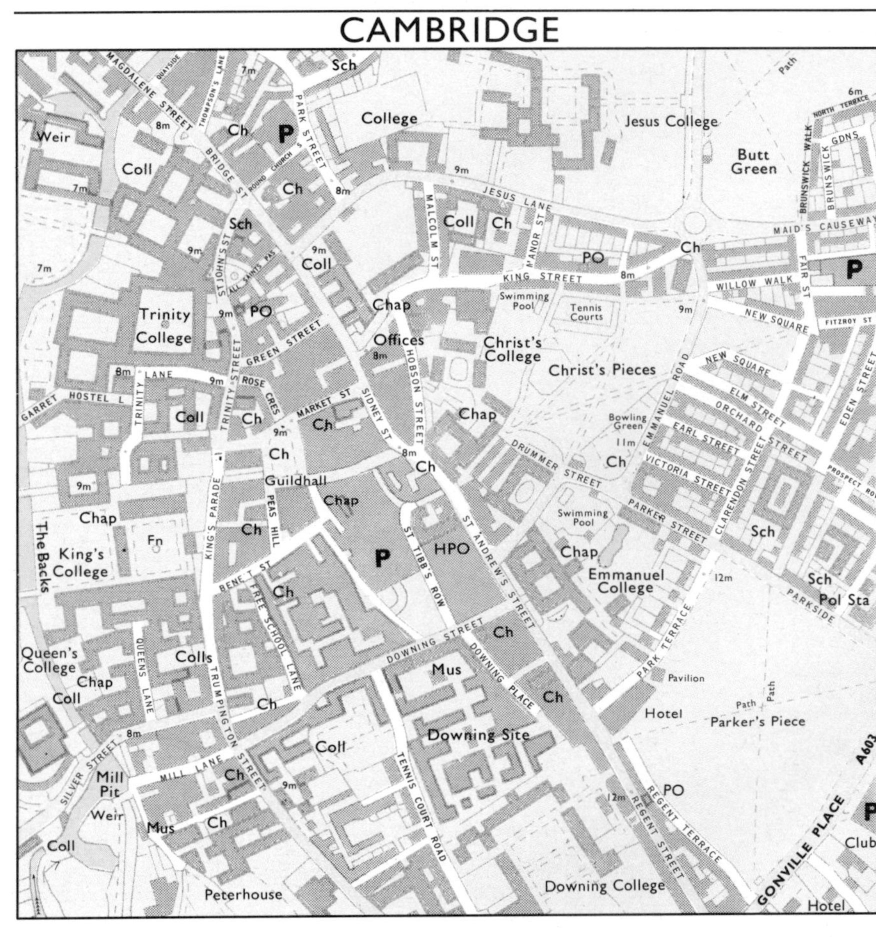

SCALE 1:10 000 (1cm = 100 metres)

CARDIFF

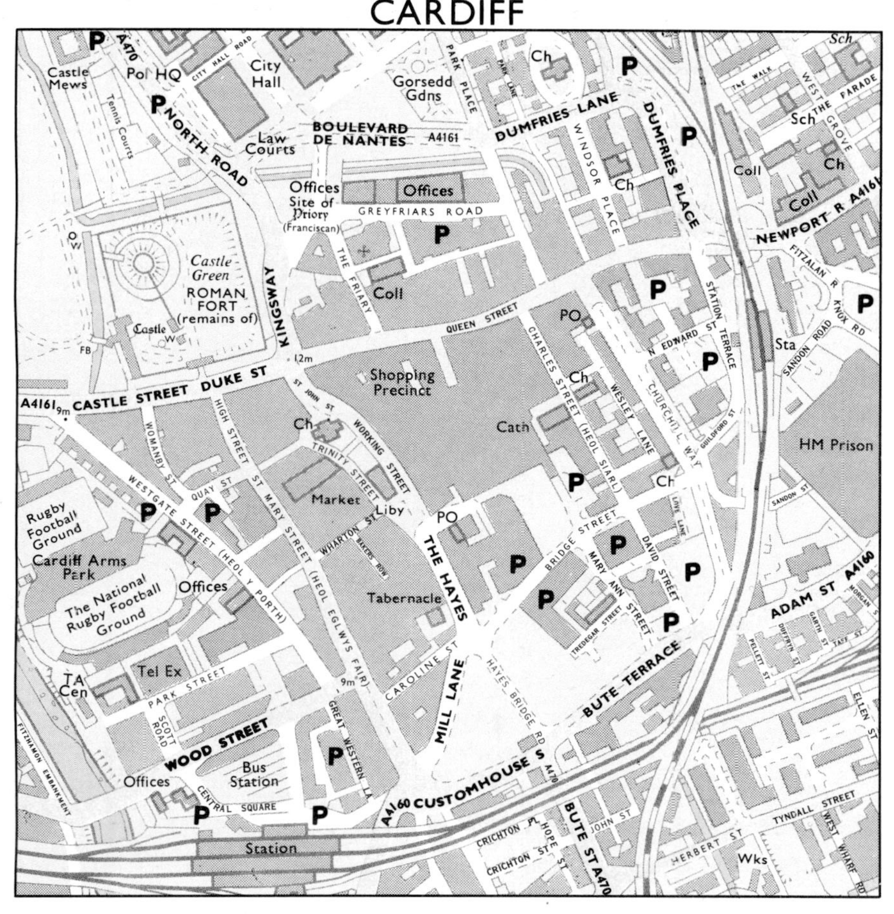

COVENTRY

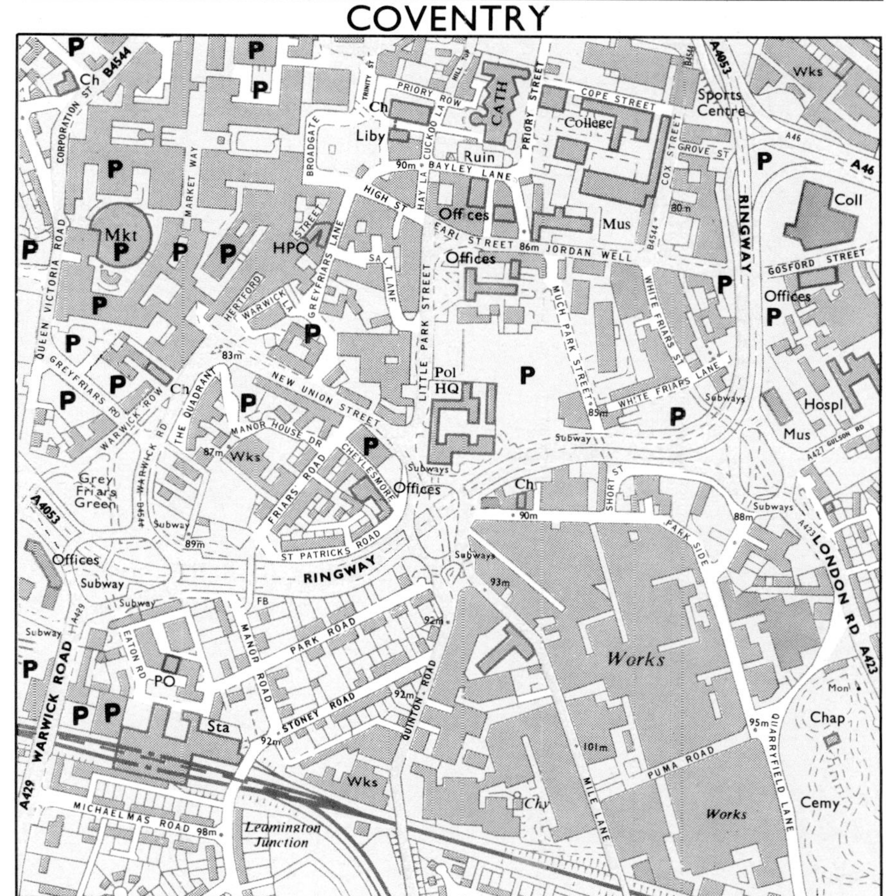

DOVER

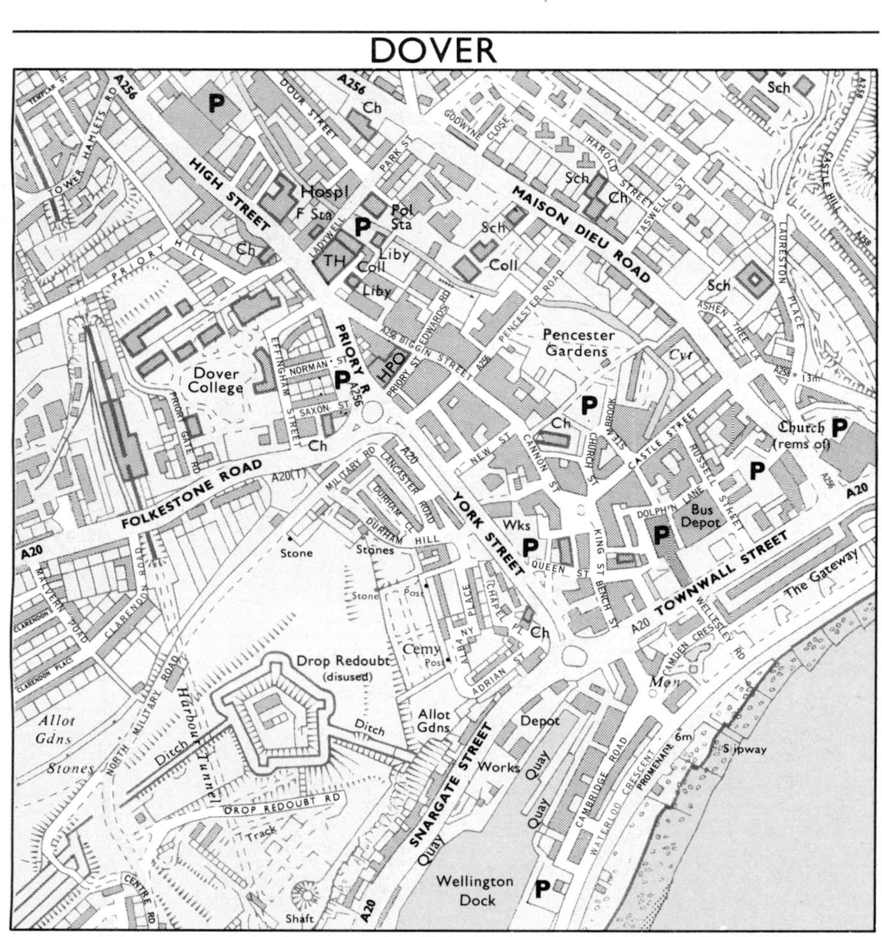

DUNDEE

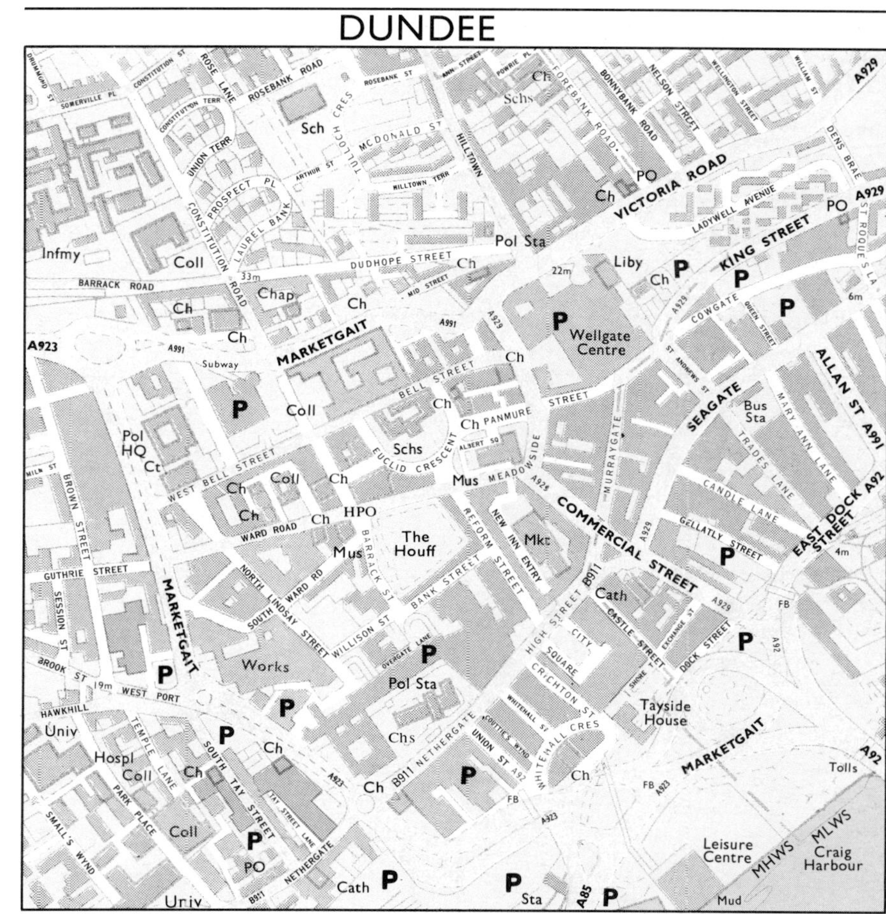

EDINBURGH

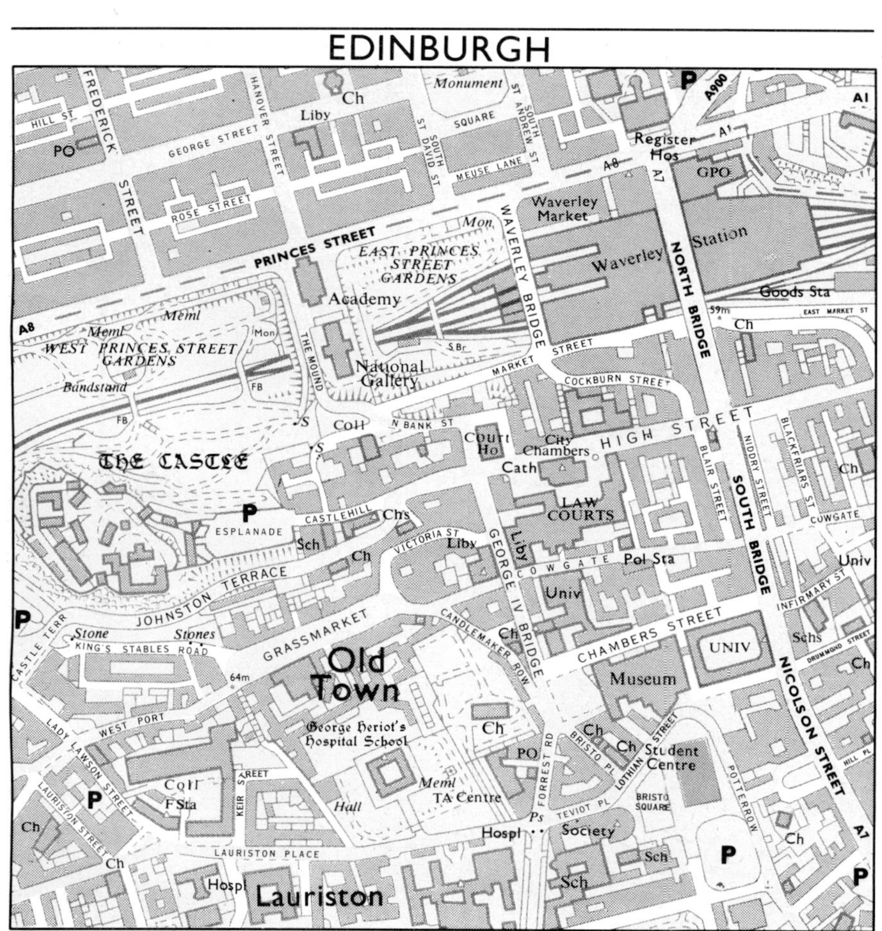

EXETER

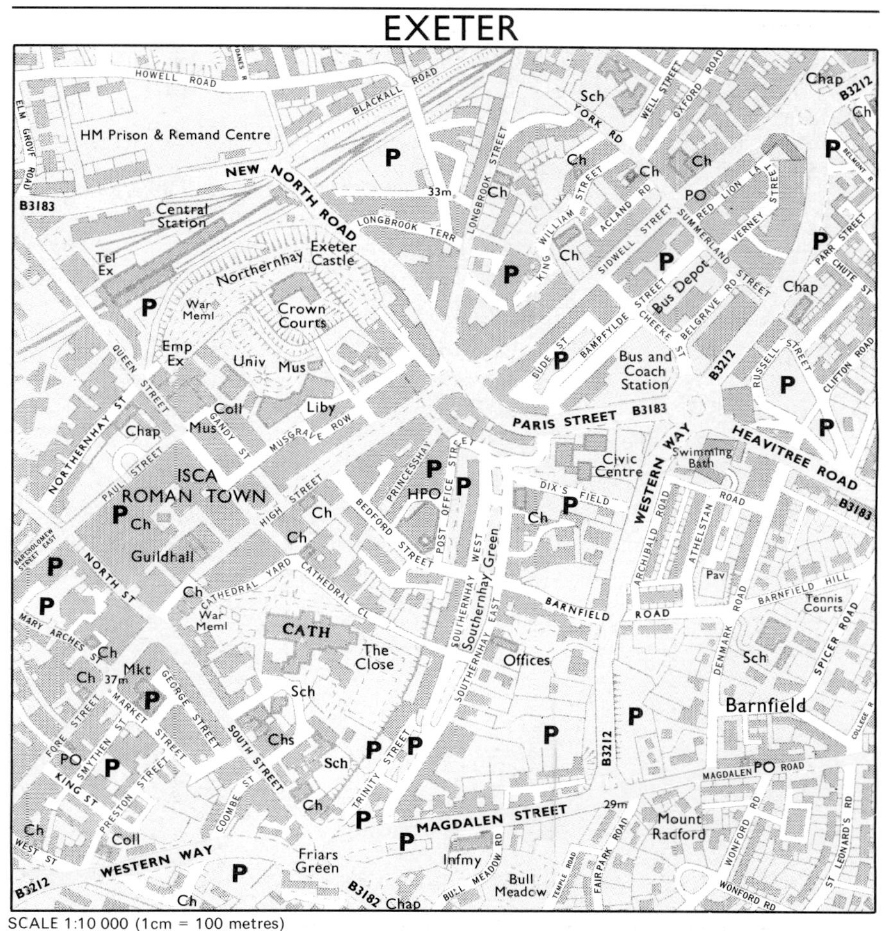

SCALE 1:10 000 (1cm = 100 metres)

GLASGOW (CENTRAL)

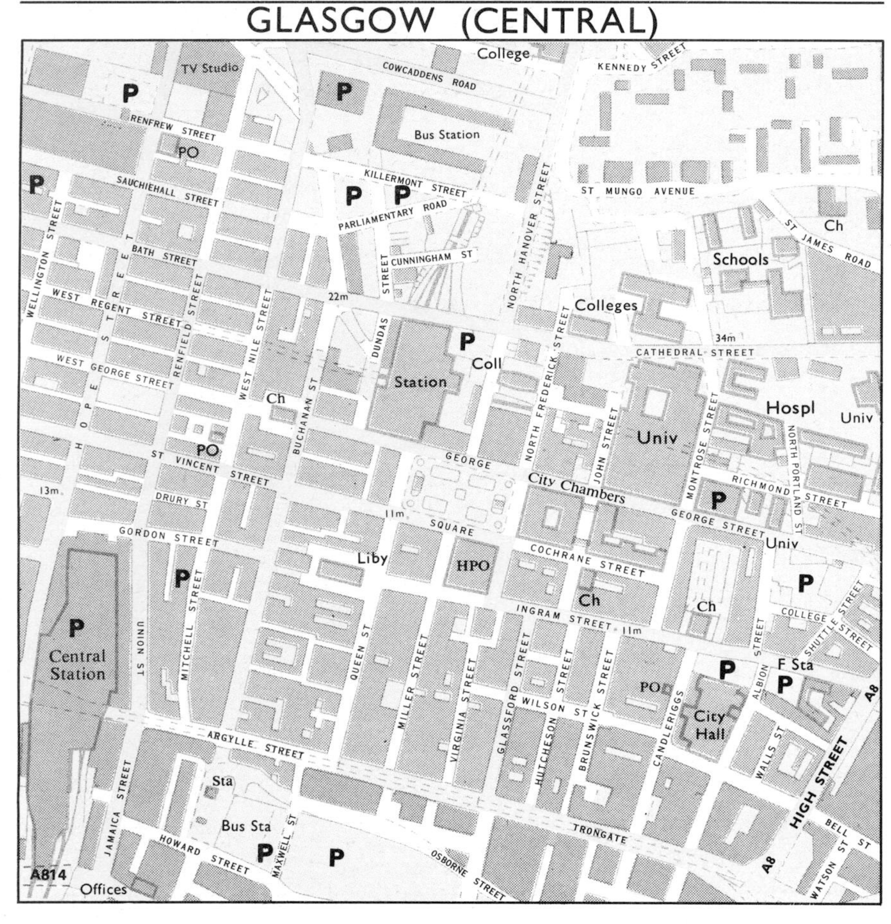

GLOUCESTER

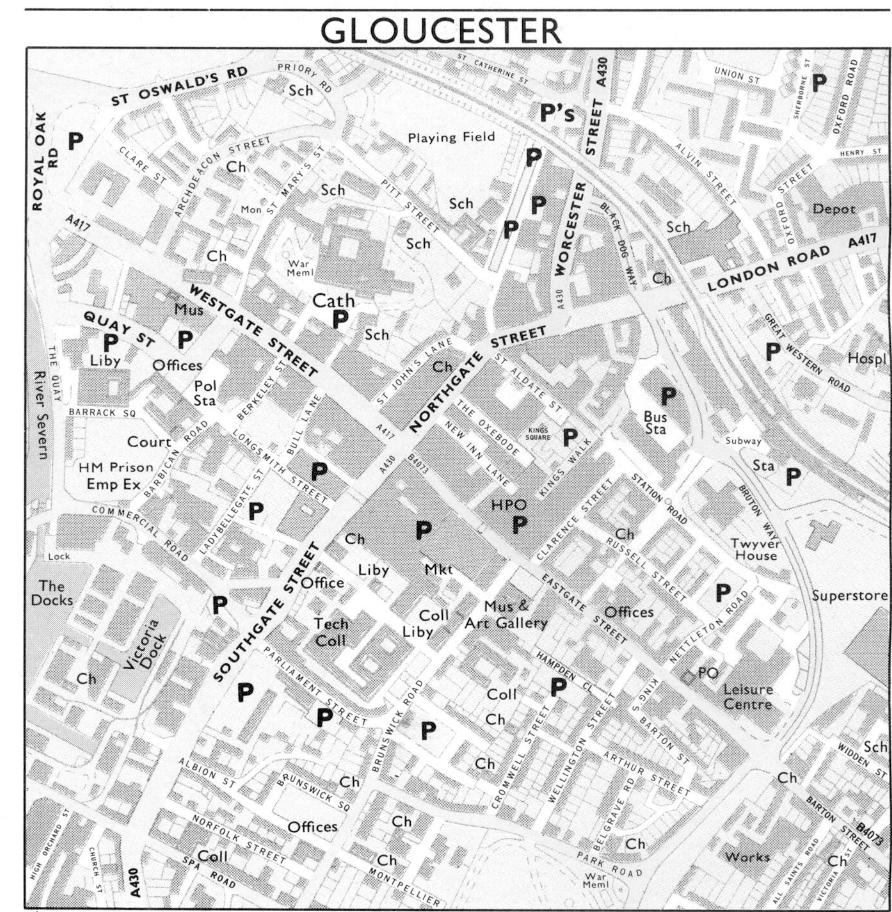

GREAT YARMOUTH

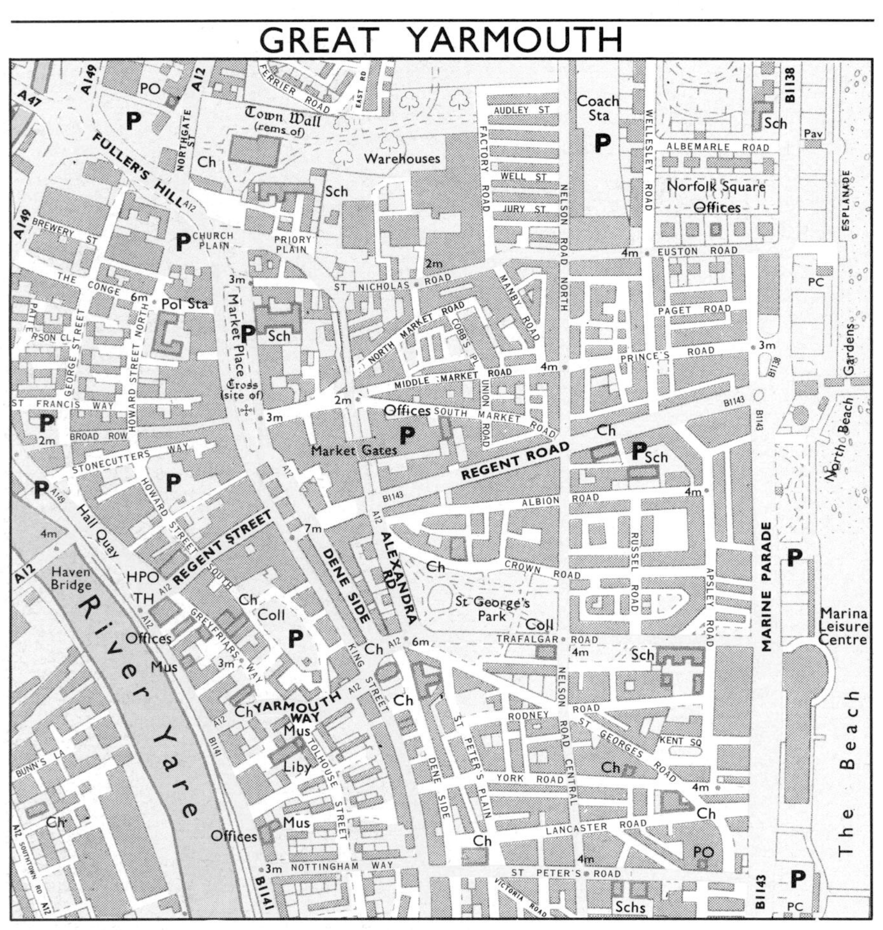

INVERNESS

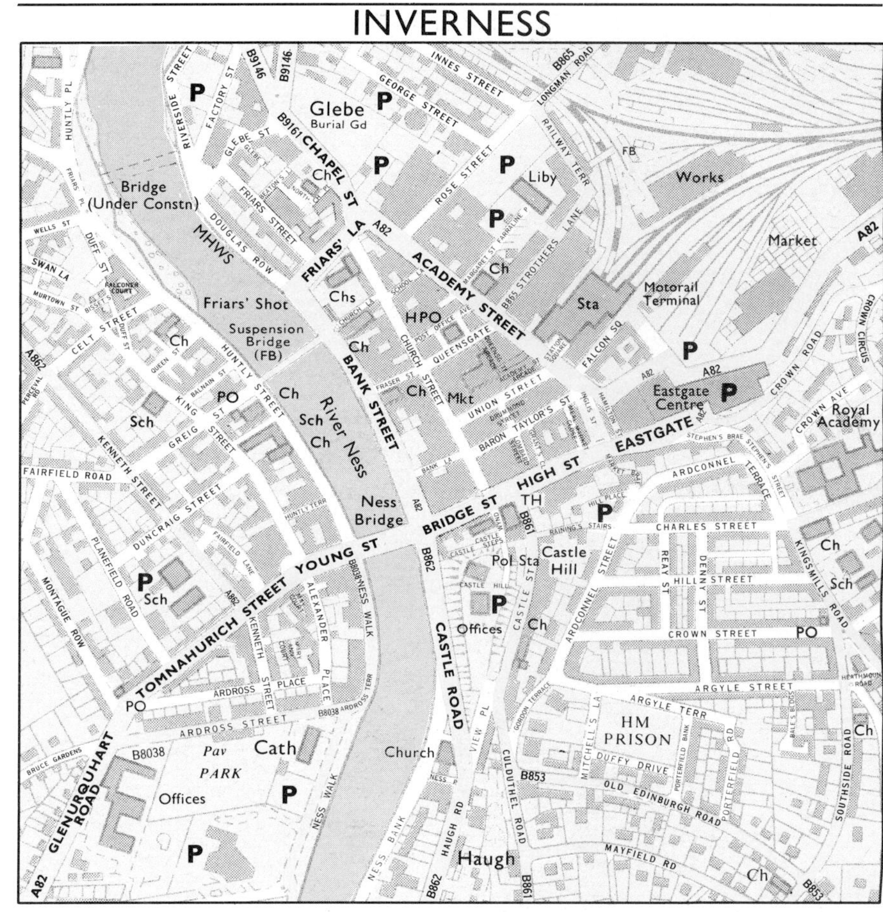

LEEDS

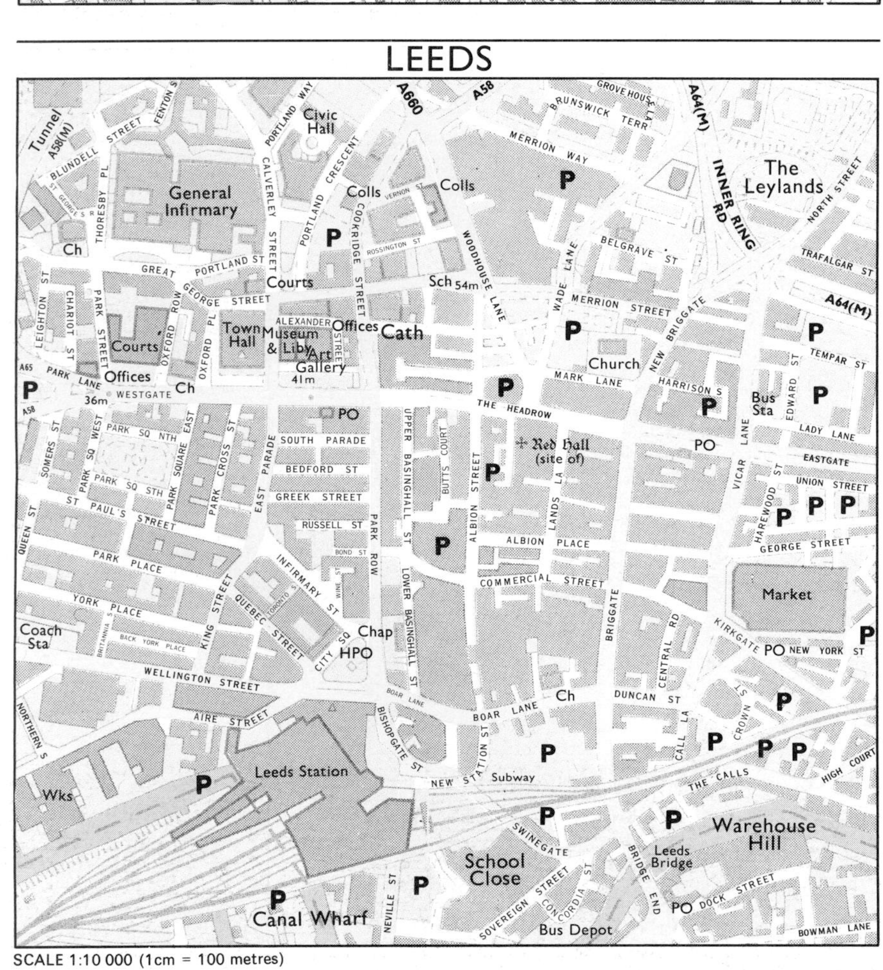

LEICESTER

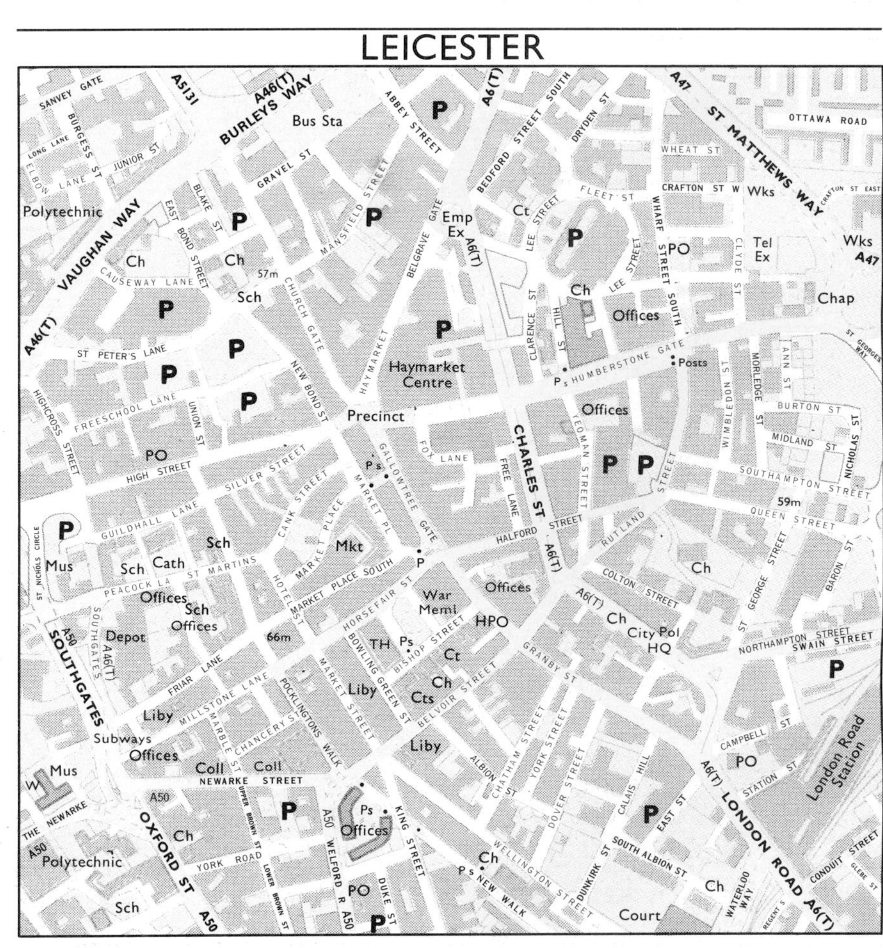

SCALE 1:10 000 (1cm = 100 metres)

LIVERPOOL

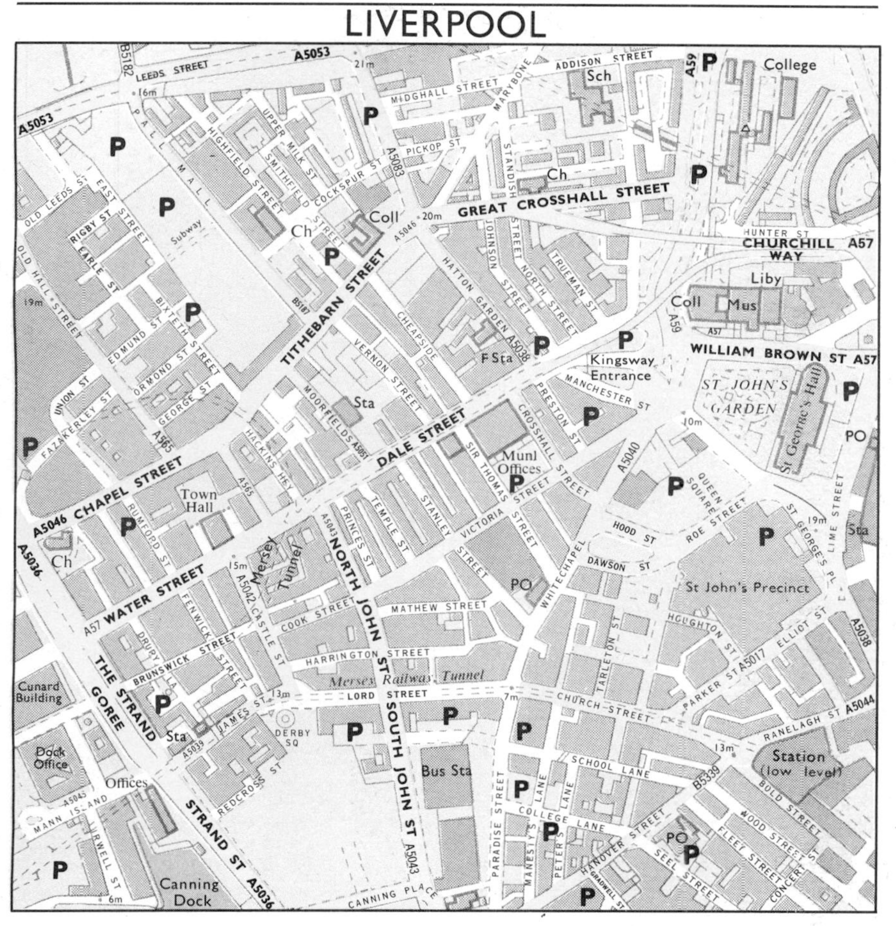

MANCHESTER

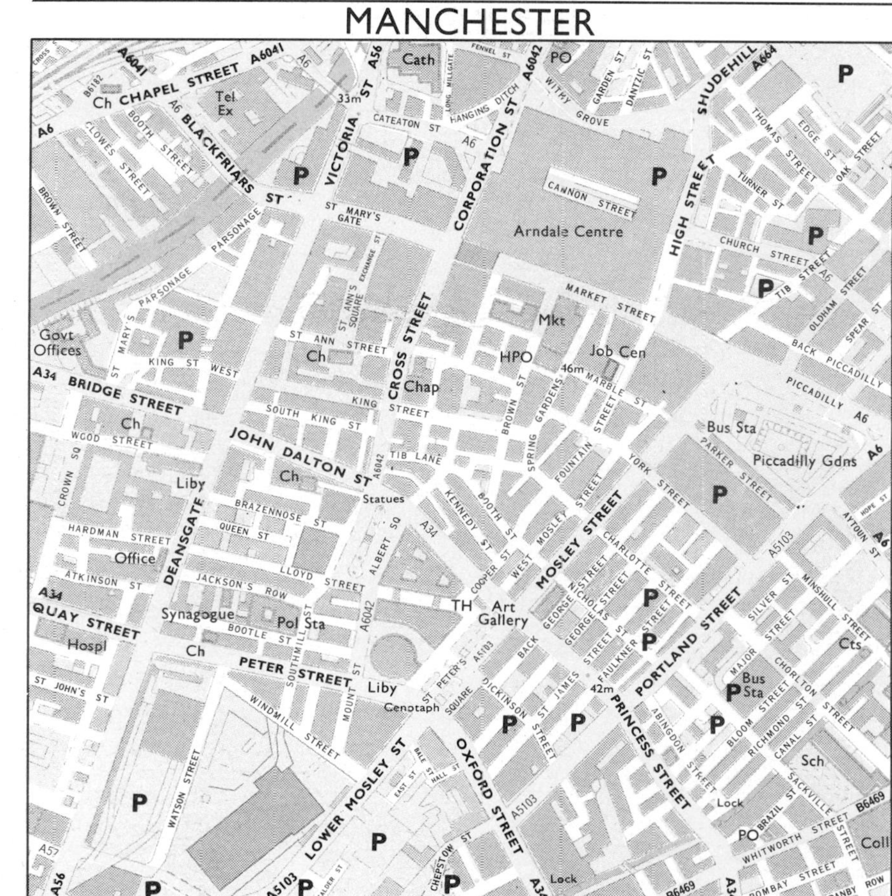

MIDDLESBROUGH

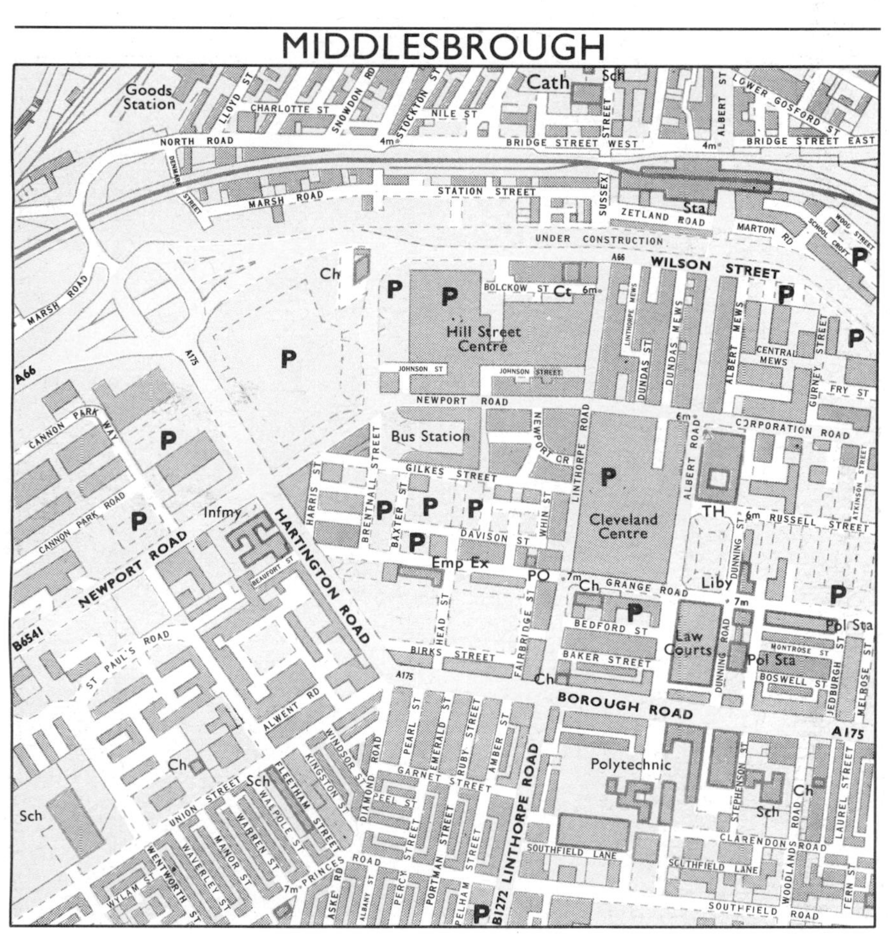

NEWCASTLE-UPON-TYNE

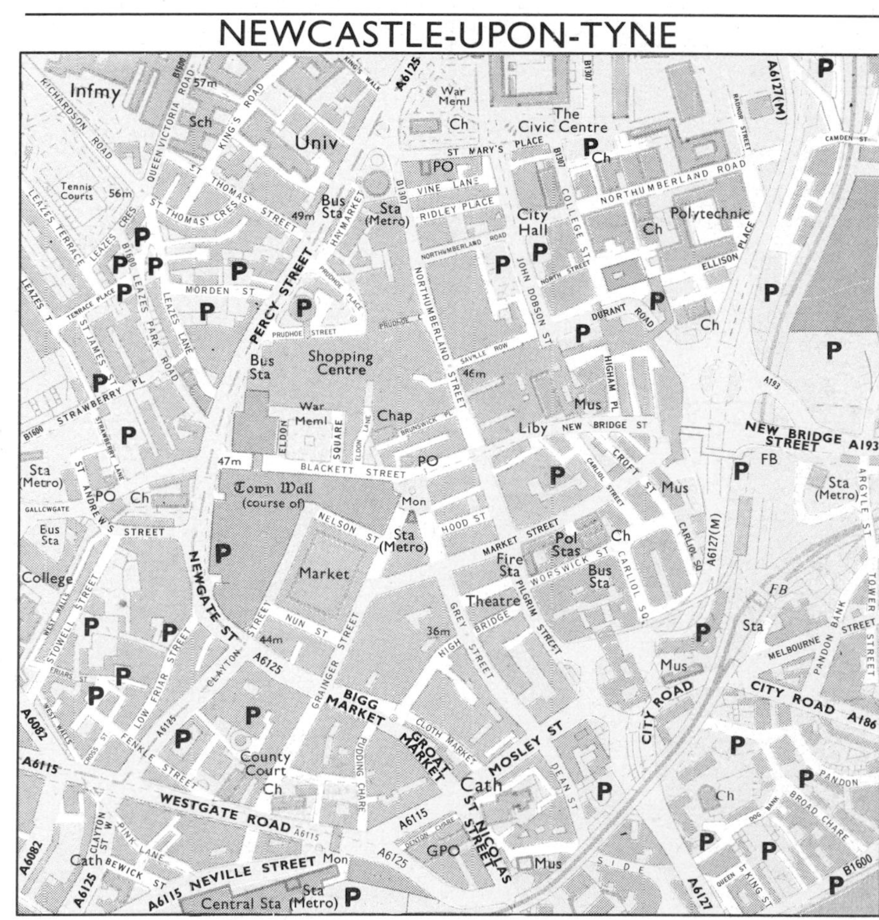

NORWICH

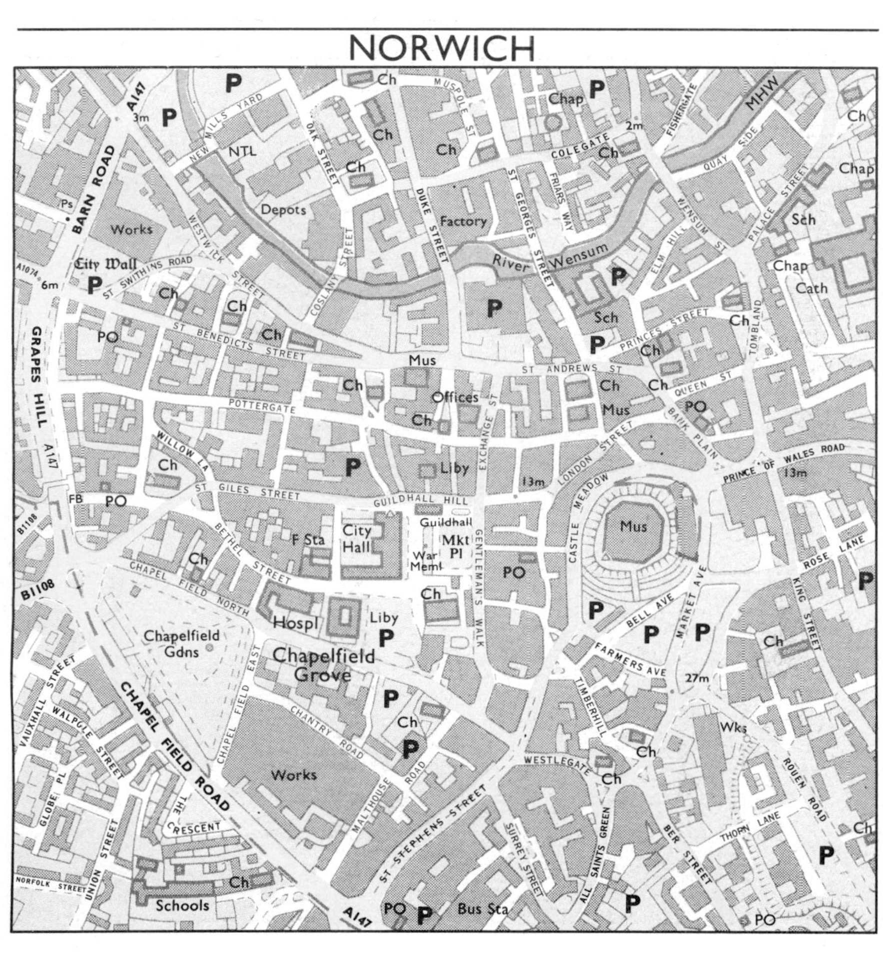

NOTTINGHAM

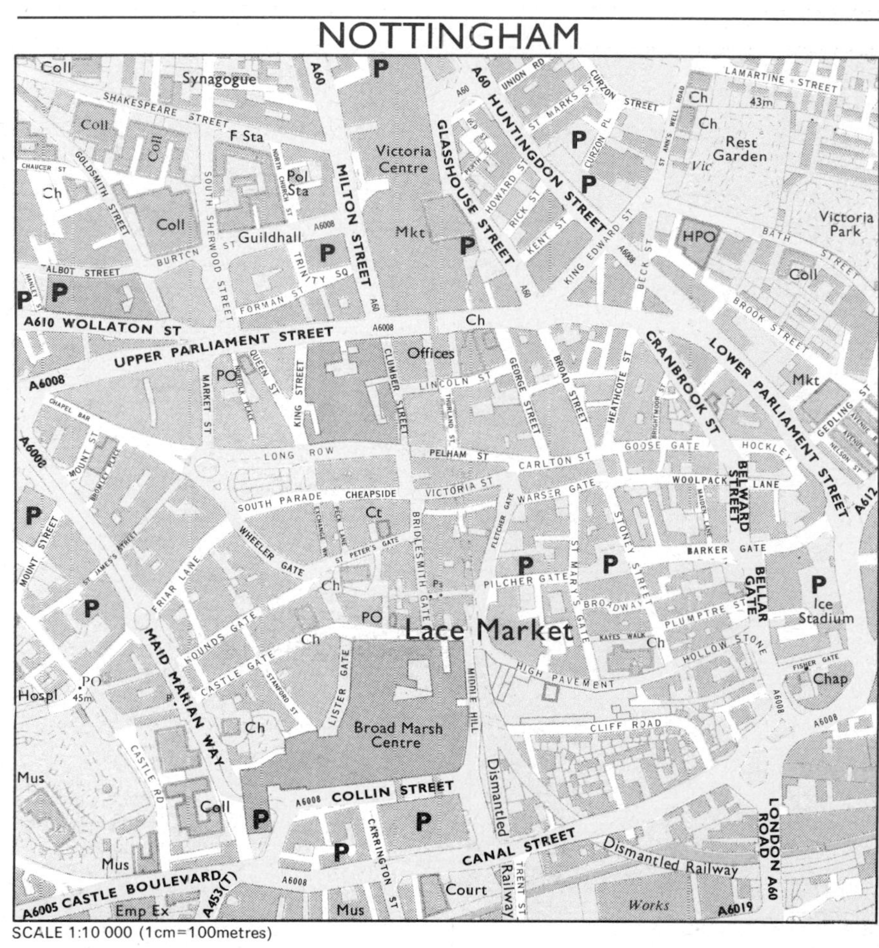

SCALE 1:10 000 (1cm=100metres)

OXFORD

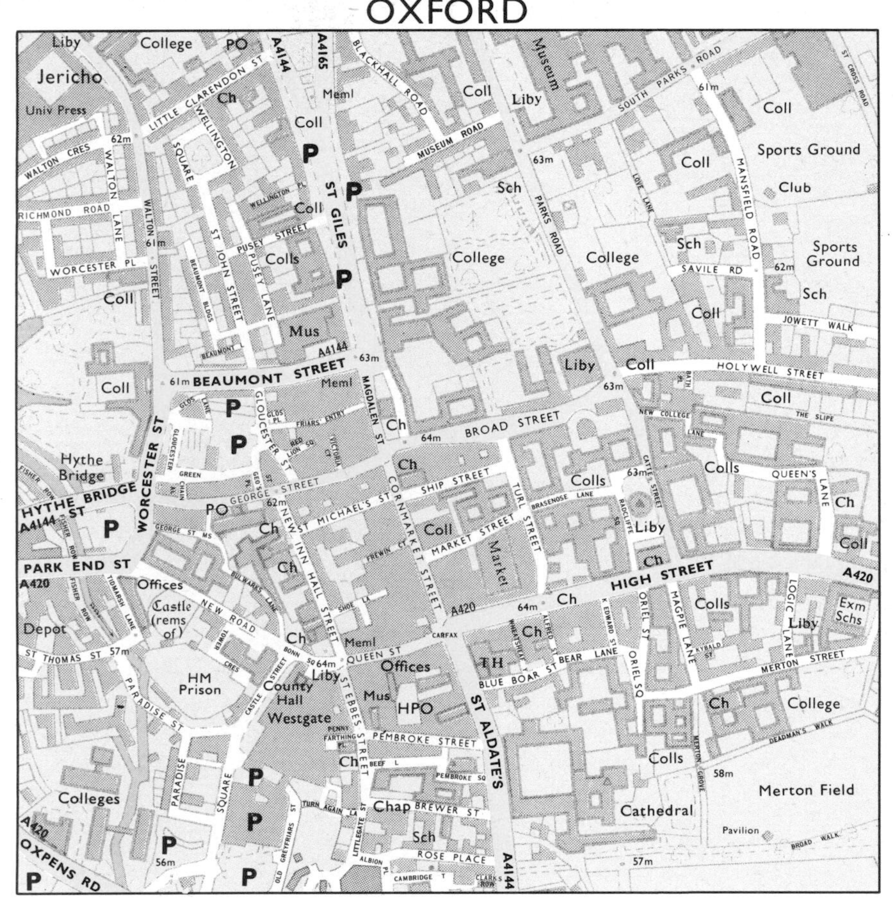

PLYMOUTH

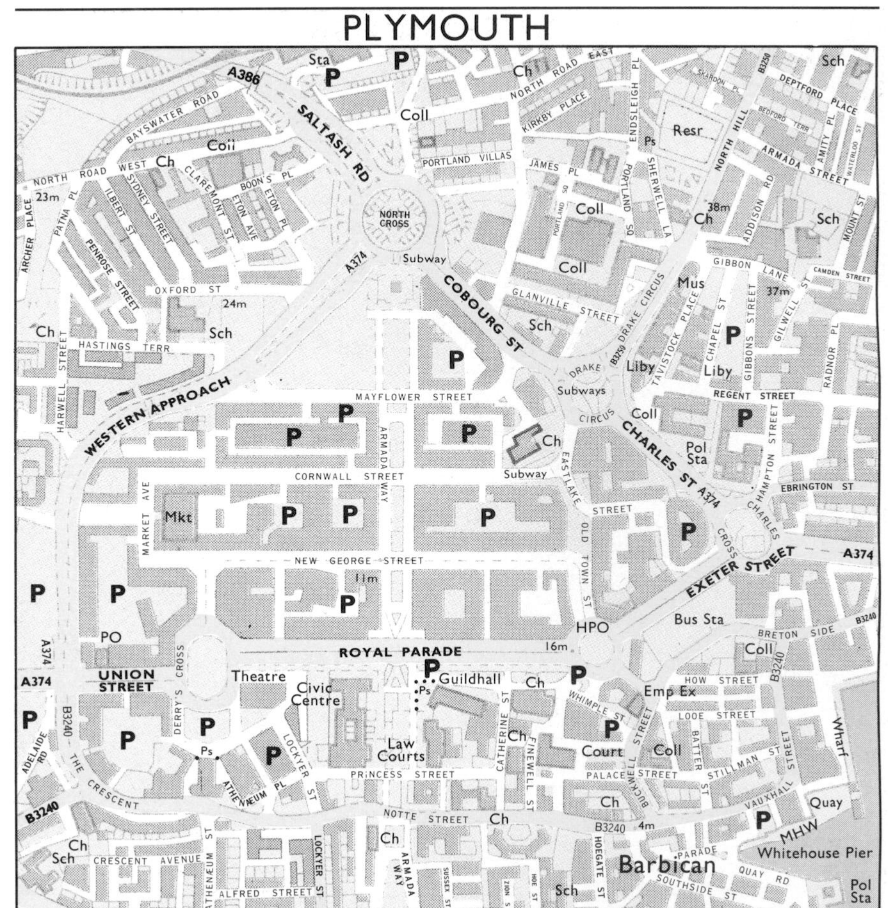

POOLE

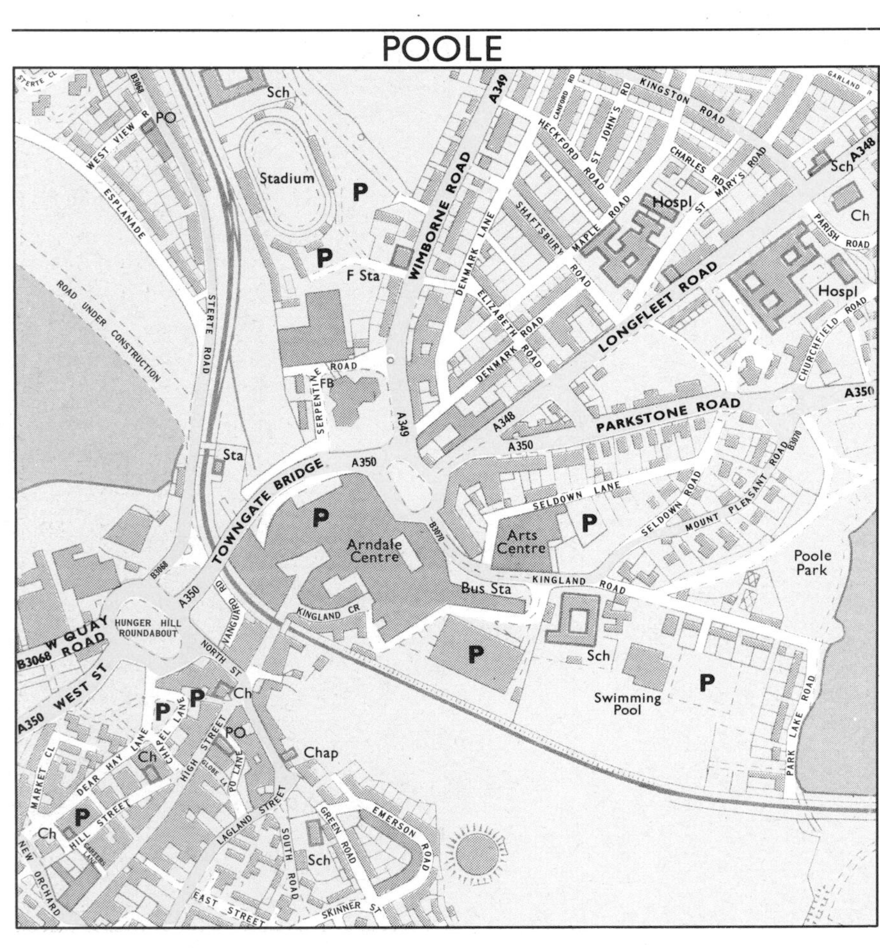

PORTSMOUTH

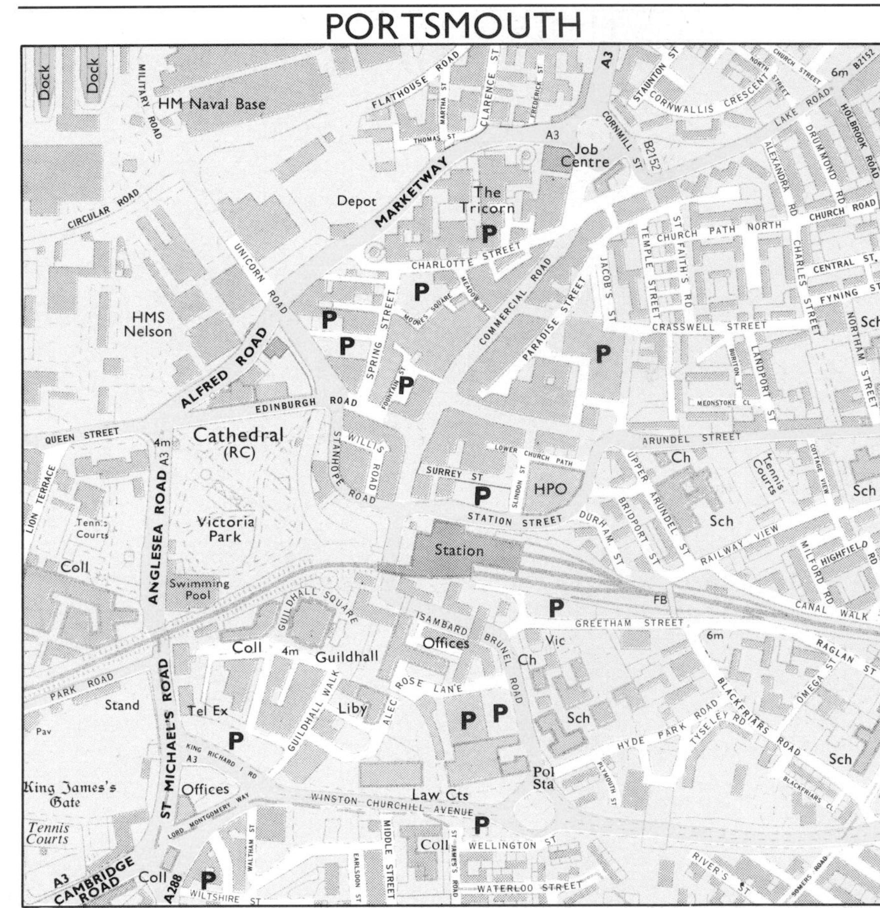

SALISBURY

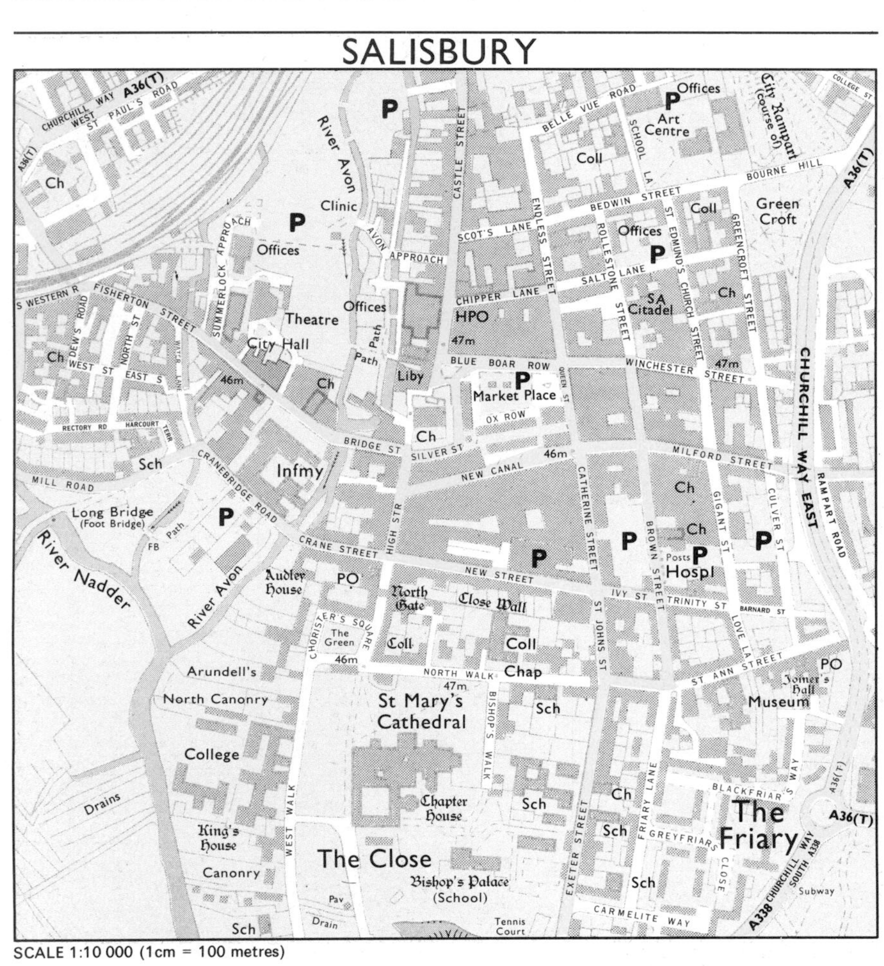

SHEFFIELD

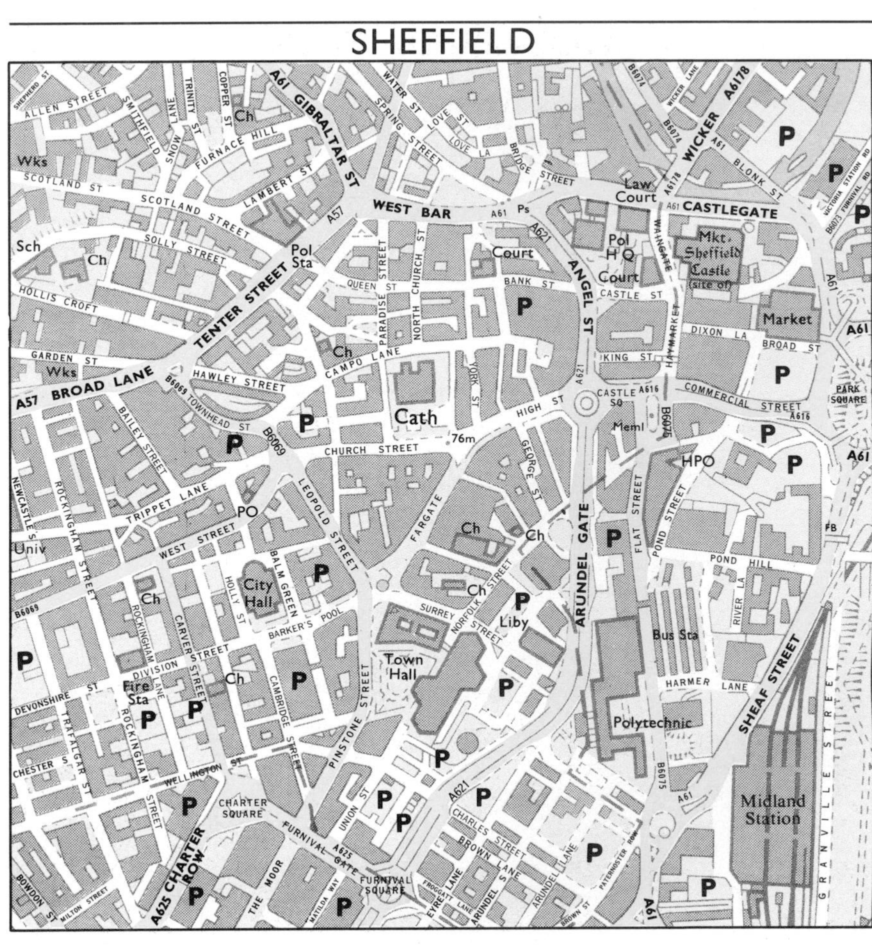

SCALE 1:10 000 (1cm = 100 metres)

SOUTHAMPTON

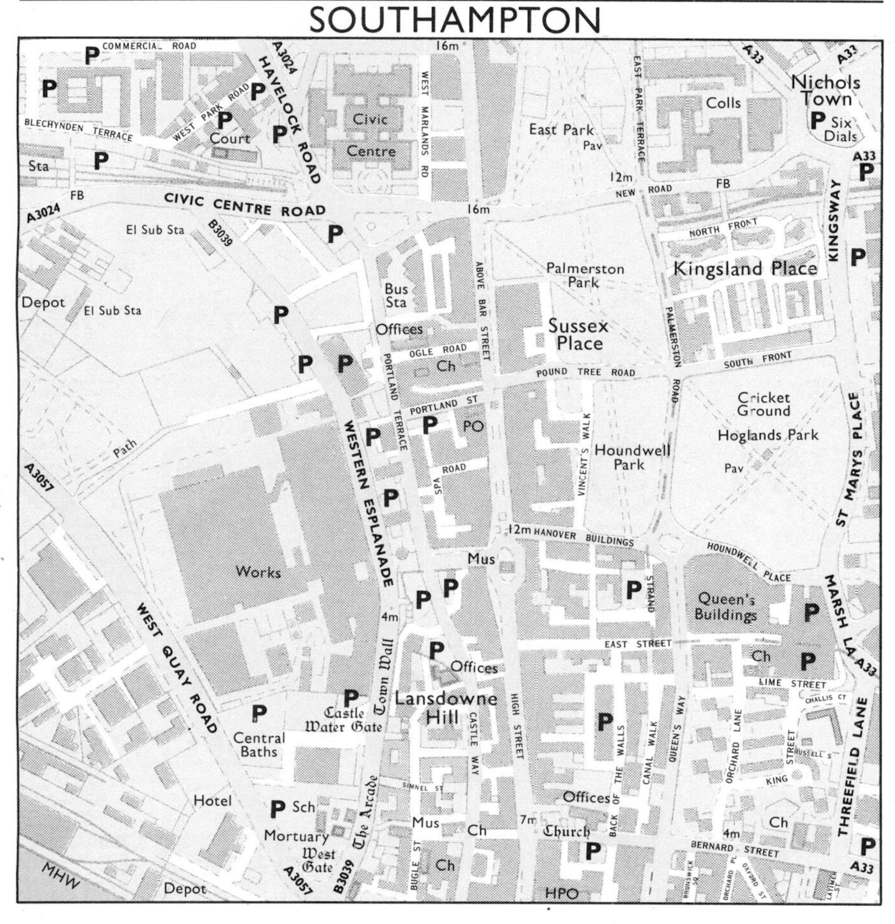

STOKE-ON-TRENT

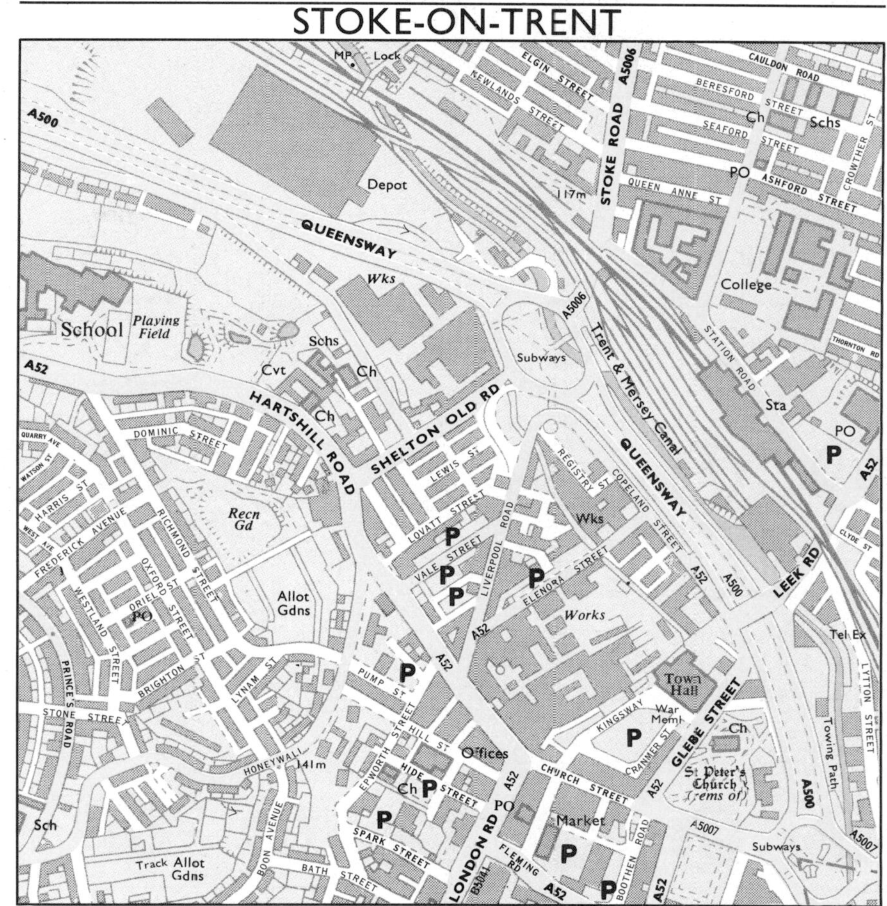

STRATFORD-UPON-AVON

SWANSEA

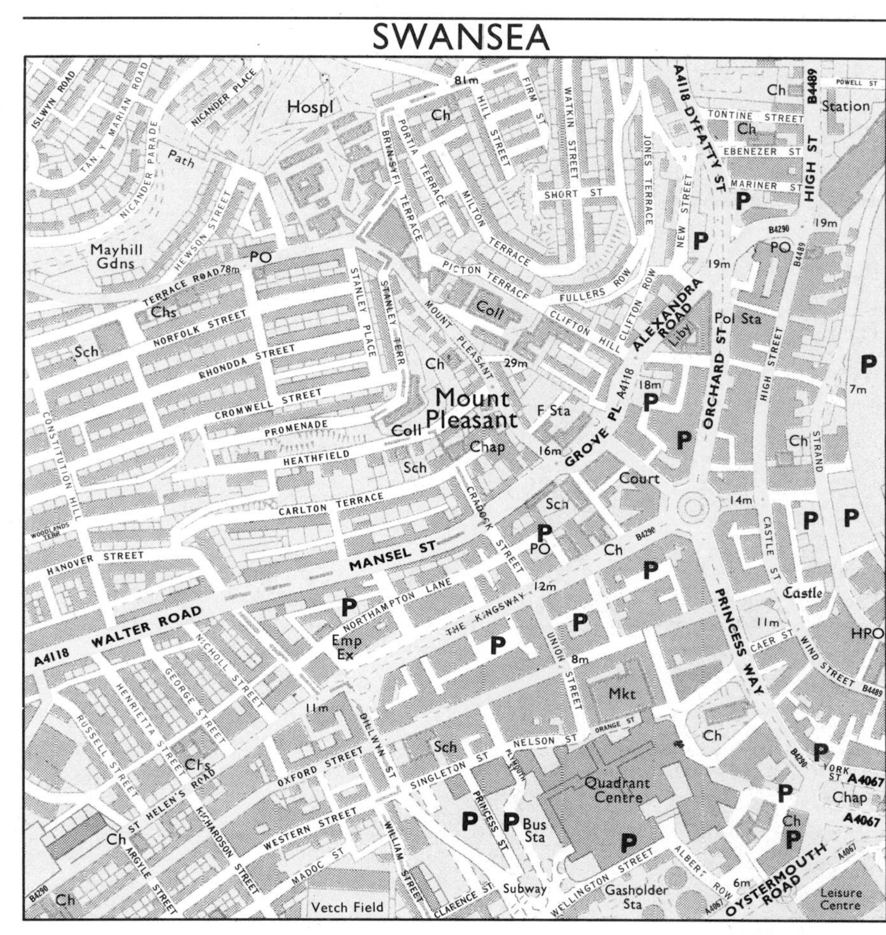

WOLVERHAMPTON

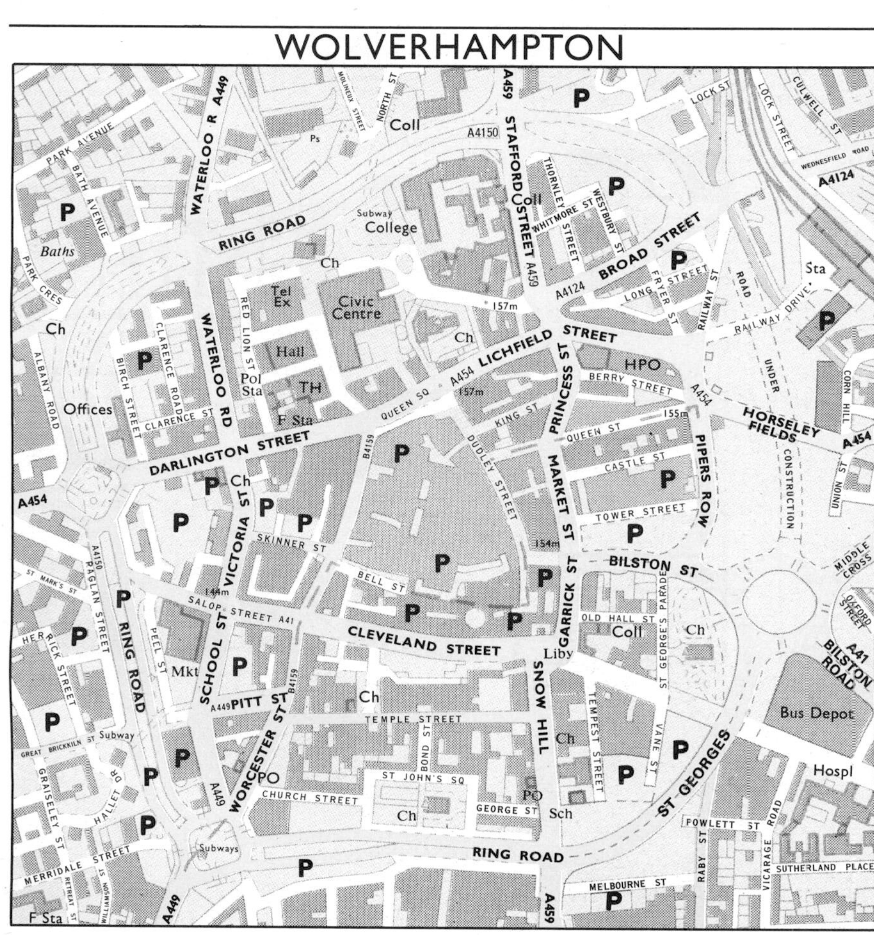

YORK

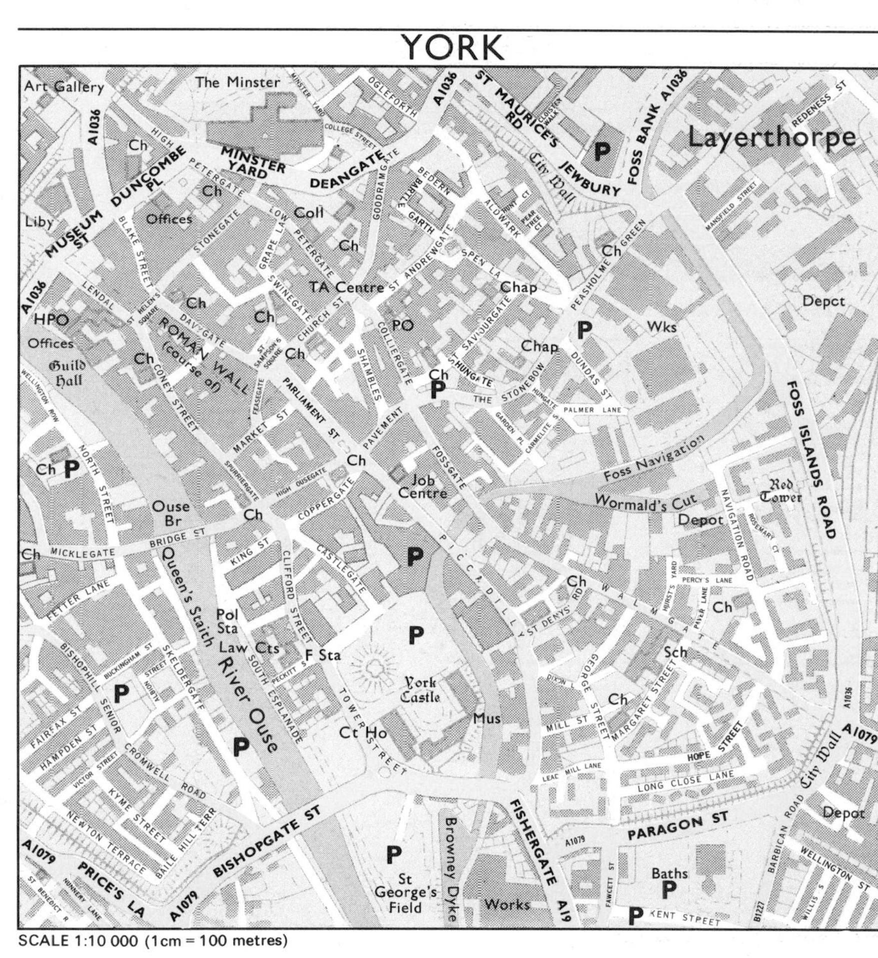

SCALE 1:10 000 (1cm = 100 metres)

Road Signs

SIGNS GIVING ORDERS

These signs are mostly circular and those with red circles are mostly prohibitive

Maximum speed

National speed limit applies

Stop and Give Way

Give way to traffic on major road

Manually operated temporary 'STOP' sign

School crossing patrol

No entry for vehicular traffic

No vehicles

No motor vehicles

No motor vehicles except solo motorcycles, scooters or mopeds

No cycling

No pedestrians

No overtaking

No stopping (Clearway)

Give priority to vehicles from opposite direction

No right turn

No left turn

No U turns

No vehicles over axle weight shown in tonnes

No vehicles including load, over weight shown (total weight limit in tonnes)

No vehicles with over 12 seats except regular scheduled, school and works buses

No vehicle or combination of vehicles over length shown

No goods vehicles over maximum gross weight shown in tonnes

Plates below some signs qualify their message

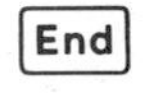
End of restriction

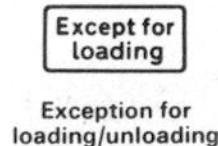
Exception for loading/unloading goods and access to off-street garaging

Exception for vehicles with over 12 seats

Exception for stage and scheduled express carriages, school and works buses

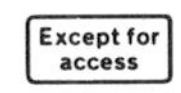
Exception for access to premises and land adjacent to the road where there is no alternative route

No vehicles over height shown

No vehicles over width shown

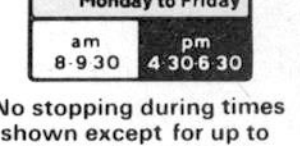
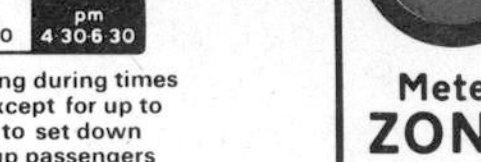
No stopping during times shown except for up to 2 mins. to set down or pick up passengers

Entrance to controlled parking zone

End of controlled parking zone

Signs with blue circles but no red border are mostly compulsory

Ahead only

Turn left ahead (right if symbol reversed)

Turn left (right if symbol reversed)

Keep left (right if symbol reversed)

Vehicles may pass either side to reach same destination

Route to be used by pedal cyclists only

Minimum speed

End of minimum speed

Mini-roundabout (roundabout circulation – give way to vehicles from the immediate right)

One-way traffic (Compare circular "Ahead only" sign)

With-flow bus lane

Contra-flow bus lane

WARNING SIGNS

Mostly triangular

Roundabout

Cross roads

Side road

T junction

Staggered junction

Traffic merges from left

Traffic merges from right

Double bend first to left (may be reversed)

Bend to right (or left if symbol reversed)

Steep hill downwards

Steep hill upwards

Gradients may be shown as a ratio i.e. 20% = 1:5

Distance to "Stop" line ahead

Distance to "Give Way" line ahead

Falling or fallen rocks

Loose chippings

Road works

Right-hand lane closed (symbols may be varied)

Two-way traffic straight ahead

Two-way traffic crosses one-way road

Dual carriageway ends

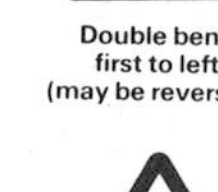
Road narrows on both sides

Road narrows on right (left if symbol reversed)

Change to opposite carriageway (may be reversed)

Children going to or from school

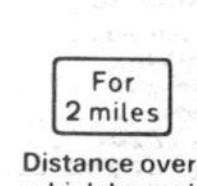
Distance over which hazard extends

Distance to hazard

Plate to indicate a level crossing equipped with automatic barriers and flashing lights

Level crossing with barrier or gate ahead

Level crossing without barrier or gate ahead

Location of level crossing without barrier or gate

"Count-down" markers approaching concealed level crossing (each bar represents ⅓ the distance from the first warning sign to the crossing)

Uneven road

Hump bridge

Opening or swing bridge ahead

Quayside or river bank

School crossing patrol ahead (Some signs have amber lights which flash when patrol is operating)

Low-flying aircraft or sudden aircraft noise

Overhead electric cable;

Cattle

Wild animals

Wild horses or ponies

Accompanied horses or ponies crossing the road ahead

Traffic signals

Pedestrian crossing

Slippery road

Height limit (e.g. low bridge)

Other danger;

Plate below some signs

Sharp deviation of route to left (or right if chevrons reversed)

DIRECTION SIGNS *Mostly rectangular*

Signs on motorways *Blue backgrounds*

Start of motorway

Direction to service area with fuel, parking, cafeteria and restaurant facilities

On approaches to junctions (junction number on black background)

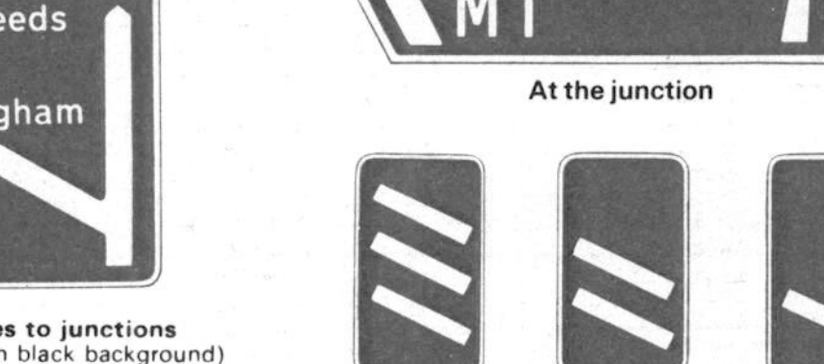
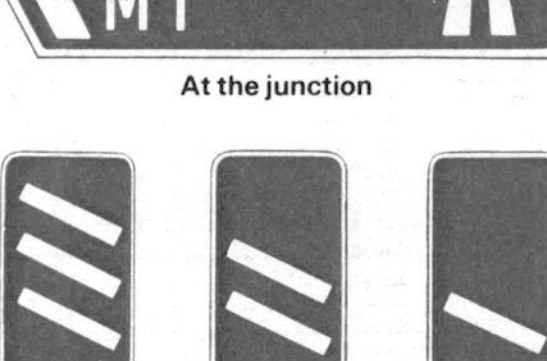

At the junction

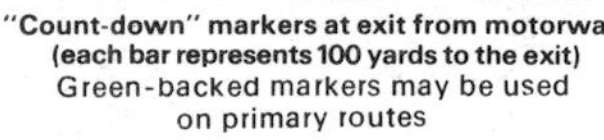
"Count-down" markers at exit from motorway (each bar represents 100 yards to the exit) Green-backed markers may be used on primary routes

A404 Marlow | Oxford M40

Downward pointing arrows mean "Get in lane"

The panel with the sloping arrow indicates the destinations which can be reached by leaving the motorway at the next junction

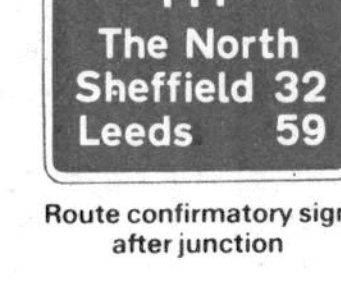

Route confirmation sign after junction

End of motorway

Signs on non-primary routes *Black borders*

At the junction

Ring road

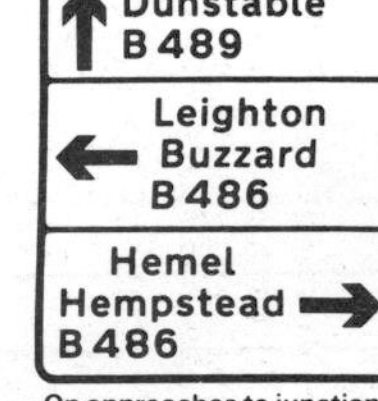

On approaches to junctions

Other direction signs

Advisory route for lorries

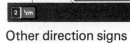

Direction to camping and caravan site

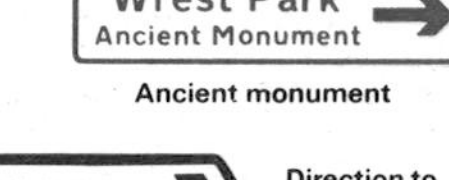

Ancient monument

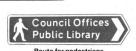

Direction to Ministry of Defence establishment

Direction to toilets with access for the disabled

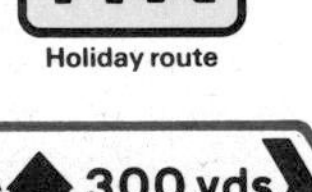

Holiday route

Route for pedestrians

Picnic site

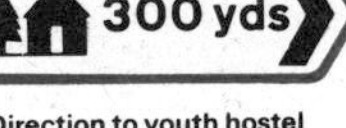

Direction to youth hostel

Airport

Local direction signs *Blue borders*

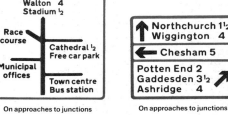

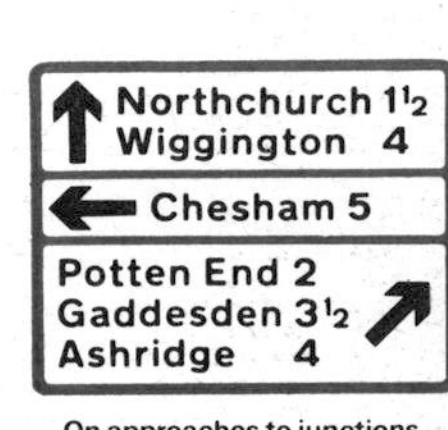
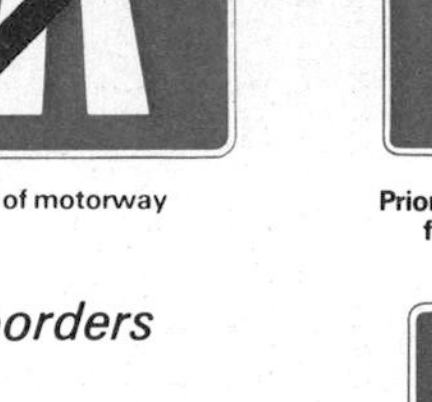

On approaches to junctions

On approaches to junctions

INFORMATION SIGNS *All rectangular*

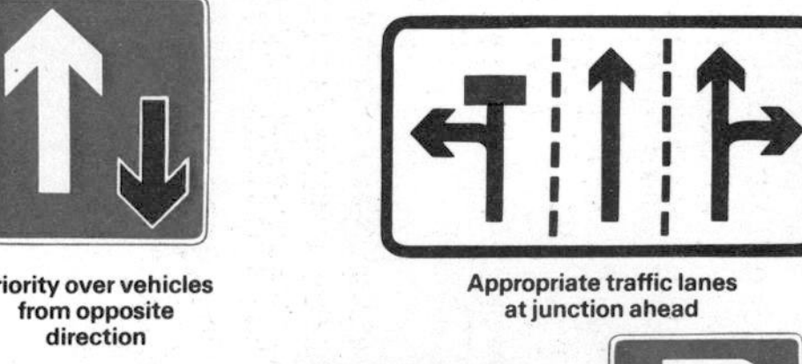
Priority over vehicles from opposite direction

Appropriate traffic lanes at junction ahead

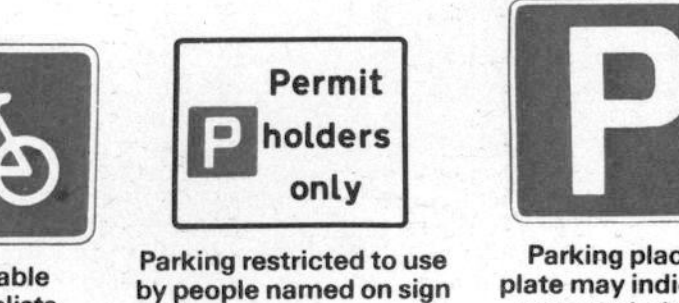

Route available for pedal cyclists

Parking restricted to use by people named on sign

Parking place; plate may indicate any restrictions on use

One-way street

No through road

Hospital ahead

Index

Content

For each entry the Atlas page number is listed and the National Grid map reference is given to the nearest kilometre of the feature to which the name applies.

Example Use of Index

To find Dorking refer to the name in the index and read off the reference 16TQ 1649. The first number indicates that Dorking is shown on page 16. The remaining two letters and four figures signify that the town lies within the 100 kilometre square TQ (see page 106) and is 16 kilometres east and 49 kilometres north of the south west corner of the square. The 10 kilometre grid numbers '1' and '4' are shown on the edges of page 16 and the exact location of Dorking is found by estimating '6' tenths eastward from the grid line '1' and '9' tenths northwards from the grid line '4'. In the National Grid Reference system the Eastings (16 for Dorking) are always stated before the Northings (49 for Dorking).

List of County Names Showing Abbreviations Used in this Index

England

Avon	Avon
Bedfordshire	Beds
Berkshire	Berks
Buckinghamshire	Bucks
Cambridgeshire	Cambs
Cheshire	Ches
Cleveland	Cleve
Cornwall	Corn
Cumbria	Cumbr
Derbyshire	Derby
Devon	Devon
Dorset	Dorset
Durham	Durham
East Sussex	E. Susx
Essex	Essex
Gloucestershire	Glos
Greater London	G. Lon
Greater Manchester	G. Man
Hampshire	Hants
Hereford & Worcester	H. & W
Hertfordshire	Herts
Humberside	Humbs
Isle of Wight	I. of W
Kent	Kent
Lancashire	Lancs
Leicester	Leic
Lincolnshire	Lincs
Merseyside	Mers
Norfolk	Norf
North Yorkshire	N. Yks
Northamptonshire	Northnts
Northumberland	Northum
Nottinghamshire	Notts
Oxfordshire	Oxon
Shropshire	Shrops
Somerset	Somer
South Yorkshire	S. Yks
Staffordshire	Staffs
Suffolk	Suff
Surrey	Surrey
Tyne and Wear	T. & W
Warwickshire	Warw
West Midlands	W. Mids
West Sussex	W. Susx
West Yorkshire	W. Yks
Wiltshire	Wilts

Wales

Clwyd	Clwyd
Dyfed	Dyfed
Gwent	Gwent
Gwynedd	Gwyn
Mid Glamorgan	M. Glam
Powys	Powys
South Glamorgan	S. Glam
West Glamorgan	W. Glam

Other Areas

Isle of Man	I. of M
Isles of Scilly	I. Scilly

Region & Island Area Names
Scotland
Regions

Borders	Border
Central	Central
Dumfries & Galloway	D. & G
Fife	Fife
Grampian	Grampn
Highland	Highl
Lothian	Lothn
Strathclyde	Strath
Tayside	Tays

Island Areas

Orkney	Orkney
Shetland	Shetld
Western Isles	W. Isles

A

B

F

G

H

I

M

Munsley 37 SO 6640
Munslow 36 SO 5287
Murch 29 ST 1671
Murcott 35 SP 5815
Murkle 103 ND 1668
Murlaggan, Highld 90 NN 0192
Murlaggan, Highld 90 NN 3181
Murrow 51 TF 3707
Mursley 40 SP 8128
Murthly 92 NO 0938
Murton, Cumbr 71 NY 7221
Murton, Durham 73 NZ 3947
Murton, Northum 85 NT 9648
Murton, N. Yks 67 SE 6552
Musbury 12 SY 2794
Muscoates 68 SE 6880
Musselburgh 89 NT 3472
Muston, Leic 50 SK 8237
Muston, N. Yks 69 TA 0979
Mustow Green 37 SO 8774
Mutford 43 TM 4888
Muthill 88 NN 8616
Mutterton 12 ST 0205
Mybster 103 ND 1652
Myddfai 29 SN 7730
Myddle 46 SJ 4623
Mydroilyn 31 SN 4555
Mylor Bridge 7 SW 8036
Mynachlog-ddu 30 SN 1430
Myndtown 36 SO 3989
Mynydd-bach 33 ST 4894
Mynydd Isa 56 SJ 2564
Mynydd Llandegai 54 SH 6065
Mynydd Mechell 54 SH 3690
Mynytho 54 SH 3031
Myrebird 93 NO 7493
Mytchett 23 SU 8855
Mytholm 66 SD 9827
Mytholmroyd 66 SE 0126
Myton-on-Swale 67 SE 4366

N

Naast 102 NG 8283
Naburn 67 SE 6045
Nackington 19 TR 1554
Nacton 43 TM 2240
Nafferton 69 TA 0559
Nailsea 21 ST 4770
Nailstone 48 SK 4107
Nailsworth 34 ST 8499
Nairn 95 NH 8856
Nancegollan 6 SW 6332
Nancledra 6 SW 4936
Nanhoron 54 SH 2831
Nannerch 56 SJ 1669
Nanpantan 49 SK 5017
Nanpean 7 SW 9656
Nanstallon 7 SX 0366
Nant-ddû 29 SO 0015
Nanternis 31 SN 3756
Nantgaredig 31 SN 4921
Nantgarw 29 ST 1285
Nant Glâs 45 SN 9965
Nantglyn 55 SJ 0062
Nantlle 54 SH 5153
Nantmawr 46 SJ 2524
Nantmel 45 SO 0366
Nantmor 54 SH 6046
Nant Peris 54 SH 6058
Nantwich 47 SJ 6552
Nant-y-derry 33 SO 3306
Nantyffyllon 29 SS 8592
Nantyglo 29 SO 1910
Nant-y-moel 29 SS 9393
Naphill 24 SU 8596
Nappa 66 SD 8553
Napton on the Hill 39 SP 4661
Narberth 30 SN 1114
Narborough, Leic 49 SP 5497
Narborough, Norf 52 TF 7412
Nasareth 54 SH 4750
Naseby 39 SP 6877
Nash, Bucks 39 SP 7834
Nash, Gwent 20 ST 3483
Nash, H. & W 36 SO 3062
Nash, Shrops 37 SO 6071
Nash Lee 24 SP 8408
Nassington 50 TL 0696
Nasty 25 TL 3524
Nateby, Cumbr 71 NY 7706
Nateby, Lancs 65 SD 4644
Natland 71 SD 5289
Naughton 42 TM 0249
Naunton, Glos 34 SP 1123
Naunton, H. & W 37 SO 8739
Naunton Beauchamp 38 SO 9652
Navenby 60 SK 9857
Navestock Heath 25 TQ 5397
Navestock Side 25 TQ 5697
Nawton 67 SE 6584
Nayland 42 TL 9734
Nazeing 25 TL 4106
Neacroft 14 SZ 1896
Neal's Green 38 SP 3384
Neasham 72 NZ 3310
Neath 29 SS 7497
Neatishead 53 TG 3421
Nebo, Dyfed 44 SN 5465
Nebo, Gwyn 54 SH 4750
Nebo, Gwyn 55 SH 8356
Necton 52 TF 8709
Nedd 102 NC 1332
Nedging Tye 42 TM 0149
Needham 43 TM 2281
Needham Market 43 TM 0954
Needingworth 41 TL 3472
Neen Savage 37 SO 6777
Neen Sollars 37 SO 6672
Neenton 37 SO 6388
Nefyn 54 SH 3040
Neilston 81 NS 4756
Nelson, Lancs 65 SD 5637
Nelson, M. Glam 29 ST 1195
Nelson Village 79 NZ 2577
Nemphlar 83 NS 8544
Nempnett Thrubwell 21 ST 5360
Nenthead 71 NY 7843
Nenthorn 84 NT 6837
Nercwys 56 SJ 2361
Nereabolls 99 NR 2255
Nerston 82 NS 6456
Nesbit 85 NT 9833
Ness, Ches 56 SJ 3076
Ness, N. Yks 68 SE 6978
Nesscliffe 46 SJ 3819
Neston, Ches 56 SJ 2977
Neston, Wilts 21 ST 8668
Nether Alderley 57 SJ 8476
Netheravon 22 SU 1449
Nether Blainslie 84 NT 5443
Netherbrae 97 NJ 7959
Nether Broughton 49 SK 6925
Netherburn 83 NS 8047
Nether Burrow 65 SD 6175
Netherbury 13 SY 4799
Nether Cerne 13 SY 6698
Nether Compton 13 ST 5917
Nether Dallachy 96 NJ 3664
Netherend 33 SO 5900
Nether Exe 9 SS 9300
Netherfield 17 TQ 7118
Netherhampton 14 SU 1129
Nether Haugh 59 SK 4196
Nether Heyford 39 SP 6558
Nether Howcleugh 77 NT 0312
Nether Kellet 65 SD 5068
Nether Kinmundy 97 NK 0544
Nether Kirkton 81 NS 4857
Netherlaw 75 NX 7445
Netherley 93 NO 8593
Nethermill 77 NY 0487
Nether Padley 59 SK 2578
Netherplace 81 NS 5255
Nether Poppleton 67 SE 5655
Nether Row 70 NY 3237
Netherseal 48 SK 2813
Nether Silton 73 SE 4592
Nether Stowey 20 ST 1939
Netherthird 76 NS 5718
Netherthong 58 SE 1309
Netherton, Central 87 NS 5579
Netherton, Devon 9 SX 8971
Netherton, H. & W 38 SO 9941
Netherton, Mers 56 SD 3500
Netherton, Northum 79 NT 9807
Netherton, Tays 93 NO 5457
Netherton, W. Yks 59 SE 2716
Nethertown, Cumbr 70 NX 9907
Nethertown, Highld 103 ND 3578
Nether Wallop 14 SU 3036
Nether Wasdale 70 NY 1204
Nether Whitacre 48 SP 2393
Nether Winchendon or Lower Winchendon 24 SP 7312
Netherwitton 79 NZ 0990
Nether Worton 35 SP 4230
Nethy Bridge 95 NJ 0020
Netley 15 SU 4508
Netley Marsh 14 SU 3313
Nettlebed 24 SU 7086
Nettlebridge 21 ST 6448
Nettlecombe 13 SY 5195
Nettleden 24 TL 0210
Nettleham 60 TF 0075
Nettlestead 17 TQ 6852
Nettlestead Green 17 TQ 6850
Nettlestone 15 SZ 6290
Nettleton, Lincs 63 TA 1000
Nettleton, Wilts 21 ST 8278
Neuk, The 93 NO 7397
Nevendon 26 TQ 7590
Nevern 30 SN 0840
New Abbey 76 NX 9666
New Aberdour 97 NJ 8863
New Addington 25 TQ 3863
New Alresford 15 SU 5832
New Alyth 92 NO 2447
Newark, Cambs 50 TF 2100
Newark, Orkney 104 HY 7242
Newark-on-Trent 49 SK 7953
Newarthill 82 NS 7859
New Ash Green 18 TQ 6065
New Bewick 79 NU 0620
Newbiggin, Cumbr 71 NY 4729
Newbiggin, Cumbr 71 NY 5549
Newbiggin, Cumbr 71 NY 6228
Newbiggin, Cumbr 64 SD 2669
Newbiggin, Durham 72 NY 9127
Newbiggin, N. Yks 72 SD 9591
Newbiggin, N. Yks 66 SD 9985
Newbiggin-by-the-Sea 79 NZ 3087
Newbigging, Strath 83 NT 0145
Newbigging, Tays 92 NO 2842
Newbigging, Tays 92 NO 4237
Newbigging, Tays 93 NO 4936
Newbiggin-on-Lune 71 NY 7005
Newbold, Derby 59 SK 3773
Newbold, Leic 48 SK 4019
Newbold on Avon 39 SP 4976
Newbold-on-Stour 38 SP 2446
Newbold Pacey 38 SP 2957
Newbold Verdon 49 SK 4403
New Bolingbroke 61 TF 3057
Newborough, Cambs 50 TF 2006
Newborough, Gwyn 54 SH 4265
Newborough, Staffs 48 SK 1325
Newbottle 39 SP 5237
Newbourne 43 TM 2742
New Brancepeth 72 NZ 2241
Newbridge, Clwyd 46 SJ 2841
Newbridge, Corn 6 SW 4231
Newbridge, Gwent 29 ST 2197
Newbridge, Hants 14 SU 2915
Newbridge, I. of W 14 SZ 4187
Newbridge, Lothn 88 NT 1272
Newbridge-on-Usk 33 ST 3894
Newbridge-on-Wye 32 SO 0158
New Brighton 56 SJ 3093
New Brinsley 49 SK 4650
Newbrough 78 NY 8767
New Buckenham 43 TM 0890
Newbuildings 11 SS 7903
Newburgh, Fife 89 NO 2318
Newburgh, Grampn 97 NJ 9925
Newburgh, Lancs 57 SD 4810
Newburn 79 NZ 1965
Newbury 23 SU 4767
Newby, Cumbr 71 NY 5921
Newby, N. Yks 73 NZ 5012
Newby, N. Yks 65 SD 7270
Newby Bridge 65 SD 3786
Newby East 77 NY 4758
New Byth 97 NJ 8254
Newby West 70 NY 3653
Newby Wiske 67 SE 3687
Newcastle, Gwent 33 SO 4417
Newcastle, Shrops 36 SO 2482
Newcastle Emlyn 31 SN 3040
Newcastleton 77 NY 4887
Newcastle-under-Lyme 47 SJ 8546
Newcastle upon Tyne 79 NZ 2464
Newchapel, Dyfed 31 SN 2339
Newchapel, Staffs 47 SJ 8654
Newchapel, Surrey 17 TQ 3642
New Cheriton 15 SU 5827
Newchurch, Dyfed 31 SN 3824
Newchurch, Gwent 33 ST 4597
Newchurch, I. of W 15 SZ 5685
Newchurch, Kent 19 TR 0531
Newchurch, Powys 33 SO 2150
Newchurch in Pendle 66 SD 8239
New Clipstone 59 SK 5863
New Costessey 53 TG 1809
Newcott 12 ST 2308
New Cross 45 SN 6377
New Cumnock 76 NS 6113
New Deer 97 NJ 8847
Newdigate 16 TQ 1942
New Duston 39 SP 7162
New Earswick 67 SE 6155
New Edlington 59 SK 5498
New Ellerby 63 TA 1639
Newell Green 24 SU 8871
New Eltham 25 TQ 4573
New End 38 SP 1060
Newenden 18 TQ 8327
Newent 34 SO 7226
New Farnley 67 SE 2431
New Ferry 56 SJ 3485
Newfield, Durham 72 NZ 2033
Newfield, Highld 103 NH 7877
New Fryston 67 SE 4527
Newgale 30 SM 8422
New Galloway 76 NX 6377
Newgate 52 TG 0543
Newgate Street 25 TL 3005
New Grimsby 6 SV 8815
Newhall, Ches 47 SJ 6145
Newhall, Derby 48 SK 2921
Newham 85 NU 1728
Newham Hall 85 NU 1729
New Hartley 79 NZ 3076
Newhaven 17 TQ 4401
New Hedges 30 SN 1302
Newhey 57 SD 9311
New Holland 62 TA 0823
Newholm 73 NZ 8610
New Horndean 85 NT 8949
New Houghton, Derby 59 SK 4965
New Houghton, Norf 52 TF 7927
Newhouse 82 NS 7961
New Houses 66 SD 8073
New Hutton 71 SD 5691
New Hythe 18 TQ 7159
Newick 17 TQ 4121
Newington, Kent 18 TQ 8564
Newington, Kent 19 TR 1837
Newington, Oxon 35 SU 6096
New Inn, Dyfed 31 SN 4736
New Inn, Gwent 33 SO 4800
New Inn, Gwent 33 ST 3099
New Invention 36 SO 2976
New Kelso 101 NG 9342
New Lanark 83 NS 8842
Newland, Glos 33 SO 5509
Newland, H. & W 37 SO 7948
Newland, N. Yks 62 SE 6924
Newlandrig 84 NT 3662
Newlands, Grampn 96 NJ 3051
Newlands, Highld 95 NH 7645
Newlands, Northum 72 NZ 0955
Newlands of Geise 103 ND 0865
New Lane 56 SD 4213
New Leake 61 TF 4057
New Leeds 97 NJ 9954
New Longton 65 SD 5025
New Luce 74 NX 1764
Newlyn 6 SW 4628
Newmachar 97 NJ 8819
Newmains 83 NS 8256
New Malden 25 TQ 2168
Newmarket, Suff 42 TL 6463
Newmarket, W. Isles 98 NB 4235
New Marske 73 NZ 6220
New Marton 46 SJ 3434
Newmill, Border 77 NT 5010
New Mill, Corn 6 SW 4534
Newmill, Grampn 96 NJ 4352
New Mill, Herts 24 SP 9212
New Mill, W. Yks 58 SE 1609
Newmill of Inshewan 92 NO 4260
New Mills, Ches 57 SJ 7782
New Mills, Corn 7 SW 9052
New Mills, Derby 58 SJ 9985
New Mills, Gwent 33 SO 5107
New Mills, Powys 45 SJ 0901
Newmiln 88 NO 1230
Newmilns 81 NS 5237
New Milton 14 SZ 2495
New Moat 30 SN 0625
Newnham, Glos 34 SO 6911
Newnham, Hants 23 SU 7153
Newnham, Herts 41 TL 2437
Newnham, H. & W 37 SO 6469
Newnham, Kent 18 TQ 9557
Newnham, Northnts 39 SP 5759
New Ollerton 59 SK 6668
New Pitsligo 97 NJ 8856
New Polzeath 7 SW 9379
Newport, Devon 11 SS 5632
Newport, Dyfed 30 SN 0539
Newport, Essex 41 TL 5233
Newport, Glos 34 ST 7097
Newport, Gwent 20 ST 3188
Newport, Highld 103 ND 1324
Newport, Humbs 62 SE 8530
Newport, I. of W 15 SZ 5089
Newport, Norf 53 TG 5016
Newport, Shrops 47 SJ 7419
Newport-on-Tay 89 NO 4227
Newport Pagnell 40 SP 8743
Newpound Common 16 TQ 0627
New Prestwick 81 NS 3424
Newquay, Corn 7 SW 8161
New Quay, Dyfed 31 SN 3959
New Rackheath 53 TG 2812
New Radnor 36 SO 2161
New Romney 19 TR 0624
New Rossington 59 SK 6197
New Row 65 SD 6438
New Sauchie 88 NS 8994
New Scone 88 NO 1326
Newseat 97 NJ 7032
Newsham, Northum 79 NZ 3079
Newsham, N. Yks 72 NZ 1010
Newsholme, Humbs 62 SE 7229
Newsholme, Lancs 66 SD 8451
New Silksworth 73 NZ 3753
Newstead, Border 84 NT 5634
Newstead, Northum 85 NU 1527
Newstead, Notts 49 SK 5252
New Stevenston 82 NS 7659
Newthorpe 67 SE 4632
New Tolsta 98 NB 5348
Newton, Border 78 NT 5920
Newton, Cambs 51 TF 4314
Newton, Cambs 41 TL 4349
Newton, Ches 57 SJ 5059
Newton, Ches 57 SJ 5375
Newton, Cumbr 64 SD 2371
Newton, D. & G 77 NY 1194
Newton, Grampn 96 NJ 1663
Newton, Highld 103 ND 3449
Newton, Highld 95 NH 7448
Newton, Highld 95 NH 7766
Newton, H. & W 33 SO 3433
Newton, H. & W 33 SO 5054
Newton, Lancs 65 SD 4431
Newton, Lancs 65 SD 5974
Newton, Lancs 65 SD 6950
Newton, Lincs 50 TF 0436
Newton, Lothn 88 NT 0977
Newton, M. Glam 29 SS 8477
Newton, Norf 52 TF 8315
Newton, Northnts 40 SP 8883
Newton, Northum 79 NZ 0364
Newton, S. Glam 20 ST 2478
Newton, Staffs 48 SK 0325
Newton, Strath 86 NS 0498
Newton, Strath 82 NS 6660
Newton, Strath 83 NS 9331
Newton, Suff 42 TL 9140
Newton, Warw 39 SP 5378
Newton, W. Glam 28 SS 6088
Newton, Wilts 14 SU 2322
Newton, W. Isles 98 NF 8977
Newton Abbot 9 SX 8671
Newton Arlosh 70 NY 1955
Newton Aycliffe 72 NZ 2724
Newton Bewley 73 NZ 4626
Newton Blossomville 40 SP 9251
Newton Bromswold 40 SP 9965
Newton Burgoland 48 SK 3709
Newton by Toft 60 TF 0587
Newton Ferrers 9 SX 5448
Newtonferry 98 NF 8978
Newton Flotman 53 TM 2098
Newtongarry Croft 96 NJ 5735
Newtongrange 84 NT 3364
Newton Harcourt 49 SP 6397
Newtonhill 93 NO 9193
Newton Kyme 67 SE 4645
Newton-le-Willows, Mers 57 SJ 5894
Newton-le-Willows, N. Yks 72 SE 2189
Newton Longville 40 SP 8431
Newton Mearns 81 NS 5455
Newtonmore 91 NN 7199
Newton of Ardtoe 101 NM 6470
Newton of Balcanquhal 88 NO 1510
Newton-on-Ouse 67 SE 5159
Newton-on-Rawcliffe 68 SE 8190
Newton on the Moor 79 NU 1705
Newton on Trent 60 SK 8374
Newton Poppleford 12 SY 0889
Newton Purcell 39 SP 6230
Newton Regis 48 SK 2707
Newton Reigny 71 NY 4731
Newton Solney 48 SK 2825
Newton Stacey 22 SU 4140
Newton St Cyres 9 SX 8797
Newton Stewart 74 NX 4065
Newton St Faith 53 TG 2217
Newton St Loe 21 ST 7064
Newton St Petrock 10 SS 4112
Newton Tony 22 SU 2140
Newton Tracey 11 SS 5226
Newton under Roseberry 73 NZ 5613
Newton upon Derwent 68 SE 7249
Newton Valence 15 SU 7232
Newtown, Ches 47 SJ 6248
Newtown, Ches 58 SJ 9784
Newtown, Cumbr 77 NY 5062
Newtown, Derby 58 SJ 9984
Newtown, Dorset 14 SZ 0493
Newtown, Grampn 95 NJ 1469
Newtown, Hants 14 SU 2710
Newtown, Hants 14 SU 3023
Newtown, Hants 23 SU 4763
Newtown, Hants 15 SU 6113
Newtown, Highld 94 NH 3504
Newtown, H. & W 33 SO 6145
Newtown, I. of M 64 SC 3273
Newtown, I. of W 14 SZ 4290
New Town, Lothn 89 NT 4470
Newtown, Northum 85 NT 9731
Newtown, Northum 79 NU 0300
Newtown, Northum 85 NU 0425
Newtown, Powys 36 SO 1191
Newtown, Shrops 47 SJ 4731
Newtown, Staffs 57 SJ 9060
Newtown, Wilts 13 ST 9128
Newtown-in-St Martins 6 SW 7423
Newtown Linford 49 SK 5110
Newtown St Boswells 84 NT 5731
New Tredegar 29 SO 1403
Newtyle 92 NO 2941
New Waltham 63 TA 2804
New Wimpole 41 TL 3449
New Winton 89 NT 4271
New Yatt 35 SP 3713
New York, Lincs 51 TF 2455
New York, T. & W 79 NZ 3270
Neyland 30 SM 9605
Nibley 21 ST 6982
Nicholashayne 12 ST 1016
Nicholaston 28 SS 5288
Nidd 67 SE 3060
Nigg, Grampn 97 NJ 9403
Nigg, Highld 103 NH 8071
Nine Ashes 26 TL 5902
Ninebanks 71 NY 7853
Ninemile Bar or Crocketford 76 NX 8372
Ninfield 17 TQ 7012
Ningwood 14 SZ 4088
Nisbet 84 NT 6725
Niton 15 SZ 5076
Nitshill 81 NS 5160
Noak Hill 25 TQ 5493
Nobottle 39 SP 6763
Nocton 60 TF 0664
Noke 35 SP 5413
Nolton 30 SM 8618
Nolton Haven 30 SM 8518
No Man's Heath, Ches 47 SJ 5148
No Man's Heath, Warw 48 SK 2909
Nomansland, Devon 11 SS 8313
Nomansland, Wilts 14 SU 2517
Noneley 47 SJ 4828
Nonington 19 TR 2552
Noonsbrough 105 HU 2957
Nor 85 NT 9047
Noranside 93 NO 4760
Norbury, Ches 47 SJ 5647
Norbury, Derby 48 SK 1242
Norbury, Shrops 46 SO 3693
Norbury, Staffs 47 SJ 7823
Nordelph 51 TF 5500
Norden, Dorset 14 SY 9483
Norden, G. Man 57 SD 8514
Nordley 47 SO 6996
Norham 85 NT 9047
Norley 57 SJ 5772
Norleywood 14 SZ 3597
Normanby, Humbs 62 SE 8816
Normanby, N. Yks 68 SE 7381
Normanby-by-Spital 60 TF 0088
Normanby le Wold 61 TF 1295
Norman Cross 40 TL 1690
Normandy 16 SU 9351
Norman's Green 12 ST 0503
Normanton, Derby 48 SK 3433
Normanton, Lincs 50 SK 9446
Normanton, Notts 49 SK 7054
Normanton, W. Yks 67 SE 3822
Normanton le Heath 48 SK 3712
Normanton on Soar 49 SK 5123
Normanton-on-the-Wolds 49 SK 6233
Normanton on Trent 60 SK 7968
Normoss 65 SD 3337
Norrington Common 21 ST 8864
Norris Hill 48 SK 3216
Northallerton 73 SE 3794
Northam, Devon 10 SS 4429
Northam, Hants 14 SU 4312
Northampton 39 SP 7560
North Ascot 24 SU 9069
North Aston 35 SP 4728
Northaw 25 TL 2802
North Baddesley 14 SU 3919
North Ballachulish 90 NN 0560
North Barrow 13 ST 6029
North Barsham 52 TF 9134
North Benfleet 26 TQ 7589
North Berwick 89 NT 5585
North Boarhunt 15 SU 6010
Northborough 50 TF 1508
Northbourne 19 TR 3352
North Bovey 9 SX 7483
North Bradley 21 ST 8555
North Brentor 8 SX 4881
North Buckland 10 SS 4740
North Burlingham 53 TG 3610
North Cadbury 13 ST 6327
North Cairn 74 NW 9770
North Carlton 60 SK 9477
North Cave 62 SE 8932
North Cerney 34 SP 0208
Northchapel 16 SU 9529
North Charford 14 SU 1919
North Charlton 85 NU 1622
North Cheriton 13 ST 6925
North Chideock 13 SY 4291
Northchurch 24 SP 9709
North Clifton 60 SK 8272
North Cotes 63 TA 3500
Northcott 8 SX 3392
North Cove 43 TM 4689
North Cowton 72 NZ 2803
North Crawley 40 SP 9244
North Cray 25 TQ 4972
North Creake 52 TF 8538
North Curry 12 ST 3125
North Dalton 69 SE 9352
North Deighton 67 SE 3951
North Duffield 62 SE 6837
Northdyke 104 HY 2320
North Elkington 61 TF 2890
North Elmham 52 TF 9820
North End, Avon 20 ST 4167
Northend, Avon 21 ST 7768
Northend, Bucks 24 SU 7392
North End, Hants 22 SU 4163
North End, Hants 15 SU 6502
Northend, Warw 38 SP 3952
North End, W. Susx 16 TQ 1209
North Erradale 102 NG 7481
North Fearns 101 NG 5935
North Ferriby 62 SE 9825
Northfield, Border 85 NT 9167
Northfield, Grampn 97 NJ 9008
Northfield, W. Mids 38 SP 0279
Northfleet 18 TQ 6274
North Frodingham 69 TA 0953
North Gorley 14 SU 1611
North Green 43 TM 2288
North Grimston 68 SE 8467
North Hayling 15 SU 7303
North Heasley 11 SS 7333
North Heath 16 TQ 0621
North Hill, Cambs 41 TL 4476
North Hill, Corn 8 SX 2776
North Hinksey Village 35 SP 4905
North Holmwood 16 TQ 1647
North Huish 9 SX 7156
North Hykeham 60 SK 9466
Northiam 18 TQ 8225
Northill 40 TL 1546
Northington 15 SU 5737
North Kelsey 62 TA 0401
North Kessock 94 NH 6548
North Kilvington 67 SE 4285
North Kilworth 39 SP 6183
North Kyme 50 TF 1552
North Lancing 16 TQ 1804
Northlands 51 TF 3453
Northleach 34 SP 1114
North Lee 24 SP 8309
Northleigh, Devon 12 SY 1995
North Leigh, Oxon 35 SP 3812
North Leverton with Habblesthorpe 60 SK 7882
Northlew 8 SX 5099
North Littleton 38 SP 0847
North Lopham 42 TM 0383
North Luffenham 50 SK 9303
North Marden 15 SU 8016
North Marston 24 SP 7722
North Middleton 84 NT 3559
North Molton 11 SS 7329
Northmoor 35 SP 4203
Northmoor Green or Moorland 12 ST 3332
North Moreton 23 SU 5689
Northmuir 92 NO 3855
North Muskham 60 SK 7959
North Newbold 62 SE 9136
North Newington 38 SP 4239
North Newnton 22 SU 1257
North Newton 12 ST 2930
North Nibley 34 ST 7495
North Oakley 23 SU 5354
North Ockendon 26 TQ 5984
Northolt 25 TQ 1285
Northop 56 SJ 2468
Northop Hall 56 SJ 2767
North Ormsby 61 TF 2893
Northorpe, Lincs 60 SK 8997
Northorpe, Lincs 50 TF 0917
North Otterington 73 SE 3689
North Owersby 60 TF 0694
Northowram 66 SE 1126
North Perrott 13 ST 4709
North Petherton 12 ST 2933
North Petherwin 8 SX 2889
North Pickenham 52 TF 8606
North Piddle 38 SO 9654
Northpunds 105 HU 4022
North Queensferry 88 NT 1380
Northrepps 53 TG 2439
North Rigton 67 SE 2849
North Rode 57 SJ 8966
North Roe 105 HU 3639
North Runcton 52 TF 6415
North Sandwick 105 HU 5497
North Scale 64 SD 1870
North Scarle 60 SK 8466
North Seaton 79 NZ 2986
North Shields 79 NZ 3568
North Shoebury 26 TQ 9386
North Shore 65 SD 3038
North Side 51 TL 2799
North Somercotes 61 TF 4296
North Stainley 67 SE 2877
North Stainmore 71 NY 8315
North Stifford 26 TQ 6080
North Stoke, Avon 21 ST 7069
North Stoke, Oxon 24 SU 6186
North Stoke, W. Susx 16 TQ 0210
North Street 15 SU 6433
North Sunderland 85 NU 2131
North Tamerton 8 SX 3197
North Tawton 11 SS 6601
North Thoresby 63 TF 2998
North Tidworth 22 SU 2349
North Tolsta 98 NB 5347
Northton 98 NF 9989
Northtown 104 ND 4797
North Tuddenham 52 TG 0414
Northwall 104 HY 7544
North Walsham 53 TG 2830
North Waltham 23 SU 5646
North Warnborough 23 SU 7351
North Water Bridge 93 NO 6566
North Watten 103 ND 2458
Northway 34 SO 9233
North Weald Bassett 25 TL 4904
North Wheatley 60 SK 7585
North Whilborough 9 SX 8766
Northwich 57 SJ 6573
Northwick, Avon 21 ST 5686
North Wick, Avon 21 ST 5865
North Widcombe 21 ST 5758
North Willingham 61 TF 1688
North Wingfield 59 SK 4165
North Witham 50 SK 9221
Northwold 52 TL 7597
Northwood, Derby 59 SK 2664
Northwood, G. Lon 24 TQ 0991
Northwood, I. of W 15 SZ 4894
Northwood, Shrops 46 SJ 4633
Northwood Green 34 SO 7216
North Wootton, Dorset 13 ST 6514
North Wootton, Norf 52 TF 6424
North Wootton, Somer 21 ST 5641
North Wraxall 21 ST 8175
Norton, Ches 57 SJ 5582
Norton, Cleve 73 NZ 4421
Norton, Glos 34 SO 8524
Norton, Herts 41 TL 2334
Norton, H. & W 37 SO 8851
Norton, H. & W 38 SP 0447
Norton, I. of W 14 SZ 3489
Norton, Northnts 39 SP 6063
Norton, Notts 59 SK 5772
Norton, N. Yks 68 SE 7971
Norton, Powys 36 SO 3067
Norton, Shrops 47 SJ 5609
Norton, Shrops 47 SJ 7200
Norton, Shrops 36 SO 4681
Norton, Suff 42 TL 9565
Norton, S. Yks 59 SE 5415
Norton, S. Yks 59 SK 3682
Norton, Wilts 21 ST 8884
Norton, W. Susx 16 SU 9206
Norton Bavant 21 ST 9043
Norton Bridge 47 SJ 8730
Norton Canes 48 SK 0108
Norton Canon 33 SO 3847
Norton Disney 60 SK 8959
Norton East 48 SK 0208
Norton Ferris 13 ST 7936
Norton Fitzwarren 12 ST 1925
Norton Green 14 SZ 3488
Norton Hawkfield 21 ST 5964
Norton Heath 26 TL 6004
Norton in Hales 47 SJ 7038
Norton-in-the-Moors 47 SJ 8951
Norton-Juxta-Twycross 48 SK 3207
Norton-le-Clay 67 SE 4071
Norton Lindsey 38 SP 2263
Norton Malreward 21 ST 6065
Norton Mandeville 25 TL 5804
Norton St Philip 21 ST 7755
Norton Subcourse 53 TM 4198
Norton sub Hamdon 13 ST 4615
Norwell 60 SK 7761
Norwell Woodhouse 60 SK 7462
Norwich 53 TG 2308
Norwich Airport 53 TG 2113
Norwick 105 HP 6514
Norwood Green 25 TQ 1378
Norwood Hill 16 TQ 2443
Noseley 49 SP 7398
Noss Mayo 9 SX 5447
Nosterfield 67 SE 2780
Nostie 101 NG 8527
Notgrove 34 SP 1120
Nottage 29 SS 8278
Nottingham 49 SK 5741
Nottington 13 SY 6682
Notton, Wilts 21 ST 9169
Notton, W. Yks 59 SE 3413
Nounsley 26 TL 7910
Noutard's Green 37 SO 7966
Nox 46 SJ 4110
Nuffield 24 SU 6787
Nunburnholme 68 SE 8548
Nuneaton 38 SP 3691
Nuneham Courtenay 35 SU 5599
Nun Monkton 67 SE 5057
Nunney 21 ST 7345
Nunnington 67 SE 6679
Nunnykirk 79 NZ 0892
Nunthorpe 73 NZ 5314
Nunton, Wilts 14 SU 1526
Nunton, W. Isles 100 NF 7653
Nursling 14 SU 3716
Nursted 15 SU 7621
Nutbourne 16 TQ 0718
Nutfield 17 TQ 3049
Nuthall 49 SK 5144
Nuthampstead 41 TL 4034
Nuthurst 16 TQ 1926
Nutley 17 TQ 4427
Nutwell 59 SE 6304
Nybster 103 ND 3663
Nyetimber 15 SZ 8998
Nyewood 15 SU 8021
Nymet Rowland 11 SS 7108
Nymet Tracey 9 SS 7200
Nympsfield 34 SO 8000
Nynehead 12 ST 1422
Nyton 16 SU 9305

O

Oadby 49 SK 6200
Oad Street 18 TQ 8662
Oakamoor 48 SK 0544
Oakbank 83 NT 0766
Oakdale 29 ST 1898
Oake 12 ST 1525
Oaken 47 SJ 8502
Oakenclough 65 SD 5447
Oakengates 47 SJ 7010
Oakenshaw, Durham 72 NZ 2037
Oakenshaw, W. Yks 66 SE 1727
Oakford, Devon 11 SS 9021
Oakford, Dyfed 31 SN 4558
Oakgrove 57 SJ 9169
Oakham 50 SK 8508
Oakhanger 15 SU 7735
Oakhill 21 ST 6347
Oakington 41 TL 4164
Oaklands 25 TL 2417
Oakle Street 34 SO 7517
Oakley, Beds 40 TL 0153
Oakley, Bucks 24 SP 6312
Oakley, Fife 88 NT 0289
Oakley, Hants 23 SU 5650
Oakley, Suff 43 TM 1677
Oakley Green 24 SU 9276
Oakley Park 45 SN 9887
Oakridge 34 SO 9103
Oaks 46 SJ 4204
Oaksey 34 ST 9993
Oakthorpe 48 SK 3213
Oakwoodhill 16 TQ 1337
Oakworth 66 SE 0338
Oare, Kent 19 TR 0062
Oare, Wilts 22 SU 1563
Oasby 50 TF 0039
Oathlaw 93 NO 4756
Oban 86 NM 8530
Oborne 13 ST 6518
Occlestone Green 57 SJ 6962
Occold 43 TM 1570
Ochiltree 81 NS 5021
Ockbrook 49 SK 4236
Ockham 15 TQ 0756
Ockle 101 NM 5570
Ockley 15 TQ 1440
Ocle Pychard 33 SO 5946
Odcombe 13 ST 5015
Odd Down 21 ST 7362
Oddendale 71 NY 5913
Oddingley 37 SO 9159
Oddington, Glos 35 SP 2225
Oddington, Oxon 35 SP 5515
Odell 40 SP 9657
Odiham 23 SU 7451
Odstock 14 SU 1426
Odstone 48 SK 3907
Offchurch 38 SP 3565
Offenham 38 SP 0546
Offham, E. Susx 17 TQ 4012
Offham, Kent 17 TQ 6557
Offord Cluny 41 TL 2267
Offord D'Arcy 41 TL 2266
Offton 42 TM 0649
Offwell 12 SY 1999
Ogbourne Maizey 22 SU 1871
Ogbourne St Andrew 22 SU 1972
Ogbourne St George 22 SU 2074
Ogle 79 NZ 1378
Ogmore 29 SS 8876
Ogmore-by-Sea 29 SS 8675
Ogmore Vale 29 SS 9390
Okeford Fitzpaine 13 ST 8010
Okehampton 9 SX 5895
Okehampton Camp 9 SX 5893
Old 39 SP 7873
Old Aberdeen 97 NJ 9408
Old Alresford 15 SU 5834
Old Basing 23 SU 6752
Oldberrow 38 SP 1266
Old Bewick 85 NU 0621
Old Bolingbroke 61 TF 3565
Oldborough 11 SS 7706
Old Brampton 59 SK 3371
Old Bridge of Urr 76 NX 7767
Old Buckenham 42 TM 0691
Old Burghclere 23 SU 4657
Oldbury, Shrops 37 SO 7192
Oldbury, Warw 48 SP 3194
Oldbury, W. Mids 38 SO 9889
Oldbury-on-Severn 21 ST 6192
Oldbury on the Hill 21 ST 8188
Old Byland 67 SE 5585
Oldcastle 33 SO 3224
Old Cleeve 20 ST 0341
Old Clipstone 59 SK 6064
Old Colwyn 55 SH 8678
Oldcotes 59 SK 5988
Old Dailly 74 NX 2299
Old Dalby 49 SK 6723
Old Deer 97 NJ 9747
Old Denaby 59 SK 4899
Old Ellerby 63 TA 1636
Old Felixstowe 43 TM 3135
Oldfield 37 SO 8465
Oldford 21 ST 7850
Old Hall, The 63 TA 2717
Oldham 57 SD 9204
Oldhamstocks 84 NT 7370
Old Heath 27 TM 0123
Oldhurst 41 TL 3077
Old Hutton 65 SD 5688
Old Kea 7 SW 8441
Old Kilpatrick 87 NS 4673
Old Kinnernie 97 NJ 7209
Old Knebworth 25 TL 2320
Oldland 21 ST 6771
Old Leake 51 TF 4050
Old Malton 68 SE 7972
Oldmeldrum 97 NJ 8127
Old Milverton 38 SP 3067
Old Monkland 82 NS 7163
Old Newton 42 TM 0562
Oldpark 47 SJ 6909
Old Philpstoun 88 NT 0577
Old Radnor 33 SO 2559
Old Rayne 96 NJ 6728
Old Romney 19 TR 0325
Oldshore Beg 102 NC 1959
Oldshoremore 102 NC 2058
Old Sodbury 21 ST 7581
Old Somerby 50 SK 9633
Oldstead 67 SE 5380
Old Swarland 79 NU 1601
Old Town, Cumbr 65 SD 5983
Old Town, Northum 78 NY 8891
Oldtown of Ord 96 NJ 6259
Old Warden 40 TL 1343
Oldways End 11 SS 8624
Old Weston 40 TL 1077
Oldwhat 97 NJ 8651
Old Windsor 24 SU 9874
Old Wives Lees 19 TR 0754
Olgrinmore 103 ND 0955
Oliver's Battery 15 SU 4527
Ollaberry 105 HU 3680
Ollach 101 NG 5136
Ollerton, Ches 57 SJ 7776
Ollerton, Notts 59 SK 6567
Ollerton, Shrops 47 SJ 6525
Olney 40 SP 8851
Olton 38 SP 1382
Olveston 21 ST 6087
Ombersley 37 SO 8464
Ompton 60 SK 6865
Onchan 64 SC 4078
Onecote 48 SK 0555
Ongar Hill 51 TF 5824
Ongar Street 36 SO 3967
Onibury 36 SO 4579
Onich 90 NN 0261
Onllwyn 29 SN 8410
Onneley 47 SJ 7543
Onslow Village 16 SU 9949
Opinan, Highld 102 NG 7472
Opinan, Highld 102 NG 8796
Orby 61 TF 4967
Orchard 13 ST 8215
Orchard Portman 12 ST 2421
Orcheston 22 SU 0545
Orcop 33 SO 4726
Orcop Hill 33 SO 4828
Ord 101 NG 6113
Ordhead 96 NJ 6610
Ordie 92 NJ 4501
Ordiequish 96 NJ 3357
Ore 18 TQ 8311
Oreton 37 SO 6580
Orford, Ches 57 SJ 6190
Orford, Suff 43 TM 4250
Orgreave 48 SK 1516
Orinsay 98 NB 3612
Orleton, H. & W 36 SO 4967
Orleton, H. & W 37 SO 6967
Orlingbury 40 SP 8672
Ormesby 73 NZ 5317
Ormesby St Margaret 53 TG 4915
Ormesby St Michael 53 TG 4814
Ormiscaig 102 NG 8590
Ormiston 89 NT 4169
Ormsaigmore 101 NM 4763
Ormskirk 56 SD 4108
Orpington 25 TQ 4665
Orrell 57 SD 5305
Orroland 75 NX 7746
Orsett 26 TQ 6481
Orslow 47 SJ 8015
Orston 49 SK 7741
Orton, Cumbr 71 NY 6208
Orton, Northnts 39 SP 8079
Orton Longueville 50 TL 1796
Orton-on-the-Hill 48 SK 3003
Orwell 41 TL 3650
Osbaldeston 65 SD 6431
Osbaston 48 SK 4204
Osbournby 50 TF 0638
Oscroft 57 SJ 5067
Ose 100 NG 3141
Osgathorpe 48 SK 4319
Osgodby, Lincs 60 TF 0792
Osgodby, N. Yks 67 SE 6433
Osgodby, N. Yks 69 TA 0584
Oskaig 101 NG 5438
Oskamull 99 NM 4540
Osmaston 48 SK 2043
Osmington 13 SY 7283
Osmington Mills 13 SY 7381
Osmotherley 73 SE 4597
Osnaburgh or Dairsie 89 NO 4117
Ospisdale 103 NH 7189
Ospringe 19 TR 0060
Ossett 59 SE 2820
Ossington 60 SK 7564
Ostend 26 TQ 9397
Oswaldkirk 67 SE 6279
Oswaldtwistle 65 SD 7327
Oswestry 46 SJ 2929
Otford 25 TQ 5259
Otham 18 TQ 7953
Othery 12 ST 3831
Otley, Suff 43 TM 2055
Otley, W. Yks 66 SE 2045
Otterbourne 15 SU 4623
Otterburn, Northum 78 NY 8893
Otterburn, N. Yks 66 SD 8857
Otterburn Camp 78 NY 8995
Otterden Place 18 TQ 9454
Otter Ferry 86 NR 9384
Otterham 8 SX 1690
Ottershaw 24 TQ 0264
Otterswick 105 HU 5185
Otterton 12 SY 0885
Ottery St Mary 12 SY 1095
Ottringham 63 TA 2624
Oughtershaw 66 SD 8681
Oughtibridge 59 SK 3093
Oulston 67 SE 5474
Oulton, Cumbr 70 NY 2450
Oulton, Norf 53 TG 1328
Oulton, Staffs 47 SJ 9135
Oulton, Suff 53 TM 5294
Oulton, W. Yks 67 SE 3628
Oulton Broad 43 TM 5292
Oulton Street 53 TG 1527
Oundle 40 TL 0488
Ousby 71 NY 6135
Ousden 42 TL 7459
Ouseburn 67 SE 4461
Ousefleet 62 SE 8223
Ouston 72 NZ 2554
Outertown 104 HY 2310
Outgate 70 SD 3599
Outhgill 71 NY 7801
Outlane 58 SE 0818
Out Newton 63 TA 3821
Out Rawcliffe 65 SD 4042
Outwell, Cambs 51 TF 5103
Outwell, Norf 51 TF 5103
Outwood, Surrey 17 TQ 3245
Outwood, W. Yks 67 SE 3323
Ovenden 66 SE 0827
Over, Avon 21 ST 5882
Over, Cambs 41 TL 3770
Overbister 104 HY 6940
Overbury 38 SO 9537
Overcombe 13 SY 6982
Over Haddon 58 SK 2066
Over Kellet 65 SD 5269
Over Kiddington 35 SP 4122
Over Norton 35 SP 3128
Overseal 48 SK 2915
Over Silton 73 SE 4593
Overstone 39 SP 8066
Overstrand 53 TG 2440
Overton, Clwyd 46 SJ 3741
Overton, D. & G 76 NX 9864
Overton, Grampn 97 NJ 8714
Overton, Hants 23 SU 5149
Overton, Lancs 65 SD 4358
Overton, Shrops 36 SO 5072
Overtown 83 NS 8052
Over Wallop 22 SU 2838
Over Whitacre 38 SP 2591
Oving, Bucks 24 SP 6821
Oving, W. Susx 15 SU 9005
Ovingdean 17 TQ 3503
Ovingham 79 NZ 0863
Ovington, Durham 72 NZ 1314
Ovington, Essex 42 TL 7642
Ovington, Hants 15 SU 5631
Ovington, Norf 52 TF 9202
Ovington, Northum 79 NZ 0663
Ower 14 SU 3216
Owermoigne 13 SY 7685
Owlswick 24 SP 7906
Owmby-by-Spital 60 TF 0087
Owslebury 15 SU 5123
Owston 49 SK 7707
Owston Ferry 62 SE 8000
Owstwick 63 TA 2732
Owthorpe 49 SK 6733
Oxborough 52 TF 7401
Oxenholme 71 SD 5289
Oxenhope 66 SE 0335
Oxen Park 65 SD 3187
Oxenton 34 SO 9531
Oxenwood 22 SU 3059
Oxford 35 SP 5106
Oxhill 38 SP 3145
Oxley 47 SJ 9102
Oxley's Green 17 TQ 6921
Oxnam 78 NT 6918
Oxshott 25 TQ 1460
Oxspring 59 SE 2602
Oxted 17 TQ 3952
Oxton, Border 84 NT 4953
Oxton, Notts 49 SK 6351
Oxwich 28 SS 4986
Oxwick 52 TF 9124
Oykel Bridge 102 NC 3800
Oyne 96 NJ 6725

P

Packington 48 SK 3614
Padanaram 92 NO 4251
Padbury 39 SP 7230
Paddington 25 TQ 2482
Paddlesworth 19 TR 1939
Paddockhaugh 96 NJ 2058
Paddock Wood 17 TQ 6745
Paddolgreen 47 SJ 5032
Padeswood 56 SJ 2762
Padiham 66 SD 8033
Padstow 7 SW 9175
Pagham 15 SZ 8897
Paglesham Churchend 26 TQ 9293
Paglesham Eastend 26 TQ 9492
Paible, W. Isles 100 NF 7367
Paignton 9 SX 8960
Pailton 39 SP 4781
Painscastle 33 SO 1646
Painshawfield 79 NZ 0660
Painswick 34 SO 8609
Paisley 81 NS 4864
Pakefield 43 TM 5390
Pakenham 42 TL 9267
Pale 55 SH 9836
Palestine 22 SU 2640
Paley Street 24 SU 8676
Palgrave 43 TM 1178
Palmerstown 29 ST 1369
Palnackie 75 NX 8256
Palnure 75 NX 4563
Palterton 59 SK 4768
Pamber End 24 SU 6158
Pamber Green 23 SU 6059
Pamber Heath 24 SU 6162
Pamphill 14 ST 9900
Pampisford 41 TL 4948
Panbride 89 NO 5635
Pancrasweek 10 SS 2905
Pandy, Clwyd 46 SJ 1935
Pandy, Gwent 33 SO 3322
Pandy, Powys 45 SH 9004
Pandy Tudur 55 SH 8564
Panfield 42 TL 7325
Pangbourne 24 SU 6376
Pannal 67 SE 3051
Pant 46 SJ 2722
Panteg 30 SM 9234
Pant-glas, Gwyn 54 SH 4747
Pantglas, Powys 45 SN 7798
Pantgwyn 31 SN 2446
Pant Mawr 45 SN 8582
Panton 61 TF 1778
Pant-pastynog 55 SJ 0461
Pantperthog 45 SH 7404
Pant-y-dwr 45 SN 9875
Pant-y-ffridd 46 SJ 1502
Pantyffynnon 31 SN 6210
Panxworth 53 TG 3112
Papcastle 70 NY 1131
Papley 104 ND 4691
Papple 89 NT 5972
Papplewick 49 SK 5451
Papworth Everard 41 TL 2863
Papworth St Agnes 41 TL 2664
Par 7 SX 0753
Parbold 57 SD 4911
Parbrook 13 ST 5636
Parcllyn 31 SN 2451
Parc Seymour 20 ST 4091
Pardshaw 70 NY 0924
Parham 43 TM 3060
Park Corner 24 SU 6988
Parkend, Glos 33 SO 6108
Park End, Northum 78 NY 8775
Parkeston 43 TM 2332
Parkgate, Ches 56 SJ 2878
Parkgate, Ches 57 SJ 7874
Parkgate, D. & G 76 NY 0288
Park Gate, Hants 15 SU 5208
Parkgate, Surrey 16 TQ 2044
Parkham 10 SS 3821
Parkham Ash 10 SS 3620
Parkhouse 33 SO 5003
Parkhurst 15 SZ 4991
Parkmill 28 SS 5589
Parkstone 14 SZ 0391
Parley Cross 14 SZ 0897
Parracombe 11 SS 6644
Parrog 30 SN 0439
Parson Cross 59 SK 3592
Parson Drove 51 TF 3708
Partick 81 NS 5467
Partington 57 SJ 7191
Partney 61 TF 4168
Parton, Cumbr 70 NX 9720
Parton, D. & G 76 NX 6970
Partridge Green 16 TQ 1919
Parwich 48 SK 1854
Passenham 39 SP 7939
Paston 53 TG 3234
Patcham 17 TQ 3008
Patching 16 TQ 0806
Patchole 11 SS 6142
Patchway 21 ST 6081
Pateley Bridge 66 SE 1565
Pathfinder Village 9 SX 8493
Pathhead, Fife 89 NT 2892
Pathhead, Lothn 84 NT 3964
Pathhead, Strath 76 NS 6114
Patmore Heath 41 TL 4425
Patna 81 NS 4110
Patney 22 SU 0758
Patrick 64 SC 2482
Patrick Brompton 72 SE 2290
Patrington 63 TA 3122
Patrixbourne 19 TR 2055
Patterdale 71 NY 3915
Pattingham 47 SO 8299
Pattisball 39 SP 6754
Patton Bridge 71 SD 5597
Paul 6 SW 4627
Paulerspury 39 SP 7245
Paull 63 TA 1626
Paulton 21 ST 6556
Pavenham 40 SP 8955
Pawston 85 NT 8532
Paxford 38 SP 1837
Paxton 85 NT 9352
Payhembury 12 ST 0801
Paythorne 66 SD 8352
Pcaston 84 NT 4265
Peacehaven 17 TQ 4101
Peak Dale 58 SK 0976
Peak Forest 58 SK 1179
Peakirk 50 TF 1606
Peanmeanach 101 NM 7180
Peasedown St John 21 ST 7057
Peasemore 23 SU 4577
Peasenhall 43 TM 3569
Peaslake 16 TQ 0844
Peasmarsh 18 TQ 8823
Peaston Bank 84 NT 4466
Peathill 97 NJ 9366
Peatling Magna 39 SP 5992
Peatling Parva 39 SP 5989
Peaton 36 SO 5385
Pebmarsh 42 TL 8533
Pebworth 38 SP 1346
Pecket Well 66 SD 9929
Peckforton 47 SJ 5356
Peckleton 49 SK 4701
Pedmore 37 SO 9182
Pedwell 13 ST 4236
Peebles 83 NT 2540
Peel 64 SC 2484
Pegswood 79 NZ 2287
Peinchorran 101 NG 5233
Peinlich 101 NG 4158
Pelaw 79 NZ 2962
Pelcomb Cross 30 SM 9218
Peldon 27 TL 9816
Pelsall 48 SK 0203
Pelton 72 NZ 2553
Peluth 70 NY 1249
Pelynt 7 SX 2055
Pembrey 28 SN 4201
Pembridge 33 SO 3958
Pembroke 30 SM 9801
Pembroke Dock 30 SM 9603
Pembury 17 TQ 6241
Penallt 33 SO 5209
Penally 30 SS 1199
Penare 7 SW 9940
Penarth 29 ST 1871
Pen-bont Rhydybeddau 45 SN 6883
Penbryn 31 SN 2952
Pencader 31 SN 4436
Pencaitland 84 NT 4468
Pencarreg 31 SN 5345
Pencelli 29 SO 0925
Pen-Clawdd 28 SS 5495
Pencoed 29 SS 9581
Pencombe 33 SO 6052
Pencoyd 33 SO 5126
Pencraig, H. & W 33 SO 5621
Pencraig, Powys 45 SJ 0427
Pendeen 6 SW 3734
Penderyn 29 SN 9408
Pendine 31 SN 2308
Pendlebury 57 SD 7801
Pendleton 66 SD 7639
Pendock 34 SO 7832
Pendoggett 7 SX 0279
Pendoylan 29 ST 0676
Penegoes 45 SH 7701
Penffordd 30 SN 0722
Penffridd 54 SH 5057
Penge 25 TQ 3570
Pengorffwysfa 54 SH 4692
Penhalurick 6 SW 7037
Penhow 21 ST 4290
Penhurst 17 TQ 6916
Penicuik 83 NT 2360
Peniel 55 SJ 0363
Penifiler 101 NG 4841
Peninver 80 NR 7524
Penisa'r Waun 54 SH 5564
Penistone 59 SE 2403
Penketh 57 SJ 5687
Penkridge 47 SJ 9213
Penley 46 SJ 4140
Penllergaer 28 SS 6198
Pen-llyn, Gwyn 54 SH 3582
Penllyn, S. Glam 29 SS 9776
Penmachno 55 SH 7950
Penmaen, Gwent 29 ST 1897
Penmaen, W. Glam 28 SS 5388
Penmaenmawr 55 SH 7176
Penmaenpool 45 SH 6918
Penmark 29 ST 0568
Penmon 55 SH 6380
Penmorfa 54 SH 5440
Penmynydd 54 SH 5174
Penn 24 SU 9193
Pennal 45 SH 7000
Pennan 97 NJ 8465
Pennant, Dyfed 44 SN 5163
Pennant, Powys 45 SN 8797
Pennant-Melangell 45 SJ 0226
Pennard 28 SS 5688
Pennerley 46 SO 3599
Pennington 64 SD 2677
Pennjerick 6 SW 7730
Penn Street 24 SU 9295
Penny Bridge 65 SD 3083
Pennycross 99 NM 5026
Pennymoor 11 SS 8611
Penparc 31 SN 2148
Penparcau 44 SN 5980
Penperlleni 33 SO 3204
Penpillick 7 SX 0756
Penpol 7 SW 8139
Penpoll 7 SX 1454
Penpont 76 NX 8494
Penrherber 31 SN 2939
Penrhiwceiber 29 ST 0598
Penrhiw-llan 31 SN 3742
Penrhiwpal 31 SN 3445
Penrhos, Gwent 33 SO 4111
Penrhos, Gwyn 54 SH 2781
Penrhos, Gwyn 54 SH 3433
Penrhos, Powys 29 SN 8011
Penrhyn Bay 55 SH 8281
Penrhyn-coch 45 SN 6484
Penrhyndeudraeth 54 SH 6139
Penrhyn-side 55 SH 8181
Penrice 28 SS 4988
Penrith 71 NY 5130
Penrose 7 SW 8770
Penruddock 71 NY 4227
Penryn 7 SW 7834
Pensarn, Clwyd 55 SH 9578
Pen-sarn, Gwyn 54 SH 4344
Pen-sarn, Gwyn 44 SH 5828
Pensax 37 SO 7269
Pensby 56 SJ 2683
Penselwood 13 ST 7531
Pensford 21 ST 6263
Penshaw 72 NZ 3253
Penshurst 17 TQ 5243
Pensilva 8 SX 2969
Pentewan 7 SX 0147
Pentir 54 SH 5767
Pentire 7 SW 7961
Pentney 52 TF 7213
Penton Mewsey 22 SU 3347
Pentraeth 54 SH 5278
Pentre, Clwyd 55 SJ 0862
Pentre, Clwyd 46 SJ 1334
Pentre, Clwyd 46 SJ 2940
Pentre, Powys 45 SO 0686
Pentre, Shrops 46 SJ 3617
Pentre-bâch, Dyfed 31 SN 5547
Pentrebach, M. Glam 29 SO 0604
Pentre-bach, Powys 29 SN 9133
Pentre Berw 54 SH 4772
Pentre-bont 55 SH 7352
Pentre-celyn 46 SJ 1553
Pentre-cwrt 31 SN 3838
Pentre Dolau Honddu 32 SN 9943
Pentredwr, Clwyd 46 SJ 1946
Pentre-dwr, W. Glam 28 SS 6996
Pentrefelin, Gwyn 54 SH 5239
Pentrefelin, Gwyn 55 SH 8074
Pentrefoelas 55 SH 8751
Pentregat 31 SN 3552
Pentre-Gwenlais 31 SN 6116
Pentre Halkyn 56 SJ 2072
Pentre-llyn-cymmer 55 SH 9752
Pentre'r beirdd 46 SJ 1914
Pentre'r-felin 29 SN 9230
Pentre-tafarn-y-fedw 55 SH 8162
Pentre-ty-gwyn 29 SN 8135
Pentrich 48 SK 3852
Pentridge 14 SU 0317
Pentwyn 29 ST 2081
Pentyrch 29 ST 1082
Penuwch 44 SN 5962
Penwithick 7 SX 0256
Penybanc 31 SN 6124
Pen-y-bont, Clwyd 46 SJ 2123
Pen-y-bont, Dyfed 37 SN 3027
Penybont, Powys 36 SO 1164
Penybontfawr 45 SJ 0824
Pen-y-bryn, Gwyn 45 SH 6919
Penybryn, M. Glam 29 ST 1396
Penycae, Clwyd 46 SJ 2845
Pen-y-cae, Powys 29 SN 8413
Pen-y-cae-mawr 33 ST 4196
Pen-y-cefn 56 SJ 1175
Pen-y-clawdd 33 SO 4507
Pen-y-coedcae 29 ST 0687
Penycwm 30 SM 8523
Penyffordd 56 SJ 3061
Pen-y-garn 31 SN 5731
Pen-y-garnedd, Gwyn 54 SH 5376
Penygarnedd, Powys 45 SJ 1023
Penygraig 29 SS 9991
Pen-y-groes, Dyfed 31 SN 5813
Penygroes, Gwyn 54 SH 4753
Penysarn 54 SH 4690
Pen-y-stryt 46 SJ 1951
Penywaun 29 SN 9704
Penzance 6 SW 4730
Peopleton 37 SO 9350
Peover Heath 57 SJ 7973
Peper Harow 16 SU 9344
Peplow 47 SJ 6324
Percie 93 NO 5992
Percyhorner 97 NJ 9665
Perivale 25 TQ 1682
Perlethorpe 59 SK 6571
Perranarworthal 6 SW 7738
Perranporth 6 SW 7554
Perranuthnoe 6 SW 5329
Perranzabuloe 6 SW 7752
Perry Barr 38 SP 0692
Perry Green 25 TL 4317
Pershore 37 SO 9446
Pert 93 NO 6565
Pertenhall 40 TL 0865
Perth 88 NO 1123
Perthy 46 SJ 3633
Perton 47 SO 8598
Peterborough 50 TL 1998
Peterburn 102 NG 7483
Peterchurch 33 SO 3438
Peterculter 93 NJ 8401
Peterhead 97 NK 1346
Peterlee 73 NZ 4240
Petersfield 15 SU 7423
Peter's Green 25 TL 1419
Peters Marland 10 SS 4713
Peterstone Wentlooge 20 ST 2680
Peterston-super-Ely 29 ST 0876
Peterstow 33 SO 5624
Peter Tavy 8 SX 5177
Petertown 104 HY 3004
Petham 19 TR 1251
Petrockstowe 10 SS 5109
Pett 18 TQ 8714
Pettaugh 43 TM 1659
Pettinain 83 NS 9542
Pettistree 43 TM 2954
Petton, Devon 11 ST 0024
Petton, Shrops 46 SJ 4326
Petty 97 NJ 7636
Pettycur 89 NT 2686
Pettymuick 97 NJ 9024
Petworth 16 SU 9721
Pevensey Bay 17 TQ 6504
Pewsey 22 SU 1660
Philham 10 SS 2522
Philiphaugh 84 NT 4427
Phillack 6 SW 5638
Philleigh 7 SW 8739
Philpstoun 88 NT 0476
Phoenix Green 23 SU 7555
Pica 70 NY 0222
Piccotts End 24 TL 0509
Pickering 68 SE 7984
Picket Piece 22 SU 3947
Pickhill 67 SE 3483
Picklescott 46 SO 4399
Pickmere 57 SJ 6977
Pickwell, Devon 10 SS 4540
Pickwell, Leic 49 SK 7811
Pickworth, Leic 50 SK 9913
Pickworth, Lincs 50 TF 0433
Picton, Ches 56 SJ 4371
Picton, N. Yks 73 NZ 4107
Piddinghoe 17 TQ 4303
Piddington, Northnts 39 SP 8054
Piddington, Oxon 24 SP 6417
Piddlehinton 13 SY 7197
Piddletrenthide 13 SY 7099
Pidley 41 TL 3377
Piercebridge 72 NZ 2015
Pierowall 104 HY 4348
Pigdon 79 NZ 1588
Pikehall 58 SK 1959
Pilgrims Hatch 25 TQ 5895
Pilham 60 SK 8693
Pill 21 ST 5275
Pillaton 8 SX 3664
Pillerton Hersey 38 SP 3048
Pillerton Priors 38 SP 2947
Pilleth 36 SO 2568
Pilley 59 SE 3300
Pilling 65 SD 4048
Pilling Lane 65 SD 3749
Pilning 21 ST 5585
Pilsbury 58 SK 1163
Pilsdon 12 SY 4199
Pilsley, Derby 59 SK 2471
Pilsley, Derby 59 SK 4262
Pilton, Leic 50 SK 9102
Pilton, Northnts 40 TL 0284
Pilton, Somer 21 ST 5940
Pimperne 13 ST 9009
Pinchbeck 51 TF 2325
Pinchbeck West 50 TF 2024
Pinfold 56 SD 3811
Pinhoe 9 SX 9694
Pinmore 74 NX 2091
Pinner 25 TQ 1289
Pinvin 38 SO 9549
Pinwherry 74 NX 1936
Pinxton 49 SK 4554
Pipe and Lyde 33 SO 5044
Pipe Gate 57 SJ 7360
Piperhill 95 NH 8651
Pipewell 40 SP 8485
Pippacott 11 SS 5237
Pirbright 16 SU 9455
Pirnmill 80 NR 8744
Pirton, Herts 40 TL 1431
Pirton, H. & W 37 SO 8847
Pishill 24 SU 7289
Pistyll 54 SH 3242
Pitblae 97 NJ 9865
Pitcairngreen 88 NO 0627
Pitcalnie 103 NH 8072
Pitcaple 97 NJ 7225
Pitchcombe 34 SO 8508
Pitchford 47 SJ 5303
Pitch Green 24 SP 7703
Pitchott 24 SP 7720
Pitch Place 16 SU 9852
Pitcombe 13 ST 6733
Pitcox 89 NT 6475
Pitfichie 96 NJ 6716
Pitfour Castle 89 NO 1920
Pitgrudy 103 NH 7991
Pitlessie 89 NO 3309
Pitlochry 91 NN 9458
Pitmedden 97 NJ 8927
Pitminster 12 ST 2219
Pitmunie 96 NJ 6615
Pitney 13 ST 4528
Pitscottie 89 NO 4113
Pitsea 26 TQ 7388
Pitsford 39 SP 7563
Pitstone Green 24 SP 9315
Pittendreich 96 NJ 1961
Pittentrail 103 NC 7202
Pittenweem 89 NO 5402
Pittington 72 NZ 3244
Pitton 14 SU 2131
Pixey Green 43 TM 2475
Place Newton 69 SE 8872
Plains 82 NS 7966
Plaish 47 SO 5396
Plaistow 16 TQ 0030
Plaitford 14 SU 2819
Plâs 31 SN 4827
Plas Gogerddan 45 SN 6383
Plas Isaf 55 SJ 0542
Plâs Llwyngwern 45 SH 7504
Plas Llysyn 45 SN 9597
Plastow Green 23 SU 5361
Platt 17 TQ 6257
Plawsworth 72 NZ 2647
Plaxtol 17 TQ 6053
Playden 18 TQ 9221
Playford 43 TM 2147
Play Hatch 24 SU 7475
Playing Place 7 SW 8141
Plealey 46 SJ 4206
Plean 87 NS 8386
Pleasington 65 SD 6426
Pleasley 59 SK 5064
Plenmeller 78 NY 7163
Pleshey 26 TL 6614
Plockton 101 NG 8033
Plocrapool 98 NG 1793
Plocrapool Point 98 NG 1893
Ploughfield 33 SO 3841
Plowden 36 SO 3887
Ploxgreen 46 SJ 3603
Pluckley 18 TQ 9245
Plumbland 70 NY 1539
Plumley 57 SJ 7175
Plumpton, Cumbr 71 NY 4937
Plumpton, E. Susx 17 TQ 3613
Plumpton, Lancs 65 SD 3833
Plumpton Green 17 TQ 3616
Plumpton Head 71 NY 5035
Plumstead 53 TG 1334
Plumtree 49 SK 6133
Plungar 49 SK 7633
Plush 13 ST 7102
Plwmp 31 SN 3652
Plymouth 8 SX 4755
Plymstock 8 SX 5152
Plymtree 12 ST 0502
Pockley 67 SE 6386
Pocklington 68 SE 8049
Pode Hole 50 TF 2122
Podimore 13 ST 5424
Podington 40 SP 9462
Podmore 47 SJ 7835
Point Clear 27 TM 0915
Pointon 50 TF 1131
Pokesdown 14 SZ 1292
Polapit Tamar 8 SX 3389
Polbain 102 NB 9910
Polbathic 8 SX 3456
Polbeth 83 NT 0364
Polebrook 40 TL 0787
Polegate 17 TQ 5704
Pole of Itlaw, The 96 NJ 6756
Polesworth 48 SK 2602
Polglass 102 NC 0307
Polgooth 7 SW 9950
Poling 16 TQ 0404
Polkerris 7 SX 0952
Pollington 59 SE 6119
Polloch 101 NM 7968
Pollockshields 82 NS 5763
Pollokshaws 81 NS 5561
Polmassick 7 SW 9745
Polnessan 81 NS 4111
Polperro 7 SX 2050
Polruan 7 SX 1250
Polsham 21 ST 5142
Polstead 42 TL 9938
Poltalloch 99 NR 8196
Poltimore 9 SX 9696
Polwarth 84 NT 7450
Polyphant 8 SX 2681
Polzeath 7 SW 9378
Ponde 32 SO 1037
Pondersbridge 41 TL 2692
Ponders End 25 TQ 3695
Ponsanooth 6 SW 7537
Ponsworthy 9 SX 7073
Pontamman 31 SN 6412
Pontantwn 31 SN 4413
Pontardawe 28 SN 7204
Pontardulais 31 SN 5903
Pontarsais 31 SN 4428
Pont Creuddyn 31 SN 5552
Pont Cyfyng 55 SH 7357
Pontefract 67 SE 4521
Ponteland 79 NZ 1673
Ponterwyd 45 SN 7581
Pontesbury 46 SJ 4006
Pontfadog 46 SJ 2338
Pontfaen, Dyfed 30 SN 0234
Pont-faen, Powys 29 SN 9934
Pont Henri 31 SN 4809
Ponthir 20 ST 3292
Ponthirwaun 31 SN 2645
Pontllanfraith 29 ST 1795
Pontlliw 28 SN 6101
Pont Llogel 45 SJ 0315
Pontlottyn 29 SO 1106
Pontlyfni 54 SH 4352
Pontneddfechan 29 SN 9007
Pont Pen-y-benglog 55 SH 6560
Pontrhydfendigaid 45 SN 7366
Pont Rhyd-y-cyff 29 SS 8789
Pontrhydyfen 29 SS 7994
Pont-rhyd-y-groes 45 SN 7372
Pontrilas 33 SO 3927
Pontrobert 46 SJ 1112

Q

R

S

Shernborne 52 TF 7132
Sherrington 22 ST 9639
Sherston 21 ST 8586
Sherwood Green 11 SS 5520
Sheshader 98 NB 5534
Shettleston 82 NS 6463
Shevington 57 SD 5408
Shevington Moor 57 SD 5410
Sheviock 8 SX 3755
Shiel Bridge 101 NG 9318
Shieldaig, Highld 102 NG 8072
Shieldaig, Highld 101 NG 8153
Shieldhill 88 NS 8976
Shielfoot 101 NM 6670
Shifnal 47 SJ 7508
Shilbottle 79 NU 1908
Shildon 72 NZ 2325
Shillingford, Devon 11 SS 9824
Shillingford, Oxon 23 SU 5992
Shillingford St George 9 SX 9087
Shillingstone 13 ST 8210
Shillington 40 TL 1234
Shillmoor 78 NT 8807
Shiltenish 98 NB 2819
Shilton, Oxon 35 SP 2608
Shilton, Warw 38 SP 4084
Shimpling, Norf 43 TM 1583
Shimpling, Suff 42 TL 8651
Shimpling Street 42 TL 8752
Shiney Row 72 NZ 3252
Shinfield 24 SU 7368
Shinness 102 NC 5314
Shipbourne 17 TQ 5952
Shipdham 52 TF 9507
Shipham 21 ST 4457
Shiphay 9 SX 8965
Shiplake 24 SU 7678
Shipley, Shrops 47 SO 8195
Shipley, W. Susx 16 TQ 1421
Shipley, W. Yks 66 SE 1537
Shipmeadow 43 TM 3890
Shippon 35 SU 4898
Shipston-on-Stour 38 SP 2540
Shipton, Glos 34 SP 0418
Shipton, N. Yks 67 SE 5558
Shipton, Shrops 36 SO 5692
Shipton Bellinger 22 SU 2345
Shipton Gorge 13 SY 4991
Shipton Green 15 SZ 8099
Shipton Moyne 21 ST 8989
Shipton-on-Cherwell 35 SP 4816
Shiptonthorpe 62 SE 8543
Shipton-under-Wychwood 35 SP 2717
Shirburn 24 SU 6995
Shirdley Hill 56 SD 3613
Shirebrook 59 SK 5267
Shirehampton 21 ST 5377
Shiremoor 79 NZ 3171
Shirenewton 33 ST 4893
Shire Oak 48 SK 0504
Shireoaks 59 SK 5581
Shirkoak 18 TQ 9436
Shirland 59 SK 3958
Shirley, Derby 48 SK 2141
Shirley, Hants 14 SU 4013
Shirley, W. Mids 38 SP 1279
Shirl Heath 33 SO 4359
Shirrell Heath 15 SU 5714
Shirwell 11 SS 5937
Shiskine 80 NR 9130
Shobdon 36 SO 4062
Shobrooke 11 SS 8601
Shocklach 46 SJ 4449
Shoeburyness 26 TQ 9385
Sholden 19 TR 3552
Sholing 15 SU 4511
Sholver 58 SD 9507
Shop, Corn 10 SS 2214
Shop, Corn 7 SW 8773
Shoreditch 25 TQ 3282
Shoreham 25 TQ 5161
Shoreham-by-Sea 16 TQ 2204
Shoresdean 85 NT 9546
Shoreswood 85 NT 9446
Shoretown 94 NH 6161
Shorncote 34 SU 0296
Shorne 18 TQ 6970
Shortgate 17 TQ 4915
Short Heath, Leic 48 SK 3115
Short Heath, W. Mids 48 SP 1093
Shortlanesend 7 SW 8047
Shortlees 81 NS 4335
Shortley Bridge 72 NZ 0852
Shorwell 15 SZ 4583
Shoscombe 21 ST 7156
Shotesham 53 TM 2499
Shotgate 26 TQ 7692
Shotley 43 TM 2335
Shotley Gate 43 TM 2433
Shottenden 19 TR 0454
Shottermill 15 SU 8832
Shottery 38 SP 1855
Shotteswell 38 SP 4245
Shottisham 43 TM 3244
Shottle 48 SK 3149
Shotton, Clwyd 56 SJ 3068
Shotton, Durham 73 NZ 4139
Shotton, Northum 85 NT 8430
Shotts 83 NS 8760
Shotwick 56 SJ 3371
Shoughlaige-e-Caine 64 SC 3187
Shouldham 52 TF 6709
Shouldham Thorpe 52 TF 6508
Shoulton 37 SO 8158
Shrawardine 46 SJ 4015
Shrawley 37 SO 8064
Shrewley 38 SP 2267
Shrewsbury 47 SJ 4912
Shrewton 22 SU 0643
Shripney 16 SU 9302
Shrivenham 22 SU 2489
Shropham 52 TL 9893
Shroton or Iwerne Courtney 13 ST 8512
Shrub End 27 TL 9723
Shucknall 33 SO 5842
Shudy Camps 42 TL 6244
Shulishader 98 NB 5335
Shurdington 34 SO 9218
Shurlock Row 24 SU 8374
Shurrery 103 ND 0458
Shurton 20 ST 2044
Shustoke 38 SP 2290
Shute 12 SY 2597
Shutford 38 SP 3840
Shuthonger 34 SO 8835
Shutlanger 39 SP 7249
Shuttington 48 SK 2505
Shuttlewood 59 SK 4672
Sibbertoft 39 SP 6882
Sibdon Carwood 36 SO 4183
Sibertswold or Shepherdswell 19 TR 2647
Sibford Ferris 38 SP 3537
Sibford Gower 38 SP 3537
Sible Hedingham 42 TL 7834
Sibsey 51 TF 3551
Sibson, Cambs 50 TL 0997
Sibson, Leic 48 SK 3500
Sibthorpe 49 SK 7645
Sibton 43 TM 3669
Sicklesmere 42 TL 8760
Sicklinghall 67 SE 3648
Sidbury, Devon 12 SY 1391
Sidbury, Shrops 37 SO 6885
Sidcup 25 TQ 4672
Siddington, Ches 57 SJ 8471
Siddington, Glos 34 SU 0399
Sidestrand 53 TG 2639
Sidford 12 SY 1390
Sidinish 100 NF 8763
Sidlesham 15 SZ 8598
Sidley 17 TQ 7309
Sidmouth 12 SY 1287
Sigford 9 SX 7773
Sigglesthorne 63 TA 1545
Silchester 24 SU 6261
Sileby 49 SK 6015
Silecroft 64 SD 1381
Silian 31 SN 5751
Silkstone 59 SE 2905
Silkstone Common 59 SE 2904
Silksworth 73 NZ 3752
Silk Willoughby 50 TF 0543
Silloth 70 NY 1153
Sillyearn 96 NJ 5254
Siloh 32 SN 7437
Silpho 69 SE 9692
Silsden 66 SE 0446
Silsoe 40 TL 0735
Silton 13 ST 7829
Silverburn 83 NT 2060
Silverdale, Cumbr 65 SD 4675
Silverdale, Staffs 47 SJ 8146
Silver End 26 TL 8119
Silverford 97 NJ 7763
Silverley's Green 43 TM 2975
Silverstone 39 SP 6644
Silverton 11 SS 9502
Silwick 105 HU 2942
Simonburn 78 NY 8773
Simonsbath 11 SS 7739
Simonstone 66 SD 7734
Simprim 85 NT 8545
Simpson 40 SP 8835
Simpson Cross 29 SN 8919
Sinclairston 81 NS 4716
Sinderby 67 SE 3481
Sinderhope 71 NY 8451
Sindlesham 24 SU 7769
Singleton, Lancs 65 SD 3838
Singleton, W. Susx 15 SU 8713
Singlewell 18 TQ 6471
Sinnahard 96 NJ 4713
Sinnington 68 SE 7485
Sinton Green 37 SO 8160
Sipson 24 TQ 0778
Sirhowy 29 SO 1410
Sissinghurst 18 TQ 7937
Siston 21 ST 6875
Sithney 6 SW 6328
Sittingbourne 18 TQ 9063
Six Ashes 37 SO 7988
Sixhills 61 TF 1787
Sixpenny Handley 14 ST 9917
Sizewell 43 TM 4762
Skares 81 NS 5217
Skateraw 84 NT 7375
Skaw 105 HU 5966
Skeabost 101 NG 4148
Skeabrae 104 HY 2720
Skeeby 72 NZ 1902
Skeffington 49 SK 7402
Skeffling 63 TA 3719
Skegby 59 SK 4961
Skegness 61 TF 5663
Skelberry 105 HU 3916
Skelbo 103 NH 7995
Skeldyke 51 TF 3337
Skellingthorpe 60 SK 9271
Skellister 105 HU 4654
Skellow 59 SE 5210
Skelmanthorpe 59 SE 2310
Skelmersdale 56 SD 4605
Skelmorlie 81 NS 1967
Skelpick 103 NC 7256
Skelton, Cleve 73 NZ 6518
Skelton, Cumbr 71 NY 4335
Skelton, N. Yks 72 NZ 0900
Skelton, N. Yks 67 SE 3668
Skelton, N. Yks 67 SE 5756
Skelwick 104 HY 4844
Skelwith Bridge 70 NY 3403
Skendleby 61 TF 4369
Skenfrith 33 SO 4520
Skerne 69 TA 0455
Skerray 103 NC 6563
Sketty 28 SS 6293
Skewen 28 SS 7297
Skewsby 67 SE 6271
Skeyton 53 TG 2425
Skidbrooke 61 TF 4492
Skidby 62 TA 0133
Skigersta 98 NB 5461
Skilgate 11 SS 9827
Skillington 50 SK 8925
Skinburness 70 NY 1255
Skinflats 88 NS 9083
Skinidin 100 NG 2247
Skinningrove 73 NZ 7119
Skipness 80 NR 9057
Skipsea 69 TA 1655
Skipton 66 SD 9951
Skipton-on-Swale 67 SE 3679
Skipwith 67 SE 6638
Skirling 83 NT 0739
Skirmett 24 SU 7790
Skirpenbeck 68 SE 7457
Skirwith 71 NY 6132
Skirza 103 ND 3868
Skulamus 101 NG 6622
Skullomie 103 NC 6161
Skyehouse 59 SE 6317
Skye of Curr 95 NH 9924
Slack 66 SD 9728
Slackhall 58 SK 0781
Slackhead 96 NJ 4063
Slacks of Cairnbanno 97 NJ 8446
Slad 34 SO 8707
Slade 10 SS 5146
Slade Green 25 TQ 5276
Slaggyford 71 NY 6752
Slaidburn 65 SD 7152
Slaithwaite 58 SE 0814
Slaley 72 NY 9757
Slamannan 88 NS 8573
Slapton, Bucks 24 SP 9320
Slapton, Devon 9 SX 8245
Slapton, Northnts 39 SP 6446
Slaugham 16 TQ 2527
Slawston 49 SP 7794
Sleaford, Hants 23 SU 8038
Sleaford, Lincs 50 TF 0645
Sleagill 71 NY 5919
Sleapford 47 SJ 6315
Sledge Green 34 SO 8134
Sledmere 69 SE 9364
Sleightholme 72 NY 9510
Sleights 68 NZ 8607
Slepe 13 SY 9293
Slickly 103 ND 3066
Sliddery 80 NR 9322
Slimbridge 34 SO 7403
Slindon, Staffs 47 SJ 8232
Slindon, W. Susx 16 SU 9608
Slinfold 16 TQ 1131
Slingsby 68 SE 6974
Slip End 24 TL 0818
Slipton 40 SP 9579
Slochd 95 NH 8424
Slockavullin 99 NR 8297
Sloley 53 TG 2924
Sloothby 61 TF 4970
Slough, Berks 24 SU 9780
Slough, Powys 36 SO 3063
Slyne 65 SD 4765
Smailholm 84 NT 6436
Smallbridge 57 SD 9115
Smallburgh 53 TG 3324
Smallburn, Grampn 97 NK 0141
Smallburn, Strath 82 NS 6826
Small Dole 16 TQ 2112
Smalley 48 SK 4044
Smallfield 17 TQ 3143
Small Hythe 18 TQ 8930
Smallridge 12 ST 3000
Smardale 71 NY 7308
Smarden 18 TQ 8842
Smeatharpe 12 ST 1910
Smeeth 19 TR 0739
Smeeton Westerby 39 SP 6792
Smerclate 100 NF 7515
Smerral 103 ND 1733
Smethwick 38 SP 0288
Smirisary 101 NM 6477
Smisby 48 SK 3419
Smithfield 77 NY 4465
Smithincott 12 ST 0611
Smithton 95 NH 7146
Snailbeach 46 SJ 3702
Snailwell 42 TL 6467
Snainton 69 SE 9282
Snaith 67 SE 6422
Snape, N. Yks 67 SE 2684
Snape, Suff 43 TM 3958
Snarestone 48 SK 3409
Snarford 60 TF 0582
Snargate 19 TQ 9828
Snave 19 TR 0129
Snead 36 SO 3192
Sneaton 69 NZ 8907
Sneatonthorpe 69 NZ 9006
Snelland 60 TF 0780
Snelston 48 SK 1543
Snettisham 52 TF 6834
Snishival 100 NF 7634
Snitter 79 NU 0203
Snitterby 60 SK 9894
Snitterfield 38 SP 2160
Snitton 36 SO 5575
Snodhill 33 SO 3240
Snodland 18 TQ 7061
Snowshill 34 SP 0933
Soberton 15 SU 6116
Soberton Heath 15 SU 6014
Soham 42 TL 5973
Soldon Cross 10 SS 3210
Soldridge 15 SU 6535
Sole Street, Kent 18 TQ 6567
Sole Street, Kent 19 TR 0949
Solihull 38 SP 1579
Sollas 98 NF 8174
Sollers Dilwyn 33 SO 4255
Sollers Hope 33 SO 6033
Sollom 56 SD 4518
Solva 30 SM 8024
Somerby 49 SK 7710
Somercotes 48 SK 4253
Somerford Keynes 34 SU 0295
Somerley 15 SZ 8198
Somerleyton 53 TM 4796
Somersal Herbert 48 SK 1335
Somersby 61 TF 3472
Somersham, Cambs 41 TL 3678
Somersham, Suff 43 TM 0848
Somerton, Norf 53 TG 4719
Somerton, Oxon 35 SP 4928
Somerton, Somer 13 ST 4828
Sompting 16 TQ 1704
Sonning 24 SU 7575
Sonning Common 24 SU 7080
Sopley 14 SZ 1697
Sopworth 21 ST 8286
Sorbie 75 NX 4346
Sordale 103 ND 1561
Sorisdale 100 NM 2763
Sorn 81 NS 5526
Sortat 103 ND 2863
Sotby 61 TF 2078
Sots Hole 61 TF 1164
Sotterley 43 TM 4584
Soudley 47 SJ 7229
Soughton or Sychdyn 56 SJ 2466
Soulbury 40 SP 8827
Soulby 71 NY 7410
Souldern 35 SP 5231
Souldrop 40 SP 9861
Sound, Shetld 105 HU 3850
Sound, Shetld 105 HU 4640
Soundwell 21 ST 6575
Sourhope 78 NT 8420
Sourin 104 HY 4331
Sourton 9 SX 5390
Soutergate 64 SD 2281
South Acre 52 TF 8114
Southall 25 TQ 1280
South Allington 9 SX 7938
South Alloa 88 NS 8791
Southam, Glos 34 SO 9725
Southam, Warw 38 SP 4161
South Ambersham 16 SU 9120
Southampton 14 SU 4112
South Bank 73 NZ 5320
South Barrow 13 ST 6027
South Benfleet 26 TQ 7785
Southborough 17 TQ 5842
Southbourne, Dorset 14 SZ 1491
Southbourne, W. Susx 15 SU 7705
South Brent 9 SX 6960
Southburgh 52 TG 0004
South Burlingham 53 TG 3707
South Cadbury 13 ST 6325
South Carlton 60 SK 9576
South Cave 62 SE 9231
South Cerney 34 SU 0597
South Chard 12 ST 3205
South Charlton 79 NU 1620
South Cheriton 13 ST 6925
Southchurch 26 TQ 9085
South Cliffe 62 SE 8736
South Clifton 60 SK 8270
South Cove 43 TM 4980
South Creake 52 TF 8536
South Croxton 49 SK 6810
South Dalton 62 SE 9645
South Darenth 25 TQ 5669
South Duffield 62 SE 6833
Southease 17 TQ 4205
South Elkington 61 TF 2988
South Elmsall 59 SE 4711
Southend, Berks 23 SU 5970
South End, Cumbr 64 SD 2063
Southend, Strath 80 NR 6908
Southend-on-Sea 26 TQ 8785
Southerndown 29 SS 8874
Southerness 70 NX 9754
South Erradale 102 NG 7471
Southery 52 TL 6294
South Fambridge 26 TQ 8595
South Fawley 22 SU 3980
South Ferriby 62 SE 9820
Southfleet 18 TQ 6171
South Garvan 90 NM 9977
Southgate, G. Lon 25 TQ 3094
Southgate, Norf 52 TF 6833
Southgate, Norf 53 TG 1424
Southgate, W. Glam 28 SS 5588
South Godstone 17 TQ 3648
South Gorley 14 SU 1610
South Green 26 TQ 6893
South Hanningfield 26 TQ 7497
South Harting 15 SU 7819
South Hayling 15 SZ 7299
South Heath 24 SP 9102
South Heighton 17 TQ 4503
South Hetton 73 NZ 3745
South Hiendley 59 SE 3912
South Hill 8 SX 3372
South Hole 10 SS 2219
South Holmwood 16 TQ 1745
South Hornchurch 25 TQ 5283
South Hylton 73 NZ 3556
Southill 40 TL 1542
South Kelsey 62 TF 0498
South Kilvington 67 SE 4284
South Kilworth 39 SP 6881
South Kirkby 59 SE 4510
South Kirkton 97 NJ 7405
South Kyme 50 TF 1749
South Lancing 16 TQ 1803
Southleigh, Devon 12 SY 2093
South Leigh, Oxon 35 SP 3908
South Leverton 60 SK 7881
South Littleton 38 SP 0746
South Lochboisdale 100 NF 7717
South Lopham 42 TM 0481
South Luffenham 50 SK 9401
South Malling 17 TQ 4111
South Marston 22 SU 1988
South Milford 67 SE 4931
South Milton 9 SX 6942
South Mimms 25 TL 2201
Southminster 26 TQ 9599
South Molton 11 SS 7125
South Moor, Durham 72 NZ 1851
Southmoor, Oxon 35 SU 4098
South Moreton 23 SU 5688
South Mundam 15 SU 8700
South Muskham 60 SK 7957
South Newington 35 SP 4033
South Newton 14 SU 0834
South Normanton 49 SK 4456
South Norwood 25 TQ 3468
South Nuffield 17 TQ 3049
South Ockendon 26 TQ 5982
Southoe 40 TL 1860
Southolt 43 TM 1968
South Ormsby 61 TF 3775
Southorpe 50 TF 0803
South Otterington 67 SE 3787
Southowram 66 SE 1123
South Oxhey 25 TQ 1193
South Perrott 13 ST 4706
South Petherton 13 ST 4316
South Petherwin 8 SX 3182
South Pickenham 52 TF 8504
South Pool 9 SX 7740
Southport 56 SD 3316
South Raynham 52 TF 8724
Southrepps 53 TG 2536
South Reston 61 TF 4083
Southrey 61 TF 1366
Southrop 35 SP 2003
Southrope 23 SU 6744
South Runcton 52 TF 6308
South Scarle 60 SK 8463
Southsea 15 SZ 6498
South Shields 79 NZ 3666
South Shore 65 SD 3033
South Skirlaugh 63 TA 1439
South Somercotes 61 TF 4193
South Stainley 67 SE 3063
South Stainmore 71 NY 8413
Southstoke, Avon 21 ST 7461
South Stoke, Oxon 23 SU 5983
South Stoke, W. Susx 16 TQ 0210
South Street 17 TQ 3917
South Tawton 9 SX 6594
South Thoresby 61 TF 4076
South Tidworth 22 SU 2448
South Town, Hants 15 SU 6536
Southtown, Orkney 104 ND 4895
Southwaite 71 NY 4545
South Walsham 53 TG 3613
South Warnborough 23 SU 7247
Southwater 16 TQ 1525
Southway 21 ST 5142
South Weald 25 TQ 5793
Southwell, Dorset 13 SY 6870
Southwell, Notts 49 SK 7054
South Weston 24 SU 7098
South Wheatley 8 SX 2492
Southwick, Hants 15 SU 6208
Southwick, Northnts 40 TL 0292
Southwick, T. & W 79 NZ 3758
Southwick, Wilts 21 ST 8355
Southwick, W. Susx 16 TQ 2405
South Widcombe 21 ST 5856
South Wigston 49 SP 5898
South Willingham 61 TF 1983
South Wingfield 48 SK 3755
South Witham 50 SK 9219
Southwold 43 TM 5076
South Wonston 15 SU 4635
Southwood 53 TG 3905
South Woodham Ferrers 26 TQ 8097
South Wootton 52 TF 6422
South Zeal 9 SX 6593
Soutra Mains 84 NT 4559
Sowerby, N. Yks 67 SE 4381
Sowerby, W. Yks 66 SE 0423
Sowerby Bridge 66 SE 0623
Sowerby Row 71 NY 3940
Sowton 9 SX 9791
Spa Common 53 TG 2930
Spalding 51 TF 2422
Spaldington 62 SE 7633
Spaldwick 40 TL 1272
Spalford 60 SK 8369
Sparham 52 TG 0719
Spark Bridge 65 SD 3084
Sparkford 13 ST 6026
Sparkwell 9 SX 5857
Sparrowpit 58 SK 0980
Sparsholt, Hants 14 SU 4331
Sparsholt, Oxon 22 SU 3487
Spaunton 68 SE 7289
Spaxton 12 ST 2237
Spean Bridge 90 NN 2281
Speen, Berks 23 SU 4668
Speen, Bucks 24 SU 8499
Speeton 69 TA 1574
Speke 56 SJ 4483
Speldhurst 17 TQ 5541
Spellbrook 25 TL 4817
Spelsbury 35 SP 3521
Spencers Wood 24 SU 7166
Spennithorne 66 SE 1388
Spennymoor 72 NZ 2534
Spetchley 37 SO 8954
Spetisbury 13 ST 9102
Spexhall 43 TM 3780
Spey Bay 96 NJ 3565
Speybridge 95 NJ 0326
Spilsby 61 TF 4066
Spindlestone 85 NU 1533
Spinningdale 103 NH 6789
Spirthill 22 ST 9975
Spithurst 17 TQ 4217
Spittal, Dyfed 30 SM 9723
Spittal, Highld 103 ND 1654
Spittal, Lothn 89 NT 4677
Spittal, Northum 85 NU 0051
Spittalfield 92 NO 1040
Spittal of Glenmuick 92 NO 3085
Spittal of Glenshee 92 NO 1070
Spixworth 53 TG 2415
Spofforth 67 SE 3651
Spondon 48 SK 4035
Spooner Row 53 TM 0997
Sporle 52 TF 8411
Spott 89 NT 6775
Spratton 39 SP 7170
Spreakley 23 SU 8341
Spreyton 9 SX 6996
Spridlington 60 TF 0084
Springburn 82 NS 6068
Springcorrie 98 NB 2332
Springfield, Fife 89 NO 3411
Springfield, Grampn 95 NJ 0560
Springfield, W. Mids 38 SP 0981
Springholm 76 NX 8069
Springside 81 NS 3738
Springthorpe 60 SK 8789
Sproatley 63 TA 3419
Sproston Green 57 SJ 7366
Sprotbrough 59 SE 5402
Sproughton 40 TL 1244
Sprouston 84 NT 7535
Sprowston 53 TG 2411
Sproxton, Leic 50 SK 8524
Sproxton, N. Yks 67 SE 6181
Spurstow 57 SJ 5557
Square and Compass 30 SM 8531
Stackhouse 66 SD 8165
Stackpole 30 SR 9895
Stacksteads 66 SD 8421
Staddiscombe 8 SX 5151
Staddlethorpe 62 SE 8423
Stadhampton 35 SU 6098
Staffield 71 NY 5442
Staffin 101 NG 4867
Stafford 47 SJ 9223
Stagsden 40 SP 9849
Stainacre 69 NZ 9103
Stainburn 67 SE 2443
Stainby 50 SK 9022
Staincross 59 SE 3310
Staindrop 72 NZ 1220
Staines 24 TQ 0471
Stainfield, Lincs 50 TF 0725
Stainfield, Lincs 61 TF 1073
Stainforth, N. Yks 66 SD 8267
Stainforth, S. Yks 59 SE 6411
Staining 65 SD 3536
Stainland 58 SE 0719
Stainsacre 69 NZ 9103
Stainton, Cleve 73 NZ 4814
Stainton, Cumbr 71 NY 4823
Stainton, Cumbr 65 SD 5285
Stainton, Durham 72 NZ 0713
Stainton, N. Yks 72 SE 1096
Stainton, S. Yks 59 SK 5593
Stainton by Langworth 60 TF 0677
Staintondale 69 SE 9993
Stainton le Vale 61 TF 1794
Stainton With Adgarley 64 SD 2572
Stair, Cumbr 70 NY 2321
Stair, Strath 81 NS 4323
Staithes 73 NZ 7818
Stakeford 79 NZ 2785
Stake Pool 65 SD 4143
Stalbans 25 TL 1407
Stalbridge 13 ST 7317
Stalbridge Weston 13 ST 7216
Stalham 53 TG 3725
Stalham Green 53 TG 3824
Stalisfield Green 18 TQ 9552
Stallingborough 63 TA 2011
Stalling Busk 66 SD 9185
Stalmine 65 SD 3745
Stalybridge 58 SJ 9698
Stambourne 42 TL 7238
Stambourne Green 42 TL 7038
Stamford 50 TF 0307
Stamford Bridge 68 SE 7155
Stamfordham 79 NZ 0872
Stanborough 25 TL 2211
Stanbridge, Beds 24 SP 9624
Stanbridge, Dorset 14 SU 0004
Stand 82 NS 7668
Standburn 88 NS 9274
Standeford 47 SJ 9108
Standen 18 TQ 8540
Standford 15 SU 8134
Standish 57 SD 5610
Standlake 35 SP 3903
Standon, Hants 14 SU 4226
Standon, Herts 25 TL 3922
Standon, Staffs 47 SJ 8235
Stane 83 NS 8859
Stanfield 52 TF 9320
Stanford, Beds 40 TL 1641
Stanford, Kent 19 TR 1238
Stanford Bishop 37 SO 6851
Stanford Bridge 37 SO 7165
Stanford Dingley 23 SU 5771
Stanford in the Vale 35 SU 3493
Stanford-le-Hope 26 TQ 6882
Stanford on Avon 39 SP 5878
Stanford on Soar 49 SK 5422
Stanford on Teme 37 SO 7066
Stanford Rivers 25 TL 5300
Stanghow 73 NZ 6715
Stanhoe 52 TF 8036
Stanhope, Border 83 NT 1229
Stanhope, Durham 72 NY 9939
Stanion 40 SP 9187
Stanley, Derby 48 SK 4140
Stanley, Durham 72 NZ 1952
Stanley, Staffs 47 SJ 9352
Stanley, Tays 88 NO 1033
Stanley, W. Yks 67 SE 3424
Stanley Crook 72 NZ 1638
Stanmer 17 TQ 3309
Stanmore, Berks 23 SU 4778
Stanmore, G. Lon 25 TQ 1692
Stannington, Northum 79 NZ 2179
Stannington, S. Yks 59 SK 3088
Stansbatch 36 SO 3561
Stansfield 42 TL 7852
Stanstead 42 TL 8449
Stanstead Abbotts 25 TL 3911
Stansted 18 TQ 6062
Stansted Mountfitchet 25 TL 5124
Stanton, Derby 48 SK 2719
Stanton, Glos 34 SP 0734
Stanton, Gwent 33 SO 3121
Stanton, Staffs 48 SK 1246
Stanton, Suff 42 TL 9673
Stanton by Bridge 48 SK 3727
Stanton-by-Dale 49 SK 4638
Stanton Drew 21 ST 5963
Stanton Fitzwarren 22 SU 1790
Stanton Harcourt 35 SP 4105
Stanton Hill 59 SK 4860
Stanton in Peak 59 SK 2464
Stanton Lacy 36 SO 4978
Stanton Long 36 SO 5790
Stanton-on-the-Wolds 49 SK 6330
Stanton Prior 21 ST 6762
Stanton St Bernard 22 SU 0962
Stanton St John 35 SP 5709
Stanton St Quintin 21 ST 9080
Stanton Street 42 TL 9566
Stanton under Bardon 49 SK 4610
Stanton upon Hine Heath 47 SJ 5724
Stanton Wick 21 ST 6162
Stanwardine in the Fields 46 SJ 4124
Stanway, Essex 26 TL 9424
Stanway, Glos 34 SP 0632
Stanwell 24 TQ 0574
Stanwell Moor 24 TQ 0474
Stanwick 40 SP 9771
Stanwick-St-John 72 NZ 1811
Stanydale 105 HU 2850
Stape 68 SE 7993
Stapehill 14 SU 0507
Stapeley 47 SJ 6749
Staple 19 TR 2756
Staplecross 18 TQ 7822
Staplefield 16 TQ 2728
Staple Fitzpaine 12 ST 2618
Stapleford, Cambs 41 TL 4751
Stapleford, Herts 25 TL 3116
Stapleford, Leic 50 SK 8118
Stapleford, Lincs 60 SK 8757
Stapleford, Notts 49 SK 4837
Stapleford, Wilts 14 SU 0737
Stapleford Abbotts 25 TQ 5095
Stapleford Tawney 25 TQ 5099
Staplegrove 12 ST 2126
Staplehay 12 ST 2121
Staplehurst 18 TQ 7843
Staplers 15 SZ 5189
Stapleton, Avon 21 ST 6176
Stapleton, Cumbr 77 NY 5071
Stapleton, H. & W 36 SO 3265
Stapleton, Leic 48 SP 4398
Stapleton, N. Yks 72 NZ 2612
Stapleton, Shrops 47 SJ 4704
Stapleton, Somer 13 ST 4621
Stapley 12 ST 1813
Staploe 40 TL 1460
Star, Dyfed 31 SN 2435
Star, Fife 89 NO 3103
Star, Somer 21 ST 4358
Starbotton 66 SD 9574
Starcross 9 SX 9781
Starkigarth 105 HU 4329
Starston 43 TM 2384
Startforth 72 NZ 0316
Startley 22 ST 9482
Stathe 12 ST 3728
Stathern 49 SK 7731
Station Town 73 NZ 4036
Staughton Highway 40 TL 1364
Staunton, Glos 33 SO 5512
Staunton, Glos 34 SO 7929
Staunton in the Vale 49 SK 8043
Staunton on Arrow 33 SO 3760
Staunton on Wye 33 SO 3645
Staveley, Cumbr 71 SD 4698
Staveley, Derby 59 SK 4374
Staveley, N. Yks 67 SE 3662
Staveley-in-Cartmel 65 SD 3886
Staverton, Devon 9 SX 7964
Staverton, Glos 34 SO 8923
Staverton, Northnts 39 SP 5361
Staverton, Wilts 21 ST 8560
Stawell 20 ST 3638
Staxigoe 103 ND 3852
Staxton 69 TA 0179
Staylittle 45 SN 8892
Staythorpe 49 SK 7553
Stean 66 SE 0873
Stearsby 67 SE 6171
Steart 20 ST 2745
Stebbing 26 TL 6624
Stedham 15 SU 8622
Steele Road 78 NY 5293
Steen's Bridge 33 SO 5457
Steep 15 SU 7425
Steeple, Dorset 13 SY 9181
Steeple, Essex 26 TL 9303
Steeple Ashton, Oxon 35 SP 4725
Steeple Ashton, Wilts 21 ST 9056
Steeple Barton 35 SP 4425
Steeple Bumpstead 42 TL 6841
Steeple Claydon 39 SP 6926
Steeple Gidding 40 TL 1381
Steeple Langford 14 SU 0437
Steeple Morden 41 TL 2842
Steeton 66 SE 0344
Steinmanhill 97 NJ 7642
Steisay 100 NF 8544
Stelling Minnis 19 TR 1446
Stemster 103 ND 1861
Stenalees 7 SX 0157
Stenhousemuir 88 NS 8783
Stenton 89 NT 6274
Stepney 25 TQ 3581
Steppingley 40 TL 0135
Stepps 82 NS 6568
Sternfield 43 TM 3961
Stert 22 SU 0359
Stetchworth 42 TL 6458
Stevenage 25 TL 2324
Stevenston 81 NS 2642
Steventon, Hants 23 SU 5447
Steventon, Oxon 23 SU 4791
Stevington 40 SP 9853
Stewartby 40 TL 0242
Stewarton 81 NS 4246
Stewkley 40 SP 8526
Stewton 61 TF 3686
Steyning 16 TQ 1811
Steynton 30 SM 9107
Stibb 10 SS 2210
Stibbard 52 TF 9828
Stibb Cross 10 SS 4214
Stibb Green 22 SU 2262
Stibbington 50 TL 0898
Stichill 84 NT 7138
Sticker 7 SW 9750
Stickford 61 TF 3559
Sticklepath 9 SX 6494
Stickney 51 TF 3456
Stiffkey 52 TF 9742
Stifford's Bridge 37 SO 7348
Stilligarry 100 NF 7638
Stillingfleet 67 SE 5941
Stillington, Cleve 73 NZ 3723
Stillington, N. Yks 67 SE 5867
Stilton 40 TL 1689
Stinchcombe 34 ST 7398
Stinsford 13 SY 7191
Stirchley 47 SJ 7006
Stirling 87 NS 7993
Stisted 26 TL 8024
Stithians 6 SW 7336
Stittenham 103 NH 6574
Stivichall 38 SP 3376
Stixwould 61 TF 1766
Stoak 56 SJ 4273
Stobo 83 NT 1837
Stoborough 13 SY 9286
Stoborough Green 13 SY 9285
Stock 26 TQ 6998
Stockbridge 14 SU 3635
Stockbriggs 82 NS 7936
Stockbury 18 TQ 8461
Stockcross 22 SU 4368
Stockdalewath 71 NY 3845
Stockeinteignhead 9 SX 9170
Stockerston 50 SP 8397
Stock Green 38 SO 9959
Stockingford 38 SP 3491
Stocking Pelham 41 TL 4529
Stockinish Island 98 NG 1390
Stockland 12 ST 2404
Stockland Bristol 20 ST 2443
Stockleigh English 11 SS 8506
Stockleigh Pomeroy 11 SS 8703
Stockley 22 SU 0067
Stockport 57 SJ 8990
Stocksbridge 59 SK 2698
Stocksfield 79 NZ 0561
Stockton, H. & W 36 SO 5161
Stockton, Norf 53 TM 3894
Stockton, Shrops 47 SO 7299
Stockton, Warw 38 SP 4363
Stockton, Wilts 22 ST 9838
Stockton Heath 57 SJ 6186
Stockton-on-Tees 73 NZ 4419
Stockton on Teme 37 SO 7167
Stockton on the Forest 67 SE 6555
Stock Wood 38 SP 0058
Stodmarsh 19 TR 2160
Stoer 102 NC 0428
Stoford, Somer 13 ST 5613
Stoford, Wilts 14 SU 0835
Stogumber 12 ST 0937
Stogursey 20 ST 2042
Stoke, Devon 10 SS 2324
Stoke, Hants 22 SU 4051
Stoke, Hants 15 SU 7202
Stoke, Kent 18 TQ 8275
Stoke Abbott 13 ST 4500
Stoke Albany 39 SP 8088
Stoke Ash 43 TM 1170
Stoke Bardolph 49 SK 6441
Stoke Bliss 37 SO 6562
Stoke Bruerne 39 SP 7449
Stoke by Clare 42 TL 7443
Stoke-by-Nayland 42 TL 9836
Stoke Canon 9 SX 9397
Stoke Charity 23 SU 4839
Stoke Climsland 8 SX 3674
Stoke D'Abernon 25 TQ 1259
Stoke Doyle 40 TL 0286
Stoke Dry 50 SP 8596
Stoke Ferry 52 TF 7000
Stoke Fleming 9 SX 8648
Stokeford 13 SY 8687
Stoke Gabriel 9 SX 8457
Stoke Gifford 21 ST 6280
Stoke Golding 48 SP 3997
Stoke Goldington 40 SP 8748
Stokeham 60 SK 7876
Stoke Hammond 40 SP 8829
Stoke Heath 47 SJ 6529
Stoke Holy Cross 53 TG 2301
Stoke Lacy 33 SO 6249
Stoke Lyne 35 SP 5628
Stoke Mandeville 24 SP 8310
Stokenchurch 24 SU 7696
Stoke Newington 25 TQ 3286
Stokenham 9 SX 8042
Stoke on Tern 47 SJ 6428
Stoke-on-Trent 47 SJ 8745
Stoke Orchard 34 SO 9228
Stoke Poges 24 SU 9884
Stoke Prior, H. & W 33 SO 5256
Stoke Prior, H. & W 37 SO 9467
Stoke Rivers 11 SS 6335
Stoke Rochford 50 SK 9127
Stoke Row 24 SU 6884
Stokesay 36 SO 4381
Stokesby 53 TG 4310
Stokesley 73 NZ 5208
Stoke St Gregory 12 ST 3427
Stoke St Mary 12 ST 2622
Stoke St Michael 21 ST 6646
Stoke St Milborough 36 SO 5782
Stoke sub Hamdon 13 ST 4717
Stoke Talmage 24 SU 6799
Stoke Trister 13 ST 7428
Stolford 20 ST 2245
Stondon Massey 25 TL 5800
Stone, Bucks 24 SP 7812
Stone, Glos 34 ST 6895
Stone, H. & W 37 SO 8675
Stone, Kent 25 TQ 5774
Stone, Staffs 47 SJ 9033
Stone Allerton 20 ST 4051
Ston Easton 21 ST 6253
Stonebroom 59 SK 4159
Stone Cross 17 TQ 6204
Stonefield 82 NS 6857
Stonegate 17 TQ 6628
Stonegate Crofts 97 NK 0339
Stonegrave 67 SE 6577
Stonehaugh 78 NY 7976
Stonehaven 93 NO 8786
Stone House, Cumbr 66 SD 7686
Stonehouse, Glos 34 SO 8005
Stonehouse, Northum 78 NY 6958
Stonehouse, Strath 82 NS 7546
Stone in Oxney 18 TQ 9427
Stoneleigh 38 SP 3372
Stonely 40 TL 1067
Stonesby 50 SK 8224
Stonesfield 35 SP 3917
Stones Green 43 TM 1626
Stoneybridge 100 NF 7433
Stoneyburn 83 NS 9762
Stoney Cross 14 SU 2611
Stoneygate 49 SK 6002
Stoneyhills 26 TQ 9597
Stoneykirk 74 NX 0953
Stoney Middleton 59 SK 2375
Stoney Stanton 49 SP 4994
Stoney Stratton 21 ST 6539
Stoney Stretton 46 SJ 3809
Stoneywood 97 NJ 8911
Stonham Aspal 43 TM 1359
Stonnall 48 SK 0704
Stonor 24 SU 7388
Stonton Wyville 49 SP 7395
Stonybreck 104 HZ 2071
Stony Stratford 39 SP 7940
Stoodleigh 11 SS 9218
Stopham 16 TQ 0219
Stopsley 25 TL 1023
Storeton 56 SJ 3084
Stornoway 98 NB 4233
Storridge 37 SO 7548
Storrington 16 TQ 0814
Storrs 71 SD 4094
Storth 65 SD 4779
Stotfold 40 TL 2136
Stottesdon 37 SO 6782
Stoughton, Leic 49 SK 6402
Stoughton, Surrey 16 SU 9851
Stoughton, W. Susx 15 SU 8011
Stoul 101 NM 7594
Stoulton 37 SO 9049
Stourbridge 37 SO 9084
Stourpaine 13 ST 8609
Stourport-on-Severn 37 SO 8171
Stour Provost 13 ST 7921
Stour Row 13 ST 8221
Stourton, Staffs 37 SO 8685
Stourton, Warw 38 SP 2936
Stourton, Wilts 13 ST 7734
Stourton Caundle 13 ST 7115
Stoven 43 TM 4481
Stow 60 SK 8882
Stow Bardolph 52 TF 6205
Stow Bedon 52 TL 9596
Stowbridge 52 TF 6007
Stow cum Quy 41 TL 5160
Stowe 36 SO 3073
Stowe-by-Chartley 48 SK 0027
Stowell 13 ST 6822
Stowford 8 SX 4386
Stowlangtoft 42 TL 9668
Stow Longa 40 TL 1070
Stow Maries 26 TQ 8399
Stowmarket 42 TM 0458
Stow-on-the-Wold 35 SP 1925
Stowting 19 TR 1242
Stowupland 40 TL 0660
Straad 80 NS 0462
Strachan 93 NO 6792
Strachur 86 NN 0901
Stradbroke 43 TM 2374
Stradishall 42 TL 7452
Stradsett 52 TF 6605
Stragglethorpe 50 SK 9152
Straiton, Lothn 83 NT 2766
Straiton, Strath 81 NS 3804
Straloch 92 NO 0463
Stramshall 48 SK 0835
Stranraer 74 NX 0660
Strata Florida 45 SN 7465
Stratfield Mortimer 24 SU 6664
Stratfield Saye 24 SU 6861
Stratfield Turgis 24 SU 6960
Stratford 25 TQ 3884
Stratford St Andrew 43 TM 3560
Stratford St Mary 42 TM 0434
Stratford Tony 14 SU 0926
Stratford-upon-Avon 38 SP 2055
Strath 102 NG 7977
Strathan, Highld 102 NC 0821
Strathan, Highld 90 NM 9791
Strathaven 82 NS 7044
Strathblane 87 NS 5679
Strathdon 96 NJ 3512
Strath Kanaird 102 NC 1501
Strathkinness 89 NO 4616
Strathmiglo 89 NO 2110
Strathpeffer 94 NH 4858
Strathrannoch 102 NH 3874
Strathwhillan 80 NS 0235
Strathy 103 NC 8365
Strathyre 87 NN 5617
Stratton, Corn 10 SS 2206
Stratton, Dorset 13 SY 6593
Stratton, Glos 34 SP 0103
Stratton Audley 35 SP 6026
Stratton-on-the-Fosse 21 ST 6550
Stratton St Margaret 22 SU 1787
Stratton St Michael 53 TM 2093
Stratton Strawless 53 TG 2220
Streat 17 TQ 3515
Streatham 25 TQ 2972
Streatley, Beds 40 TL 0728
Streatley, Berks 23 SU 5980
Street, Lancs 65 SD 5252
Street, N. Yks 68 NZ 7304
Street, Somer 13 ST 4836
Street End 15 SZ 8599
Streethay 48 SK 1410
Streetly 48 SP 0898
Strefford 36 SO 4485
Strensall 67 SE 6360
Strensham 37 SO 9140
Stretcholt 20 ST 2944
Strete 9 SX 8347
Stretford 57 SJ 7994
Stretford Court 33 SO 4455
Strethall 41 TL 4839
Stretham 41 TL 5174
Strettington 15 SU 8907
Stretton, Ches 46 SJ 4453
Stretton, Ches 57 SJ 6182
Stretton, Derby 59 SK 3961
Stretton, Leic 50 SK 9415
Stretton, Staffs 47 SJ 8811
Stretton, Staffs 48 SK 2526
Stretton en le Fields 48 SK 3011
Stretton Grandison 33 SO 6344
Stretton Heath 46 SJ 3610
Stretton-on-Dunsmore 38 SP 4172
Stretton-on-Fosse 38 SP 2238
Stretton Sugwas 33 SO 4642
Stretton under Fosse 39 SP 4581
Stretton Westwood 47 SO 5998
Strichen 97 NJ 9455
Stringston 20 ST 1742
Strixton 40 SP 9061
Stroat 33 ST 5797
Stromeferry 101 NG 8634
Stromemore 101 NG 8635
Stromness 104 HY 2509
Stronachlachar 87 NN 4010
Strond 98 NG 0384
Strone, Highld 94 NH 5228
Strone, Highld 90 NN 1481
Strone, Strath 86 NS 1980
Stronenaba 90 NN 2084
Stronmilchan 86 NN 1528
Strontian 101 NM 8161
Strood 18 TQ 7269
Stroud, Glos 34 SO 8505
Stroud, Hants 15 SU 7223
Struan, Highld 101 NG 3438
Struan, Tays 91 NN 8065
Strubby 61 TF 4582
Strumpshaw 53 TG 3507
Strutherhill 82 NS 7649
Struy 94 NH 4039
Stuartfield 97 NJ 9746
Stubbington 15 SU 5503
Stubbins 57 SD 7918
Stubhampton 13 ST 9113
Stubton 50 SK 8748
Stuckton 14 SU 1613
Studham 24 TL 0215
Studland 14 SZ 0382
Studley, Warw 38 SP 0763
Studley, Wilts 22 ST 9671
Studley Roger 67 SE 2970
Stuntney 41 TL 5578
Sturbridge 47 SJ 8330
Sturmer 42 TL 6944
Sturminster Marshall 14 SY 9499
Sturminster Newton 13 ST 7814
Sturry 19 TR 1760
Sturton by Stow 60 SK 8880
Sturton le Steeple 60 SK 7884
Stuston 43 TM 1377
Stutton, N. Yks 67 SE 4841
Stutton, Suff 43 TM 1434
Styal 57 SJ 8383
Suckley 37 SO 7251
Sudborough 40 SP 9682
Sudbourne 43 TM 4153
Sudbrook, Gwent 21 ST 5087
Sudbrook, Lincs 60 TF 0375
Sudbury, Derby 48 SK 1632
Sudbury, Suff 42 TL 8741
Sudgrove 34 SO 9303
Suffield 53 TG 2332
Sugnall 47 SJ 8031
Sulby 64 SC 3894
Sulgrave 39 SP 5545
Sulham 24 SU 6474
Sulhamstead 24 SU 6368
Sullington 16 TQ 0913
Sullom 105 HU 3573
Sully 29 ST 1568
Sumburgh 105 HU 4009
Summerbridge 66 SE 2062
Summercourt 7 SW 8856
Summerleaze 21 ST 4285
Summerseat 57 SD 7914
Summit 57 SD 9418
Sunbiggin 71 NY 6503
Sunbury 24 TQ 0769
Sunderland, Cumbr 70 NY 1835
Sunderland, T. & W 73 NZ 3957
Sunderland Bridge 72 NZ 2637
Sundhope 84 NT 3325
Sundon Park 40 TL 0525
Sundridge 17 TQ 4755
Sunk Island 63 TA 2619
Sunningdale 24 SU 9567
Sunninghill 24 SU 9467
Sunningwell 35 SP 4900
Sunniside, Durham 72 NZ 1438
Sunniside, T. & W 79 NZ 2058
Sunnylaw 87 NS 7898
Sunnyside 17 TQ 3937
Surbiton 25 TQ 1867
Surfleet 51 TF 2528
Surfleet Seas End 51 TF 2729
Surlingham 53 TG 3106
Sustead 53 TG 1936
Susworth 62 SE 8302
Sutcombe 10 SS 3411
Suton 53 TM 0998
Sutors of Cromarty 95 NH 8067
Sutterton 51 TF 2835
Sutton, Beds 41 TL 2247
Sutton, Cambs 50 TL 0998
Sutton, Cambs 41 TL 4479
Sutton, G. Lon 25 TQ 2564
Sutton, Kent 19 TR 3349
Sutton, Norf 53 TG 3823
Sutton, Notts 60 SK 6884
Sutton, Notts 49 SK 7637
Sutton, N. Yks 67 SE 4841
Sutton, Oxon 35 SP 4106
Sutton, Shrops 47 SJ 6631
Sutton, Shrops 36 SO 5183
Sutton, Shrops 37 SO 7286
Sutton, Staffs 47 SJ 7622
Sutton, Suff 43 TM 3145
Sutton, Surrey 16 TQ 1046
Sutton, W. Susx 16 SU 9715
Sutton at Hone 25 TQ 5570
Sutton Bassett 39 SP 7790
Sutton Benger 22 ST 9478
Sutton Bridge 51 TF 4721
Sutton Cheney 48 SK 4100
Sutton Coldfield 48 SP 1296
Sutton Courtenay 35 SU 5093
Sutton Crosses 51 TF 4321
Sutton Grange 67 SE 2874
Sutton Hill 47 SJ 7003
Sutton Howgrave 67 SE 3179
Sutton in Ashfield 59 SK 4959
Sutton-in-Craven 66 SE 0144
Sutton Lane Ends 57 SJ 9271
Sutton Leach 57 SJ 5292
Sutton Maddock 47 SJ 7201
Sutton Mallet 12 ST 3736
Sutton Mandeville 14 ST 9828
Sutton Montis 13 ST 6224
Sutton-on-Hull 63 TA 1232
Sutton on Sea 61 TF 5281
Sutton-on-the-Forest 67 SE 5864
Sutton on the Hill 48 SK 2333
Sutton on Trent 60 SK 7965
Sutton Scotney 23 SU 4439
Sutton St Edmund 51 TF 3613
Sutton St James 51 TF 3918
Sutton St Nicholas 33 SO 5345
Sutton-under-Brailes 38 SP 3037
Sutton-under-Whitestonecliffe 67 SE 4882
Sutton upon Derwent 62 SE 7046
Sutton Valence 18 TQ 8149
Sutton Veny 21 ST 8941
Sutton Waldron 13 ST 8615
Sutton Weaver 57 SJ 5479
Swaby 61 TF 3877
Swadlincote 48 SK 3020
Swaffham 52 TF 8208
Swaffham Bulbeck 41 TL 5562
Swaffham Prior 41 TL 5764
Swafield 53 TG 2832
Swainbost 98 NB 5162
Swainby 73 NZ 4701
Swainshill 33 SO 4641
Swainsthorpe 53 TG 2200
Swalcliffe 38 SP 3737
Swalecliffe 19 TR 1367
Swallow 63 TA 1703
Swallowcliffe 14 ST 9627
Swallowfield 24 SU 7264
Swanage 14 SZ 0378
Swanbister 104 HY 3505
Swanbourne 39 SP 8027
Swan Green 57 SJ 7373
Swanland 62 SE 9927
Swanley 25 TQ 5168
Swanmore 15 SU 5716
Swannington, Leic 48 SK 4116
Swannington, Norf 53 TG 1319
Swanscombe 18 TQ 6074
Swansea 28 SS 6593
Swanton Abbot 53 TG 2625
Swanton Morley 52 TG 0116
Swanton Novers 52 TG 0232
Swanwick, Derby 48 SK 4053
Swanwick, Hants 15 SU 5109
Swarby 50 TF 0440
Swardeston 53 TG 2002
Swarister 105 HU 5284
Swarkestone 48 SK 3628
Swarland 79 NU 1603
Swaton 50 TF 1337
Swavesey 41 TL 3668
Sway 14 SZ 2798
Swayfield 50 SK 9922
Swaythling 14 SU 4315
Sweffling 43 TM 3463
Swepstone 48 SK 3610
Swerford 35 SP 3731
Swettenham 57 SJ 8067
Swffyd 29 ST 2199
Swilland 43 TM 1852
Swillington 67 SE 3830
Swimbridge 11 SS 6229
Swinbrook 35 SP 2812
Swinderby 60 SK 8663
Swindon, Glos 34 SO 9325
Swindon, Staffs 37 SO 8690
Swindon, Wilts 22 SU 1585
Swine 63 TA 1335
Swinefleet 62 SE 7722
Swineshead, Lincs 51 TF 2340
Swineshead, Northnts 40 TL 0565
Swineshead Bridge 50 TF 2142
Swiney 103 ND 2335
Swinford, Leic 39 SP 5779
Swinford, Oxon 35 SP 4408
Swingfield Minnis 19 TR 2142
Swinhoe 85 NU 2028
Swinhope 61 TF 2196
Swinithwaite 72 SE 0489
Swinscoe 48 SK 1348
Swinside Hall 78 NT 7216
Swinstead 50 TF 0122
Swinton, Border 85 NT 8347
Swinton, G. Man 57 SD 7701
Swinton, N. Yks 66 SE 2179
Swinton, N. Yks 68 SE 7573
Swinton, S. Yks 59 SK 4598
Swintonmill 85 NT 8145
Swithland 49 SK 5413
Swordale 94 NH 5765
Swordland 101 NM 7891
Swordly 103 NC 7363
Sworton Heath 57 SJ 6884
Swyddffynnon 45 SN 6966
Swynnerton 47 SJ 8535
Swyre 13 SY 5288
Sychdyn or Soughton 56 SJ 2466
Syde 34 SO 9511
Sydenham, G. Lon 25 TQ 3571
Sydenham, Oxon 24 SP 7301
Sydenham Damerel 8 SX 4076
Syderstone 52 TF 8332
Sydling St Nicholas 13 SY 6399
Sydmonton 23 SU 4857
Syerston 49 SK 7447
Syke 57 SD 8915
Sykes 65 SD 6351
Syleham 43 TM 2178
Sylen 31 SN 5107
Symbister 105 HU 5462
Symington, Strath 81 NS 3831
Symington, Strath 83 NS 9935
Symondsbury 13 SY 4493
Symonds Yat 33 SO 5516
Synod Inn 31 SN 4054
Syre 103 NC 6943
Syreford 34 SP 0320
Syresham 39 SP 6341
Syston, Leic 49 SK 6211
Syston, Lincs 50 SK 9240
Sytchampton 37 SO 8466
Sywell 40 SP 8267

T

Tackley 35 SP 4820
Tacolneston 53 TM 1495
Tadcaster 67 SE 4843
Tadden 14 ST 9901
Taddington 58 SK 1471
Tadley 23 SU 6061
Tadlow 41 TL 2847
Tadmarton 38 SP 3937
Tadworth 16 TQ 2356
Tafarnaubach 29 SO 1210
Tafarn-y-Gelyn 56 SJ 1861
Taff's Well 29 ST 1283
Tafolwern 45 SH 8902
Tai-bach, Clwyd 46 SJ 1528
Taibach, W. Glam 29 SS 7789
Tain, Highld 103 ND 2266
Tain, Highld 103 NH 7882
Tai'n Lôn 54 SH 4450
Takeley 25 TL 5621
Talachddu 29 SO 0833
Talacre 56 SJ 1284
Talaton 12 SY 0699
Talbenny 30 SM 8412
Talerddig 45 SH 9300
Talgarreg 31 SN 4251
Talgarth 29 SO 1533
Taliesin 45 SN 6591
Talisker 100 NG 3230
Talke 47 SJ 8253
Talkin 71 NY 5457
Talladale 101 NG 9170
Tallantire 70 NY 1035
Tallarn Green 46 SJ 4444
Talley 31 SN 6332
Tallington 50 TF 0908
Talmine 103 NC 5863
Talog 31 SN 3325
Tal-sarn 31 SN 5456
Talsarnau 54 SH 6136
Talskiddy 7 SW 9165
Talwrn 54 SH 4877
Talybont, Dyfed 45 SN 6589
Tal-y-bont, Gwyn 44 SH 5921
Tal-y-Bont, Gwyn 55 SH 7668
Talybont-on-Usk 29 SO 1122
Tal-y-cafn 55 SH 7871
Tal-y-llyn, Gwyn 45 SH 7109
Talyllyn, Powys 29 SO 1027
Talysarn 54 SH 4853
Talywern 45 SH 8200
Tamerton Foliot 8 SX 4761
Tamworth 48 SK 2104
Tandridge 17 TQ 3750
Tanfield 72 NZ 1855
Tangasdale 100 NF 6400
Tangley 22 SU 3252
Tangmere 15 SU 9006
Tangwick 105 HU 2377
Tankerness 104 HY 5210
Tankersley 59 SK 3499
Tannach 103 ND 3247
Tannadice 93 NO 4758
Tannington 43 TM 2467
Tansley 59 SK 3259
Tansor 40 TL 0590
Tantobie 72 NZ 1754
Tanton 73 NZ 5210
Tanworth-in-Arden 38 SP 1170
Tan-y-fron 55 SH 9564
Tanygrisiau 55 SH 6945
Tan-y-groes 31 SN 2849
Taplow 24 SU 9182
Tarbert, Strath 99 NR 6182
Tarbert, Strath 80 NR 8668
Tarbert, W. Isles 98 NB 1500
Tarbet, Highld 102 NC 1648
Tarbet, Highld 101 NM 7992
Tarbet, Strath 86 NN 3104
Tarbock Green 56 SJ 4687
Tarbolton 81 NS 4327
Tarbrax 83 NT 0255
Tarfside 93 NO 4979
Tarland 96 NJ 4804
Tarleton 65 SD 4521
Tarlogie 103 NH 7583
Tarlscough 56 SD 4314
Tarlton 34 ST 9699
Tarnbrook 65 SD 5855
Tarporley 57 SJ 5562
Tarr 12 ST 1030
Tarrant Crawford 13 ST 9203
Tarrant Gunville 13 ST 9212
Tarrant Hinton 14 ST 9310
Tarrant Keyneston 13 ST 9204
Tarrant Launceston 14 ST 9409
Tarrant Monkton 14 ST 9408
Tarrant Rawston 14 ST 9306
Tarrant Rushton 14 ST 9305
Tarrel 103 NH 8981
Tarring Neville 17 TQ 4403
Tarrington 33 SO 6140
Tarskavaig 101 NG 5809
Tarves 97 NJ 8631
Tarvie 94 NH 4258
Tarvin 57 SJ 4967
Tasburgh 53 TM 2095
Tasley 47 SO 6994
Taston 35 SP 3621
Tatenhill 48 SK 2022
Tatham 65 SD 6069
Tathwell 61 TF 3282
Tatsfield 17 TQ 4157
Tattenhall 57 SJ 4858
Tatterford 52 TF 8628
Tattersett 52 TF 8429
Tattershall 61 TF 2157
Tattershall Bridge 50 TF 1956
Tattershall Thorpe 61 TF 2159
Tattingstone 43 TM 1337
Tatworth 12 ST 3205
Tauchers 96 NJ 3749
Taunton 12 ST 2224
Taverham 53 TG 1614
Tavernspite 31 SN 1812
Tavistock 8 SX 4774
Taw Green 9 SX 6596
Tawstock 11 SS 5529
Taxal 58 SK 0079
Tayinloan 80 NR 6946
Taynish 99 NR 7283
Taynton, Glos 34 SO 7321
Taynton, Oxon 35 SP 2313
Taynuilt 86 NN 0031
Tayport 89 NO 4528
Tay Road Bridge, Fife 89 NO 4129
Tay Road Bridge, Tays 89 NO 4129
Tayvallich 99 NR 7487
Tealby 61 TF 1590
Teanamachar 100 NF 7762
Teangue 101 NG 6609
Tebay 71 NY 6104
Tebworth 40 SP 9926
Tedburn St Mary 9 SX 8194
Teddington, G. Lon 25 TQ 1671
Teddington, Glos 34 SO 9633
Tedstone Delamere 37 SO 6958
Tedstone Wafre 37 SO 6759
Teeton 39 SP 6970
Teffont Evias 14 ST 9931
Teffont Magna 14 ST 9832
Tegryn 31 SN 2333
Teigh 50 SK 8616
Teigngrace 9 SX 8473
Teignmouth 9 SX 9473
Telford 47 SJ 6910
Tellisford 21 ST 8055
Telscombe 17 TQ 4003
Templand 77 NY 0886
Temple, Corn 7 SX 1473
Temple, Lothn 84 NT 3158
Temple, Strath 87 NS 5469
Temple Bar 31 SN 5354
Temple Cloud 21 ST 6257
Templecombe 13 ST 7022
Temple Ewell 19 TR 2844
Temple Grafton 38 SP 1255
Temple Guiting 34 SP 0928
Temple Hirst 67 SE 6025
Temple Normanton 59 SK 4167
Temple Sowerby 71 NY 6127
Templeton, Devon 11 SS 8813
Templeton, Dyfed 30 SN 1111
Tempsford 40 TL 1753
Tenbury Wells 37 SO 5968
Tenby 30 SN 1300
Tendring 27 TM 1424
Ten Mile Bank 52 TL 6096
Tenston 104 HY 2716
Tenterden 18 TQ 8833
Terling 26 TL 7715
Ternhill 47 SJ 6332
Terregles 76 NX 9376
Terril 71 NY 5026
Terrington 67 SE 6770
Terrington St Clement 51 TF 5520
Terrington St John 51 TF 5314
Teston 17 TQ 7053
Testwood 14 SU 3514
Tetbury 34 ST 8993
Tetbury Upton 34 ST 8895
Tetchill 46 SJ 3932
Tetcott 8 SX 3396
Tetford 61 TF 3374
Tetney 63 TA 3101
Tetney Lock 63 TA 3402
Tetsworth 24 SP 6601
Tettenhall 47 SJ 8800
Teversal 59 SK 4861
Teversham 41 TL 4958
Teviothead 77 NT 4005
Tewin 25 TL 2714
Tewkesbury 34 SO 8932
Teynham 18 TQ 9562
Thainston 93 NO 6375
Thakeham 16 TQ 1017
Thame 24 SP 7005
Thames Ditton 25 TQ 1567
Thamesmead 25 TQ 4780
Thaneston 93 NO 6374
Thanington 19 TR 1356
Thankerton 83 NS 9738
Tharston 53 TM 1894
Thatcham 23 SU 5167
Thatto Heath 57 SJ 5093
Thaxted 42 TL 6131
Theakston 67 SE 3085
Thealby 62 SE 8917
Theale, Berks 24 SU 6471
Theale, Somer 21 ST 4645
Thearne 62 TA 0736
Theberton 43 TM 4365
Thedden Grange 23 SU 6839
Theddingworth 39 SP 6685
Theddlethorpe All Saints 61 TF 4688
Theddlethorpe St Helen 61 TF 4788
Thelbridge Barton 11 SS 7812
Thelnetham 42 TM 0178
Thelwall 57 SJ 6487
Themelthorpe 52 TG 0523
Thenford 39 SP 5241
Therfield 41 TL 3377
Thetford 42 TL 8783
Theydon Bois 25 TQ 4598
Thickwood 21 ST 8272
Thimbleby, Lincs 61 TF 2369
Thimbleby, N. Yks 73 SE 4595
Thirkleby 67 SE 4778
Thirlby 67 SE 4884
Thirlestane 84 NT 5647
Thirn 66 SE 2186
Thirsk 67 SE 4382
Thistleton 50 SK 9117
Thistley Green 42 TL 6676
Thixendale 68 SE 8461
Tholomas Drove 51 TF 4006
Tholthorpe 67 SE 4766
Thomas Chapel 30 SN 1008
Thomastown 96 NJ 5736
Thompson 52 TL 9296
Thomshill 96 NJ 2157
Thong 18 TQ 6770
Thoralby 66 SE 0086
Thoresway 61 TF 1696
Thorganby, Lincs 61 TF 2197
Thorganby, N. Yks 62 SE 6942
Thorington 43 TM 4274
Thorington Street 42 TM 0135
Thorlby 66 SD 9652
Thorley 25 TL 4718
Thormanby 67 SE 4974
Thornaby-on-Tees 73 NZ 4516
Thornage 52 TG 0536
Thornborough, Bucks 39 SP 7433
Thornborough, N. Yks 67 SE 2979
Thornbury, Avon 21 ST 6490
Thornbury, Devon 10 SS 4008
Thornbury, H. & W 33 SO 6259
Thornby 39 SP 6775
Thorncliffe 58 SK 0158
Thorncombe 12 ST 3703
Thorncombe Street 16 TQ 0042
Thorndon 43 TM 1369
Thorndon Cross 9 SX 5393
Thorne 62 SE 6913
Thorner 67 SE 3840
Thorne St Margaret 12 ST 0921
Thorney, Cambs 51 TF 2804
Thorney, Notts 60 SK 8573
Thorney Hill 14 SZ 2099
Thornfalcon 12 ST 2823
Thornford 13 ST 6013
Thorngumbald 63 TA 2026
Thornham 52 TF 7343
Thornham Magna 43 TM 1071
Thornham Parva 43 TM 1172
Thornhaugh 50 TF 0600
Thornhill, Central 87 NS 6699
Thornhill, Derby 58 SK 1983
Thornhill, D. & G 76 NX 8795
Thornhill, Hants 15 SU 4712
Thornhill, M. Glam 29 ST 1584
Thornhill Edge 59 SE 2518
Thornicombe 13 ST 8703
Thornley, Durham 72 NZ 1137
Thornley, Durham 73 NZ 3639
Thornliebank 81 NS 5559
Thorns 42 TL 7455
Thornthwaite, Cumbr 70 NY 2225
Thornthwaite, N. Yks 66 SE 1758
Thornton, Bucks 39 SP 7535
Thornton, Fife 89 NT 2897
Thornton, Humbs 62 SE 7645
Thornton, Humbs 62 TA 0817
Thornton, Lancs 65 SD 3442
Thornton, Lincs 61 TF 2467
Thornton, Mers 56 SD 3300
Thornton, Northum 85 NT 9547
Thornton Dale 68 SE 8382
Thorntonhall 82 NS 5955
Thornton Hough 56 SJ 3081
Thornton-in-Craven 66 SD 9048
Thornton-le-Beans 73 SE 3990
Thornton-le-Clay 68 SE 6865
Thornton le Moor, Lincs 60 TF 0596
Thornton-le-Moor, N. Yks 67 SE 3988
Thornton-le-Moors 56 SJ 4474
Thorntonloch 84 NT 7574
Thornton Rust 66 SD 9788
Thornton Steward 66 SE 1787
Thornton Watlass 67 SE 2385
Thornwood Common 25 TL 4704
Thoroton 49 SK 7642
Thorp Arch 67 SE 4345
Thorpe, Cumbr 71 NY 4926
Thorpe, Derby 48 SK 1550
Thorpe, Lincs 61 TF 4982
Thorpe, Norf 53 TM 4398
Thorpe, Notts 49 SK 7649
Thorpe, N. Yks 66 SE 0161
Thorpe, Surrey 24 TQ 0268
Thorpe Abbotts 43 TM 1979
Thorpe Acre 49 SK 5120
Thorpe Arnold 49 SK 7720
Thorpe Audlin 59 SE 4716
Thorpe Bassett 68 SE 8673
Thorpe Bay 26 TQ 9185
Thorpe by Water 50 SP 8996
Thorpe Constantine 48 SK 2609
Thorpe End 53 TG 2811
Thorpe Fendykes 61 TF 4560
Thorpe Green 42 TL 9354
Thorpe Hesley 59 SK 3796
Thorpe in Balne 59 SE 5910
Thorpe Langton 39 SP 7492
Thorpe Larches 73 NZ 3826
Thorpe le Fallows 60 SK 9180
Thorpe-le-Soken 27 TM 1822
Thorpe Malsor 40 SP 8379
Thorpe Mandeville 39 SP 5344
Thorpe Market 53 TG 2435
Thorpe Morieux 42 TL 9453
Thorpeness 43 TM 4759
Thorpe on the Hill 60 SK 9065
Thorpe Salvin 59 SK 5281
Thorpe Satchville 49 SK 7311
Thorpe St Andrew 53 TG 2609
Thorpe Thewles 73 NZ 4023
Thorpe Underwood 67 SE 4659
Thorpe Waterville 40 TL 0281
Thorpe Willoughby 67 SE 5730

Thorp St Peter 61 TF 4860
Thorrington 27 TM 0920
Thorverton 11 SS 9202
Thrandeston 43 TM 1176
Thrapston 40 SP 9978
Threapwood 46 SJ 4445
Three Bridges 17 TQ 2837
Three Cocks 33 SO 1737
Three Crosses 28 SS 5794
Three Holes 51 TF 5000
Threekingham 50 TF 0836
Three Leg Cross 17 TQ 6831
Three Legged Cross 14 SU 0506
Three Mile Cross 24 SU 7167
Threemilestone 7 SW 7844
Threlkeld 70 NY 3125
Threshfield 66 SD 9863
Thrigby 53 TG 4612
Thringarth 72 NY 9322
Thringstone 48 SK 4217
Thrintoft 72 SE 3293
Thriplow 41 TL 4346
Throcking 41 TL 3330
Throckley 79 NZ 1566
Throckmorton 38 SO 9849
Throphill 79 NZ 1385
Thropton 79 NU 0202
Throwleigh 9 SX 6690
Throwley 19 TQ 9955
Throwley Forestal 19 TQ 9854
Thrumpton 49 SK 5031
Thrumster 103 ND 3345
Thrunton 79 NU 0810
Thrupp, Glos 34 SO 8603
Thrupp, Oxon 35 SP 4815
Thrushelton 8 SX 4487
Thrushgill 65 SD 6562
Thruxton, Hants 22 SU 2945
Thruxton, H. & W 33 SO 4334
Thrybergh 59 SK 4695
Thundersley 26 TQ 7988
Thurcaston 49 SK 5610
Thurcroft 59 SK 4988
Thurgarton, Norf 53 TG 1834
Thurgarton, Notts 49 SK 6949
Thurgoland 59 SE 2901
Thurlaston, Leic 49 SP 5099
Thurlaston, Warw 39 SP 4670
Thurlby, Lincs 60 SK 9061
Thurlby, Lincs 50 TF 0916
Thurleigh 40 TL 0558
Thurlestone 9 SX 6742
Thurloxton 12 ST 2730
Thurlstone 59 SE 2303
Thurlton 53 TM 4198
Thurmaston 49 SK 6109
Thurnham, Kent 18 TQ 8057
Thurnham, Lancs 65 SD 4554
Thurning, Norf 53 TG 0829
Thurning, Northnts 40 TL 0883
Thurnscoe 59 SE 4505
Thursby 70 NY 3250
Thursford 52 TF 9833
Thursley 23 SU 9039
Thurso 103 ND 1168
Thurstaston 56 SJ 2484
Thurston 42 TL 9265
Thurstonfield 70 NY 3156
Thurstonland 58 SE 1610
Thurton 53 TG 3200
Thurvaston 48 SK 2437
Thuxton 52 TG 0307
Thwaite, N. Yks 72 SD 8998
Thwaite, Suff 43 TM 1168
Thwaite St Mary 53 TM 3395
Thwing 69 TA 0570
Tibbermore 88 NO 0523
Tibberton, Glos 34 SO 7622
Tibberton, H. & W 37 SO 9057
Tibberton, Shrops 47 SJ 6820
Tibshelf 59 SK 4360
Tibthorpe 69 SE 9655
Ticehurst 17 TQ 6930
Tichborne 15 SU 5730
Tickencote 50 SK 9809
Tickenham 21 ST 4471
Tickhill 59 SK 5893
Ticklerton 36 SO 4890
Ticknall 48 SK 3523
Tickton 62 TA 0641
Tidcombe 22 SU 2958
Tiddington, Oxon 24 SP 6504
Tiddington, Warw 38 SP 2255
Tidebrook 17 TQ 6129
Tideford 8 SX 3459
Tidenham 33 ST 5596
Tideswell 58 SK 1575
Tidmarsh 24 SU 6374
Tidmington 38 SP 2638
Tidpit 14 SU 0719
Tiers Cross 30 SM 9010
Tiffield 39 SP 6951
Tifty 97 NJ 7740
Tigerton 93 NO 5464
Tigharry 100 NF 7172
Tighnabruaich 86 NR 9772
Tighnafiline 102 NG 8789
Tigley 9 SX 7560
Tilbrook 40 TL 0869
Tilbury 18 TQ 6376
Tile Cross 38 SP 1686
Tile Hill 38 SP 2878
Tilehurst 24 SU 6673
Tilford 23 SU 8743
Tillathrowie 96 NJ 4735
Tillicoultry 88 NS 9196
Tillingham 27 TL 9903
Tillington, H. & W 33 SO 4645
Tillington, W. Susx 16 SU 9621
Tillington Common 33 SO 4546
Tillycorthie 97 NJ 9023
Tillydrine 93 NO 6098
Tillyfourie 96 NJ 6412
Tillygreig 97 NJ 8823
Tilmanstone 19 TR 3051
Tilney All Saints 51 TF 5617
Tilney High End 51 TF 5617
Tilney St Lawrence 51 TF 5413
Tilshead 22 SU 0347
Tilstock 47 SJ 5437
Tilston 46 SJ 4651
Tilstone Fearnall 57 SJ 5660
Tilsworth 24 SP 9724
Tilton on the Hill 49 SK 7405
Timberland 61 TF 1258
Timbersbrook 57 SJ 8962
Timberscombe 11 SS 9542
Timble 66 SE 1853
Timperley 57 SJ 7888
Timsbury, Avon 21 ST 6658
Timsbury, Hants 14 SU 3424
Timsgarry 98 NB 0534
Timworth Green 42 TL 8669
Tincleton 13 SY 7791
Tindale 78 NY 6159
Tingewick 39 SP 6532
Tingley 67 SE 2826
Tingrith 40 TL 0032
Tinhay 8 SX 3985
Tinshill 67 SE 2539
Tinsley 59 SK 4090
Tintagel 8 SX 0588
Tintern Parva 33 SO 5301
Tintinhull 13 ST 4919
Tintwhistle 58 SK 0297
Tinwald 76 NY 0081
Tinwell 50 TF 0006
Tipperty 97 NJ 9627
Tipton 38 SO 9592
Tipton St John 12 SY 0991
Tiptree 26 TL 8916
Tirabad 32 SN 8841
Tiree Aerodrome 100 NM 0045
Tirley 34 SO 8328
Tirphil 29 SO 1303
Tisbury 14 ST 9429
Tissington 48 SK 1752
Titchberry 10 SS 2427
Titchfied 15 SU 5305
Titchmarsh 40 TL 0279
Titchwell 52 TF 7643
Titley 33 SO 3360
Titlington 79 NU 0915
Tittensor 47 SJ 8738
Tittleshall 52 TF 8921
Tiverton, Ches 57 SJ 5560
Tiverton, Devon 11 SS 9512
Tivetshall St Margaret 43 TM 1686
Tivetshall St Mary 43 TM 1686
Tixall 48 SJ 9722
Tixover 50 SK 9700
Toab, Orkney 104 HY 5106
Toab, Shetld 105 HU 3811
Tobermory 99 NM 5055
Toberonochy 99 NM 7408
Tobson 98 NB 1338
Tocher 97 NJ 6932
Tockenham 22 SU 0479
Tockenham Wick 22 SU 0381
Tockholes 65 SD 6623
Tockington 21 ST 6086
Tockwith 67 SE 4752
Todber 13 ST 7920
Toddington, Beds 40 TL 0028
Toddington, Glos 34 SP 0332
Todenham 38 SP 2436
Todhills 77 NY 3663
Todmorden 66 SD 9324
Todwick 59 SK 4984
Toft, Cambs 41 TL 3656
Toft, Lincs 50 TF 0617
Toft Hill 72 NZ 1528
Toft Monks 53 TM 4294
Toft next Newton 60 TF 0488
Toftrees 52 TF 8927
Toftwood 52 TF 9911
Togston 79 NU 2401
Tokavaig 101 NG 6011
Tokers Green 24 SU 6977
Tolland 12 ST 1032
Tollard Royal 14 ST 9417
Toll Bar 59 SE 5508
Toller Fratrum 13 SY 5797
Toller Porcorum 13 SY 5697
Tollerton, Notts 49 SK 6034
Tollerton, N. Yks 67 SE 5164
Tollesbury 26 TL 9510
Tolleshunt D'Arcy 26 TL 9211
Tolleshunt Major 26 TL 9011
Tolpuddle 13 SY 7994
Tolsta Chaolais 98 NB 1937
Tolworth 25 TQ 1965
Tomatin 95 NH 8029
Tombreck 95 NH 6934
Tomchrasky 94 NH 2512
Tomdoun 90 NH 1501
Tomich, Highld 94 NH 3027
Tomich, Highld 103 NH 7071
Tomintoul, Grampn 96 NJ 1618
Tomintoul, Grampn 92 NO 1490
Tomnavoulin 96 NJ 2126
Tonbridge 17 TQ 5947
Tondu 29 SS 8984
Tong, Shrops 47 SJ 7907
Tong, W. Isles 98 NB 4436
Tonge 48 SK 4123
Tongham 23 SU 8849
Tongland 75 NX 6953
Tongue 103 NC 5956
Tongwynlais 29 ST 1382
Tonna 29 SS 7799
Ton-teg 29 ST 0986
Tonwell 25 TL 3317
Tonypandy 29 SS 9992
Tonyrefail 29 ST 0188
Toot Baldon 35 SP 5600
Toot Hill, Essex 25 TL 5102
Toothill, Hants 14 SU 3818
Topcliffe 67 SE 4026
Topcroft 43 TM 2692
Topcroft Street 43 TM 2691
Toppesfield 42 TL 7337
Toppings 57 SD 7213
Topsham 9 SX 9688
Torbay 9 SX 8962
Torbeg 80 NR 9029
Torbryan 9 SX 8166
Torcross 9 SX 8242
Tore 94 NH 6052
Torksey 60 SK 8378
Torlum 100 NF 7851
Torlundy 90 NN 1477
Tormarton 21 ST 7778
Tormitchell 74 NX 2394
Tormore 80 NR 8932
Tornagrain 95 NH 7649
Tornahaish 96 NJ 2908
Tornaveen 96 NJ 6106
Torness 94 NH 5827
Torpenhow 70 NY 2039
Torphichen 88 NS 9672
Torphins 93 NJ 6202
Torpoint 8 SX 4355
Torquay 9 SX 9164
Torquhan 84 NT 4447
Torran 101 NG 5948
Torrance 87 NS 6274
Torridon 101 NG 8956
Torrin 101 NG 5720
Torrisdale 103 NC 6761
Torrisholme 65 SD 4564
Torroble 103 NC 5904
Torry, Grampn 96 NJ 4340
Torry, Grampn 97 NJ 9505
Torrylin 80 NR 9521
Torterston 97 NK 0747
Torthorwald 77 NY 0378
Tortington 16 TQ 0005
Tortworth 34 ST 7093
Torvaig 101 NG 4944
Torver 70 SD 2894
Torworth 59 SK 6586
Toscaig 101 NG 7138
Toseland 41 TL 2362
Tosside 66 SD 7756
Tostock 42 TL 9563
Totaig 100 NG 2050
Totarol 98 NB 1834
Tote, Highld 101 NG 4149
Tote, Highld 101 NG 5159
Totegan 103 NC 8268
Totland 14 SZ 3287
Totley 59 SK 3079
Totnes 9 SX 8060
Totscore 101 NG 3866
Tottenham 25 TQ 3390
Tottenhill 52 TF 6410
Totteridge, Bucks 24 SU 8793
Totteridge, G. Lon 25 TQ 2494
Totternhoe 24 SP 9821
Tottington 57 SD 7712
Totton 14 SU 3613
Tournaig 102 NG 8783
Toux, Grampn 96 NJ 5459
Toux, Grampn 97 NJ 9850
Tovil 17 TQ 7554
Toward 76 NS 6812
Towcester 39 SP 6948
Towednack 6 SW 4838
Towersey 24 SP 7305
Towie 96 NJ 4412
Towiemore 96 NJ 3945
Tow Law 72 NZ 1139
Town End 51 TL 4195
Townhead, Cumbr 71 NY 6334
Townhead, D. & G 75 NX 6946
Townhead of Greenlaw 76 NX 7464
Townhill 88 NT 1089
Townshend 6 SW 5932
Town Yetholm 85 NT 8228
Towthorpe 67 SE 6258
Towton 67 SE 4839
Towyn 55 SH 9779
Toynton All Saints 61 TF 3964
Toynton Fen Side 61 TF 3962
Toynton St Peter 61 TF 4063
Toy's Hill 17 TQ 4651
Trabboch 81 NS 4321
Trabbochburn 81 NS 4621
Traboe 6 SW 7421
Tradespark, Highld 95 NH 8656
Tradespark, Orkney 104 HY 4508
Trafford Park 57 SJ 7896
Trallong 29 SN 9629
Trallwng or Welshpool 46 SJ 2207
Tranent 89 NT 4072
Trantlemore 103 NC 8953
Tranwell 79 NZ 1883
Trapp 31 SN 6519
Traprain 89 NT 5975
Traquair 84 NT 3334
Trawden 66 SD 9138
Trawsfynydd 55 SH 7035
Trealaw 29 ST 0092
Treales 65 SD 4433
Trearddur 54 SH 2579
Treaslane 101 NG 3953
Trebartha 8 SX 2677
Trebetherick 7 SW 9377
Treborough 12 ST 0136
Trebudannon 7 SW 8961
Treburley 8 SX 3477
Trecastle 29 SN 8829
Trecwn 30 SM 9632
Trecynon 29 SN 9903
Tredavoe 6 SW 4528
Tredegar 29 SO 1409
Tredington 38 SP 2543
Tredinnick 7 SW 9270
Tredomen 29 SO 1231
Tredrizzick 7 SW 9576
Tredunnock 33 ST 3894
Treen 6 SW 3923
Treeton 59 SK 4387
Trefdraeth 54 SH 4070
Trefeca 29 SO 1432
Trefeglwys 45 SN 9790
Trefenter 44 SN 6068
Treffgarne 30 SM 9523
Treffynnon 30 SM 8428
Trefil 29 SO 1212
Trefilan 31 SN 5557
Trefnanney 46 SJ 2015
Trefnant 55 SJ 0570
Trefonen 46 SJ 2527
Trefor 54 SH 3780
Treforest 29 ST 0889
Trefriw 55 SH 7863
Tregadillett 8 SX 2983
Tregaian 54 SH 4579
Tregare 33 SO 4110
Tregaron 32 SN 6860
Tregarth 54 SH 6068
Tregeare 8 SX 2486
Tregeiriog 46 SJ 1733
Tregele 54 SH 3592
Tregidden 6 SW 7522
Treglemais 30 SM 8229
Tregole 8 SX 1998
Tregonetha 7 SW 9563
Tregony 7 SW 9244
Tregoyd 33 SO 1937
Tre-groes 31 SN 4044
Tregurrian 7 SW 8565
Tregynon 45 SO 0998
Trehafod 29 ST 0491
Treharris 29 ST 0997
Treherbert 29 SS 9498
Treknow 8 SX 0586
Trelan 6 SW 7418
Trelawnyd 55 SJ 0979
Trelech 31 SN 2830
Treleddyd-fawr 30 SM 7527
Trelewis 29 ST 1097
Treligga 8 SX 0584
Trelights 7 SW 9979
Trelill 7 SX 0478
Trelissik 7 SW 8339
Trelleck 33 SO 5005
Trelleck Grange 33 SO 4901
Trelogan 56 SJ 1180
Tremadog 54 SH 5640
Tremail 8 SX 1686
Tremain 31 SN 2348
Tremaine 8 SX 2388
Tremar 7 SX 2568
Trematon 8 SX 3959
Tremeirchion 55 SJ 0873
Trenance 7 SW 8567
Trenarren 7 SX 0348
Trench 47 SJ 6913
Treneglos 8 SX 2088
Trenewan 7 SX 1753
Trent 13 ST 5918
Trentham 47 SJ 8741
Trentishoe 11 SS 6448
Treoes 29 SS 9478
Treorchy 29 SS 9596
Tre'r-ddôl 45 SN 6692
Tresaith 31 SN 2851
Trescott 47 SO 8497
Trescowe 6 SW 5730
Tresham 21 ST 7991
Tresillian 7 SW 8646
Tresinwen 30 SM 9040
Tresmeer 8 SX 2387
Tressait 91 NN 8160
Tresta 105 HU 3651
Treswell 60 SK 7879
Trethewey 6 SW 3823
Trethomas 29 ST 1889
Trethurgy 7 SX 0355
Tretio 30 SM 7829
Tretire 33 SO 5224
Tretower 29 SO 1821
Treuddyn 56 SJ 2558
Trevalga 8 SX 0890
Trevanson 7 SW 9772
Trevarren 7 SW 9160
Trevarrick 7 SW 9843
Trevellas 6 SW 7452
Treverva 6 SW 7531
Trevethin 33 SO 2802
Trevigro 8 SX 3369
Trevine 30 SM 8432
Treviscoe 7 SW 9456
Trevone 7 SW 8975
Trevor 54 SH 3746
Trewarmett 8 SX 0686
Trewarthenick 7 SW 9044
Trewassa 8 SX 1486
Trewellard 6 SW 3733
Trewen 8 SX 2583
Trewidland 7 SX 2559
Trewint 8 SX 1897
Trewithian 7 SW 8737
Trewoon 7 SW 9952
Treyarnon 7 SW 8673
Treyford 15 SU 8218
Trickett's Cross 14 SU 0901
Trimdon 73 NZ 3633
Trimdon Grange 73 NZ 3635
Trimingham 53 TG 2738
Trimley St Martin 43 TM 2738
Trimley St Mary 43 TM 2836
Trimpley 37 SO 7978
Trimsaran 31 SN 4504
Trimstone 10 SS 5043
Trinant 29 SO 2000
Tring 24 SP 9211
Trinity 93 NO 6062
Trislaig 90 NN 0874
Trispen 7 SW 8450
Tritlington 79 NZ 2092
Trochry 92 NN 9740
Troedyraur 31 SN 3245
Troedyrhiw 29 SO 0702
Trofarth 55 SH 8571
Trondavoe 105 HU 3770
Troon, Corn 6 SW 6638
Troon, Strath 81 NS 3230
Troston 42 TL 8972
Trottiscliffe 18 TQ 6460
Trotton 15 SU 8322
Troutbeck 71 NY 4003
Troutbeck Bridge 71 NY 4000
Trowbridge 21 ST 8557
Trow Green 33 SO 5706
Trowle Common 21 ST 8458
Trows 84 NT 6932
Trowse Newton 53 TG 2406
Trudoxhill 21 ST 7443
Trull 12 ST 2122
Trumisgarry 98 NF 8675
Trumpan 100 NG 2261
Trumpet 37 SO 6539
Trumpington 41 TL 4454
Trunch 53 TG 2834
Truro 7 SW 8244
Trusham 9 SX 8582
Trusley 48 SK 2535
Trusthorpe 61 TF 5183
Trysull 47 SO 8594
Tubney 35 SU 4398
Tuckenhay 9 SX 8156
Tuckhill 37 SO 7888
Tuddenham, Suff 42 TL 7371
Tuddenham, Suff 43 TM 1948
Tudeley 17 TQ 6245
Tudhoe 72 NZ 2635
Tudweiliog 54 SH 2336
Tuffley 34 SO 8315
Tufton 30 SN 0428
Tugby 49 SK 7600
Tugford 36 SO 5587
Tullibody 88 NS 8695
Tullich 86 NN 0815
Tullich Muir 103 NH 7373
Tulloch 93 NO 7771
Tullynessle 96 NJ 5519
Tumble 31 SN 5411
Tumby Woodside 61 TF 2657
Tummel Bridge 91 NN 7659
Tunbridge Wells, Royal 17 TQ 5839
Tunstall, Humbs 63 TA 3031
Tunstall, Kent 18 TQ 8961
Tunstall, Lancs 65 SD 6073
Tunstall, Norf 53 TG 4108
Tunstall, N. Yks 72 SE 2196
Tunstall, Staffs 47 SJ 8651
Tunstall, Suff 43 TM 3655
Tunstead 53 TG 2921
Tunworth 23 SU 6748
Tupsley 33 SO 5340
Tupton 59 SK 3966
Turgis Green 24 SU 6959
Turkdean 34 SP 1017
Tur Langton 49 SP 7194
Turnastone 33 SO 3536
Turnberry 81 NS 2005
Turnditch 48 SK 2946
Turners Hill 17 TQ 3135
Turners Puddle 13 SY 8393
Turnworth 13 ST 8207
Turriff 97 NJ 7250
Turton Bottoms 57 SD 7415
Turves 51 TL 3396
Turvey 40 SP 9452
Turville 24 SU 7691
Turville Heath 24 SU 7491
Turweston 39 SP 6037
Tutbury 48 SK 2128
Tutnall 38 SO 9970
Tutshill 33 ST 5494
Tuttington 53 TG 2227
Tuxford 60 SK 7370
Twatt, Orkney 104 HY 2724
Twatt, Shetld 105 HU 3253
Twechar 87 NS 7075
Tweedmouth 85 NT 9952
Tweedsmuir 83 NT 1024
Twelveheads 6 SW 7642
Twemloe Green 57 SJ 7868
Twenty 50 TF 1520
Twerton 21 ST 7264
Twickenham 25 TQ 1473
Twigworth 34 SO 8522
Twineham 16 TQ 2519
Twinhoe 21 ST 7459
Twinstead 42 TL 8636
Twitchen, Devon 11 SS 7830
Twitchen, Shrops 36 SO 3779
Two Bridges 9 SX 6074
Two Dales 59 SK 2863
Two Gates 48 SK 2101
Twycross 48 SK 3305
Twyford, Berks 24 SU 7975
Twyford, Bucks 39 SP 6626
Twyford, Hants 15 SU 4825
Twyford, Leic 49 SK 7210
Twyford, Norf 52 TG 0124
Twyford Common 33 SO 5135
Twynholm 75 NX 6654
Twyning 37 SO 9037
Twyning Green 37 SO 9036
Twynllanan 29 SN 7524
Twyn-y-Sheriff 33 SO 4005
Twywell 40 SP 9578
Tyberton 33 SO 3839
Tyburn 38 SP 1391
Tycroes 31 SN 6010
Tycrwyn 45 SJ 1018
Tydd Gote 51 TF 4517
Tydd St Giles 51 TF 4216
Tydd St Mary 51 TF 4418
Tŷ-hen 54 SH 1731
Tyldesley 57 SD 7001
Tyler Hill 19 TR 1460
Tylers Green 24 SU 9094
Tylorstown 29 ST 0195
Tylwch 45 SN 9780
Ty-nant, Clwyd 55 SH 9944
Ty-nant, Gwyn 45 SH 9026
Tyndrum 86 NN 3330
Tyneham 13 SY 8880
Tynehead 84 NT 3959
Tynemouth 79 NZ 3669
Tynewydd 29 SS 9399
Tyninghame 89 NT 6079
Tynribbie 90 NM 9346
Tynron 76 NX 8092
Tyn-y-ffridd 46 SJ 1130
Tynygraig, Dyfed 45 SN 6969
Tyn-y-graig, Powys 32 SO 0250
Ty'n-y-groes 55 SH 7771
Ty Rhiw 29 ST 1284
Tyringham 40 SP 8547
Tythby 49 SK 6936
Tythegston 29 SS 8578
Tytherington, Avon 21 ST 6688
Tytherington, Ches 57 SJ 9175
Tytherington, Somer 21 ST 7645
Tytherington, Wilts 21 ST 9141
Tytherleigh 12 ST 3103
Tywardreath 7 SX 0854
Tywyn, Gwyn 44 SH 5800
Tywyn, Gwyn 55 SH 7978

U

Uachdar 100 NF 8055
Uags 101 NG 7234
Ubbeston Green 43 TM 3272
Ubley 21 ST 5258
Uckerby 72 NZ 2402
Uckfield 17 TQ 4721
Uckington 34 SO 9124
Uddingston 82 NS 6960
Uddington 83 NS 8633
Udimore 18 TQ 8619
Udny Green 97 NJ 8826
Udny Station 97 NJ 9124
Uffcott 22 SU 1277
Uffculme 12 ST 0612
Uffington, Lincs 50 TF 0607
Uffington, Oxon 22 SU 3089
Uffington, Shrops 47 SJ 5213
Ufford, Cambs 50 TF 0904
Ufford, Suff 43 TM 2952
Ufton 38 SP 3762
Ufton Nervet 24 SU 6367
Ugadale 80 NR 7828
Ugborough 9 SX 6755
Uggeshall 43 TM 4480
Ugglebarnby 69 NZ 8807
Ugley 41 TL 5228
Ugley Green 41 TL 5227
Ugthorpe 73 NZ 7911
Uig, Highld 100 NG 1952
Uig, Highld 101 NG 3963
Uigshader 101 NG 4246
Uisken 99 NM 3919
Ulbster 103 ND 3241
Ulceby, Humbs 63 TA 1215
Ulceby, Lincs 61 TF 4272
Ulcombe 18 TQ 8449
Uldale 70 NY 2537
Uley 34 ST 7998
Ulgham 79 NZ 2392
Ullapool 102 NH 1294
Ullenhall 38 SP 1267
Ullenwood 34 SO 9416
Ulleskelf 67 SE 5240
Ullesthorpe 39 SP 5087
Ulley 59 SK 4687
Ullingswick 33 SO 5950
Ullinish 100 NG 3238
Ullock 70 NY 0724
Ulpha 70 SD 1993
Ulsta 105 HU 4680
Ultrome 69 TA 1656
Ulverston 65 SD 2877
Ulzieside 76 NS 7708
Umberleigh 11 SS 6023
Unapool 102 NC 2333
Underbarrow 71 SD 4691
Underriver 17 TQ 5552
Underwood, Gwent 20 ST 3889
Underwood, Notts 49 SK 4750
Undy 21 ST 4387
Unifirth 105 HU 2856
Union Mills 64 SC 3577
Unstone 59 SK 3777
Unthank 71 NY 4536
Upavon 22 SU 1355
Up Cerne 13 ST 6502
Upchurch 18 TQ 8467
Upcott 33 SO 3251
Upend 42 TL 7058
Up Exe 11 SS 9402
Uphall 88 NT 0672
Uphall Station 88 NT 0670
Upham, Devon 11 SS 8808
Upham, Hants 15 SU 5320
Up Hatherley 34 SO 9120
Uphill 20 ST 3158
Up Holland 57 SD 5105
Uplawmoor 81 NS 4355
Upleadon 34 SO 7527
Upleatham 73 NZ 6319
Uploders 13 SY 5093
Uplowman 12 ST 0115
Uplyme 12 SY 3293
Upminster 25 TQ 5686
Up Nately 23 SU 6951
Upnor 18 TQ 7570
Upottery 12 ST 2007
Upper Affcot 36 SO 4486
Upper Ardchronie 103 NH 6188
Upper Arley 37 SO 7680
Upper Astrop 39 SP 5137
Upper Basildon 23 SU 5976
Upper Bayble 98 NB 5331
Upper Beeding 16 TQ 2010
Upper Benefield 40 SP 9889
Upper Boddington 39 SP 4853
Upper Borth 44 SN 6088
Upper Breinton 33 SO 4640
Upper Broughton 49 SK 6826
Upper Bucklebury 23 SU 5468
Upper Caldecote 40 TL 1645
Upper Chapel 32 SO 0040
Upper Chute 22 SU 2953
Upper Clatford 22 SU 3543
Upper Clynnog 54 SH 4646
Upper Coll 98 NB 4539
Upper Dallachy 96 NJ 3662
Upper Dean 40 TL 0467
Upper Denby 59 SE 2207
Upper Derraid 95 NJ 0233
Upper Dicker 17 TQ 5510
Upper Dunsforth 67 SE 4463
Upper Elkstone 58 SK 0559
Upper End 58 SK 0976
Upper Ethie 95 NH 7663
Upper Farringdon 15 SU 7135
Upper Framilode 34 SO 7510
Upper Froyle 23 SU 7543
Upper Gravenhurst 40 TL 1136
Upper Green 22 SU 3763
Upper Hackney 59 SK 2961
Upper Hale 23 SU 8449
Upper Hambleton 50 SK 9007
Upper Hardres Court 19 TR 1550
Upper Hartfield 17 TQ 4734
Upper Heath 36 SO 5685
Upper Helmsley 68 SE 6956
Upper Heyford, Northnts 39 SP 6659
Upper Heyford, Oxon 35 SP 4926
Upper Hill 33 SO 4753
Upper Hopton 58 SE 1918
Upper Hulme 58 SK 0161
Upper Inglesham 35 SU 2096
Upper Killay 28 SS 5892
Upper Knockando 96 NJ 1843
Upper Lambourne 22 SU 3180
Upper Lochton 93 NO 6997
Upper Longdon 48 SK 0614
Upper Longwood 47 SJ 6007
Upper Lydbrook 33 SO 6015
Upper Maes-coed 33 SO 3334
Uppermill 58 SD 9905
Upper Minety 22 SU 0090
Upper North Dean 24 SU 8498
Upper Poppleton 67 SE 5554
Upper Quinton 38 SP 1746
Upper Sanday 104 HY 5403
Upper Sapey 37 SO 6863
Upper Seagry 22 ST 9480
Upper Shelton 40 SP 9943
Upper Sheringham 53 TG 1441
Upper Skelmorlie 81 NS 1967
Upper Slaughter 35 SP 1523
Upper Soudley 34 SO 6610
Upper Stondon 40 TL 1435
Upper Stowe 39 SP 6456
Upper Street, Hants 14 SU 1518
Upper Street, Norf 53 TG 3517
Upper Sundon 40 TL 0427
Upper Swainswick 21 ST 7568
Upper Swell 35 SP 1726
Upper Tean 48 SK 0139
Upperthong 58 SE 1308
Upper Tillyrie 88 NO 1006
Upperton 16 SU 9522
Upper Tooting 25 TQ 2772
Uppertown 103 ND 3576
Upper Tysoe 38 SP 3343
Upper Upham 22 SU 2277
Upper Wardington 39 SP 4945
Upper Weald 39 SP 8037
Upper Weedon 39 SP 6258
Upper Wield 23 SU 6238
Upper Winchendon 24 SP 7414
Upper Woodford 14 SU 1237
Uppingham 50 SP 8699
Uppington 47 SJ 5909
Upsall 67 SE 4587
Upshire 25 TL 4101
Up Somborne 14 SU 3932
Upstreet 19 TR 2263
Up Sydling 13 ST 6201
Upton, Berks 24 SU 9879
Upton, Bucks 24 SP 7711
Upton, Cambs 50 TF 1000
Upton, Cambs 40 TL 1778
Upton, Ches 56 SJ 4169
Upton, Dorset 14 SY 9693
Upton, Hants 22 SU 3655
Upton, Hants 14 SU 3717
Upton, Leic 48 SP 3699
Upton, Lincs 60 SK 8686
Upton, Mers 56 SJ 2788
Upton, Norf 53 TG 3912
Upton, Northnts 39 SP 7160
Upton, Notts 49 SK 7354
Upton, Notts 60 SK 7476
Upton, Oxon 23 SU 5186
Upton, Somer 11 SS 9929
Upton, W. Yks 59 SE 4713
Upton Bishop 34 SO 6527
Upton Cheyney 21 ST 6969
Upton Cressett 37 SO 6592
Upton Cross 8 SX 2872
Upton Grey 23 SU 6948
Upton Hellions 11 SS 8403
Upton Lovell 22 ST 9440
Upton Magna 47 SJ 5512
Upton Noble 21 ST 7139
Upton Pyne 9 SX 9197
Upton Scudamore 21 ST 8647
Upton Snodsbury 37 SO 9454
Upton St Leonards 34 SO 8615
Upton upon Severn 37 SO 8540
Upton Warren 37 SO 9367
Upwaltham 16 SU 9413
Upware 41 TL 5370
Upwell, Cambs 51 TF 5002
Upwell, Norf 51 TF 5002
Upwey 13 SY 6684
Upwood 41 TL 2682
Urafirth 105 HU 3078
Urchfont 22 SU 0457
Urdimarsh 33 SO 5249
Urgha 98 NG 1799
Urishay Common 33 SO 3137
Urlay Nook 73 NZ 4014
Urmston 57 SJ 7594
Urquhart 96 NJ 2862
Urra 73 NZ 5701
Urray 94 NH 5052
Urswick 64 SD 2673
Ushaw Moor 72 NZ 2242
Usk 33 SO 3701
Usselby 61 TF 0993
Utley 66 SE 0542
Uton 9 SX 8298
Utterby 61 TF 3093
Uttoxeter 48 SK 0933
Uwchmynydd 44 SH 1525
Uxbridge 24 TQ 0583
Uyeasound 105 HP 5901
Uzmaston 30 SM 9714

V

Valleyfield 88 NT 0086
Valsgarth 105 HP 6413
Valtos, Highld 101 NG 5163
Valtos, W. Isles 98 NB 0937
Vange 26 TQ 7287
Varteg 33 SO 2606
Vatersay 100 NL 6394
Vatten 100 NG 2843
Vauld, The 33 SO 5349
Vaynor 29 SO 0510
Vaynor Park 46 SJ 1700
Veensgarth 105 HU 4244
Velindre 33 SO 1836
Veness 104 HY 5729
Vennington 46 SJ 3409
Venn Ottery 12 SY 0791
Ventnor 15 SZ 5677
Vernham Dean 22 SU 3456
Vernham Street 22 SU 3557
Vernolds Common 36 SO 4780
Verran Island 100 NF 7234
Verwig 31 SN 1849
Verwood 14 SU 0908
Veryan 7 SW 9139
Vicarage 12 SY 2088
Vickerstown 64 SD 1868
Victoria 7 SW 9861
Vidlin 105 HU 4765
Viewpark 82 NS 7161
Village Abberley, The 37 SO 7567
Village, The 37 SO 8989
Vinehall Street 17 TQ 7520
Vines Cross 17 TQ 5917
Virginia Water 24 SU 9967
Virginstow 8 SX 3792
Vobster 21 ST 7049
Voe 105 HU 4062
Vowchurch 33 SO 3636

W

Waberthwaite 70 SD 1093
Wackerfield 72 NZ 1522
Wacton 43 TM 1791
Wadborough 37 SO 9047
Waddesdon 24 SP 7416
Waddingham 60 SK 9896
Waddington, Lancs 65 SD 7243
Waddington, Lincs 60 SK 9764
Wadebridge 7 SW 9872
Wadeford 12 ST 3110
Wadenhoe 40 TL 0183
Wadesmill 25 TL 3517
Wadhurst 17 TQ 6332
Wadshelf 59 SK 3171
Wadworth 59 SK 5797
Waen-fâch 46 SJ 2017
Wainfleet All Saints 61 TF 4958
Wainfleet Bank 61 TF 4759
Wainhouse Corner 8 SX 1895
Wainscott 18 TQ 7471
Wainstalls 66 SE 0428
Waitby 71 NY 7508
Wakefield 59 SE 3320
Wakerley 50 SP 9599
Wakes Colne 42 TL 8928
Walberswick 43 TM 4974
Walberton 16 SU 9705
Walcot, Lincs 50 TF 0635
Walcot, Shrops 47 SJ 5912
Walcot, Shrops 36 SO 3485
Walcot, Warw 38 SP 1258
Walcote 39 SP 5683
Walcott, Lincs 50 TF 1356
Walcott, Norf 53 TG 3632
Walden 66 SE 0083
Walden Head 66 SD 9880
Walden Stubbs 59 SE 5516
Walderslade 18 TQ 7663
Walderton 15 SU 7810
Walditch 13 SY 4892
Waldridge 72 NZ 2550
Waldringfield 43 TM 2844
Waldron 17 TQ 5419
Wales 59 SK 4882
Walesby, Lincs 61 TF 1392
Walesby, Notts 60 SK 6870
Walford, H. & W 36 SO 3972
Walford, H. & W 33 SO 5820
Walford, Shrops 46 SJ 4320
Walgherton 47 SJ 6949
Walgrave 39 SP 8072
Walkden 57 SD 7403
Walker 79 NZ 2964
Walkerburn 84 NT 3637
Walker Fold 65 SD 6741
Walkeringham 60 SK 7692
Walkerith 60 SK 7893
Walkern 41 TL 2826
Walker's Green 33 SO 5247
Walkhampton 9 SX 5369
Walkington 62 SE 9937
Walk Mill 66 SD 8630
Wall, Northum 78 NY 9169
Wall, Staffs 48 SK 1006
Wallacetown 81 NS 3522
Wallasey 56 SJ 2992
Wallingford 23 SU 6089
Wallington, G. Lon 25 TQ 2863
Wallington, Hants 15 SU 5806
Wallington, Herts 41 TL 2933
Wallis 30 SN 0125
Walliswood 16 TQ 1238
Walls 105 HU 2449
Wallsend 79 NZ 2966
Wall under Heywood 36 SO 5092
Wallyford 89 NT 3672
Walmer 19 TR 3750
Walmer Bridge 65 SD 4824
Walmersley 57 SD 8013
Walmley 48 SP 1393
Walpole 43 TM 3674
Walpole Highway 51 TF 5113
Walpole St Andrew 51 TF 5017
Walpole St Peter 51 TF 5016
Walsall 48 SP 0198
Walsall Wood 48 SK 0503
Walsden 66 SD 9322
Walsgrave on Sowe 38 SP 3881
Walsham le Willows 42 TM 0071
Walsoken 51 TF 4710
Walston 83 NT 0545
Walter's Ash 50 SP 8398
Walterstone 33 SO 3425
Waltham, Humbs 63 TA 2603
Waltham, Kent 19 TR 1048
Waltham Abbey 25 TL 3300
Waltham Chase 15 SU 5615
Waltham Cross 25 TL 3601
Waltham on the Wolds 49 SK 8025
Waltham St Lawrence 24 SU 8276
Walthamstow 25 TQ 3788
Walton, Bucks 40 SP 8836
Walton, Cumbr 78 NY 5264
Walton, Derby 59 SK 3569
Walton, Leic 39 SP 5986
Walton, Powys 33 SO 2559
Walton, Shrops 47 SJ 5918
Walton, Somer 13 ST 4636
Walton, Suff 43 TM 2935
Walton, Warw 38 SP 2853
Walton, W. Yks 59 SE 3517
Walton, W. Yks 67 SE 4447
Walton Cardiff 34 SO 9032
Walton East 30 SN 0223
Walton Highway 51 TF 4912
Walton-in-Gordano 21 ST 4273
Walton-le-Dale 65 SD 5527
Walton-on-Thames 25 TQ 1066
Walton-on-the-Hill, Staffs 48 SJ 9521
Walton on the Hill, Surrey 16 TQ 2254
Walton-on-the-Naze 27 TM 2521
Walton on the Wolds 49 SK 5919
Walton-on-Trent 48 SK 2118
Walton West 30 SM 8612
Walworth 72 NZ 2318
Walwyn's Castle 30 SM 8711
Wambrook 12 ST 2908
Wanborough 22 SU 2183
Wandsworth 25 TQ 2673
Wangford 43 TM 4679
Wanlip 49 SK 5910
Wanlockhead 76 NS 8712
Wansford, Cambs 50 TL 0799
Wansford, Humbs 69 TA 0656
Wanstead 25 TQ 4087
Wanstrow 21 ST 7141
Wanswell 34 SO 6801
Wantage 22 SU 4088
Wapley 21 ST 7179
Wappenbury 38 SP 3769
Wappenham 39 SP 6245
Warbleton 17 TQ 6118
Warborough 35 SU 5993
Warboys 41 TL 3080
Warbstow 8 SX 2090
Warburton 57 SJ 7089
Warcop 71 NY 7415
Warden 19 TR 0271
Ward Green 42 TM 0463
Wardington 39 SP 4946
Wardle, Ches 57 SJ 6157
Wardle, G. Man 57 SD 9116
Wardley 50 SK 8300
Wardlow 58 SK 1874
Wardy Hill 41 TL 4782
Ware 25 TL 3514
Wareham 13 SY 9287
Warehorne 19 TQ 9832
Warenford 85 NU 1328
Waren Mill 85 NU 1434
Warenton 85 NU 1030
Wareside 25 TL 3915
Waresley 41 TL 2554
Warfield 24 SU 8872
Wargrave 24 SU 7878
Warham 52 TF 9441
Wark, Northum 85 NT 8238
Wark, Northum 78 NY 8677
Warkleigh 11 SS 6422
Warkton 40 SP 8979
Warkworth 79 NU 2406
Warlaby 73 SE 3591
Warland 57 SD 9420
Warleggan 7 SX 1569
Warlingham 25 TQ 3458
Warmfield 59 SE 3720
Warmingham 57 SJ 7161
Warmington, Northnts 40 TL 0791
Warmington, Warw 38 SP 4147
Warminster 21 ST 8644
Warmsworth 59 SE 5400
Warmwell 13 SY 7585
Warndon 37 SO 8857
Warnford 15 SU 6223
Warnham 16 TQ 1533
Warninglid 16 TQ 2526
Warren, Ches 57 SJ 8970
Warren, Dyfed 30 SR 9397
Warren Row 24 SU 8180
Warren Street 18 TQ 9253
Warrington, Bucks 40 SP 8953
Warrington, Ches 57 SJ 6088
Warsash 15 SU 4906
Warslow 58 SK 0858
Warsop 59 SK 5667
Warter 69 SE 8750
Warthill 67 SE 6755
Wartling 17 TQ 6509
Wartnaby 49 SK 7123
Warton, Lancs 65 SD 4028
Warton, Lancs 65 SD 5072
Warton, Northum 79 NU 0002
Warton, Warw 48 SK 2803
Warwick, Cumbr 71 NY 4656
Warwick, Warw 38 SP 2865
Warwick Bridge 71 NY 4756
Wasbister 104 HY 3932
Wasdale Head 70 NY 1808
Washaway 7 SX 0369
Washbourne 9 SX 7954
Washfield 11 SS 9315
Washford 20 ST 0441
Washford Pyne 11 SS 8111
Washingborough 60 TF 0270
Washington, T. & W 72 NZ 3056
Washington, W. Susx 16 TQ 1212
Wasing 23 SU 5764
Waskerley 72 NZ 0545
Wasperton 38 SP 2658
Wass 67 SE 5579
Watchet 20 ST 0743
Watchfield, Oxon 22 SU 2590
Watchfield, Somer 20 ST 3446
Watchgate 71 SD 5299
Watendlath 70 NY 2716
Water 66 SD 8425
Waterbeach 41 TL 4965
Waterbeck 77 NY 2477
Waterden 52 TF 8836
Water End, Herts 24 TL 0310
Water End, Herts 25 TL 2204
Waterfall 48 SK 0851
Waterfoot, Lancs 66 SD 8321
Waterfoot, Strath 82 NS 5655
Waterford 25 TL 3114
Waterhead, Cumbr 71 NY 3703
Waterhead, Strath 81 NS 5411
Waterhouses, Durham 72 NZ 1841
Waterhouses, Staffs 48 SK 0850
Wateringbury 17 TQ 6853
Waterlip 21 ST 6544
Waterloo, Dorset 14 SZ 0094
Waterloo, Mers 56 SJ 3198
Waterloo, Norf 53 TG 2219
Waterloo, Strath 83 NS 8054
Waterloo, Tays 92 NO 0536
Waterlooville 15 SU 6809
Watermeetings 76 NS 9512
Watermillock 71 NY 4422
Water Newton 50 TL 1097
Water Orton 38 SP 1891
Waterperry 24 SP 6206
Watersfield 16 TQ 0115
Waterside, Strath 81 NS 4308
Waterside, Strath 81 NS 4843
Waterside, Strath 81 NS 5160
Waterside, Strath 87 NS 6773
Waterstock 24 SP 6305
Waterston 30 SM 9306
Water Stratford 39 SP 6534
Waters Upton 47 SJ 6319
Waterthorpe 59 SK 4382
Water Yeat 70 SD 2889
Watford, Herts 25 TQ 1097
Watford, Northnts 39 SP 6068
Wath, N. Yks 66 SE 1467
Wath, N. Yks 67 SE 3276
Wath upon Dearne 59 SE 4300
Watlington, Norf 52 TF 6110
Watlington, Oxon 24 SU 6894
Watnall 49 SK 5045
Watten 103 ND 2454
Watterow 12 ST 0525
Wattisfield 42 TM 0174
Wattisham 42 TM 0151
Watton, Humbs 69 TA 0150
Watton, Norf 52 TF 9100
Watton at Stone 25 TL 3019
Wattston 87 NS 7769
Wattstown 29 ST 0294
Wattsville 29 ST 2091
Waunarlwydd 28 SS 6095
Waunfawr 54 SH 5259
Wavendon 40 SP 9037
Waverton, Ches 56 SJ 4564
Waverton, Cumbr 70 NY 2247
Wawne 63 TA 0937
Waxham 53 TG 4326
Waxholme 63 TA 3229
Wayford 12 ST 4006
Way Village 11 SS 8810
Wealdstone 25 TQ 1689
Weare 20 ST 4152
Weare Giffard 10 SS 4721
Wearhead 71 NY 8539
Weasdale 71 NY 6903
Weasenham All Saints 52 TF 8421
Weasenham St Peter 52 TF 8522
Weaverham 57 SJ 6174
Weaverthorpe 69 SE 9670
Webheath 38 SP 0266
Wedderlairs 97 NJ 8532
Weddington 48 SP 3693
Wedhampton 22 SU 0657
Wedmore 21 ST 4347
Wednesbury 48 SO 9995
Wednesfield 48 SJ 9500
Weedon 24 SP 8118
Weedon Bec 39 SP 6359
Weedon Lois 39 SP 6047
Weeford 48 SK 1404
Week 11 SS 7316
Weekley 40 SP 8880
Week St Mary 8 SX 2397
Weeley 27 TM 1422
Weeley Heath 27 TM 1520
Weem 91 NN 8449
Weeping Cross 47 SJ 9421
Weeting 42 TL 7788
Weeton, Lancs 65 SD 3834
Weeton, N. Yks 67 SE 2847
Weir 66 SD 8725
Welbeck Abbey 59 SK 5574
Welborne 52 TG 0609
Welbourn 50 SK 9654
Welburn 68 SE 7268
Welbury 73 NZ 3902
Welby 50 SK 9738
Welches Dam 41 TL 4686
Welcombe 10 SS 2218
Weldon 40 SP 9289
Weldrake 62 SE 6845
Welford, Berks 22 SU 4173
Welford, Northnts 39 SP 6480
Welford-on-Avon 38 SP 1552
Welham 39 SP 7692
Welham Green 25 TL 2305
Well, Hants 23 SU 7646
Well, Lincs 61 TF 4473
Well, N. Yks 67 SE 2681
Welland 37 SO 7940
Wellbank 93 NO 4736
Wellesbourne 38 SP 2855
Well Hill 25 TQ 4963
Welling 25 TQ 4775
Wellingborough 40 SP 8967
Wellingham 52 TF 8722
Wellingore 50 SK 9856
Wellington, H. & W 33 SO 4948
Wellington, Shrops 47 SJ 6511
Wellington, Somer 12 ST 1320
Wellington Heath 37 SO 7140
Wellow, Avon 21 ST 7358
Wellow, I. of W 14 SZ 3888
Wellow, Notts 59 SK 6766
Wells 21 ST 5445
Wellsborough 48 SK 3602
Wells-next-the-Sea 52 TF 9143
Wellwood 88 NT 0989
Welney 51 TL 5293
Welshampton 46 SJ 4335
Welsh Bicknor 33 SO 5917
Welsh End 47 SJ 5136
Welsh Frankton 46 SJ 3633
Welsh Hook 30 SM 9327
Welsh Newton 33 SO 5018
Welshpool or Trallwng 46 SJ 2207
Welsh St Donats 29 ST 0276
Welton, Cumbr 70 NY 3544
Welton, Humbs 62 SE 9527
Welton, Lincs 60 TF 0179
Welton, Northnts 39 SP 5866
Welton le Marsh 61 TF 4768
Welton le Wold 61 TF 2787
Welwick 63 TA 3421
Welwyn 25 TL 2316
Welwyn Garden City 25 TL 2313
Wem 47 SJ 5129
Wembdon 12 ST 2837
Wembley 25 TQ 1985
Wembury 8 SX 5148
Wembworthy 11 SS 6609
Wemyss Bay 86 NS 1969
Wendens Ambo 41 TL 5135
Wendlebury 35 SP 5619
Wendling 52 TF 9312
Wendover 24 SP 8607
Wendron 6 SW 6731
Wendy 41 TL 3247
Wenhaston 43 TM 4275
Wennington, Cambs 41 TL 2379
Wennington, G. Lon 25 TQ 5381
Wennington, Lancs 65 SD 6170
Wensley, Derby 59 SK 2661
Wensley, N. Yks 72 SE 0989
Wentbridge 59 SE 4817
Wentnor 36 SO 3892
Wentworth, Cambs 41 TL 4878
Wentworth, S. Yks 59 SK 3898
Wenvoe 29 ST 1273
Weobley 33 SO 4051
Weobley Marsh 33 SO 4151
Wereham 52 TF 6801
Wergs 47 SJ 8701
Wernrheolydd 33 SO 3912
Werrington, Cambs 50 TF 1603
Werrington, Corn 8 SX 3287
Werrington, Staffs 47 SJ 9447
Wervin 56 SJ 4272
Wesham 65 SD 4232
Wessington 59 SK 3757
West Acre 52 TF 7815
West Allerdean 85 NT 9646
West Alvington 9 SX 7243
West Anstey 11 SS 8527
West Ashby 61 TF 2672
West Ashling 15 SU 8107
West Ashton 21 ST 8755
West Aukland 72 NZ 1726
West Bagborough 12 ST 1633
West Barns 89 NT 6578
West Barsham 52 TF 9033
West Bay 13 SY 4690
West Beckham 53 TG 1339
Westbere 19 TR 1961
West Bergholt 42 TL 9627
West Bexington 13 SY 5386
West Bilney 52 TF 7115
West Blatchington 17 TQ 2806
Westborough 50 SK 8544
Westbourne, Dorset 14 SZ 0791
Westbourne, W. Susx 15 SU 7507
West Bradford 65 SD 7444
West Bradley 13 ST 5536
West Bretton 59 SE 2813
West Bridgford 49 SK 5837
West Bromwich 38 SP 0092
West Buckland, Devon 11 SS 6531
West Buckland, Somer 12 ST 1720
West Burrafirth 105 HU 2657
West Burton, Lancs 66 SD 9961
West Burton, N. Yks 66 SE 0186
West Burton, W. Susx 16 SU 9913
Westbury, Bucks 39 SP 6235
Westbury, Shrops 46 SJ 3509
Westbury, Wilts 21 ST 8751
Westbury Leigh 21 ST 8650
Westbury-on-Severn 34 SO 7214
Westbury-sub-Mendip 21 ST 5048
Westby 65 SD 3831
West Caister 53 TG 5111
West Calder 83 NT 0163
West Camel 13 ST 5724
West Challow 22 SU 3688
West Charleton 9 SX 7542
West Chelborough 13 ST 5405
West Chevington 79 NZ 2297
West Chiltington 16 TQ 0918
West Chinnock 13 ST 4613
West Clandon 16 TQ 0452
West Cliffe 19 TR 3544
Westcliffe-on-Sea 26 TQ 8685
West Clyne 103 NC 8805
West Coker 13 ST 5113
Westcombe 21 ST 6739
West Compton, Dorset 13 SY 5694
West Compton, Somer 21 ST 5942
Westcote 35 SP 2220
Westcott, Bucks 24 SP 7117
Westcott, Devon 12 ST 0204
Westcott, Surrey 16 TQ 1448
Westcott Barton 35 SP 4225
West Cross 28 SS 6189
West Cullerley 97 NJ 7603
West Curthwaite 70 NY 3248
Westdean, E. Susx 17 TV 5299
West Dean, Hants 14 SU 2527
West Dean, W. Susx 15 SU 8612
West Deeping 50 TF 1008
West Derby 56 SJ 3993
West Dereham 52 TF 6500
West Ditchburn 79 NU 1320
West Down 10 SS 5142
West Drayton, G. Lon 24 TQ 0679
West Drayton, Notts 60 SK 7074
West End, Avon 21 ST 4469
West End, Beds 40 SP 9853
West End, Hants 15 SU 4614
West End, Humbs 62 SE 9130
West End, Norf 53 TG 4911
West End, N. Yks 66 SE 1457
West End, Oxon 35 SP 4204
West End, Surrey 24 SU 9460
West End Green 24 SU 6661
Wester Culbeuchly Crofts 96 NJ 6562
Westerdale, Highld 103 ND 1251
Westerdale, N. Yks 73 NZ 6605
Westerfield, Shetld 105 HU 3551
Westerfield, Suff 43 TM 1747
Wester Fintray 97 NJ 8116
Westergate 16 SU 9305
Wester Gruinards 102 NH 5192
Westerham 17 TQ 4454
Westerleigh 21 ST 7079
Wester Quarff 105 HU 4135
Wester Skeld 105 HU 2943
Westerton 93 NO 6654
Westerwick 105 HU 2842
West Farleigh 17 TQ 7152
West Felton 46 SJ 3425
Westfield, E. Susx 18 TQ 8115
Westfield, Highld 103 ND 0664
Westfield, Lothn 88 NS 9472
Westfield, Norf 52 TF 9909
West Firle 17 TQ 4707
West Fleetham 85 NU 1928
Westgate, Durham 72 NY 9038
Westgate, Humbs 62 SE 7707
Westgate, Norf 52 TF 9740
Westgates on Sea 19 TR 3270
West Gerinish 100 NF 7741
West Ginge 23 SU 4486
West Grafton 22 SU 2460
West Green 23 SU 7456
West Grimstead 14 SU 2126
West Grinstead 16 TQ 1720
West Haddlesey 67 SE 5626
West Haddon 39 SP 6371
West Hagbourne 23 SU 5187
West Hall, Cumbr 78 NY 5667
Westhall, Suff 43 TM 4181
West Hallam 48 SK 4341
West Halton 62 SE 9021
Westham, E. Susx 17 TQ 6304
West Ham, G. Lon 25 TQ 4083
Westham, Somer 20 ST 4046
Westhampnett 15 SU 8806
West Handley 59 SK 3977
West Hanney 22 SU 4092
West Hanningfield 26 TQ 7399
West Hardwick 59 SE 4118
West Harptree 21 ST 5656
West Hatch 12 ST 2820
Westhay 21 ST 4342
Westhead 56 SD 4307
West Heath 23 SU 8556
West Helmsdale 103 ND 0115
West Hendred 23 SU 4488
West Heslerton 69 SE 9175
Westhide 33 SO 5844
West Hill, Devon 12 SY 0693
Westhill, Grampn 97 NJ 8307
West Hoathly 17 TQ 3632
West Holme 13 SY 8885
Westhope, H. & W 33 SO 4651
Westhope, Shrops 36 SO 4786
West Horndon 26 TQ 6288
Westhorpe, Lincs 50 TF 2131
Westhorpe, Suff 42 TM 0569
West Horrington 21 ST 5747
West Horsley 16 TQ 0752
West Hougham 19 TR 2640
Westhoughton 57 SD 6505
Westhouse 65 SD 6774
Westhouses 59 SK 4258
Westhumble 16 TQ 1651
West Hyde 24 TQ 0391
West Ilsley 23 SU 4782
Westing 105 HP 5705
West Itchenor 15 SU 7901
West Kennett 22 SU 1168
West Kilbride 81 NS 2147
West Kingsdown 25 TQ 5762
West Kington 21 ST 8177
West Kirby 56 SJ 2186
West Knighton 13 SY 7387
West Knoyle 13 ST 8532
Westlake 9 SX 6253
West Langdon 19 TR 3247
West Langwell 103 NC 6909
West Lavington, Wilts 22 SU 0053
West Lavington, W. Susx 15 SU 8920
West Layton 72 NZ 1409
West Leake 49 SK 5226
Westleigh, Devon 10 SS 4728
Westleigh, Devon 12 ST 0616
Westleton 43 TM 4469
West Lexham 52 TF 8417
Westley, Shrops 46 SJ 3607
Westley, Suff 42 TL 8264
Westley Waterless 42 TL 6156
West Lilling 67 SE 6465
Westlington 24 SP 7610
West Linton, Border 83 NT 1551
Westlinton, Cumbr 77 NY 3964
West Littleton 21 ST 7675
West Lulworth 13 SY 8280
West Lutton 69 SE 9369
West Malling 17 TQ 6757
West Malvern 37 SO 7646
West Marden 15 SU 7713
West Markham 60 SK 7272
Westmarsh 19 TR 2761
West Marton 66 SD 8950
West Meon 15 SU 6423
West Mersea 27 TM 0112
Westmeston 17 TQ 3313
Westmill 41 TL 3627
West Milton 13 SY 5096
Westminster 25 TQ 2979
West Monkton 12 ST 2628
West Moors 14 SU 0802
Westmuir, Tays 92 NO 3652
West Muir, Tays 93 NO 5661
Westnewton, Cumbr 70 NY 1344
West Newton, Humbs 63 TA 1937
West Newton, Norf 52 TF 6927
West Norwood 25 TQ 3171
West Ogwell 9 SX 8270
Weston, Avon 21 ST 7266
Weston, Berks 22 SU 4073
Weston, Ches 57 SJ 5080
Weston, Ches 47 SJ 7352
Weston, Dorset 13 SY 6871
Weston, Hants 15 SU 7221
Weston, Herts 41 TL 2630
Weston, Lincs 51 TF 2925
Weston, Northnts 39 SP 5847
Weston, Notts 60 SK 7767
Weston, N. Yks 66 SE 1747
Weston, N. Yks 68 SE 7565
Weston, Shrops 47 SJ 5629
Weston, Shrops 47 SO 5993
Weston, Staffs 48 SJ 9727
Weston Bampfylde 13 ST 6124
Weston Beggard 33 SO 5841
Weston by Welland 39 SP 7791
Weston Colville 42 TL 6153
Weston Green 42 TL 6252
Weston Heath 47 SJ 7713
Weston Hills 51 TF 2720
Westoning 40 TL 0332
Weston-in-Gordano 21 ST 4474
Weston Jones 47 SJ 7624
Weston Longville 53 TG 1115
Weston Lullingfields 46 SJ 4224
Weston-on-the-Green 35 SP 5318
Weston-on-Trent 48 SK 4028
Weston Patrick 23 SU 6946
Weston Rhyn 46 SJ 2835
Weston Subedge 38 SP 1241
Weston-super-Mare 20 ST 3261
Weston Turville 24 SP 8511
Weston-under-Lizard 47 SJ 8010
Weston under Penyard 33 SO 6323
Weston under Wetherley 38 SP 3669
Weston Underwood, Bucks 40 SP 8650
Weston Underwood, Derby 48 SK 2942
Westonzoyland 12 ST 3534
West Overton 22 SU 1367
West Parley 14 SZ 0898
West Peckham 17 TQ 6452
West Pennard 21 ST 5438
West Pentire 6 SW 7760
West Perry 40 TL 1466
Westport 12 ST 3820
West Putford 10 SS 3515
West Quantoxhead 20 ST 1141
West Rainton 72 NZ 3146
West Rasen 60 TF 0689
West Raynham 52 TF 8725
Westrigg 83 NS 9067
West Row 42 TL 6775
West Rudham 52 TF 8127
West Runton 53 TG 1842
Westruther 84 NT 6350
Westry 51 TL 3998
West Saltoun 84 NT 4667
West Sandwick 105 HU 4588
West Scrafton 66 SE 0783
West Stafford 13 SY 7289
West Stockwith 60 SK 7994
West Stoke 15 SU 8308
West Stonesdale 72 NY 8802
West Stoughton 20 ST 4148
West Stour 13 ST 7822
West Stourmouth 19 TR 2562
West Stow 42 TL 8170
West Stowell 22 SU 1362
West Street 18 TQ 9054
West Tanfield 67 SE 2678
West Tarbert 80 NR 8467
West Thorney 15 SU 7602
West Thurrock 25 TQ 5877
West Tilbury 18 TQ 6677
West Tisted 15 SU 6529
West Tofts 88 NO 1034
West Torrington 61 TF 1382
West Town 21 ST 4868
West Tytherley 14 SU 2729
West Tytherton 22 ST 9574
West Walton 51 TF 4713
Westward 70 NY 2744
Westward Ho[10 SS 4329
Westwell, Kent 19 TQ 9947
Westwell, Oxon 35 SP 2210
Westwell Leacon 19 TQ 9647
West Wellow 14 SU 2919
West Wemyss 89 NT 3294
West Wick, Avon 20 ST 3661
Westwick, Cambs 41 TL 4265
Westwick, Norf 53 TG 2726
West Wickham, Cambs 42 TL 6149
West Wickham, G. Lon 25 TQ 3866
West Winch 52 TF 6315
West Winterslow 14 SU 2332
West Wittering 15 SZ 7898
West Witton 66 SE 0688
Westwood, Devon 12 SY 0198
Westwood, Wilts 21 ST 8059
West Woodburn 78 NY 8986
West Woodhay 22 SU 3963
West Woodlands 21 ST 7743
Westwoodside 62 SK 7499
West Worldham 15 SU 7436
West Wratting 42 TL 6051
West Wycombe 24 SU 8394
West Yell 105 HU 4583
Wetheral 71 NY 4654
Wetherby 67 SE 4048
Wetherden 42 TM 0062
Wetheringsett 43 TM 1266
Wethersfield 42 TL 7131
Wethersta 105 HU 3665
Wetherup Street 43 TM 1464
Wetley Rocks 48 SJ 9649
Wettenhall 57 SJ 6261
Wetton 48 SK 1155
Wetwang 69 SE 9359
Wetwood 47 SJ 7733
Wexcombe 22 SU 2759
Weybourne 53 TG 1143
Weybread 43 TM 2480
Weybridge 24 TQ 0764
Weydale 103 ND 1564
Weyhill 22 SU 3146
Weymouth 13 SY 6779
Whaddon, Bucks 39 SP 8034
Whaddon, Cambs 41 TL 3546
Whaddon, Glos 34 SO 8313
Whaddon, Wilts 14 SU 1926
Whale 71 NY 5221
Whaley 59 SK 5171
Whaley Bridge 58 SK 0181
Whaley Thorns 59 SK 5371
Whalley 65 SD 7336
Whalton 79 NZ 1381
Wham 66 SD 7762
Whaness 104 HY 2502
Whaplode 51 TF 3224
Whaplode Drove 51 TF 3113
Wharfe 66 SD 7869
Wharles 65 SD 4435
Wharncliffe Side 59 SK 2994
Wharram le Street 68 SE 8666
Wharton, Ches 57 SJ 6666
Wharton, H. & W 33 SO 5055
Whashton 72 NZ 1406
Whatcombe 13 ST 8301
Whatcote 38 SP 3044
Whatfield 42 TM 0246
Whatley 21 ST 7347
Whatlington 17 TQ 7518
Whatstandwell 48 SK 3354
Whatton 49 SK 7439
Whauphill 74 NX 4049
Wheatacre 53 TM 4693
Wheathampstead 25 TL 1713
Wheathill 37 SO 6282
Wheatley, Hants 23 SU 7840
Wheatley, Oxon 35 SP 5905
Wheatley Hill 73 NZ 3738
Wheatley Lane 66 SD 8338
Wheaton Aston 47 SJ 8512
Wheddon Cross 11 SS 9238
Wheedlemont 96 NJ 4726
Wheelerstreet 16 SU 9440
Wheelock 57 SJ 7559
Wheelton 65 SD 6021
Whelford 35 SU 1799
Whelpley Hill 24 SP 9904
Whenby 67 SE 6369
Whepstead 42 TL 8358
Wherstead 43 TM 1540
Wherwell 22 SU 3840
Wheston 58 SK 1376
Whetsted 17 TQ 6545
Whetstone 49 SP 5597
Whicham 64 SD 1382
Whichford 35 SP 3134
Whickham 79 NZ 2061
Whiddon Down 9 SX 6992
Whigstreet 93 NO 4844
Whilton 39 SP 6364
Whimple 12 SY 0497
Whimpwell Green 53 TG 3829
Whinburgh 52 TG 0009
Whinnyfold 97 NK 0833
Whippingham 15 SZ 5193
Whipsnade 24 TL 0118
Whipton 9 SX 9493
Whissendine 50 SK 8214
Whissonsett 52 TF 9123
Whistley Green 24 SU 7974
Whiston, Mers 57 SJ 4791
Whiston, Northnts 40 SP 8460
Whiston, Staffs 47 SJ 8914
Whiston, Staffs 48 SK 0347
Whiston, S. Yks 59 SK 4590
Whitbeck 64 SD 1184
Whitbourne 37 SO 7256
Whitburn, Lothn 83 NS 9464
Whitburn, T. & W 79 NZ 4062
Whitby, Ches 56 SJ 3975
Whitby, N. Yks 69 NZ 8910
Whitchurch, Avon 21 ST 6167
Whitchurch, Bucks 24 SP 8020
Whitchurch, Devon 8 SX 4972
Whitchurch, Dyfed 30 SM 8025
Whitchurch, Hants 23 SU 4648
Whitchurch, H. & W 33 SO 5517
Whitchurch, Oxon 24 SU 6377
Whitchurch, S. Glam 29 ST 1580
Whitchurch, Shrops 47 SJ 5441
Whitchurch Canonicorum 12 SY 3995
Whitchurch Hill 24 SU 6478
Whitcott Keysett 36 SO 2782
Whitebridge 94 NH 4815
Whitebrook 33 SO 5306
Whitecairns 97 NJ 9218
Whitechapel 65 SD 5541
White Coppice 57 SD 6119
Whitecraig 89 NT 3570
Whitecroft 33 SO 6206
Whiteface 103 NH 7089
Whitefield 57 SD 8105
Whiteford 97 NJ 7226
Whitegate 57 SJ 6369
Whitehall 104 HY 6528
Whitehaven 70 NX 9717